HEGEL'S
Philosophy of Nature

BEING PART TWO OF THE
*ENCYCLOPAEDIA OF
THE PHILOSOPHICAL SCIENCES* (1830)
TRANSLATED FROM NICOLIN AND
PÖGGELER'S EDITION (1959)
AND FROM THE *ZUSÄTZE* IN
MICHELET'S TEXT (1847)

BY
A. V. MILLER

WITH FOREWORD BY
J. N. FINDLAY, F.B.A.

OXFORD
AT THE CLARENDON PRESS

*This book has been printed digitally and produced in a standard specification
in order to ensure its continuing availability*

OXFORD
UNIVERSITY PRESS

Great Clarendon Street, Oxford OX2 6DP

Oxford University Press is a department of the University of Oxford.
It furthers the University's objective of excellence in research, scholarship,
and education by publishing worldwide in

Oxford New York

Auckland   Cape Town Dar es Salaam Hong Kong Karachi
Kuala Lumpur Madrid Melbourne Mexico City Nairobi
New Delhi Shanghai Taipei Toronto
With offices in
Argentina Austria Brazil Chile Czech Republic France Greece
Guatemala Hungary Italy Japan South Korea Poland Portugal
Singapore Switzerland Thailand Turkey Ukraine Vietnam

Oxford is a registered trade mark of Oxford University Press
in the UK and in certain other countries

Published in the United States
by Oxford University Press Inc., New York

ISBN 978-0-19-927267-9

FOREWORD

J. N. FINDLAY

THE present translation of Hegel's *Philosophy of Nature* is part of an attempt to complete the translation of his *Encyclopaedia of the Philosophical Sciences* of which two parts already exist in W. Wallace's translation of the *Logic* (with editorial *Zusätze*) and of the *Philosophy of Mind* (without editorial *Zusätze*), both published by the Clarendon Press. Though published towards the end of the last century, these translations have held their ground, and have a liveliness and a literary sparkle not found in other English versions, which atones for their occasional looseness and use of periphrasis, and which points to what can only be described as a spiritual identification with the genius of Hegel. The present translation is of the whole *Philosophy of Nature*, together with the editorial *Zusätze*. It is hoped in an ensuing volume to present Wallace's translation of the numbered paragraphs of the *Philosophy of Mind* (or *Philosophy of Spirit*), the third part of the *Encyclopaedia*, together with the *Zusätze* which, in the first collected editions, accompany only its first section. The *Philosophy of Nature* has been translated throughout by Mr. A. V. Miller, a dedicated Hegelian, though I have considered all his renderings and have given him what help I could with many difficult terms and passages. The translation of *Zusätze* to the *Philosophy of Mind* (*Spirit*) will also be Mr. Miller's work.

The translation has been made from Karl Ludwig Michelet's edition of the *Naturphilosophie*, published in 1847 in the Second Edition of Hegel's Collected Works, but Nicolin and Pöggeler's 1959 edition of the *Encyclopaedia* (without *Zusätze*) has been consulted for the text of the numbered paragraphs. The translation of the *Zusätze* raises many problems, fortunately not peculiar to the present translation. The *Zusätze* for the *Naturphilosophie* were compiled by Michelet, a devoted pupil of Hegel's but also an original philosopher of some standing, from written

material connected with eight courses of lectures on the subject
given (respectively) in Jena in 1805–6, in Heidelberg in the summer of 1818, and in Berlin in the years 1819–20, 1821–2, 1823–4,
1825–6, 1828, and 1830. Some of this written material was Hegel's
own, e.g. his Jena notes for 1805–6 reprinted by Hoffmeister
in 1931 as the second volume of the *Jenenser Realphilosophie*,
the notes written or placed in his copies of the 1817 and 1827
editions of the *Encyclopaedia*, his lecture notes for his various
Berlin courses: in these much of the earlier material was taken
over into the later versions. Other written material was afforded
by students' lecture-notes taken down by Michelet himself (two
sets) and by three others. The way in which Michelet conflated
this material has been harshly judged, particularly in regard to the
colourful fragments taken over from the Jena material. As Hoffmeister remarks (*Realphilosophie*, vol. ii, 1931, p. ix):

> This working together of thoughts separated in part by decades,
> however much the individual passages taken over were tested for their
> suitability in support of the systematics of the mature work, must
> injure the latter. And, on the other hand, since the passages taken over
> are not distinguished, they afford no insight into Hegel's youthful
> work. Through this dubious method, Michelet robs the words of Hegel's
> youth of their originality: he simply omits difficult passages, generally
> introduces only what is easy to read, and often amends far too idio-
> syncratically. He fits single statements into other contexts, indeed he
> often quite turns them round since they would otherwise not fit later
> paragraphs, he has, in short, to round things off.

Nicolin and Pöggeler remark in similar vein: 'The procedure of
Hegel's friends and pupils can only be properly understood as
springing from their basic philosophical attitude. They were
looking for the complete, closed system on which they could
build and to which they could make their additions. They therefore brought to their task no interest in the development of
Hegel's thought and the documents of its development' (Intro. to
Encyclopaedia, 1959, pp. xlv–vi).

It must be admitted that Michelet (like the other editors) took
more liberties with his material than would now be taken by
editors in a similar position. He would perhaps have been wise to
base himself on one version, rather than try to do justice to all.

Occasionally the drift of a sentence is completely changed by Michelet. Thus in the Jena manuscript (*Realphilosophie*, vol. ii, p. 33) Hegel writes: 'what is only inner is just as much outer; for it is the Other as this outer existence.' The latter part of this is changed by Michelet to 'for it is the Other of this outer existence'. It must, however, be remembered that Hegel's *Encyclopaedia* was a condensed, arid compendium, put out as a foundation for detailed comment and explanation in lectures. Without such material as is provided by the editorial *Zusätze* it would be largely uninterpretable, a monumental inscription in Linear B. Many scholars have written as if those who first published the *Zusätze* deserved blame, whereas they deserve boundless gratitude. No doubt we shall some day see *all* the versions of Hegel's lecture-material and students' notes published separately by the Hegel-Archiv, but it is not clear *when* this will happen, and whether the whole vast array of material will ever, or ought ever, to be translated into English. The *Zusatz*-method probably represented the best that could be done at the time, and it made Hegel intelligible and established his philosophical image for the ensuing century. It is still unclear whether that image will be substantially altered by the new labours of source-disentanglement, or that the alterations made by Hegel's pupils and friends were of anything but minor philosophical importance. It must be remembered, further, that not only the *Encyclopaedia*, but the *Philosophy of Right* has had a large body of useful *Zusätze* added to it, and that the text of Hegel's lectures on Aesthetics, the Philosophy of Religion, the Philosophy of History, and the History of Philosophy is in every case the product of a conflation of materials from different lecture-courses similar to that which has produced the *Zusätze*.

It may, further, be wondered whether the concern for Hegel's 'development' displayed by many writers, is not excessive, especially in a situation where there are no reliable, detailed commentaries on his major works. The Juvenilia of Berne and Frankfurt have been studied exhaustively for very many decades, and have thrown very little light on any major notion or position in Hegel's mature work: they remain writings, interesting as reflections of their time and place, which give absolutely no indication that their writer was ever destined to be a great philosopher, let alone one of the greatest of all philosophers. Hegel, like many another young philosopher faced with a teaching situation, and with names like 'metaphysics' and 'logic' to channel his effort, matured overnight from the (to my mind) rather dreary lucubrations of his years of tutorship to the astounding writings of the Jena period (those available in Lasson's *Jenenser Logik* and in the *Realphilosophie* published by Hoffmeister). These writings everywhere anticipate the positions and method of the mature system, and are obviously the work of a very great thinker. There is undoubtedly development in the passage from these writings to the later mature works, but not the sort of causally explanatory, psychological development which those who have devoted attention to the Juvenilia seem to have been looking for. It is even arguable that the great interest shown in these Juvenilia stems, in part, from an unwillingness to scale the main crags of the system: men linger among its foothills because these resemble the lower-lying territories in which they feel best able to work and think.

It is not, however, our wish to offer further argument for publishing a translation of Hegel's *Philosophy of Nature* which includes the *Zusätze* of Michelet, and of the *Philosophy of Spirit* which will include the *Zusätze* of Boumann, just as W. Wallace's historic translation of the *Logic* included the *Zusätze* of Leopold von Henning. Our aim is to be useful, to make Hegel's thought accessible to students and teachers, particularly in regions where prejudiced simplifications might otherwise be their only route of access to it. It was our intention to supplement the present volume with a volume of Notes, in which the scientific interpretation and historical background of Hegel's treatment of nature would be given, and it would be made plain how deeply informed he was on all matters scientific, and how remote from the prejudiced picture of him as a merely *a priori* thinker. Circumstances of an extremely unfortunate character have, however, made it impossible for us to carry out this part of our task, but we believe none the less that Hegel can be allowed to speak for himself, and that the purport of his scientific views, and the wealth and depth of his empiricism (as one facet of his philosophical habit) will come clearly through. It will, in fact, be plain that Hegel, like Aristotle and Descartes and Whitehead, is one of the great philosophical interpreters of nature, as steeped in its detail as he is audacious in his treatment of it. It only remains for me, in the remainder of this short Introduction, to 'liberate my soul' much as Wallace did in the essays which accompany his translations (though at briefer length), and to indicate what I think is the place of the *Naturphilosophie* in Hegel's absolutism, and how I conceive that it has contributed to the philosophical understanding of the natural world.

The most enlightening way to approach Hegelianism as a system, and the Philosophy of Nature as one of its essential parts (which in a sense also includes the whole in itself), is to regard it as an essay in Absolute-theory, an attempt to frame the notion or work out the logic of an Absolute, by which is to be understood something whose existence is both *self*-explanatory and *all*-explanatory, an inheritor, in short, of the religious conception of a God, as of the various materialisms, idealisms, spiritualisms, etc., whose objects have been given some of the notional ultimacy and uniqueness of a God. It has recently been questioned whether the notion of an Absolute played the central part in Hegel's philosophy that most interpreters had supposed; certainly the Absolute of Hegel is not at all like the Absolute of many modern idealists, but that his whole philosophy is an attempt to work out the notion of something that he calls 'the Absolute' will, on a careful reading, admit of no question. All the categories of the Logic are confessedly an ascending series of definitions of 'the Absolute', which ends up in the supreme category of the Absolute Idea: the other parts of the system show us the same Absolute functioning more concretely, but still notionally, in other fields than 'the medium of pure thought'. To manners of thought to which the conception of an Absolute is alien and superfluous, and to which everything that is not an empty piece of formalism is simply an encountered piece of fact, whose relation to other such pieces is no more than another encountered piece of such fact, there is no logic in the workings of the Hegelian system, no inherent unrest or self-contradiction in any of its notions or phases that fail of total explanation, no need to pass beyond them to a more satisfactory embodiment of absoluteness. It is only if one belongs to a 'speculative' tradition, and finds something logically absurd, imperatively requiring supplementation, in any mere fact, or collocation of mere facts, or even mere collocation of necessities, and one will only admit ultimate contingencies if one has some basic conception which enables one to see, in general terms, just why and how there can and must be such contingencies, that Hegel can hope to achieve some 'bite' on one's thinking, though it is of course open to the speculative thinker to argue that *all* the constructive enterprises of science, *all* the appeals of morality, etc., only 'make sense' on such a basis. Hegel is, however, singular as an Absolutist, not only in holding that an element of contingency, of brute, empirical fact, is *demanded* (not, of course, as regards its detailed content, but in respect of its general presence) by the very notion of his Absolute, but also that, even in the regions where unity and total explanation 'in the end' prevail, there must yet be an initial, lower-level element of disunity and external irrelevance for such unity and total explanation to overcome, and that it is only in overcoming such initial, and in a sense 'merely apparent', disunity and irrelevance, that it can *be* a unique, unified, all-explanatory Absolute at all. And so much is this so, that even in the overcoming of such merely apparent disunity and irrelevance, its appearance, *qua* appearance, is preserved: the Absolute must, after a fashion, have an Other, and an Other incorporating an indefinite amount of lower-level otherness in itself, in order that it may in detail show, if one may so abuse language, that its Other is no other than itself, and in order that it may in truth *be* itself in that seeming Other. The preceding sentences have expounded Hegel by adopting his language: in an absolutism like Hegel's there is, in the last resort, nothing else one can do. One must use his language, and the characteristic logic it embodies, if one is fully to understand or to communicate what he is maintaining. But, whether one thinks such an absolutist logic crazy or cogent, it was certainly at all times the most important and characteristic 'message' of Hegel. The Absolute is said, even in the Jena manuscripts, to be 'so like self in what appears unlike self as to be the absolute ground of this unlike element' (Lasson, *Jenenser Logik*, p. 159), and in the *Encyclopaedia* (§ 214) to be 'the eternal vision of itself *in the other*', while in § 386 Hegel writes characteristically: 'Mind (*Geist*) is the infinite Idea: thus finitude here means the disproportion between the concept and the reality—but with the qualification that it is a shadow cast by the mind's own light—a show or illusion which the mind implicitly imposes as a barrier to itself, in order, by its removal, actually to realize and become conscious of freedom as its very being, i.e. to be fully manifest' (Wallace's translation in the last two cases). The use of the notion of *Geist*, Mind or Spirit, in the last quotation must not mislead us: Hegel believes in a spiritual, self-thinking Absolute rather than in some other sort of one, because in conscious life one has a better realization of the *logical* properties of an Absolute, of its complete explanatoriness even of what is most seemingly alien, than one has in any other sort of Absolute. The place of the definite, limited, not self-explanatory in Hegel's Absolutism, as the permanent foil and contrast and raw material, if one may so speak, of the Absolute, is uniquely characteristic of Hegelianism: one here has Spinozism with the mutilation and transience of the modes necessarily built into the unbrokenness and eternity of the One Substance, and in fact conditioning the latter.

It is the inner tension involved in Hegel's notion of his Absolute that explains why its unity expresses itself in subjectivity rather than in substantiality, a unity and an identity which actively achieves and maintains itself in the face of, and in self-identification with, the most boundless variety, and which is not bound down to one inert, fixed character or position, whether outward or inward, and why, when it is conceived by Hegel in Platonic terms as an eternal Idea, it is also credited with an inherent dynamism or ideal causality, so that it can be said to 'let itself go', to *give* itself specific forms and instances. These last conceptions may seem to be merely mythic imaginations masquerading as logical relations: if Hegel is right, they are, however, strictly logical relations of which there are many more or less adequate empirical illustrations. All this may seem very strange from the point of view of philosophers who are not in quest of the total explanatoriness which is another name for absolutism, but, granted this aspiration, the paradoxical character of Hegelian concepts will vanish. They are, arguably, the concepts that one *has* to frame if one is to have an absolutism which is contentful and not empty, and if one's absolutism is to leave nothing whatever unexplained and outside of itself. The Idea of an infinite activity which is its own end, and which consummates itself in the conscious spirituality which, whether in theory or practice, deprives objects of their 'otherness', their independence and externality, and which further consummates itself in the consciousness of this consummating consciousness and its work, and which, in so subordinating the objective world to its theory and its practice, reveals itself and knows itself as the true *raison d'être* of that world, and in so doing reduces the latter to a mere adjunct and externalized form of itself—the concept here involved, though arduous and even terrifying in its complex recursiveness, yet really seems to achieve a perfect re-entrance, and the possibility of a perpetual tying up of all loose threads back again into itself. Meditated upon, it is plainly logically superior, *qua* absolutism, to a mechanistic or an emergent or a dialectical materialism, to a transcendent theism, to a Platonic realism, to a Berkeleyan or other subjectivism, or to the modern doctrine of a boundless contingency and open empirical possibility which is arguably an inverted form of absolutism. All this cannot, however, be persuasively argued in the present Introduction.

To characterize Hegel's Absolute most helpfully for our purpose, we may adopt his comparison or identification of it with a syllogism, in which there are distinct terms which only have a complete sense in their mutual interconnection, and which form a reasoned whole in which each term mediates the connection of the others. These terms are, severally, in Hegel's absolutism, the Idea, Nature and Spirit (Mind or *Geist*). The absolute Idea is the abstracted notion of absoluteness, i.e. of the return to self in and through otherness, and it contains within itself all that leads up to such a consummation: the 'descriptive' surface categories of the Doctrine of Being, with their coverage of mere quality and quantity, the 'explanatory' categories of the Doctrine of Essence, with their reference of everything to everything *else* for explanation which in its turn refers back to the point of origin, and the 'self-explanatory' or absolutist categories of the Doctrine of the Notion, where all is a commerce of self with self, and a development of self into self, until we end up with the self-explanatory teleological conceptions of Life, Cognition, and Practice, and of the practical-theoretical Absolute Idea. The Absolute Idea leads on to the greater concreteness of nature and Spirit, because instantiation, concrete embodiment is part and parcel of its sense: it would not *be* the Absolute Idea were it not thus instantiated and embodied, and it may in *this* sense be credited with a power of self-release, of ideal or formal causality. Nature, on the other hand, is the Idea self-externalized, lost or sunk in otherness, and having its whole being and function in the gradual setting aside of this self-externalization and otherness, in ever more 'evolved' or spiritual-seeming natural forms. Nature leads on to Mind or Spirit, because it is the whole sense of Nature to achieve a kind of self-dependent unity which is only adequately realized in Spirit. Spirit, on the other hand, is the Idea asserting its intrinsic unity in ever clearer, and therefore more complex, conscious forms, and overcoming various forms of 'alienation', various natural and social barriers, until it achieves absoluteness, and a consciousness of absoluteness, in the spiritual transformations of the world and life and experience involved in Art, Religion, and Philosophy. The syllogism which is the Absolute can accordingly be read as the Idea perfecting itself in self-conscious Spirit by way of its self-alienation in Nature, but it can equally be read, Hegel tells us at the end of the *Encyclopaedia* (§§ 575-7), as Nature using conscious Spirit to bring out its inherent Idea, or as Spirit using the Idea to achieve theoretical and practical mastery over Nature. What these final *Encyclopaedia* passages tell us is that there is a place for Nature and naturalism in the philosophy of Hegel, just as there is a place for a dynamic Platonic realism and for a teleological, social subjectivism. Despite the somewhat relegated position of Nature, as the 'Other' of the Idea and Spirit, it is an Other whose final apotheosis into Spirit makes it coequal with the other forms of the Absolute. There is, for Hegel, nothing ideal or spiritual which does not have its roots in Nature, and which is not nourished and brought to full fruition by Nature. And it is arguable that if one wants to call one's absolutism a 'dialectical materialism', then such a 'dialectical materialism' is to be found in a more coherent and intelligibly worked-out form in Hegel's Philosophy of Nature and Spirit than in the imperfectly coherent 'dialectics' of Marx, Engels, and the Marxists generally. The true classless society is certainly a high form of the Hegelian Absolute, but it is a society in which every class or group reflects, and is, the whole of the society in and for which it lives, rather than one characterized by a mere negation of class-structure. It is to the way that Hegel treats Nature in the second part of his system that we now turn, though we shall have to content ourselves with a characterization as general as the one just applied to the system as a whole.

In the Introduction to the *Philosophy of Nature*, as elsewhere throughout the work, Hegel apologizes for his deficiencies as a philosopher of Nature by dwelling on the inherent difficulties of his task, the exploration of a realm where fundamental explanatory notions are buried under the rubble of mere contingencies, senseless diversifications, for which no notional justification can, or ought to be, given. It is also a region where externalization, and therefore untruth, prevails; though it is always being attenuated: things that belong notionally together are given in a grotesque manner as apart, and things that are notionally fluid and indistinct acquire a misplaced rigidity, which our thought must reduce to a new fluidity. Everything is in fact constructed as if designed to give comfort to the analytic Understanding, and all suggests those happy theories of special stuffs, elements, components, agencies, or linking media which the understanding of science devises and which a rational philosophy must demolish. Nature may be said to be a realm of exteriorized thoughts, but of thoughts petrified and dismembered by exteriorization: it is, as Hegel romantically says, a Bacchic god unrestrained and unmindful of itself, and the task of bringing what is thus romantically distraught to the sober coherence of rational discourse must necessarily be an arduous and often unsuccessful one. The philosophical interpretation of Nature, must, Hegel tells us, consist in seeing in it a series of stages which evince the gradual triumph of self-explanatory unity over mutual externality and otherness (§ 249); these stages can be run through in two directions, either from the extreme or integrated organization that we have in life to the opposite extreme of mechanical interaction, or in precisely the opposite sense, from the extreme of mechanism to the extreme of organism. The ordering actually followed by Hegel is the latter, and it accords with the whole habit of his system, but the fact that he thought a reverse ordering possible throws light on the nature of his whole dialectical method. Either mode of viewing Nature and its stages can, however, in Hegel's view, be given a misleading temporal form: we can be emanationists, who see Nature as involved in a slow degeneration from more fully integrated to more hopelessly disintegrated forms, or we can be evolutionists, who see the trend of things as more agreeably progressive. Hegel, though amazingly well acquainted with the facts of the geological record, then quite widely known, thought it false and, worse than false, philosophically irrelevant and misleading, to temporalize Nature and its notional stages into a temporally arranged, evolutionary picture. The natural stages in question were all logically necessary to the existence of Nature as a facet of the self-explanatory Absolute, and it did not make their serial order more intelligible to imagine them as following on one another in time. In general, Hegel thinks that no light is won by imagining the time of Nature as an infinitely long-drawn-out affair only complete over its whole extent: its completeness lies in the ever-living *Now* of present existence, in which Nature in all its forms is always totally present. But as Hegel was willing to temporalize the spiritual history of Man, without denying the living totality of the present, it is not clear why he was not prepared to do the same for Nature. Plainly the only reason was that he lived in a pre-Darwinian age, and was, moreover, a somewhat timid conservative in regard to the detail of science.

In the Mechanics which follows Hegel first introduces us to the self-externality of Space and Time: in these mutual outsideness and indifference seem paramount, but we still have a deep continuity, a mutual holding together, which belies this. Hegel is concerned to stress the *necessary* three-dimensionality of space, though his arguments amount to little more than that, whether or not more or less than three spatial dimensions can be abstractly conceived, three dimensions can be seen to be both necessary and sufficient for *fully concrete* side-by-sideness. He also believes in the necessary integration of space and time, time having a punctiformity, a concentration of spread-out diversity into the undivided Now, which alone can dirempt the otherwise unbroken continuity of space. Time, it would seem, can successively high-light various continuously blending spatial positions, which in their turn, it would seem, enable time to give a space-like to-getherness to its past and its future. Whatever the success of these not very lucid contentions, they are certainly 'after' some-thing deep and true, a mutual entailment that we 'feel with our bones'. Thus also deep and true are his characterization of time as the 'abstraction of destruction', and his statement that the Idea and Spirit only transcend time because they are the very notion of time. (§ 258). Even in the realm of mutual externality, we are infinitely removed from that barren succession of complete, mutually independent existences that empiricist analyses have usually given us, and that the scientific understanding has further corrupted into stretches on 'world-lines', etc. Obviously Hegel is also right in his next step which sees time and space as alike empty and meaningless without a matter and a motion which give them content. 'Motion', he tells us (*Zus.* § 261), 'is the transition of time into space and of space into time: matter, on the other hand, is the relation of space and time as a peaceful entity'. This leads on to his organic view of matter, based on Kant's *Metaphysical Elements of Natural Science*, as essentially combining a mutual repulsiveness which holds the parts of matter apart, and gives meaning to their occupation of space, and a mutual attraction which enables them to hold together, and is likewise necessary for such occupation. This combination of attraction and repulsion in matter illustrates the *logical* differentiation and reintegration which together constitute Hegel's Absolute: the terms 'attraction' and 'repulsion' are accordingly used in many purely logical and non-physical contexts, e.g. in regard to society. The various notions and laws of inertia and motion are then dealt with, and shown to have a profound philosophical foundation.

Hegel goes on, in his Absolute Mechanics, to maintain that the distribution of matter into large centres, with subordinate centres clustered around them, having further satellite centres around these last, and loose cometary members wandering in and out on the fringes of the system, has something necessary about it, which conforms to 'the Notion'. The arrangement of bodies in a solar system is a rough forthshowing, in the medium of inert externality, of the self-explanatory unity which is the source and goal of Nature: in it wandering, separated bodies all have a common centre outside of themselves, which brings them all together. The Newtonian and Laplacian view according to which this is all a great accident, and matter need not have been distributed in this centralistic fashion, is repugnant to Hegelianism, and it is arguable that it is inherently absurd. Those modern cosmologies which conceive of matter as spontaneously generated in the empty regions of expanding space, certainly suggest that the centrality of cosmic matter, its grouping about large, continuous aggregations, is part and parcel of its existence. There can be loose, wandering bits of matter only because there are orderly, centrally situated bits. Hegel of course did not believe in a plurality of solar centres, the fixed stars being for him a mere backcloth to the central stage, on which we are the supreme performers, a Judaic-Christian opinion in which it now looks as if he may regrettably be proved right. We may, however, plead that Hegel's conceptions should have been given a hearing, and that philosophers at least should have paid attention to his passionate advocacy of Kepler as opposed to Newton, and to the possibility of taking a more 'organic' view of the internal economy of a solar system. If the belief that 'anything is possible', and that only experience can show us what is actual, can be held to be productive of many more difficulties than it resolves, we may well begin to look for categorical frameworks in regions now given over to chance and empiricism.

In the second section of the *Naturphilosophie*, the Physics, we change to a philosophical consideration of the concepts involved in such natural phenomena as concentrate in themselves, as it were, the complex balanced unity that we find in a solar system. We thus take a further step towards the self-explanatory, absolute unity, totally present in each of its phases, which it is the task of Nature to implement, and a further step away from the irrelevant side-by-sideness and external interference characteristic of the mechanical level. The Physics is by far the hardest part of Hegel's Nature-philosophy on account of its close engagement with the physical theory of his time, and the immense difficulty of tracing the sort of notional pattern that Hegel believed in through this wealth of ramifying material. This part of Hegel's work requires a detailed, paragraph-by-paragraph commentary by one as much versed in physical science and its history as in Hegelian concepts: it is not possible for me to provide such a commentary, and, even if I could, I could not do so within the limits of the present Introduction. The most I can hope to do is to hint at the philosophical point of the various stages distinguished. The Physics falls into three parts, concerned, respectively, with *pervasively universal* qualities of physical being, then with the various *specific* qualities which differentiate one sort of matter from another, and, lastly, with phenomena that exhibit *physical 'totality'*, i.e. situations in which different natural bodies act in a concert which anyone who is not a Hegelian philosopher tends to find 'mysterious'.

The universal side of physical individuality begins with Light, which is for Hegel a more telling denial of the possibility of mere side-by-sideness and externality that we have in a gravitating assembly like the solar system. There heavy bodies have a unifying centre outside of themselves, towards which and around which they clumsily tend, whereas in Light they have an immaterial, ideal manifestation of all to all, which is grotesquely misunderstood as involving the rays, particles, and pencils, and other barbarities of Newtonian optics. Light is no contingent feature of the material world: it may seem to be no more than a peculiar 'stuff' that travels, but its true essence lies in the necessary disclosure of everything to everything else. There are of course aspects of modern physics which endorse Hegel's view of the central place of light in the world. Light, further, is nothing without the presence of the various contrasting *dark* bodies which it makes manifest to one another, and whose differences as regards the light and the dark come out in the complex phenomena of colour.

The mention of the dark bodies which are the foil to light, leads Hegel on to consider their 'elements', in which connection he is reactionary enough to put in a plea for the four classical elements of Air, Fire, Water, and Earth, the new-fangled, modern elements such as Oxygen, Nitrogen, etc., being regarded as abstract aspects of the natural elements unnaturally forced into isolation. Air and Fire are said to exhibit a negative universality, passively receptive in the case of Air, and destructively active in the case of Fire, while Water represents a wholly characterless neutrality, and Earth a developed differentiation and definiteness of structure. It is not easy to make much of all this, though plainly there are basic phenomenological differences between the solid, the liquid, and the gaseous which are arguably necessary to any possible natural world. But just as the various bodies into which the solar system differentiates itself engage in an elaborate ballet which expresses their notional interdependence, so too the four elementary material substances engage in a meteorological ballet that expresses their basic unity and identity. Hegel here takes us back to a refreshing, Ionian stage of physics, and he also defends the Aristotelian view of a complete transmutation of element into element, and remorselessly attacks the view that water, air, etc., when they vanish, are in some latent way really present. This he holds to be a fiction of the reflective understanding, which is always bent on turning genuine transformations into mere jugglings with unchanging elements.

In the Physics of Specific Individuality we go on to the many ways in which matter varies its spatio-temporal occupancy, and so differentiates itself into many *sorts* of body. We have the Specific Gravity whereby matter ceases to be merely outside of itself, and varies the *intensity* of its heavy presence in space, a variation which the scientific understanding loves to distort into a mere change in the ratio of occupancy to void. In similar fashion matter varies in the degree of its cohesion or holding together: it is more or less brittle, more or less rigid, more or less ductile or malleable. It also varies in its capacity both to yield to the thrust of other bodies and then to recover its spread; we have the very Hegelian property of elasticity. Elasticity carried to a further extreme carries us over into sound, where, according to Hegel, extended body craves a momentary remission from extension, transforming itself into something purely qualitative, which again reverts to tranquil spreadoutness. This organic inner shiver (*Erzittern*) which despatializes and respatializes bodies, then gives rise to the secondary air or water vibration which merely transmits the sound. From elasticity and sound, matter, exhausted, swings back to the relaxed, formless fluidity of Heat. Highly coherent metallic bodies are more susceptible to such thermal collapse than less coherent bodies like wool. Specific heat shows us matter, even when thus reduced, still specifying and differentiating itself. Hegel makes merry over the substantialist theories of Heat which prevailed in his time.

The diremption of matter into the various species of bodies, leads, however, to a necessary reintegration of the same, and we have the Physics of Total Individuality, in which no body lives to itself alone, but necessarily functions and fulfils itself in a total community of bodies. Magnetism is the first manifestation of this essential community of dispersed matter. Here there are differences so essentially interdependent, and in a deep sense 'identical', as to reveal themselves in a paradoxical coming together of 'unlike' poles and a mutual repulsion of 'like' ones. The phenomena of magnetism were for Hegel, as for Schelling, of inexhaustible import, and it would be pardonable exaggeration to see in the whole of Hegel's philosophy an interpretation of magnetism. Hegel further points to magnetism as an instance of the *naïveté* of Nature, and its use of *existent abstraction* (*seiende Abstraktion*). Nature, like a child that misunderstands syntax, separates the inseparable, and gives each part of it a distinct location: it thus engenders the mystery of a motion which astonishes the abstract Understanding. This mystery of motion consists in the overcoming by Nature of a conceptual absurdity, a gambit which will of course not recommend itself to a contemporary logician. The regular structure of crystals, according to Hegel, manifests the same principles as magnetism, except that tranquil three-dimensionality has in them taken the place of urgent linearity (§ 315).

Hegel then goes on to discuss the varying relation of crystalline bodies to light shown in the phenomena of refraction and prismatic separation. In the case of the latter we have, as is to be expected, a passionate defence of Goethe's 'organic' colour-theory as against the mechanistic, pictorial thought of Newton. The details of Goethe's theory seem to us strange and unconvincing, but the belief that there is something both exhaustive and necessary in the arrangements of what we call 'colour-space' has become a commonplace in modern philosophy.

From colour we go on to electricity, which Hegel, like his time, sees more in the context of static electricity, of galvanic flashes and peals, than of the as yet largely unexplored and technologically unused, marvels of current-electricity. This leads Hegel on, however, to the still deeper engagement of chemical interaction, where we have the interdependent aspects of one unity masquerading as separate bodies, and then revealing their deeper identity in the dramatic act of chemical coming together and its resultant compound product. Hegel is of course unremittingly hostile to the analytic notion of the chemical elements as latently persisting in their compounds: like Aristotle, he believes in their temporary resolution into new forms of unity. Chemical interaction reveals, however, the deep notional *naïveté* of turning its elements into separately existent substances, and it therefore permits a return to the original state of separation *after* the elements have been united in what is their 'truth'. Chemical interaction being external, likewise depends on externalities, the chance conditions which make union and separation possible and necessary. Chemical interaction is, for Hegel, a stage towards the spontaneously self-differentiating, self-sustaining unity that we have in life, but a stage still dominated by a mechanical externality which the living organism more smoothly subordinates. It is to life, the supreme manifestation of Nature, that the dialectic of the natural Idea accordingly turns.

Hegel's Organics can fortunately be treated more summarily than his Physics, since its foundations are in Aristotelian teleology, and since in it Hegel is in his home territory, finding in Life an inherent intelligibility that is with difficulty coaxed out of the lifelessness of Mechanism or the half-life of Physics. The Organics divides into a geological, a botanical, and a zoological subsection. The first is interesting as showing Hegel's quasi-animistic view of the earth and its structure, as also his command of the facts of the geological record, which do not lead him to shrink from admitting that the earth existed for untold ages before life, and *a fortiori* before mind, arose upon it. This indefinite temporal pre-history is for Hegel philosophically uninteresting, since it is only when life and mind emerge that a true dialectic can begin: this should not, however, permit us to think that Hegel did not really *believe* in the facts of geological pre-history, or that he held a merely constructive, subjective view of the same. The truth of dispersed, mutually irrelevant matter lies in united, internally relevant spirit. Philosophically the latter is the Alpha, the former the Omega; *temporally*, however, matter is the Alpha and spirit the Omega, as is made clear at several points in the *Encyclopaedia* (§ 248 *Zus.* and § 448 *Zus.*), and the dependence of both matter and spirit on the Absolute Idea is not a dependence on any conscious mind. Hegel, however, was so set in his anti-evolutionism as to believe that the fossils found in the geological record were really expressions of an 'organic-plastic' impulse operating in inorganic matter, which anticipated, though it did not achieve, life. (The sex-life of plants is in the same way a mere anticipation of the true sex-life of animals.) True self-explanatory unity only gleams through unorganized, geological Nature: it makes its first, explicit appearance in the vegetable organism.

Hegel tells us that the vegetable organism is imperfectly organic because imperfectly individualized: the parts of a plant are separable without damage to the whole, and the whole plant can often be regenerated from an inconsiderable fragment. This vaguely extensible individualization makes sexual reproduction a superfluity for plants, a rite whose full meaning presupposes the definite individualization that we find in the animal world. A plant's lack of true unity also makes it incapable of gathering the dispersed world together in sensation, or of modifying it through independent bodily movement. And the plant's self, like the centre of gravitating bodies, is located outside of it in the sun, towards whose light and warmth it must perpetually turn. Plants are best understood as imperfect anticipations of animals, to whose form of life the dialectic accordingly moves.

Hegel's account of animal life involves a vast amount of classification and detailed documentation into which we cannot enter. The Kantian view of the organism as a self-sustaining, immanently teleological system, in which every organ and function is both a means and an end to every other, and the whole only aims at itself and its continued being and functioning, is persuasively argued for, and the varied bodily organs studied in the light of this conception. The animal organism, further, presupposes an environment, an environing 'Other', which it is its task to receive sensitively, to transform practically, and in some cases to absorb and assimilate to itself. The environment, on Hegel's view, is really an adjunct of the organism, an adjunct whose whole destiny lies in its use by the latter: in generating sensations, stimulating reactions, and, in the last resort, being absorbed and eaten, it fulfils its true self. It is not our business to adjust ourselves to environmental bodies: they exist to be seen, handled, and in the ultimate devoured by us. It is curious and touching that a dialectical idealism such as Hegel's should lay so much stress on eating.

The animal organism also has its 'Other' in other organisms of the same species, for the species, like the individual, has a real, dynamic meaning in Nature. In sexual intercourse and reproduction we have the animal species, as a living reality exemplified in various limited, transitory individual specimens, actively exhibiting itself in a creative connection among such individuals, and instantiating itself in an open infinity of ever new generations. The ever-unfinished character of the generative series thus arising, and the loss of successful livingness which also sets in from the very first moment of each individual's existence, and terminates in disease and death, points, however, to the 'contradiction' in the embodiment of the species in finite corporeal individuals, and thereby also points to the more perfect, interior, conscious realization of self-explanatory unity that we have in Spirit or Mind. In Spirit or Mind, ultimately understood as something that transcends the vanishing individual, and is common to all individuals, the dispersion of spatio-temporal existence can truly be overcome, as it cannot be in corporeal, perishing organisms. With this Nature has had its say in the Absolute Dialectic, and the syllogism of which it is the Middle Term (in one of its readings) passes on to its third, Major Term, Spirit of Mind.

There are a great number of general reflections prompted by Hegel's Philosophy of Nature. It points, in the first place, to the necessity of having a philosophy of Nature as such, or of the Idea of *a* Nature in general, if we are to understand the detail of Nature as learnt from experience. A natural world has more to its meaning and being than the mere joint existence of a large number of entities, whose classification and arrangement is all a matter of detailed empirical encounter: one can learn from experience only within the bounds of a framework which makes learning from experience possible. One must know what sort of thing a Nature in general terms is, in order to plot and document the ways of the particular Nature in which one's lot is cast. This is not only the doctrine of Hegel and of classical German idealism generally, but also of Husserl in the Second Book of his *Ideas towards a Pure Phenomenology*. Within the limits of his basic rationalism, Hegel is infinitely willing to learn from experience, either by conceding the existence of innumerable factual details of which no precise philosophical understanding is possible, and which are necessary only in the higher-order sense in which there must be contingencies, or, more importantly, by allowing that our understanding of a notionally basic distinction may in the first case be empirical. It is by *seeing* unity-in-differentiation differently at work in Light, Magnetism, Electricity, Reproduction, etc., that we become aware of what the Absolute as an articulate, living piece of concrete dialectic is trying to do or to say, or if one likes the static phrase, what it is.

The particular analysis that Hegel gives of Nature as such would of course be profoundly suspect from the point of view of the transcendent, creative absolutism of the Jewish-Christian tradition, or that of the mechanistic materialism which has dominated natural science since the time of Descartes, or from the standpoint of the absolutistic non-absolutism which prevails in modern philosophy. Hegel's view of Nature is, in fact, a carrying to the limit of an immanent, Aristotelian teleology, in which Nature is to be understood as throughout working towards an end which will ultimately carry it beyond itself. It is arguable that this immanent teleology is a better and less prejudiced foundation for empirical investigations than the half-formulated absolutisms current in natural science. Thus in investigating the working of the nervous system, especially in its non-conscious phases, we shall be open to the possibility of finding something that is not to be found at the merely chemical level, but which also is not to be found at the fully conscious level, but represents a stage in between. Nervous matter has undoubtedly some of the properties of fully conscious discrimination and decision, and can be held to be responsive even to universals and their ideal connections, but this does not mean that it can do all that is done in the focus of inner enjoyment, vision, and creation. It is arguable, further, that the teleological absolutism of Hegel is more satisfactory internally than the alternative absolutisms mentioned above. For it *requires* the lower forms of being which lead up to the higher, conscious forms of integration, whereas they, if taken as absolute, do not require these last. One has, in fact, the old choice of regarding the higher integrations as queer offthrows of an infinitely improbable lower-order accident, or as the explanatory foundation of all that leads up to them. The audacious anthropocentricism of the latter opinion may give one pause, but the sheer dualism of the former gives one more than pause: it is, from the standpoint of a logic that demands explanation, not as a luxury but a necessity, logically impossible.

We may admire Hegel, further, for the thoroughgoing realism of his approach to Nature. The ultimate ground of nature may be in the Absolute Idea, but it is not to be found in the mental constructions of conscious beings, even of a supreme conscious being. The mythology of the original, chaotic 'manifold', and of the synthetic mental activities which organized it, a mythology infinitely more obscure and dubious than the mythology of Hesiod or the Ionians or the eighteenth-century cosmogonists, has simply no place in Hegel. It is nowhere in evidence, and, where mentioned, it is denied. This part of the doctrine of Kant, Fichte, and Schelling Hegel never took over. His idealism is that of the Greeks, and in this idealism Nature, though subordinate, has an indefeasible place and right, and is to be interpreted in terms of its own categories, which, though essentially linked with the ideal and the subjective, are reducible to neither. We may also admire Hegel for his willingness, unusual in philosophers, to read, digest, and take full account of so much detailed scientific material, a willingness which puts him on a pinnacle of scientific information and understanding shared only by Aristotle.

J. N. FINDLAY

Yale University
September 1968

TRANSLATOR'S FOREWORD

This translation of Hegel's *Philosophy of Nature* was begun many years ago, but for various reasons had to be laid aside when less than a fifth part of the whole work had been completed. It was Professor J. N. Findlay who encouraged me to complete the translation in order that this neglected but important work should be made accessible to English-speaking students. The translation has greatly benefited from his invaluable assistance, and I wish to record my indebtedness to him for his unstinted help so generously given. I am also greatly indebted to Sir Malcolm Knox for many suggestions in connection with the translation of the *Introduction* and *Mechanics* which have been adopted in the text. Vera's French translation of the *Naturphilosophie* made in 1863 with its valuable footnotes on the science of that period has also been consulted with advantage.

CONTENTS

---

* *Note.* In the third edition of the *Encyclopaedia* (1830) these Paragraphs appear in the following order:

INTRODUCTION

Zusatz. It can be said perhaps that in our time, philosophy does not enjoy any special favour and liking. At least, it is no longer recognized, as it was formerly, that the study of philosophy must constitute the indispensable introduction and foundation for all further scientific education and professional study. But this much may be assumed *without hesitation* as correct, that the *Philosophy of Nature* in particular is in considerable disfavour. I do not intend to deal at length with the extent to which this prejudice against the Philosophy of Nature in particular, is justified; and yet I cannot altogether pass it over. What is seldom absent from a period of great intellectual ferment has, of course, happened in connection with the *idea of the Philosophy of Nature* as recently expounded. It can be said that in the first satisfaction afforded by its discovery, this idea met with crude treatment at unskilled hands, instead of being cultivated by thinking Reason; and it has been brought low not so much by its opponents as by its friends. It has in many respects, in fact for the most part, been transformed into an external formalism and perverted into a thoughtless instrument for superficial thinking and fanciful imagination. I do not want to characterize in any further detail the eccentricities for which the Idea, or rather its lifeless forms, have been used. I said more about this some while ago in the preface to the *Phenomenology of Spirit.* It is, then, not to be wondered at that a more thoughtful examination of Nature, as well as crude empiricism, a knowing led by the Idea, as well as the external, abstract Understanding, alike turned their backs on a procedure which was as fantastic as it was pretentious, which itself made a chaotic mixture of crude empiricism and uncomprehended thoughts, of a purely capricious exercise of the imagination and the most commonplace way of reasoning by superficial analogy, and which passed off such a hotchpotch as the Idea, Reason, philosophical science, divine knowledge, and pretended that the complete lack of method and scientific procedure was the acme of scientific procedure. It is on account of such charlatanism that the Philosophy of Nature, especially Schelling's has become discredited.

It is quite another thing, however, to reject the Philosophy of Nature itself because of such aberration and misunderstanding of the Idea. It not infrequently happens that those who are obsessed by a hatred of philosophy, welcome abuses and perversions of it, because they use the perversion to disparage the science itself and they hope to make their reasoned rejection of the perversion a justification in some vague way for their claim to have hit philosophy itself.

It might seem appropriate first of all, in view of the existing misunderstandings and prejudices in regard to the Philosophy of Nature, to set forth the *true* Notion of this science. But this opposition which we encounter at the outset, is to be regarded as something contingent and external, and all such opposition we can straightway leave on one side. Such a treatment of the subject tends to become polemical and is not a procedure in which one can take any pleasure. What might be instructive in it falls partly within the science itself, but it would not be so instructive as to justify reducing still further the available space which is already restricted enough for the wealth of material contained in an *Encyclopaedia*. We shall therefore content ourselves with the observation made above; it can serve as a kind of protest against that style of philosophizing about Nature, as an assurance that such a style is not to be expected in this exposition. That style, it is true, often appears brilliant and entertaining, arousing astonishment at least; but it can only satisfy those who openly confess to seeing in the Philosophy of Nature simply a brilliant display of fireworks, thus sparing themselves the effort of thought. What we are engaged on here, is not an affair of imagination and fancy, but of the Notion, of Reason.

In keeping with this standpoint, we do not propose to discuss here the Notion, the task, the manner and method, of the Philosophy of Nature; but it is quite in place to preface a scientific work with a statement of the specific character of its subject-matter and purpose, and what is to be considered in it, and how it is to be considered. The opposition between the Philosophy of Nature and a perverted form of it, disappears of its own accord when we determine its Notion more precisely. The science of philosophy is a circle in which each member has an antecedent and a successor, but in the philosophical encyclopaedia, the Philosophy of Nature appears as only one circle in the whole, and therefore the procession of Nature from the eternal Idea, its creation, the proof that there necessarily is a Nature, lies in the preceding exposition (§ 244); here we have to presuppose it as known. If we do want to determine what the Philosophy of Nature is, our best method is to separate it off from the subject-matter with which it is contrasted; for all determining requires two terms. In the first place, we find the Philosophy of Nature in a peculiar relationship to natural science in general, to physics, natural history, and physiology; it is itself physics, but *rational physics*. It is at this point that we have to grasp what the Philosophy of Nature is and, in particular, to determine its relationship to physics. In so doing, one may imagine that this contrast between natural science and the Philosophy of Nature is something new. The Philosophy of Nature may perhaps be regarded prima facie as a new science; this is certainly correct in one sense, but in another sense it is not. For it is ancient, as ancient as any study of Nature at all; it is not distinct from the latter and it is, in fact, older than physics; Aristotelian physics, for example, is far more a Philosophy of Nature than it is physics. It is only in modern times that the two have been separated. We already see this separation in the science which, as cosmology, was distinguished in Wolff's philosophy from physics, and though supposed to be a metaphysics of the world or of Nature was confined to the wholly abstract categories of the Understanding. This metaphysics was, of course, further removed from physics than is the Philosophy of Nature as we now understand it. In connection with this distinction between physics and the Philosophy of Nature, and of the specific character of each as contrasted with the other, it must be noted, right from the start, that the two do not lie so far apart as is at first assumed. Physics and natural history are called empirical sciences *par excellence*, and they profess to belong entirely to the sphere of perception and experience, and in this way to be opposed to the Philosophy of Nature, i.e. to a knowledge of Nature from thought. The fact is, however, that the principal charge to be brought against physics is that it contains much more thought than it admits and is aware of, and that it is better than it supposes itself to be; or if, perhaps, all thought in physics is to be counted a defect, then it is worse than it supposes itself to be. Physics and the Philosophy of Nature, therefore, are not distinguished from each other as perception and thought, but only by *the kind and manner of their thought*; they are both a thinking apprehension of Nature.

It is this which we shall consider *first*, i.e. how thought is present in physics: then, *secondly*, we have to consider what Nature is: and, *thirdly*, to give the divisions of the philosophy of Nature.

A. *Ways of considering Nature*

In order to find the *Notion of the Philosophy of Nature*, we must *first* of all indicate the Notion of the knowledge of Nature in general, and *secondly*, develop the *distinction between physics and the Philosophy of Nature*.

What is Nature? We propose to answer this general question by reference to the knowledge of Nature and the Philosophy of Nature. Nature confronts us as a riddle and a problem, whose solution both attracts and repels us: attracts us, because Spirit is presaged in Nature; repels us, because Nature seems an alien existence, in which Spirit does not find itself. That is why Aristotle said that philosophy started from wonder. We start to perceive, we collect facts about the manifold formations and laws of Nature; this procedure, on its own account, runs on into endless detail in all directions, and just because no end can be perceived in it, this method does not satisfy us. And in all this wealth of knowledge the question can again arise, or perhaps come to us for the first time: What is Nature? It remains a problem. When we see Nature's processes and transformations we want to grasp its simple essence, to compel this Proteus to cease its transformations and show itself to us and declare itself to us; so that it may not present us with a variety of ever new forms, but in simpler fashion bring to our consciousness in language what it *is*. This inquiry after the *being* of something has a number of meanings, and can often refer simply to its name, as in the question: What kind of a plant *is* this? or it can refer to perception if the name is given; if I do not know what a compass is, I get someone to show me the instrument, and I say, now I know what a compass is. 'Is' can also refer to status, as for example when we ask: What is this man? But this is not what we mean when we ask: What is Nature? It is the meaning to be attached to this question that we propose to examine here, remembering that we want to acquire a knowledge of the Philosophy of Nature.

We could straightway resort to the philosophical Idea and say that the Philosophy of Nature ought to give us the Idea of Nature. But to begin thus might be confusing. For we must grasp the Idea itself as concrete and thus apprehend its various specifications and then bring them together. In order therefore to possess the Idea, we must traverse a series of specifications through which it is first there for us. If we now take these up in forms which are familiar to us, and say that we want to approach Nature as thinkers, there are, in the first place, other ways of approaching Nature which I will mention, not for the sake of completeness, but because we shall find in them the elements or moments which are requisite for a knowledge of the Idea and which individually reach our consciousness earlier in other *ways of considering Nature*. In so doing, we shall come to the point where the characteristic feature of our inquiry becomes prominent. Our approach to Nature is partly practical and partly theoretical. An examination of the theoretical approach will reveal a contradiction which, thirdly, will lead us to our standpoint; to resolve the contradiction we must incorporate what is peculiar to the practical approach, and by this means practical and theoretical will be united and integrated into a totality.

§ 245

In man's *practical* approach to Nature, the latter is, for him, something immediate and external; and he himself is an external and therefore sensuous individual, although in relation to natural objects, he correctly regards himself as *end*. A consideration of Nature according to this relationship yields the standpoint of *finite* teleology (§ 205). In this, we find the correct presupposition that Nature does not itself contain the absolute, final end (§§ 207–11). But if this way of considering the matter starts from particular, *finite* ends, on the one hand it makes them into presuppositions whose contingent content may in itself be even insignificant and trivial. On the other hand, the end-relationship demands for itself a deeper mode of treatment than that appropriate to external and finite relationships, namely, the mode of treatment of the Notion, which in its own general nature is immanent and therefore is immanent in Nature as such.

Zusatz. The practical approach to Nature is, in general, determined by appetite, which is self-seeking; need impels us to use Nature for our own advantage, to wear her out, to wear her down, in short, to annihilate her. And here, two characteristics at once stand out. (a) The practical approach is concerned only with individual products of Nature, or with individual aspects of those products. The necessities and the wit of man have found an endless variety of ways of using and mastering Nature. Sophocles says:

> οὐδὲν ἀνθρώπου δεινότερον πέλει,—
> ἄπορος ἐπ' οὐδὲν ἔρχεται.

Whatever forces Nature develops and lets loose against man—cold, wild beasts, water, fire—he knows means to counter them; indeed, he takes these means from Nature and uses them against herself. The cunning of his reason enables him to preserve and maintain himself in face of the forces of Nature, by sheltering behind other products of Nature, and letting these suffer her destructive attacks. Nature herself, however, in her universal aspect, he cannot overcome in this way, nor can he turn her to his own purposes. (β) The other characteristic of the practical approach is that, since it is *our* end which is paramount, not natural things themselves, we convert the latter into means, the destiny of which is determined by us, not by the things themselves; an example of this is the conversion of food into blood. (γ) What is achieved is our satisfaction, our self-feeling, which had been disturbed by a lack of some kind or another. The negation of myself which I suffer within me in hunger, is at the same time present as an other than myself, as something to be consumed; my act is to annul this contradiction by making this other identical with myself, or by restoring my self-unity through sacrificing the thing.

The teleological standpoint which was formerly so popular, was based, it is true, on a reference to Spirit, but it was confined to external purposiveness only, and took Spirit in the sense of finite Spirit caught up in natural ends; but because the finite ends which natural objects were shown to subserve were so trivial, teleology has become discredited as an argument for the wisdom of God. The notion of end, however, is not merely external to Nature, as it is, for example, when I say that the wool of the sheep is there only to provide me with clothes; for this often results in trivial reflections, as in the *Xenia*,* where God's wisdom is admired in that He has provided cork-trees for bottle-stoppers, or herbs for curing disordered stomachs, and cinnabar for cosmetics. The notion

* Goethe–Schiller, *Xenien* (1796), No. 286.

of end as immanent in natural objects is their simple determinateness, e.g. the seed of a plant, which contains the real possibility of all that is to exist in the tree, and thus, as a purposive activity, is directed solely to self-preservation. This notion of end was already recognized by Aristotle, too, and he called this activity the *nature of a thing*; the true teleological method—and this is the highest—consists, therefore, in the method of regarding Nature as free in her own peculiar vital activity.

§ 246

What is now called *physics* was formerly called *natural philosophy*, and it is also a *theoretical*, and indeed a *thinking* consideration of Nature; but, on the one hand, it does not start from determinations which are external to Nature, like those ends already mentioned; and secondly, it is directed to a knowledge of the *universal* aspect of Nature, a universal which is also *determined* within itself —directed to a knowledge of forces, laws and genera, whose content must not be a simple aggregate, but arranged in orders and classes, must present itself as an organism. As the Philosophy of Nature is a *comprehending* (*begreifend*) treatment, it has as its object the same *universal*, but *explicitly*, and it considers this universal in its *own immanent necessity* in accordance with the self-determination of the Notion.

Remark

The relation of philosophy to the empirical sciences was discussed in the general introduction [to the *Encyclopaedia*]. Not only must philosophy be in agreement with our empirical knowledge of Nature, but the *origin* and *formation* of the Philosophy of Nature presupposes and is conditioned by empirical physics. However, the course of a science's origin and the preliminaries of its construction are one thing, while the science itself is another. In the latter, the former can no longer appear as the foundation of the science; here, the foundation must be the necessity of the Notion.

It has already been mentioned that, in the progress of philosophical knowledge, we must not only give an account of the object *as determined by its Notion*, but we must also name the *empirical* appearance corresponding to it, and we must show that the appearance does, in fact, correspond to its Notion. However, this is not an appeal to experience in regard to the necessity of the content. Even less admissible is an appeal to what is called *intuition* (*Anschauung*), which is usually nothing but a fanciful and sometimes fantastic exercise of the imagination on the lines of *analogies*, which may be more or less significant, and which impress determinations and schemata on objects only *externally* (§ 231, Remark).

Zusatz. In the theoretical approach to Nature (α) the first point is that we stand back from natural objects, leaving them as they are and adjusting ourselves to them. Here, we start from our sense-knowledge of Nature. However, if physics were based solely on perceptions, and perceptions were nothing more than the evidence of the senses, then the physical act would consist only in seeing, hearing, smelling, etc., and animals, too, would in this way be physicists. But what sees, hears, etc., is a spirit, a thinker. Now if we said that, in our theoretical approach to Nature, we left things free, this applied only partly to the outer senses, for these are themselves partly theoretical and partly practical (§ 358); it is only our ideational faculty (*Vorstellen*), our intelligence, that has this free relationship to things. We can, of course, consider things practically, as means; but then knowing is itself only a means, not an end in itself. (β) The second bearing of things on us is that things acquire the character of universality for us or that we transform them into universals. The more thought enters into our representation of things, the less do they retain their naturalness, their singularity and immediacy. The wealth of natural forms, in all their infinitely manifold configuration, is impoverished by the all-pervading power of thought, their vernal life and glowing colours die and fade away. The rustle of Nature's life is silenced in the stillness of thought; her abundant life, wearing a thousand wonderful and delightful shapes, shrivels into arid forms and shapeless generalities resembling a murky northern fog. (γ) These two characteristics are not only opposed to the two practical ones, but we also find that the theoretical approach is self-contradictory, for it seems to bring about the direct opposite of what it intends; for we want to know the Nature that really is, not something that is not. But instead of leaving Nature as she is, and taking her as she is in truth, instead of simply perceiving her, we make her into something quite different. In thinking things, we transform them into something universal; but things are singular and the Lion as Such does not exist. We give them the form of something subjective, of something produced by us and belonging to us, and belonging to us in our specifically human character: for natural objects do not think, and are not presentations or thoughts. But according to the second characteristic of the theoretical approach referred to above, it is precisely this inversion which does take place; in fact, it might seem that what we are beginning is made impossible for us at the outset. The theoretical approach begins with the arrest of appetite, is disinterested, lets things exist and go on just as they are; with this attitude to Nature, we have straightway established a duality of object and subject and their separation, something here and something yonder. Our intention, however, is rather to grasp, to comprehend Nature, to make her ours, so that she is not something alien and yonder. Here, then, comes the difficulty: How do we, as subjects, come into contact with objects? If we venture to bridge this gulf and mislead ourselves along that line and so think this Nature, we make Nature, which is an Other than we are, into an Other than she is. Both theoretical approaches are also directly opposed to each other: we transform things into universals, or make them our own, and yet as natural objects they are supposed to have a free, self-subsistent being. This, therefore, is the point with which we are concerned in regard to the nature of cognition—this is the interest of philosophy.

But the Philosophy of Nature is in the unfavourable position of having to demonstrate its existence, and, in order to justify it, we must trace it back to something familiar. Mention must be made here of a special solution of the contradiction between subjectivity and objectivity, a solution which has been made familiar both by science and religion—in the latter case in the past—and which makes short shrift of the whole difficulty. The union of the two determinations is, namely, what is called the *primal state of innocence*, where Spirit is identical with Nature, and the spiritual eye is placed directly in the centre of Nature; whereas the standpoint of the divided consciousness is the fall of man from the eternal, divine unity. This unity is represented as a primal intuition (*Anschauung*), a Reason, which is at the same time one with fantasy, i.e. it forms sensuous shapes, and in so doing gives them a rational significance. This intuitive Reason is the divine Reason; for God, we are entitled to say, is that Being in whom Spirit and Nature are united, in whom intelligence at the same time also has being and shape. The eccentricities of the Philosophy of Nature originate partly in such an idea, namely in the idea that, although nowadays we no longer dwell in this paradisal state, there still are favoured ones, seers to whom God imparts true knowledge and wisdom in sleep; or that man, even without being so favoured, can at least by faith in it, transport himself into a state where the inner side of Nature is immediately revealed to him, and where he need only let fancies occur to him, i.e. give free play to his fancy, in order to declare prophetically what is true. This visionary state, about the source of which nothing further can be said, has, in general, been regarded as the consummation of the scientific faculty; and it is, perhaps, added that such a state of perfect knowledge preceded the present history of the world, and that, since man's fall from his unity with Nature, there has remained for us in myths, traditions or in other vestiges, still some fragments and faint echoes of that spiritual, illuminated state. These fragments have formed the basis for the further religious education of humanity, and are the source of all scientific knowledge. If it had not been made so difficult to know the truth, but one needed only to sit on the tripod and utter oracles, then, of course, the labour of thought would not be needed.

In order to state briefly what is the defect of this conception, we must at once admit that there is something lofty in it which at first glance makes a strong appeal. But this unity of intelligence and intuition, of the inwardness of Spirit and its relation to externality, must be, not the beginning, but the goal, not an immediate, but a resultant unity. A natural unity of thought and intuition is that of the child and the animal, and this can at the most be called feeling, not spirituality. But man must have eaten of the tree of the knowledge of good and evil and must have gone through the labour and activity of thought in order to become what he is, having overcome this separation between himself and Nature. The immediate unity is thus only an abstract, implicit truth, not the actual truth; for not only must the content be true, but the form also. The healing of this breach must be in the form of the knowing Idea, and the moments of the solution must be sought in consciousness itself. It is not a question of betaking oneself to abstraction and vacuity, of taking refuge in the negation of knowing; on the contrary, consciousness must preserve itself in that we must use the ordinary consciousness itself to refute the assumptions which have given rise to the contradiction.

The difficulty arising from the one-sided assumption of the theoretical consciousness, that natural objects confront us as permanent and impenetrable objects, is directly negatived by the practical approach which acts on the absolutely idealistic belief that individual things are nothing in themselves. The defect of appetite, from the side of its relationship to things, is not that it is realistic towards them, but that it is all too idealistic. Philosophical, true idealism consists in nothing else but laying down that the truth about things is that as such immediately single, i.e. sensuous things, they are only a show, an appearance (*Schein*). Of a metaphysics prevalent today which maintains that we cannot know things because they are absolutely shut to us, it might be said that not even the animals are so stupid as these metaphysicians; for they go after things, seize and consume them. The same thing is laid down in the second aspect of the theoretical approach referred to above, namely, that we think natural objects. Intelligence familiarizes itself with things, not of course in their sensuous existence, but by thinking them and positing their content in itself; and in, so to speak, adding form, universality, to the practical ideality which, by itself, is only negativity, it gives an affirmative character to the negativity of the singular. This universal aspect of things is not something subjective, something belonging to us: rather is it, in contrast to the transient phenomenon, the noumenon, the true, objective, actual nature of things themselves, like the Platonic Ideas, which are not somewhere afar off in the beyond, but exist in individual things as their substantial genera. Not until one does violence to Proteus—that is not until one turns one's back on the sensuous appearance of Nature—is he compelled to speak the truth. The inscription on the veil of Isis, 'I am that which was, is, and will be, and my veil no mortal hath lifted', melts away before thought. 'Nature', Hamann therefore rightly says, 'is a Hebrew word written only with consonants and the understanding must point it.'

Now although the empirical treatment of Nature has this category of universality in common with the Philosophy of Nature, the empiricists are sometimes uncertain whether this universal is subjective or objective; one can often hear it said that these classes and orders are only made as aids to cognition. This uncertainty is still more apparent in the search for distinguishing marks, not in the belief that they are essential, objective characteristics of things, but that they only serve our convenience to help us to distinguish things. If nothing more than that were involved, we might, e.g., take the lobe of the ear as the sign of man, for no animal has it; but we feel at once that such a characteristic is not sufficient for a knowledge of the essential nature of man. When, however, the universal is characterized as law, force, matter, then we cannot allow that it counts only as an external form and a subjective addition; on the contrary, objective reality is attributed to laws, forces are immanent, and matter is the true nature of the thing itself. Something similar may be conceded in regard to genera too, namely that they are not just a grouping of similarities, an abstraction made by us, that they not only have common features but that they are the objects' own inner essence; the orders not only serve to give us a general view, but form a graduated scale of Nature itself. The distinguishing marks, too, should be the universal, substantial element of the genus. Physics looks on these universals as its triumph: one can say even that, unfortunately, it goes too far in its generalizations. Present-day philosophy is called the philosophy of identity: this name can be much more appropriately given to that physics which simply ignores specific differences (*Bestimmtheiten*), as occurs, for example, in the current theory of electro-chemistry in which magnetism, electricity, and chemistry are regarded as one and the same. It is the weakness of physics that it is too much dominated by the category of identity; for identity is the fundamental category of the Understanding.

The Philosophy of Nature takes up the material which physics has prepared for it empirically, at the point to which physics has brought it, and reconstitutes it, so that experience is not its final warrant and base. Physics must therefore work into the hands of philosophy, in order that the latter may translate into the Notion the abstract universal transmitted to it, by showing how this universal, as an intrinsically necessary whole, proceeds from the Notion. The philosophical way of putting the facts is no mere whim, once in a way to walk on one's head for a change, after having walked for a long while on one's legs, or once in a way to see our everyday face bedaubed with paint: no, it is because the method of physics does not satisfy the Notion, that we have to go further.

What distinguishes the Philosophy of Nature from physics is, more precisely, the kind of metaphysics used by them both; for metaphysics is nothing else but the entire range of the universal determinations of thought, as it were, the diamond net into which everything is brought and thereby first made intelligible. Every educated consciousness has its metaphysics, an instinctive way of thinking, the absolute power within us of which we become master only when we make it in turn the object of our knowledge. Philosophy in general has, as philosophy, other categories than those of the ordinary consciousness: all education (*Bildung*) reduces to the distinction of categories. All revolutions, in the sciences no less than in world history, originate solely from the fact that Spirit, in order to understand and comprehend itself with a view to possessing itself, has changed its categories, comprehending itself more truly, more deeply, more intimately, and more in unity with itself. Now the inadequacy of the thought-determinations used in physics can be traced to two points which are closely bound up with each other. (a) The universal of physics is abstract or only formal; its determination is not immanent in it and it does not pass over into particularity. (β) The determinate content falls for that very reason outside the universal; and so is split into fragments, into parts which are isolated and detached from each other, devoid of any necessary connection, and it is just this which stamps it as only finite. If we examine a flower, for example, our understanding notes its particular qualities; chemistry dismembers and analyses it. In this way, we separate colour, shape of the leaves, citric acid, etheric oil, carbon, hydrogen, etc.; and now we say that the plant consists of all these parts.

> If you want to describe life and gather its meaning,
> To drive out its spirit must be your beginning,
> Then though fast in your hand lie the parts one by one
> The spirit that linked them, alas is gone
> And 'Nature's Laboratory' is only a name
> That the chemist bestows on't to hide his own shame.[1]

as Goethe says. Spirit cannot remain at this stage of thinking in terms of detached, unrelated concepts (*Verstandesreflexion*) and there are two ways in which it can advance beyond it. (a) The naïve mind (*der unbefangene Geist*), when it vividly contemplates Nature, as in the suggestive examples we often come across in Goethe, feels the life and the universal relationship in Nature; it divines that the universe is an organic whole and a totality pervaded by Reason, and it also feels in single forms of life an

---

[1] *Faust*, part I, sc. 4. (Wallace's rendering, but see his note on p. 398 of his translation of the *Encyclopaedia Logic*. Only the last four lines are quoted, though in a different order, by Hegel, and a prose version of them would run: 'Nature's laboratory' the chemist calls it, mocking himself and confessing his ignorance. The parts, certainly, he holds in his hand, but alas the spiritual link is missing.)

intimate oneness with itself; but even if we put together all those ingredients of the flower the result is still not a flower. And so, in the
Philosophy of Nature, people have fallen back on intuition (*Anschauung*)
and set it above reflective thought; but this is a mistake, for one cannot
philosophize out of intuition. (β) What is intuited must also be thought,
the isolated parts must be brought back by thought to simple universality; this thought unity is the Notion, which contains the specific
differences, but as an immanent self-moving unity. The determinations
of philosophical universality are not indifferent; it is the universality which
fulfils itself, and which, in its diamantine identity, also contains difference.

The true infinite is the unity of itself and the finite; and this, now, is
the category of philosophy and so, too, of the Philosophy of Nature. If
genera and forces are the inner side of Nature, the universal, in face of
which the outer and individual is only transient, then still a third stage is
demanded, namely, the inner side of the inner side, and this, according to
what has been said, would be the unity of the universal and the particular.

> To Nature's heart there penetrates no mere created mind:
> Too happy if she but display the outside of her rind.

* * * *

> I swear—of course but to myself—as rings within my ears
> That same old warning o'er and o'er again for sixty years,
> And thus a thousand times I answer in my mind:—
> With gladsome and ungrudging hand metes Nature from her store:
> She keeps not back the core,
> Nor separates the rind,
> But all in each both rind and core has evermore combined.[1]

In grasping this inner side, the one-sidedness of the theoretical and
practical approaches is transcended, and at the same time each side
receives its due. The former contains a universal without determinateness,
the latter an individuality without a universal; the cognition which comprehends (*begreifendes Erkennen*) is the middle term in which universality
does not remain on *this* side, in *me*, over against the individuality of the
objects: on the contrary, while it stands in a negative relation to things and
assimilates them to itself, it equally finds individuality in them and does
not encroach upon their independence, or interfere with their free self-
determination. The cognition which comprehends is thus the unity of the
theoretical and practical approaches: the negation of individuality is, as
negation of the negative, the affirmative universality which gives permanence to its determinations; for the true individuality is at the same time
within itself a universality.

As regards the objections which can be raised against this standpoint,

---

[1] Goethe, *Zur Morphologie*, vol. i, part 3, 1820. (Wallace's rendering in the
Encyclopaedia Logic, pp. 421-2.)

the first question which can be asked is: How does the universal determine itself? How does the infinite become finite? A more concrete form
of the question is: How has God come to create the world? God is, of
course, conceived to be a subject, a self-subsistent actuality far removed
from the world; but such an abstract infinity, such a universality which had
the particular outside it, would itself be only one side of the relation, and
therefore itself only a particular and finite: it is characteristic of the
Understanding that it unwittingly nullifies the very determination it
posits, and thus does the very opposite of what it intends. The particular
is supposed to be separate from the universal, but this very separateness,
this independence, makes it a universal, and so what is present is only the
unity of the universal and the particular. God reveals Himself in two different ways: as Nature and as Spirit. Both manifestations are temples of
God which He fills, and in which He is present. God, as an abstraction,
is not the true God, but only as the living process of positing His Other,
the world, which, comprehended in its divine form is His Son; and it is
only in unity with His Other, in Spirit, that God is Subject. This, now,
is the specific character and the goal of the Philosophy of Nature, that
Spirit finds in Nature its own essence, i.e. the Notion, finds its counter-
part in her. The study of Nature is thus the liberation of Spirit in her, for
Spirit is present in her in so far as it is in relation, not with an Other, but
with itself. This is also the liberation of Nature; implicitly she is Reason,
but it is through Spirit that Reason as such first emerges from Nature
into existence. Spirit has the certainty which Adam had when he looked
on Eve: 'This is flesh of my flesh, and bone of my bone.' Thus Nature is
the bride which Spirit weds. But is this certainty also truth? Since the
inner being of Nature is none other than the universal, then in our thoughts
of this inner being we are at home with ourselves. Truth in its subjective
meaning is the agreement of thought with the object: in its objective
meaning, truth is the agreement of the object with its own self, the
correspondence of its reality with its Notion. The Ego in its essence is
the Notion, which is equal to itself and pervades all things, and which,
because it retains the mastery over the particular differences, is the
universal which returns into itself. This Notion is directly the true Idea,
the divine Idea of the universe which alone is the Actual. Thus God
alone is the Truth, in Plato's words, the immortal Being whose body and
and soul are joined in a single nature. The first question here is: Why has
God willed to create Nature?

B. *The Notion of Nature*

§ 247

Nature has presented itself as the Idea in the form of *otherness*.
Since therefore the Idea is the negative of itself, or is *external to*

itself, Nature is not merely external in relation to this Idea (and to its subjective existence Spirit); the truth is rather that *externality* constitutes the specific character in which Nature, as Nature, exists.

Zusatz. If God is all-sufficient and lacks nothing, why does He disclose Himself in a sheer Other of Himself? The divine Idea is just this: to disclose itself, to posit this Other outside itself and to take it back again into itself, in order to be subjectivity and Spirit. The Philosophy of Nature itself belongs to this path of return; for it is that which overcomes the division between Nature and Spirit and assures to Spirit the knowledge of its essence in Nature. This, now, is the place of Nature in the whole; its determinateness is this, that the Idea determines itself, posits difference within itself, an Other, but in such a way that in its indivisible nature it is infinite goodness, imparting to its otherness and sharing with it its entire fullness of content. God, therefore, in determining Himself, remains equal to Himself; each of these moments is itself the whole Idea and must be posited as the divine totality. The different moments can be grasped under three different forms: the universal, the particular, and the individual. First, the different moments remain preserved in the eternal unity of the Idea; this is the Logos, the eternal Son of God as Philo conceived it. The other to this extreme is individuality, the form of finite Spirit. As a return into itself individuality is, indeed, Spirit; but, as otherness with exclusion of all others, it is finite or human Spirit; for finite spirits other than human beings do not concern us here. The individual man grasped as also in unity with the divine essence is the object of the Christian religion; and this is the most tremendous demand that can be made on him. The third form which concerns us here, the Idea in the mode of particularity, is Nature, which lies between the two extremes. This form presents the least difficulty for the Understanding; Spirit is posited as the contradiction existing explicitly, for the Idea in its infinite freedom, and again in the form of individuality, are in objective contradiction; but in Nature, the contradiction is only implicit or for us, the otherness appearing in the Idea as a quiescent form. In Christ, the contradiction is posited and overcome, as His life, passion, and resurrection: Nature is the son of God, but not as the Son, but as abiding in otherness—the divine Idea as held fast for a moment outside the divine love. Nature is Spirit estranged from itself; in Nature, Spirit lets itself go (*ausgelassen*), a Bacchic god unrestrained and unmindful of itself; in Nature, the unity of the Notion is concealed.

A rational consideration of Nature must consider how Nature is in its own self this process of becoming Spirit, of sublating its otherness—and how the Idea is present in each grade or level of Nature itself; estranged from the Idea, Nature is only the corpse of the Understanding. Nature is, however, only implicitly the Idea, and Schelling therefore called her a petrified intelligence, others even a frozen intelligence; but God does not remain petrified and dead; the very stones cry out and raise themselves to Spirit. God is subjectivity, activity, infinite actuosity, in which otherness has only a transient being, remaining implicit within the unity of the Idea, because it is itself this totality of the Idea. Since Nature is the Idea in the form of otherness, the Idea, comformable to its Notion, is not present in Nature as it is in and for itself, although nevertheless, Nature is one of the ways in which the Idea manifests itself, and is a necessary mode of the Idea. However, the fact that this mode of the Idea is Nature, is the second question to be discussed and demonstrated; to this end we must compare our definition with the ordinary idea of Nature and see whether the two correspond; this will occur in the sequel. In other respects, however, philosophy need not trouble itself about ordinary ideas, nor is it bound to realize in every respect what such ideas demand, for ideas are arbitrary; but still, generally speaking, the two must agree.

In connection with this fundamental determination of Nature, attention must be drawn to the metaphysical aspect which has been dealt with in the form of the question of the *eternity of the world*. It might be thought that we need pay no attention to metaphysics here; but this is the very place to bring it to notice, and we need not hesitate to do so, for it does not lead to prolixity and is readily dealt with. Now the metaphysics of Nature, i.e. Nature's essential and distinctive characteristic, is to be the Idea in the form of otherness, and this implies that the being of Nature is essentially ideality, or that, as only relative, Nature is essentially related to a First. The question of the eternity of the world (this is confused with Nature, since it is a collection of both spiritual and natural objects) has, in the first place, the meaning of the conception of time, of an eternity as it is called, of an infinitely long time, so that the world had no beginning in time; secondly, the question implies that Nature is conceived as uncreated, eternal, as existing independently of God. As regards this second meaning, it is completely set aside and eliminated by the distinctive character of Nature to be the Idea in its otherness. As regards the first meaning, after removing the sense of the absoluteness of the world, we are left only with eternity in connection with the conception of time.

About this, the following is to be said: (a) eternity is not before or after time, not before the creation of the world, nor when it perishes; rather is eternity the absolute present, the Now, without before and after. The world is created, is now being created, and has eternally been created; this presents itself in the form of the preservation of the world. Creating is the activity of the absolute Idea; the Idea of Nature, like the Idea as such, is eternal. (β) In the question whether the world or Nature, in its finitude, has a beginning in time or not, one thinks of the world or Nature as such, i.e. as the universal; and the true universal is the Idea, which we have already said is eternal. The finite, however, is temporal, it has a before and an after; and when the finite is our object we are in time. It has a beginning but not an absolute one; its time begins with it, and time belongs only to the sphere of finitude. Philosophy is timeless comprehension, of time too and of all things generally in their eternal mode. Having rid oneself of the conception of the absolute beginning of time, one assumes the opposite conception of an infinite time; but infinite time, when it is still conceived as time, not as sublated time, is also to be distinguished from eternity. It is not this time but another time, and again another time, and so on (§ 258), if thought cannot resolve the finite into the eternal. Thus matter is infinitely divisible; that is, its nature is such that what is posited as a Whole, as a One, is completely self-external and within itself a Many. But matter is not in fact so divided, as if it consisted of atoms; on the contrary, this infinite divisibility of matter is a possibility and only a possibility: that is, this division *ad infinitum* is not something positive and actual, but is only a subjective idea. Similarly, infinite time is only an idea, a going into the beyond, which remains infected with the negative; a necessary idea so long as one is confined to a consideration of the finite as finite. However, if I pass on to the universal, to the non-finite, I leave behind the standpoint where singularity and its alternate variations have their place. In our ordinary way of thinking, the world is only an aggregate of finite existences, but when it is grasped as a universal, as a totality, the question of a beginning at once disappears. Where to make the beginning is therefore undetermined; a beginning is to be made, but it is only a relative one. We pass beyond it, but not to infinity, but only to another beginning which, of course, is also only a conditioned one; in short, it is only the nature of the relative which is expressed, because we are in the sphere of finitude.

This is the metaphysics which passes hither and thither from one abstract determination to another, taking them for absolute. A plain, positive answer cannot be given to the question whether the world has, or has not, a beginning in time. A plain answer is supposed to state that *either* the one *or* the other is true. But the plain answer is, rather, that the question itself, this 'either-or', is badly posed. If we are talking of the finite, then we have both a beginning and a non-beginning; these opposed determinations in their unresolved and unreconciled conflict with each other, belong to the finite: and so the finite, because it is this contradiction, perishes. The finite is preceded by an Other, and in tracing out the context of the finite, its antecedents must be sought, e.g., in the history of the earth or of man. There is no end to such an inquiry, even though we reach an end of each finite thing; time has its power over the manifoldness of the finite. The finite has a beginning, but this beginning is not the First; the finite has an independent existence, but its immediacy is also limited. When ordinary thinking forsakes this determinate finite, which is preceded and followed by other finites, and goes on to the empty thought of time as such, or the world as such, it flounders about in empty ideas, i.e. merely abstract thoughts.

§ 248

In this externality, the determinations of the Notion have the show of an *indifferent subsistence* and *isolation* (*Vereinzelung*) in regard to each other, and the Notion, therefore, is present only as something inward. Consequently, Nature exhibits no freedom in its existence, but only *necessity* and *contingency*.

Remark

For this reason, Nature in the determinate existence which makes it Nature, is not to be deified; nor are sun, moon, animals, plants, etc., to be regarded and cited as more excellent, as works of God, than human actions and events. *In itself*, in the Idea, Nature is divine: but as it *is*, the being of Nature does not accord with its Notion; rather is Nature the *unresolved contradiction*. Its characteristic is *positedness*, the negative, in the same way that the ancients grasped matter in general as the *non-ens*. Thus Nature has also been spoken of as the *self-degradation of the Idea*, in that the Idea, in this form of externality, is in a disparity with its own self. It is only to the external and immediate stage of consciousness, that is, to *sensuous* consciousness, that Nature appears as the First, the immediate, as mere being (*das Seiende*). But because, even in this element of externality, Nature is a representation of the *Idea*, one may, and indeed ought, to admire in it the wisdom of God. Vanini said that a stalk of straw suffices to demonstrate God's being: but every mental image, the slightest fancy of mind, the play of its most capricious whims, every word, affords a superior ground for a knowledge of God's being than any single object of Nature. In Nature, not only is the play of forms a prey to boundless and unchecked contingency, but each separate entity is without the Notion of itself. The highest level to which Nature attains is life; but this, as only a natural mode of the Idea, is at the mercy of the unreason of externality, and the living creature is throughout its whole life entangled with other alien existences, whereas in every expression of Spirit there is contained the moment of free, universal self-relation. It is equally an error to regard the products of mind as inferior to natural objects, and to regard the latter as superior to *human works of art*, on the ground that these must take their material from outside, and that they are not alive. As if the spiritual form did not contain a higher kind of life, and were not more worthy of the Spirit, than the natural form, and as though form generally were not superior to matter, and throughout the ethical sphere even what can be called matter did not belong to Spirit alone: as if in Nature the higher form, the living creature, did not also receive its matter from outside. It is put forward as a further superiority of Nature that throughout all the contingency of its manifold existence it remains obedient to eternal laws. But surely this is also true of the realm of self-consciousness, a fact which finds recognition in the belief that human affairs are governed by Providence; or are the laws of this Providence in the field of human affairs supposed to be only contingent and irrational? But if the contingency of Spirit, the free will (*Willkür*) does *evil*, this is still infinitely superior to the regular motions of the celestial bodies, or to the innocence of plant life; for what thus errs is still Spirit.

Zusatz. The infinite divisibility of matter simply means that matter is external to itself. The immeasurableness of Nature, which at first excites our wonder, is precisely this same externality. Because each material point seems to be entirely independent of all the others, a failure to hold fast to the Notion prevails in Nature which is unable to bring together its determinations. The sun, planets, comets, the Elements, plants, animals, exist separately by themselves. The sun is an individual other than the earth, connected with the planets only by gravity. It is only in *life* that we meet with subjectivity and the counter to externality. The heart, liver, eye, are not self-subsistent individualities on their own account, and the hand, when separated from the body, putrefies. The organic body is still a whole composed of many members external to each other; but each individual member exists only in the subject, and the Notion exists as the power over these members. Thus it is that the Notion, which at the stage of Notionlessness (*Begrifflosigkeit*) is only something inward, first comes into existence in life, as soul. The spatiality of the organism has no truth whatever for the soul; otherwise there would be as many souls as material points, for the soul feels in each point of the organism. One must not be deceived by the show of mutual externality, but must comprehend that mutually external points form only one unity. The celestial bodies only *appear* to be independent of each other, they are the guardians of *one* field. But because the unity in Nature is a relation between things which are apparently self-subsistent, Nature is not free, but is only necessary and contingent. For necessity is the inseparability of different terms which yet appear as indifferent towards each other; but because this abstract state of externality also receives its due, there is contingency in Nature, i.e. external necessity, not the inner necessity of the Notion. There has been a lot of talk in physics about polarity. This concept is a great advance in the metaphysics of the science; for the concept of polarity is simply nothing else but the specific relation of necessity between two different terms which are one, in that when one is given, the other is also given. But this polarity is restricted to the opposition. However, through the opposition there is also given the return of the opposition into unity, and this is the third term which the necessity of the Notion has over and above polarity. In Nature, as the otherness [of the Idea], there also occur the square or the tetrad, for example, the four Elements, the four colours, etc., and even the pentad, e.g. the fingers and the senses. In Spirit, the fundamental form of necessity is the triad. The totality of the disjunction of the Notion exists in Nature as a tetrad because the first term is the universal as such, and the second, or the difference, appears itself as a duality—in Nature, the Other must exist explicitly as Other; with the result that the subjective unity of the universal and the particular is the fourth term which then has a separate existence in face of the other three terms. Further, as the monad and the dyad themselves constitute the entire particularity, the totality of the Notion can go as far as the pentad.

Nature is the negative because it is the negative of the Idea. Jacob Boehme says that God's first-born is Lucifer; and this son of Light centred his imagination on himself and became evil: that is the moment of difference, of otherness held fast against the Son, who is otherness within the divine love. The ground and significance of such conceptions which occur wildly in an oriental style, is to be found in the negative nature of Nature. The other form of otherness is immediacy, which consists in the moment of difference existing abstractly on its own. This existence, however, is only momentary, not a true existence; the Idea alone exists eternally, because it is being in and for itself, i.e. being which has returned into itself. Nature is the first in point of time, but the absolute *prius* is the Idea; this absolute *prius* is the last, the true beginning, Alpha is Omega. What is unmediated is often held to be superior, the mediated being thought of as dependent. The Notion, however, has both aspects: it is mediation through the sublation of mediation, and so is immediacy. People speak, for example, of an immediate belief in God; but this is the inferior mode of being, not the higher; the primitive religions were religions of nature-worship. The affirmative element in Nature is the manifestation of the Notion in it; the nearest instance of the power of the Notion is the perishableness of this outer existence; all natural existences form but a single body in which dwells the soul [the Notion]. The Notion manifests itself in these giant members, but not *qua* Notion; this occurs only in Spirit where the Notion exists as it is.

§ 249

Nature is to be regarded as a *system of stages*, one arising necessarily from the other and being the proximate truth of the stage from which it results: but it is not generated *naturally* out of the other but only in the inner Idea which constitutes the ground of Nature. *Metamorphosis* pertains only to the Notion as such, since only *its* alteration is development. But in Nature, the Notion is partly only something inward, partly existent only as a living individual: *existent* metamorphosis, therefore, is limited to this individual alone.

Remark

It has been an inept conception of ancient and also recent Philosophy of Nature to regard the progression and transition of one natural form and sphere into a higher as an outwardly-actual production which, however, to be made *clearer*, is relegated to the *obscurity* of the past. It is precisely externality which is characteristic of Nature, that is, differences are allowed to fall apart and to appear as indifferent to each other: the dialectical Notion which leads forward the *stages*, is the inner side of them. A thinking consideration must reject such nebulous, at bottom, sensuous ideas, as in particular the so-called *origination*, for example, of plants and animals from water, and then the *origination* of the more highly developed animal organisms from the lower, and so on.

Zusatz. The consideration of the utility of natural objects contains this truth, that they are not an absolute end in and for themselves. This negative aspect, however, is not external to them but is the immanent moment of their Idea, which effects their perishability and transition into another existence, but at the same time into a higher Notion. The Notion timelessly and in a universal manner posits all particularity in existence. It is a completely empty thought to represent species as developing successively, one after the other, in time. Chronological difference has no interest whatever for thought. If it is only a question of enumerating the series of living species in order to show the mind how they are divided into classes, either by starting from the poorest and simplest terms, and rising to the more developed and richer in determinations and content, or by proceeding in the reverse fashion, this operation will always have a general interest. It will be a way of arranging things as in the division of Nature into three kingdoms; this is preferable to jumbling them together, a procedure which would be somewhat repellent to an intelligence which had an inkling of the Notion. But it must not be imagined that such a dry series is made dynamic or philosophical, or more intelligible, or whatever you like to say, by representing the terms as producing each other. Animal nature is the truth of vegetable nature, vegetable of mineral; the earth is the truth of the solar system. In a system, it is the most abstract term which is the first, and the truth of each sphere is the last; but this again is only the first of a higher sphere. It is the necessity of the Idea which causes each sphere to complete itself by passing into another higher one, and the variety of forms must be considered as necessary and determinate. The land animal did not develop *naturally* out of the aquatic animal, nor did it fly into the air on leaving the water, nor did perhaps the bird again fall back to earth. If we want to compare the different stages of Nature, it is quite proper to note that, for example, a certain animal has one ventricle and another has two; but we must not then talk of the fact as if we were dealing with parts which had been put together. Still less must the category of earlier spheres be used to explain others: for this is a formal error, as when it is said that the plant is a carbon pole and the animal a nitrogen pole.

The two forms under which the serial progression of Nature is conceived are *evolution* and *emanation*. The way of evolution, which starts from the imperfect and formless, is as follows: at first there was the liquid element and aqueous forms of life, and from the water there evolved plants, polyps, molluscs, and finally fishes; then from the fishes were evolved the land animals, and finally from the land animals came man. This gradual alteration is called an explanation and understanding; it is a conception which comes from the Philosophy of Nature, and it still flourishes. But though this quantitative difference is of all theories the easiest to understand, it does not really explain anything at all. The way of emanation is peculiar to the oriental world. It involves a series of degradations of being, starting from the perfect being, the absolute totality, God. God has created, and from Him have proceeded splendours, lightnings and likenesses in such fashion that the first likeness is that which most resembles God. This first likeness in its turn, is supposed to have generated another but less perfect one, and so on, so that each created being has become, in its turn, a creative being, down to the negative being, matter, the extreme of evil. Emanation thus ends with the absence of all form. Both ways are one-sided and superficial, and postulate an indeterminate goal. That which proceeds from the perfect to the imperfect has this advantage, that then we have before us the type of the complete organism; and this is the type which picture-thinking must have before it in order to understand the imperfect organisms. What appear in the latter as subordinate, for example, organs which have no functions, is first understood through the more developed organisms which enable one to see the place the organ fills. The perfect, if it is to have the advantage over the imperfect, must exist not only in picture-thinking but also in reality.

The basis of the idea of metamorphosis is also a single Idea which persists in the various genera and even in each particular organ, so that these genera and organs are only the diverse forms of a single, self-same type. Similarly, one speaks of the metamorphosis of an insect, in that the caterpillar, the pupa and the butterfly, are one and the same individual. In the case of individuals, the development certainly takes place in time, but it is otherwise with the genus. With the existence of the genus in a particular form, the other modes of its existence are necessarily postulated. Water being given, then air, fire, etc., too, are necessarily postulated. It is important to hold fast to identity; but to hold fast to difference is no less important, and this gets pushed into the background when a change is conceived only quantitatively. This makes the mere idea of metamorphosis inadequate.

Under the same heading, too, comes the idea of the *series* formed by things, and especially living things. The desire to know the necessity of this development leads to the search for a law of the series, a basic determination which, while positing difference, repeats itself in such difference and in so doing also produces a fresh difference. But to enlarge a series merely by the successive addition of elements similarly determined, and to see only the same relationship between all the members of the series, is not the way in which the Notion generates its determinations. It is this very fact of imagining a *series* of stages and the like, which has been such a hindrance to any progress in understanding the necessity of the various forms of Nature. To seek to arrange in serial form the planets, the metals or chemical substances in general, plants and animals, and then to ascertain the law of the series, is a fruitless task, because Nature does not arrange its forms in such articulate series: the Notion differentiates things according to their own specific qualitative character, and to that extent advances by leaps. The old saying, or so-called law, *non datur saltus in natura*, is altogether inadequate to the diremption of the Notion. The continuity of the Notion with itself is of an entirely different character.

§ 250

The *contradiction* of the Idea, arising from the fact that, as Nature, it is external to itself, is more precisely this: that on the one hand there is the *necessity* of its forms which is generated by the Notion, and their rational determination in the organic totality; while on the other hand, there is their indifferent *contingency* and indeterminable irregularity. In the sphere of Nature contingency and determination from without has its right, and this contingency is at its greatest in the realm of concrete individual forms, which however, as products of Nature, are concrete only in an *immediate* manner. The *immediately* concrete thing is a group of properties, external to one another and more or less indifferently related to each other; and for that very reason, the simple subjectivity which exists for itself is also indifferent and abandons them to contingent and external determination. This is the *impotence* of Nature, that it preserves the determinations of the Notion only *abstractly*, and leaves their detailed specification to external determination.

Remark

The infinite wealth and variety of forms and, what is most irrational, the contingency which enters into the external arrangement of natural things, have been extolled as the sublime freedom of Nature, even as the divinity *of* Nature, or at least the divinity present *in* it. This confusion of contingency, caprice, and disorder, with freedom and rationality is characteristic of sensuous and unphilosophical thinking. This impotence of Nature sets limits to philosophy and it is quite improper to expect the Notion to comprehend—or as it is said, construe or deduce—these contingent products of Nature. It is even imagined that the more trivial and isolated the object, the easier is the task of deducing it.* Undoubtedly, traces of determination by the Notion are to be found even in the most particularized object, although these traces do not exhaust its nature. Traces of this influence of the Notion and of this inner coherence of natural objects will often surprise the investigator, but especially will they seem startling, or rather incredible, to those who are accustomed to see only contingency in natural, as in human, history. One must, however, be careful to avoid taking such trace of the Notion for the total

* It was in this—and other respects too—quite naïve sense that Herr Krug once challenged the Philosophy of Nature to perform the feat of deducing *only* his pen. One could perhaps give him hope that *his* pen would have the glory of being deduced, if ever philosophy should advance so far and have such a clear insight into every great theme in heaven and on earth, past and present, that there was nothing more important to comprehend.

determination of the object, for that is the route to the analogies previously mentioned.

In the impotence of Nature to adhere strictly to the Notion in its realization, lies the difficulty and, in many cases, the impossibility of finding fixed distinctions for classes and orders from an empirical consideration of Nature. Nature everywhere blurs the essential limits of species and genera by intermediate and defective forms, which continually furnish counter examples to every fixed distinction; this even occurs within a specific genus, that of man, for example, where monstrous births, on the one hand, must be considered as belonging to the genus, while on the other hand, they lack certain essential determinations characteristic of the genus. In order to be able to consider such forms as defective, imperfect and deformed, one must presuppose a fixed, invariable type. This type, however, cannot be furnished by experience, for it is experience which also presents these so-called monstrosities, deformities, intermediate products, etc. The fixed type rather presupposes the self-subsistence and dignity of the determination stemming from the Notion.

§ 251

Nature is, in itself, a living Whole. The movement through its stages is more precisely this: that the Idea *posits* itself as that which it is *in itself*; or what is the same thing, that it returns *into itself* out of its immediacy and externality which is *death*, in order to be, first a *living creature*, but further, to sublate this determinateness also in which it is only Life, and to give itself an existence as Spirit, which is the truth and the final goal of Nature and the genuine actuality of the Idea.

Zusatz. The development of the Notion towards its destination, its end or, if you like, its purpose, is to be grasped as a positing of what it is in itself, so that these determinations of its content come into existence, are manifested, but at the same time not as independent and self-subsistent, but as moments which remain in the unity of the Notion, as ideal, i.e. posited moments. This positing can therefore be grasped as an utterance or expression, a coming forth, a setting forth, a coming-out-of-self, in so far as the subjectivity of the Notion is lost in the mutual outsideness of its determinations. But it preserves itself in them, as their unity and ideality; and this going out of the centre from itself to the periphery is therefore, looked at from the opposite side, equally a taking up again of this outer into the inner, an inwardizing or remembering (*Erinnern*) that it is it, the Notion, that exists in this externality. Starting therefore from the externality in which the Notion at first exists, its progress is a movement into itself, into the centre, i.e. a bringing of immediate and external existence which is inadequate to itself, to subjective unity, to being-within-self: not in such a way that the Notion withdraws itself from this externality, leaving it behind like a dead shell, but rather that existence as such is within self or conforms to the Notion, that the being-within-self itself exists, which is Life. The Notion strives to burst the shell of outer existence and to become for itself. Life is the Notion which has attained to the manifestation of itself, which has explicated, set forth, what it is in itself; but the Understanding finds this the most difficult of things to grasp because what it finds easiest to grasp is the most simple of things, i.e. the abstract and the dead.

c. *Division*

§ 252

The Idea as Nature is:

I. in the determination of asunderness or mutual outsideness, of infinite separatedness, the unity of form being outside it; this unity, as *ideal*, is only *in itself* and is consequently a unity which is only *sought*. This is *matter* and its ideal system—Mechanics;

II. in the determination of *particularity*, so that reality is posited with an immanent determinateness of form and with an existent difference in it. This is a relationship of Reflection (*Reflexionsverhältnis*) whose being-within-self is natural *individuality*—Physics;

III. in the determination of *subjectivity*, in which the real differences of form are also brought back to the *ideal* unity which has found itself and is for itself—Organics.

Zusatz. The division is made from the standpoint of the Notion grasped in its totality, and it indicates the diremption of the Notion into its determinations; and since in this diremption the Notion explicates its determinations and gives them a self-subsistence, though only as moments, the process is one of self-realization in which the Notion posits itself as Idea. But the Notion not only sets forth its moments, and not only articulates itself in its differences, but it also brings these apparently self-subsistent stages back to their ideality and unity, to itself; and only then, in fact, has it made itself the concrete Notion, the Idea and the Truth. It seems, therefore, that there are two ways of presenting both the Division and the scientific exposition: one way would start from the concrete Notion, and in Nature this is Life, which would be considered on its own account. It would then be led to consider the externalized forms of the Notion, the forms being thrown out by the Notion to exist separately as spheres of Nature, the Notion being related to them as to other—consequently more abstract—modes of its existence; this way would close with the complete extinction of life. The other way is the reverse of this. It starts with the, at first, only immediate mode of the Notion's existence, with its uttermost self-externality, and it closes with the true existence of the Notion, with the truth of the whole course of its exposition. The first way can be compared to the process implied in the conception of emanation, the second, to the process implied in the conception of evolution (§ 249, *Zusatz*). Each of these forms taken separately is one-sided, but they exist together; the eternal divine process is a flowing in two opposite directions which meet and permeate each other in what is simply and solely *one*. The First, let it be called by the loftiest name, is only an immediate, even though we mean by it something concrete. Matter, for example, negates itself as an untrue existence and from this negation emerges a higher existence. From one aspect, it is by an evolution that the earlier stages are cancelled but from another aspect matter remains in the background and is produced anew by emanation. Evolution is thus also an involution, in that matter interiorizes itself to become life. In virtue of the urge of the Idea to become objective to itself, the self-subsistent becomes a moment: the senses of the animal, for example, made objective and external, are the Sun and the lunar and cometary bodies. Even in the sphere of Physics these bodies lose their independence although they still retain the same form with some modifications; they are the Elements [air, fire, and water]. The subjective sense of sight existing outwardly is the Sun, taste is water, and smell is the air. But as our task here is to posit the determinations of the Notion, we must not start from the most concrete, the true sphere, but from the most abstract.

Matter is the form in which the self-externality of Nature achieves its first being-within-self, an abstract being-for-self which is exclusive and therefore a plurality, which has its unity, as what brings the independent many into a universal being-for-self, at once within and outside itself: gravity. In the sphere of Mechanics, being-for-self is not yet an individual, stable unity having the power to subordinate plurality to itself. Heavy matter does not yet possess the individuality which preserves its determinations; and since in matter the determinations of the Notion are still external to each other, its differences are not qualitative but indifferent or purely quantitative, and matter, merely as mass, has no form. Form is acquired by individual bodies in Physics, and with this we have at once gravity revealed for the first time as the mastery of being-for-self over multiplicity, a being-for-self which is no longer merely a striving but which has come to rest, although at first only in the mode of appearance (*nur auf erscheinende Weise*). Each atom of gold, for example, contains all the determinations or properties of the whole lump of gold, and matter is immanently specified and particularized. The second determination is that here, still, particularity as qualitative determinateness, and being-for-self as the point of individuality, fall together in unity, and therefore body is finitely determined; individuality is still bound to definite exclusive specific properties, does not yet exist as totality. If such a body enters into a process in which it loses such properties, then it ceases to be what it is; the qualitative determinateness is therefore affirmatively posited, but not at the same time also negatively. The organic being is totality as found in Nature, an individuality which is for itself and which internally develops into its differences: but in such a way that first, these determinations are not only specific properties but also concrete totalities; secondly, they remain also qualitatively determined against each other, and, as thus finite, are posited as ideal moments by Life, which preserves itself in the process of these members. Thus we have a number of beings-for-self which, however, are brought back to the being-for-self which is for itself and which, as its own end (*Selbstzweck*), subdues the members and reduces them to means: this is the unity of qualitatively determined being and gravity, which finds itself in Life.

Each stage is a specific realm of Nature and all appear to have independent existence, But the last is the concrete unity of all the preceding ones, just as, in general, each successive stage embodies the lower stages, but equally posits these, as its non-organic nature, over against itself. One stage is the power of the other, and this relation is reciprocal. Here can be seen the true meaning of *powers* (*Potenzen*). The non-organic Elements are powers opposed to what is individual, subjective—the non-organic destroys the organic. But equally the organism, in its turn, is the power which subdues its universal powers, air, water; these are perpetually liberated and also perpetually subdued and assimilated. The eternal life of Nature consists in this: first, that the Idea displays itself in each sphere so far as it can within the finitude of that sphere, just as each drop of water provides an image of the sun, and secondly, that the Notion, through its dialectic, breaks through the limitation of this sphere, since it cannot rest content with an inadequate element, and necessarily passes over into a higher stage.

SECTION ONE ✦ MECHANICS

§ 253

Mechanics treats of:

A. self-externality in its complete abstraction—Space and Time;
B. self-externality as individualized and its relation in that state of abstraction, i.e. *Matter* and *Motion—Finite* Mechanics;
C. Matter in the freedom of its intrinsic Notion, in its *free motion—Absolute* Mechanics.

Zusatz. Self-externality splits at once into two forms, positively as Space, and negatively as Time. The first concrete thing, the unity and negation of these abstract moments, is Matter; this is related to its moments, and these consequently are themselves related to each other, i.e. in Motion. When this relation is not external, we have the absolute unity of Matter and Motion, self-moving Matter.

A. SPACE AND TIME

(I) SPACE

§ 254

The first or immediate determination of Nature is *Space*: the abstract *universality of Nature's self-externality*, self-externality's mediationless indifference. It is a wholly ideal *side-by-sideness* because it is self-externality; and it is absolutely *continuous*, because this asunderness is still quite *abstract*, and contains no specific difference within itself.

Remark

A number of different theories have been put forward about the nature of space. I will mention only the Kantian definition that space, like time, is a form of *sensuous intuition*. It has also become usual elsewhere to lay down as a principle that space must be regarded only as something subjective in our ideas. Disregarding what belongs in the Kantian conception to subjective idealism and its determinations, there remains the correct definition that space is a mere form, i.e. an *abstraction*, that of immediate *externality*. It is not permissible to speak of *points of space*, as if they constituted the positive element of space, since space, on account of its lack of difference, is only the possibility and not the actual *positedness* of being-outside-of-one-another and of the negative, and is therefore absolutely continuous; the point, the being-for-self, is consequently rather the *negation* of space, a negation which is posited in space. This also settles the question of the infinitude of space (§ 100, Remark). Space is simply pure Quantity, only no longer as a logical determination, but as existing immediately and externally. Nature, consequently, does not begin with the qualitative but with the quantitative, because its determination is not, like Being in Logic, the abstractly First and immediate, but a Being already essentially *mediated* within itself, an external- and other-being.

Zusatz. Our procedure consists in first fixing the thought demanded by the necessity of the Notion and then in asking how this thought appears in our ordinary ideas. The further requirement is that in intuition, space shall correspond to the thought of pure self-externality. Even if we were mistaken in this, it would not affect the truth of our thought. In the empirical sciences the reverse method is followed; there the first thing is the empirical intuition of space, and only thereafter do we come to the thought of space. In order to prove that space accords with our thought, we must compare the idea of space with the determination of our notion. The filling of space does not affect space itself; the Heres are side by side and do not interfere with each other. The Here is not yet place, but only the possibility of Place; the Heres are completely the same, and this abstract plurality without real interruption or limit is, precisely, externality. The Heres are also different; but the difference is equally no difference, i.e. it is an abstract difference. Space is therefore punctiformity, but a negative punctiformity, and so perfect continuity. To fix a point is to interrupt space: but space is absolutely uninterrupted thereby. The point has meaning only in so far as it is spatial, and so external both to itself and to others; Here contains within itself an Above, Below, Right, and Left. Something which was not external in its own self but only to an Other, would be a point; but there is no such point, because no Here is ultimate. However remotely I place a star, I can go beyond it, for the universe is nowhere nailed up with boards. This is the complete externality of space. But the Other of the point is just as much a self-externality as the point is, and therefore the two are undistinguished and unseparated. Beyond its limit, as its *otherness*, space is still in community with itself, and this unity in asunderness is continuity. The unity of these two moments, discreteness and continuity, is the objectively determined Notion of space. This Notion, however, is only the abstraction of space, which is often regarded as absolute space. This is thought to be the truth of space; but relative space is something much higher, for it is the determinate space of some material body. It is rather the truth of abstract space to exist as a material body.

One main question of metaphysics was whether space is real on its own account, or is only a property of things. If it is said that space is something substantial in its own right, then it must be like a box which, even when empty, still maintains a particular being of its own. Space, however, is absolutely penetrable, it offers no resistance whatever; but we demand that what is real should be incompatible with something else. Nowhere can a space which is space *per se* be demonstrated; it is always a filled space and never distinct from what fills it. It is thus both a non-sensuous sensuousness and a sensuous non-sensuousness. Natural objects are in space, which remains their basis, because Nature lies in the bonds of externality. If, like Leibniz, one says that space is an arrangement of things which does not concern the noumena, and which has its substrate in things, we are still sure that when the things which fill space are removed, the spatial relationships will remain independently of the things. Certainly it can be said that space is an arrangement, for it is of course an external determination; but it is not merely an external determination, but is rather in its very self externality.

§ 255

Space, as in itself the Notion as such, contains within itself the *differences* of the Notion. (a) In the indifference of space, these are immediately the three *dimensions*, which are merely *diverse* and possess no determination whatever.

Remark

Geometry is not required to deduce that space necessarily has just three dimensions, because it is not a philosophical science, and may presuppose as its subject-matter space with its universal determinations. But apart from this, no thought is given to the necessity of such a deduction. The necessity is based on the nature of the Notion, whose determinations in this first form of asunderness, in *abstract* Quantity, are altogether superficial and a completely empty difference. The reason, therefore, why it cannot be said how *height*, *length*, and *breadth* differ from each other is that these three dimensions only *ought* to be different, but that they *are* not yet differences. It is not at all fixed whether a direction is called height, length, or breadth. The more precise definition of *height* is to be in the direction of the centre of the earth; but this more concrete determination does not concern the nature of space in itself. Even assuming this definition, it is still immaterial whether this direction is called height or depth; and it also does not serve to determine length and breadth, which is also often called depth.

§ 256

(β) The difference of space is, however, essentially a determinate, qualitative difference. As such, it is (α), first, the *negation* of space itself, because this is immediate *differenceless* self-externality, the *point*. (β) But the negation is the negation *of space*, i.e. it is itself spatial. The point, as essentially this relation, i.e. as sublating itself, is the *line*, the first other-being, i.e. spatial being, of the point. (γ) The truth of other-being is, however, negation of the negation. The line consequently passes over into the plane, which, on the one hand, is a determinateness opposed to line and point, and so surface, simply as such, but, on the other hand, is the sublated negation of space. It is thus the restoration of the spatial totality which now contains the negative moment within itself, an *enclosing surface* which separates off a *single* whole space.

Remark

That the line does not consist of points, nor the plane of lines, follows from their Notion; for the line is rather the point existing *outside* of itself, i.e. *relating* itself to space and sublating itself, and the plane, similarly, is the sublated line existing outside of itself. Here the point is conceived as the primary and positive element which forms the starting-point. But the converse is also true; inasmuch as space, not point, is in fact the positive element, the plane is the first negation, and the line the second; but as the second negation of space the line is, in its truth, the negation which relates self to self, the point. The necessity of the transition is the same. In the external way of understanding and defining the point, line, etc., no thought is given to the necessity of this transition. It is true that the first kind of transition is envisaged, though only as something contingent, in the form of the definition that when the point *moves*, the line is formed, etc. The other configurations of space considered by geometry are further qualitative limitations of an abstract division of space, of the plane, or of a bounded spatial whole. Here, too, there enters an element of necessity; e.g. that the triangle is the first rectilinear figure, that all other figures can only be determined by reducing them to the triangle or the square, and so on. The principle of these constructions is the identity of the Understanding, which subordinates figures to a *regularity*, and so establishes relationships between them which it is thereby possible to know.

We may note in passing that it was a singular opinion of Kant's that the definition of the *straight line* as the shortest distance between two points is a synthetic proposition, since my *concept* of *straight* involves nothing of quantity, but only a quality. In this sense every definition is a synthetic proposition. What is defined, *the straight line*, is at first only intuition or figurate conception; the definition that it is the shortest distance between two points, first constitutes the *notion* (that is, as it appears in such definitions. See § 229). That the *notion* is not already given in *intuition*, is the difference between them which makes a definition necessary. However, the definition is obviously analytic, since the straight line can be reduced to simplicity of direction; and simplicity with reference to *manifoldness* yields the determination of the *least* manifold, here of the shortest distance.

Zusatz. The first determination of spatiality is only the straight line, curved lines being in themselves at once in two dimensions. In the circle we have the line raised to the second power. As second negation, the plane has two dimensions, for what is second is no less double than Two.

The science of geometry sets out to find what determinations follow when certain others are presupposed. The main object is then that the presupposed and derived determinations should form a single developed totality. The cardinal propositions of geometry are those where a whole is postulated, and this is expressed in terms of its determinate elements. In regard to the triangle there are two such cardinal propositions whereby the triangle is completely determined. (α) If we take three parts of a triangle, one of which must be a side (there are three cases), then the triangle is completely determined. Now geometry goes the roundabout way of taking two triangles, which in these circumstances are supposed to be congruent; this is an easier mode of presentation, but also a super-fluous one. The truth of the matter is this, that the proposition only requires one triangle, which is in itself such a relationship that, when its first three parts are determined, the remaining three parts also are; the triangle is determined by two sides and one angle, or by two angles and one side, and so on. The first three parts are the determinateness or the Notion of the triangle; the other three parts belong to its outer reality, and are superfluous for the Notion. In such postulation, the determination is still quite abstract, and only the general dependence of the parts is given; we still lack the relation of specific determinateness, i.e. the magnitude of the parts of the triangle. (β) This is achieved in Pythagoras' theorem. Here we have the complete determinateness of the triangle, since only the right-angle is completely determined, its supplementary angle being equal to it. This proposition is consequently superior to all others as a symbol of the Idea. It represents a Whole self-divided into its parts, just as each form in philosophy is self-divided into Notion and reality. We have the same magnitude, first as square of the hypotenuse, then again as distributed in the squares of the other two sides. A higher definition of the circle than that based on the equality of the radii, is that which takes account of the difference in it, and so reaches a complete determinateness of the circle. This occurs in the analytic treatment of the circle which contains nothing but what is found in Pythagoras' theorem; the other two sides are sine and cosine, or abscissa and ordinate—the hypotenuse is the radius. The relationship of these three is the determinateness of the circle, not simple as in the first definition, but a relation of differentiated elements. With Pythagoras' theorem, Euclid also closes his first book. Subsequently, aiming at the reduction of differences to equality, he concludes his second book with the reduction of the rectangle to the square. Just as there are an infinite number of right-angled triangles possible on one hypotenuse, so to a square there correspond a multi-tude of rectangles; both have their place in the circle. This is the way in which geometry, as an abstract science of the Understanding, proceeds scientifically.

(2) TIME

§ 257

Negativity, as point, relates itself to space, in which it develops its determinations as line and plane; but in the sphere of self-externality, negativity is equally *for itself* and so are its determinations; but, at the same time, these are posited in the sphere of self-externality, and negativity, in so doing, appears as indifferent to the inert side-by-sideness of space. Negativity, thus posited for itself, is Time.

Zusatz. Space is the immediate existence of Quantity in which everything subsists, even the limit having the form of subsistence; this is the defect of space. Space is this contradiction, to be infected with negation, but in such wise that this negation falls apart into indifferent subsistence. Since space, therefore, is only this inner negation of itself, the self-sublating of its moments is its truth. Now time is precisely the existence of this perpetual self-sublation; in time, therefore, the point has actuality. Difference has stepped out of space; this means that it has ceased to be this indifference, it is for itself in all its unrest, is no longer paralysed. This pure Quantity, as self-existent difference, is what is negative in itself, Time; it is the negation of the negation, the self-relating negation. Negation in space is negation attached to an Other; the negative in space does not therefore yet receive its due. In space the plane is indeed a negation of the negation, but in its truth it is distinct from space. The truth of space is time, and thus space becomes time; the transition to time is not made subjectively by us, but made by space itself. In pictorial thought, space and time are taken to be quite separate: we have space and *also* time; philosophy fights against this 'also'.

§ 258

Time, as the negative unity of self-externality, is similarly an out-and-out abstract, ideal being. It is that being which, inasmuch as it *is*, is *not*, and inasmuch as it is *not*, *is*: it is Becoming directly *intuited*; this means that differences, which admittedly are purely *momentary*, i.e. directly self-sublating, are determined as *external*, i.e. as external to *themselves*.

Remark

Time, like space, is a *pure form* of *sense* or *intuition*, the non-sensuous sensuous; but, as in the case of space, the distinction of objectivity and a subjective consciousness confronting it, does not apply to time. If these determinations were applied to space and time, the former would then be abstract objectivity, the latter abstract subjectivity. Time is the same principle as the I = I of pure self-consciousness, but this principle, or the simple Notion, still in its uttermost externality and abstraction—as intuited mere *Becoming*, pure being-within-self as sheer coming-out-of-self.

Time is *continuous*, too, like space, for it is the negativity abstractly relating self to self, and in this abstraction there is as yet no real difference.

Everything, it is said, *comes to be* and *passes away* in time. If abstraction is made from *everything*, namely from what fills time, and also from what fills space, then what we have left over is empty time and empty space: in other words, these abstractions of externality are posited and represented as if they were for themselves. But it is not *in* time that everything comes to be and passes away, rather time itself is the *becoming*, this coming-to-be and passing away, the *actually existent abstraction, Chronos*, from whom everything is born and by whom its offspring is destroyed. The real is certainly distinct from time, but is also essentially identical with it. What is real is limited, and the Other to this negation is *outside* it; therefore the determinateness in it is self-external and is consequently the contradiction of its being; the abstraction of this externality and unrest of its contradiction is time itself. The finite is perishable and *temporal* because, unlike the Notion, it is not in its own self total negativity; true, this negativity is immanent in it as its universal essence, but the finite is not adequate to this essence: it is *one-sided*, and consequently it is related to negativity as to the power that dominates it. The Notion, however, in its freely self-existent identity as I = I, is in and for itself absolute negativity and freedom. Time, therefore, has no power over the Notion, nor is the Notion in time or temporal; on the contrary, *it* is the power over time, which is this negativity only *qua* externality. Only the natural, therefore, is subject to time in so far as it is finite; the True, on the other hand, the Idea, Spirit, is *eternal*. But the notion of eternity must not be grasped negatively as abstraction from time, as existing, as it were, outside of time; nor in a sense which makes eternity come *after* time, for this would turn eternity into futurity, one of the moments of time.

Zusatz. Time is not, as it were, a receptacle in which everything is placed as in a flowing stream, which sweeps it away and engulfs it. Time is only this abstraction of destruction. It is because things are finite that they are in time; it is not because they are in time that they perish; on the contrary, things themselves are the temporal, and to be so is their objective determination. It is therefore the process of actual things themselves which makes time; and though time is called omnipotent, it is also completely impotent. The Now has a tremendous right; it *is* nothing as the individual Now, for as I pronounce it, this proudly exclusive Now dissolves, flows away and falls into dust. *Duration* is the universal of all these Nows, it is the sublatedness of this process of things which do not endure. And though things endure, time still passes away and does not rest; in this way, time appears to be independent of, and distinct from, things. But if we say that time passes away even though things endure, this merely means that although some things endure, change is nevertheless apparent in others, as for example in the course of the sun; and so, after all, things are in time. A final shallow attempt to attribute rest and duration to things is made by representing change as gradual. If everything stood still, even our imagination, then we should endure, there would be no time. But all finite things are temporal, because sooner or later they are subject to change; their duration is thus only relative.

Absolute timelessness is distinct from duration; the former is eternity, from which natural time is absent. But in its Notion, time itself is eternal; for time as such—not any particular time, nor Now—is its Notion, and this, like every Notion generally, is eternal, and therefore also absolute Presence. Eternity will not come to be, nor was it, but it *is*. The difference therefore between eternity and duration is that the latter is only a relative sublating of time, whereas eternity is infinite, i.e. not relative, duration but duration reflected into self. What is not in time is that in which there is no process. The worst and the best are not in time, they endure. The former because it is an abstract universality: such are space, time itself, the sun, the Elements, stones, mountains, inorganic Nature generally, and even works of man, e.g. the pyramids; their duration is no virtue. What endures is esteemed higher than what soon perishes; but all bloom, all beautiful vitality, dies early. But what is best also endures, not only the lifeless, inorganic universal, but the other universal, that which is concrete in itself, the Genus, the Law, the Idea, Spirit. For we must distinguish between what is the whole process and what is only a moment of the process. The universal, as law, also has a process within it, and lives only as a process; but it is not a *part* of the process, is not in process, but contains its two sides, and is itself processless. On its phenomenal side, law enters into the time-process, in that the moments of the Notion have a show of self-subsistence; but in their Notion, the excluded differences are reconciled and co-exist in peace again. The Idea, Spirit, transcends time because it is itself the Notion of time; it is eternal, in and for itself, and it is not dragged into the time-process because it does not lose itself in one side of the process. In the individual as such, it is otherwise, for on one side it is the genus; the most beautiful life is that in which the universal and its individuality are completely united in a single form. But the individual is then also separated from the universal, and as such it is only one side of the process, and is subject to change; it is in respect of this moment of mortality that it falls into time. Achilles, the flower of Greek life, Alexander the Great, that infinitely powerful individuality, do not survive. Only their deeds, their effects remain, i.e. the world which they brought into being. Mediocrity endures, and in the end rules the world. There is also a mediocrity of thought which beats down the contemporary world, extinguishes spiritual vitality, converts it into mere habit and in this way endures. Its endurance is simply this: that it exists in untruth, does not receive its due, does not honour the Notion, that truth is not manifest in it as a process.

§ 259

The dimensions of time, *present*, *future*, and *past*, are the *becoming* of externality as such, and the resolution of it into the differences of being as passing over into nothing, and of nothing as passing over into being. The immediate vanishing of these differences into *singularity* is the present as *Now* which, as singularity, is *exclusive* of the other moments, and at the same time completely *continuous* in them, and is only this vanishing of its being into nothing and of nothing into its being.

Remark

The *finite* present is the *Now* fixed as *being* and distinguished as the concrete unity, and hence as the affirmative, from what is *negative*, from the abstract moments of past and future; but this being is itself only abstract, vanishing into nothing. Furthermore, in Nature where time is a *Now*, being does not reach the *existence* of the difference of these dimensions; they are, of necessity, only in subjective imagination, in *remembrance* and *fear* or *hope*. But the past and future of time as *being* in Nature, are space, for space is negated time; just as sublated space is immediately the point, which developed for itself is time.

There is no *science of time* corresponding to the *science of space*, to *geometry*. The differences of time have not this *indifference* of self-externality which constitutes the immediate determinateness of space, and they are consequently not capable of being expressed, like space, in configurations. The principle of time is only capable of being so expressed when the Understanding has paralysed it and reduced its negativity to the *unit*. This inert One, the uttermost externality of thought, can be used to form external combinations, and these, the numbers of *arithmetic*, can in turn be brought by the Understanding under the categories of equality and inequality, of identity and difference.

One could also conceive the idea of a philosophical mathematics knowing by Notions, what ordinary mathematics deduces from hypotheses according to the method of the Understanding. However, as mathematics is the science of finite determinations of magnitude which are supposed to remain fixed and valid in their finitude and not to pass beyond it, mathematics is essentially a science of the Understanding; and since it is able to be this in a perfect manner, it is better that it should maintain this superiority over other sciences of the kind, and not allow itself to become adulterated either by mixing itself with the Notion, which is of a quite different nature, or by empirical applications. There is nothing in that to hinder the Notion from establishing a more definite consciousness alike of the leading principles of the Understanding and also of order and its necessity in arithmetical operations (see § 102) as well as in the theorems of geometry.

Furthermore, it would be a superfluous and thankless task to try to express *thoughts* in such a refractory and inadequate medium as spatial figures and numbers, and to do violence to these for this purpose. The simple elementary figures and numbers, on account of their simplicity, can be used for *symbols* without fear of misunderstanding; but even so, these symbols are too heterogeneous and cumbersome to express thought. The first efforts of pure thought had recourse to such aids, and the Pythagorean system of numbers is the famous example of this. But with richer notions these means become completely inadequate, because their *external* juxtaposition and their contingent combination do not accord at all with the nature of the Notion, and it is altogether ambiguous which of the many possible relationships in complex numbers and figures should be stuck to. Besides, the fluid character of the Notion is dissipated in such an external medium, in which each determination is indifferent to and outside the others. This ambiguity could be removed only by an *explanation*; but then the essential expression of the thought is this explanation, so that the representation by symbols becomes a worthless superfluity.

Other mathematical determinations such as the *infinite and its relationships*, the *infinitesimal, factors, powers*, etc., have their true notions in philosophy itself; it is inept to employ these determinations in philosophy, borrowing them from mathematics where they are employed in a notionless, often meaningless way; rather must they await their justification and meaning from philosophy. It is only indolence which, to spare itself the labour of thought and notional determination, takes refuge in formulae which are not even an immediate expression of thought, and in their ready-made schemata.

The truly philosophical science of mathematics as *theory of magnitude*, would be the science of *measures*; but this already presupposes the real particularity of things, which is found only in concrete Nature. On account of the *external* nature of magnitude, this would certainly also be the most difficult of all sciences.

Zusatz. The dimensions of time complete the determinate content of intuition in that they posit for intuition the Notion of time, which is *becoming*, in its totality or reality; this consists in positing each of the abstract moments of the unity which becoming is, as the whole, but under opposite determinations. Each of these two determinations is thus itself a unity of being and nothing; but they are also distinguished. This difference can only be that of coming-to-be and passing away. In the one case, in the Past (in Hades), being is the foundation, the starting point; the Past has been actual as history of the world, as natural events, but posited under the category of non-being which is added to it. In the other case, the position is reversed; in the Future, non-being is the first determination, while being is later, though of course not in time. The middle term is the indifferent unity of both, so that neither the one nor the other is the determinant. The Present *is*, only because the Past is not; conversely, the being of the Now is determined as not-being, and the non-being of its being is the Future; the Present is this negative unity. The non-being of the being which is replaced by the Now, is the Past; the being of the non-being which is contained in the Present, is the Future. In the positive meaning of time, it can be said that only the Present *is*, that Before and After are not. But the concrete Present is the result of the Past and is pregnant with the Future. The true Present, therefore, is eternity.

The name of mathematics could also be used for the philosophical treatment of space and time. But if it were desired to treat the forms of space and the unit philosophically, they would lose their peculiar significance and pattern; a philosophy of them would become a matter of logic, or would even assume the character of another concrete philosophical science, according as a more concrete significance was imparted to the notions. Mathematics deals with these objects only *qua quantitative*, and among them it does not—as we noted—include time itself but only the unit variously combined and linked. No doubt in the theory of motion time *is* an object considered, but applied mathematics is, on the whole, not an immanent science, simply because it is the application of pure mathematics to a given material and to its empirically derived determinations.

(3) PLACE AND MOTION

§ 260

Space is within itself the contradiction of indifferent asunderness and differenceless continuity, the pure negativity of itself, and the *transition, first of all, into time*. Similarly, time is the immediate *collapse* into indifference, into undifferentiated asunderness or *space*, because its opposed moments which are held together in unity, immediately sublate themselves. In this way, the *negative* determination in space, the *exclusive* point, no longer only implicitly [or in itself] conforms to the Notion, but is *posited* and *concrete* within itself, through the total negativity which is time; the point, as thus concrete, is *Place* (§ 255, 256).

Zusatz. If we refer back to the exposition of the notion of duration, we see that this immediate unity of space and time is already the ground of their being; for the negative of space is time, and the positive, i.e. the being of the differences of time, is space. But space and time are posited unequally therein, in other words, their unity is manifested only as a movement of transition of the one into the other, so that the beginning and the realization, the result, fall asunder. But it is precisely the result which enunciates their ground and truth. What persists is the equality-with-self into which time has retreated; this is space, for the characteristic of space is to be indifferent existence in general. The point exists here in its truth, namely as a universal, and for this reason it is a whole space as a totality of dimensions. This Here is now equally time, a Present which immediately sublates itself, a Now which has been. The Here is at the same time a Now, for it is the point of duration. This unity of Here and Now is Place.

§ 261

Place, as this *posited* identity of space and time is equally, at first, the posited *contradiction* which space and time are each in themselves. Place is spatial, and therefore indifferent, *singularity*; and it is this only as a *spatial Now*, as time, so that place is immediately indifferent towards itself as *this* place, is external to itself, the negation of itself, and is *another place*. This *vanishing* and *self-regeneration* of space in time and of time in space, a process in which time posits itself spatially as *place*, but in which place, too, as indifferent spatiality, is immediately posited as *temporal*: this is *Motion*. This becoming, however, is itself just as much the collapse within itself of its contradiction, the *immediately identical* and *existent* unity of both, namely, *Matter*.

Remark

The transition from ideality to reality, from abstraction to concrete existence, in this case from space and time to reality, which appears as matter, is incomprehensible to the Understanding; consequently, the transition always presents itself to the Understanding as an external affair, as something already given. The usual conception of space and time takes them to be *empty* and indifferent to what fills them, and yet they are to be considered as always filled, that is, *empty* space and time are *filled* with matter from outside. In this way, material things are, on the one hand, regarded as indifferent to space and time, and yet at the same time as essentially spatial and temporal.

It is said of matter: (α) that it is *composite*; this refers to its abstract asunderness, to space. In so far as abstraction is made from time and all forms generally, it is asserted that matter is eternal and immutable. This, in fact, follows immediately; but such a matter is also only an untrue abstraction. It is said (β) that it is *impenetrable* and *offers resistance*, is tangible, visible, and so on. These predicates signify nothing else than that matter exists, partly for specific forms of perception, in general, for an Other, and partly that it exists just as much *for itself*. Both these determinations belong to matter precisely because it is the *identity* of space and time, of immediate *asunderness* and of *negativity* or *self-subsistent* singularity.

The *transition of ideality into reality* is explicitly demonstrated in the familiar mechanical phenomena, namely, that ideality can take the place of reality, and vice versa; and only the notionless thinking of the imagination and the Understanding are to blame if the identity of both is not inferred from their interchangeability. In connection with the *lever*, for instance, *distance* can take the place of *mass*, and vice versa, and a quantum of ideal moment produces the same effect as the corresponding real amount. Similarly, in connection with the *magnitude of motion*, *velocity*, which is simply the quantitative relationship of space and time, can take the place of *mass*; and conversely, the real effect is the same if the mass is increased and the velocity proportionately decreased. A brick does not kill a man just because it is a brick, but brings about such a result only by virtue of the velocity it has acquired; that is to say, the man is killed by space and time. It is *Force*, a category of reflection fixed by the Understanding, which presents itself here as ultimate, and prevents the Understanding from inquiring further into the relationship of its categories. But this at least is adumbrated, that the *effect* of force is something real, appealing to sense, also that *force* and its *expression* have the same content and that the *real expression of* this force is achieved through the relation of its ideal moments, space and time.

It is also in keeping with this notionless reflection that the so-called forces are regarded as *implanted* in matter, that is to say, as originally *external* to it, with the result that this very identity of time and space which is vaguely present in the reflective category of Force, and which in truth constitutes the *essence* of matter, is posited as something *alien* to it and *contingent*, something introduced into it from outside.

Zusatz. One place only points to another place, and so sublates itself and becomes another; but the difference is likewise sublated. Each place, taken by itself, is only *this* place, that is, they are all the same as each other; in other words, Place is simply the universal Here. Something occupies its place, then changes it; another place arises, but, both before and after, something occupies its place and does not leave it. This dialectic which is inherent in Place was enunciated by Zeno when he showed that nothing moves: for motion would be a change of place, but the arrow does not leave its place. This dialectic is precisely the infinite Notion which the Here is; for time is posited in its own self. There are three different places: the present place, the place about to be occupied, and the place which has just been vacated; the vanishing of the dimensions of time is paralysed. But at the same time there is only *one* place, a universal of these places, which remains unchanged through all the changes; it is duration, existing immediately in accordance with its Notion, and as such it is Motion. That Motion is what we have expounded, is self-evident; this Notion of it conforms to our intuition of it. Its essence is to be the immediate unity of Space and Time; it is Time which has a real existence through Space, or Space which is first truly differentiated by Time. Thus we know that Space and Time pertain to Motion; the velocity, the quantum of Motion, is Space in relation to a specific Time elapsed. It is also said that Motion is a relation of Space and Time; but the specific nature of this relation has to be comprehended. It is in Motion that Space and Time first acquire actuality.

Just as Time is the purely formal soul of Nature, and Space, according to Newton, is the sensorium of God, so Motion is the Notion of the veritable soul of the world. We are accustomed to regard it as a predicate or a state; but Motion is, in fact, the Self, the Subject as Subject, the abiding of vanishing. The fact that Motion appears as a predicate is the immediate necessity of its self-extinction. Rectilinear motion is not Motion in and for itself, but Motion in subjection to an Other in which it has become a predicate or a sublated moment. The restoration of the duration of the Point, as opposed to its motion, is the restoration of Place as unmoved. But this restored Place is not immediate Place, but Place which has returned out of alteration, and is the result and ground of Motion. As forming a dimension, i.e. as opposed to the other moments, it is the centre. This return of the line is the circle; it is the Now, Before and After which have closed together in a unity in which these dimensions are indifferent, so that Before is equally After, and vice versa. It is in circular motion that the necessary paralysis of these dimensions is first posited in space. Circular motion is the spatial or subsistent unity of the dimensions of time. The point proceeds towards a place which is its future, and leaves one which is the past; but what it has left behind is at the same time what it has still to reach: it has been already at the place which it is reaching. Its goal is the point which is its past; and this is the truth of time, that the goal is not the future but the past. The motion which relates itself to the centre is itself the *plane*, motion as the synthetic whole in which exist its moments, the extinction of the motion in the centre, the motion itself and its relation to its extinction, namely the radii of the circle. But this plane itself moves and becomes the other of itself, a complete space; or the reversion-into-self, the immobile centre, becomes a universal point in which the whole is peacefully absorbed. In other words, it is motion in its essence, motion which has sublated the distinctions of Now, Before and After, its dimensions or its Notion. In the circle, these are in a unity; the circle is the restored Notion of duration, Motion extinguished within itself. There is posited *Mass*, the persistent, the self-consolidated, which exhibits motion as its possibility.

Now this is how we conceive the matter: since there is motion, something moves; but this something which persists is matter. Space and Time are filled with Matter. Space does not conform to its Notion; it is therefore the Notion of Space itself which gives itself existence in Matter. Matter has often been made the starting-point, and Space and Time have then been regarded as forms of it. What is right in this standpoint is that Matter is what is real in Space and Time. But these, being abstract, must present themselves here as the First, and then it must appear that Matter is their truth. Just as there is no Motion without Matter, so too, there is no Matter without Motion. Motion is the process, the transition of Time into Space and of Space into Time: Matter, on the other hand, is the relation of Space and Time as a peaceful identity. Matter is the first reality, existent being-for-self; it is not merely the abstract being, but the positive existence of Space, which, however, excludes other spaces. The point *should* also be exclusive: but because it is only an abstract negation, it does not yet exclude. Matter is exclusive relation-to-self, and is thus the first real limit in Space. What is called the filling of Space and Time, the palpable and tangible, what offers resistance and what, in its being-for-other, is also for itself, all this is attained simply in the unity of Space and Time.

B. MATTER AND MOTION

FINITE MECHANICS

§ 262

Through the moment of its negativity, of its abstract *separation into parts*, matter holds itself asunder in opposition to its self-identity; this is the *repulsion* of matter. But since these different parts are one and the same, matter is no less essentially the negative unity of this sundered being-for-self and is therefore continuous; this is its *attraction*. Matter is inseparably both and is the negative unity of these two moments, singularity. But this singularity as still *distinguished* from the *immediate* asunderness of matter and consequently *not yet posited* as *material*, is an *ideal* singularity, a *centre*: *gravity*.

Remark

By his attempt at a so-called *construction* of matter in his *Meta-physical Elements of Natural Science*, Kant has, among other things, the merit of having started towards a *notion* of matter, and of having revived with this attempt, the concept of a *philosophy of Nature*. But in so doing he postulated the forces of attraction and repulsion, determinations of the reflective Understanding, as fixed mutual opposites, and whereas he should have made matter result from them he presupposed it as something ready-made, so that what is to be attracted and repelled is already matter. I have demonstrated in detail the confusion which prevails in this Kantian exposition, in my system of Logic, vol. i, pp. 119 ff.[1] Besides, only *heavy* matter is that totality and real existence in which attraction and repulsion can occur; it possesses the ideal moments of the Notion, of singularity or subjectivity. For this reason, attraction and repulsion are not to be taken as independent of each other or as forces on their own account; matter results from them only as moments of the Notion; but it is the presupposition of their manifestation.

It is essential to distinguish *gravity* from mere *attraction*. The latter is only the sublating of discreteness and yields only continuity. Gravity, on the other hand, is the reduction of both discrete and continuous particularity to unity as a negative relation to self, to *singularity*, to a *subjectivity* which, however, is still quite abstract. Now in the sphere of the first *immediacy* of Nature, this self-external continuity is still posited as the *existent*; it is first in the sphere of Physics that material reflection-into-self begins. Consequently, *singularity*, although present as a determi-nation of the Idea, is here *outside* the material element. In the first place, therefore, matter itself is essentially *heavy*; this is not an external property, nor can it be separated from matter. Gravity constitutes the substantiality of matter; this itself is the *nisus*, the striving to reach the *centre*; but—and this is the other essential determination of matter—this centre falls *outside it*. It can be said that matter is attracted by the centre, i.e. its existence as a self-external continuum is negated; but if the centre itself is conceived as material, then the attraction is merely reciprocal, is at the same

[1] See pp. 178–84 in my Translation of Hegels' *Science of Logic*. Translator.

time a being-attracted, so that the centre again exists in distinction from them both. The centre, however, is not to be taken as material; for the characteristic of the material object is, precisely, to posit its centre *outside itself*. It is not the centre, but the striving to reach it, which is immanent in matter. Gravity is, so to speak, the confession of the nullity of the self-externality of matter in its being-for-self, of its lack of self-subsistence, of its contradiction.

It can also be said that gravity is the being-within-self of matter, in this sense, that just because it is not yet in its own self a centre or subjectivity, it is still indeterminate, undeveloped, and undisclosed, the form is not yet material.

Where the centre lies, is determined by the heavy matter of which it is the centre; matter, as mass, is determinate, and so also, therefore, is its *nisus*, which is the positing—and so a determinate positing—of the centre.

Zusatz. Matter is spatial separation; it offers resistance and in doing so repels itself from itself: this is repulsion, by which matter posits its reality and fills space. But the separated parts which mutually repel each other are only a One, many Ones; each is what the other is. The One repels itself only from itself; this is the sublating of the separation of what is for itself: attraction. These two together, as gravity, constitute the Notion of matter; gravity is the predicate of matter and constitutes the substance of this Subject. The unity of gravity is only an Ought, a longing, the most unhappy *nisus* to which matter is eternally condemned; for this unity does not come to itself or reach itself. If matter attained what it seeks in gravity, it would melt into a single point. The reason why this unity is not realized here, is because repulsion, no less than attraction, is an essential moment of matter. The dull, obscure unity does not become free; but since, all the same, matter has as its specific character the positing of the Many in the One, it is not so foolish as those would-be philosophers who keep the One and the Many apart, and in this respect they are refuted by matter itself. The two unities of attraction and repulsion, although forming the inseparable moments of gravity, do not unite to form a single, ideal unity; this unity first attains its explicit existence in Light, as we shall see later. Matter seeks a place outside the Many; and since there is not yet any difference between the parts which are seeking this place, there is no reason why one should be nearer than another. They are at equal distances on the periphery; the point they seek is the centre, and this extends in every dimension so that the next determination we have is the *sphere*. Although gravity is a mode of the inwardness of matter and not its lifeless externality, nevertheless this inwardness does not yet have its place here; matter is still that which is without inwardness, is the Notion of the Notionless.

Accordingly, the second sphere which we have now to consider is finite mechanics, because here, matter still does not conform to its Notion. This finitude of matter lies in the separation between motion and matter as such; in other words, matter is finite in so far as its life, i.e. motion, is external to it. The body is at rest, or else motion is communicated to it from outside; this is the first difference in matter as such; this difference is then sublated by the nature of matter, by gravity. Here, therefore, we have the three determinations of finite mechanics: *first*, inert matter; *secondly*, thrust; and *thirdly*, the motion of falling, which forms the transition to absolute mechanics where matter in its existence, too, conforms to the Notion. Gravity belongs to matter not only in itself, but in so far as the 'in-itself' is already manifested; this is falling, where, consequently, gravity will first make its appearance.

(I) INERT MATTER

§ 263

Matter, as simply universal and immediate, has at first only a *quantitative* difference and is particularized into different quanta or *masses* which, in the superficial determination of a whole or a One, are *bodies*. The body, too, is immediately distinguished from its ideality; it is *essentially* spatial and temporal, but as being *in* space and *in* time, and it appears as their *content*, indifferent to this form.

Zusatz. Matter fills space; this simply means that it is a real limit in space because, as a being-for-self, it is exclusive, as space as such is not. With being-for-self there at once enters the determination of plurality, a difference, however, which is quite indeterminate and is not yet a difference of matter in its own self; material bodies are mutually exclusive.

§ 264

In accordance with the spatial determination in which time is sublated, the body *endures*, and in accordance with the temporal determination in which indifferent spatial existence is sublated, it is *transitory*; in general, it is a wholly *contingent* One. It is, indeed, the unity which holds together the two moments *in their opposition*, i.e. *motion*; but because the body is indifferent to space and time (preceding §), and so to their relation, motion, the latter is *external* to it, as is also *rest*, the negation of motion in body: the body is *inert*.

Remark

The finitude of the body, i.e. its inadequacy to its Notion, consists here in this: as matter, the body is only the *abstract*, immediate unity of time and space, but their developed and restless unity, motion, is not here posited as a unity *immanent* in it. This is the character given to body by ordinary (*physikalischen*) mechanics, which postulates as an axiom that a body is set in motion or comes to rest only through an *external cause*, motion or rest constituting only a *state* of the body. What this mechanics has in view is only the selfless bodies of the earth for which such characterizations are, of course, true. But here we have only immediate materiality which, for that very reason, is only *abstract* and finite. Body *qua* body means this abstraction of body. But the untruth of this abstract existence is sublated in bodies which have a concrete existence and this sublation begins to be posited already in the selfless body. The determinations of inertia, thrust, pressure, falling, etc., which are proper to the sphere of ordinary mechanics, and so to *finite motion*, are improperly carried over into absolute mechanics in which, on the contrary, matter and motion exist in their free Notion.

Zusatz. In mass, as immediately posited, motion is present as *resistance*; for this immediacy is a being-for-other. The real moment of difference is outside mass, which contains motion as this Notion or as sublated. Mass, fixed in this sense, is inert: but this inertia is not equivalent to rest. Duration is rest, in the relationship in which the former, as Notion, is opposed to its realization, to motion. Mass is the unity of the moments of rest and motion; both moments are present in mass but as sublated, or in other words, mass is indifferent to them both and is equally capable of motion or rest, and is itself neither of them. Mass itself is neither at rest nor in motion, but only passes from one state to the other through an external impulse; in other words, rest and motion are posited in it by an Other. When at rest it remains in that state and does not spontaneously set itself in motion; and conversely, when in motion it remains in motion and does not spontaneously pass over into a state of rest. *In itself*, matter is inert, i.e. matter as its Notion, opposed to its reality. It is only when this reality has acquired a separate existence in opposition to the Notion of matter, that the reality of matter is sublated, or that matter exists only as an abstraction; and for those to whom sensuous reality is the real, and the form of abstraction is the 'in-itself', this abstraction is always what is meant by the 'in-itself' or essence.

While, therefore, motion is communicated to finite matter from outside, free matter moves spontaneously; it is therefore infinite within its sphere, for in the whole system, matter stands at the level of finitude. Similarly, the good man is free *in* his obedience to the law, and it is only the bad man for whom the law is something *external* to him. Each sphere of Nature exists not simply in its infinitude, but also as a finite relationship. Finite relationships like pressure and thrust, have the advantage of being familiar to our ordinary reflection and of being drawn from experience. The defect is simply that other relationships are subsumed under this empirically fixed rule. It is presumed that what holds good for us on earth, also holds good in the heavens. But finite relationships cannot exhibit a sphere in its infinitude.

(2) THRUST

§ 265

The inert body externally set in motion—hence a finite motion— and so connected with another body, momentarily constitutes with this other, one body, for they are only quantitatively distinguished masses. In this way, there is a *single* motion of both bodies (*communication of motion*). But equally, the bodies offer resistance to each other, since each is likewise presupposed as an immediate One. This being-for-self of each against the other, which is further particularized by the quantum of mass, is their relative *heaviness*: *weight* as the *heaviness* of a quantitatively distinct mass (extensively as an aggregate of heavy parts, intensively as a specific pressure, see § 103, Remark). This weight, as the real determinateness, together with the ideal or the quantitative determinateness of motion, of velocity, constitutes a single determinateness (*quantitas motus*) within which weight and velocity can each take the place of the other (cf. § 261, Remark).

Zusatz. The second moment from this standpoint is that matter is set in motion and in this motion forms contact with itself. Now because matter is indifferent to place, it follows that it is also set in motion. This is contingent, but here, every necessary moment is posited in the mode of contingency. Later on, we shall see that the motion of matter in the sphere of existence is necessary too. In the thrust of two bodies on each other, both are to be regarded as moving themselves, for it is the struggle for one and the same place. The body exerting thrust takes the place of the body at rest, and this, the one being pushed, is retaining its place and therefore moves, too, in its effort to reoccupy the place taken up by the other. But there is no empty space between the bodies (*Massen*) which are thrusting and pressing against each other, they are in *contact*; and it is in this contact now that the ideality of matter begins; and the interest lies in seeing how this inwardness of matter emerges into existence, just as the attainment of existence by the Notion is always the interesting thing. Thus, two masses come into contact, that is to say, are for each other; this means that there are two material points or atoms, coinciding in a single point or in an identity: their being-for-self is *not* a being-for-self. No matter how hard and brittle the matter is imagined to be, one can imagine that there is still some space between them; but as soon as they touch each other they exist as *one* body, however small this point is conceived to be. This is the higher, materially existing continuity, a continuity which is not external and merely spatial, but real. Similarly, the point of time is a unity of past and future: the two points are in one, and at the same time they are also not in one. Motion is precisely this: to be in one place, and at the same time to be in another place, and yet not to be in another place but only in this place.

Though the two masses form a single body at their point of contact, they equally retain their being-for-self; and this is the other moment— repulsion, or in other words, matter is elastic. This unity of the two masses is only the surface, that is to say, the whole is continuous, and therefore the body is absolutely *hard*. But since it is only the whole that is a One and the One is therefore not posited, the body simply yields or is absolutely *soft*. But in leaving its whole, the body is by that very fact a more intensive One. The very softness which is the sublating of the body's outwardly exerted force is, through the return-into-self of that force, the latter's restoration. The immediate inversion of these two sides is *elasticity*. What is soft also repels, is elastic; it yields, but only *so* far, for there is one place from which it cannot be expelled. In elasticity, we have the first appearance of the being-for-self of matter, through which it asserts itself as an inwardness (also called force) in opposition to its externality, which means here a being-for-other, that is, the being of an Other in it. The ideality of being-for-self consists in this, that an Other prevails in the body (*Masse*), and the body also prevails in this Other. This determination of ideality, which seemed to come from outside, shows itself to be the very essence of matter, an essence which at the same time belongs to matter's inwardness. This is the reason why Physics turns to the conception of Force, a category of reflective thought.

The intensity of thrust, as magnitude of the effect, is simply that through which matter preserves its being-for-self, or resists; for thrust is equally resistance: resistance, however, simply means matter. What resists is material, and conversely, is material in so far as it offers resistance;

resistance is the motion of both bodies, determinate motion and determinate resistance are the same. Bodies only act on each other in so far as they are self-subsistent; and they are such only through gravity. Thus it is only through their heaviness that bodies resist each other; but this heaviness is not the absolute heaviness which expresses the Notion of matter, but relative heaviness. One of the moments of the body is its weight, whereby in its striving towards the centre of the earth it presses on another body which resists it. Pressure is therefore the motion of cancelling the separation of the body from the other mass [the earth]. The other moment of the body is the motion communicated to it in a direction oblique to, and so deviating from, the quest for the centre of the earth. The magnitude of its motion is determined by these two moments: by mass, and by the specific tangential motion as velocity. If this magnitude is posited as something internal, it is what we call force; however, we can dispense with this realm of forces, for the theorems of mechanics about them are very tautological. Because there is only one determinateness, that of force, we have, it is true, the same material effect when the amount of material parts and the velocity are interchanged (for the material effect exists only as self-moving); but the ideal and real factors can only be partly, not wholly, interchangeable. If the mass is six pounds and the velocity four units, then the force is twenty-four; but it is the same, too, if eight pounds moves with a velocity of three units, and so on; similarly, the length of the arm on the one side of the ὑπομόχλιον [fulcrum] where the (motive) weight hangs has its counterpoise on the other side where the weight (to be moved) hangs. Pressure and thrust are the two causes of external, mechanical motion.

§ 266

This weight, concentrated as intensive magnitude into a point of the body itself, is its *centre of gravity*; but the characteristic of a body as heavy, is to posit and to have its centre *outside itself*. Consequently, thrust and resistance, like the motion produced by them, have an essential basis in a *centre* common to and lying outside the separate bodies, and the contingent motion externally communicated to them passes over into *rest* in this centre. At the same time, because the centre is *outside* matter, this rest is only an *effort* to reach the centre; and in accordance with the relationship (*Verhältnisse*) of matter particularized in bodies striving in common to reach the centre, is a *pressure* of the bodies on each other. When the body is *separated* from the centre of its gravity [i.e. the centre of the earth] by a relatively empty space, this effort becomes the motion of *falling*, the *essential* motion; contingent motion, in conformity with the Notion, *passes over* into this *essential* motion, and on its existential side *passes over* into rest.

Remark

In regard to *external*, finite motion, it is an axiom in mechanics that a body at rest would remain at rest, and a body in motion would continue in motion, for ever, *if they were not* made to pass from one state to the other by an *external* cause. This means no more than that motion and rest are enunciated in accordance with the principle of identity (§ 115): motion *is* motion, and rest *is* rest; the two determinations are external to each other.* It is on these abstractions of motion and rest, each taken in isolation from the other, that is based the empty assertion of a motion continuing *for ever*, *unless*, etc. The nullity of the principle of identity on which this assertion is based has been specifically demonstrated in its place. That assertion has no *empirical* foundation; even thrust as such is conditioned by gravity, i.e. by the determination of falling. Throwing shows *contingent* motion in contrast to the *essential* motion of falling; but the abstraction, body *qua* body, is inseparably connected with its gravity, and one is thus forced to take this gravity into account in throwing. Throwing cannot be demonstrated as something separate, *existing on its own*. The usual example given of the motion supposedly produced by centrifugal force is that of a stone held in a sling and whirled round in a circle: the stone tries all the time to fly off at a tangent (Newton, *Phil. Nat. Princ. Math.*, Defin. V). But the question is not whether such a tendency *exists*, but whether it exists *on its own*, *apart from gravity*, as in the conception of [centrifugal] *force* where it is represented as wholly self-subsistent. Newton, in the same place, maintains that a lead bullet '*in coelos abiret et motu abeundi pergeret in infinitum*', *if* (certainly *if*) *only* one could impart to it the appropriate velocity. Such a separation of external and essential motion belongs neither to experience nor to the

---

* Descartes' proposition that the quantum of motion in the universe is constant, belongs to this same standpoint. [This is in the text of the 2nd edition only.]

Notion, but only to abstractive reflection. It is one thing to *distinguish* them, to represent them mathematically as separate lines and to treat them as distinct quantitative factors, all this is necessary; but it is another thing to regard them as physically independent existences.*

But in this unending flight of the lead bullet, one is also supposed to abstract from the resistance of the air, from *friction*. The fact that a *perpetuum mobile*, no matter how correctly calculated and proved in theory, nevertheless in its time, which does not fail to appear, passes over into a state of rest, is attributed solely to friction, gravity being left out of account. To this same hindrance is ascribed the gradual decrease in the *motion of the pendulum* and its final cessation from motion; it is said of this motion, too, that it would continue without ever stopping, *if* friction could be prevented. This resistance which the body encounters in its contingent motion belongs, of course, to the necessary manifestation of its lack of self-subsistent being. But in the same way that a body meets with hindrances in its effort to reach the centre of its central body, without these hindrances destroying its pressure, or its gravity, so too the resistance of friction checks the motion of throwing, without thereby destroying the weight of the body, or friction taking the weight's place. Friction is a hindrance, but not the *essential* hindrance of external, contingent motion. The fact remains that finite motion is inseparably connected with gravity, and as accidental, it passes over into and is subjected to the latter, to the substantial determination of matter.

---

* Newton expressly says (op. cit., Defin. VIII): '*Voces Attractionis, Impulsus vel Propensionis cujuscunque in centrum, indifferenter et pro se mutuo promiscue usurpo, has vires non Physice sed Mathematice tantum considerando. Unde caveat lector, ne per hujusmodi voces cogitet me speciem vel modum actionis causamve aut rationem Physicam alicubi definire, vel centris (quae sunt puncta Mathematica) vires vere et Physice tribuere; si forte aut centra trahere, aut vires centrorum esse dixero.*' But by introducing the conception of forces, Newton has shifted them away from physical reality and made them essentially self-subsistent. At the same time, in these descriptions, he himself has everywhere spoken of physical objects: and so in those descriptions of the universe which are supposed to be physical, not metaphysical, he has also spoken of such self-subsistent and mutually independent forces, of their attractions, impulses and the like, as if they were physical existences and has treated them on the basis of the principle of identity.

Zusatz. It is here that gravity itself enters as the mover, as movement pure and simple, though movement determined as cancelling the separation, i.e. distance, from the centre. Motion here, as self-generative, is motion whose determinateness in [the realm of] appearance is posited by itself. The first determinateness is direction, the second, the law of falling. The *direction* is the bearing on the One which in gravity is sought and presupposed; this search is not a searching around, a vague, indeterminate wandering to and fro in space; on the contrary, it is matter which itself posits this One in space as a place which, however, it never reaches. This centre is not present to itself only, as it were, like a nucleus round which matter is gathered and towards which it would be drawn; on the contrary, the gravity of bodies generates such a centre; material points in seeking each other have in so doing posited a common centre of gravity. Gravity is the positing of such a One; each particular mass is the positing of it, it seeks a One within itself and gathers its entire quantitative relationship to others into a single point. This subjective One which, as only questing, is the objective One, is the centre of gravity of a body. Every body has a centre of gravity, in order, as a centre to have its centre in an Other; and mass is such an actual One or a body, in so far as it has a centre of gravity. The centre of gravity is the first reality of the One of gravity, the effort in which the whole weight of the body is concentrated; for the body to be at rest, its centre of gravity must be supported. It is just as if the rest of the body did not exist; its gravity has returned into this one point. This point, as a line, each part of which belongs to this centre, is the *lever*, the centre of gravity as the middle dividing itself into end-points whose continuity is the line. The whole is equally this One of gravity; the surface constitutes the One, but the One which, as a whole, has returned into the centre. What is here externalized in dimensions is immediately a One; that is, gravity develops itself in this way into a whole, single body.

Now each separate mass is such a body which strives to reach its centre, the absolute centre of gravity. In so far as matter fixes a centre and strives to reach it, and this centre is a unifying point while matter remains a multiplicity, matter is determined as coming outside itself from out of its place. It thus comes out of its self-externality and this, as a sublation of the externality, constitutes its first true inwardness. Every mass belongs to such a centre and each separate mass is something non-self-subsistent and contingent in contrast to this its truth. Now it is because of this contingency that a single mass can be separated from this central body. If between these two there is another specific mass which gives way to the first body in its tendency towards the centre, then this body is not impeded by the other mass and it moves: that is, the body is determined as being unsupported and it falls. The rest in which the external motion culminates in falling is, it is true, still an effort [a striving to reach the centre]; but it is not contingent nor a mere state or externally posited, as was rest in the first instance. The rest which we have now is rest posited by the Notion, just as falling, as a motion posited by the Notion, sublates external, contingent motion. Here, inertia has disappeared because we have now arrived at the Notion of matter. Since each mass, as heavy, strives to reach the centre and therefore exerts pressure, the motion is only an attempted motion which makes itself felt in another mass, and posits it as an ideal moment; just as the second mass posits the first as an ideal moment by resisting it and maintaining itself. In finite mechanics, both kinds of rest and motion are placed on the same level. Everything is reduced to forces standing in relation to each other and differing in direction and velocity; the main concern is then the *result*. Thus the motion of falling which is posited by the force of gravity and the motion resulting from throwing, are put on the same level.

It is imagined that, if a cannon-ball were projected with a force greater than that of gravity, it would fly off at a tangent—*if*, it is added, there were no resistance from the air. Similarly, the pendulum would swing for ever if the air offered no resistance. 'The pendulum', it is said, 'in its fall describes an arc of a circle. Arrived at the vertical position, it has acquired a velocity through its descent, by virtue of which it must reach the same height on the other side of the circle as it had previously; thus it must oscillate perpetually in both directions.' On the one hand, the pendulum follows the direction of gravity. By raising it, it is taken out of the direction of gravity and given another determination. It is this second determination which gives rise to the oscillatory motion. It is now asserted that 'resistance is the *principal* cause of the oscillations becoming smaller and smaller, until finally, the pendulum comes to rest; otherwise the oscillatory motion in itself would continue for ever.' But the motion due to gravity and the transversal motion are related to each other, not simply as two kinds of motion: the former is the essential motion, to which the latter, the contingent motion succumbs. Friction itself, however, is not contingent but is a result of gravity, even though it can be diminished. This was recognized by Francoeur (*Traité élémentaire de mécanique*, p. 175, nn. 4–5), when he said: 'Friction does not depend on the extent of the surfaces in contact, the weight of the body remaining the same: friction is proportional to *pressure*.' Friction, therefore, is gravity in the form of an external resistance—pressure, as a mutual drawing towards the centre. Now in order in the pendulum to check the variable motion of the body, it must be fixed to another body; this material connection is necessary, but it disturbs its motion and so gives rise to friction. This, then, is itself a necessary factor in the construction of a pendulum and cannot be eliminated, nor thought away. It is an empty thought to think of the pendulum as if it were free from friction. But also, it is not only friction which brings the motion of the pendulum to a standstill, for even if friction ceased, the pendulum would still have to come to rest. Gravity is the power which, through the Notion of matter, brings the pendulum to rest; as the universal, it prevails over the foreign element, and the oscillation terminates in the direction of falling. But in this sphere of externality the necessity of the

Notion appears as an external check, or as friction. A man can be killed; but this external circumstance is contingent; the truth is that man dies through his own nature.

The combinations of falling with contingent motion, e.g. in [the motion of] throwing, do not concern us here; what we have to consider here is the sublation of purely contingent motion. In throwing, the magnitude of the motion is the product of the force of the throw and the weight of the mass. But this same weight is also gravity; this, as the universal, retains the preponderance and overcomes the determinateness posited in it. The body is thrown only by gravity; when thrown, its motion is at first determined contingently, but it returns into the determination posited by the universal and becomes a simple falling. This return introduces a new determinateness into gravity, or the motion is made more closely one with gravity. In the motion of throwing, weight is only one moment of the motive force; or there is posited the transition into gravity of the force which was external to it. In accordance with this transition, gravity is now the entire motive force; true, the principle of the motion is still external to gravity, but only formally so, as simple thrust, in the same way that, in the motion of falling, this principle appears simply as distance [from the centre]. In this way, throwing is also a falling, and the motion of the pendulum is both falling and throwing at the same time. Gravity is separation and distance from itself, a presentation of itself as sundering itself into two—but all this is still external. The fixed point, the deviation from the direction of falling, the holding at a distance of the moved point, the moments of the actual motion, these belong to an Other. The return into the direction of falling, from the motion given in throwing is itself a throwing; and the oscillation of the pendulum is the motion in which throwing spontaneously transforms itself into falling.[1]

(3) FALLING

§ 267

Falling is *relatively free* motion. It is *free*, because it is posited by the *Notion* of body and is thus the manifestation of the body's own gravity; it is therefore *immanent* in the body. But at the same time, as only the *first* negation of externality, it is *conditioned*; consequently the separation of the body from its connection with the centre is still a *contingent* determination, *externally* posited.

[1] Michelet has taken this passage from the manuscript of Hegel's Jena lectures on *Realphilosophie* in 1805/6. The corrupt version in the *Werke* has been corrected by Hoffmeister in his edition of the *Realphilosophie* (vol. ii, p. 39) to read: '*und die Schwingung* [*ist*] *die Bewegung des fallend sich erzeugenden Aufhebens des Wurfs*'.

Remark

The laws of motion concern *magnitude*, and essentially that of the time elapsed and the space traversed therein; they are immortal discoveries which redound to the greatest honour of the analysis of the Understanding. The next step concerns their *proof* independently of empirical methods; and this proof has also been furnished by mathematical mechanics, so that even a science based on empirically ascertained facts is not satisfied with the merely empirical *pointing out* (demonstration). The *a priori* proof in question rests on the presupposition that the velocity of a falling body is *uniformly* accelerated; the proof, however, consists in the conversion of the moments of the *mathematical* formula into *physical* forces, into an *accelerating* force imparting one and the same impulse in each unit of time,* and into a force of *inertia* which perpetuates the (greater) velocity acquired in each moment of time—determinations utterly devoid of empirical sanction and equally inconsistent with the Notion. More precisely, the determination of magnitude, which here contains a relation of *powers*, is reduced to the form of a *sum* of two independent elements, and in this way, the qualitative determination dependent on the Notion is destroyed. From the law thus supposedly proved, it is *concluded* 'that in the uniformly accelerated motion velocities are proportional to times'. In point of fact, however, this proposition is nothing but the quite simple definition of uniformly accelerated motion itself. The simply *uniform* motion is one in which the spaces traversed are proportional to the times elapsed: the *accelerated* motion is one in which the *velocity* increases in every successive unit of time; hence, the *uniformly accelerated* motion is a motion in which the velocities are proportional to the times elapsed: hence V/t, i.e.

---

* It might be said that this so-called accelerating force is very inappropriately named, for the effect which it is supposed to produce in each moment of time is *constant*—the *empirical* factor in the magnitude of the fall, the unit of 15 feet at the earth's surface. The acceleration consists solely in the *addition* of this empirical unit in each moment of time. But in the same way, at least, *acceleration* belongs also to the force of *inertia*, for this is credited with *preserving the velocity attained* at the end of each moment of time, i.e. the force of inertia for its part *adds* this velocity to the said empirical magnitude: and this velocity is greater at the end of each moment of time than at the end of the preceding moment.

s/t^2. This is the simple, genuine proof. V stands for velocity *as such*, as still *indeterminate*, and consequently for the *abstract*, i.e. purely uniform velocity. The difficulty in connection with the proof in question lies in this, that V at first stands for indeterminate velocity as such, but in the mathematical formula it presents itself as s/t, i.e. as purely uniform velocity. The indirect method of proof derived from the mathematical exposition, serves the need for treating velocity as purely uniform velocity s/t, and making the transition to s/t^2. In the statement that velocity is proportional to time, it is primarily velocity as such that is referred to; so it is superfluous to convert it into s/t, purely uniform velocity, and to introduce the force of inertia, and then to attribute to this the moment of purely uniform velocity. But if velocity is to be proportional to time, then it must be uniformly accelerated velocity, s/t^2, so that the determination of s/t is out of place and is excluded.*

As against the abstract, uniform velocity of lifeless, externally determined mechanism, the law of descent of a falling body is a *free* law of Nature, i.e. it involves an element which is determined by the *Notion* of body. Since it follows that the law must be deducible from this Notion, what has to be done is to show the way in which Galileo's law, 'that the traversed spaces are propor-

---

* Lagrange in his *Théorie des fonctions, part III, Application de la théorie à la mécanique*, chap. I, follows, as is his way, the simple, quite correct procedure: he presupposes the mathematical treatment of functions and then *finds* in the application to mechanics that among the motions represented by the general equation $s = ft$, ft and also bt^2 are found in Nature; $s = ct^3$ does not occur in Nature. Quite properly, there is no question here of wanting to set up a proof of $s = bt^2$; this ratio is simply accepted as *occurring* in Nature. In the development of the function where t becomes $t+\theta$, the series expressing the space traversed in θ time only makes use of the first two terms, the others being omitted, and this circumstance is disposed of by Lagrange in his usual way from the analytical standpoint. But the first two terms are only treated as important for the object because they alone have a real determination ('one sees that the first and second functions occur *naturally* in mechanics where they have a specific value and significance', ibid., 4. 5). At this point Lagrange, it is true, resorts to the Newtonian expressions of abstract, i.e. simply uniform velocity which comes from the law of inertia, and to an accelerating force, thus introducing mental fictions of an infinitely small period of time (θ) and of its beginning and end. But this has no influence on the aforesaid correct procedure, which does not use these determinations *to prove the law*, but properly takes them from experience and then subjects them to mathematical treatment.

tional to the squares of the elapsed times', coheres with the determination of the Notion.

This connection lies simply in this, that because it is the Notion that now determines motion, time and space, as determinations of the Notion, become *free* in regard to each other; that is to say, their quantitative relationships conform to their *notional* determinations. Now seeing that *time* is the moment of *negation*, of being-for-self, the principle of the One, its magnitude (any empirical number) in relation to space is to be taken as the unit or denominator. Space, on the contrary, is asunderness, and its magnitude is no other than that of time; for the velocity of this *free* motion means precisely that space and time are not *external* or *contingent* in relation to each other, but that they form a *single* determination. But the form of the mutual externality of space, the form opposed to unity as the form of time, and without the intermixture of any other determinateness whatever, is the *square*: magnitude as *coming outside itself*, raising itself into a second dimension and thus expanding itself, but *solely in accordance with its own determinateness*; in this expansion it sets its own self as limit, and thus in becoming an Other, it is related solely to itself.

This is the proof of the law of descent of a falling body as derived from the Notion of the thing. The relation of *powers* is essentially a *qualitative* relation and the only relation belonging to the Notion. There remains this to be added with reference to what follows, that because the motion of *falling* is still *conditioned* in its freedom, time remains only an abstract unit, as an *immediate* number; similarly, the quantitative determination of space only attains to the second dimension.

Zusatz. In the motion of falling, it is only the quest for the centre which is the absolute factor. Later, we shall see how the other moment, the diremption or differentiation, the placing of the body in an unsupported position, also derives from the Notion. In falling, the body does not become separated from the centre through its own act; but when it is so separated, it returns into the unity. The motion of falling thus forms the transition and middle term between inert matter and matter whose Notion is absolutely realized, that is, absolutely free motion. While mass, as the merely quantitative, indifferent difference is one factor in external motion, here, on the contrary, where the motion is posited by the Notion of matter, the quantitative difference between bodies has no significance; bodies fall simply as matter, not as masses. In other words, bodies fall simply on account of their heaviness, and in this respect a large body and a smaller one, i.e. one smaller in weight, are equally heavy. We are well aware that a feather does not fall like a lead bullet; but this is on account of the medium which has to give way, so that the bodies behave according to the qualitative difference of the resistance they encounter. For example, a stone falls faster in air than in water; but in a vacuum, bodies fall with equal velocity. Galileo put forward this proposition and demonstrated it to monks; only one of them recorded agreement—but in his own way, saying that scissors and knives reached the ground at the same time: but the matter is not to be decided in this easy fashion. Galileo's knowledge is worth more than thousands of so-called brilliant thoughts.

The empirical magnitude of a falling body is that the body falls a little more than 15 feet in the first second; in other latitudes there is a slight variation. In two seconds, the body falls, not twice but four times the distance, i.e. 60 feet; in three seconds it falls 9×15 feet, and so on. That is to say, if one body falls for three seconds and another for nine seconds, the spaces traversed are not in the ratio of $3 : 9$, but $9 : 81$. Purely uniform motion is the ordinary, mechanical motion; motion which is not uniformly accelerated is capricious. It is in uniformly accelerated motion that we first have the living motion of Nature conforming to law. Thus the velocity increases with the time; i.e. $t : s/t$, i.e. $s : t^2$; for $s : t^2$ is the same as s/t^2. In mechanics this is proved mathematically by representing the so-called force of inertia by a square, and the so-called force of acceleration by a triangle fitted on to it. This method is of interest and is perhaps necessary for the mathematical exposition; but it is necessary only because of that exposition, a tortuous one. These mathematical proofs always presuppose what they set out to prove. They then, of course, describe what has already been admitted. This mathematical procedure comes from the need to convert the relation of powers into one more amenable to mathematical treatment, e.g. to reduce it to addition or subtraction or multiplication. In this way, the motion of a falling body is analysed into two parts. But this division has no reality and is merely an empty fiction introduced only to aid the mathematical exposition.

§ 268

Falling is the merely *abstract* positing of a centre in whose unity the distinction of particular masses and bodies is posited as sublated; consequently mass, weight, exercises no influence on the magnitude of this motion. But the simple being-for-self of the centre is, as this *negative* self-relation, essentially a *repulsion* of itself: a *formal* repulsion into the many immobile (*ruhende*) centres (*stars*); a *living* repulsion as a determination of them in accordance with the *moments of the Notion*, and an essential interrelationship of these centres thus differentiated according to the Notion. This relation is the *contradiction* of their independent being-for-self and their *notional* interconnectedness; the manifestation of this contradiction between their reality and their ideality is motion, the *absolutely free motion*.

Zusatz. The defect of the law of descent of a falling body is at once obvious in the fact that in this motion, space is posited only in the first power (*Potenz*) that is, abstractly as line; this is because the motion of falling is partly free and partly conditioned (see prec. §). Falling is only the first manifestation of gravity because its condition, namely, distance from the centre, is still contingent, is not posited by gravity. This contingency has still to be eliminated. The Notion must become completely immanent in matter; and this is the third main division, absolute mechanics, absolutely free matter which, in its existence, is completely adequate to its Notion. Inert matter is completely inadequate to its Notion. Heavy matter in the motion of falling, is only partly adequate to its Notion, namely, through the sublation of the Many, as the effort of matter to reach one place, as centre. The other moment, however, the differentiation of the centre within itself is not yet posited by the Notion: in other words, the defect is that attracted matter, as heavy, has not yet repelled itself, the diremption into many bodies is not yet the act of gravity itself. Such matter which, as a Many, is both extended and continuous within itself, and which contains a centre, must also be repelled; this is real repulsion where the centre repels itself, multiplies itself so that masses are posited as a Many, each with its centre. The logical One is infinite self-reference, which is self-identity, but as a self-relating negativity and thus self-repulsion: this is the other moment contained in the Notion. In order to be a reality, matter must posit itself in the determinations of its moments. Falling is the one-sided positing of matter as attraction: the next step is that it must now also appear as repulsion. Formal repulsion must also receive its due; for it is characteristic of Nature to do just this, to let an abstract, separate moment exist independently. The stars are such an existence of formal repulsion, in so far as they are still undifferentiated, simply a plurality of bodies; here, we are not yet concerned with them as luminous, for this is a *physical* determination.

We may suppose the stars in their interrelationships to exhibit a formal rationality, but they belong to the sphere of dead repulsion. Their *groupings* may express essential relations; these, however, do not belong to living matter where the centre is self-differentiated. The host of stars is a formal world because in it the one-sided determination of repulsion holds sway alone. We must certainly not set this system on the same level as the solar system, in which we first discern the system of Reason as a reality in the heavens. The stars can be admired on account of their repose, but they are not to be reckoned as equal in dignity to the concrete individual bodies. Matter, in filling space, erupts into an infinite plurality of masses, but this, which may delight the eye, is only the first manifestation of matter. This eruption of light is as little worthy of wonderment as an eruption on the skin or a swarm of flies. The tranquillity of the stars interests the heart more keenly; in contemplating their repose and simplicity the passions are calmed. Philosophy, however, does not find the interest in this sphere that feeling does. The multitude of stars in immeasurable space means nothing to Reason; this is externality, the void, the negative infinitude to which Reason knows itself to be superior. The wonderment is purely negative, an uplifting which remains confined within its limited standpoint. What is rational in regard to the stars, is to ascertain how they are grouped in relation to each other. The eruption of space into abstract matter, itself proceeds according to an inner law, the stars representing crystallizations which have an inner connection. It is an idle curiosity which would seek to satisfy itself about this. Now there is not much to be said about the necessity of these groupings. Herschel has observed forms in the nebulae which hint at regularity. There are fewer stars in those regions which are more distant from the Milky Way. From this it has been inferred (Herschel and Kant) that the stars form the shape of a lens. This is something quite indeterminate and general. The dignity of science must not be held to consist in the comprehension and explanation of all the multiplicity of forms in Nature; we must be content with what we can, in fact, comprehend at present. There is plenty that cannot be comprehended yet; this is something we must grant in the Philosophy of Nature. At present, the only rational interest offered by the stars lies in their geometrical forms; the stars are the realm of this abstract, infinite diremption, and on their constellations contingency has an essential influence.

C. ABSOLUTE MECHANICS

§ 269

(1) UNIVERSAL GRAVITATION

Gravitation is the true and determinate *Notion* of material corporeality which is *realized* into the *Idea*. *Universal* corporeality essentially sunders itself (*sich urteilt*) into *particular* bodies and achieves conclusion with itself in the moment of *individuality* or subjectivity as manifested existence in *motion* which thus is immediately a system of *several bodies*.

Remark

Universal gravitation must be recognized as a profound thought in itself, though it is especially by reason of the quantitative determinations bound up with it that it has attracted attention and credit, and its verification has been based on *experience*, from the solar system down to the phenomenon of the capillary tube; so that, as understood by the reflective Understanding, it has only the significance of abstraction generally, and more concretely, only that of gravity in the quantitative determination of falling, not the significance stated above, of the Idea developed in its reality. Gravitation directly contradicts the law of inertia; for, by virtue of the former, matter strives to get away *out of itself* to an Other.

In the *Notion of gravity*, as has been shown, there are included the two moments: being-for-self, and the continuity that sublates it. It has been the fate of these two moments of the Notion to be regarded as separate *forces*, corresponding to the forces of attraction and repulsion, more precisely determined as *centripetal* and *centrifugal* forces, which are supposed, like gravity, to *act on bodies*, and—independently of each other and contingently—to meet together in a third something, the body. In this way, whatever deeper meaning there were in the thought of universal gravitation is destroyed again; and the Notion and Reason will be unable to penetrate into the theory of absolute motion, so long as the much vaunted discoveries of *forces* prevail there. In the syllogism which contains the *Idea* of gravity—gravity itself, namely, as the Notion which, through the different particular bodies, develops into an outer reality, and at the same time shows itself in the ideality and reflection-into-self of these bodies, i.e. in motion, to be *in a unity with itself*—in this syllogism are contained the rational identity and inseparability of the moments, which elsewhere are conceived as independent. Motion as such has meaning and existence simply and solely in a system of *several* bodies that stand in relation to each other, but in a differently *specified* relation. This more precise specification in the syllogism of totality, which syllogism is itself a system of three syllogisms, has been indicated in the Notion of Objectivity (§ 198).

Zusatz. The solar system is in the first place a group of independent bodies which stand in an essential relationship to each other and are heavy, but which in this relationship maintain themselves and posit their unity in an other outside them. The plurality of bodies is thus no longer indeterminate as it is in the stars, but the difference is posited; the determinateness of this difference is solely that of absolutely *universal* centrality and *particular* centrality. These two determinations yield the forms of motion in which the Notion of matter is fulfilled. The motion falls into the relative central body which is the universal determinateness of place; at the same time, the place of this central body is also not determined, in so far as it has its centre in an other and this indeterminateness must also have an existence, whereas the place which is determined in and for itself is only One. It is therefore a matter of indifference as regards the particular central bodies where their place is, and this is manifested in the fact that they seek their centre, i.e. they leave their place and occupy another one. Thirdly, they could be equidistant from their centre; if this were so they would not be distant from one another; if they all moved in the same orbit, they would not be distinguished from one another at all, but would be one and the same, each a mere repetition of the other, and so their difference would be an empty word. Fourthly, in altering their distances from one another they describe a curve and return into themselves. For it is only in this way that they express their independence in regard to the central body; just as their unity with the central body finds expression in their motion round it in this same curve. But as independent in face of the central body, they no longer fall onto it but keep their own place.

Altogether, then, there exist three motions: (α) mechanical motion which is communicated from outside and is uniform; (β) the partly conditioned and partly free motion of falling, where the separation of a body from its gravity is still posited contingently but where the motion already belongs to the gravity itself; (γ) the unconditionally free motion, the principal moments of which have been indicated, the great mechanics of the heavens. This motion is a curve. In it, the positing of a central body by the particular bodies, and conversely, the positing of these by the central body, occur simultaneously. The centre has no meaning apart from the periphery nor the periphery apart from the centre. This puts to rout those physical hypotheses which start now with the centre and now with the particular bodies, sometimes making the former and sometimes the latter the original factor. Both points of view are necessary, but, taken separately, they are one-sided. The diremption into different bodies, and the positing of the moment of subjectivity, is a single act, a free motion, nothing external like pressure and thrust. It is said that in gravity we have a force of attraction which can be demonstrated as a real force on its own account. Gravity, as the cause of falling, is certainly the Notion of matter, but the Notion as still abstract and as not yet differentiating itself within itself; falling is an imperfect manifestation of gravity, and is therefore not real. The centrifugal force, as the tendency to fly off at a tangent, is weakly supposed to be communicated to the celestial bodies by a fling to one side, a swing, a push, which it is assumed they received in the beginning. Such contingency of externally communicated motion, as when a stone whirled round on a string tends to fly off from it, belongs only to inert matter. We must not therefore speak of forces. If we want to speak of force, then there is but *one* force, and its moments do not, as two forces, pull in different directions. The motion of the celestial bodies is not any such pulling this way and that but is free motion; they go on their way, as the ancients said, like blessed gods. Celestial corporeality is not a corporeality which could have the principle of rest or motion outside it. A stone is inert; the entire earth consists of stones; therefore the other celestial bodies are the same; this is a conclusion which sets the qualities of the whole equal to those of the parts. Thrust, pressure, resistance, friction, pulling and the like, apply to an existence of matter other than celestial corporeality. It is true that both are matter, as a good thought and a bad one are both thoughts; but the bad one is not good just because the good one is a thought.

(2) KEPLER'S LAWS

§ 270

As regards the bodies in which the Notion of gravity is freely realized explicitly, they have as the determinations of their diverse natures the moments of their Notion. One body, therefore, is the *universal* centre of abstract self-relation. Over against this extreme, there is that of *immediate*, self-external, centreless *singularity*, appearing as likewise independent corporeality. But the *particular* bodies are those which, characterized as well by self-externality as by being-within-self, are centres for themselves, and are related to the first-mentioned body as to their essential unity.

Remark

The *planetary* bodies are, as the directly *concrete* ones, the most perfect in their existence. Usually, the *sun* is given pride of place, inasmuch as the Understanding prefers the abstract to the concrete, the fixed stars, for example, even being more esteemed than the bodies of the solar system. The centreless corporeality, as belonging

to externality, is sundered in its own self into the opposition of
the *lunar* and the *cometary* body.

The *laws* of absolutely free motion were discovered, as is well
known, by Kepler—a discovery of immortal fame. Kepler *proved*
them, too, in the sense that he found for the empirical data their
general expression (§ 227). It has since become a commonplace
to say that Newton first found the proofs of these laws. Seldom
has fame been more unjustly transferred from a first discoverer
to another person. I comment on this as follows:

1. It is admitted by mathematicians themselves that the Newtonian formulae may be deduced from Kepler's laws. The
   quite abstract derivation, however, is simply this: In Kepler's
   third law, the constant is A^3/T^2. If this is put in the form
   $A.A^2/T^2$, and we call A/T^2 with Newton, universal gravitation,
   then we have his expression for the action of this so-called
   gravitation, in the inverse ratio of the square of the distances.

2. Newton's proof of the proposition that a body in subjection
   to the law of gravitation moves round the central body in an
   ellipse, gives simply a *conic section*, whereas the main point
   which was to be proved consists precisely in this, that the
   path of such a body is not *a circle or any other conic section*,
   but *solely* the *ellipse*. There are other objections to be made
   to this proof, as a proof (*Princ. Math.* 1. I. Sect. II, prop. 1);
   and though it is the basis of the Newtonian theory, analysis
   no longer uses it. The conditions which make the path of the
   body a *specific* conic section are, in the analytical formula,
   constants, and their determination is referred to an *empirical*
   circumstance, namely, to a particular position of the body at
   a certain point of time, and to the *fortuitous* strength of an
   impulse which it is supposed to have received in the beginning;
   so that the circumstance which determines the curve to be
   an ellipse falls outside the formula that is supposed to be
   proved, and no one has ever dreamt of proving this circumstance.

3. Newton's so-called law of the force of gravity has likewise
   only been inductively demonstrated from experience.

The only difference to be seen is that what Kepler, in a simple and sublime manner, enunciated as *laws of celestial motion*, Newton converted into the *reflective* form of *force of gravity* and into the form of this force as it yields the law of magnitude in the motion of a falling body. If Newton's form has not only its convenience but also its necessity for the method of analysis, this is a mere difference of the mathematical formula; analysis has long understood the derivation of Newton's expression and the propositions connected with it from the form of Kepler's laws (I refer here to the elegant exposition in Francoeur's *Traité élém. de mécanique*, Liv. II, ch. 11, n. iv).—In general, the older manner of the so-called proof exhibits a tangled tissue of *lines* of merely geometrical construction, to which a physical meaning of *independent forces* is given, and of the empty reflective forms of the *force of acceleration* and the *force of inertia* already mentioned, but especially of the relation of so-called gravity itself to the centripetal and centrifugal forces, and so on.

The observations made here require a more detailed discussion than can have place in a compendium. Propositions which do not accord with what is received appear as assertions, and, in contradicting such high authorities, as something still worse, namely as pretensions.* Nevertheless, what have been adduced are not so much propositions as bare facts; and the requisite reflection is only this, that the distinctions and determinations brought forward by mathematical analysis, and the course it has to follow in accordance with its method, are wholly distinct from what is supposed to have a physical reality. The presuppositions, the course, and the results, which analysis requires and affords, remain quite outside the objections, which concern the *physical* value and the *physical* meaning of that method and its categories. It is to this that attention should be directed; what is wanted is an awareness that physical mechanics is steeped in an *unspeakable metaphysics* which, contrary to experience and the Notion, has the said mathematical determinations alone as its source.

It is acknowledged that—apart from the basis of analytical treatment, the development of which, moreover, has rendered superfluous, in fact, rejected, much that belonged to Newton's

* I shall not appeal to the fact that, moreover, an interest in these subjects has occupied me for 25 years. [2nd edition, 1827.]

essential principles and fame—the really material addition made by Newton to Kepler's laws is the principle of *perturbation*, a principle whose importance is to be mentioned here, since it rests on the proposition that attraction, so-called, is an effect of all the individual parts of bodies as material. There is implied in this that matter as such posits its own centre. Consequently, the mass of the particular body is to be considered as a moment in the *determination of its place*, and the bodies of the system collectively posit their own sun; but even the particular bodies, too, according to the relative positions occupied by them as a result of their universal motion, form a momentary gravitational relationship *with one another*; and they do not merely stand in the abstract spatial relation of their distance from one another, but jointly give themselves a *particular* centre; this, however, is partly resolved again in the universal system, and partly, at least when such relation is permanent (in the mutual perturbations of Jupiter and Saturn), remains in subjection to it.

If now in this way some main features are indicated of the way in which the main characteristics of free motion are connected *with the Notion*, this connection cannot be developed into any further detail and must therefore, at present, be left to its fate. The principle concerned is, that the proof of Reason in regard to the quantitative determinations of free motion can only be based on space and time as *determinations of the Notion*, i.e. on moments whose relation (but not an external one) is motion. When will science ever become aware of the nature of the metaphysical categories it employs and base its reasoning on the Notion of the thing, instead of on these categories?

That in the *first* place, the motion in general is one that *turns back into itself*, lies in the determination of the bodies of particularity and singularity generally (§ 269), i.e. that of having, on the one hand, a centre in themselves, and a self-subsistent existence, and also, at the same time, having their centre in another than themselves. These are the determinations of the Notion which underlie the conceptions of *centripetal and centrifugal forces*, but they are perverted into that form, as if each of them existed and acted *independently* on its own, apart from the other, and as if they encountered each other only in their effects, only *externally* and consequently contingently. They are, as already pointed out, the lines which must be drawn for the mathematical demonstration, converted into physical realities.

Further, this motion is *uniformly accelerated* (and, as returning into itself, in turn uniformly *retarded*). In the motion which is *free*, space and time reach the point of validating themselves as what they are, i.e. as *different* in determining the magnitude of the motion (§ 267, Remark), instead of being related as they are in the abstract, purely uniform velocity. In the so-called *explanation* of the uniformly accelerated and retarded motion, by the *alternate decrease* and *increase* in the magnitude of the centripetal and centrifugal forces, the *confusion* introduced by the assumption of such self-subsistent forces appears at its worst. According to this explanation, in the motion of the planet from aphelion to perihelion, the centrifugal force is *less* than the centripetal one, while in the perihelion itself, the centrifugal force is supposed to become immediately *greater* again than the centripetal one; for the motion from perihelion to aphelion the forces are, in similar fashion, supposed to pass into the opposite relationship. It is evident that such a *sudden reversal* of the attained preponderance of the one force into its overthrow by the other one, is not something drawn from the nature of the forces. On the contrary, the conclusion ought to have been that a preponderance obtained by the one force over the other should not only maintain itself, but go on to destroy the other force completely; and that the motion should pass, either through the preponderance of the centripetal force into rest, namely, by the fall of the planet into the central body, or through the preponderance of the centrifugal force, into a straight line. The conclusion drawn is simply this: because from its perihelion onwards, the body moves farther away from the sun, the centrifugal force becomes greater again; and because in aphelion, it is farthest from the sun, it is there at its maximum. This metaphysical monstrosity of a self-subsistent force, centrifugal or centripetal, is a presupposition; upon these fictions of the Understanding, however, no further understanding is to be applied —the question is not to be asked how either of these forces, being self-subsistent, is, *out if its own self*, to make itself or be made, now weaker, now stronger than the other, and then again to destroy, or allow to be destroyed, its own preponderance. Should this, in itself unfounded, alternate increase and decrease be looked at more closely, there will be found in the mean distance from the apsides, points in which the forces are in *equilibrium*. The supposed ensuing emergence from this equilibrium is just as unmotived as the suddenness of their reversal. It is quite obvious that, with such a mode of explanation, the mending of a false position by the introduction of a further determination leads to new and worse difficulties.

An analogous confusion occurs in the explanation of the phenomenon of the slowing of the oscillations of the pendulum under the equator. This is ascribed to the greater centrifugal force which is supposed to obtain there; it might quite as well be ascribed to the increased gravity drawing the pendulum more strongly to the perpendicular line of rest.

Now as regards the *form of the path*, the circle is to be grasped only as the path of a *purely uniform* motion. Certainly, it is *conceivable* (as the saying goes) that a uniformly *increasing* or *decreasing* motion also should take place in a circle. But this conceivability or possibility is only an abstract imaginableness which ignores the specific feature concerned, and is therefore not only superficial but false. The circle is the line returning into itself in which all the radii are *equal*; that is to say, it is completely determined by the radius; there is only a *single* determinateness and that is the *entire* determinateness. But in free motion, where the determinations of space and time come together in a *diversity*, in a qualitative relation, this relation necessarily emerges in the *space-element* itself as a *difference* of it, which accordingly demands *two* determinations. For this reason, the form of the path that returns into itself is essentially an *ellipse*—the first of Kepler's laws.

The abstract determinateness that constitutes the circle, manifests itself also in this way, that the arc or angle contained between two radii, is *independent of them*, is, as regards them, a purely empirical quantity. But in motion which is determined by the Notion, the distance from the centre, and the arc described in a certain unit of time, must be embraced in a *single* determinateness, must constitute *a Whole* (moments of the Notion are not contingently related); thus we have a space-determination of two dimensions—the *sector*. The arc is in this way essentially a function of the radius vector, and as in equal times unequal, involves the inequality of the radii. That the determination of space by time appears as a determination of two dimensions, as a *plane*, is connected with what was said above (§ 267) about the same determinateness as displayed in the motion of falling: now as time in the root, and again as space in the *square*. Here, however, the *quadraticity* of space is, through the return of the line of motion into itself, confined to the sector.—These clearly, are the general principles on which rests Kepler's second law, that *equal sectors are swept out in equal times*.

This law concerns only the relation of the arc to the radius vector, and here time is an abstract unity in which the various sectors are equalized, because it is the determinant as a unity. But the further relation is that of time, not as unity, but as quantum generally, as period of revolution, to the magnitude of the path, or what is the same thing, to that of the distance from the centre. We saw time and space related to each other as root and square in the motion of falling, the half-free motion, which on one side is certainly determined by the Notion, but on the other side, externally. But in absolute motion, the realm of *free* measures, each determinateness attains its totality. Time as root is a purely empirical magnitude, and as qualitative is only an abstract unity. But as *moment* of the developed totality, time is also therein a determinate unity, a totality on its own, producing itself and *therein* relating *itself to itself*: since it contains no dimensions, it attains in its production only a formal identity with itself—the *square*. Space, on the other hand, as the positive asunderness attains the dimensions of the Notion—the *cube*. Their realization thus retains at the same time their original difference. This is Kepler's third law, the relation of the *cubes of the distances to the squares* of the times; the greatness of this law is that it so simply and directly demonstrates the *Reason of the thing*. The formula of Newton, on the contrary, which transforms it into a law for the *force* of gravity, exhibits the perversion and inversion of a reflective thinking which has stopped half-way.

Zusatz. It is here, in the sphere of mechanics, that laws, in the strict sense, first appear; for law means the combination of two simple determinations such that merely their simple interconnection constitutes the whole relationship and yet each must have the show of freedom in regard to the other. In magnetism, on the other hand, the inseparability of the two determinations is already posited; consequently this is not called a law. In higher forms the individualized term constitutes the Third in which the determinations are conjoined, and we no longer have the direct determinations of two things which are in relationship with each other. The next sphere in which we find laws again is Spirit, because there we have self-subsistent entities confronting each other. Now the laws of this motion concern two things: the form of the path and the velocity of the motion. The thing to be done is to develop this from the Notion. This would give rise to a far-reaching science and the difficulty of the task is such that this has not yet been fully accomplished.

Kepler discovered his laws empirically by induction, based on the investigations of Tycho Brahe. To elicit the universal law from these isolated phenomena is the work of genius in this field.

1. Copernicus still assumed that the path was circular but the motion eccentric. But equal arcs are not traversed in equal times; now such a motion cannot take place in a circle for it is against its nature. The circle is the curve of the Understanding which posits equality. Motion in a circle can only be uniform; to equal arcs there can only correspond equal radii. This is not universally accepted, but a closer examination would show that the contrary opinion is an empty assertion. The circle has only one constant, while other curves of the second order have two constants, the major and the minor arcs. If different arcs are traversed in the same time, then they must differ not only empirically but in regard to their function; that is to say the difference must lie in their function itself. Actually, however, in a circle such arcs would only differ from each other empirically. The radius belongs essentially to the function of an arc, the relation of the circumference to the centre. If the arcs differ, then so must the radii too, and thus the Notion of the circle is transcended So, too, the assumption of an acceleration directly implies a difference in the radii: arc and radius are inseparably connected. The path must therefore be an ellipse, for it is a motion which returns into itself. Observation shows that even the ellipse does not exactly correspond to the path of the planets, and so other perturbations must be assumed. It will be for future astronomy to decide whether the path has not functions more profound than the ellipse, whether it is not perhaps an oval, etc.

2. The determinateness of the arc lies here in the radii by which it is intersected; these three lines together form a triangle, a determinate whole of which they are the moments. The radius is thus a function of the arc and the other radius. In this triangle the determinateness of the whole does not reside in the arc as such, as an empirical magnitude and separate determinateness which can be externally compared: this point is not to be lost sight of. The one, empirical determinateness of the whole curve,

of which the arc is any part, lies in the relation of its axes; the other determinateness lies in the law of the variability of the vectors; and, as part of the whole, the arc, like the triangle, has its determinateness in that which constitutes the determinateness of the whole path as such. A line can be grasped as a *necessary* determinateness only when it is a moment of a whole. The magnitude of the line is only empirical, only the triangle is the Whole. In this is to be found the origin of the mathematical conception of the parallelogram of forces in finite mechanics, where the space traversed is represented as a diagonal which thus, as part of a whole, as function, is susceptible of mathematical treatment. The centripetal force is the radius, the centrifugal force is the tangent; the arc is the diagonal of the tangent and the radius. These however, are only mathematical lines; to envisage them as *physically* separate is an empty idea. In the abstract motion of falling, the squares, that is, the plane aspect of the time factor, are only numerical determinations; the square is not to be taken in a spatial sense, because in this motion, what is traversed is only a straight line. It is this that constitutes the formal element in falling; consequently, the construction of the traversed space as a plane surface, as a quadratic relation of space, as is done even in the case of a falling body, is only a formal construction. But here [in free motion], time which has raised itself to a square corresponds to a plane, and so this production of itself attains reality here. The sector is a plane which is the product of the arc and the radius vector. The two determinations of the sector are the space traversed and the distance from the centre. The radii which emanate from the focus occupied by the central body vary. Of two equal sectors, that which has the longer radii has a smaller arc. Both sectors are supposed to be traversed in the same time; therefore the space traversed is less, and consequently the velocity is slower, in the sector which has the longer radii. Here, the arc or the space traversed is no longer something immediate but is reduced to a moment, to a factor therefore of a product, through its relation to the radius. In the motion of falling, this has not yet taken place. But here, the spatial element, which is determined by time, forms two determinations of the path itself, namely, the space traversed and the distance from the centre. Time determines the whole, of which the arc is only a moment. From this it follows that equal sectors correspond to equal times: the sector is determined by time, that is to say, the space traversed is reduced to the status of a moment. A similar thing happens in the lever, where the weight and the distance from the fulcrum form the two moments of the equilibrium.

3. For twenty-seven years Kepler sought the law that the cubes of the mean distances of the different planets are proportional to the squares of their periods of revolution; had it not been for an error in calculation when he was quite near to discovering the law, he would have discovered it earlier. He had absolute faith that Reason must be there and through this faith he arrived at this law. It is already to be expected from what has preceded that time has one dimension less than space. Since space and

time are here bound up with each other, each is posited in its own specific character and it is their quality which determines them quantitatively.

These laws are among the most beautiful to be found in the natural sciences, and they are the purest and the least entangled with heterogeneous elements; a [philosophical] comprehension of them is consequently of the greatest interest. These laws of Kepler's are, as presented, in their purest and clearest form. The Newtonian form of the law is that the motion is controlled by gravity, the force of which is inversely proportional to the squares of the distances.* To Newton is ascribed the glory of having discovered the law of universal gravitation. Kepler's glory has been obscured by Newton who has obtained for himself, in the general opinion, the greater part of the glory due to Kepler. The English have often arrogated to themselves such authority and the Germans have not protested. Voltaire brought the Newtonian theory into honour in France and the Germans then followed suit. Newton's merit, of course, is that his form of the law possesses great advantages for mathematical treatment. It is often envy which seeks to belittle the glory of great men; but on the other hand, it is superstitious to regard their fame as ultimate.

An injustice has been done to Newton in so far as mathematicians themselves understand gravity in two different ways. First of all, it means only the direction of the force which, at the surface of the earth, makes a stone fall fifteen feet in a second; this is a purely empirical determination. Newton applied the law of descent of a falling body, which is ascribed principally to gravity, to the revolution of the moon, for this also has the earth for its centre. The magnitude of fifteen feet is thus also laid down as a basis for the moon's revolution. Since the distance of the moon from the earth is sixty times the earth's radius,† this serves to determine the moment of attraction in the moon's motion. It is then found that that which produces the attraction of the earth on the moon (the *sinus versus*, the *sagitta*) also determines the entire revolution of the latter; and so the moon falls. This may be correct. In the first place, however, it is only a particular case of falling, an extension to the moon of empirical falling on the earth. This is not meant to apply to the planets, or would apply only to their relation to their satellites. It is therefore a limited point. It is said that the heavenly bodies fall. Yet they do not fall into the sun; they are therefore given another motion which checks their fall. This is effected quite simply. It is like the way in which boys whip a top to prevent it from falling over. The adoption of such childish devices to explain this free motion does not commend itself to us. It is the

* La Place, *Exposition du système du monde*, t. ii, p. 12 (Paris, année IV): Newton trouva qu'en effet cette force est réciproque au carré du rayon vecteur. Newton says (*Phil. Nat. Princ. Math.* I prop. XI seq.): When a body moves in an ellipse, hyperbola or parabola [but the ellipse passes over into the circle], the centripetal force is *reciproce in duplicata ratione distantiae*. [The words in brackets have been interpolated by Hegel.]

† *Durchmesser* in the text is a slip.

second meaning of gravity which is universal gravitation, and Newton saw in gravity the law of all motion. He thus grafted gravitation on to the law of the celestial bodies and named it the law of gravity. It is this generalization of the law of gravity which is Newton's merit and we have a visible example of the law in the motion with which we see a stone falling. An apple falling from a tree is supposed to have occasioned this generalization. According to the law of its fall, the body moves towards the centre of its gravity and the planets (*Körper*) have a tendency to move towards the sun. The direction of their motion is a combination of this tendency and the tangential direction, the resultant of these two being the diagonal.

Here, therefore, we believe we have a law which has for its moments: 1. the law of gravitation as the force of attraction; 2. the law of the tangential force. But if we examine the law of planetary revolution we find only one law of gravitation; the centrifugal force is something superfluous and thus disappears entirely, although the centripetal force is supposed to be only one of the moments. This shows that the construction of the motion from the two forces is useless. The law of one of the moments—what is attributed to the law of attraction—is not the law of this force only, but reveals itself to be the law of the entire motion, the other moment becoming an empirical coefficient. Nothing more is heard of the centrifugal force. Elsewhere, the two forces are readily granted a separate existence. It is said that the centrifugal force is an impulse which the bodies have received, both in regard to direction and magnitude. But such an empirical magnitude can no more be the moment of a law than can the fifteen feet. Any attempt to determine the laws of centrifugal force as such runs into contradictions, as is always the case with such opposed determinations. Sometimes the same laws are given to centrifugal force as to centripetal force, and sometimes different ones. The greatest confusion prevails if one attempts to separate the effects of the two forces when they are no longer in equilibrium but one is greater when the other is smaller and one is supposed to increase when the other decreases. 'In the aphelion', it is said, 'the centrifugal force is at its maximum, and in the perihelion the centripetal force.' But the opposite could equally well be asserted. For if, when the planet is nearest the sun, the force of attraction is greatest, then as the distance from the sun again begins to increase, the centrifugal force must also overcome the centripetal force and therefore, in its turn, have attained its maximum. If, however, instead of the sudden reversal of the relative preponderance, a gradual increase of the force in question is premised, then, since it was the other force which was presupposed as increasing, the opposition between the two which was assumed for the purpose of explanation is destroyed, even though the increase in one is taken to be different from that of the other (as is done in some explanations). This play at explaining how each force is supposed repeatedly to gain the ascendancy only results in confusion. The same thing happens in medicine when irritability and sensibility are regarded as in inverse ratio to each other. This form of reflective thinking is therefore to be rejected altogether.

The experience that because the pendulum swings more slowly under the equator than it does in higher latitudes, it must be made shorter in order to make it swing faster, is brought back to the stronger action of centrifugal force, in that the equatorial region describes a greater circle than does the pole in the same time, and the centrifugal force therefore checks the force of gravity which makes the pendulum fall. But the converse can equally well be said and with more truth. Slower oscillation means that the direction towards the vertical or towards rest is stronger here and therefore retards the oscillation. Since the motion is a deviation from the direction of gravity, it is rather gravity which is increased here. That is how it is with such antitheses.

At first, the thought that the planets stood in an immanent connection with the sun was not present in Newton's mind, although Kepler already had it. It is absurd, therefore, to cite this as a new conception of Newton's. Besides, 'attracted' is an inept expression; rather do the planets impel themselves towards the sun. Everything turns on the proof that the path is an ellipse, but Newton did not prove this, although it is the nerve of Kepler's law. Laplace (*Exposition du système du monde*, t. ii. pp. 12–13) admits that 'infinitesimal analysis which, on account of its generality, embraces all that can be deduced from a given law, shows us that not only the ellipse but *any conic section* can be described by virtue of the force which keeps the planets in their orbits'. This essential fact reveals the complete inadequacy of the Newtonian proof. In the geometrical proof, Newton employs the infinitely small. This proof is not rigorously exact and for this reason modern analysis has discarded it. Therefore Newton, instead of proving Kepler's laws, has rather done the reverse; he wanted to give them a ground and was satisfied with a bad one. The conception of the infinitely small is misleading in this proof, which rests on the fact that in the infinitely small, Newton treats all triangles as equal to each other. The sine and cosine, however, are unequal; but if we are going to say that as infinitely small quanta they are equal, then with such a proposition we can do anything we like. At night all cows are black. The quantum is to vanish; but if with its vanishing, the qualitative element, too, is effaced, then we can prove anything we like. Now the Newtonian proof rests on such a proposition and is therefore thoroughly bad. From the ellipse, analysis then deduces the two other laws; this it has accomplished in a different way from that employed by Newton; but this was done later and it is the first law which is not proved. In the Newtonian law gravity, as diminishing with distance, is only the velocity with which bodies move. It is this mathematical determination S/T^2 to which Newton gave prominence, in that he so arranged Kepler's laws that they yielded the law of gravitation; but this was already implied in Kepler's laws. The procedure is similar when we have the definition of the circle $a^2 = x^2 + y^2$, as the relation of the invariable hypotenuse (the radius) to the two other sides which are variable (abscissa or cosine, ordinate or sine). Now if we wish to deduce, for example, the abscissa from this equation, we say: $x^2 = a^2 - y^2, = (a+y)(a-y)$; or the ordinate, then $y^2 = a^2 - x^2, = (a+x)(a-x)$. Thus from the original function of the curve we can deduce all the other determinations. It is in the same way that we are also supposed to find A/T^2 as gravitation; we have only to arrange the formula of Kepler in such a way as to yield this determination. This can be effected from any of Kepler's laws, from the law of ellipses, from that of the proportionality of times and sectors, and most simply and directly from the third law, for which the formula is $A^3/T^2 = a^3/t^2$. From this let us now extract S/T^2. S is the space traversed as a part of the orbit and A is the distance from the sun. Each, however, can take the place of the other because the distance (diameter) and the orbit as a constant function of the distance, stand in relationship to each other. The diameter being determined, I know also the curve of revolution, and conversely; for there is only a single determinateness. Now if I write the formula as $(A^2.A/T^2) = (a^2.a/t^2)$, i.e. $A^2.(A/T^2) = a^2.(a/t^2)$ and replace gravitation (A/T^2) by G and a/t^2 by g (the different gravitations), I then have $A^2.G = a^2.g$. If now I express these as a ratio, I have $A^2:a^2 = g:G$; and this is the Newtonian law.

Hitherto in celestial motion we have had two bodies. One of these, the central body, as subjectivity and the absolute determinedness of place (*Anundfürsichbestimmtsein des Orts*), has its centre absolutely within itself. The other moment is the objectivity confronting this absolutely determined centre: the particular bodies which have a centre not only in themselves but also in an Other. Since they are no longer the body which expresses the abstract moment of subjectivity, their place is, of course, determined, they are outside it; their place is, however, not absolutely determined, but its determinateness is indeterminate. The various possibilities are realized by the body in its curvilinear motion. That is, the various places on the curve are all the same to the body, and it gives expression to this fact by just moving through them round the central body. In this first relationship, gravity is not yet developed into the *totality* of the Notion; for this, it is necessary that the differentiation into a number of bodies by which the subjectivity of the centre objectifies itself, be further determined within itself. First of all, we have the absolute, central body, then dependent bodies without a centre in themselves, and lastly, relative central bodies. It is only with these three kinds of bodies that the system of gravity is completed into a totality. Thus it is said that to distinguish which of two bodies is moving, a third body is necessary, as when we are in a ship and the bank flies past us. The plurality of planets could be said already to possess determinateness; but this plurality is just plurality, not a differentiated determinateness. Whether it is the sun or the earth which moves is a matter of indifference for the Notion if there are only these two bodies. This led Tycho Brahe to say that the sun goes round the earth and the planets go round the sun; there is no objection to this except that it makes calculation more difficult. It was Copernicus who found the truth of the matter; but when astronomy gave as the reason for it that it is more fitting that the earth should move round the sun because the latter is the larger body, this was no reason at all. If mass, too, is to be taken into account, then the question arises whether the larger body also has as great a specific density as the smaller one. The main thing is the law of motion. The central body exhibits abstract rotatory motion. The particular bodies have a simple motion round a centre without an independent rotatory motion of their own. The third kind in the system of free motion is now motion round a centre simultaneously with a rotatory motion independent of this centre.

1. The *centre* is supposed to be a point, but as a body it is extended, i.e. it consists of points seeking [a centre]. This dependent matter contained in the central body necessitates the rotation of the latter round itself. For the dependent points which are at the same time held at a distance from the centre, do not have a self-related, i.e. fixedly determined place: they are merely falling matter, and so are determined as moving only in one direction. The other determinateness is lacking; each point must therefore occupy every place that it can. What is absolutely determined is the centre alone; the remaining asunderness is indifferent. For it is only the distance of each point from the centre which is determined here, not the point's own place. This contingency of the determination is manifested in the fact that matter changes its place and this is expressed by the *rotatio of the sun round its centre*. This sphere is therefore mass in its immediacy as a unity of rest and motion, that is, it is a self-related motion. The axial rotation is not a change of place, for all the points retain the same position in relation to each other. Thus the whole is a motion which is equally at rest. The motion could be real only if the axis were not indifferent in relation to the mass; it could not stay at rest while the mass was in motion. The difference between rest and motion we have here is not a real difference, not a difference of mass. What is at rest is not a mass but a line; and what moves is differentiated not by masses but solely by places.

2. The *dependent* bodies which also have an apparently free existence and do not constitute the connected parts of the extension of a body endowed with a centre, but hold themselves at a distance from it, also have a rotatory motion, but not round their own axis, for they have no centre in themselves. They rotate, therefore, round a centre belonging to another, separate body from which they are repelled. Their place is simply this or that place, here or there, and this contingency is expressed, too, by rotation. But their motion is an inert and rigid one round the central body, their determinate position in relation to the latter remaining always the same, as for example, in the relation of the moon to the earth. Any position A in the peripheral body always remains in the straight line joining the absolute centre and the relative centre; and every other point B preserves its fixed angle throughout the rotation. Thus the dependent bodies only move round the central body simply as mass, not as self-

related, individual bodies. The dependent celestial bodies form the side of particularity; that is why they are split into a diversity, for in Nature particularity exists as a duality, and not as a unity, as in Spirit. If we consider this twofold mode of existence of the dependent bodies only with respect to the difference of motion, we have the two aspects of the motion as follows:

(a) The moment which is posited first is this, that the motion which is equally at rest becomes this restless motion, a sphere of *aberration* or the effort to get away from its immediate existence into something beyond itself. This moment of self-externality, as a mass and a sphere, is itself a moment of substance (*Moment der Substanz*); for here each moment acquires an existence of its own or has in it the reality of the whole which is a sphere. This second sphere, the *cometary* sphere, expresses this whirl (*Wirbel*); comets are always on the point of dispersing and scattering themselves to infinity or into the void of space. In this connection there is to be put out of mind first, the bodily shape of comets, and secondly, that way of thinking about comets and celestial bodies generally, which knows that they exist simply because they are seen, and concerns itself only with their contingency. According to this standpoint, there could equally well not be any comets; and to recognize them as necessary and to grasp their Notion, may even appear ridiculous, customary as it is to consider such things as something quite beyond the reach of our intelligence and so, too, of the Notion. To the same standpoint belongs all those conceptions grouped under the heading 'Explanation of origin', namely, whether the comets have been thrown out by the sun, or are atmospheric vapours and the like. Such explanations may well set out to say what the comets are, but it leaves on one side the main point, namely, their necessity; and this necessity is just the Notion. Here, too, what we have to do is not to pick up phenomena and apply a tinge of thought to them. The cometary sphere threatens to escape from the universal, self-related order and to lose its unity; it is the formal freedom which has its substance (*Substanz*) outside itself, a pushing out into the future. But in so far as the cometary sphere is a necessary moment of the whole, it cannot escape from this whole and remains enclosed within the first sphere. However, it is uncertain whether such spheres, i.e. comets, are dissolved as single bodies while other single bodies come into existence in their place, or whether, as motions having their rest outside themselves in the first [solar] sphere, they continually move round the latter. Both possibilities belong to the contingency of Nature; and this division, or transition by stages, from the determinateness of this sphere into another is to be put to the account of sensuous existence. But the extreme limit of the aberration itself consists necessarily in the fact that the comet first approaches the subjectivity of the central body indefinitely and then yields to repulsion.

(b) This unrest, however, is precisely the moment of rotation which moves towards its centre. The transition is not merely a simple alteration, but this otherness is immediately, in its own self, the opposite of itself. The opposition is the duality of the immediate otherness, and the sublating of this otherness. But it is the opposition, not as such, not a pure unrest, but as the quest for its centre, its rest: the sublated future, the past as a moment in which the opposition is sublated, but only in its Notion, not yet in reality. This is the *lunar* sphere which is not the aberration from immediate existence, the process away from this, but the relation to what has (already) become, or to being-for-self, to the self [the planet]. Thus, while the cometary sphere is related only to the immediate sphere of rotation round an axis [the sun], the lunar sphere is related to the new centre which is reflected into itself, to the planet. Therefore the moon, too, does not yet possess a being in and for itself, does not have an axial rotation of its own; its axis is outside it, but is not the axis of the first [solar] sphere. The lunar sphere, regarded as a passive motion, is only a *satellite* and is rigidly controlled by a single centre. But the comet, too, is equally non-self-subsistent; the former is an abstract obedience, motion directed by an other: the latter is a meant (or intended) freedom. The cometary sphere is an eccentric motion governed by the abstract totality; the lunar sphere is restful inertia (*ruhige Trägheit*).*

3. Lastly, the sphere which is in and for itself, the planetary, is related both to itself and to an Other. It rotates round its axis and also has its centre outside it. The planet thus also has its centre within itself, but this is only a relative centre; it has not its absolute centre within itself and so is also dependent. It contains both determinations and expresses them as an alteration of place. Its independence is expressed merely by its parts themselves changing their position in relation to the straight line joining the absolute and the relative centres; this is the basis of the rotatory motion of the planets. The shifting of the orbital axis produces the precession of the equinoxes. (Similarly the axis of the earth also has a rotatory motion, its poles describing an ellipse.) The planet, as the third sphere, is the syllogism which presents us with the Whole. This quadruplicity of the celestial bodies forms the complete system of rational corporeality. This belongs to a solar system and is the developed disjunction of the Notion; these four display in the skies the moments of the Notion outside one another. It may seem strange to want to fit the comets into this system; but what exists must necessarily be embraced by the Notion. Here the differences still enjoy a free, separate existence. We shall pursue the solar, planetary, lunar, and cometary natures through all the further stages of Nature. The deepening of Nature is nothing but the progressive transformation of these four. Because the planetary nature is the totality, the unity of the oppositions, whereas the other bodies, as its non-organic nature, only exhibit these moments in their

* Vera doubts the correctness of the text and suggests it should read: 'unruhige Trägheit'. 'Restless inertia' would be more fitting in the context than 'restful inertia'.

separation, therefore the planetary nature is the most perfect, even in regard to motion, and it is this alone which is under consideration here. Consequently, it is only on the planet that life can appear. Ancient peoples worshipped the sun and made it higher [than the other celestial bodies]. We do the same kind of thing, too, when we make the abstraction of the Understanding supreme, and so, for example, define God as the supreme Being.

This totality is the ground and the universal substance on which is borne what follows. Everything is this totality of motion but as brought back under a higher being-within-self or, what is the same thing, as realized into a higher being-within-self. The being-within-self contains this totality, but the latter remains indifferently and separately in the background as a particular existence, as a history, or as the origin against which the being-for-self is turned, just so that it can be for itself. It lives therefore in this element but also liberates itself therefrom, since only weak traces of this element are present in it. Terrestrial being, and still more organic and self-conscious being, has escaped from the motion of absolute matter, but still remains in sympathy with it and lives on in it as in its inner element. The alternation of the seasons and of day and night, the transition from waking to sleep, is this life of the earth in the organic sphere. Each is itself a sphere of going forth from self and return into its centre, i.e. into its power; this life gathers up within itself and subdues all the manifold elements of consciousness. Night is the negative into which all has returned and from which therefore organic life draws its power to re-enter with renewed strength into the manifold activities of waking existence. And thus this universal sphere is present in each, is a sphere periodically returning into itself, which expresses the universal sphere according to the mode of its determinate individuality. It finds expression in the periodic deviations of the magnetic needle; and in man there is, according to Fourcroy's observations, a four-day cycle of decrease and increase, an increase during three days and a return on the fourth day to the original point; diseases, too, run a periodic course. The more developed totality of this sphere appears in general in the circulation of the blood, which has a different rhythm from that of respiration, and thirdly in the peristaltic movement. But the higher nature of the physical realm generally suppresses the proper expression of freedom in this sphere; consequently, it is not in these partial manifestations that universal motion must be studied, but in the sphere where it exists in its freedom. In the individuality it is only something inward, i.e. something only intended (*ein Gemeintes*), it is not there in its free existence.

The exposition of the solar system is not exhausted by what has been said. There may be still further determinations resulting from those already set forth, although the fundamental ones have been expounded. The relation of the planetary orbits to each other, their reciprocal inclinations, also the inclinations of the comets and satellites in relation to those of the planets, all this could attract our interest. The planetary orbits do not lie in a single plane, and the cometary orbits cut those of the planets at very different angles. The latter orbits do not go beyond the ecliptic but they vary their angle in relation to each other, and their nodes have a secular motion. To develop these points is a more difficult matter and we have not as yet got so far. Then the intervals between the planets would have to be considered, for here we have only been concerned with the planet as such. A law is wanted for the *series* formed by the distances between the planets, although it has not yet been found. Astronomers, on the whole, are disdainful of such a law and will have nothing to do with it; but it is a necessary problem. Kepler, for example, has taken up again the numbers in Plato's *Timaeus*. What might be said in the present state of our knowledge in this connection would be somewhat as follows: if the distance from the sun of Mercury, the first planet, is taken as a, then the orbit of Venus is $a+b$, that of the earth $a+2b$, and that of Mars $a+3b$. It is clear that these four planets together constitute a Whole, if you like, one system, as the four bodies of the solar system, and after them another order begins both as regards numbers and physical constitution. These four move in a uniform manner and it is noteworthy that there are four planets with such a homogeneous nature. The earth alone of them has a satellite and is, therefore, the most perfect planet. Between Mars and Jupiter there is a sudden wide gap, and there was no planet corresponding to $a+4b$ until recently, when four smaller planets were discovered, Vesta, Juno, Ceres, and Pallas, which fill this gap and form a new group. Here the unity of the planet is disintegrated into a host of asteroids which all have approximately the same path. In this fifth place, dispersion and separation predominate. Then comes the third group. Jupiter with its many satellites is $a+5b$, and so on. This is only approximately true and the rational element in all this is so far not known. This large mass of satellites, too, is another mode of the satellite than that which obtains in the group of the first four planets. Then comes Saturn with its rings and seven satellites, and Uranus, discovered by Herschel, with a host of satellites which only a few people have seen. This offers a starting-point for the more precise determination of the relationship of the planets. It is plain that by proceeding on these lines the law will be discovered.

Philosophy has to start from the Notion, and even if it does not assert much, we must be content with this. The Philosophy of Nature is in error when it wants to account for every phenomenon; this is what happens in the finite sciences, which try to trace everything back to general conceptions, the hypotheses. In these sciences, the sole verification of the hypothesis lies in the empirical element and consequently everything must be explained. But what is known through the Notion is clear by itself and stands firm; and philosophy need not feel any embarrassment about this, even if all phenomena are not yet explained. I have therefore set down here only the rudiments of a rational procedure in the comprehension of the mathematical and mechanical laws of Nature as this free realm of measures. This standpoint, I know, is ignored by professional astronomers; but a time will come when this science will require for its satisfaction the philosophical Notion.

(3) TRANSITION TO PHYSICS

§ 271

The substance of matter, gravity, developed into the *totality* of form, no longer has the self-externality of matter outside it. At first, *form* is manifested in the ideal determinations of space, time, and motion, that is, in accordance with its differences, and also, in accordance with its being-for-self, as a *centre* which is determined as lying *outside* self-external matter; but in the developed totality, this asunderness is posited as determined simply and solely by the totality, and matter, apart from this its asunderness, is nothing. The form is in this way materialized. Regarded from the opposite point of view matter, in this negation of its self-externality in the totality, has now acquired within itself what it previously only sought, namely, the centre, its self, determinateness of form. Its abstract, torpid being-within-self, as simply heavy, has resolved itself into form: it is *qualified matter*—the sphere of *Physics*.

Zusatz. Thus terminates the first part of the Philosophy of Nature, Mechanics constituting a complete sphere by itself. Descartes treated the standpoint of mechanics as the *prius* when he said: 'Give me matter and motion and I will construct the universe.' However deficient the mechanical standpoint may be, these words of Descartes unmistakably reveal the greatness of his mind. In motion, bodies exist only as points; what gravity determines is only the spatial inter-relationships of points. The unity of matter is only a unity of the place it seeks, not a concrete One, a self. That is the nature of this sphere; and the externality of the determining of matter constitutes the peculiar determinateness of matter. Matter is heavy, is for itself, a quest for its being-within-self; the point of this infinitude is only a place, and consequently the being-for-self is not yet real. The totality of the being-for-self [of matter] is posited only in the solar system as a whole; what the solar system is as a whole, matter is now to be in detail. In the solar system, the totality of the form is the Notion of matter in general; but now the self-externality is to be the whole, developed Notion in each determinate existence. Matter is to be for itself throughout the whole of its reality—that is, it finds its unity; this is the being-for-self which is for itself. In other words, the solar system as self-moving is the sublating of the merely ideal being-for-self, of the mere spatiality of the determination, i.e. of the non-being-for-self. In the Notion, the negation of place is not again only a determining of place; on the contrary, the negation of the non-being-for-self is a negation of the negation, an affirmation, and thus there emerges real being-for-self. This is the abstractly logical determination of the *transition*. Real being-for-self is just this, a totality of the development of being-for-self, and this can also be expressed as a liberation of the form in matter. The determinations of form which constitute the solar system are the determinations of matter itself and they constitute the being of matter. The determination and the being are thus essentially identical; but this is the nature of the qualitative, for here, if the determination is removed, the being, too, is destroyed. This is the transition from Mechanics to Physics.

SECTION TWO ✦ PHYSICS

§ 272

Matter has *individuality*, in so far as it has being-for-self developed within itself, and is therefore determined within itself. Matter thus wrests itself from gravity, manifests itself, and determines itself within itself. Previously, the spatial element in it was determined by gravity, i.e. by a centre other than matter itself, a centre which matter only sought; but now, by virtue of the form immanent in it, matter develops the spatial element out of itself and in opposition to gravity.

Zusatz. Bodies now come under the might of individuality. What ensues is the subjection of the free bodies to the might of the individual point of unity which assimilates them. Gravity, as the inward essence of matter, its merely inner identity, passes over—since its Notion is essential outwardness—into the manifestation of this essence. As such, it is the totality of the determinations of Reflection, but these as cast asunder, so that each appears as a particular, qualified matter which, as not yet determined to individuality, is a formless element. These materialized form-determinations exist in two ways: once as immediate, and again as posited. In the solar system they appear as immediate existences, and again as essentially posited: just as parents, *qua* parents, have an immediate existence, but exist also as children, as offspring. Light exists, therefore, once as the sun, and also as the product of external conditions. The former is generated intrinsically in the Notion; but this must also be posited, and so this reality distinguishes itself as a particular mode of existence.

§ 273

Physics has for its content:

A. the Universal Individuality, the immediate, free, physical Qualities;
B. the Particular Individuality, the relation of form, as a physical determination, to gravity, and the determination of gravity by this form;
C. the total, free Individuality.

Zusatz. This part is the most difficult in Nature, for it embraces finite corporeality. The sphere of difference always presents the greatest difficulty, because the Notion is no longer present in immediate fashion, as in the first part [Mechanics], nor has it yet shown itself as real, as in the third part [Organics]. Here the Notion is concealed; it shows itself only as the connecting bond of necessity, while what is manifest is notionless. In the first part, differences of form are unconnected and mutually independent; in the second, individuality is in a state of difference, of opposition; it is only in the third part that individuality is mistress over differences of form.

PHYSICS OF THE UNIVERSAL INDIVIDUALITY

§ 274

Physical Qualities exist *first* as *immediate*, as separate and self-subsistent existences—the now physically determined *celestial* bodies; secondly, as related to the *individual* unity of their totality —the *physical Elements*; thirdly, as the *process* which engenders what is individual in these Elements—the *meteorological process*.

A. THE FREE PHYSICAL BODIES

Zusatz. The determinations of the Notion now receive materiality; the being-for-self of matter finds its point of unity. As matter is thus a being-for-self which is for itself, and the transition of the determinations, their vanishing into one another, has itself vanished, we enter logically into the sphere of Essence. Essence is return-to-self in one's other, reflection of determinations into one another which, as thus reflected into self, now develop as forms. These forms are Identity, Difference, Opposition, and Ground. That is to say, matter leaves its first immediacy behind where space and time, matter and motion, passed over into each other, until finally, in Free Mechanics, matter appropriated the determinations as its own, and thus revealed itself as self-mediating and self-determining. Thrust is no longer external to matter; on the contrary, matter's differentiation is its internal, immanent thrust; matter differentiates and determines itself by itself, is reflection-into-self. Its determinations are material and express the nature of material being; in them it manifests its own self, for it is merely these determinations. They are material qualities which belong to the substance (*Substanz*) of matter; what matter is, it is only through its qualities. In the first sphere (Mechanics) the determinations are still divorced from the substance, they are not material determinations; substance as such is still shut up within itself, unmanifest, and that is why such substance was only a *quest* for its unity.

1. *Light*

§ 275

Matter in its first qualified state is *pure identity*-with-self, unity of *reflection-into-self*, and hence the first, still quite abstract *manifestation*. As *existent* in Nature, it is the reference to itself as *independent* in face of the other determinations of the totality. This existent, universal *self* of matter is *Light*—as an individuality it is a *star*; as a star which is a moment of a totality, it is the *sun*.

Zusatz. The first point now is the *a priori* notional determination of light: the second point is to find out the mode and manner in which this notional determination occurs in our ordinary thinking. Matter as immediate, free, self-subsistent motion which has returned into self, is simple, uniform compactness. Motion having returned into self, the celestial sphere has accomplished and enclosed in itself its own independent, ideal life. It is precisely this realized being-within-self (*Insichsein*) which constitutes its compactness. As existent it is within itself; that is to say, this being-within-self of the totality itself exists. It contains in itself the moment of being-for-another. What is *for itself* is the force of its centre, or its self-containedness. But this simple force is itself there, itself exists outwardly; what is only inner is just as much outer: for it is the other of this outer existence. Matter, as immediate, pure totality, thus enters into the opposition of what it is inwardly and what it is for another, or as an outer existence: for its inwardness is not yet overtly present in its outer reality. Matter which has revealed itself as this unresting whirlpool of self-relating motion, and as the return to a being which is in and for itself, and this being-within-self which is there in contrast to outer existence: such matter is Light. It is the self-contained totality of matter, only as pure force, an intensive life which holds itself within itself, the celestial sphere which has withdrawn into itself, whose whirling is precisely this direct opposition of the directions of the self-relating motion, in whose flux and reflux every distinction is extinguished. As *existent* identity, it is a pure line which refers itself only to itself. Light is this pure *existent* force of space-filling, its being is absolute velocity, pure materiality which is everywhere present, real existence which remains within itself, or actuality as a transparent possibility. To speak of space being filled is, however, ambiguous; for if this filling consists in being-for-self, light cannot be said to fill space, since the hardness which offers resistance has passed away. On the contrary, light is only *present* in space, and then not as something individual. Space is only abstract subsistence or virtual being (*Ansichsein*); but light, as existent being-within-self (*Insichsein*), or existence which is in itself and hence is pure, is the power of universal actuality to be outside itself, and as the possibility of coalescing with all things it enters into community with all and yet abides in itself, so that the self-subsistence of objects is in no way affected by it.

When matter, as light, passes into being-for-another, and hence begins to manifest itself, heavy matter also manifests itself. The quest for unity, as a striving towards an other, as pressure, is only a discordant, hostile manifestation; matter is in it a being-for-another but as an exclusion and separation of the other from it. While the Many are negatively related to one another, we now have affirmative manifestation, for the being-for-another is here the sharing of a common existence. Light brings us into the universal interrelation; everything exists for us in theoretical, unresistant fashion because it is in light.

This manifestation is to be grasped in its *first* determinateness; as such it is the wholly universal manifestation, as yet devoid of any determination within itself. Its determinateness is indeterminateness, identity, a reflection-into-self, complete physical ideality in contrast to the reality of heavy matter, in that this latter connotes differentiation and exclusion. This abstract manifestation, material identity-with-self, does not yet oppose itself to an other; it is a determinateness, *oscillation*, but only in itself. The being-for-self of being-for-self, as self-referring affirmative identity, is no longer exclusive: the hard One has melted and, as a continuity of manifestation lacking all determination, has lost its opposition. This is the pure reflection-into-self which, in the higher form of spirit, is the Ego. The Ego is infinite space, the infinite likeness of self-consciousness to itself, the abstraction of the empty certainty of myself and of my pure self-identity. The Ego is only the identity of my own attitude as subject to myself as object. With this identity of self-consciousness, light is parallel and is its faithful image. The reason why it is not the Ego is simply that it does not inwardly obscure and disrupt itself, but is only an abstract appearing. If the Ego could maintain itself in pure, abstract sameness as the Hindus wish, it would pass away into light, into an abstract transparency. But self-consciousness exists only as consciousness: this latter posits determinations within itself, and self-consciousness is the pure reflection of the Ego of consciousness into itself, in so far as it is object to itself. Like light, the Ego is pure self-manifestation, only it is at the same time the infinite negativity of the return-to-self out of itself as object, and is hence the infinite point of subjective individuality, of the exclusion of another. Because, therefore, it lacks the infinitude of the return into self, light is not self-consciousness; it is only the manifestation *of* itself, not *for itself*, but for another.

Light thus lacks the concrete unity with itself possessed by self-consciousness as an infinite point of being-for self, and is consequently only a manifestation of Nature, not of spirit. For this reason, this abstract manifestation is *secondly*, also spatial, an absolute *expansion* in *space*, and not the taking back of this expansion into the unifying point of infinite subjectivity. Light is infinite spatial dispersion, or rather it is an infinite *generation of space*. Now since in Nature the determinations, as sundered, fall outside one another, this pure manifestation also exists separately, but as an untrue existence. Spirit, as infinitely concrete, does not give pure identity such a separate, detached existence; in self-consciousness, on the contrary, this thought is subjected to the absolute subjectivity of the Self.

Thirdly, light must arrive at its limit. However, this necessity of encountering an other differs from the absolute limitation of being-for-self, in virtue of which matter offers resistance. As abstract identity, light has difference outside it, as the Not of light; this is constituted by the other reflected determinations of Essence, existing as physical corporealities. As the universal principle of making-manifest, light is the first satisfaction. Only the abstract Understanding gives this universal physical Element the highest place. The self-determining, concrete thought of Reason demands a principle distinguished within itself, a universal immanently self-determined, which does not lose its universality in its particularization. Light, as the beginning of material manifestation, is excellent only in the sense of an abstraction. Because of this abstraction, light has a limit, a defect or lack; and it is only through this its limit that it manifests itself. The specific content must come from elsewhere; in order that something may be manifested, something different from light is required. Light as such is invisible; in pure light nothing is seen, just as little as in pure *darkness*; it is dark, nightlike. If we see in pure light, we are a pure act of seeing; we do not as yet see anything. It is first in the limit that the moment of negation—and therefore of determination—is found; and it is in the limit that reality first begins. Since only the concrete is true, existence demands not only the *one* abstract element, but also the other. It is only after light has distinguished itself as light, as against darkness, that it manifests itself as light.

Having developed the Notion of light, we must now, *secondly*, inquire into its *reality*. To say that we have to consider the existence of light, is to say that we have to consider the being-for-another of light. But light is itself the positing of being-for-another; in the existence of light, we must therefore set forth the being-for-another of this being-for-another. How is visibility made visible? How is this process of manifestation itself made manifest? Manifestation demands a Subject, and the question is how this Subject exists. Light can only be called matter in so far as it exists independently in an individualized form; this individualization consists in the fact that light exists as a body. Light constitutes the real existence or the physical import of the Body of Abstract Centrality, which real existence is in the form of a *luminous body*: this is the Sun, the *self-luminous* body. This fact is empirically ascertained, and at first it is all we have to say about the Sun. This body is the primordial, uncreated light, which does not arise from the conditions of finite existence, but *immediately* is. The stars also are self-luminous bodies, their existence constituted by the physical abstraction of light; abstract matter exists precisely as this abstract identity of light. This existence of the stars as points of light means that they stay at this level of abstraction. This inability to pass to concrete existence, far from being worthy of admiration, is rather a defect. It is therefore absurd to regard the stars as superior, e.g., to plants. The Sun is not yet anything concrete. Piety wants to populate the Sun and Moon with men, animals and plants, but only a planet can rise to this. Natures which have withdrawn into themselves, such concrete forms as preserve independence in face of the universal, are not yet to be found in the Sun; only luminous matter (*Lichtmaterie*) is present in Sun and stars. The connection between the Sun as a moment of the Solar System, and the Sun as self-luminous, is that in both cases it has the same determination. In the mechanical sphere, the Sun is matter related only to itself; this determination is also the physical determination of the identity of the abstract manifestation, and this is the reason why the Sun shines.

Further, one can inquire into the *finite causes* of the existence of that which shines in this way. To ask how we receive the light of the Sun, is to regard this light as something *produced*. Light so determined we see connected with fire and heat in our usual experience of earthly light which appears as combustion. We may therefore think we must say how the solar fire is maintained, in order to explain the shining of the Sun by analogy with the earthly process of light, where fire must consume material in order to exist. As against this, it must be remembered that the conditions of the earthly process which occurs in individualized matter, do not yet occur in the relation of Free Physical Qualities. This first light must be distinguished from fire. Earthly light is usually connected with heat; sunlight also is warm, but this heat does not belong to sunlight as such, which first warms when near the Earth. Sunlight, by itself, is cold, as shown by high mountains and balloon ascents. Even empirically we know light without flame, phosphorescent light, e.g. in rotting wood, also electric light; for the fusion effected by electricity is due, not to light, but shock. There are, as cases of earthly light, metals which emit light without burning when stroked with a piece of iron, or when scratched; the minerals which do this are perhaps more numerous than those that do not. We also have analogies here with a luminous body, as a shining without chemical process.

Light must also show itself as a product. The physical conditions of the solar light do not concern us inasmuch as they are not determinations of the Notion, but only matters of empirical fact. We can, however, say that Sun and stars, as rotating centres, generate internal friction as they rotate. In its motion, the life of the Sun is merely to be this process of phosphorescence which emits light. The mechanical origin of the solar light is to be sought in the axial rotation of the Sun, because this is abstract reference-to-self. In so far as light must be physically produced, we can say that all bodies belonging to the solar system produce a centre and make a luminous body for themselves; neither of these two moments is without the other, but the one involves the other.

General Alix, a Frenchman who lived for some time at Cassel, explained the origin of the solar light in an essay in the following way. Since the Sun in shining is always emitting light, it is therefore always losing it. If one now asks what becomes of the hydrogen which is continually being formed on the planets, General Alix would reply that, since it is the lightest gas, it is not to be found in the atmosphere, but that it furnishes the material whereby the losses of the Sun are made good. In this conception there is this amount of truth, that the planets project their material development out of themselves and give it an objective shape in the Sun. In this case, however, we must exclude physical and chemical relationships and processes in their ordinary acceptation. The life of the Star is eternally kindled and renewed by the planets which posit their plurality ideally in their centre, and epitomize themselves in this unity of their existence. As in the earthly process, the reduction of what is individual is the simplicity of flame, so too in the Sun, plurality is reduced to unity. The Sun is therefore the process of the entire Solar System which bursts forth in this point of light.

§ 276

As the abstract self of matter, light is *absolutely weightless (das absolut Leichte)*, and as matter, it is an *infinite* self-externality; but as pure making manifest, as material ideality, it is *inseparable* and *simple self-externality*.

Remark

In the oriental intuition of the substantial identity of the spiritual and the natural, the pure selfhood of consciousness—self-identical thought in the abstract form of the True and the Good—is one with light. When so-called *realistic* thinking (*Vorstellung*) denies that identity is *present* in Nature, it can be referred among other things to light, to this pure making manifest which is nothing but a *making manifest*.

The proof that this thought-determination, identity-with-self or the initially abstract self of Centrality which now contains matter in itself, the proof that this simple ideality exists as *light* is, as our Introduction said, to be conducted empirically. The immanent philosophical element is here, as everywhere, the inherent necessity of the notional determination, which must then be pointed out as *some* natural existence. Here I only want to add a few remarks on the empirical existence of pure manifestation as light.

Heavy matter is *divisible* into *masses*, since it is concrete being-for-self and quantity; but in the quite *abstract* ideality of light there is no such distinction; a limitation of light in its infinite expansion does not destroy its absolute continuity in itself. The conception of discrete, simple *rays* of light, and of *particles* and *bundles* of them, which are supposed to constitute a limited expansion of light, is of a piece with those other barbarous categories for whose prevalence in physics Newton is chiefly responsible. The narrowest experience teaches that light can no more be isolated into rays, and put together into bundles of rays, than it can be packed up into bags. The Understanding should be the last to treat as incomprehensible this indivisibility of light in its infinite expansion, a physical asunderness that remains self-identical, for its own principle is this very abstract identity.

Astronomers speak of celestial phenomena which are perceived by us 500 years and more after their actual occurrence. In this one can see, on the one hand, empirical phenomena of the *propagation of light*, carried over from a sphere where they obtain into another sphere where they have no significance—although such determination of the materiality of light does not contradict its simple indivisibility; on the other hand, we can see in it a Past which has become a Present in ideal fashion as in memory.

Light is also represented in Optics as being emitted in rays in every direction from each *point* of a visible surface (which each person sees at another place) so that from each point, a material hemisphere of infinite dimensions is formed; the direct result of this would be that all these infinitely many hemispheres would interpenetrate like hedgehogs. If this were so, a dense confused mass would be formed between the eye and the object, and from such a theory one ought rather to expect invisibility than an explanation of visibility; the whole conception reduces to an absurdity, as is also the case when a concrete body is represented as composed of various matters, each matter existing and circulating through the pores of the other matters. This universal penetration destroys the assumed discrete materiality of the supposedly real matters, and establishes an entirely ideal relationship between them, between the illuminated and manifested and that which illuminates and makes it manifest. This relationship, like reflection-into-self which in itself is relationless, excludes all further forms of *mediations* (such as corpuscles, waves, oscillations, etc., no less than rays, i.e. fine rods and bundles) which are usually called explanations and elucidations.

Zusatz. The self-like nature of light by which natural objects are vitalized and individualized, and their unfoldment strengthened and controlled, first becomes manifest in the individualization of matter, for it is only as return-into-self, and as sublation of particularity, that light's identity which is at first merely abstract, becomes the negative unity of individuality. Gravity, acidity, sound are also manifestations of matter but not, like light, pure manifestations, for they contain specific modifications within themselves. We cannot hear sound as such, but only a specific tone, that is higher or lower; nor can we taste an acid as such, but only specific acids. Only light itself exists as this pure manifestation, as this abstract unindividualized universality. Light is incorporeal, in fact, immaterial matter; this seems a contradiction, but this can be of no consequence to us. Physicists say that light can be weighed. But light has been focused through large lenses on to one pan of the finest scales, which was either not depressed or, if it were, it was found that the effect depended only on the heat concentrated in the focus. Matter is heavy in so far as it still seeks unity as Place; but light is matter which has found itself.

Light was one of the first objects of worship because it contains the moment of union-with-self, and in it the rift of finitude has vanished; light has therefore been seen as that in which man was conscious of the Absolute. The extreme oppositions of Thought and Being, Subject and Object, were not yet made; man had to reach the deepest self-consciousness to oppose himself to Nature. The religion of light is more sublime than that of the Indians and Greeks, but it is also the religion in which man has not yet risen to a consciousness of opposition, to self-knowing spirituality.

Light is an interesting theme to treat; for we think that in Nature we have only the individual, *this* particular reality. But light is the very opposite of this, it is simply Thought itself, present in natural mode. For there is Understanding in Nature, i.e. the forms of the Understanding exist in it. In thinking of light, one must renounce all conceptions of composition and the like. The physics of light as particles is no whit better than the efforts of a man who, having built a house without windows, wants to carry light into it in bags. The expression 'bundles of rays' is merely one of convenience, it means nothing; the bundles are light in its entirety, which is only outwardly limited; it is no more divided into bundles of rays than is the Ego or pure self-consciousness. It is the same when I say: in *my* time, or in Caesar's time. This was also the time of everyone else; but here I am speaking of it in relation to Caesar, and restrict it to him without meaning that he really had a separate ray or parcel of time. The Newtonian theory according to which light is propagated in straight lines, or the wave theory which makes it travel in waves, are, like Euler's aether or the vibration of sound, materialistic representations quite useless for the comprehension of light. The dark element in light is supposed to run through the movement in a series of curves which can be mathematically calculated; this abstract determination has been introduced into the theory, and is nowadays thought to be a great triumph over Newton. But this is nothing physical; and neither of these two ideas is in place, since nothing empirical obtains here. There no more exist particles of light or aether than the nerves consist of series of globules, each receiving an impulse and setting others in motion.

The propagation of light occurs in time, since, being an activity and an alteration, it cannot dispense with this moment. Light has immediate expansion; but in so far as it is matter, a luminous body in relationship with another body, a separation is present, in any case, a kind of interruption of its continuity. The sublation of this separation is motion and then time, too, enters in relation to what is thus interrupted. The distances which light is supposed to travel involve time; for illumination, whether through a medium or by reflection, is a modification of matter requiring time. In our planetary system, i.e. in a more or less transparent medium, the propagation of light involves a time-determination since the rays are broken by the atmosphere. But this propagation in the airless, or as it were empty, stellar spaces is another matter; such spaces, so to speak, are filled only by interstellar distances, i.e. they have no filling, but are mere negations of union. Laws regarding the propagation of light which were plainly observed in connection with Jupiter's satellites were tranferred by Herschel to the stellar spaces; these distances are, however, somewhat hypothetical, as he himself admits. In the case of the periodical disappearance and reappearance of certain stars and nebulae, Herschel declared that the time taken by light to reach us means that these events occurred 500 years before we saw them: there is something eerie about being thus affected by what has long since ceased to be. One must admit that time is a condition of propagation without involving oneself in these far-fetched conclusions.

§ 277

Light, as the universal physical identity, enters into relation with matter qualified by the other moments of the Notion, in the first place, as *different* from it (§ 275) and therefore as something else, external to it; such matter, being thus the negative of light, is specified as *dark*. In so far as this equally exists on its own account, light is in relation only with its surface which is hereby made manifest, the matter being in the first place opaque: but equally, this surface, if it lacks further particularization, i.e. is *smooth*, inseparably manifests itself, i.e. becomes a showing or shining in *something else*. Since, then, each appears in *something else*, and thus it is only something else which appears in each, this manifestation which places things outside themselves is the abstractly infinite reflection-into-self, by which nothing, as yet, is manifested *in its own self for itself*. In order, therefore, that something finally can appear, can be made visible, some further particularization must be physically present (e.g. roughness, colour, etc.).

Zusatz. Matter, in contrast to this pure self, is what is just as purely selfless, darkness. Its relation to light is that of sheer opposition, so that the one is positive and the other negative. For darkness to be positive, corporeal individualization is required; body is individualized, and as such only considered from an aspect in which it is a negative of its abstract self-identity. Darkness vanishes before light; only a dark body remains over, as a body, against light, and this body now becomes visible. Before I can see, not only light, but also a body is requisite; *something* must be seen. Light is therefore visible only as a luminous body. The dark element, however, which becomes visible through light, is, taken affirmatively, shape as an abstract aspect of body. Light and darkness have an external relationship to each other; it is only at their common limit that light attains to existence, for it is in this being-for-another that something is lit up. The limitation of light in space is to be grasped only as light's being kept to the direction it has; if its connection with the central body were severed, then light would cease to be. The limit, therefore, is posited by the dark body which is lit up. The dark body, which is heavy matter, is, as the other to which light stands in relation, specified matter. But the first specification is here the spatial difference of surfaces; matter is rough, smooth, pointed, thus placed, and so on. The difference of things visible is a difference of spatial shapes; only thus do light and shade arise. There is as yet no question of colour. In this first abstract manifestation, corporeality, otherwise particularized into a manifold variety of shapes, is reduced to surface. What we have here is not the manifesting of something, but only manifesting as such, the determination of which is, therefore, merely spatial.

§ 278

The manifestation of objects to each other, as limited by their opacity, is a self-external, *spatial* relationship, which, not being further determined by anything, is therefore *direct* or rectilinear. Since surfaces are so related to each other and can occupy various positions, it follows that the manifestation of a visible object to another (a smooth surface) is manifest to a third, and so on. Its image, whose location is ascribed to the *mirror*, is reflected in another surface, the eye or another mirror, and so on. In these particularized spatial determinations the law of manifestation can only be that of *equality*—the equality of the angles of incidence and reflection, and the *unity* of the plane of these angles. Nothing whatever is present which could in any way alter the identity of the relation.

Remark

The determinations of this Paragraph, which might readily seem to belong to a more determinate stage of physics, contain the transition of the general limitation of light by darkness to the more specific limitation of light by the particular spatial determinations of the latter. This determination is usually associated with the representation of light as ordinary matter; but what is here involved is simply this, that abstract ideality, this pure process of manifestation, as inseparable *self-externality*, is intrinsically *spatial*, and hence is capable of limitation by external determinations. This capacity of light to be limited by particularized spatiality is a necessary determination which involves this and no more; all material categories of transmission, physical reflection of light and the like are therefore excluded.

With the determinations of this Paragraph are associated the phenomena which have led to the crude conception of the so-called *fixed* polarization, or polarity of light. In simple reflection, the so-called angles of incidence and reflection fall in *one* plane. None the less, when a *second* mirror is introduced which again communicates the illumination reflected by the first mirror, the position of the first plane in regard to the second (the one formed by the direction of the first and second reflections) has an influence on the position, clarity or obscurity of the object as it appears after the second reflection. Consequently, for the brightness (light) which has been twice reflected to retain its natural, undisturbed clarity, a normal position is necessary, that is, the planes of the several respective angles of incidence and reflection must all fall in *one plane*. On the other hand, it also necessarily follows that the twice-reflected light is obscured and disappears when the two planes are—as one must call it—*negatively* related to each other, i.e. when one is perpendicular to the other (cf. Goethe, *Zur Naturwissenschaft*, vol. i, part 1, bottom of p. 28 ff. and 3 Heft, *Entopt. Farben*, xviii, xix, pp. 144 et seq.). From the modification in the clarity of the reflection resulting from this relation, Malus has inferred that the molecules of light possess *in themselves*, even on their different sides, different physical powers, as a corollary of which the so-called *rays of light* are regarded as *four-sided*. On this foundation, in conjunction with the further associated phenomena of entoptic colours, there has been built a vast maze of most complicated theory which forms one of the most characteristic examples in physics of *drawing conclusions* from experiments. The only conclusion to be drawn from the phenomenon of reflection on which Malus based his theory of polarization is simply this, that the condition governing the brightness of the second reflection is that the angle in this reflection must fall in the *same plane* as the angles formed by the first reflection.

Zusatz. Light, by coming into contact with matter which it makes visible, becomes generally more specifically determined as to difference of direction, and as to quantitative differences of the more or less bright. This *reflection* of light is a more difficult determination than is believed. To say that objects are visible means that light is reflected in all directions. For as visible, objects are for an other, and therefore are in relation to an other; that is to say, they have this their visible aspect in the other, light is not present to itself but to an other; thus objects are in the other, and this precisely is the reflection of light. When the sun shines, its light is for an other; this other, e.g. a surface, then becomes as large a surface of sunlight as its own size. The surface now shines, but is not originally self-luminous, its shining is derived; since the surface at each point behaves like the sun it is a being-for-another, hence outside itself and so in the other. That is the chief characteristic of reflection.

Now we only see anything on a surface if the surface exhibits spatial

E

shapes, is uneven for example; if it is smooth, no visible distinction is present. What is here visible is not any part of the surface itself, for this is undifferentiated. Only something else becomes visible, not any feature of the surface; i.e. the surface mirrors or reflects something. To be smooth is to lack spatial distinctions. And as, when unevenness is lacking, we see nothing definite on the surface of the object, all that we see on the smooth surface is a gleam, which is a general abstract shining, an indefinite illumination. The smooth, therefore, is that which manifests the undistorted image of something else. Consequently, what is seen on the smooth surface is another determinate form; this is visible in so far as it is for an other. If this other is placed opposite, and if the surface is opaque—although transparent objects also reflect; we shall refer to this later, § 320 *Zusatz*—but smooth, then this other is visible in it; for to be visible means to be in an other. If we have another mirror opposite, and a light in between, the light is visible in both mirrors at once, but in each only as reflected in the other mirror: and similarly each mirror's own image is also visible because visible in the other mirror: and so on to infinity, if the mirrors are placed at an angle to each other, since the object is then seen as many times as the width of the mirrors allows. Any attempt to explain this mechanically results only in the wildest confusion. If we call the two mirrors A and B, and ask what is visible in A, the answer is B: but B is A's visibility in B, so that what is visible in A is A as visible in B. Now what is visible in B? A itself, and A as visible in B. What more is visible in A? B and that which is visible in B; i.e. A itself and A as visible in B, and so on. Thus we have the continual repetition of the same thing, but so that each repeated image exists separately. Much light can also be concentrated by a mirror on one point.

Light is the active identity which posits everything as identical. As this identity, however, is still wholly abstract, things are not yet really identical, but are for an other, positing their identity with the other in the other. This positing of things as identical is thus for the things themselves something external, their being illumined is for them a matter of indifference. But it is necessary that things should be posited in their own proper character as concretely identical; light must become the thing's own light, must fulfil and realize itself. Light is selfhood still wholly abstract, which is therefore the not-self, a free identity with self devoid of any inner opposition. The other with which light stands in relationship (and light as the solar body has a free existence) is external to light, just as the Understanding has its material external to it. This negative, we have at first only called darkness, but it also has an immanent determinate character of its own. It is this physical opposition in its abstract determination, and so still enjoying independent being, which we now have to consider.

2. *The Bodies of Opposition*

§ 279

Darkness, as immediately the negative of light, is the opposition to light's abstractly identical ideality; it is this *opposition* in its own self. It has material reality and falls apart into a *duality*, namely (1) corporeal *difference*, i.e. material being-for-self, *rigidity*; (2) *opposition* as such which, existing independently and uncontrolled by individuality, is merely sunk within itself and is thus a dissolution and *neutrality*: the former is the *lunar*, the latter the *cometary*, body.

Remark

The peculiarity of these two bodies as *relative central bodies* in the system of gravity is based on the same Notion as their physical peculiarity (which may be here stated more exactly): they do not rotate on their axes. The *body of rigidity* has only a formal being-for-self and its independence is caught up in the opposition. It is, therefore, not individuality, but *subservient* to another body whose *satellite* it is, and in which it has its *axis*. The body of dissolution, the opposite to the body of rigidity, on the other hand, behaves *aberrantly*; it exhibits contingency in its eccentric path as in its physical existence. The cometary bodies present themselves as a superficial concretion, which in the same chance fashion may again reduce itself to dust.

The moon has no atmosphere and therefore lacks the meteorological process. It exhibits only high, conical mountains, the craters of which correspond to valleys, and the combustion of this rigidity in itself. It has the form of a crystal which Heim (one of the few profound geologists) has also indicated as the primitive form of the earth as a merely solid or rigid body.

The comet appears as a formal process, an unstable mass of vapour; nothing of a solid nature, such as a nucleus, has been observed in any of them. Astronomers have of late been less supercilious of the opinion of the ancients that comets are merely momentarily formed meteors, like fire-balls and shooting stars.

Till now, the return of only some of them has been demonstrated; the return of others has been calculated and expected but they have not appeared. If we think of the solar system as in fact a system, as in essence an intrinsically coherent totality, we must discard the formal point of view which regards comets, in all their crisscross manifestations, as contingencies within the whole system. For we can then accept the idea that the other bodies of the system *protect* themselves against them, i.e. that they (the other bodies) function as necessary organic moments of the system, and as such must preserve themselves. This point of view can afford better grounds for comfort against cometary dangers than those based mainly on the fact that comets have so much celestial space for their paths, that they should not really hit the earth— which 'should not really' is transformed into a learned theory of probability.

Zusatz. These two logical sides of the opposition here exist apart, since the opposition is free. The presence of them both in the solar system is therefore not a chance matter; if we have thoroughly grasped the nature of the Notion, it will not seem strange that even such things must be represented as entering within the sphere of the Idea, from which alone they derive all their rights. They constitute the self-subsistent moments of the dissolving earth: the moon is the earth's hard interior, the comet is the earth's atmosphere which has acquired independent existence, an enduring meteor (see below, § 287). Now on the one hand, the earth, being ensouled, can and certainly must give freedom to its crystal, its dead essence, separating off from itself this moment of its inwardness, so that this becomes the regent of its individual process, as the sun is of its universal process; on the other hand, the Notion of dissolution implies that this moment has freely detached itself and, as independent, has ceased to have connection with the earth, but has escaped from it.

Rigid being-for-self means to remain shut up within oneself, an opaque, neutral existence on one's own. This being-for-self, as an independent self-subsistence, is still inert (*ruhend*), and is as such rigid. Whatever is rigid, hard, has for principle the point; each point is a separate individual on its own. This is the mechanical phenomenon of pure rigidity; the physical determination of the same is combustibility. Now real being-for-self is self-relating negativity, the process of fire which, in consuming an other, consumes itself; but that which has rigidity for its principle is only potentially combustible, it is not yet fire as an active process, but the possibility of fire. Here, therefore, we have not yet the *process* of fire. This requires the organic relation of differences to one another, but here the physical Qualities are as yet free in their mutual relationship. Now whereas clouds and active atmospheric changes have been seen on Mercury and Venus, there are neither clouds, seas nor rivers on the moon; and yet water surfaces, or the silver threads of watercourses, would be very clearly observable on it. Momentary points of light are often seen on the moon, and they are believed to be volcanic eruptions; such things certainly imply an atmosphere, but one devoid of water. Heim, brother of the physician Heim, tried to show that if we imagine the earth as it was prior to demonstrable geological revolutions, it must be given the form of the moon. The moon is the waterless crystal, which strives, as it were, to unite itself with our sea and so to quench the thirst of its rigid, immobile nature, and which so produces the ebb and flow of the tides. The sea raises itself, is minded to escape to the moon, and the moon, in its turn, is on the verge of snatching the sea away to itself. Laplace (*Exposition du système du monde*, vol. ii, pp. 136–8) finds from observation and theory that the lunar tide is thrice as strong as the solar tide, but that the tide is strongest when both coincide. The position of the moon, in its conjunctions and oppositions, is thus, as a qualitative relation, of the greatest importance in this connection.

That which is rigid and shut up within itself is just as impotent as that which has melted away, become abstractly neutral and capable of being determined. Since the opposition exists only as opposition, it loses grip and merely collapses internally. To make such opposition an active determination, a middle term is required which shall carry both extremes and hold them together. If the rigid and the neutral were united in this third term, we should then have a real totality. A comet is a translucent, transparent, fluid body (*Wasserkörper*) which certainly does not belong to our atmosphere. If it had a solid nucleus, this would inevitably reveal its presence by a shadow; comets, however, are completely transparent, and the stars can be seen through their tails and even through the comet itself. An astronomer once thought he had seen a nucleus but it turned out to be only a flaw in his telescope. The comet describes an almost parabolic orbit round the sun (the ellipse is very elongated); it then disperses, and another is formed. The most certain and regular return is that of Halley's comet, which last appeared in 1758, and is again expected in 1835. An astronomer showed by calculation that several appearances could be reduced to a single path which might belong to one and the same comet. This comet has been observed two or three times but, according to calculation, it should have appeared five times. Comets intersect the planetary orbits in all directions; they were supposed to be so self-subsistent as to be able to touch the planets. If people are uneasy about this, there can be no comfort to them in the thought that this is made improbable by the vastness of the sky; for each point can as well be touched as another. If, however, one bears in mind, as one necessarily must, that comets are parts of our solar system, then it will be seen that they do not come as alien visitors but are generated in the solar system, which fixes their orbits; since the other bodies in the solar system are equally necessary moments, these therefore preserve their independence in face of the comets.

Comets have their centre in the sun. The moon, as the rigid body, is more akin to the planet, for as independently representing the earth's nucleus, it contains in itself the principle of abstract individuality. Comet and moon thus reproduce in abstract fashion sun and planet. The planets form the middle term of the system, the sun being one of the extremes, and the other being formed by the dependent bodies (comet and moon) as the opposition in which the two sides still fall apart (U-I-P). This, however, is the immediate, merely formal syllogism; but it is not the only one. The other, more determinate relation, is that where the dependent bodies form the mediating term, the sun the one extreme, and the earth the other (I-P-U); the earth, being itself dependent, is connected with the sun. But the dependent bodies as the middle term must contain both moments of the extremes; and, since the middle term constitutes their unity, it must be divided within itself. Each moment must belong to one of the extremes; since the moon belongs to the planet, the comet must belong to the sun. The comet, having no internal fixity, must relate itself to the formal centre. Just so, courtiers who are closer to the sovereign are made less independent by their relation, while ministers and their subordinates display as officials more regularity and hence more uniformity. The third syllogism is that in which the sun itself is the middle term (P-U-I).

This physical relationship of the heavenly bodies, taken together with their mechanical relations, constitutes cosmic Nature. This cosmic relation is the foundation, the wholly universal life in which all living Nature participates (see above, § 270, *Zusatz*). But one must not talk as if the moon had an influence on the earth, an influence which operated externally on it. On the contrary, the universal life is passive towards the individual; and the more powerful the latter becomes, the more impotent are the sidereal powers. It is through our share in this universal life that we sleep and wake, and that we are differently disposed in the morning and evening. The periodicity of the moon's phases, too, reproduces itself in living creatures and especially in animals when sick; but the healthy, and more especially minded, creature withdraws itself from this universal life and opposes itself to it. The position of the moon is, however, supposed to have an influence on, e.g., insane persons and lunatics. The weather also makes itself felt in the scars of wounds which have left behind a local weakness. But although recently much has been made of cosmic conditions and relationships, yet for the most part the subject has remained at the level of empty phrases, vague generalities, or quite isolated instances. The influences of comets should by no means be denied. I once wrung a groan from Herr Bode by saying that experience shows that comets are followed by good vintage years, as in the years 1811 and 1819, and that this double experience is as good as and even better than that regarding the return of comets. What makes comet-wine so good is that the water-process detaches itself from the earth and thus brings about an altered state in the planet.

3. The Body of Individuality

§ 280

The opposition which has gone back into itself is the *Earth*, or the *Planet* as such. It is the body of the *individual* totality where rigidity opens up into a separation into real differences and this resolution is held together by a *selflike point of unity*.

Remark

The axial rotation of the planets combined with their motion round the sun is the most concrete form of motion and so the expression of their livingness. Just so, the luminous nature of the central body is an *abstract* identity which finds its truth, like the truth of thought, in the concrete Idea, i.e. in individuality.

As regards the first determinateness of the series of planets, i.e. their *relative distances*, astronomy has as yet discovered no real law. Just so, the attempts of a philosophy of Nature to demonstrate the rationality of the planetary series as regards *physical* constitution, and by analogy with a series of metals, can hardly be regarded as an approach to discovering a requisite point of view.

It is, however, irrational to look on contingency as the governing factor here and to see, with Laplace, only the *confusion* of a visionary *imagination* in Kepler's attempt to arrange the solar system in accordance with the laws of musical harmony, and not to esteem his deep faith in the presence of *Reason in this system*; a faith which was the sole basis of this great man's brilliant discoveries. The wholly inept, factually quite false application of the numerical relations of sounds to colours made by Newton has, on the other hand, retained credence and fame.

Zusatz. The planet is the veritable *prius*, the Subject in which the differences exist only as ideal moments, where life first has a real existence. The sun is the *servant* of the planet; and sun, moon, comets, and stars generally are mere conditions of the earth. The sun therefore has not produced the planet, nor thrown it off; on the contrary, the whole solar system exists together, since the sun is as much produced by the other bodies as *they* are produced by it. Similarly, the Ego is not yet Spirit, but finds its truth in the latter in the same way that light does in the concrete planet. I, alone by myself, to esteem this as the highest, is a negative vanity which is not Spirit. The Ego is certainly an absolute moment of Spirit, but not in so far as it isolates itself.

There is little more to be said here of the individual body (the earth), because what follows is nothing but the explication of this individuality, whose abstract determination we have here reached. The function of the earth, of the organic, is to assimilate the purely universal astral powers which, as celestial bodies, have a show of self-subsistence, to subdue them to the violence of the individuality in which these giant members are demoted to the rank of moments. Quality, in its totality, is individuality, as the infinite form which is one with itself. If there is a question of pride of place, we must give the place of honour to the earth we live on. Quantitatively regarded, we may indeed let the earth sink beneath our notice, seeing it as 'a drop in the ocean of the infinite'; magnitude, however, is a very external determination. We have now come therefore to stand on the earth as our home, and not only our physical home but the home of Spirit too.

There are a number of earths or planets which together form an organic unity; many correspondences and resemblances can be adduced in connection with them, though this has not yet been achieved in entire conformity with the Idea. Schelling and Steffens have likened the series of planets to the series of metals in a clever and ingenious fashion. This mode of representation is an old one: Venus bears the sign of copper, Mercury of quicksilver, the earth of iron, Jupiter of tin, and Saturn of lead; as the sun and moon bore the names of gold and silver respectively. There is something natural about this, for the metals are the most compact, solid, self-subsistent bodies to be found on earth. The planets, however, belong to another sphere from the metals or the chemical process. Such allusions and analogies are external comparisons which decide nothing. Knowledge is not advanced by their means; only non-philosophical thinking is dazzled by them. The Linnaean classification of plants, and the successive ordering of animal species is the work of intellect or instinct; the metals are arranged according to their specific gravity. But the arrangement of the planets in space is the act of the planets themselves. If, now, a law is sought for this series as in the case of mathematical series, then each term only repeats the same law. But the whole conception of series is unphilosophical and contrary to the Notion; for Nature does not dispose its forms on such ladders, one after the other, but in masses. The universal disjunction comes first, and then follows the further subdivision within each genus. Linnaeus's twenty-four classes of plants are no system derived from Nature itself. On the other hand, the Frenchman Jussieu had a better sense of big differences, when he divided plants into monocotyledons and dicotyledons. Aristotle proceeded in a similar way in regard to animals. The same is the case with the planets, which do not exist out there as such a series. Kepler, in his *Harmonia mundi*, treated the intervals of the planets as the ratios of notes in the musical scale; but this thought was already entertained by the Pythagorean school.

A historical observation is that Paracelsus made all terrestrial bodies consist of four elements: mercury, sulphur, salt, and virgin earth, just as there were also four cardinal virtues. Mercury is the metallic element as fluid likeness to itself; it corresponds to light, since metal is abstract matter. Sulphur is the rigid element, the *possibility* of combustion; fire is not alien to it, but is sulphur's self-consuming *actuality*. Salt corresponds to water, to the cometary element; its solution is the indifferent reality, the resolution of fire into self-subsistent moments. Finally, virgin earth is the simple innocence of this movement, the Subject which is the extinction of these moments. By virgin earth was understood earth in its abstract form, e.g. pure silica. If this theory is interpreted in a chemical sense, there are many bodies which contain neither mercury nor sulphur. The deeper sense of such assertions is not that these substances are present *realiter*, but that real corporeality has four moments. Consequently such elements are not to be regarded as physical existences; otherwise Jacob Boehme and others can be charged with absurd ideas and lack of experience.

B. THE ELEMENTS

§ 281

The determinations of the elemental totality which have an immediate existence as free, independent bodies, are contained in the body of individuality as subordinate moments. As such, they constitute its universal, *physical Elements*.

In recent times, *chemical simplicity* has been arbitrarily accepted as the definition of an element. This chemical simplicity has nothing to do with the Notion of a *physical* Element, which is a real matter, a matter which has not yet been volatilized or dissipated into a chemical abstraction.

Zusatz. We have just considered the cosmic powers (as we have seen to be the case in Nature generally), fixed as independent but interrelated corporealities on high; we now pass on to consider what they are as moments of individuality, through which their existence is raised to a higher truth. Light, as positing the identical, no longer merely illuminates darkness but advances to become a really active agent. The particularized matters not only show in each other in such a way that each remains what it is, but they change into one another, and this positing of themselves as ideal and identical moments is also the activity of light. Light kindles the process of the Elements, arouses and governs it generally. This process belongs to the individual Earth which is at first, however, only an abstractly universal individuality and must acquire a much more concrete nature before becoming a true individuality. The universal individuality which is not yet reflected into self, still has the principle of individuality as subjectivity and as infinite self-relation outside of itself. This latter principle is light, the activating and animating agent in Nature. For the present, we will note that such a relationship occurs; but before dealing with the process of the Elements, we have to consider the nature of these differences themselves, in their own independent individuality. At first, it is only we who determine the body of individuality as having the moments of the solar system within it: the next step is that the planet must posit these determinations itself. In the planet, the bodies of the solar system are no longer self-subsistent but are predicates of a single Subject. These Elements are *four*, arranged in the following order. Air corresponds to light; it is passive light which has sunk to the level of a moment. The Elements of opposition are Fire and Water. Rigidity (*Starrheit*), the lunar principle, is no longer indifferent, existing by itself alone; but as an Element entering into relation with an other, namely the individuality, it is an active, unstable being-for-self which is in ceaseless process, and thus is liberated negativity—Fire. The third Element corresponds to the cometary principle and is Water. The fourth is the earth again. As the history of philosophy teaches us, it was the main importance of Empedocles to have been the first definitely to grasp and distinguish these universal basic physical forms.

The Elements are universal natural existences which are no longer self-subsistent and yet are still not individualized. From the standpoint of chemistry, we are, it is held, required to understand by an 'element' a general constituent of bodies which are all supposed to consist of a definite number of these elements. Men start by assuming that all bodies are composite, and the concern of thought is then to reduce the infinite variety of qualified and individualized corporealities to a few simple incomposite and therefore general qualities. Based on this supposition, the conception of the four Elements which has been general since the time of Empedocles, is nowadays rejected as a childish belief because, forsooth, the Elements are composite. No physicist or chemist, in fact no educated person, is any longer permitted to mention the four Elements anywhere. To search for a simple, universal existence in the sense now current is a matter only for chemistry, a standpoint which will not be dealt with until later on. The standpoint of chemistry presupposes the individuality of bodies and then seeks to tear apart this individuality, this point of unity which holds differences in itself, and to liberate the latter from the violence that has been done to them. The combination of acid and base gives rise to a salt, their unity, the third term. But there is still something else in this third term, namely shape, crystallization, the *individual* unity of form which is not the merely abstract unity of the chemical elements. If the body is only the neutrality of its differences, then the latter can of course be demonstrated by decomposing the body; but they are not universal Elements and primary principles, but only qualitatively, i.e. specifically determined, constituents. The individuality of a body, however, is much more than the mere neutrality of these sides: the infinite form is the main thing, especially in the living creature. When we have exhibited the constituents of the vegetable or animal organism, what we have are no longer the constituents of the vegetable or animal, since the organism is destroyed. Chemistry in its effort to reach what is simple thus destroys individuality. If the individual thing is neutral like a salt, then chemistry succeeds in exhibiting its sides separately, since the unity of the difference is only a formal unity which alone is destroyed. If, however, the thing to be decomposed is an organic being, then not only do we destroy the unity but also the organic nature we wanted to know. In dealing with the physical Elements, we are not in the least concerned with elements in the chemical sense. The chemical standpoint is by no means the only one; it is only a peculiar sphere which has no right at all to extend itself to other spheres as if it were their essential principle. We are here dealing only with the becoming of individuality and at first, only with that of the universal individual, the Earth: the Elements are the differentiated matters which constitute the moments of this becoming of the universal individual. We must not therefore confuse the standpoint of chemistry with that of the still wholly universal individuality. The chemical elements cannot be ordered at all and are quite heterogeneous as regards one another. The physical Elements, on the other hand, are universal matters particularized solely in conformity with the moments of the Notion; consequently, there are only four of them. The ancients were right in saying that all things were composed of these four Elements; but the elements they had before them were only 'thoughts' of such Elements.

These physical Elements must now be considered more closely. They are not individualized in themselves but are without form and consequently sunder themselves into chemical abstractions: Air into oxygen and nitrogen, Water into oxygen and hydrogen; Fire does not do so because it is process itself, from which only luminous matter remains over as material. At the other extreme of subjectivity, living substances such as the sap of plants and, still more, animal organisms, can be decomposed into these abstract chemical substances; and the specific residue is a minor part. But the intermediate stage of physical, individual inorganic matter is the most refractory to deal with, since here, though matter is specified by its individuality, this latter is still at the same time immediate, not alive and not sentient, and so, as quality, directly identical with the universal.

1. *Air*

§ 282

The Element of undifferentiated simplicity is no longer the positive identity-with-self and self-manifestation which light as such is; on the contrary, it is only a *negative universality*, reduced to the selfless moment of an *other* and therefore also *heavy*. As *negative* universality, this identity is the harmless-seeming but insidious and consuming power over what is individual and organic. In its relationship to light, this Element behaves as a passive, *transparent* fluid, although everything individual is *sublimated* in it; in its outward relationships it is a mechanically *elastic* fluid which pervades everything—Air.

Zusatz. (α) The bond of individuality, the relation of the moments to each other, is the inner Self of the individual body. This selflike nature, taken as a free independent existence without any *posited* individualization, is Air, although this Element contains *in principle* the determination of being-for-self, of the point. Air is the universal posited as in relation to subjectivity, to infinite, self-relating negativity, to being-for-self: consequently, the universal as a subordinate moment, determined as relative. Air is indeterminate but absolutely determinable: it is not yet immanently determined, but is only capable of being determined by its other; this other is light, because light is the free universal. Air thus stands in relationship to light; it is absolutely penetrable by light, and is passive light: in general, it is the universal posited as passive. Similarly the Good, as the universal, is also passive in that it is first actualized by subjectivity and is not self-active. Light *in itself* is also passive, but it is not yet *posited* as such. Air is not dark but transparent because it is only in principle an individuality; opacity is first manifest in the Element of earth.

(β) The second determination is that air is the absolutely active in opposition to the individual, is the active identity whereas light was only an abstract identity. The illumined object posits itself only ideally in an other; but air is this identity which is now among its equals, and is in relation to physical materials which exist for one another and touch one another in accordance with their specific nature. This universality of air is thus the urge to posit the other to which it is related as actually identical with itself; but the other which air posits as identical with itself is individualized, particularized matter in general. Because, however, air itself is only a universality, it does not come forward in its activity as an individual body which has power to decompose this individualized matter: air is purely corrosive, the enemy of all that is individual which it posits as a universal Element. The destruction, however, is invisible, motionless, and does not manifest itself as violence, but stealthily enters everywhere without any apparent connection with air: in the same way that Reason insinuates itself into what is individual and breaks it up. Air thus renders bodies odorous; for being odorous is only this invisible, ceaseless process between what is individual and air. Everything evaporates and turns to fine dust, and the residue is odourless. Through its breathing, the organism is also in conflict with air as it is with all the Elements generally. A wound, for example, only becomes dangerous through exposure to air. Organic life alone is characterized by its perpetual self-restoration in the process of its own destruction. Inorganic matter which cannot withstand this struggle must fall into decay; more solid things, it is true, preserve themselves, but they too are unceasingly attacked by air. Animal forms which are no longer alive are preserved from decay if they are kept away from air. This destruction can be mediated as, for example, when moisture brings the process to a particular product; but then this is *only* a mediation, since air *as such* is already this wasting activity. As the universal, air is pure, but not an inert purity; for what evaporates into air is not preserved therein but is reduced to a simple universality. It is supposed in mechanical physics that the fine particles of these bodies which are dissolved in air continue to float about in it, but can no longer be smelt simply because they are so finely divided. Physicists therefore do not wish these bodies to cease to exist; but we must not be so tender towards matter. It is only in the Understanding's 'system of identity' that matter perdures. Air purifies itself, converts everything into air; it is not a jumbled collection of materials; this assumption is justified neither by smell not chemical examination. The Understanding, it is true, brings forward the quibble of 'fineness' and has an invincible prejudice against the word 'transmutation'. Still, empirical physics has no right to credit the imperceptible with existence; and if it wishes to proceed purely empirically, it must admit that matter passes away.

(γ) Air, as matter, offers resistance but merely quantitatively as mass, not as a point or an individual as other bodies do. Thus Biot says (*Traité de phys.* vol. i, p. 188): 'Tous les gaz permanents, exposés à des températures égales, sous la même pression, se dilatent exactement de la même quantité.' Since air offers resistance only as mass, it is indifferent to the space it occupies. It is not rigid but is without cohesion, and has no external shape. It is to a certain extent *compressible*, for it is not absolutely spaceless: i.e. it is a case of mutual externality but not atomistically so, as if the principle of individuation had a real existence in it. Hence it follows that different gases can occupy the same space: this manifestation of the penetrability of air belongs to its universality, in virtue of which it is not individualized within itself. If, for example, two globes are taken, one filled with air and the other with steam, then the latter can be poured out into the first, which can receive as much steam as if it were void of air. Air, forcefully and mechanically compressed so as to give it an intensive existence, can reach the stage where its spatial asunderness is

completely subdued. This is one of the finest discoveries. Apparatus for
producing fire in this way is familiar. A cylinder is fitted with a piston and
a piece of tinder at the bottom. When the piston is forced into the cylinder,
the compressed air gives off a spark which lights the tinder. If the cylinder is transparent the spark can be seen. Here the whole nature of air
as this self-identical, destructive Element is manifest. This invisible
Element which renders bodies odorous is here reduced to a point, so
that the active being-for-self which was only *implicit* or *in itself* is here
expressly posited as *realized* being-for-self. This is the absolute origin of
Fire: the active, destructive universality achieves form, where indifferent
subsistence ceases; it is no longer universal, but unstable self-relation.
The above experiment is admirable because it shows the connection
between air and fire in their very nature. Air is slumbering fire; in order
to make this fire apparent, it is only necessary to modify the way in
which air exists.

2. *The Elements of Opposition*

§ 283

a. The Elements of opposition are first, being-for-self, but not the
indifferent being-for-self of rigidity but being-for-self posited in
individuality as a moment, as the unrest of individuality existing
on its own account: *Fire*. Air is *in itself* fire (as is shown by com-
pressing it) and fire is air *posited* as a *negative* universality or a
self-relating negativity. It is materialized time or selfhood (light
identical with heat), the absolutely restless and consuming
Element; just as this Element destroys a body when attacking it
from without, so too, conversely, does the self-consumption of
body, e.g. in friction, burst into flame. In consuming an other it
also consumes itself and thus passes over into neutrality.

Zusatz. Air, too, is this negativity of particularity, but it is inconspicuous
because still posited in the form of an undifferentiated sameness: as an
isolated, individual and localized existence distinct from other modes of
existence, it is fire. Fire exists only as this relation to a particular body.
It does not merely drain the body, leaving it tasteless and odourless, as
indeterminate and savourless matter, but it destroys its particularity as
matter. Heat is only the manifestation of such destruction in the individual body and is thus identical with fire. Fire is the existent being-
for-self, negativity as such: only not the negativity of an other but the
negation of the negative which results in universality and exact likeness.
The first universality (air) is a dead affirmation; the veritable affirmation is

fire. In fire, that which is not is posited as being, and vice versa; fire is accordingly active (*rege*) Time. As a single moment fire is absolutely conditioned and, like air, it only has being in its connection with particularized matter. It is an activity which exists *only in an opposition*, unlike the activity of Spirit; to consume, fire must have something to consume and without material it vanishes. The life-process is also a fire-process for it consists in the consumption of particularized existences; but it perpetually reproduces its material.

What is consumed by fire is, in the first place, the concrete, secondly its opposed sides. To consume the concrete means to bring it into opposition, to energize or kindle it: oxidation or the process of making an acid caustic belongs here. The concrete is thus given an edge, is raised to a pitch where it consumes itself; this is its bracing of self against another. The other side of the matter is that the element of determinateness, of difference, of individuality and particularity, which is present in everything concrete, is reduced to a unity, to an indeterminate, neutral state. So it is that all chemical process produces water just as it produces opposition. Fire is air posited as different, a negated unity, an opposition which is just as much reduced to neutrality. The neutrality in which fire is submerged, extinguished fire, is Water. The triumph of the ideal identity to which particularized matter is brought is, as a manifest unity, light, abstract selfhood. Since the Element of earth remains over as the ground of the process, all the Elements make their appearance here.

§ 284

b. The *other* [Element] of the opposition is the *neutral* Element, the opposition returned into itself. As devoid of independent individuality and therefore without rigidity and determination within itself, it is a thorough-going equilibrium that resolves any determinateness mechanically placed in it; limitation of shape it receives only externally and seeks it from outside (adhesion). It does not have the unrest of process in itself but is only the possibility of process, namely, solubility. It is capable of assuming a gaseous and a solid form as a state apart from its characteristic state, that of internal indeterminateness: this Element is *Water*.

Zusatz. Water is the Element of selfless opposition; it is a passive being-for-another, while fire is an active being-for-another. Water, therefore, exists as a being-for-another. It is quite without internal cohesion, without smell, taste, or shape; its character is to fall short of particularized being. It is an abstract neutrality, not, like salt, an individualized neutrality; for this reason it was early called 'the mother of everything

particular'. Water is fluid, like air; but not elastically fluid, so as to ex-
pand in all directions. It is more earthy than air; it seeks a centre of
gravity, is most akin to what is individual and is impelled towards it,
because in itself it is a concrete neutrality although not yet posited as
concrete. Air, on the other hand, is not even in principle concrete. Water
is thus the real possibility of difference, a difference, however, which does
not as yet exist in it. Because water has no centre of gravity, it is subject
only to the direction of gravity, and since it lacks cohesion, each point is
pressed in a vertical, i.e. a linear, direction; since, then, no part of it can
offer resistance, water takes up a *horizontal* position. Consequently each
mechanical pressure from outside has only a passing effect: the point under
pressure cannot hold its own, but communicates itself to the others, and
these cancel out the pressure. Water is indeed transparent but, since it is
already more earthy than air it is also not so transparent. As the neutral
Element, it is the *solvent* of salts and acids. What is dissolved in water
loses its shape; the mechanical relationship is sublated, and only the
chemical remains. Water is indifferent to the various states of matter: it
is the possibility of being elastically fluid as steam, liquid in drops, and
also solid as ice. All these, however, are merely states and formal transitions. These states do not depend on water itself but on something else,
inasmuch as they are produced externally by alterations in the temperature of the air. This is the *first* consequence of the *passivity* of water.

A *second* consequence is that water is not compressible or only very
slightly so; for there is no absolute determination in Nature. Water
offers resistance, not as individualized particles but only in mass, in its
usual state, that is, where it tends to form liquid drops. It might be
thought that compressibility would be a consequence of passivity; water,
on the contrary, is not compressible on account of its passivity, that is,
does not alter its spatial magnitude. Since air is an active intensity,
though only as the universal power of being-for-self, it is indifferent to
its asunderness, to its determinate space, and can therefore be compressed. A spatial change in water would therefore be an intensity in it
which it does not possess; but if, nevertheless, its spatial magnitude is
changed, this is at the same time bound up with a change of its state. As
an elastic fluid (steam) and as ice, water occupies more space just because its chemical quality has changed. Physicists are wrong when they
attribute the larger space filled up by ice to the air-bubbles present in it.

A *third* consequence of this passivity is the ease of separation, and the
tendency of water to *adhere*, that is, to make *wet*. It clings to everything,
and is in closer connection with anything it touches than with itself. It
separates itself off from its whole: it is not only able to receive any
externally impressed shape, but essentially seeks such external support
and connection, in order to divide itself, since it lacks firm internal
cohesion and stability. Its relation to oily and fatty substances is of course
an exception.

Summarizing the character of the three Elements considered, we must say that air is a universal ideality of everything that is other to it, the universal in relation to what is other, by which everything particular is destroyed. Fire is this same universality but as *manifest* and consequently in the form of being-for-self; it is therefore an existent ideality, the *existent* nature of air, the becoming-manifest of the reduction-to-show of what is other. The third Element is a passive neutrality. These are the necessary thought-determinations of these Elements.

3. *The Individual Element*

§ 285

The Element of *developed* difference and its *individual* determination is *Earth*: as distinct from the other moments, it is in the first instance *earthiness* as such, and as yet indeterminate; but, as the totality which holds together the different moments in individual unity, it is the power which kindles them into a process which it also sustains.

C. PROCESS OF THE ELEMENTS

§ 286

The individual identity which binds together the different Elements, as well as their difference from one another and from their unity, is a dialectic which constitutes the physical life of the Earth, the *meteorological process*. It is in this process alone that the Elements, as subordinate moments, have their existence, being *generated* in it and *posited* as existent, after first being developed out of the *in-itself* as moments of the Notion.

Remark

Just as the determinations of ordinary mechanics and dependent bodies are applied to absolute mechanics and the free central bodies of the solar system, so, too, the *finite* physics of *single* individual bodies is taken to be the same as the free, independent physics of the process of Earth. It is seen as a triumph of science that one recognizes and demonstrates the same determinations in the universal process of Earth as are found in the processes of isolated bodies. In the realm of these isolated bodies, however, the determinations immanent in the free existence of the Notion are deposed to a relationship in which they are mutually *external* and exist as mutually independent circumstances; the activity, too, appears as externally conditioned, and hence as contingent, so that its products also remain external formations of bodies presupposed as self-subsistent, and as remaining so. The demonstration of this likeness, or rather analogy, is effected by making abstraction from specific differences and conditions; such abstraction thus leads to superficial generalities like attraction, to forces and laws in which particularity and specific conditions are lacking. In applying the *concrete* modes of activity obtaining in the realm of *isolated* bodies to the sphere where the differentiated bodies are only *moments*, the necessary external circumstances belonging to the former sphere are usually overlooked in part, and in part added by analogical invention. In general, we have the applications of categories from a sphere of *finite* relationships to a sphere where such relationships are *infinite*, that is, where they conform to the Notion.

The fundamental defect in the consideration of this sphere rests on the fixed conception of the substantial immutable *difference* of the Elements, a conception based by Understanding on the processes of *isolated* materials and once for all established. Where higher transitions occur in these finite processes, where, for instance, water is solidified in a crystal, where light and heat vanish, and so on, Reflection has recourse to the nebulous and meaningless conceptions of *solution*, of *becoming bound* or *latent*, and the like (see below, § 305, Remark and *Zusatz*). It is chiefly this mode of explanation, too, which converts each relationship in physical phenomena into 'matters' and 'stuffs', in part *imponderable*, so that each physical existence becomes the *chaos*, previously mentioned, of 'matters' passing in and out of each other's imaginary pores; a supposition which conflicts not only with the Notion, but even with ordinary thinking. Above all, *experience* itself is extinguished: an empirical existence is still assumed though it no longer shows itself empirically.

Zusatz. The main difficulty in grasping the meteorological process comes from confusing physical Elements with individual bodies; the former are abstract determinatenesses still lacking in subjectivity-status; consequently, what is true of them is not yet true of subjectivized matter. Neglect of this distinction leads to the greatest confusion in the natural sciences. People want to put everything on the same level. Certainly, everything can be dealt with chemically, but then things can just as well be dealt with mechanically or as cases of electricity. But by this treatment of bodies on one level, the nature of other bodies is not exhausted: e.g. when vegetable or animal bodies are treated from the standpoint of chemistry. This separation and division, so that each body is dealt with according to its particular sphere, is the principal thing. Air and water show themselves to be quite different in their free elemental connection with the whole Earth, from what they are in their isolated connection with individual bodies, when they are therefore subordinated to the conditions of a wholly different sphere. It is as if one wished to study the human Spirit, and for this purpose observed customs officials or sailors; one is then dealing with Spirit under finite conditions and rules which do not exhaust its nature. Water is supposed to reveal its nature in the retort, and to be unable in its free existence as a physical Element to show any other characteristics. Usually, when men wish to demonstrate universal manifestations of physical objects such as water, air, or heat, they start by asking: *What* are they? *What* do they do? And this 'what' is supposed to be, not a thought-determination, but a phenomenon, a sensuous mode of existence. To this, however, there belong two factors: first air, water, or heat, and then some other object; and the phenomenon is the result of both combined. The second object in this combination is always a particular, and consequently the effect depends also on its particular nature. In this way, therefore, it cannot be said what the Elements in their universal manifestations are, but only what they are in relation to particular objects. If one asks: What does heat do? the answer is given that it expands; but it likewise also contracts. It is impossible to indicate a universal manifestation to which there are no exceptions: with some bodies one thing results, with other bodies another. Consequently, the manner in which air, fire, etc., appear in another sphere, determines nothing in regard to the sphere under consideration. Phenomena in their finite, individual relationships, are generalized, and on this basis the free meteorological process is explained by analogy; this is a $\mu\epsilon\tau\alpha\beta\alpha\sigma\iota\sigma$ $\epsilon\grave{\iota}s$ $\ddot{\alpha}\lambda\lambda o$ $\gamma\acute{\epsilon}\nu os$. Lightning, for instance, is held to be only the spark of the electric discharge produced by friction among the clouds. But in the skies there is no glass, no sealing-wax, no resin, no cushion, no rotation, etc. Electricity is the scapegoat which must do service everywhere; but it is a familiar fact that electricity is completely dispelled by moisture, whereas lightning originates in quite moist air. Such assertions transfer finite conditions to the free life of Nature: this occurs chiefly in regard to living things, but is out of place, and a man of sound intelligence rejects such explanations.

This transmutation of the Elements into one another is the specific character of the physical process. Finite physics, an exercise of the Understanding, is unaware of this: always holds fast to the abstract identity of persistence, so that the Elements, being composite, are only decomposed, separated, set apart, but not actually transmuted. In this process of the Elements, water, air, fire, and earth are in conflict: water is the existent material of this process and plays the chief part because it is neutral, mutable, and capable of being determined; air, as the secretly destructive, ideally positing Element is the active Element which sublates determinate existence; fire is the manifestation of being-for-self, the ideality made manifest, the manifested process of destruction. The simple relationship is just this, that water is transformed into air and vanishes; air conversely becomes water and swings over from being-for-self into its opposite, the inert neutrality which, on its side, tensed itself to become being-for-self. It was thus that the ancients, e.g. Heraclitus and Aristotle, regarded the process of the Elements. There is no difficulty in recognizing this, since experience and observation show it to us. The *formation of rain* is the main point; physics itself admits that rain has not been adequately explained. The difficulty, however, comes from reflective physics alone which, against all observation, sticks to its double presupposition: '(α) what takes place in a free context must also be capable of reproduction in conditioned and external circumstances; (β) what takes place in a conditioned context also takes place in a free one. So that what maintains self-identity in the former case, has strict identity in itself as well.' We maintain, on the other hand, that when water evaporates, the form of vapour vanishes altogether.

Now if mechanical determinations and determinations of finite phenomena are applied to this process, then, on one theory, water is supposed to be preserved, and only its form suffers a change of state. Thus Gren says (*Physics*, § 945): 'Evaporation can take place in the complete absence of air. At equal temperature and absolute elasticity, air charged with water-vapour has, as Saussure has shown, a lesser specific weight than dry air, which could not be so if water were dissolved in air, as salt is in water. Water can accordingly only be contained in the air as an elastic vapour having lesser specific weight.' It is therefore said that water-particles in the form of vapour are filled up with air, and so only quantitatively driven apart, only finely divided. This vapour depends on a certain temperature; if this goes, then it turns to water again. Rain, therefore, is held to be merely a coming together again of things formerly present, but on account of their smallness, imperceptible. It is by such nebulous ideas that rain and mist have to be explained. This theory has been completely refuted by Lichtenberg in his criticism of a prize essay on the formation of rain, crowned by the Berlin Academy; he robbed the theory of its crown, and made it appear absurd. Lichtenberg proved, following Deluc (who, though fantastically basing his argument on the creation of the world, here made correct observations), that the hygrometer showed that the air on the highest mountains in Switzerland is, or can be, quite dry immediately before mists and clouds are formed, which then turn to rain. The rain comes, so to speak, from dry air; this fact physics fails to explain. So it is in summer and winter; it is precisely in summer when evaporation is at its most intense, and when, consequently, air should be moistest, that it is driest. On this theory it is quite impossible to indicate where the water stays. It might be thought that water-vapour, on account of its elasticity, would rise; since, however, it is even colder in higher regions, vapour would there very soon be reduced to water again. Air, therefore, is not only dry through external removal of moisture, as when a body is dried in an oven; on the contrary, the drying-up of water is comparable to the vanishing of the so-called water of crystallization in the crystal; but as it vanishes, so, too, does it reappear.

The *second* theory is that of chemistry, that water is decomposed into its simple materials, hydrogen and oxygen. In this gaseous form it cannot, of course, act on the hygrometer, since warmth comes to its hydrogen and makes it a gas. Against this theory, the old question may be put: Does water really *consist* of oxygen and hydrogen? It is true that both are turned into water by an electric spark; but water is not composed of them. More correctly, it must be said that oxygen and hydrogen are only different forms assumed by water. If water were such a mere *compositum*, it would always necessarily be separable into these parts. Ritter, however, a physicist who died in Munich, made a galvanic experiment which irrefutably proved that water cannot be thought of as composed of parts. He took a bent tube which he filled with water, and put mercury in the bend, thus dividing the water in the two limbs of the tube. Communication being maintained by a metal wire through the tube and the water brought into contact with a galvanic pile, the water in the one limb was converted into hydrogen, in the other limb, into oxygen, so that only one gas was present in each limb of the tube. In the absence of the barrier of mercury in this experiment it would be said of this phenomenon that the hydrogen and the oxygen passed over from one limb of the tube to the other. This so-called explanation—though no one sees the alleged transference of the two gases—is impossible here. If in evaporation, too, water is held to be decomposed, one may ask, where do the gases go? The oxygen could augment the air: but this almost always reveals the same quantity of oxygen and nitrogen. Humboldt chemically decomposed air from high mountains, and so-called foul air from a ballroom (which should therefore have contained more nitrogen), and found the same amount of oxygen in each. In summer, especially, with the intense evaporation, the air should contain more oxygen, but this is not the case. Hydrogen, too, is nowhere to be found, neither in the upper nor lower strata of the atmosphere, nor in the region of cloud-formation, which is not so very high up. Though streams dry up for months at a time, and the soil has lost all moisture, yet none of this moisture is found in the atmosphere. These theories therefore contradict observation and rest on inferences and analogies from another sphere. When Alix, therefore, in explaining where the sun gets the material it perpetually consumes, makes it feed on hydrogen, his conception, too, is empty though it has this amount of sense in it, that Alix thought he should show where the hydrogen has to go.

It is a similar conception which looks on heat, water of crystallization, etc., as reduced to latency. Heat, for example, is no longer seen, felt, and so forth; yet it is said to be still there, though not perceptible. But what is not subject to observation does not exist in this sphere; for to exist is precisely to be for an other, to make oneself perceptible; and this sphere is precisely the sphere of existence. Consequently, this *reduction to latency* is the hollowest of forms, it keeps what has been transformed as something no longer existent, and yet supposes it to exist. The greatest contradiction thus appears when through the abstract thought of identity, the thing is still held to exist: such things of thought are false—false in thought and false in experience. Philosophy does not therefore ignore conceptions of this kind but recognizes them in their entire emptiness. Similarly, where Spirit is concerned: a man with a weak character *is* weak; virtue is not latent in him, it is not in him at all.

§ 287

The process of the earth is perpetually kindled and stimulated by its *universal self*, the activity of light, its primary relationship to the sun; and it is then further particularized according to the position of the earth in relation to the sun (climates, seasons, etc.). One *moment* of this process is the *diremption* of individual identity, the development of the moments of the self-subsistent opposition into a tension between them as embodying rigidity and selfless neutrality. Through this tension, first, the earth is on the way to resolving itself into a crystalline form, into a moon, on the one hand, and into a fluid body, i.e. a comet, on the other; and secondly, the moments of the individuality seek to realize their connection with their *self-subsistent* roots.

Zusatz. Light, as the universal principle of identity, is here no longer merely, as the opposition to darkness, the ideal positing of the being-for-another, but the positing of real existence as ideal, the positing of real ideality. This real, active, relationship of the solar light to the earth produces the difference of day and night, and so on. Without its connection with the sun, the earth would be devoid of process. The more precise manner in which this effect appears is to be considered under two aspects. One alteration is simply a change of state; the other is the qualitative alteration in the actual process .

Under the first aspect, comes the difference of heat and cold, of winter and summer; it gets warmer or colder according to the position of the earth in relation to the sun. This alteration of state, however, is not merely quantitative, but shows itself also as an inward determinateness. In summer, since the earth's axis always forms the same angle with the plane of its orbit, the advance to winter is, in the first place, merely a quantitative difference, the sun visibly mounting higher and higher day by day, and when it has reached the highest point, sinking again to the lowest point. But if the greatest heat and greatest cold depended solely on this quantitative difference, and on solar radiation, these extremes would have to fall in June and December at the time of the solstices. The alteration of state, however, is focused into specific nodal points; the equinoxes, etc. form qualitative points where not merely a quantitative decrease and increase of heat occurs. Thus, the greatest cold occurs between the 15th of January and the 15th of February, and the greatest heat in July or August. In regard to the former, it might be said that the greatest cold first comes to us from the poles; but even at the poles, as Captain Parry asserts, the position is the same. At the beginning of November, after the autumnal equinox, we have cold and storms; then the cold abates in December until, just in the middle of January, it reaches its maximum degree. Similarly, cold and storms occur at the spring equinox, after fine weather at the end of February, March and April being similar to November in this respect; and so, too, in July, after the summer solstice, there is often a drop in temperature.

Now the essential point is the qualitative alteration: the tension within the earth itself, and between the earth and the atmosphere. The process is the alternation between the lunar and cometary moments. Cloud-formation is thus not merely the result of evaporation, but is essentially this striving of earth toward one extreme. Cloud-formation is a play of reduction of the air to neutrality; but clouds can be formed for weeks at a stretch without thunderstorms or rain. The true disappearance of water is not merely a privative determination, but is a conflict within water itself, an impulse and urge toward the consuming Element of fire which, as being-for-self, is the edge on which earth tears itself asunder. Heat and cold are here only accessory states which do not belong to the determination of the process itself, and so only exert an accidental influence as in the formation of hail.

Associated with this tension is a greater specific gravity of the air; for the greater air-pressure which produces a raised level of mercury in the barometer, only shows a greater intensity or density of the air—the quantity of air has not increased. The raised level in the barometer might be accounted for by the water absorbed by the air; but it is just when air is filled with mist or rain that its specific gravity is diminished. Goethe says (*Zur Naturwissenschaft*, vol. ii, part 1, p. 68): 'When the barometer is high, the formation of water ceases. The atmosphere can carry moisture or can decompose it into its elements. A low barometer permits the formation of water, a process which often seems limitless. When earth exercises its power, increasing its force of attraction,[1] it conquers the atmosphere, and completely appropriates its contents. Whatever arises in the atmosphere must come down as *dew* or *hoar frost*, but the sky remains relatively clear. Furthermore, there is a constant relationship between barometric level and winds. A high mercury level indicates winds from the north and east, a low level winds from the west and south. In the first case, moisture is cast onto the mountains, in the second, from the mountains onto the lowlands.'

§ 288

The *other moment* of the process is that the being-for-self towards which the sides of the opposition strive, becomes, as negativity pushed to its extreme, self-sublating; in other words, it becomes the *self-kindling* destruction of the separate existence sought by the two sides. Through this process, the essential linkage of the sides is restored and the earth has made itself into a real and *fecund individuality*.

Remark

Earthquakes, volcanoes, and their eruptions may be regarded as belonging to the process of fire in which *rigidity* passes over into the negativity of being-for-self set free; such phenomena are also supposed to occur on the moon. Clouds, on the other hand, may be regarded as rudimentary *comets*. But the complete manifestation of this process is the *thunderstorm*, to which the other meteorological phenomena attach themselves as rudiments, moments, or unripe realizations. Physics has so far been unable to propound a satisfactory explanation of the formation of rain (in spite of the conclusions drawn by Deluc from observations and put forward in Germany by the gifted Lichtenberg in opposition to the *dissolution theories*), or of *thunder* and *lightning*. It has had as little success in explaining other meteorological phenomena, especially *meteorites*, where the process even gets as far as a rudimentary earthy core. For these quite everyday phenomena,

---

[1] Michelet here refers to his footnote (§ 293 *Zusatz*) on the force of attraction and specific gravity. The footnote has not been translated.

physics has not yet provided an explanation which is at all satisfactory.

Zusatz. The easing of the tension is, as rain, earth's reduction to neutrality, its relapse into unresisting indifference. But the strained cometary
formlessness also enters into the process and passes over into being-for-
self. Pushed to this extreme of opposition, the opposed sides collapse
into each other. But the unity which springs forth from them is an insubstantial fire having as its moments, not formed matter, but pure fluids; it
has no sustenance, but is the lightning which at once suffers extinction,
an aerial fire. Thus both sides sublate themselves within themselves;
their being-for-self is, in other words, simply the destruction of their
existence. In lightning, this self-destruction achieves existence; this
spontaneous ignition of the air is the extreme point of the tension, which
then collapses.

This moment of self-destruction can be demonstrated also in the
tensed earth itself. The earth *makes itself inwardly tense*, like the organic
bodies; it converts itself into the living activity of fire and likewise into
the neutrality of water, into volcanoes and springs, and so both the
principles of vulcanism and neptunism assumed in geology are, of course,
essential and belong to the process of the earth's formation. The fire
submerged within the earth's crystal is its melting, its spontaneous
combustion, in which this crystal becomes volcanic. Volcanoes, therefore,
are not to be understood as mechnical phenomena but as subterranean
thunderstorms with earthquakes; the thunderstorm, conversely, is a
volcano in the clouds. External circumstances are, of course, also needed
before an eruption takes place; but assumptions such as the release of
imprisoned gases, etc., put forward in explanation of earthquakes, are
arbitrary inventions, or else ideas taken from the sphere of ordinary
chemistry. One sees rather that earthquakes belong to the life of the total
earth; thus it is that animals, birds in the air, feel them even several days
in advance, just as we feel the sultriness before a thunderstorm. In such
phenomena the whole organism of the earth comes into play, as is also
the case in the formation of clouds, where mountain ranges are determining factors. A host of circumstances therefore shows that none of
these phenomena is isolated, but that each is a happening bound up with
the whole earth-process. Barometric level is also a factor, since the air
either acquires or loses a great specific gravity with these atmospheric
changes. Goethe compared barometric readings from the same latitudes
on different meridians in Europe, America, and Asia, and from these
found that around the entire globe their variations are simultaneous (see
below *Zusatz*, to § 293). This result is more noteworthy than any other:
only it is difficult to carry this comparison further as there are only
isolated data. The scientists have not yet been able to make simultaneous
observations; and what the poet has done is rejected by them as is the
case, too, with the theory of colours.

Explanations on mechanical lines are also inadequate to account for the formation of springs, which is a peculiar process, though, of course, determined by the nature of the terrain. The hot springs are supposedly explained by the continued combustion of carboniferous deposits which have caught fire; but hot springs are living eruptions, as are the others too. The reservoirs of such springs are supposed to be on high mountains; rain and snow, of course, play their part, and in a severe drought springs may dry up. Springs, however, must be likened to clouds which turn to rain without lightning, while volcanoes are comparable to the lightnings of the atmosphere. The crystal of the earth is always reducing itself to this abstract neutrality of water, as it is also transforming itself into the living activity of fire.

The total state of the atmosphere, likewise, including the trade-winds, forms a vast living Whole. The direction of storms, on the contrary, according to Goethe (*Zur Naturwissenschaft*, vol. ii, part 1, p. 75) is more local. In Chili, the entire meteorological process occurs daily; at 3 o'clock in the afternoon, there is always a thunderstorm; below the equator generally, winds and also the barometer are constant. The trade-winds are constant east winds between the tropics. If one enters the region of these winds from Europe, they blow from the north-east; the nearer one gets to the equator, the more they come from the east. Below the equator, calms are usually to be feared. Beyond the equator, the winds gradually take on a southerly direction till they are south-east. Beyond the tropics, one loses the trade-winds and again gets into the region of variable winds as in our European seas. In India, the barometer almost always stands at the same level; with us it is more irregular. No thunderstorms were found by Parry in the polar regions, but almost every night he saw the *northern lights* in all directions, often in opposite quarters at once. All these phenomena are isolated, formal moments of the total process, appearing within its totality as contingencies. The northern lights are merely a dry shining without the remaining material features of the thunderstorm.

Goethe has said the first sensible word about clouds. He distinguishes three main forms: finely curled-up or fleecy clouds (cirrus), which mark the stage of dissolution or the beginning of the formation of water; the rounder form seen on summer evenings which is the form of the cumulus; lastly, the outspread form (stratus) which immediately yields rain.

Shooting stars, meteors, are also such isolated forms of the total process. For just as air goes on to become water, the clouds being rudiments of cometary bodies, so this self-subsistence of the atmosphere can advance to other material forms, to the lunar form, to meteoric stones or metals. At first, there is only something watery in the clouds, but later there is quite individualized matter. These results transcend all conditions attaching to processes in isolated bodies. Livy says *lapidibus pluit*, but no one believed it till thirty years ago when stones fell on people's heads at Aigle in France; then it was believed. The phenomenon was now observed more often; the stones were examined and compared with older masses which had also passed for meteorites and were found to be of similar constitution. One must not ask where the fragments of nickel and iron in meteorites come from. Some people say they have dropped from the moon; others mention the dust from the roads, horse-shoes, etc. Meteorites come with an explosion in the clouds. The transition is accomplished by a ball of fire which is extinguished and bursts with a report, followed by a shower of stones. These stones all have identical constituents, an amalgam, which is also found in the earth. Pure iron is not found in the fossil state; but everywhere, in Brazil, Siberia, and also Baffins Bay, masses of iron, like those which fell at Aigle, are combined with a stony substance in which nickel is also found. The outer construction of these stones also compels one to recognize their atmospheric origin.

This water and fire, darkened into metal, are rudimentary moons, the retreat of individuality into itself. As meteorites represent the earth in process of becoming lunar, so do *meteors*, transient shapes, represent its cometary character. The main thing is the resolution of the real moments of the earth. The meteorological process is the manifestation of this origin of individuality, dominating the free Qualities in their efforts at self-isolation and bringing them back to the concrete point of unity. These Qualities were, at first, still determined as immediate: Light, rigidity, fluidity, earthiness; gravity had one quality, and then another. In this partition (*Urteilen*), heavy matter is the subject and the Qualities are the predicates; this has been our subjective act of judgement. Now this form has attained to existence, inasmuch as the earth itself is the infinite negativity of these differences; and so the earth is for the first time posited as an individuality. Previously, individuality was an empty word since it was only immediate, not yet self-producing. This return, and with it this total self-supporting subject, this process, is the fructified earth, the universal individual which, completely at home in its moments, no longer has anything foreign to it, whether inner or outer, but has only completely realized moments; its abstract moments are themselves the physical Elements and these are themselves processes.

§ 289

In the first place, the Notion of matter, gravity, sets forth its moments as self-subsistent but elemental realities, and the earth therefore is only the *abstract* ground of individuality. In its process, the earth posits itself as the *negative unity* of these abstract, mutually external Elements, and consequently as a *real* individuality.

Zusatz. Through the selfhood by which the earth proves itself to be real, it distinguishes itself from gravity. Whereas previously we had only matter simply determined as heavy, the Qualities are now distinct from heavy matter; heavy matter, that is, now stands in a relation to the determinateness, and this is a new development. This selfhood of light which was previously opposed to heavy matter, is now the selfhood of matter itself; this infinite ideality is now the nature of matter itself: a relation of this ideality is thus posited to the torpid being-within-self of gravity. The physical Elements are thus no longer mere moments of a single subject, but are now pervaded by this principle of individuality which is the same at each point of this physical existence. Instead, therefore, of one universal individuality, we have a multiplication of individualities, each likewise possessing the total form. The earth separates itself into individualities possessing the entire form in themselves; this constitutes the second sphere which we have now to consider.

PHYSICS OF THE PARTICULAR INDIVIDUALITY

§ 290

Since the former elemental determinatenesses are in subjection to the individual unity, this unity is now the immanent form which, acting independently, determines matter *in opposition to* its gravity. As a quest for the point of unity, heaviness does not prejudice the *asunderness* of matter: space, or rather a specific quantity of space, is the measure of the particularizations of the differences of heavy matter, of its masses. The determinations of the physical Elements are not yet *in themselves* a *concrete being-for-self*; thus they are not yet opposed to the being-for-self sought for by heavy matter. Now, however, through its *posited* individuality, matter is in its very asunderness a centralizing of itself in opposition to its asunderness and to the latter's *quest* for individuality; it differentiates itself from the ideal, centralizing activity of gravity and is an immanent determining of material spatiality, distinct in character and direction from the determinations due to gravity. This part of physics is *individualizing mechanics*, matter here being spatially determined by the immanent form. This yields, at first, a *relation* between the two, i.e. between the spatial determinateness as such and the matter belonging to it.

Zusatz. Whereas the One (the centre) of gravity is distinct from the other material parts, the individual point of unity, as selfhood, pervades the differences and is their soul. The differences are thus no longer outside their centre, but this is the light they possess within themselves; the selfhood of light is thus the selfhood of matter itself. The standpoint of individuality now arrived at consists in the return of Quality into itself. The One is here present in two modes which at first stand mutually related: we have not yet reached their absolute identity, since selfhood is itself still conditioned. Here, for the first time, the asunderness and inwardness of matter appear mutually opposed, the former determined by the latter; and thus another centre, another unity, is posited by the inwardness of matter. With this, there is liberation from gravity.

§ 291

This individualizing determination of form is at first *in itself* or immediate, and so not yet posited as a totality. The particular moments of the form consequently attain only to an indifferent, mutually external existence and their form-relation is a *relationship* of distinct terms. Here, body is finitely determined, is conditioned by external factors and falls asunder into many particular bodies. Difference thus becomes manifest, partly in the *comparison* of different bodies with each other, partly in a *more real* connection of them, a connection, however, which remains *mechanical*. It is in Shape (*Gestalt*) that we first have the self-subsistent manifestation of form which needs neither comparison with other bodies nor solicitation by them.

Remark

What is true of the sphere of finite and conditioned being generally, is true here in the sphere of conditioned individuality, which is a subject-matter most hard to separate from the other determinations of the Concrete and to hold fast by itself, especially as the *finitude* of its content is opposed to, and contradicts, the speculative unity of the Notion, which alone can be the determining principle.

Zusatz. Individuality, as at first only *for us*, is itself only primary individuality, and is therefore a conditioned, still unrealized individuality, mere universal selfhood. It has come straight out of the non-individual and so is abstract; also, as different only in relation to what is other, it is not yet inwardly fulfilled. The otherness is not yet its own otherness and is therefore passive; it is an other, gravity, determined by individuality, just because this is not yet totality. To be free, individuality must posit the difference as its own, whereas it is now merely something presupposed. It has not yet set forth its determinations within itself, whereas *total* individuality has set forth the determinations of the heavenly bodies within itself; this is Shape (*Gestalt*), but here we have only the becoming of Shape. Individuality, as the determining principle, is at first the mere positing of single determinations; it is only when these are posited both singly and in their totality that we have an individuality developed into its entire determinateness. The goal of the process therefore is that selfhood shall become the whole; this fulfilled selfhood we shall meet with in *Sound*. However, since as non-material this passes away, it is again abstract; but in unity with what is material it is Shape. Here we must deal with physics in its most finite, external aspects; these do not offer the interest found in dealing with the Notion, or with the realized Notion, the totality.

§ 292

The determinateness imposed on gravity is (*a*) an abstract, *simple* determinateness and so is present in it as a merely quantitative relationship, namely, *specific gravity*; (*b*) a specific mode of the *connection* of the material parts—*cohesion*. (*c*) This connection of the material parts as an independently *existing ideality* is (α) their merely *ideal* sublation—*Sound*; (β) the *real* sublation of cohesion—*Heat*.

A. SPECIFIC GRAVITY

§ 293

The *simple*, abstract specification is the *specific gravity* or *density* of matter, a relation of the *weight* of its mass to the *volume*. In this relation, matter, in its selfhood, tears itself free from its abstract relation to the central body, from universal gravity, ceases to be the uniform filling of space and opposes a specific inwardness to abstract asunderness.

Remark

The varying density of matter is explained by the assumption of *pores*—a densification by the invention of empty interstices which are spoken of as *actually existent*, though physics does not demonstrate them despite its claim to be based on experience and observation.—An example of the *existent* specification of gravity is furnished by the following phenomenon: when a bar of iron, evenly balanced on its fulcrum, is magnetized, it loses its equilibrium and shows itself to be heavier at one pole than at the other. Here the one part is so affected that without changing its volume it becomes heavier; the matter, without increase in its mass, has thus become *specifically* heavier. The axioms presupposed by physics in its mode of representing density are: (1) that equal amounts of equally large material parts weigh the same; so that (2) the measure of the number of parts is the amount of weight, but (3) also of space, so that bodies which weigh the same occupy equal amounts of space; consequently (4) when equal weights are found in different volumes, the equality of the spaces is preserved by the assumption of pores, though the spaces should have been *filled* with matter. The invention of pores in the fourth axiom is necessitated by the first three axioms, which rest, not on experience, but on the mere principle of identity as formulated by the Understanding, and are consequently formal *a priori* inventions like the pores. Kant has already opposed *intensity* to the quantitative determination of *amount*, and instead of explaining the different densities of bodies which occupy the same volume by assuming that the heavier body contains *more* particles, he has assumed that in the heavier body the same number of particles *fill space* to a greater *degree*: in this way, he founded a so-called *dynamic physics*. The determination of an *intensive* quantum would, at least, be just as correct as that of an *extensive* quantum, to which latter category the usual theory of density above-mentioned is restricted. But here, the determination of *intensive* magnitude has this in its favour, that it points to the category of Measure and begins to hint at an *inwardness* which, as a determination of the Notion, is an *immanent determinateness of form*, which only appears as a quantum by way of *comparison*. But the differences of quantum

as extensive or intensive—and dynamic physics goes no further—
do not express any reality. (§ 103, Remark.)

Zusatz. In the determinatenesses hitherto considered, gravity and space
were an undivided unity: the difference between bodies was only one of
mass, which is only a difference of one body from another, a difference
measured by the amount of space filled, the greater number of parts
corresponding to the larger space filled. In the inwardness (*Insichsein*) of
bodies, there now enters a different measure and equal volumes have
different weights, or equal weights have different volumes. This immanent relation, constituting the selfhood of a material thing is, precisely, specific gravity; it is this independent, self-subsistent being which
is related to itself alone, and is quite indifferent to mass. As density is the
ratio of weight to volume, either of the two sides can be taken as unity. A
cubic inch can be of water or gold, and as regards this their volume we
treat them as equal; but their weights are quite different, the gold
weighing nineteen times more than the water. Or a pound of water
occupies nineteen times more space than a pound of gold. Here the
merely quantitative gives place to the qualitative, since matter has now
its peculiar determination within itself. Specific gravity is thus an all-
pervasive, fundamental determination of bodies. Corporeal stuff in all
its parts is charged with this specific determinateness, whereas in the
sphere of gravity such centrality belonged only to a single point.

Specific gravity belongs to the earth generally, to the universal individual, no less than to particular bodies. In the process of the Elements,
the earth was only an abstract individual; the first indication of individuality is specific gravity. The earth is, as process, the ideality of particular existences. But this its individuality also shows itself as a simple
determinateness, and its manifestation is specific gravity which, in the
form of barometric level, is an index of the meteorological process.
Goethe has occupied himself a good deal with meteorology; barometer
readings interested him particularly and he enjoys airing his views on
the subject. What he says is important: the main thing is that he gives a
comparative table of barometric readings during the whole month of
December, 1822, at Weimar, Jena, London, Boston, Vienna, Töpel
(near Töplitz, and situated at a high altitude); he represents this 'graphi-
cally'. He claims to deduce from it that the barometric level varies in the
same proportion not only in each zone but that it has the same variation,
too, at different altitudes above sea-level. For it is well known that the
barometer on a high mountain stands much lower than at sea-level.
From this difference in barometric level (at the same temperature,
consequently the thermometer, too, must be brought into account), the
height of mountains can be measured. Therefore, after subtracting the
height of the mountain, the barometric variation there corresponds to
the variation at sea-level. 'If', says Goethe (*Zur Naturwissenschaft,*

vol. ii, part 1, p. 74), 'from Boston to London, and thence through Karlsruhe to Vienna, and so on, the rise and fall of the barometer always follows a similar course, this cannot possibly depend on an external cause but must be attributed to an inner one.' And on p. 63: 'When one looks at the records of the rise and fall of the barometer (even in the numerical ratios the close agreement is noticeable) one is struck by the perfectly proportionate rise and fall of the column of mercury from the highest point to the lowest. If, for the moment, we assume the sun's action to be only productive of heat, we are finally left with that of the earth only. We therefore now look for the causes of barometric changes not outside but inside the terrestrial sphere; they are not cosmic nor atmospheric, but terrestrial. The earth alters its attractive force and consequently attracts the atmosphere either more or less. This latter has no weight, nor does it exert any pressure; but when it is more strongly attracted it seems to press and weigh down more.' According to Goethe, the atmosphere has no weight: but to be attracted and to have weight are in fact, the same.[1] 'The attractive force proceeds from the mass of the entire earth, probably from the centre to the familiar surface, and then from sea-level up to the highest peaks and beyond in diminishing degree, at the same time revealing itself through a teleologically limited pulsation.' The main point is that Goethe correctly ascribes the change in specific gravity to the earth. We have already noted (§ 287, *Zusatz*) that a higher barometric level puts a stop to the formation of water, while a low level permits it. The specific gravity of the earth is the way in which it shows itself as a determinant and so as an individuality. With a higher barometric level, there is a greater tension, and intensification of the earth's inwardness with a corresponding withdrawal of matter from its abstract gravity; for specific gravity must be seen as a withdrawal by individuality from the grip of universal gravity.

It was formerly thought that a pound of gold contained as many parts as a pound of water, only the parts were nineteen times more closely compressed, so that the water had nineteen times more pores, empty space, air, etc. Such empty conceptions are the stock devices of Reflection, which is incapable of grasping an immanent determinateness but wants to maintain the numerical equality of the parts and yet finds it necessary to fill the remaining space. In current physics, specific gravity has also been derived from the opposition of repulsion and attraction: bodies are held to be denser where there is more attraction of matter, less dense where repulsion predominates. These factors no longer have any sense here. The opposition of attraction and repulsion as two separate, self-subsistent forces is a product only of reflective Understanding. If attraction and repulsion were not in absolute equilibrium, one would be involved in contradictions which would show up the falsity of this

---

[1] Michelet's footnote here on the force of attraction and specific gravity is not translated.

conception, as has already been shown in connection with the motions
of the heavenly bodies (§ 270, Remark and *Zusatz*).

§ 294

Density is at first only a *simple* determinateness of heavy matter;
but as matter remains the essential asunderness, the determination
of the form is again a specific mode of the spatial interrelation of
its manifold parts—*Cohesion*.

Zusatz. Cohesion, like specific gravity, is a determinateness which
distinguishes itself from gravity; but it is wider than specific gravity,
being not simply another centrality, but a centre with reference to a
plurality of parts. Cohesion is not merely a comparison of bodies according to their specific gravity, but their determinateness is now so posited
that they have a real relationship to each other and touch one another.

B. COHESION

§ 295

In *Cohesion*, the immanent form posits a mode of the spatial
juxtaposition of the material parts distinct from that determined
by gravity. This, consequently specific, mode of the holding
together of the material parts is at first posited in these parts as
merely different, as not yet withdrawn into a self-enclosed totality
(Shape); it is therefore manifest only in the relationship between
masses which are similarly different and different in respect of
cohesion, and it thus shows itself to be a peculiar *mode of resistance*
in the mechanical response to *other* masses.

Zusatz. We saw that the purely mechanical response of bodies was
pressure and thrust; bodies now react in pressure and thrust not merely
as masses, as in the mechanical relationship, but independently of this
quantity; they exhibit a particular way of maintaining themselves, of
positing themselves in unity. The first, immediate mode of this holding
together of the material parts was gravity, bodies having a centre of
gravity; now the mode is an immanent one which they show to one
another according to their particular weight.

Now cohesion is a word which has been used in a very indefinite
sense in a number of philosophies of Nature. There has been a great deal
of chatter about it with no better outcome than mere opinions and

obscure adumbrations of an indefinite Notion. Total cohesion is magnetism which does not appear until we have Shape (*Gestalt*). Abstract cohesion, however, is not yet the syllogism of magnetism which distinguishes extremes and also posits their point of unity, but so that extremes and unity are distinct from each other. For this reason, magnetism, too, is not yet in place here. Nevertheless Schelling has embraced magnetism and cohesion under the same head, although the former belongs to an entirely different stage. Magnetism, namely, is totality within itself, even though still an abstract one; for it is linear, admittedly, but extremes and unity are already developed as differences. This is not yet the case with cohesion, which belongs to the becoming of individuality as totality, whereas magnetism belongs to the total individuality. Consequently, cohesion is still in conflict with gravity, is still only a moment of the determination opposed to gravity, not yet the total determination opposed to gravity.

§ 296

In cohesion, this unity of form of the manifold asunderness is in its own self manifold. (*a*) Its *first* determinateness is the wholly indeterminate holding-together, and so is the cohesion of what itself is without cohesion and is consequently *adhesion* to an other. (*β*) The coherence of matter *with its own self* is, in the first place, merely *quantitative*—ordinary cohesion, the strength of matter's holding-together in resistance to the influence of weight; secondly, however, it is *qualitative*, the characteristic property of yielding to the pressure and thrust of external violence, and at the same time showing itself to be independent in its form. The inwardly mechanizing geometry, operating in accordance with the specific mode of the forms of space, produces the peculiarity of maintaining a specific *dimension* of bodily cohesion: *punctiformity*—which is brittleness; *linearity*—which is rigidity generally and, more exactly, tenacity; *superficiality*—which is ductility and malleability.

Zusatz. Adhesion, as passive cohesion, is not the inwardness of body, but its greater affinity with an other than with itself, just as light is a showing or shining in an other. For this reason, and more particularly on account of the absolute displaceability of its parts, water, too, as the neutral Element adheres, i.e. makes wet. In addition, solid bodies which definitely have inner cohesion also adhere, provided only that their surfaces are not rough but quite smooth so that all their parts can make complete contact with each other: these surfaces then lack all distinction either in themselves or in relation to others which are likewise smooth, and both can therefore posit themselves as identical. Glass plates, e.g., stick together very strongly especially if water is poured between them so as to fill up any possible unevennesses completely; it then requires great force to pull them apart. Gren therefore says: 'The strength of adhesion depends in general on the number of points in contact.' (*Physics*, §§ 149–50.) Adhesion has various modifications: e.g. water in a glass sticks to the sides and stands higher on the sides than in the middle of the glass; in a capillary tube, the water rises quite of its own accord, and so on.

But as regards matter's coherence with itself as its specific being-within-self, this, as mechanical cohesion, is only the holding together of a homogeneous mass in itself in opposition to the placing of another body in it, i.e. a ratio of the intensity of its coherence to the weight of the other body. If, therefore, a mass is pulled or pressed by a weight it reacts with a quantum of its 'in-itself'. The amount of the weight determines whether the mass retains its coherence or gives it up: glass, wood, etc. can therefore bear a certain number of pounds before breaking and the pressure need not be in the direction of gravity. The serial arrangement of bodies in respect of their cohesion bears no relation to their serial relation in respect of specific gravity: gold and lead, for example, have greater specific gravities than iron and copper, but are not so firm. The resistance, too, offered by a body to a thrust is not the same as when the body has to resist only in one direction, that, namely, of the gravitational pull: breaking and thrust, on the other hand, occur at an angle, and their force, therefore, is two-dimensional; hence the infinite force of thrust.

Qualitative cohesion proper is a holding-together of homogeneous masses by an immanent characteristic form or limitation, which here explicates itself as the abstract dimensions of space. The characteristic configuration, namely, can be none other than a mode of specific spatiality which the body displays in itself. For cohesion is the identity of the body in the mutual externality of its parts; qualitative cohesion is therefore a specific mode of asunderness, i.e. a determination of space. This unity, as present in individual matter itself, is a holding-together in opposition to the universal unity which it seeks in gravity. Matter now tends to follow a variety of peculiar directions other than the vertical direction of gravity. This cohesion, although an individuality, is at the same time still a conditioned individuality, because brought out only through the action of other bodies: it is not yet the free individuality of Shape, i.e. not yet the individuality as a totality of the forms it posits. For the total shape is actually there, mechanically determined, with such and such sides and angles. Here, however, the character of matter is at first only its inner shape, i.e. the latter is not yet actually present in its developed determinateness. This again finds expression in the circumstance that it shows its character only through an other. Cohesion is thus only a mode of resistance to an other, just because its determinations are only isolated forms of individuality, which are not yet manifested as totality. The brittle body is neither malleable nor ductile in linear fashion but maintains itself as a point and is not continuous; this is hardness fashioned inwardly. Glass is so brittle that it shatters: combustible substances, too, are generally brittle. One of the properties which distinguishes steel from iron is brittleness: it has a granular fracture; so too has cast iron. Glass which is cooled quickly is very brittle, but not when it is cooled slowly; the former when smashed turns to powder. Metals, on the other hand, are more continuous within themselves but they, too, vary in their degrees of brittleness. Tough bodies are fibrous and do not fracture but hold together; iron can be drawn out into wire, but not every kind of iron: forged iron is more malleable than cast iron and can be given a linear form. This is the ductility of bodies. Lastly, malleable bodies can be beaten into thin sheets; some metals can be beaten into sheets, while others crack. Iron, copper, gold, and silver can be beaten out; they are soft and yielding, neither brittle nor tough. Some forms of iron can be worked only into sheets, some only drawn out into lines of wire, others like cast iron have for their principle the point. As the sheet of metal becomes a surface, or the point in it becomes the whole, so malleability as such is, in its turn, ductility of the whole—an unformed inwardness which maintains its cohesion generally as togetherness of the mass. It must be noted that these moments are only single dimensions, each of which is a moment of the real, shaped body; but Shape is not any one of these moments.

§ 297

(γ) It is *another individual body* to whose violence a body gives way, at the same time maintaining its own character. But as cohesive, body is in its own self a materiality of mutually external parts; and when the whole suffers violence, the parts do violence to, and give way to, *each other*. However, as they are no less self-subsistent, they sublate the negation they have suffered and reinstate themselves. Consequently, the yielding of body with the simultaneous self-preservation of its own character in face of *outer* objects, is directly bound up with this *inner* activity of yielding and preserving itself in face of itself: *Elasticity*.

Zusatz. Elasticity is cohesion displaying itself in motion, the totality of cohesion. We had elasticity even in the First Part [Mechanics] in treating of matter as such, where a number of bodies, in resisting each other, press against and touch each other, negating their spatiality but equally reinstating it. That was abstract elasticity directed outwards. Here, elasticity is internal to the self-individualizing body.

§ 298

Ideality here attains the existence which the material parts, as matter, *only sought*, the independent, self-subsistent point of unity in which the material parts, if really attracted, would only be negated. This point of unity, in so far as the parts are merely heavy, is in the first instance *outside* them, and so at first only *in itself*; in the demonstrated negation suffered by the parts, this ideality is now *posited*. But it is still conditioned, being only one of the sides of the relation, the other side of which is the persistence (*Bestehen*) of the *mutually external* parts, so that the negation of these gives place to their re-establishment. Elasticity, therefore, is only a change in specific gravity which reinstates itself.

Remark

When here and elsewhere mention is made of material *parts*, these are not to be understood as atoms or molecules, i.e. as having a separate existence of their own, but only as quantitatively or contingently distinguished, so that their continuity is essentially inseparable from their distinctness; elasticity is just the existence of the dialectic of these moments. The place of the material object is its *indifferent* specific *persistence*, and the *ideality* of this persistence is thus its *continuity* posited as a *real* unity; i.e. that two material parts which formerly *persisted* as outside each other and which therefore must be conceived as occupying different places, now occupy *one and the same* place. This is the *contradiction*, and it exists here in a material form. It is the same contradiction which lies at the base of the Zenonian dialectic of motion, except that in motion the contradiction concerns abstract places, but here *material* places, material parts, are involved. In motion, space posits itself temporally and time posits itself spatially (§ 260). Motion falls into the Zenonian antinomy, insoluble if the places are *isolated* as points of space, and the time-moments as points of time; and the solution of the antinomy, i.e. motion, is reached only when space and time are grasped as in themselves continuous, and the moving body as being at once in and *not* in the same place, i.e. as being at once in *another* place; just as the same point of time at once is and is not, i.e. is at once *another* point of time. Thus in elasticity, the material part, atom, or molecule is posited as affirmatively occupying its space, as *persisting*, and yet at the same time as not persisting—as a quantum which is at once an extensive and also only an intensive magnitude. In contrast to this putting of the material parts into a unity in elasticity, the so-called explanation has recourse to the oft-mentioned invention of *pores*. True, it is admitted in principle that matter is perishable, not absolute, yet in practice this admission is resisted when matter has to be grasped as *in fact* negative, when the negation has to be posited *in* matter. The pores are certainly the negative moment—for it is no use, the advance to this determination must be made—but they are the negative only *alongside* matter, the negative, *not of matter itself*, but present *where matter is not*, so that in point of fact, matter is regarded only as affirmative, as *absolutely self-subsistent, eternal*. This error springs from the general error of the Understanding, viz. that what is metaphysical is only a 'thought-thing' *alongside*, i.e. *outside* actuality; and so, *along* with the belief in the *non-absoluteness* of matter, there is *also* a belief in its absoluteness. The former belief, when admitted, is admitted outside the sphere of science, but it is the latter belief which really prevails in science.

Zusatz. When one body is posited in another, the two bodies having a certain density, the specific gravity of the second body is altered: this is the first moment. The second moment is the resistance offered by the latter, its negating of, and abstract bearing toward, the first body. The third moment is that the second body reacts, and repels the first. These are the three moments familiar as *softness, hardness*, and elasticity. The body no longer yields in purely mechanical fashion, but inwardly through alteration of its density; this softness is *compressibility*. Matter is thus not immutable, impenetrable. When the weight of the body remains the same and its volume diminishes, its density increases; but this can also be decreased, e.g. by heat. The hardening of steel, which as contractility is the opposite of elasticity, is also an increase of density. Elasticity is the retreat of body into itself so as immediately to reinstate itself. The cohesive body when struck, pushed, or pressed by another body, suffers a negation of its material being as occupying space, and so of its occupation

of a particular place. We are thus in the presence of the negation of
material asunderness, but equally, too, of the negation of this negation,
of the reinstatement of materiality. This reinstatement is no longer the
former general elasticity in which matter was merely reinstated as mass;
this elasticity is rather an inward reaction—it is the immanent form of
matter which makes itself felt therein in accordance with its qualitative
nature. Each particle of cohesive matter thus behaves as a centre, and
there is a single form of the whole which permeates the matter, not tied
to the asunderness, but fluid. If now pressure is exerted on the matter,
i.e. if the body receives a negation from without, which affects its inner
determinateness, the specific form of the body posits an inner reaction in
it so that the pressure imparted to it is nullified. Each particle has its
own particular place by way of the form, and is the preserving of this
particular relationship. In general elasticity, the body acts merely as a
mass; but here the motion persists within itself, not as a reaction outwards, but as a reaction inwards till form has reinstated itself. This is the
oscillation and vibration of the body which now continues itself inwardly even though the abstract reinstatement of general elasticity has
resulted: the motion, it is true, originated externally, but the impact
touched its inner form. This inner fluidity of the body is total cohesion.

§ 299

The ideality posited in elasticity is an alteration which is a double
negating. The negating of the persistence of the material parts in
their mutual externality is itself negated as the re-establishing of
their asunderness and their cohesion; there is a *single* ideality as
an alternation of the two mutually sublating determinations, the
inner oscillation of the body within itself—*Sound*.

Zusatz. The outer reality (*Dasein*) of this inner oscillation seems different
from the determination which we had, viz. elasticity: its being-for-
another is *Sound*, which is thus the third determinateness [after specific
gravity and cohesion].

C. SOUND

§ 300

The specific *simplicity* of the determinateness possessed by body
in density and in the principle of its cohesion, this at first *inward
form*, emerging from its submergence in material asunderness,
becomes *free* in the *negation* of the self-subsistence of this its

asunderness. This is the transition of materialized *space* into materialized *time*. In the *vibration* of the material body—i.e. through the momentary negation of its parts and, equally, the negation of this negation of them, the two negations being so linked that one evokes the other, and through an oscillation between the subsistence and the negation of specific gravity and cohesion—this simple form, as the *ideality* of material body, achieves *independent existence* and mechanically soul-like manifestation.

Remark

The purity or impurity of sound proper and its distinction from mere noise (resulting from a blow on a solid body), rustling, etc. is bound up with the homogeneity of the vibrating body, and also with its specific cohesion and other spatial determinations, i.e. whether it is a material line, a material surface, and then again whether it is a bounded line and surface, or a solid body.—Water, being without cohesion, makes no sound, and its movement, as merely *external* friction of its freely displaceable parts, yields only a murmuring sound. The continuity of glass, despite its inner brittleness, manages to ring, and the continuity of metal, lacking all brittleness, rings through and through, even more so than glass, and so on.

The *possibility of transmitting* sound, its so to speak *soundless* propagation—without the repetition and oscillation of vibration—through all bodies, no matter how varying in brittleness, etc. (through solid bodies better than through air, through the earth to a distance of many miles, through metals, according to calculation, ten times faster than through air), this possibility reveals the ideality which freely passes through all these bodies, and which takes account only of their *abstract* materiality, not of the specific determinations of their density, cohesion, and further structure, and which brings their parts into negation, that is into vibration. This idealizing process is itself nothing but the transmission of sound.

The *qualitative* side of sound in general and also of self-articulating sound, namely *tone*, depends on the density, cohesion, and further specified forms of cohesion of the sonorous body; this is because the ideality or subjectivity which vibration is, is a negation of these specific qualities, and therefore has them for its content and its determinateness; so it is that vibration and sound are themselves specified accordingly, and that instruments have their own characteristic sound and *timbre*.

Zusatz. Sound belongs to the sphere of mechanism since it is associated with heavy matter. Form, as wresting itself from heavy matter but as still attached to it, is for that reason still conditioned: it is the free physical utterance of ideality still linked to the mechanical sphere—the freedom *from* heavy matter which is at the same time *in* heavy matter. Bodies do not as yet sound spontaneously as organic bodies do, but only when they are struck. Movement, external impact, propagates itself since the inner cohesion of body bears witness to self-preservation of body in the face of the merely mechanical impulse, from which standpoint it now has to be treated. These bodily phenomena are very familiar and are moreover very varied, and this makes it difficult to exhibit their necessary connection through the Notion. Because we find them trivial we pay no attention to them; but they, too, must show themselves to be necessary moments with a place in the Notion. When a body sounds, we feel we are entering a higher sphere; sound affects our innermost feeling. It speaks to the inner soul since it is itself inner and subjective. Sound, by itself, is the self of the individuality, not an abstractly ideal something like light, but as it were a mechanical light, manifest only as the time of movement in cohesion. Individuality includes matter and form; sound is this total form which announces itself in time—the whole individuality which is merely this: that this soul is now posited as one with the material body and dominating it as a stable existence. What is here revealed is not based on matter for it does not have its objectivity in anything material. It is only the Understanding which, for purposes of explanation, assumes an objective being and speaks of sound-matter as it does of heat-matter. The natural man marvels at sound since in it an inner being is revealed; he does not presuppose a material basis for it but rather something psychic. We have here a phenomenon similar to that met with in motion, where mere velocity or, in the case of the lever, distance, shows itself as a mode that can be put in the place of quantitative materiality. This phenomenon of an inner being coming into physical existence cannot astonish *us*; for the basis of the Philosophy of Nature is that thought-determinations show themselves to be active principles.

In running through the empirical manifestations of this thought-determination only a brief account can be given of the detailed nature of Sound. We have many expressions: sound, tone, noise, also to creak, hiss, rustle, and so on. This wealth of language for the characterization of sensuous phenomena is quite superfluous; the sound being given, it is no trouble to make a sign for it which directly corresponds to it. Liquids as such do not sound: an impact or impression is indeed transmitted to the whole but this transmission springs from the entire formlessness, the entire lack of any inner determination; sound, on the other hand, presupposes the identity of the determination and intrinsically has the nature of form. Pure sound requires compact continuity and homogeneity of matter, and so metals—especially precious metals—and glass, give out a clear sound, a property developed by smelting. If, on the other hand, a bell is cracked, we hear not only the vibration but also other forms of material resistance, the brittleness and irregularities of shape, then we have an impure sound, a noise. Stone slabs, though brittle, also give out sound; air and water, on the contrary, though not themselves resonant, can propagate sound.

The origin of Sound is hard to grasp. Sound is the emergence of the specific inner being freed from gravity; it is the plaint of the ideal in the midst of violence, but also its triumph over the latter since it preserves itself therein. Sound is produced in two manners: (a) by friction, (b) by vibration proper, by elasticity of inner being. Vibration is also present in friction, for while it lasts a manifold is brought into unity, the various separately existing parts being brought momentarily into contact. The place of each part, and hence its materiality, is sublated; but it is just as much restored. It is precisely this elasticity which announces itself in sound. But when the body is rubbed, the rubbing itself is heard and this sound corresponds rather to what we call noise. If the vibration of the body is caused by an external body, we hear the vibrations of each; each works on the other and prevents purity of sound. In that case the vibration is not so much independent as forced on each by the other; then we call it noise. Thus in bad musical instruments one hears the clatter, the mechanical striking of the instrument: e.g. the scratching of the bow on the violin, just as, in a bad voice, the vibration of the muscles can be heard. The other, higher sound is the inward vibration of the body, its inner negation and self-restoration. Sound, properly speaking, is reverberation, the unhindered inner vibration of a body which is freely determined by the nature of its cohesion. There is still a third form where the outer excitation and the sound emitted by the body are like in kind, and that is the singing voice of man. It is in the voice that we first have this subjectivity or independence of form; this merely vibratory movement thus has something spiritual about it. The violin too does not reverberate; it sounds only while the strings are being rubbed.

Now if we ask with reference to sound as such why it is connected with hearing, we must answer that it is because this sense belongs to the mechanical sphere and is moreover the sense connected with the flight from materiality, with the transition to the immaterial and ideal. On the other hand, everything associated with specific gravity and cohesion relates to the sense of feeling; the sense of touch is thus the other sense of the mechanical sphere, in so far, namely, as this sphere contains the determinations of materiality itself.

The particular sound produced by matter depends on the nature of its cohesion, and these specific differences also are connected with the pitch of the sound. But the peculiar determinateness of the sound can strictly speaking only be manifested through a comparison of the intrinsic sounds of bodies. As regards the first point, metals for example have their own specific sound, like the sound of silver and of brass. Rods of different substances of equal thickness and length emit different sounds; as Chladni has observed, whalebone emits *a*, tin, *b*, silver, *d* in the upper octave, Cologne pipes, *e*, copper, *g*, glass, *c* in a still higher octave, deal, *c* sharp, and so on. Ritter, I remember, investigated at some length the various parts of the head where the sound is more hollow, and by tapping its different bones he found a variety of tones, which he arranged in a definite scale. There are also entire heads which sound hollow, but this kind of hollow noise he did not consider. One might well ask whether the heads of those we call 'empty-heads' do actually sound more hollow.

Biot's researches show that not only air, but all other bodies, transmit sound. If, e.g., one strikes the earthenware or metal pipe of a water supply, the sound can be heard several miles away at the other end of the pipe; then two sounds can be distinguished, of which the one carried by the material of the pipe is heard before the one transmitted by the air in the pipe. The sound is not held up by mountains, water, or forests. The transmission of sound by the earth is remarkable: e.g. by putting one's ear to the ground, a bombardment ten to twenty miles away can be heard; sound, too, is transmitted by the earth ten times faster than by air. This transmission is also noteworthy in that it shows the complete untenability of the sound-matter postulated by physicists, which is thought to move rapidly through the pores of bodies.

§ 301

In the vibration we must distinguish the oscillation as an *external* change of place, an alteration of spatial relationship to *other* bodies, which is movement in the ordinary, proper sense. But such oscillation, though distinct from, is at the same time identical with, the inner movement characterized above, which is subjectivity in process of liberation, the manifestation of sound as such.

This ideality, since its universality is abstract, is only *quantitatively* differentiated in its existence. Consequently, the further distinctions of sounds and tones, their harmony and disharmony, rest on *numerical relationships*, and on the simpler or more complex and remoter agreement of these.

Remark

The vibration of strings, air-columns, reeds, etc, is an alternating transition from the straight line to the arc, and vice versa; with this mere show of an external change of place in relation to other bodies, there is directly connected the inner alternating change of specific gravity and cohesion: the side of the material line lying against the centre of the arc of oscillation is shortened, while the outer side is lengthened. The specific gravity and the cohesion of the latter side are therefore diminished, while those of the former side are at the same time increased.

As regards the power of the quantitative factor in this ideal sphere, we may recall the fact that when a vibrating line or surface is mechanically interrupted, the quantitative determination thus introduced communicates *itself* to the previously communicated vibration of the entire line or surface beyond the point of interruption, giving rise to *nodes of vibration* in it; in Chladni's experiments this phenomenon is made visible to the eye. To this class of phenomena also belongs the arousal of harmonizing notes in neighbouring strings, which are brought into specific quantitative relationships to the sounding string. But of most interest in this connection are the phenomena to which Tartini first drew attention, namely, that notes standing in specific numerical ratios to each other give rise, when sounded together, to notes different from the original notes and produced only by these ratios.

Zusatz. Vibrations are the inner oscillations of matter which, *qua* sonorous, preserves itself in this negativity and is not destroyed. A sonorous body must be a material physical surface or line, and limited at that, so that the vibrations travel along the whole line, are checked, and then return. A blow on a stone produces only a noise, not a sonorous vibration, since the shock, though propagated, does not return to itself.

The modifications of sound produced by the recurrent regularity of the vibrations are tones; this is the more important diversity of sounds which we have in music. *Unison* occurs when two strings perform the same number of vibrations in the same time. The difference between tones, on the other hand, depends on differences in the thickness, length, and tension of the strings or columns of air, according as the instrument is a stringed or wind instrument. If, for example, of the three determinations of thickness, length, and tension two are the same in different instruments, their difference in sound will depend on the third factor; and since variation in tension is easiest to observe in strings, it is mainly chosen as a basis for calculating differences in vibration. Variation in tension is effected by carrying the string over a bridge and attaching a weight to it. If only the length is varied, then the shorter a string is, the more vibrations it performs in the same time. In wind instruments the shorter the pipe in which a column of air is made to vibrate, the higher-pitched the tone; to shorten the column of air, all that is needed is to insert a piston. In a monochord where the string can be divided, the number of vibrations of any part in the same period of time is inversely proportional to the size of parts having this fixed length; one-third of the string makes thrice as many vibrations as the whole string. Small vibrations in the case of high notes can no longer be counted on account of their great speed; but the numbers can be quite accurately determined by proportionately dividing the string.

Since tones are a mode of our sensation, they are for us either pleasant or unpleasant; this objective mode of harmony is a determinateness which enters into this mechanical sphere. What is most interesting here is the coincidence between what the ear finds harmonious and numerical ratios. It was Pythagoras who first discovered this coincidence and this induced him to determinations of thought, too, in the form of numbers. Harmony is based on the ease of concords, and is a felt unity in difference like symmetry in architecture. But can harmony and melody which so enchant us, appealing to our feelings and passions, depend on abstract numbers? This seems remarkable, astonishing even; but only this determination is present and we may see in it a transfiguration of numerical ratios. The simpler ratios which form the ideal basis of harmony are those which are more readily grasped, and these are primarily those based on the number two. Half of the string vibrates to the upper octave of the note of the whole string which is the fundamental. If the lengths of two strings are in the ratio of 2:3, or if the shorter is two-thirds the length of the other, and therefore performs three vibrations in the same time as the other performs two, then the shorter gives out the *fifth* of the longer string. When three-fourths of a string vibrates this yields the fourth, which has four vibrations to the fundamental's three; four-fifths yields the major third with five vibrations against four; five-sixths yields the minor third with six vibrations against five, and so on. When a third of the whole string is made to vibrate, this yields the fifth of the higher octave. If a quarter is made to vibrate this yields the next octave above. A fifth of the string yields a third of the third octave above or the double octave of the major third; two-fifths yield the third of the next octave and three-fifths yield the sixth. A sixth of the string yields the fifth of the third octave, and so on. The fundamental, therefore, has one vibration while its octave has two; the third has one and a quarter: the fifth has one and a half and is the dominant. The fourth presents a more difficult ratio: the string makes one and a third vibrations, which is more complicated than one and a half and one and a quarter, and the fourth is therefore a livelier note. The ratio of the numbers of vibrations in an octave is therefore as follows: if c makes one vibration, d makes 9/8, e 5/4, f 4/3, g 3/2, a 5/3, b 15/8, c 2; or the ratio is 24/24, 27/24, 30/24, 32/24, 36/24, 40/24, 45/24, 48/24. If one imagines a string divided into five parts, and one-fifth part which alone is actually divided off is made to vibrate, nodes are formed in the rest of the string which spontaneously divides itself into the remaining parts. If paper riders are put on the points of division they remain there, but if put elsewhere on the string they fall off; at the former points, therefore, the string is at rest. These points are the nodes of vibration which bring other consequences in their train. An air-column also makes such nodes, e.g. a flute when the vibrations are interrupted by holes. Now the ear takes pleasure in sounds based on the simple ratios of 2, 3, 4, 5; these can express specific relationships ana-logous to the determinations of the Notion, whereas the other numbers, being intrinsically complex combinations, become indeterminate. One produces Two from itself, Three is the unity of One and Two; this led Pythagoras to use them as symbols for the determinations of the Notion. If the string is divided into two, there will be neither difference nor harmony, because the sound is too monotonous. But when the string is divided by two and by three, harmony is produced as the fifth; similarly in the case of the third, which is divided by four and five, and in the case of the fourth, which is divided by three and four.

The harmonic triad is the fundamental together with the third and the fifth; this gives a definite system of tones but is still not the scale. The ancients held mostly to the triad but now something further is required. If, for example, we start with an empirical note c, then g is the fifth. But since the start with c is arbitrary, every note must be exhibited as the fundamental of a system. In any system, therefore, whatever its fundamental may be, there occur notes which also occur in other systems; but what in one system is the third, in another system is the fourth or the fifth. Thus it comes about that one and the same note, which fulfils different functions in different scales and so runs through them all, is separated out and described by a neutral name like g, and so on, and is given a general position. This need for an abstract consideration of tone also appears as another formal need, namely, that the ear requires to pass through a series of notes which ascend and descend by equal intervals; this, com-bined with the harmonic triad, first yields the scale. How as a matter of history we have arrived at our present customary way of regarding as fundamental the succession of notes c, d, e, f and so on, I do not know; the organ perhaps has played its part. The relationship of third and fifth has no significance here; arithmetical uniformity alone is the determining factor here, and to this, as such, there is no limit. The harmonic limit to this ascent is given by the ratio 1:2, the fundamental and its octave; between these two, therefore, we must now also insert the absolutely determined notes. The parts of the string which are to give forth such notes must be greater than half the string, for if they were less, the notes would be higher than the octave. Now in order to produce the said uniformity we must insert between the notes of the harmonic triad notes which have roughly the ratio to each other of the fourth to the fifth; thus we get the whole tones which form a whole interval like that between the fourth and fifth. The interval between the fundamental and the third is filled by the second if eight-ninths of the string vibrate; this interval from fundamental to second (from *c* to *d*) is the same as that from fourth to fifth (from *f* to *g*), and that from sixth to seventh (*a* to *b*). The second (*d*) has then also a relation to the third (*e*): this too is roughly a whole tone, but the ratio is only approximately the same as that of *c* to *d*, the two ratios not being in exact agreement. The fifth bears the same ratio to the sixth (*g* to *a*) as *d* to *e*. But the ratio of the seventh (by eight-fifteenths of the string) to the higher octave (*b* to *c*) is like the ratio of the third to the fourth (*e* to *f*). Now in this advance from *e* to *f* and from *b* to *c*, there is a greater inequality than there is between the other notes, the intervals between which are filled up by the so-called half-notes, i.e. the black notes on the pianoforte: the succession is interrupted precisely by the advance from *e* to *f* and from *b* to *c*. Thus we have a uniform succession, although it is not completely uniform. The other intervals, too, which are called whole tones are, as remarked, not perfectly equal but distinguished from each other as greater and lesser tones (major and minor tones). The former comprise the intervals from *c* to *d*, from *f* to *g* and from *a* to *b*, all of which are equal; the latter, on the other hand, include the intervals from *d* to *e* and from *g* to *a* which, although equal to each other, differ from the former in not being quite a whole tone. This small difference between the intervals is what is called the *comma* in musical theory. The basic determinations of fifth, fourth, third, etc., must remain the foundation; the formal uniformity of the progression of notes must be regarded as of secondary importance. The ear which holds fast to the, so to speak, merely mechanical progression of an arithmetical advance (1, 2, 3, 4) from which ratios are absent and goes simply from 1 to 2, must yield to the ear which holds to the ratios of the absolute division of sounds. The difference is, after all, very slight and the ear yields to the internal, predominant harmonic ratios.

In this way, the harmonic basis and the uniformity of advance form the first opposition which presents itself here. And because these two principles are not in exact agreement, it is to be feared that with a further development of the system of tones, this difference will become more apparent: namely, when a note in a particular scale is made the tonic of another scale (any note can be so treated since each has the same right to be a tonic), and for this other scale the same notes are to be used, and for several octaves too. Thus, if *g* is the tonic, then *d* is the fifth; but if *b* is the tonic, *d* is the third, and for *a* it is the fourth, and so on. Since the same note is supposed to be in turn third, fourth, and fifth, this cannot be perfectly achieved in instruments with fixed notes. In these, the further the development is carried the more pronounced are the differences. Notes which are correct in one key are not so in another, which would not be the case if the intervals were equal. The keys thereby acquire an inner diversity, i.e. one which rests on the nature of the ratios of the notes in their scale. We know that if, for example, the fifth of *c* (viz. *g*) is now made the tonic, and the fifth of this is taken (*d*), and again the fifth of this, and so on, then on the pianoforte the eleventh and twelfth fifths are not pure and no longer fit in the system where these notes were tuned from *c*; thus in relation to *c* they are false fifths. And from this results, too, an alteration of further tones, of the half-tones, etc. in which the impurities, differences and discords emerge much earlier on. So far as this confusion can be remedied, it is made good by a fair and equal distribution of the inequalities. In this way, perfectly harmonic harps have been invented in which each system *c*, *d*, and so on, has its own half-notes. Formerly, (a) each fifth was slightly diminished from the start so that the difference was uniformly distributed; but as, again, this jarred on those with fine hearing, (b) the instrument had to be restricted to a range of six octaves (although here too there occur enough deviations in instruments with fixed, neutral notes). Generally, scales in which such dissonances occur are less frequently used or else those particular combinations are avoided where the notes are noticeably impure.

What remains now to be made explicit is how harmony is manifest *objectively*—its objective effect. Here we are presented with phenomena which at first sight are paradoxical, since what is merely audible in the notes provides no ground for them: they can be understood solely through numerical ratios. In the first place, when a string is made to vibrate it spontaneously divides itself in its vibrations into these ratios; this is an immanent, characteristic ratio of Nature, an activity of form within itself. Not only is the fundamental (1) heard, but also the fifth of the higher (3) octave and the third of the still higher (5) octave; a practised ear also hears the second octave of the fundamental and its double octave. Thus notes are heard which are represented by the whole numbers 1, 2, 3, 4, 5. When a string is fixed by two points, a node of vibration is formed in the middle; this again is in relationship with the end points, and so we have the phenomenon of different sounds which are harmonious.

Secondly, notes can be aroused from a string without striking it but by striking another. It is thought understandable that a string emits its own note when struck; but it is not so easy to see why, when a number of notes are played, often only one note is heard; or when two notes are played, a third can be heard. This, too, rests on the nature of these numerical relationships. (α) One phenomenon is that when strings which have a certain relationship to each other are plucked simultaneously, only the fundamental is heard. There is, for example, in the organ a stop which makes a single key produce five tones, and although each pipe has its own tone yet these five tones result in only one. This occurs when these five pipes or tones are the following: (1) the fundamental *c*; (2) the octave of *c*; (3) the fifth (*g*) of the next octave; (4) the third *c*; (5) the third (*e*) of the still higher octave. Only the fundamental *c* is then heard and this because the vibrations coincide. The different notes must, of course, be taken within a certain range, not too low and not too high. The reason for this coincidence is as follows. When the lower c has one vibration, the octave has two. The g of this octave has three vibrations whereas the fundamental has one; for the next fifth has one-and-a-half vibrations and this g therefore has three. The third c has four vibrations. The third of that octave has five vibrations whereas the fundamental has one. For the third makes $5/4$ times as many vibrations as the fundamental, but the third of the third octave four times as many; and that is five vibrations. The nature of these vibrations is therefore such that the vibrations of the other notes coincide with those of the fundamental. The strings of these notes are in the numerical ratio of 1, 2, 3, 4, 5; and all their vibrations finish simultaneously, since after five vibrations of the highest note, the lower have completed exactly four, three, two, or one vibration. Because of this coincidence only one c is heard.

(β) The case is similar with the other phenomenon, a really remarkable one, discovered by Tartini, namely, that when two different strings of a guitar are plucked, not only are their notes heard but also a third note which, however, is not merely the mixture of the first two, is not merely an abstractly neutral note. If, for example, c and g of a certain octave are plucked together then c of the next lower octave is also heard. The reason for this is as follows: when the fundamental has one vibration, the fifth has one-and-a-half; or three when the fundamental has two. When the fundamental makes one vibration, and this first vibration still persists, the second vibration of the fifth has already begun. But the second vibration of c which begins during the period of the second vibration of g, finishes at the same time as the third vibration of g; so that the next vibrations of the two notes begin simultaneously. 'There are periods', says Biot therefore (*Traité de physique*, vol. ii, p. 47), 'when vibrations reach the ear simultaneously and others when they reach it separately.' It is as when a person makes three steps in the same time in which another person makes two: after the first has taken three steps and the second two, both begin the next step together. In this way there occurs a periodic coincidence after two vibrations of c. This coincidence is twice as slow or half as fast as the vibration of c. But when the vibration of one tone is half as fast as that of the other, we have the lower octave which vibrates once while the other tone vibrates twice. This can best be demonstrated on a well-tuned organ. The lower octave can be heard and on a monochord, too, though that instrument cannot itself produce the note. Abt Vogler has based a special system of organ-building on this fact; in such an organ several pipes, each of which has its own tone, together produce another pure tone which requires neither a particular pipe nor a special key.

If harmony is considered only from the standpoint of hearing, and no attention is paid to numerical relationships, it is quite impossible to account for the fact that notes heard simultaneously are heard as one note though they are separate and distinct notes. In harmony, therefore, we must not limit ourselves to mere hearing, but must learn to know the objective determinateness of sounds. Further details of the subject are a matter for physics and musical theory. But what has been said is in place here in so far as the musical tone is this ideality in the sphere of mechanics, and the determinateness of the sound must therefore be grasped as a mechanical one, and the precise nature of this mechanical determinateness must be apprehended.

§ 302

Sound is the *alternation* of the specific asunderness of the material parts and of their mutual negatedness; it is only the *abstract*, or so to say, only ideal *ideality* of this specific asunderness. But this alternation is thus itself directly the negation of the material, specific subsistence. This negation, therefore, is the *real ideality* of specific gravity and cohesion—heat.

Remark

The generation of heat in sonorous bodies and in those which are struck or rubbed together, is the manifestation of heat originating with sound in conformity with its Notion.

Zusatz. The inwardness which reveals itself in sound is itself materialized; it dominates matter and acquires a sensuous existence in that matter is subjected to violence. Because the inwardness, as sound, is only a conditioned individuality, not yet a real totality, its self-preservation is only one aspect of its being; the other is the fact that the matter pervaded by this inwardness is also destructible. With this convulsion of body within itself there occurs not merely an ideal sublation of matter but a real sublation of it by heat. Instead of the body displaying itself specifically as preserving itself, it is now manifest rather as negating itself. The reciprocity of its cohesion within itself is, at the same time, a positing of the opposite of cohesion, an incipient sublating of its rigidity; and this precisely is heat. Sound and heat are thus directly related; heat is the consummation of sound, the manifestation in matter of matter's negativity: sound itself can even shatter or fuse an object, in fact a glass can be shattered by a sharp cry. To picture-thinking, sound and heat are widely separated phenomena and it may seem odd to associate them in this way. But if, for example, a bell is struck it gets hot; and this heat is not external to it but results from its own inner vibrations. Not only the musician gets warm, his instruments do also.

D. HEAT

§ 303

Heat is the self-restoration of matter to its formlessness, its fluidity, the triumph of its abstract homogeneity over specific determinatenesses; its abstract, merely *implicit continuity*, as negation of the negation, is here *posited* as an activity, as an existent dissolution. Heat therefore appears formally, i.e. in relation to spatial determination as such, as an *expansion* of matter in which it sublates or overcomes the boundedness which is the *specifying* of the *indifferent* occupation of space.

Zusatz. The disruption and shattering of real cohesion as such when it yields to force and is dissolved by it, is only the dissolution of passive, quantitative cohesion, although here, too, real cohesion showed itself to be determined in its own characteristic fashion (§ 296). But heat, which is the other form of dissolution, is bound up solely with specific, qualitative cohesion. Whereas in sound the main thing is the repelling of an outer force, as the subsistence of the form and the parts pervaded by the form, in heat it is attraction which comes to the fore: in such wise that the specifically cohesive body, while repelling the force, at the same time inwardly yields to it. If cohesion and rigidity are overpowered, the subsistence of the parts becomes ideally posited and they therefore suffer alteration. This inner melting of the body is the birthplace of heat in which sound perishes; for the fluid body as such resounds no more, any more than the merely rigid, brittle, or powdery body. Heat is not a disruption of bodies into masses, but one only in which the parts stay clinging together: it is this intimate, inner dissolution of body's repelling, of its holding apart of its parts. Heat, therefore, makes body even more a unity than form does; but this unity is devoid of determination. This dissolution is the triumph of the form itself; outer force, which constitutes the strength of inert matter under the sway of repulsion, destroys itself. This dissolution is *mediated* by cohesion; otherwise force only shatters into bits as is the case with a stone. Mere rigidity opposes an obstacle to the communication of heat; this demands cohesion as inner fluidity and expansibility—really, inner elasticity, whereby the particles posit themselves in each other: i.e. a non-rigidity, a non-fixity, which is at the same time a destroying of the particles as subsisting in their togetherness. The form preserves itself as a soul (*Seele*) in the body's melting; yet equally a destruction of the form by fire is posited.

The repelling of outer force and the yielding to it as an inner state—sound and heat—are thus opposed to each other; but equally, the former also switches round into the latter. In higher natures, too, this opposition is still suggested, in the organic sphere, namely, where the self has and holds itself within itself as an ideality, and where it is forced *outwards* by heat into real existence. To plants and flowers belong *par excellence* the variety as well as the pure, abstract development of the individual colours and their brilliance; their self, drawn outwards by outward light, is poured into existence as light. The colouring of animals, on the other hand, is in general duller. And in the bird creation which is pre-eminent in its gorgeous colouring, it is the tropical birds whose selfhood is drawn out by the light and the heat of the climate, plantwise, into their vegetative covering, their plumage; whereas the birds of northern lands are inferior to them in colouring but sing better, as e.g. the nightingale and the lark, which are not to be found in the tropics.* In the birds of the tropics it is therefore heat which fails to preserve this inwardness, this launching forth of their inner ideality as voice, but melts it and drives it forth in the metallic splendour of colour; that is to say, sound perishes in heat. Voice, it is true, is superior to mere sound; but voice, too, reveals itself as in this opposition to the heat of climate.

§ 304

This real negation of the body's own nature is therefore its state of not belonging affirmatively to itself in its existence; this the body's existence is rather a community with *others* and the *communication* of itself to them—*external* heat. The passivity of body in regard to heat rests on the continuity of matter which is present *in principle* in specific gravity and cohesion; and in virtue of this primary ideality, the modification of specific gravity and cohesion cannot form a real barrier for such communication, for the positing of a community with other bodies.

* Spix and Martius' *Travels*, vol. i, p. 191: 'In these forests (of Brazil, behind Santa Cruz) we heard for the first time the note of a greyish-brown bird, probably a thrush, which lives in the undergrowth and on the damp earth of the forests and repeatedly sings through the scale from b^1 to a^2 with such regularity that not even a single tone is missed. Usually it sings each note four or five times and then goes on unnoticeably to the following quarter-tone. It is customary to deny all harmonious sounds to the songsters of the American forests and to concede them a superiority only in respect of their splendid plumage. Though, generally speaking, the tender inhabitants of the tropics are distinguished more by their splendid plumage than by the richness and power of their notes, and although their notes seem to be inferior to the clear and melodious singing of our nightingale, still this little bird, apart from all others, proves that they too possess at least the fundamentals of melody.—It is conceivable, too, that if ever the almost inarticulate sounds of degenerate men cease to echo through the forests of Brazil, many of these feathered songsters will pour forth their delicate melodies.'

Remark

Substances like wool which are non-cohesive and those which are *intrinsically* non-cohesive (i.e. brittle substances like glass or stones) are worse conductors of heat than metals, which are characterized by the internal possession of compact, unbroken continuity. Air and water likewise are bad conductors of heat on account of their lack of cohesion, and in general, as being matters which are still non-corporeal. The conception of heat as having a separate existence of its own, as *heat-matter* or *caloric*, rests mainly on two things: first, on the fact that heat can be transmitted, and so appears to be separable from the body in which it is present in the first instance, and therefore as existing independently of it, and also as coming to the body from *outside*; secondly, on the various mechanical determinations connected with this which can be introduced into the *transmission* of heat (e.g. reflection by concave mirrors), and also on the quantitative determinations which occur in connection with heat (cf. § 286, Remark). But at least, one will hesitate to call heat a *body*, or even something corporeal; for this already implies that a *manifestation* of a *particular existence* is at once capable of various categories. So, too, with heat, its limited particularity and the fact that it can be distinguished from the bodies in which it is present, are not sufficient to warrant applying to it the category of matter, which is so essentially a totality in itself as to be at least *heavy*. The said appearance of particularity is mainly due only to the *external* way in which heat, in its *transmission*, appears in relation to the bodies concerned. Rumford's experiments on the heating of bodies by friction, in the boring of cannon, for example, should have sufficed long since to dismiss the conception of heat as a particular, independent existence; these demonstrate irrefutably that heat is in its origin and nature a mere condition or state of body. The abstract conception of matter implies of itself the determination of *continuity*, which is the possibility of transmission, and, as activity, the actuality of it; and this implicit continuity becomes activity as the negation of form, i.e. of specific gravity and cohesion, as it will subsequently be the negation of Shape.

Zusatz. In the world of appearance (*Erscheinung*) sound and heat are themselves appearances. The chief characteristic of a state is that it is communicable and has been communicated; for 'state' is essentially a common determination and a dependence on environment. Heat therefore is communicable because it is determined as an appearance, and not merely as such, but within the fields where the reality of matter is presupposed; it is a being which is at the same time an illusory being (*Schein*), or an illusory being which is still a being. The being is the cohesive body: its dissolution, the negation of cohesion, is the illusory being. Thus heat is not matter but the negation of this reality: yet no longer the abstract negation which is sound, nor as yet the completed negation which is fire. As a materialized negation, or a negative materialization, it is something present, and present in the shape of universality, community (*Gemeinschaft*): just as much a still real subsistence as a negation—an existent passivity in general. As this merely apparent negation, heat is not self-subsistent but is dependent on an other.

Heat, then, is essentially diffusible, and, in diffusing itself, posits exact likeness of a body with other bodies. This diffusion can be externally determined through the surfaces of bodies: thus heat can be concentrated by burning glasses and concave mirrors; the same can be done even with cold—I believe the experiment is one of Professor Pictet's of Geneva. Now since bodies are themselves capable of being posited as apparent, they cannot keep off heat from themselves, for it is implied in their nature that their cohesion can be negated. They are thus in themselves or implicitly, that which in heat comes to exist outwardly; and this 'in-itself' or implicit nature is precisely their passivity. For that is passive which is only 'in itself' or implicit: just as a man, e.g., who is only virtually or in principle rational, is a passive creature. The communicated state is therefore a determinateness posited by an other in accordance with this implicit aspect—a manifestation simply of its mere implicit being; but this state, as an activity, must also be actual. The mode of manifesting is thus twofold: as an active, incipient manifestation, and as passive. Thus a body can have an inner source of heat: others receive heat from outside, not as generated in them. The transition from the primary origin of heat in the alteration of cohesion, into the external relationship where something already in existence is added to something else, as occurs in the diffusion of heat, is the revelation of the absence of selfhood in such determinations; heaviness, weight, on the other hand, cannot be communicated.

Because the nature of heat generally is to convert into an ideality the specific, real asunderness, and we assert that it is based on this negation, we must not here think in terms of a heat-matter or caloric. The assumption of such a caloric, like that of a sound-matter, rests on the category that what makes a sensible impression must also have a sensible existence. Now even though here the concept of matter was so stretched that gravity, its fundamental determination, was abandoned—for the question was raised whether such matter can be weighed or not—nevertheless the objective existence of a material stuff was still presupposed, one which was supposed to be indestructible, independent, and self-subsistent, coming and going, increasing and diminishing in a particular place. It is this conception of external accretion at which the metaphysics of the Understanding stops short, making it the original relationship, especially of heat. Heat-matter is supposed to be added to a body, to be accumulated or be latent, where it does not appear and yet subsequently heat is manifested. Now if experiments are thought fit to decide the question of the materiality of heat, experiments in which sophistical conclusions are often drawn from trivial circumstances, Count Rumford's[1] experiment, in which he aimed at accurately measuring the heat generated in the boring of cannon, had a particularly telling result. For whereas it was maintained that the great heat produced in the metal fragments was called forth from the surrounding bodies by the intense friction, Rumford himself said that it was generated in the metal itself, since, when he enclosed the whole in wood which, being a bad conductor, did not let the heat through, the metal fragments came out just as glowing hot as when there was no such covering. It is thus that the Understanding makes itself substrates which are not recognized through the Notion. Sound and heat do not exist on their own account like heavy matter, and so-called sound-matter and heat-matter are merely physical fictions of the metaphysics of the Understanding. Sound and heat are conditioned by material existences and constitute their negativity; they are no more than moments, but being determinations of what is material they are quantitative, and so are intensive or to be determined by *degrees*.

§ 305

The communication of heat to different bodies contains in itself only the abstract continuation of this determination through indeterminate materiality; heat is, to this extent, not capable of qualitative dimensions within itself, but only of the abstract opposition of positive and negative, and of quantum and degree, in the form of an abstract equilibrium, an equalization of temperature in the bodies among which varying degrees of temperature are distributed. Since, however, heat is an alteration of specific gravity and cohesion, it is at the same time bound up with these determinations, and the outside communicated temperature is conditioned and determined in its existence in the body to which it is transmitted, by the particular specific gravity and cohesion of that body: *specific thermal capacity*.

[1] Count Benjamin Rumford: 'An Inquiry concerning the Source of the Heat which is excited by Friction.' In *Philosophical Transactions of the Royal Society of London*, 1798, part i, pp. 80–102.

Remark

Specific thermal capacity, associated with the category of *matter* and *stuff*, has led to the conception of *latent, imperceptible, heat-matter* or *caloric*. As *imperceptible*, such a determination lacks the warrant of *observation* and *experience*, and as inferred, it rests on the *assumption of a material self-subsistence* of heat (cf. Remark § 286 and *Zusatz*). This assumption, precisely because it is itself non-empirical, serves in its way to make the self-subsistence of heat as a material substance *empirically* irrefutable. When the disappearance of heat, or its appearance where formerly it was not, is pointed out, the former is explained as a mere concealment or *fixation* of heat in an imperceptible state, while the latter is explained as an emergence from mere imperceptibility. The metaphysics of self-subsistence is *opposed* to the said *experience* and is indeed presupposed *a priori*.

The important point in regard to the characterization of heat which has been given here, is that it be *empirically* confirmed that the determination itself demanded by the Notion, that, namely, of an *alteration* of specific gravity and cohesion, is manifest as *heat*. In the first place, the close connection of both is easily perceived in the numerous ways of generating heat (and in the equally numerous ways in which it disappears), in fermentations and other chemical processes, in crystallizations and decrystallizations, in the mechanical phenomena already mentioned of internal (coupled with external) shock, the striking of bells and metals, various kinds of friction, etc. Friction (e.g. of two pieces of wood among savages or in the ordinary striking of a light) brings the material asunderness of the one body through the pressure of the other, momentarily together into a *single* point—a negation of the spatial subsistence of the material particles which bursts forth into heat and flame in the body, or into a spark which detaches itself from the latter.—The further difficulty is to grasp the connection of heat with specific gravity and cohesion as the *existent* ideality of what is material—moreover, an existence of what is negative, which itself contains the determinateness of what is negated, which furthermore has the determinateness of a quantum, and which, as the ideality of an existence, is the latter's self-externality and self-positing in an other, that is, the communication of itself.—Here, as throughout the whole of the Philosophy of Nature, all that we have to do is to substitute for the categories of the Understanding the thought-relationships of the speculative Notion, and to grasp and determine the phenomenon in terms of the latter.

Zusatz. Just as each body has a specific mode of sound according to its specific cohesion, so heat too is specific. If qualitatively different bodies are brought to the same temperature, i.e. the same heat is applied to them, they are variously heated. Thus each body differs in its reception of the temperature of the air: iron, e.g., becomes colder in cold air than a stone does; in warm air water is always cooler than the air. It is calculated that to give water the same temperature as mercury, about thirteen times more heat must be applied to the former, or, if both are exposed to the same temperature, then water is thirteen times less warm than mercury. Similarly, the melting-point produced by transmitted heat varies; mercury, e.g., melts at a much lower temperature than all other metals. Since the behaviour of a body in its reception of heat is specific, the question arises, which form of the inwardness (*Insichsein*) of a body is manifest here. The inwardness is in the forms of cohesion, punctiformity, linearity, and superficiality: as a simple determinateness, it is specific gravity. The inwardness manifested in specific heat can be only a simple mode of the inwardness. For heat is the sublating of the specific asunderness of cohesion; but the body as subsisting is also still preserved in its specific inwardness: now inwardness with self-sublating cohesion is still only a universal, abstract inwardness—specific gravity. Thus specific gravity reveals itself as the inwardness which makes itself effective here.

In this way, thermal capacity stands in a relationship to specific gravity, which is the inwardness of bodies in contrast to mere gravity. This relation is an inverse one: bodies of higher specific gravity warm up much more easily, i.e. get hotter in the same temperature, than others of lower specific gravity. It is then said that in the latter bodies caloric or heat-matter becomes latent, in the former free. Similarly, it is maintained that caloric has been latent when it is evident that the heat did not come from outside but was generated internally (see § 304, *Zusatz*). Heat is also supposed to become latent when cold is produced by the evaporation of naphtha. Frozen water standing at zero loses, so it is said, the heat which is applied to melt it: for since its temperature is not raised thereby, the caloric is said to have become latent in it. The same is said to occur in the elastic steam into which it is transformed; for water does not get hotter than 80 degrees, and at a higher temperature only evaporates. Conversely, vapours, elastic fluids, of a specific temperature generate a greater heat in precipitation than in their elastic state; i.e. expansion does duty for temperature as intensity (cf. § 103, *Zusatz*). Latency then is the expedient adopted whenever the phenomena shout aloud that it is an inner alteration in cohesion—e.g., the freezing of water which was several degrees below zero, and which in freezing rises to zero —which gives rise to heat. Caloric is supposed to be always being added and subtracted; but it will not be admitted that heat, as a material substance, passes away, since it is self-subsistent; it is said therefore to be merely latent and still present. But how can something be present and yet not exist? That sort of thing is an empty thought-figment; the transmissibility of heat would, moreover, rather prove that this deter-mination is, in fact, not self-subsistent.

It might be thought that a high specific gravity must also produce more heat. But the bodies of higher specific gravity are those whose determinateness is still simple, i.e. have an undeveloped, non-individua-lized inwardness; they have not yet advanced to further immanent determinations. Individuality, on the other hand, is a higher resistance to heat. For this reason, the organic body is far less receptive to external heat. Thus in higher organic natures, plants and animals, specific gravity and thermal capacity generally lose their importance and interest; in this respect, the differences, therefore, between the various woods are, on the whole, without significance. In metals, on the other hand, specific gravity is, like thermal capacity, a fundamental determination. Specific gravity is not yet cohesion, much less individuality, but on the contrary only an abstract, general inwardness not immanently specified and, consequently, most penetrable by heat; an inwardness which is most easily and most readily receptive to the negation of specific cohesion. On the other hand, the cohesive body which is more individualized endows its determinations with a much greater permanence so that they are not readily receptive to heat.

We have seen the *origin* of heat from the side of cohesion for we started from the material inwardness as specifically determined. This is (α) the origin proper of heat which can become manifest as vibration or even as spontaneous combustion, e.g. in certain fermentations. A frigate of the Empress Catherine caught fire in this way: roast coffee ferments, the heat increasing until the coffee bursts into flames; this was probably what happened to the ship. Flax, hemp, tarred rope end up in spontaneous combustion. The fermentation of wine or vinegar also generates heat. The same occurs in chemical processes; for the dissolution of crystals is always an alteration of the state of cohesion. But it is known that in this sphere of mechanical relationships, in the relation to gravity, heat origi-nates in two ways. (β) The other way is through friction as such. Friction keeps to the surface, is a disturbance or shaking of the parts of the surface, not a vibration throughout the whole body. This friction is the common, usual origin of heat. But it, too, must not be conceived as a purely mechanical phenomenon as is done in the *Göttinger gelehrten Anzeigen* (1817, p. 161): 'It is known that any body under strong pressure is deprived of a part of its specific heat, or rather, when subjected to strong pressure, cannot hold the same amount of specific heat as when the pressure is less; hence the production of heat by the striking and rubbing of bodies, by the rapid compression of air and the like.' This liberation of the form is therefore not yet the truly self-subsistent totality of the self, but is still conditioned, is not yet an immanent self-preserving activity of the unity. This is why heat can be produced mechanically and externally by friction. Heat intensified to the point of flame is the free triumph of pure ideality over this material asunderness. With steel and flint, it is only a spark which leaps *out*: in other words, the more the inner hardness holds out against heat, the stronger is the shock in the *outwardly* affected parts; wood, on the other hand, is *consumed* because it is a material which can let the heat pass through it.

§ 306

Heat, as temperature in general, is in the first place the as yet abstract dissolution of specified materiality, a dissolution conditioned in its determinateness and its existence. But in realizing itself or as actually realized, this consumption of bodily peculiarity comes to exist as a pure physical ideality, as the negation of materiality set free and issuing forth as *light*, though in the form of *flame*, a negation of matter still tied to matter. As fire first developed itself out of its '*in-itself*', air, (§ 283): so here, fire is *posited* as externally conditioned, as self-produced out of its existent notional moments within the sphere of conditioned existence. Furthermore, as thus finite, fire consumes itself together with the conditions whose consumption it is.

Zusatz. Light as such is cold; and the light which in summer gives such heat, does so first in the atmosphere, on the earth. In midsummer, high mountain peaks are quite cold and are covered by eternal snow though they are nearer the sun; it is only through contact with other bodies that heat arises. For light is the principle of selfhood and what is touched by it also acquires selfhood, that is to say, displays incipient dissolution, that is, heat.

§ 307

The development of real matter, i.e. matter imbued with *form*, thus passes over in its totality into the pure ideality of its determinations, into abstractly self-identical selfhood, which in this sphere of *external* individuality itself becomes external as flame, and so disappears. The *conditioned* character of this sphere consists in the *form* being a *specifying* of heavy matter, and individuality as totality being at first only *implicit*. In heat is posited the moment of the real *dissolution* of the *immediacy* of specified material things with their initial mutual indifference. The form *as a totality* is consequently now immanent in matter which does not resist it.— Selfhood as the infinite self-relating form has, as such, entered existence; it maintains itself in the externality subjected to it and is, as *totality* which freely determines these material things, *free individuality*.

Zusatz. From this stage the *transition* must be made to real individuality, to Shape, whose moments we have seen in the preceding paragraphs. The gathering of form into itself, the soul (*Seele*) of matter which escaped as sound, and the fluidity of matter, are the two moments constituting the real Notion of individuality. Gravity, as subject to infinite form, is the total free individuality, where matter is completely permeated and determined by form. The immanently developed Shape which determines the multitude of material parts is the absolute centrality which, unlike gravity, no longer has multitude *outside* itself. Individuality as an urge is so constituted as to posit its moments in the first instance as separate configurations. But whereas in space the configurations of point, line, and surface were only negations of space, these configurations are now inscribed by the form in a matter determined solely by the form itself and no longer as mere spatial outlines but as differentiations of the material body, real spatial configurations in matter which complete themselves into the totality of the surface. In order that sound, as matter's soul, should not escape from it, but should be a formative force in it, the negation of the stability and permanence of matter must be posited; this occurs in the dissolution of matter by heat. The penetrability of matter originally posited by the Notion is now posited as existent. We started with the inwardness of matter as specific gravity where matter was taken to be immediately so constituted that the form could build itself into it. This '*in-itself*' of matter, its capacity for being penetrated and dissolved, had, however, also to be shown up as existent, namely through cohesion. The dissolution in cohesion of the asunderness of matter annuls cohesion itself, and what remains is specific gravity. This, as the first stage of subjectivity, was an abstract, simple determinedness which, raised to immanent totality, is sound, and, as fluid, is heat. The first immediacy must show itself as sublated, as posited; thus, as always, we must return to the beginning. Cohesion constituted the form's being conditioned by matter. It is itself the intermediary which, opposing this conditioned state, produces internally the negation of matter, heat. In this way, cohesion negates its own self, i.e. negates this mere 'in-itselfness', the merely conditioned mode of existence of the form. It is easy to indicate these moments: but it is hard to consider them separately, if one wants to discover the existence which corresponds to the thought-determination, for to each thought-determination an existence corresponds. This difficulty is especially great in those sections where the whole is present only as a tendency, and where, therefore, the determinations emerge only as separate properties (*Beschaffenheiten*). The abstract moments of individuality—specific gravity, cohesion, etc.—must, through their very Notion, precede free individuality, in order that this may result from them. In total individuality where form becomes dominant, all the moments are now realized, and form dwells in them as a determinate unity. To Shape there belongs soul (*Seele*), unity of form with itself, and then, as a being-for-another, the determinations of the Notion. In this positing, the form is at the same time free, as the unconditioned unity of these differences. Specific gravity is only abstractly free, for the reference to another is not its own act but a matter of external comparison. But genuine form is reference to another on the form's own part, not in some third thing. Matter, melting under heat, is receptive to form; the conditionedness of sound as infinite form is therefore sublated and this form no longer encounters opposition as if still referring itself to an other. Heat is Shape in process of liberating itself from Shape, a light which gives itself substance, and which contains the moment of passive shape as sublated within itself.

PHYSICS OF THE TOTAL INDIVIDUALITY

§ 308

Matter, *qua heavy*, is at first only *in itself* (*an sich*) the totality of the Notion; as such it is without intrinsic form; the Notion posited in it with its particular determinations, at first manifests the finite individuality whose particular moments fall asunder. The totality of the Notion being now *posited*, the centre of gravity is no longer a subjectivity merely *sought* by matter, but a subjectivity immanent in it as the ideality of those form-determinations which were at first immediate and conditioned, but which are from now on moments developed from within outwards. Material individuality, being thus identical with itself in its development, is infinitely *for itself*, but is at the same time conditioned: it is the subjective totality, but at first only in immediate fashion. Therefore, though infinitely for itself, it involves relationship to *another*; only as it develops are this externality and this conditionedness posited as self-sublating. Individuality thus becomes the existent totality of material being-for-self, which is then Life in principle, and in the Notion passes over into Life.

Zusatz. The two moments of real physical body—form as an abstract whole and determinable matter confronting it—are in themselves identical; therein lies their transition into one another in conformity with the Notion. For just as form is the pure, physical self-related identity-with-self which lacks determinate being, so matter, too, as fluid, is this universal identical existent which offers no resistance. Matter, like form, is without internal distinction, and is thus itself form. As universal, matter's destiny is to become inwardly determinate and this is precisely what form, whose 'in-itself' (*Ansich*) matter is, is obliged to be. At first, we had individuality in general; the next stage was the positing of this individuality as distinct from gravity, in its finite, restricted determinateness: the third stage is the return of individuality out of difference to itself. Now this itself, in turn, has three forms or determinations.

§ 309

Total individuality is:

(a) immediately *Shape* as such and the freely manifested existence of its abstract principle—Magnetism;

(b) it determines itself to *difference*, the particular forms of corporeal totality; this particularization carried to extremes is *Electricity*.

(c) the *reality* of this particularization is the *chemically* differentiated body and its relationships, the individuality which has bodies for its moments, and which realizes itself as a totality—*Chemical Process*.

Zusatz. In Shape, the infinite form is the determining principle of the material parts, the connectedness of which is now no longer only the indifferent relationship of space. Shape, then, does not remain at the stage of this its Notion, because this itself is not a stable, inert subsistence (*ein ruhiges Bestehen*), but, as self-differentiating, it essentially develops into real properties not ideally contained in the unity but also endowed with separate existence. These differences, determined as having qualitative individuality, are the Elements, but these as belonging to the sphere of individuality, i.e.—as specified—as united with individualized matter, or rather as transformed into it. In itself, i.e. in the Notion, the defect still attaching to Form has in this way been made good. But now necessity again demands the positing of this 'in-itself', or the self-begetting of Shape; that is, the transition must also be made into existence. The result therefore is this, that Shape is generated. This is the return to the first stage which now, however, appears as *produced*. This return now is at the same time the transition into something further; thus the Chemical Process contains in its Notion the transition into the organic sphere. At first we had process as motion in the sphere of Mechanics, then as process of the Elements; now we have the process of individualized matter.

A. SHAPE

§ 310

Body as total individuality, is—*immediately*—*quiescent* totality and thus a form of the spatial togetherness of matter; consequently, at first a *mechanism* again. Shape is thus a material mechanism of the now unconditioned and freely determining individuality:—body, whose external limitation *in space* as well as specific kind of inner connectedness, is determined by the *immanent* and *developed* form. In this way, form manifests itself *through its own activity*, and does not show itself merely as a characteristic mode of *resistance* to *outside* force.

Zusatz. Whereas inwardness previously revealed itself only through an outer stimulus and as a reaction against it, here, on the other hand, form manifests itself neither through an outer force nor as destruction of materiality; but without stimulus, body contains in itself a secret, silent, geometrician which, as an all-pervading form, organizes it both outwardly and inwardly. This limitation, both outward and inward, is necessary to individuality. Thus the surface, too, of body is bounded by form; it is shut off from other bodies and shows its specific determinateness, without external action, in its quiescent subsistence. A crystal indeed is not mechanically compounded; nevertheless mechanism is resumed here, an individual mechanism, just because this sphere is the quiescent subsistence of the separated parts even though the connection of the parts with the centre is determined by immanent form. Body so formed is removed from [the influence of] gravity; it grows, for example, upwards. The examination of natural crystals reveals them to be articulated through and through. However, we have not soul here yet—this we shall find in Life—since individuality here is not yet objective to itself; and that is the difference of the inorganic from the organic. Individuality is not yet subjectivity; if it were, the infinite form, which differentiates itself and holds its differences together, would also be for itself. This takes place only in the sentient creature; but here individuality is still submerged in matter—it is not yet free, it only *is*.

We pass on to the *determinateness* which belongs to the shape of the inorganic in distinction from the organic. The shape we have here is one whose spatial determinations of Form are at first only those characteristic of the Understanding (*verständige Bestimmungen*): straight lines, plane surfaces, and definite angles. The reason for this must be given here. The form disclosed in crystallization is a dumb life which, in merely mechanical objects, stones and metals, which apparently are determinable from outside, stirs and moves in marvellous fashion, expressing itself in characteristic formations as an organic and organizing impulse. These grow freely and independently; and anyone unused to the sight of these regular, ornamental shapes does not take them to be products of Nature, but attributes them rather to human art and effort. But the regularity of art comes from a purposive activity outside the object. Here one must not think in terms of external purposiveness, as when one moulds an external material in accordance with one's ends. On the contrary, in the crystal form is not external to matter; the latter is itself the end, freely active on its own account. In water there is thus an invisible germ, a force which constructs. This shape is regular in the strictest sense; but because it is not yet a process in its own self, it is a regularity only in the body as a whole, its one form being constituted by the parts taken together. It is not yet an organic formation whose determinations no longer conform to the Understanding; since it is not yet subjective, it is still inorganic. In the organic sphere on the other hand, the nature of the formation is such that in each part the whole of the form is manifest, not such that each part can only be understood through the whole. In the living organism, therefore, each point of the periphery is the whole, just as I am sentient in every part of my body. From this it follows that the shape of the organism is not based on straight lines and plane surfaces, which belong only to the abstract direction of the whole, and are not immanent totalities. But in the living shape we have curves, since each part of a curve can only be grasped through the whole law of the curve; this is definitely not the case with the shape characteristic of the Understanding (*verständige Gestalt*). But the roundness of the organism is neither circular nor spherical; for these too again are curves of the Understanding (*verständige Curven*), since the relation of all points of the periphery to the centre is once more abstract identity. The curved line which we have in organisms must have difference immanent in it, but so that the differences are in turn subordinated to equality. The line of the living organism must therefore be the ellipse, where the equality of both parts appears again and that, too, in the direction of the major and of the minor axis. But more accurately, it is the oval which dominates in the organism, the line which has such equality only in one direction. Möller therefore aptly remarks that all organic forms, e.g., of feathers, wings, of the head, all the lines of the face, all the shapes of leaves, of insects, birds, fishes, etc. are modifications of the oval or else of the undulant line which for this reason he also calls the line of beauty (*Schönheitslinie*). But curved lines do not yet appear in the inorganic, but geometrically regular shapes with equal and correspondent angles, where all necessarily follows from continued identity. Formation therefore is such a secret drawing of lines, a determining of surfaces and a bounding by parallel angles.

We have now to consider this shape further in its particular *determinations*, three of which should be distinguished: *first*, the abstractions of shape, therefore, strictly speaking, the Shapeless; *secondly*, Shape in its strict meaning, Shape in process of becoming, Shaping as an activity, Shape as not yet achieved—Magnetism; thirdly, real Shape, the Crystal.

§ 311

(α) The *immediate* Shape, i.e. Shape which is posited as *formless* within itself, is on the one hand the extreme of the *punctiform principle*, of brittleness (*Sprödigkeit*), and on the other hand the extreme of the *spherical* shape assumed by liquids—Shape as an inner shapelessness.

Zusatz. The determinations of form as this inner master geometrician are first the point, then the line and surface, and lastly the total volume. The brittle (*spröde*) body is pulverizable and singular (*Singulare*), properties we have already encountered as a simple mode of cohesion. It is granular as is particularly shown in platinum grains. Opposed to this is sphericity, the general self-rounding fluidity which effaces every dimension within itself and which, therefore, although carried out in all three dimensions, is a totality in which determinateness is not developed. The spherical shape is the universal shape endowed with a formal regularity; it is freely poised and is therefore also the shape of the free, heavenly bodies as universal individuals. Fluid matter assumes a spherical shape since, being inwardly indeterminate, it has equal atmospheric pressures on all sides; the shape therefore is equally determined in all directions and no difference is as yet posited in it. Shape, however, is not merely this abstract determination but a real principle, i.e. a real totality of form.

§ 312

(β) The brittle body, as *implicitly* the totality of formative individuality, deploys the difference of the Notion. The point first becomes the line where the form posits itself as opposed extremes which, as moments, lack an existence of their own, but are held only in their relation which appears as their middle term and as the point of indifference in their opposition. This syllogism constitutes the *principle of formation* in its developed determinateness, and is, in this still abstract rigour, *Magnetism.*

Remark

Magnetism is one of the determinations which inevitably became prominent when the presence of the *Notion* was suspected in specific natural phenomena, and the idea of a *Philosophy of Nature* was grasped. For the magnet exhibits in simple, naïve fashion the nature of the Notion, and the Notion moreover in its developed form as syllogism (§ 181). The poles are the sensibly existent ends of a real line (of a bar or also in a body extending further in every dimension); but as poles, they have no sensible, mechanical reality but an ideal one, and are absolutely inseparable. The point of indifference, where they have their substance, is the unity where they exist as determinations of the Notion, so that they have meaning and existence solely in this unity; polarity is the relation only of such moments. Apart from the determination here explicated, magnetism has no further special property. That the individual magnetic needle points to the *north*, and so to the *south* as well, is a manifestation of general *terrestial magnetism.*— But the statement that all bodies are magnetic is sadly ambiguous. The correct meaning is that every real, not merely brittle (*spröde*), shape involves this principle of determinateness; the incorrect meaning is that all bodies also show forth this principle as it *exists* in its pure *abstraction*, i.e. as magnetism. It would be unphilosophical to try to show that a form of the Notion *exists universally* in Nature in the determinateness in which it is as an abstraction. Nature is rather the Idea in the element of asunderness, so that like the Understanding it, too, holds fast to the moments of the Notion in their *dispersion*, and represents them thus in reality; but in higher things the differentiated forms of the Notion are unified to the extreme of concretion (see Remark to following §).

Zusatz. It is when the spherical and the brittle are put together that we first have real Shape as such; the infinite form, posited as centrality in the brittle body, posits its differences, gives them an existence, and yet contains them in unity. Space, it is true, is still the element of their existence; but the Notion is this simplicity of character, this tone, which in its diremption, remains this pervasive universal, which, freed from the general being-within-self of gravity, has made itself the substance of its differences or their existence. The merely internal shape had as yet no existence within itself, but only when the mass broke up: but the determination now posited comes from Shape itself. This individualizing principle is the End which translates itself into reality but is still distinct from it, is not yet the completed End. It thus expresses itself only as the process of the two principles of brittleness and fluidity; in this process the determinable but indeterminate fluid is impregnated by the form. This is the *principle of magnetism*, the *tendency towards Shape* which has not yet come to rest, or the formative form still as tendency. Magnetism, therefore, is in the first place only this bare subject-status of matter, the formal existence of differences in the unity of the subject—cohesion as the activity of bringing distinct material points under the form of unity. The sides of magnetism are, therefore, still completely dominated by the unity of the subject; their opposition has not yet risen to independence of existence. In the separable point as such, the moment of difference is as yet by no means posited. But since we now have the total individuality which is supposed to be spatially present, and which, as concrete, must posit itself in difference, the point now connects itself with a point and distinguishes itself from it; this is the line, not yet the plane, or the totality of three dimensions, since the tendency does not yet exist as a totality, and also the two dimensions immediately become three, a surface, in reality. Thus we have wholly abstract spatiality as linearity; this is the *first* general determination. But the straight line is the natural line—so to speak, the line as such; for with the curved line we already have a second determination and that would at once involve the positing of the plane.

How is magnetism *manifest*? The movements present here may be grasped only in an ideal way; for magnetism cannot be interpreted sensuously. The manifold, as sensuously apprehended, is only externally conjoined; admittedly this is also true of the two poles and the point of indifference connecting them. But this is only the *magnet*, not yet magnetism. In order to ascertain what is contained in this *Notion* we must, in the first instance, completely forget the sensuous image of a lodestone or of iron stroked with the lodestone. But then we must also compare the phenomena of magnetism with its Notion to see whether they correspond to it. The identity of the differences is not posited here in external fashion: on the contrary, their identity is posited by the differences themselves. The movement of the magnet is, no doubt, still an external one, simply because the negativity has not as yet real, self-subsistent sides, or the moments of the totality are not yet set free, do not yet enter into relationship with each other as different, self-subsistent things, the centre of gravity is not yet burst asunder. Accordingly, the explication of the moments is still posited as something external, or is posited only by their *implicit* Notion. The separable point, in opening itself to differentiation by the Notion, produces the poles. In the physical line which has in it the difference of form, they are the two live ends, so posited that each only is, in its connection with its other, without which it has no meaning. But they are outside each other, each is negative relatively to the other; and their unity, in which their opposition is sublated, *also* exists *between* them in space. Such polarity is often applied indiscriminately where it does not belong at all, for nowadays everything is full of polarity. Now this physical opposition is not a sense datum; the north pole, for example, cannot be chopped off. If the magnet is chopped in two, each piece is again a whole magnet; the north pole immediately arises once more in the broken part. Each pole posits the other and also excludes it from itself. The terms of the syllogism cannot exist on their own, but only in union. We are, then, wholly in the supersensible sphere. If anyone thinks that thought is not present in Nature, he can be shown it here in magnetism. Thus magnetism is, on its own account, a highly astonishing phenomenon; but a little thought about it makes it even more wonderful, and it was therefore placed in the forefront of the Philosophy of Nature as a basic principle. Reflection, it is true, does speak of magnetic matter but this is not manifest in the phenomenon; what is active in magnetism is nothing material, but pure immaterial form.

Now if we put small unmagnetized iron bars near a magnetized iron bar whose north and south poles we distinguish, then, if the former can move freely without mechanical restraint, being balanced, e.g. on needles, etc., we observe a movement. In this case one of the ends of each small bar will attach itself to the north pole of the magnet, while the other end will be repelled by it; the small bar has thus itself become a magnet, for it has acquired a magnetic determinateness. However, this determinateness is not confined to the end-points. Iron filings attach themselves to a magnet up to its midpoint; but a neutral point comes where such *attraction* and *repulsion* cease. One can distinguish in this way a *passive* and an *active* magnetism; but one can also speak of passive magnetism where no effect on non-magnetic iron can be produced. With this neutral point a free centre is now posited, just as we earlier had the centre of the earth. If, further, the small bar is once more removed and brought up against the other pole of the magnet, then the end which was attracted by the first pole will be repelled, and vice versa. In all this no determination is yet present in which the ends of the magnet are intrinsically opposed; the difference is the empty difference of space which in itself is no difference, as little as the one end of a line is, as such, different from the other end. But if, now, we compare these two magnets with the earth, they have one end pointing more or less north, while the other points south; and now we find that both north poles of the two magnets repel each other, and likewise both south poles: but the north pole of the one and the south pole of the other attract one another. The direction north derives from the path of the sun, and is not peculiar to the magnet. Since one end of a single magnet points north, and the other end south, the Chinese are just as correct in saying that the magnet points south as we are when we say it points north; both constitute a single determination. And this, too, is only a relation of two magnets to one another since it is the earth's magnetism that determines the bar magnet; only we must be aware that what we call the north pole of a magnet (a nomenclature which nowadays changes backwards and forwards, causing much confusion) is strictly speaking the south pole according to the thing's nature; for the south pole of the magnet moves towards the north pole of the earth. This phenomenon is the *entire theory* of magnetism. The physicists say we do not yet know what magnetism may be: whether it is a current, etc. All this belongs to a metaphysics which the Notion does not recognize. There is nothing mysterious about magnetism.

If we have bits of a lodestone, not a line, the magnetic impulse still always acts along an ideal line: the axis. Now with such a fragment, whether it has the form of a cube or a sphere, etc., there can be several axes; in this way the earth has several magnetic axes, none of which directly coincides with its axis of rotation. In the earth, magnetism becomes free since the earth never arrives at being a true crystal, but, as that which gives birth to individuality, it stops short at the abstract impulse, the yearning to confer shape. Since the earth is thus a living magnet whose axis is not tied down to a definite point, the direction of the magnetic needle, though closely approximating to that of the true meridian, does not exactly coincide with the latter; hence the *declination* of the magnetic needle to east and west, which accordingly varies at different places and times—an oscillation of a more general nature. As regards generally this relation of the magnetic needle to such an axis, physicists now dispense with an iron rod or, what is the same, a specific existence in the direction of the axes. They have found that the facts are sufficiently accounted for by the assumption of a magnet at the earth's centre having infinite intensity but no extension, i.e. *not* a line stronger at one point than another: as in the case of magnetic iron, where iron filings are more strongly attracted to the poles than the middle, the attraction continually decreasing from the former to the latter. Magnetism, on the contrary, is this wholly universal feature of the earth, which at all points is magnetism in its entirety.—Two *secondary aspects* of magnetism fall to be mentioned here.

For philosophy, it is a matter of complete indifference *which bodies* manifest magnetism. It is found principally in *iron*, but also in nickel and cobalt. Richter thought he had isolated pure cobalt and nickel, and claimed that even these were magnetic. Others say that iron is still present in them, and that this is the sole reason why these metals are magnetic. That iron's cohesion and inner crystallization cause this formative urge to be manifest as such in it: all this is no affair of the Notion. Other metals, too, become magnetic at a given temperature; so that the appearance of magnetism in a body is bound up with its cohesion. Generally, however, only metals can be magnetized; for metals, without being absolutely brittle, have within them the compact continuity of simple specific gravity, which precisely is the abstract Shape we still have under consideration here; metals are thus conductors of heat and magnetism. Magnetism as such is not present in salts and minerals, since they are neutral substances in which difference is paralysed. The question now arises as to the properties of iron which make it the metal *par excellence* for the appearance of magnetism. The cohesion of iron can harbour the impulse to give itself Shape in the form of a tension which, however, falls short of achieving a result, simply because in this metal brittleness and continuity are more or less in equilibrium. It can be brought from a state of extreme brittleness to one of the greatest malleability and combines both extremes, in contrast to the compact continuity of the precious metals. But now magnetism is precisely this brittleness which has been *opened up (aufgeschlossen)*, and which possesses the peculiarity of not yet having passed over into compact continuity. Iron is thus much more *open* to the action of acids than metals of the highest specific gravity, such as gold, whose compact unity does not permit difference to emerge. Conversely, iron has no difficulty in retaining its pure form, unlike metals of lower specific gravity which are readily attacked by acids, crumble away and, in the case of metalloids (*Halbmetalle*), can hardly preserve their metallic form. That in iron, north and south poles have a distinct existence outside the point of indifference, is but another instance of the naïvety of Nature which sets forth its abstract moments just as abstractly in individual things. Thus it is that magnetism is present in iron ore; but magnetic ironstone seems to be the specific metal in which magnetism is manifested.—Some magnets act on the compass needle but do not magnetize other iron; Humboldt discovered this in a serpentine rock in the Bayreuth region. Bodies capable of magnetism, even lodestone, are not as yet magnetic while in the mine; only after they have been brought to the surface do they become so; the stimulus of light in the atmosphere is therefore needed to posit difference and tension in them.* This brings us to a further question; in what *circumstances* and under what *conditions* is magnetism manifested? Molten iron loses its magnetism; similarly, calcined iron, where the iron has been completely oxidized, lacks magnetism, since there the cohesion of the metal in its pure form has been wholly destroyed. Forging, beating, etc., also introduces modifications. Forged iron very readily becomes magnetic and as readily loses this property; steel, on the other hand, where iron

* Spix and Martius in their *Travels*, part i, p. 65, say: 'The phenomena of magnetic polarity were more distinct in this wacke' (in Madeira) 'than in the deeper layers of basalt.'—for the same reason, namely, that the higher-lying rock is more isolated from the soil (*cf. Edinburgh philos. Journ.* 1821, p. 221).

acquires an earthy, granular fracture, is much harder to magnetize, but keeps its magnetism longer; this can be attributed to the greater brittleness of steel. The process of generating magnetism shows up its fugitive character; it is not stable at all, but comes and goes. Merely to stroke iron renders it magnetic and that at both poles; but it must be stroked in the direction of the meridian. Striking or knocking iron with the bare hand, shaking it in the air, likewise makes it magnetic. The vibration of cohesion creates a tension; and this is the formative impulse. Even iron rods which have merely been stood on end in the open air become magnetic; similarly iron ovens, iron crosses on churches, weather vanes, in general any iron body readily acquires a magnetic property; and only weak magnets are necessary to elicit the magnetism in these bodies. In fact, the greatest difficulty has been found in simply making iron nonmagnetic and keeping it so; this can be done only by making it red hot.— Now when a bar of iron is stroked, there comes to be a point where one of the poles is not magnetic; the same holds of a certain point on the other side of the other pole. These are the two indifference-points of Brugmann, which differ from the general indifference-point, which does not itself fall exactly in the middle. Are we now to assume that in each of these points there is forsooth also a *latent* magnetism? The point where the action of each pole is strongest was called by van Swinden the *point of culmination.*

If an unmagnetized iron rod is balanced in horizontal equilibrium on a needle, and is then magnetized, one of its ends sinks (§ 293 Remark): in northern latitudes the north end sinks and in southern latitudes, the south end; and it sinks lower the higher the latitude, i.e. the nearer the geographical locality to the poles. Finally, when the magnetic needle at the magnetic pole stands at right-angles to the line of the magnetic meridian, it assumes a vertical position, i.e. becomes a straight line representing a pure specification and distance from earth. This is the *inclination* which thus varies as regards time and place; Parry in his expedition to the North Pole found this so strong that he could not make use of the magnetic needle any more. The inclination exhibits magnetism as gravity and that, too, in a more remarkable manner than in the attraction of iron. Magnetism, pictured as mass and lever, has a centre of gravity, and the two masses falling on either side, though in free equilibrium, are also specified, so that the one is heavier than the other. Specific gravity is here posited in the naïvest fashion; it is not changed but only determined differently. The earth's axis also has an inclination to the ecliptic; but this belongs strictly to the determination of the celestial spheres.

But the genuine mode of the distinctive manifestation of the specific and universal moments is found in the pendulum, in which definite masses at different places all over the world differ in force: at the poles, the specific weight of the masses is greater than beneath the equator; for the same masses are seen to behave differently. Bodies can only be compared with one another in these circumstances, in so far as the force of their mass shows as a dynamic power which, as free, remains equal to itself and is constant. Since in the pendulum the magnitude of the mass enters as motive force, the same mass must have a stronger motive force in the pendulum the nearer this is to the poles. Centripetal and centrifugal forces are supposed to act as separate forces on account of the earth's rotation; but it makes no difference whether we say that a body has more centrifugal force and escapes more forcefully from the direction of falling, or that it falls more strongly: for it is immaterial which motion we call falling or throwing. Now although the force of gravity does not vary when height and mass remain the same, in the pendulum gravity itself is specified; in other words, it acts as if the body fell from a greater or lesser height. The difference therefore among the varied magnitudes of the pendulum's motion in different latitudes is also a specification of gravity itself (see § 270, Remark, p. 70 *Zusatz*, p. 76).

§ 313

In so far as this self-related form exists at first in this *abstract* determination of being the identity of the *existing* differences, and is therefore not yet paralysed and reduced to a product in the totality of Shape, it is, as an *activity* in the sphere of Shape, the immanent activity of free *mechanism*, namely, the determining of relationships of *place*.

Remark

Here we must say a word regarding the *identity* of magnetism, electricity, and chemistry, an identity nowadays widely recognized and in physics even regarded as fundamental. The *opposition* of form in individualized matter also goes on in its self-determination to the more real opposition of *electricity* and to the still more real opposition of *chemical action*. At the base of all these particular forms lies one and the same universal totality of form as their substance. Electrical and chemical actions are, further, as processes, activities stemming from a more real, physically more developed, opposition; but above all, these processes also produce alterations in the spatial relationships of matter. On this side, namely, that this concrete activity is at the same time a mechanizing determination, it *implicitly* is a magnetic activity. Recently, the empirical conditions have been found which determine how far magnetism is as such also *manifest* in these more concrete processes. It is therefore to be looked on as an important advance in empirical science that the identity of these phenomena has been recognized in common thought, and goes by the name of 'electro-chemistry' or possibly of 'magneto-electro-chemistry' or something similar. It is just as important, however, to *distinguish from each other* the *particular* forms in which the universal exists and their *particular manifestations*. The name 'magnetism' should therefore be kept for the express form and for its manifestation which, being in the sphere of Shape as such, relates only to determinations of space; the name 'electricity', similarly, should be reserved for the phenomenal determinations expressly denoted by that word. Formerly, magnetism, electricity, and chemism were treated as wholly separate and uncorrelated, each being regarded as an independent force. Philosophy has grasped the idea of their *identity*, *but* with the express *proviso* that they also are *different*. Recent ideas in physics seem to have jumped to the other extreme and to emphasize only the *identity* of these phenomena, so that the need now is to assert the fact and manner of their distinctiveness. The difficulty lies in the necessity of unifying both extremes; it is only in the nature of the Notion that this difficulty finds a solution, not in the identity which merely confuses the names of these phenomena in a 'magneto-electro-chemistry'.

Zusatz. The second point in connection with the linearity of magnetism (see prev. Para, Zus., p. 164) is the inquiry into the *determinate modes of this activity*. Since we have not yet determined matter specifically, but only in its spatial relationships, its alteration can only be a movement; for movement is precisely this alteration in time of what is spatial. This activity must further have a material *substrate* which carries it, for the simple reason that it is immersed in matter and not yet brought to actuality; for in the substrate the form is present only as the direction of a straight line. In the living creature, on the other hand, matter is determined by the creature's own vitality. It is true that here, too, the determinateness is an *immanent* one, which merely determines heavy matter in immediate fashion without further physical determination. The activity, however, forces its way into matter without being communicated to it by an external mechanical impulse; as *form* immanent in matter, it is a materialized and materializing activity. And since this movement is not indeterminate but rather determined, it is either an *approach* or a *withdrawal*. Magnetism, however, differs from gravity in this, that it forces bodies into a quite different direction from the vertical one of gravity; its effect is to determine iron filings not to fall, nor to remain lying on the spot where they would have fallen, under the influence of gravity alone. This movement is not rotatory, not a curve, like the motion of the heavenly bodies which is accordingly neither attractive not repellent. Its curve is therefore an approach and a withdrawal *in one*; there, accordingly, attraction and repulsion were inseparable. Here, however, these two movements exist *separated*, as approach and withdrawal, since we are in the sphere of finite, individualized matter, where the moments contained in the Notion seek to become free; their unity, which also emerges in contrast to their difference, is only an implicit identity. The universal of the two moments is *rest*, and this rest is their indifference; for a point of rest is necessary to separate them, so that a specific movement may occur. But the opposition within the movement itself is an opposition in rectilinear activity; for all one has is the simple determinateness of withdrawal and approach along the same line. The two determinations cannot alternate or lie apart on each side, but are always together; for we are not in time, but in the element of space. It must therefore be the same body which, in being specified as attracted is, at the same time, also specified as repelled. The body approaches a certain point, and in so doing has something communicated to it; it is itself specified, and, as thus specified, must move on the other side as well.

The connection of electricity and magnetism has been viewed as typically displayed in the voltaic pile. This connection was thus discovered experimentally long after it had been grasped by thought: for just this, in general, is the business of the scientists, to search for and exhibit the identity of the Notion as the identity of phenomena. Philosophy, however, does not grasp this identity with superficial abstraction, as if magnetism, electricity, and chemical action were simply one and the same. Philosophy had said long since: magnetism is the principle of form, and electricity and chemical process are merely other forms of this principle. Formerly, magnetism stood isolated in the background; it was by no means clear to anyone—apart from navigators—what the system of Nature would lose without it. Its connection with chemical action and electricity lies in what we have said. Chemical process is the totality into which bodies enter according to their specific peculiarities; but magnetism is merely spatial. Yet in certain circumstances magnetic poles, too, differ electrically and chemically; or conversely, magnetism is easily generated by the galvanic process, the action of the closed circuit being highly sensitive to magnetism. In electro-galvanic action, in the chemical process, the moment of difference is posited; it is a process of physical opposites. Now it is quite natural that these concrete opposites should also be manifested at the lower stage of magnetism. The electrical process, too, is a movement; more than that, it is a conflict between physical opposites. In electricity, further, the two poles are free; in magnetism, they are not. In electricity accordingly the poles are related to one another as particular bodies, so that polarity exists in it in a quite different form from the merely linear polarity of the magnet. But if metallic bodies are set in motion by the electrical process without prior physical determinations, they manifest the process in their own way; this way is the activity of mere motion, and this therefore is magnetism. We must, therefore, see which is the magnetic moment and which is the electrical, etc., in each phenomenon. It has been said that all electrical action is magnetism: magnetism is the fundamental force which produces different terms, which likewise keeps them apart while also keeping them absolutely connected. This, of course, is what happens in both the electrical and the chemical processes, only more concretely than in magnetism. The chemical process is the formative process of really individualized matter. The formative urge is thus itself a moment in the chemical process; and this moment becomes free especially in the galvanic circuit where a tension is present throughout, but one which does not, as in the chemical process, issue in a product. This tension is concentrated at the extremities; and so it is here that influence is exerted on the magnet.

It is interesting to note, further, that this activity of the galvanic process, when it sets a magnetic body in motion, causes it to become inclined. This yields the opposition: the magnet inclines either to the east or west, according as the south and north pole is inclined. In regard to this, there is an ingenious apparatus by which my colleague Professor P. Erman has succeeded in freely suspending a galvanic circuit. A strip of cardboard or whalebone is so cut that a small copper or silver bowl can be brought up to one of its ends (or in the middle too?). The bowl is filled with acid, a strip of zinc or piece of zinc wire is put into the acid and wound round the strip of whalebone up to the other end and thence to the outside of the bowl. This produces galvanic action. The whole apparatus, suspended by a thread, can be brought up against the poles of a magnet so that opposition is now introduced into this mobile apparatus. This mobile suspended galvanic battery Erman calls a 'rotation battery' (*Rotations-Kette*). The $+E$ wire is in the direction south to north. 'Now', says Erman, 'if the north pole of a magnet is brought up to the north end of the apparatus from the east side, *this north end is repelled*; but if the same north pole is brought up from the west side, attraction will result. The total result is in either case the same; for whether attracted or repelled, the rotation battery when influenced by the north pole of a magnet placed outside of its arc always moves westwards, i.e. from left to right, when it was previously at rest in a south–north position. The south pole of a magnet produces the opposite effect.' Here, chemical polarity and magnetic polarity run counter; the latter has a north–south polarity, the former an east–west polarity; magnetic polarity achieves wider significance on the earth. Here, too, the transiency of magnetism is manifest. If the magnet is held over the galvanic battery, the determination is quite different from that which results when it is held in the middle: it turns completely round.

§ 314

The activity of the form is none other than that of the Notion in general, viz., to posit the *identical* as *different* and the *different* as *identical*. Here, therefore, in the sphere of material spatiality, the activity consists in positing what is identical in space as different, i.e. in removing it from itself (*repelling* it) and in positing what is different in space as identical, i.e. in bringing it closer and into contact (*attracting* it). This activity, having only an *abstract* existence in matter (and only as such is it magnetism) only ensouls a *linear* body (§ 256). In such a body, the two determinations of form can emerge separately only in the difference of the body, i.e. at the two ends, and the active magnetic difference of form consists merely in this, that one end (one *pole*) posits the same thing (a third term) as identical with itself which the other end (the other *pole*) repels from itself.

Remark

We express the law of magnetism by saying that *like* poles repel each other and *unlike* poles attract, or that like poles are *hostile* to one another whereas unlike poles are *friendly*. The expression 'like' has, however, no other determinate content except that those poles are like, both of which are equally attracted or repelled by a third. But the determination of this third consists similarly in either merely repelling or attracting the said like poles or simply some other. All these determinations are purely *relative*, without a distinct, sensible, neutral existence; as was said above (Remark § 312), terms such as north and south contain no such original, primary or immediate determination. Consequently the *attraction* of *unlike*, and the *repulsion* of *like* poles are certainly no secondary nor yet a special manifestation of a magnetism presupposed and already peculiarly determined: they express nothing else, on the contrary, but the nature of magnetism itself and so, too, the pure nature of the Notion when posited as an activity in this sphere.

Zusatz. A third question therefore arises: *what* is attracted and *what* repelled? Magnetism *is* this diremption, but this is not as yet plain in it. When one thing is put into relation with another which is as yet indifferent, then the second thing is affected in one way by one extreme of the first, and in another way by the other. The infection consists in the second body being made the opposite of the first in order that, as other (and as posited as other by the first), it may be posited by the first as identical with itself. It is therefore the activity (*Wirksamkeit*) of the form which first determines the second as opposed; the form thus exists as a process against the other. The activity enters into relation with an other, opposes this other to itself. The other was, in the first instance, only an other for us, in our comparison; now it is determined as other for the form, to be then posited as identical. Conversely, on the other side, we have the opposite side of the determination. The second body, to which, we must assume, a linear activity has also been communicated, is made opposite at one of its ends, and its other end therefore is at once identical with the first end of the first body. If now this second end of the second material line is brought into contact with the first end of the first, it is identical with it and is therefore repelled. The Understanding, no less than pictorial conception, is at a loss in trying to give an account of magnetism. For to Understanding, the identical is simply identical, the different simply different: in other words, two things which are identical in any respect are, in *that* respect, not different. But what we have in magnetism is just this, that something in being simply identical is *ipso facto* posited as different, and in being simply different is *ipso facto* posited as identical. Difference is this, to be itself and its opposite. The identical element in both poles posits itself as different, and the different element in both poles posits itself as identical; and this is the clear, active Notion, which however is not as yet realized.

This is the activity of the *total* form, as the positing of the opposed moments as identical—the concrete activity in contrast with the abstract activity of gravity where both moments are in principle (*an sich*) identical. The activity of magnetism, on the other hand, consists in first infecting the other, in making it heavy. Gravity is thus not active like magnetism though it has attraction, since the bodies which are attracted are already in principle identical; here, however, the other is first made capable of attracting and being attracted—only then is the form active. The attracting is simply a *doing*, which is just as much the other's doing as that of the first, the attracting body. Magnetism now functions as *middle* term to the extreme of subjectivity which contains itself in a point, and the extreme of fluidity which exists only as a continuum but is completely indeterminate within itself; magnetism is the abstract liberation of the form which, in the crystal, results in a material product as shown for example in the ice-needle. As this free, dialectical activity which, as such, goes on perennially, magnetism is also the *middle term* between being-in-self and accomplished self-realization. It is the impotence of Nature that separates off the motive activity in magnetism; but it is the power of thought which binds it back into a whole.

§ 315

(γ) The activity which has passed over into its product is *shape* and determined as *crystal*. In this totality, the different magnetic poles are reduced to neutrality and the abstract linearity of the place-determining activity is realized in the planes and surfaces of the entire body; more precisely, the rigid punctiform principle is, on the one hand, expanded into the developed form, while the formal expansion of the sphere is subjected to limits. It is the *one* form which is active: it crystallizes the body outwardly by setting bounds to the sphere; and it shapes the punctiform principle by crystallizing its inner continuity through and through in the natural direction of the layers (*Durchgang der Blätter*), i.e. in the basic structure.

Zusatz. In the third determination we first have shape as the unity of magnetism and sphericity; the still immaterial determining becomes material, and with this the restless activity of magnetism reaches complete rest. Here there is no longer approach and withdrawal but everything is set in its place. In the first instance, magnetism passes over into universal self-subsistence, into the crystal of the earth—the line passes over into the whole round of space. But the individual crystal, as real magnetism, is this totality in which the urge has died down and the oppositions have been neutralized into the form of indifference; magnetism then expresses its difference as a determination of surface. Thus we no longer have an inner shape which, for real existence, requires an other, but a shape which itself is the source of its real existence. All formative activity has magnetism in it; for it is a complete limitation in space posited by the immanent impulse, the *master-workman* (*Werkmeister*) of form. This is a silent activity of Nature which sets forth its dimensions timelessly—Nature's own vital principle which expounds itself without action, and of whose Shapes one can only say that they are there. The principle is everywhere at work unresisted in the fluid roundness; it is the silent formative process which links together all the indifferent parts of the whole. But since magnetism finds satisfaction in the crystal, it is not as such present in it; the inseparable sides of magnetism which, here poured out into the indifferent fluidity of the sphere, have at the same time an enduring existence, are the formative shaping which dies out in this indifference. It is therefore right in the Philosophy of Nature to treat magnetism as a wholly universal determination; but it is a mistake to try to demonstrate magnetism as magnetism in shape. The determination of magnetism as an abstract impulse is still linear; but magnetism in its realization determines spatial limitation in every dimension; shape is quiescent matter extending in every dimension— the neutrality of the infinite form and materiality. Here, therefore, is displayed the dominance of form over the entire mechanical mass. Certainly body still remains heavy in relation to the earth; this first substantial relation is preserved. Even man, who is spirit—the absolutely weightless (*das absolut Leichte*)—is still heavy. But the coherence of bodily parts is now determined from within outwards by a principle of form which is independent of heaviness. Here, therefore, we encounter for the first time the purposiveness of Nature itself: a connection of different indifferents constituting a necessity whose moments have a stable existence, or an inwardness (*Insichsein*) which is there outwardly— a spontaneous intelligent act of Nature itself. Purposiveness, therefore, is not merely an understanding which imposes a form externally on matter. The preceding forms are not as yet purposive—only an existence which, as existence, does not have in itself its relation to an other. The magnet is not yet purposive; for its two moments are not yet indifferent, only purely necessary for each other. Here, however, there is a unity of indifferent moments or of moments, each of which has free existence in relation to the other. The lines of the crystal are this indifference: one can be parted from the other and they remain; but they have meaning solely in relation to each other—the End constitutes their unity and their meaning.

But since the crystal is this quiescent End, the movement is other than its End; the End is still not a temporal matter. The divided fragments remain lying in mutual indifference; the points of the crystal can be broken off, and we then have each one separately. Now this is not the case in magnetism; so that to call the points of a crystal 'poles' since they too are opposites determined by a subjective form, would none the less be an inappropriate way of speaking. For here the differences have attained a quiescent persistence. Shape being thus the equilibrium of distinct moments, must also exhibit these differences within itself; the crystal therefore contains the moments of being-for-another (*für ein Fremdes zu sein*) and reveals its character in the shattering of its mass. In addition, shape must itself also come under the category of difference, and must be the unity of these distinct moments; the crystal has not only an *outer* but an *inner* shape, two wholes of form. This double geometry, this double formation is, as it were, Notion and reality, soul and body. The growth of the crystal takes place in layers but the *cleavage* goes right through all the layers. The inner determination of the form is no longer mere determination of cohesion, but all parts belong to this form; matter is crystalline through and through. The crystal is likewise bounded externally and is regularly enclosed in an internally differentiated unity. Its surfaces are quite smooth like mirrors; their edges and angles form shapes ranging from simply regular, equilateral prisms to those which are outwardly irregular, though a law is traceable even in these. There are, of course, fine-grained earthy crystals where the shape lies more on the surface; the nature of earth, since it has the point for principle, is the shape of shapelessness. Pure crystals such as calcite, when struck so that they are free to break in accordance with their internal structure, reveal in their smallest particles their inner, previously quite invisible shape. Thus huge rock crystals three feet long and a foot thick, found on the St. Gotthard and in Madagascar, still keep their hexagonal shape. It is this nuclear shape, permeating the entire crystal, which is most astonishing. When calcite, whose shape is rhomboidal, is fractured, the pieces are quite regular; if the fractures follow the internal structure, all the surfaces are mirrors. If the pieces are in turn fractured, the result always is the same; the ideal form which is the ensouling principle pervades the whole ubiquitously. This inner Shape is now a totality; for whereas in cohesion one dimension—point, line, or surface—dominated, shapes are now formed in all three dimensions. What were formerly called, after Werner, the natural directions of the layers (*Durchgänge der Blätter*), are now called forms of cleavage or nuclear forms. The nucleus of the crystal is itself a crystal, the inner shape as a three-dimensional whole. The shape of the nucleus may vary; there are gradations of the lamellar shape in flat and convex lamellae up to a perfectly determined nucleus. The diamond is externally crystallized in octahedral form, and though perfectly clear, is also inwardly crystalline. It breaks up into lamellae; when one polishes it, points are cut with difficulty; it can, however, be so struck that it breaks along the plane of cleavage and then its surfaces are smooth as mirrors. It is chiefly Haüy who has *described* the forms of crystals, and others after him have added to his work.

To find the connection between the inner form (*forme primitive*) and the outer form (*sécondaire*) and to deduce the latter from the former, is an interesting and delicate point in *crystallography*. All observations must be carried out in accordance with a general principle of transformation. The outer crystallization does not always accord with the inner; not all rhomboidal calcite has the same determination outwardly as inwardly, and yet there is a unity between the two formations. We know that Haüy has expounded this geometry of the relation between inner and outer shape in fossils but without showing its inner necessity, or the connection of shape with specific gravity. He assumes the nucleus, lets the *molécules intégrantes* attach themselves to the surfaces of the nucleus in a kind of serial arrangement in which the outer shape depends on a decrease in the series of the base, but in such a way that the law of this serial arrangement is determined precisely by the pre-existent shape. It is also the business of crystallography to determine the relation between the shapes of crystals and chemical substances, for one shape is more characteristic of a chemical substance than another. Salts in particular are crystalline, both outwardly and inwardly. Metals, on the contrary, not being neutral but abstractly indifferent, are generally bounded by a formal (*formelle*) shape; the presence of a nucleus in them is more hypothetical, only in bismuth has one been observed. Metal is still the substantially uniform substance. True, it shows the beginning of a crystallization, e.g., in the *moirés métalliques* of tin and iron when their surface is acted on by a weak acid, but the shaping is not regular and only the rudiment of a nuclear shape is discernible.

B. THE PARTICULARIZATION (SPECIFICATION) OF THE INDIVIDUAL BODY

§ 316

The process of shaping, the space-determining individualization of *mechanism*, passes over into *physical specification*. *In itself*, the individual body is the *physical* totality; this is to be posited in the body in the form of *difference*, but as difference determined and held in the individuality. The body, as *subject* of these determinations, contains them as *properties* or *predicates*, but in such manner that they are at the same time a relationship towards their unbound, universal Elements and form processes with them. It is their immediate, not as yet *posited*, specification—the latter constitutes the *chemical* process in which they are not yet taken back into the individuality, are not the real totality of the process, but only relations with those Elements. The differentiation of these determinations is that of their Elements, the logical determinateness of which has been indicated in their sphere (§ 282 et seq.).

Remark

In connection with the general idea of the ancients that each body consists of the four elements, or the more recent view of Paracelsus that it consists of mercury or fluid, sulphur or oil, and salt (Jacob Boehme called them the great trinity), and with many other ideas of this kind, it is to be remarked *first*, that it is easy to refute them if by such names one understands only the particular empirical substances that they primarily denote. The fact must not, however, be overlooked that the much more essential significance of these names is that of containing and expressing the determinations of the Notion. Rather should we wonder at the vehemence with which thought which was still unfree[1] perceived and held fast what was only its own peculiar nature and the universal signification in such sensuous, particular existences. It is therefore also pointless to refute such conceptions empirically (see above, *Zus.* to § 280, p. 105). *Secondly*, such a mode of conception and determination, since it has its source in the driving energy of Reason, which does not become lost or self-forgetful in the tangled interplay of sense phenomena, is raised far above the mere investigation and chaotic counting of the *properties* of bodies. In this searching, it is counted meritorious and praiseworthy to have made yet another *particular* discovery, instead of tracing back the multitude of particulars to the universal and the Notion, and recognizing the latter in them.

Zusatz. In the crystal, the infinite form has established itself in heavy matter merely spatially; what is lacking is the specification of the difference. Since the determinations of form must now themselves appear as material substances, we have the reconstruction and transformation of the physical Elements by individuality. The individual body, the Element of earth, is the unity of air, light, fire, and water; and the mode in which they exist in it constitutes the specification of individuality. Light corresponds to air; and light which, in contact with the darkness of body is individualized to a specific obscuration, is colour. The combustible, fiery Element, treated as a moment of the individual body, is the body's smell—the permanent, unsuspected process of its consumption; not combustion in the chemical sense which we call oxidation, but air individualized to the simplicity of a specific process. Water, as individualized neutrality, is salt, acid, etc.—the body's taste; the neutral body already points to solubility, a real relation to something else, i.e. to the chemical process. These properties of the individual body, colour, odour, taste, have no independent existence but belong to a substrate. As the individuality in which they are held is, in the first instance, immediate, they, too, are mutually indifferent; what therefore is a property is also a material substance, e.g. a colour-pigment. It is because individuality is still powerless to prevent it, that the properties also become free; the cohesive force of life is not as yet present, as in the organic sphere. As particular, properties also have the general signification of keeping up

[1] Reading *unfrei* for *frei*.

their connection with their source of origin. Colour consequently has a relation to light, is bleached by it; odour is a process with air; taste likewise keeps up a connection with its abstract Element, water.

In particular, the very names of odour and taste, which are also under discussion now, call to mind sensation, since they do not merely denote physical properties belonging objectively to bodies, but also denote subjectivity, i.e. the being of these properties for the subjective sense. Consequently, with this emergence of elemental qualities within the sphere of individuality, mention must also be made of their connection with the senses. Here we must first ask why is it just here that the *relation of body to subjective sense* originates: and secondly, what objective properties correspond to our five senses. The properties just mentioned, colour, odour, and taste, are only three; thus we have the three senses of sight, smell, and taste. Since hearing and touch do not appear here, the question at once arises: where is the place of the objective properties corresponding to these two other senses?

(α) With regard to that relation the following must be noted. We had the individual shape, shut up within itself, which, because as totality it has the significance of being complete in itself, is no longer involved in a difference with an other, and has therefore no practical relation to an other. The determinations of cohesion are not indifferent to an other, but are only in relation to an other; shape, on the contrary, is indifferent to this relation. Shape can, it is true, be treated mechanically; but since shape is self-relating, the relation of an other to it is not necessary but only contingent. Such a relation of an other to it can be called a theoretical relation; but only *sentient natures*, and at a higher level only thinking ones, have this relation to anything. Such a theoretical relation consists more precisely in this, that the sentient being in being related to the other is at the same time related to self, preserving its own freedom in face of the object, while the freedom of the object, too, is left inviolate. Two individual bodies, crystals for example, likewise let each other exist in freedom, but only because they have no relationship with each other: to have such a relation they would have to be chemically determined through the medium of water; otherwise it is only a Third, myself, who determines them by comparison. This theoretical relation, then, rests solely on the absence of any relation between them. The true theoretical relation exists only where there is an actual relation between the two sides, yet where each side is free in the face of the other; it is in just such a relationship that sensation stands to its object. Here, now, the closed totality is given freedom by the other and is only thus in relation to the other: in other words, the physical totality exists for sensation, and—since it once more exhibits itself in its determinate forms (to which we pass on here)— it exists for distinct modes of sensation, for the senses. It is for this reason, then, that here, in dealing with the formative process, we have noted the relation to the senses, though we need not have touched on it yet (see below, § 358), since it does not belong to the sphere of Physics.

(β) While we have here met with colour, odour, and taste as determinations of shape perceived by the three senses of sight, smell, and taste, we have already come across the sensuous properties corresponding to the two other senses (see above, *Zus.* to § 300, p. 139). Shape as such, the mechanical individuality, is for feeling in general; heat especially belongs here too. Our relationship to heat is more theoretical than it is to shape as such; for we feel the latter only in so far as it offers us resistance. This already is a practical relationship, for one side will not leave the other as it is; here one has to press, touch, whereas with heat there is still no resistance. Hearing we had in connection with sound, which is the mechanically conditioned individuality. The place of the sense of hearing in our specification is therefore where the infinite form is related to the material aspect. But this soullike element is only externally related to matter; it is only a form fleeing from mechanical materiality and is therefore vanishing and without enduring existence. Hearing's opposite is touch, the sense of the totality of mechanism in its ideal manifestation; its object is that terrestrial feature, gravity, shape which is not yet specified within itself. The two extremes, the ideal sense of hearing and the real sense of touch, were therefore contained in the total shape; the differences of shape are confined to the three other senses.

The specific physical properties of the individual shape are not themselves shape but shape's manifestations, essentially preserved in their being-for-an-other; this marks the beginning of the end of the pure indifference of the theoretical relation. The other to which these qualities are related is their universal nature or element, not as yet an individual body; on this a relationship of process and differentiation is founded which can, however, only be abstract. Since, however, the physical body is not merely *one* particular difference, is not merely separated into these qualities, but is a totality of these differences, this separation is only an internal distinction of its properties in which it remains a single whole. In this way, we have differentiated body in general, and this itself as a totality, now also enters into relationship with other similarly differentiated bodies. The difference of these total shapes is an outwardly mechanical relationship since they have to remain what they are, while their self-maintenance remains undissolved; this expression of enduringly different things is electricity, which is therefore at the same time a superficial process of this body against the Elements. Thus on the one hand we have particular differences, and on the other hand differences as such as a totality.

The division of the following Paragraphs is precisely this: *first*, relation of the individual body to light; *secondly*, the differentiated relations as such, smell and taste; *thirdly*, difference as such between two total bodies, electricity. Here we consider the physical determinatenesses of the individual body only in their relationship to their respective universal Elements, in regard to which they are individual, total bodies. Consequently, it is not individuality as such which is dissolved in this relationship; it should, on the contrary, preserve itself as such. What we are here to consider are, then, only properties. The actual dissolution of shape first occurs in the chemical process; i.e. what are here properties will there be exhibited as specific sorts of matter. Materialized colour, e.g. in the form of pigment, no longer belongs to the individual body as a total shape, but is separated off from it by chemical action and endowed with independent existence. Such a property, existing apart from its association with the self of individuality, can, it is true, be also called an individual totality, as in the case of metal, which is, however, only an indifferent, not a neutral, body. In the chemical process, then, we shall further see such bodies to be merely formal, abstract totalities. These specifications are, in the first instance, our doing, through the Notion; i.e. they have only an implicit or immediate existence, as shape has too. But they will afterwards also be posited by the *actual*, i.e. by the chemical process; and it is there, too, that we shall first discover the conditions of their existence as well as those of shape.

1. *Relationship to Light*

§ 317

The first determination of shaped corporeality is its *self-identical* selfhood (*Selbstischkeit*), the abstract self-manifestation of itself as an indeterminate, simple individuality—Light. But shape as such is not luminous, for this property is (previous §) a *relationship* to light.

(*a*) Body as *pure* crystal, in the perfect *homogeneity* of its neutrally existing inner individualization, is *transparent* and a *medium* for light.

Remark

The inner lack of cohesion in air stands to its transparency as does, in the concrete body, the *homogeneity* of the coherent crystallized shape. The individual body taken as unspecified is, indeed, as much transparent as opaque, translucent, etc.;[1] but transparency is its immediate, first *determination* as crystal, the physical homogeneity of which is not yet further specified and deepened within itself.

Zusatz. Shape is here still the quiescent individuality existing in a state of mechanical and chemical neutrality, though it does not possess the

[1] *Zusatz* of the Second Edition: Light and darkness are merely possibilities in the same thing.

latter at every point as does shape in its completeness. Shape, as the pure form by which matter is completely determined and pervaded, is therein only identical with self, and dominates matter at every point. This is the *first* determination of shape in thought. Now since this identity-with-self in matter is physical, but light represents this abstract, physical identity-with-self, the first specification of shape is its relationship to light which, however, in virtue of this identity, it has within itself. This relation through which shape posits itself for an other is strictly theoretical, not practical; it is, rather, a wholly ideal relationship. The identity which is no longer, as in gravity, posited as a mere urge, but which in light has become free, the identity now posited in the terrestrial individuality, is the dawning of the light aspect in shape itself. But since shape is still not an absolutely free, but a determinate individuality, the terrestrial specification of its universality is not yet an inner relation of the individuality to its own universality. It is only the sentient creature which possesses the universal of its determinateness as a universal within itself, i.e. is a universal for itself. Only the organism, therefore, so shows up against its other that its universality falls within itself. Here, on the contrary, the universal of this individuality is still, *qua* Element, an other, something external to the individual body. The earth, no doubt, taken only as a universal individual, has a relation to the sun, but a relation which is wholly abstract, whereas the individual body has at least a real relation to light. For though the individual body is, in the first place, dark, since this generally is the determination of abstract, independently existing matter, yet this abstract darkness is overcome by the individualization of matter, through its pervasive form. The particular modifications of this relationship to light are then the colours which must also, therefore, be mentioned here; as, on the one hand, they belong to the real, individual body so, too, on the other hand, they merely hover outside the individuality of bodies: shadowy entities generally to which no objective, material existence can as yet be ascribed—mere semblances resting simply on the relation between light and still incorporeal darkness, in short, a spectrum. Colours are thus in part quite subjective, conjured up by the eye—an action produced by a brightness or darkness in the eye and a modification of their relation; but an external brightness is, naturally, also requisite. Schulz ascribes a peculiar brightness to the phosphorus in our eye, so that it is often hard to say whether the brightness and darkness and the relation between them lie in us or not.

We have now to consider this relation of individualized matter to light, *first*, as the identity to which nothing is opposed, which is not yet posited as different from another determination—formal, general transparency. *Secondly*, we have this identity as specified with respect to an other; the comparison of two transparent media—refraction, where the medium is not purely transparent but specifically determined. *Thirdly*, we have colour as a property—metallic body, mechanically neutral but not chemically so.

First, with regard to transparency, opacity and darkness belong to the abstract individuality, to the Element of earth. Air, water, flame, on account of their elemental universality and neutrality, are transparent, not dark or opaque. Pure Shape has likewise overcome darkness, this abstract, brittle, unrevealed, being-for-self of individual matter, the non-manifestation of itself, and has therefore made itself transparent: simply because it has brought itself back to the neutrality and uniformity which is a relation to light. Material individuality is an inward darkening since it shuts itself off from ideal manifestation to another. But the individual form which, as totality, has pervaded its matter, has thereby entered into manifestation and advances to this ideality of definite being (*Dasein*). Self-manifestation is the explication of form, the positing of a being-here-for-another; but so that thus is, at the same time, held in an individual unity. It is for this reason that the body of brittleness (*das Spröde*), the moon, is not transparent, whereas the comet is so. Since this transparency is formal, the crystal has it in common with the intrinsically shapeless Elements of air and water. But the transparency of the crystal is, in keeping with its origin, also different from that of those Elements: they are transparent since they have not yet attained to immanent individuality, to the Element of earth, to obscuration. Bodies possessing shape are, it is true, not themselves light, since they are individual matter; but, since the pointlike self of individuality, as the inner fashioner, is unhindered, it no longer meets with anything alien in this dark matter: this being-within-self which has passed completely into the developed totality of the form, is here brought to the homogeneous sameness of matter. The form, as free and unrestricted, embracing both the whole and the single parts, is transparency. All the single parts are made quite like this whole and are for that very reason made quite like each other, and are separated from each other in mechanical interpenetration. The abstract identity of the crystal, its perfect mechanical unity as indifference, and its chemical unity as neutrality, are what constitutes its transparency. Now though this identity does not itself shine, it is so much akin to light that it can almost reach the stage of shining. It is the crystal to which light has given birth; light is the soul of this being-within-self, for in its ray mass is completely dissolved. The archetypal crystal is the diamond of earth in which every eye rejoices, recognizing it as the first-born son of light and gravity. Light is the abstract, perfectly free identity—Air the elemental identity; the subordinate identity is passivity to light, and this is the transparency of the crystal. Metal, on the other hand, is opaque, since in it the individual is concentrated into being-for-self through a high specific gravity (see *Zusatz* to § 320 towards the end). To be transparent, the crystal must be free from an earthy flaw; otherwise it is simply brittle. A transparent body can further be rendered opaque without chemical action simply by mechanical alteration, as we see in familiar phenomena where the body is merely divided into separate parts: powdered glass, for instance, and water made into foam, are opaque. This

is because their mechanical indifference and homogeneity have been removed; what was formerly a mechanical continuum has been disrupted and given the form of separate being-for-self. Even ice is less transparent than water, and, when crushed, is quite opaque. *White* is produced when the continuity of parts of the transparent body is destroyed and they are converted into a plurality, as, e.g., in snow; and only then, as white, does white exist for us and excite our eye. Goethe (*Zur Farbenlehre*, part i, p. 189) says: 'The *contingently* (i.e. mechanically) opaque state of the wholly transparent body could be called white. The familiar (simple) minerals are white in their pure state; but become transparent through natural crystallization.' Thus lime and silica are opaque; they have a metallic base which, however, has gone over into opposition and difference, and has consequently become a neutral substance. There are, therefore, chemically neutral substances which are opaque, but they are for that very reason not perfectly neutral: i.e. there is a residual principle in them which has not entered into relation with an other. But when we see silica crystallized without acid in rock crystal, or clay in mica, or magnesia in talc, or lime, of course, in carbonic acid, we have transparency. This phenomenon of a ready passage from transparency into opacity is frequent. A certain stone, hydrophane, is opaque; saturated with water, it becomes transparent. Water renders it neutral and so removes its discreteness. Borax, too, when dipped in olive oil becomes perfectly transparent, the parts therefore are ranged in simply continuous fashion.*
Since what is chemically neutral tends towards the transparent, metallic crystals also, such as are not pure metals but metallic salts (vitriols), become translucent by virtue of their neutrality. There are also coloured transparent bodies, e.g. precious stones; these are not perfectly transparent simply because the metallic principle to which they owe their colour is neutralized but not wholly overcome.

§ 318

(*b*) The first, simplest determinateness possessed by the physical medium is its specific gravity, whose peculiar nature is specifically manifested in comparison, and so also in regard to transparency, is manifest only in the *comparison* with the different density of another medium. To facilitate the exposition and

---

* Biot, *Traité de physique*, part iii, p. 199; 'Irregular fragments of borax' (i.e. borate of soda, a transparent crystal which in time loses some of its lustre and loses some of its water of crystallization at its surface) 'lose their transparency as a result of their unevennesses and the lack of polish on their surfaces. But they become perfectly transparent if dipped in olive oil, since this levels their unevennesses; the reflection at the surface of contact of these two substances is so slight that one can hardly distinguish the boundaries which separate them.'

illustration of this point let us assume that our two media are water and air; then the action of the first medium—let it be the one further from the eye—on the second, is solely that of *density* as what qualitatively determines place. The volume of water with the image in it is thus seen in the transparent air as if the same volume of air in which the volume of water is placed had the greater specific gravity, that of water, i.e. as if the volume of air were contracted into a correspondingly smaller space—so-called *refraction*.

Remark

The expression *refraction* of light is primarily a sensuous description, correct in so far as, e.g., a stick held in water, as is well known, appears to be broken; this expression is also naturally applied in the geometrical description of the phenomenon. But the *physical* meaning of the refraction of light and of so-called light-rays is quite another matter, and is a phenomenon much harder to understand than appears at first sight. Apart from other defects inherent in the ordinary conception, the confusion which must result from describing light-rays as if they radiated from a centre in the shape of a hemisphere is quite obvious. In regard to the theory by which the phenomenon is usually explained, we must draw attention to an important experiment in which the *flat* bottom of a vessel filled with water seems *level* and thus as *completely and uniformly raised*, a circumstance quite contradicting the theory, but which, as usually happens in such cases, is for that reason ignored or passed over in the textbooks.

It is important to note that in a single medium we merely have simple transparency as such, and that it is only the *relationship* of two media of different specific gravities that brings about a particularization of visibility—a determination which at the same time only fixes place, i.e. is posited by the wholly abstract density. But an *active relationship* of media results, not from their indifferent juxtaposition, but solely from the positing of *the one medium in the other*—here merely as something *visible*, as a visual *space*. This second medium is, so to speak, infected by the *immaterial* density of the first one posited in it, so that the space in which the image is seen in the second medium shows the same contraction as is suffered by this medium itself. The purely mechanical, physically not real but *ideal* property of density, of being merely determinative of space, is here expressly present: it seems to act *outside* the material medium to which it belongs since it acts solely on the space in which the object is seen. Without this ideality, the relationship cannot be understood.

Zusatz. Having first dealt with the transparency of the crystal which, *qua* transparent, is itself invisible, we must now deal with visibility in this transparent body, but at the same time with the visible opaque body. We have already had (§ 278) the rectilinear manifestation, the ideal self-positing of a visible body in an indeterminate transparent one—the reflection of light. But in the formal identity of the crystal, visibility is further specified. The transparent crystal, which has achieved the ideality of its opaque being-for-self, lets other opaque bodies be seen through it; it is the medium, the intermediary for the showing of one body in another. Now there are two phenomena here: refraction of light and the double images shown by a number of crystals.

The visibility here in question is that of something seen through more than one transparent medium: for since the transparency is that of the individual, specifically determined body, it appears only in relation to another transparent medium. As specifically determined, the medium has its own specific gravity and other physical qualities. But this determinateness only finds expression when the medium encounters another transparent medium, and the showing is mediated by both these media. In a single medium the mediation is a uniform showing of the object, determined merely by the expansion of light; one also sees in water (for instance), only less clearly. If the medium is in this way single, we only one density and therefore also only one fixing of place; but if there are two media there are also two different fixings of place. Here precisely the extremely remarkable phenomenon of refraction makes its appearance. It seems simple, trivial in fact; it is seen every day. Refraction, however, is a mere word. Through each medium taken separately, the object is seen in a straight line with the eye and in the same relationship with other objects; it is solely the relation between the two media which gives rise to the difference. If the eye sees an object through another medium (so as to see through two media) the object will be seen in a different place from the place it would have appeared in had it not been for the specific nature of the second medium, that is, in another place than the one it occupies for feeling in the context of material bodies—or the object in the context of light has a different place. The image of the sun is seen, for example, even when the sun is no longer on the horizon. An object in a vessel containing water is seen in a different and higher position than when the vessel is empty. Those who shoot fish, know that they must aim below the spot where they see the fish because the fish is raised.

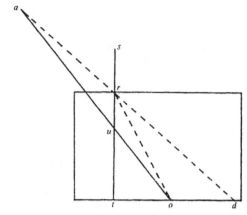

In the above figure, the angle *ars*, made by the line *ad* from the eye *a* to the object as seen *d*, with the perpendicular *st*, is greater than the angle *aus* made with the same perpendicular by the line *ao* from the eye to the point *o*, where the object actually is. It is usually said that light is refracted when, in passing from one medium to another, it is diverted from its path *or*, and the object is seen in the changed direction *ard*. But, considered more closely, this does not make sense: for one medium on its own does not refract; the cause of such refraction is to be sought solely in the relation between the two media. Light, in emerging from the one medium, has not acquired a special quality which has modified it in respect of the other medium, so that the latter would now direct it along another path. This is shown still more clearly by the following figure.

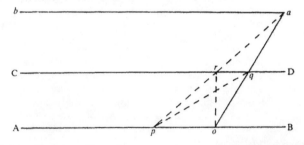

If, namely, between AB and *a*, the position of the eye, there is one medium, for example, water, then the object *o* is seen at *o* in the direction *aqo*; thus the medium CDAB does not alter the direction *qo* to *qp*. If now this medium between *ab* and CD is removed, it would be absurd to assume: (α) that *o* now leads not to *q* but to *r*, as if the light-ray *oq* had now noticed that air was above it and that it now wanted to emerge at *r*

in order that *o* could be seen by me at *r*; and similarly (β) it would not make sense to say that *o* no longer led towards and through *q*, from which point the ray could equally well reach *a*. For *o* goes out in all directions towards *q* just as well as towards *r*, and so on.

The phenomenon is thus seen to be a difficult one, difficult because here the sensible becomes ghostly (*geistermäßig*). I have often turned my attention to it and shall explain how I overcame the difficulty.

What happens, then, is that CDAB is not only transparent but that its own peculiar nature is also seen, i.e. the ideal relation mediates the act of seeing between AB and *a*. In treating of visibility we are in the field of ideality, for visibility as such is the positing of something as ideally present in an other. Since here what is ideally posited is still not in a unity with the material appearance, visibility is determined only by the ideal determinateness which is *in itself*, i.e. not embodied, namely, specific gravity: colour and other properties are not affected but only the spatial relationship. In other words, I see the immaterial determinateness of the medium CDAB without the medium with its material existence coming into play. The difference between one kind of matter and another does not concern the eye; but light-space or the medium of the eye is also material: this material nature affects only its determining of the spatial element.

The phenomenon is to be understood more exactly as follows. If we stop at the relation between water and air (although these are only elemental transparencies, i.e. not posited by the form which has overcome gravity) and if we posit them as two neighbouring media—for though in their abstract determinateness they appear prior to specific gravity, we must, if we wish to characterize them as physically concrete, have regard to all the qualities which we do not yet need to consider in the development of their own peculiar nature—we see the object in a different place from the one it occupies if the two media are between the object and our eyes. The question is, What is happening in this case? The entire medium CDAB with its object *o* is posited as ideally present in its own qualitative nature in the medium CDab. But what do I see of its qualitative nature? Or in what way can this enter into the other medium? It is this qualitative immaterial nature (of the water, for example) which enters into the other medium (the air), but *only* in its incorporeal and qualitative and not in its chemical nature: it determines visibility without actual water. This qualitative nature is now posited, in respect to visibility, as active in air: i.e. the water with its content is seen *as if it were air*; the important point is that its qualitative nature is visibly present in the air. The visual space formed by the water is transposed into another visual space, that formed by the air in which the eye is. What particular quality does it keep in this new visual space through which it announces itself as visible, i.e. is active? Not shape, for water and air as transparent are shapeless in regard to each other—not cohesion, but specific gravity. Other characteristics such as oiliness and combustibility also make a difference, but we do not want to introduce endless complications and will stick to specific gravity. It is only the specific determinateness of the one medium which shows in the other. What occasions the difficulty is that the quality of specific gravity which determines place, freed here from its matter, determines *only* the place of visibility. But what else does specific gravity mean but space-determining form? The specific gravity of water, therefore, can be here active in no other way than by endowing the second visual space, the air, with the specific gravity of water. The eye starts from the visual medium of air; this first medium in which it is, is its principle, its unity. It is now faced by a second medium, that of water, in whose place it posits the space of the air and reduces the former to the latter: consequently (since it is only this difference which comes into account), to the volume which the air-space would occupy if it had the density of water; for the water-space makes itself visible in another space, that of the air. A certain amount of water is therefore made into air which retains the specific gravity of water: the visible air-space has the same extent as the water, but as now invested with the specific gravity of water, it acquires a smaller volume though its content is the same. The water-space being now transposed into air-space—instead of the medium of water I see that of air—the quantum of air of course remains the same extensive quantum; but the volume of water appears only as large as if an equal amount, i.e. an equal volume, of air had the specific gravity of water. One can, therefore, also say conversely that this specific amount of air is qualitatively altered, i.e. is contracted into the space it would occupy were it converted into water. Since now air has a lower specific gravity, and the same volume of air consequently acquires, as water-space, a lesser volume, the space is raised and is also reduced in size on all sides. This is the sort of way in which this phenomenon is to be grasped; it may appear artificial but there is no alternative. It is said that the light-ray is propagated, passes through the medium; but here the entire medium—the transparent, illuminated water-space—is posited with its own specific quality in another medium, not as a mere radiation. The light must not be represented as a material propagation: the water, as visible, is ideally present in the air. This presence is a specific gravity; with this specific determinateness alone, the water preserves and exerts itself in that into which it has been transformed, and so transforms this its transformation into itself. It is as if a human soul placed in an animal body should maintain itself in it and amplify it to a human form. Or as if the soul of a mouse in an elephant's body should be elephantine and yet at the same time should reduce and dwarf the body to its own size. The best example is to be found in the world of ordinary thought where the relation to the object is ideal, and yet our thinking likewise achieves such belittlement. A petty soul, for example, measures the grandeur of a great man's heroic deed by its own dwarfish standards and reduces it to its own level, so that its littleness sees the deed only with such greatness as it has itself imparted to it. As the hero I imagine is actively present in me, if only in ideal fashion, *so too does the air receive within itself the visual space of the water and dwarf it to itself*. It is this *reception* which is the hardest to grasp, simply because it is an ideal, but at the same time an active, real existence. It is the medium *qua* transparent which constitutes this immaterial nature, this light-like quality which can be immaterially present in another place and yet stay as it is. Thus it is that in transparency the material body is transfigured into light.

The empirical phenomenon is that, e.g., objects in a vessel filled with water are raised. Snellius, a Dutchman, discovered the angle of refraction and Descartes took up the discovery. A line is drawn from the eye to the object; and, though light travels in a straight line, the object is seen, not at the end of the straight line, but as raised up. From the definite place where the object is seen another line is drawn to the eye. The extent of the difference between the two places is exactly determined geometrically by dropping a perpendicular from the point on the surface of the water where the first line comes out, and measuring the angle made by the line of vision with the perpendicular. Now if the medium in which we are has a lower specific gravity than the medium in which the object is, the object will seem further from the perpendicular than if we were merely seeing it through air; i.e. the angle is increased by this second medium. Mathematical physicists determine the alteration by the sine of the angle as the index of refraction. If there is no such angle, but the eye is vertically above the medium's surface, it follows directly from the determination of the sine that the object is not displaced, but seen in its true place; and this we express by saying that the ray which falls straight down on the plane of refraction is not refracted. But the other fact, that the object is none the less always raised—for though we see it in the same direction we see it nearer—is not accounted for by such a determination. Mathematical physicists and the physics textbooks only state the law of the magnitude of refraction in relation to the sine, but say nothing about the raising itself, which occurs also when the angle of incidence is $= 0$. From this it follows that the determinations of the sine of the angle are not enough, since they do not refer to the closer approach of the object. For from this law alone it would follow that I would see at its real distance only the point at the end of the perpendicular drawn from my eye, and the other points at distances gradually decreasing in such wise that the phenomenon would have the appearance of a spherical segment, the rim of which would be raised, while the depth of the bottom would increase gradually towards the middle, i.e. would be concave. But this is not so; I see the bottom quite flat, only brought closer. This is the way physics deals with things! This fact prevents us from basing our explanation, as physicists do, on the angles of incidence and refraction and their sine, i.e. we cannot regard these alone as accounting for the alteration. On the theory, when angle and sine $= 0$, the perpendicular is not affected: but since nevertheless we do have a raising of the bottom here as in other cases, the explanation should rather start from this raising, whereupon the determination of the angle of refraction among various angles of incidence would follow.

Refractive power depends on the specific gravity of media, which varies from case to case; on the whole, media with greater specific gravity have greater refractive power. The phenomenon does not, however, depend solely on specific gravity but other factors are operative such as an oily, combustible principle in one of the media. Thus Gren (*Physics*, § 700) cites examples where refractive powers are independent of densities: light in passing through alum and vitriol, for example, is perceptibly refracted though there is no perceptible difference between the specific gravities of these substances. Similarly in the case of borax saturated with olive oil, both combustible substances, the refraction does not conform to the specific gravity of the two bodies; the same holds of water and turpentine, etc. Biot too says (*Traité de physique*, vol. iii, p. 296), that while the behaviour of mineral substances conforms fairly generally to their densities, the same is not true of inflammable and gaseous substances; and on the following page: 'on voit que des substances de densités très-diverses peuvent avoir des forces réfringentes égales, et qu'une substance moins dense qu'une autre peut cependant posséder un pouvoir réfringent plus fort. Cette force dépend surtout de la *nature chimique* de chaque particule. La force réfringente la plus énergique est dans les huiles et résines, et l'eau distillée ne leur est pas inférieure.' The combustible principle is thus a specific quality which manifests itself here in a characteristic manner: oil, the diamond, and hydrogen, therefore have a higher refractive index. We must, however, content ourselves with stating and sticking to general points of view. The phenomenon is one of the most intricate there are: but the inherent nature of this intricacy is to be found in the fact that the most spiritual of Elements is here subordinated to material determinations, that the divine has commerce with the earthly, but that, in this alliance of the pure, virginal, impalpable light with corporeality, each side retains its due rights.

§ 319

The different densities which determine the visibility of objects, and which exist in different media (air, water, glass, etc.) are in the first instance only *externally* compared and unified; in the nature of crystals this comparison is *internal*. Crystals have, on the one hand, a general transparency, but, on the other hand, they possess in their *inner* individualization (their basic structure— *Kerngestalt*) a form deviating from the exact formal likeness* to

———
* Exact formal likeness here refers to the cubic shape generally. As regards the internal structure of those crystals in which double refraction of light occurs,

which this general transparency belongs. This form is also shape as basic structure, but is likewise an ideal, subjective form which, like specific gravity, actively determines space: it consequently also determines spatially manifest visibility in a specific fashion distinct from the first, abstract transparency—*double refraction*.

Remark

The category of *force* could be appropriately used here, since the rhomboidal form (the most usual among the forms deviating from exact formal likeness of shape) individualizes the crystal internally *through and through*, but, if the crystal is not accidentally split into lamellae, does not come into *existence* as shape, and does not in the least interrupt or disturb the perfect homogeneity and transparency of the crystal, but operates only as an *immaterial* determinateness.

In reference to this passage from an (at first) externally posited relationship, to its form as an internally active determinateness or force, I can quote nothing more apposite than Goethe's description of the relation between the external apparatus of two mutually facing mirrors and the phenomenon of the entoptic colours produced in the *interior* of a glass cube placed between them. In his *Zur Naturwissenschaft*, vol. i, p. 148, Goethe says *à propos* of 'natural, transparent, crystallized bodies' that 'Nature has constructed in the innermost part of such bodies a *mirroring apparatus exactly like* that we have made with *external, physico-mechanical* means' (cf. ibid., p. 147);*—an interior damask web woven by Nature. In this collation of outer and inner it is not, I repeat, a question of the refraction mentioned in this Paragraph but of an *external* double mirroring and of the phenomenon corresponding to it in the crystal's interior. A similar distinction must also be made in regard to what is said on page 147 of the same work: 'it

I quote the following passage from Biot (*Traité de physique*, vol. iii, ch. iv, p. 325) in which the matter is sufficiently described: 'This phenomenon is met with in all transparent crystals whose primitive form is neither a cube nor a regular octahedron.'

* What I have said about this *aperçu* was so favourably received by Goethe that it can be found in *Zur Naturwissenschaft*, part 4, p. 294.

could be quite distinctly observed in a rhombohedron of Iceland spar that the varying lie of the layers and *consequent* interplay of *reflection* were the immediate cause of the phenomenon'—this Paragraph is concerned with, so to speak, rhomboidal *force* or *activity*, not with the action of existent lamellae (cf. *Zur Natur-wissenschaft*, vol. i, part 1, p. 25).

Zusatz. Of the two images shown by Iceland spar, one is in the usual position, i.e. it is the result of ordinary refraction. The second image, called extraordinary, seems raised by the distortedly cubic, rhomboidal shape; the *molécules intégrantes* do not therefore have the form of a cube or double pyramid. There are two different positions and so two images, but in a single shape; for since this shape is, on the one hand, passive to light, it lets the image freely through; but its materiality then equally exercises its influence since the whole interior of the individual body forms a surface. Goethe brooded a great deal over this phenomenon which he attributes to fine fissures in the crystal, to existent lamellae; the displacement is not, however, produced by fissures but only by interior shape. For when actual discontinuities are present, colours, too, at once make their appearance (see follg. §). There are other bodies through which one sees a line not merely as doubled but even in two pairs. Recently many more bodies have been discovered which exhibit double refraction. Here, too, belongs the phenomenon called *fata morgana* and by the French, *mirage* (Biot: *Traité de physique*, part iii. p. 321) in which, on the seashore, an object is seen double. This is not reflection but refraction, since, as in the case of Iceland spar, the object is seen through layers of air which, having different temperatures have different densities.

§ 320

This immaterial *being-for-self* (force) of form, developing into *interior existence*, supersedes the neutral nature of crystallization, and we now have the determination of the immanent punctiform principle, brittleness (*Sprödigkeit*) (and with it cohesion) in a still perfect but *formal* transparency (brittle glass for example). This moment of brittleness is *difference* from *self-identical* manifestation, from light and illumination; it is, therefore, the inner beginning or *principle* of *darkening*, not as yet existent darkness but its *active principle*. (It is a familiar fact that brittle glass, though perfectly transparent, is the condition for the *entoptic* colours.)

Darkening does not remain a mere principle, but—in contrast

with the simple, indeterminate neutrality of shape and apart from darkenings and lessenings of transparency due to external and quantitative causes—it develops into the *abstract*, one-sided *extreme* of compact solidity, of passive cohesion (the metallic principle). Thus the *dark element* and the *bright element*, each separately *existent*, are at the same time posited through the intermediation of transparency in a concrete and individualized unity—the manifestation of *colour*.

Remark

Abstract darkness is the immediate opposite of light as such (§ 277 and *Zus.*). But the dark element first becomes real as physical, individualized corporeality; and the process of darkening just indicated is this *individualization* of the bright element, i.e. here, of the transparent body, of passive manifestation in the sphere of shape, culminating in the *being-for-self* of individualized matter. Transparency is homogeneous and neutral existence; the dark element is matter individualized within itself to the point of being-for-self which, however, does not exist punctiformly, but only as a *force* opposed to brightness and for that reason just as capable of perfect homogeneity.—It is well known that the metallic principle is the material principle of all colouring—one can call it the universal *pigment* if one likes. Only the high specific gravity of metals is here relevant and it is into this preponderant particularization that specified matter concentrates itself in extreme intensity as against the unlocked (*aufgeschlossen*) inner neutrality of transparent shape; in the sphere of chemistry, what is metallic is the equally one-sided, indifferent base.

In setting forth the process of darkening in the preceding paragraph, it was important that besides enumerating its moments abstractly, one should state the empirical ways in which these moments are manifested. Obviously, there are difficulties in each case; but physics creates even greater difficulties for itself by mixing up determinations or properties belonging to quite different spheres. Important as it is to find out the simple, specific determinateness among all the various conditions and circumstances associated with general phenomena like heat, colour, etc., it is just as important on the other hand to bear in mind the *differences* bound up with the manifestation of such phenomena. In empirical science, any statement as to what colour or heat, etc., is, cannot be based on the Notion but must depend on their modes of origin. These modes are, however, extremely varied. But the craze for finding only general laws, leads to neglect of essential differences while an *abstract* viewpoint leads to the chaotic lumping together of the most heterogeneous substances (as e.g. gases, sulphur, metals, etc., in chemistry). Thus the failure to consider modes of action as particularized by the differing media and spheres in which they occur, must have been prejudicial to the very desire to discover general laws and determinations. The circumstances connected with the manifestation of colour are lumped together in this chaotic fashion, and experiments tied to the most specialized conditions are usually opposed to the simple, general conditions, the archetypal phenomena (*Urphänomenen*), in which the nature of colour reveals itself to an unprejudiced intelligence. *The confusion attaching to a procedure which makes such a show of precise and well-grounded experiment, while it is in fact crude and superficial,* can only be countered by taking account of differences in the modes of origin of the phenomena: one must know what these differences are and one must keep them apart in their distinctive characters.

First of all, one must be convinced of the fundamental principle that loss of brightness is bound up with specific gravity and cohesion. These determinations are, in contrast to the abstract identity of pure manifestation (light as such), the peculiarities and specifications of corporeality; beyond these determinations, matter retreats further into itself and into the dark. These determinations directly constitute the advance from conditioned to free individuality (§ 307) and they appear here in the relation of the former to the latter. The interesting fact about the *entoptic* colours is that the darkening principle which here is brittleness, is an *immaterial* punctiform determinateness (i.e. active only as a force), which exists *outwardly* and produces opacity when a transparent crystal is reduced to powder: another example is froth on a transparent liquid, and the like (§ 317 *Zus.*). *Pressure* on a lens which gives rise to *epoptic* colours is an externally mechanical alteration of specific gravity alone, where there is no division into lamellae or suchlike *existent* obstacles to transparency.—When metals are *heated* (alteration of specific gravity) 'their surfaces exhibit a fleeting succession of colours which can even be arrested at will' (Goethe's *Farbenlehre*, part i, p. 191).—The *chemical* determination of colour by acid, however, involves an entirely different principle of the lightening of darkness, of a more immanent self-manifestation, of a fiery activity (*Befeuerung*). In considering colours as such, we should in the first instance exclude any lessening of transparency, any darkening or brightening due to chemical action; for the chemical substance, like the eye (in the subjective physiological phenomena of colour), is a *concrete* entity containing many other determinations, and those connected with colour cannot be definitely identified and isolated: on the contrary, the discovery of anything in the concrete object connected with colour presupposes a knowledge of colour in the abstract.

The preceding remarks refer to *inner* darkening in so far as this belongs to the *nature* of a body; it is interesting to demonstrate this darkening in connection with colour since the dimness it produces does not exist in externally independent fashion and cannot therefore be pointed out in that way. But even an *external* dimming is not a *diminution* of light as such, e.g., through distance: an obscuring medium which exists externally is simply less transparent, merely translucent; a quite transparent medium like water or clear glass—the Element of air lacks that concreteness present even in the neutrality of unindividualized water—begins to lose transparency as a result of a thickening of the medium, especially if the number of layers, i.e. of discontinuous boundaries increases. The most celebrated means for producing external obscuration is the *prism*, whose dimming action stems from two factors: first, from its outer boundary as such, its edges, and secondly, from its prismatic shape, from the variable transverse diameter between the whole spread of one side and the opposite edge. Among the incomprehensible features of colour-theories is the fact that men have ignored a prism's property of lessening transparency and in particular of doing so unevenly according to the varying thickness of the diameter of the different parts through which the light passes.

Darkening, however, is only *one* factor, brightness is the other; colour requires a more precise determination of their relationship. Light illumines, the day *dispels* darkness; a dim or dull light (*Verdüsterung*) as simply a mixture of light with existent darkness yields in general a *grey*. But in colour, these two determinations are in such a relationship that while they are held asunder they are just as much posited in unity; they are separate and yet each also shows in the other. Such a relationship is to be called an individualization; a similar relation was demonstrated in connection with so-called refraction, where one determination is active in the other and yet has its own separate existence. It is the way of the Notion as such which, as concrete, contains moments in their difference and at the same time in their ideality, their unity. This determination, which makes Goethe's exposition hard to grasp, is expressed by him in the sensuous manner appropriate to it. He says that in the prism, the bright *overrides* the dark or vice versa: so that the bright, though modified by the dark, still acts independently *qua* bright, though dimmed, and (in the case of the prism), disregarding the common displacement, remains in its own place at the very time of its displacement. Where the bright or dark, or rather the brightening or darkening agent (the two terms are relative), exist independently in an *obscuring medium*, this medium when set in front of a dark (or bright) background—and so serving to brighten (or darken) the latter—maintains its characteristic appearance and is as intensively bright or dark as before. The one is posited as negating the other, and so both are posited as identical. It is in this way that the difference between colour and mere grey is to be grasped (though e.g. a merely grey, colourless shadow is perhaps more rarely met with than is supposed). The difference is the same as that between green and red in the colour-square (*Farben-Viereck*); green is the *mixture* of the opposed colours, blue and yellow, while red is their individuality.

On Newton's familiar theory white light, i.e. colourless light, *consists* of *five* or *seven* colours; for the theory itself does not know the exact number. One cannot express oneself too strongly, first, regarding the conceptual barbarism which applies the category of *composition*, the worst form of reflection, even to light, and makes *brightness* consist of seven *darknesses*: one might as well say that clear water consisted of seven sorts of earth.

One may likewise censure the *ineptitude* and *incorrectness* of Newtonian observation and experiment and no less their *stupidity*, and as Goethe* has even shown, their *dishonesty*: one of the most striking as well as simplest errors is the false assertion that when a monochromatic part of the spectrum produced by a prism is passed through a second prism, it reappears as monochromatic (*Newt. Opt.*, lib. I, part I, prop. V, in fine).

Likewise one may condemn the equally bad character of the *reasoning* and *proof* based on such impure empirical data. Newton not only used the prism but was also aware of the fact that to produce colour by it a boundary of light and dark was necessary (*Opt.*, lib. II, part II, p. 230, ed. lat. Lond. 1719), and yet he could overlook darkness as an active factor in producing dimness. This *condition* for colour he only mentions by the way, in connection with a very special case—and then ineptly—long after his theory is complete. The only use made of Newton's reference to this condition by defenders of his theory is to say he was not unaware of it; but they do not see that it is an argument for treating darkness (in association with light) as a supreme *condition* in all consideration of colours. On the contrary, the textbooks do not mention the fact that darkness is present in all colour phenomena, nor the quite simple fact that a white wall (or wall of one colour) looked at through a prism shows *no* colour (in the case of a wall of one colour, no other colour than that of the wall); if, however, a nail is driven into the wall or any unevenness is made on it, then and only then and only at that spot, do others colours make their appearance. This ignoring of so many experiments which refute it must thus count as another fault of the theory.

We may further object particularly to the *thoughtless inconsistency* which abandons a number of direct inferences from the theory (e.g. the impossibility of achromatic telescopes) and yet still clings to the theory itself.

Finally, however, we may object to the *blind prejudice* which treats this theory as having a *mathematical* basis; as if measurements,

* Cf. *Farbenlehre*, part ii, p. 632: 'But I am well aware that lies are called for, and big lies.'

in part false and one-sided, merited even the name of mathematics, and as if the quantitative determinations introduced into its inferences could furnish any ground whatever for the theory and for the nature of colour itself.

Undoubtedly one of the main reasons why Goethe's illumination of this darkness in light, as lucid as it is profound and learned, has not found more general recognition is that far too much illogicality and credulity would have to be confessed. These absurd conceptions instead of declining have recently grown into an even more complicated metaphysical hotch-potch in the discoveries of Malus, the *polarization* of light, the *four-cornered* shape of light rays,[1] the rotatory movement of light corpuscles—red ones to the left and blue ones to the right,[2]—and especially in the Newtonian *Fits*, the *accès de facile transmission* and *accès de facile réflexion* (Biot, vol. iv, pp. 88 et seq.). Some of these conceptions arose from the application of the formulae of the differential calculus to the phenomena of colour; for the valid meanings which terms of these formulae have in mechanics have been illegitimately applied to determinations of an entirely different sphere.

Zusatz. In the prism, there is likewise so-called double refraction; and here we come upon the further determinateness with which transparency passes over into darkening, thus giving birth to colours. The brittleness of the glass shows itself as an obscuration of the bright element, though the glass is perfectly transparent. A milky glass, an opal, does the same; but in them, obscurations are produced which give no indication of outward existence. Light does not obscure itself, rather it is the unobscured; the idea of colour is, therefore, essentially bound up with what is individual, subjective, what spontaneously sunders itself into its differences and binds them within itself. The details of this belong to empirical physics; yet since science has not only to observe, but also to reduce observations to general laws, it therefore touches the philosophical theory of colour. There are *two* prevailing ideas about colours: the first,

[1] If two mirrors are set up at a slant—the one a weak mirror of transparent glass—and the lower mirror is rotated, one has an image of a light which vanishes when the mirrors are at right angles. Since if one continues the rotation for another 90°, the light is seen on two sides, but not seen on two other sides, Herr Prof. Mayer's Göttingen intelligence surmises sunbeams to be square.

[2] Biot, *Traité de physique*, vol. iv, p. 521: 'Lorsqu'on tourne le rhomboïde de gauche à droite, on devrait en conclure, que ces plaques *font également tourner la lumière de gauche à droite*: c.-à.-d. *en sens contraire* des précédentes, *c'est en effet ce qui m'est arrivé*' (cf. pp. 391, 523-4, 526-9).

which is ours, makes light simple. The other idea makes light composite, a conception flatly opposed to every Notion and the crudest of metaphysics; it is thoroughly bad since a whole way of treating things is in question. When dealing with light, we must lay aside any thought of separateness, of manifoldness; we must rise to the abstraction of the identical as existent. With light, therefore, we are forced to rise to the ideal, to Thought; but such thought is rendered impossible in the other idea by the sheer crudity of the conception. The object of philosophy is never the [merely] composite, but the Notion, the unity of differentiated terms, the unity being immanent in them, not external and superficial. To help out the Newtonian theory, the attempt has been made to eliminate this composition by saying that light determines itself immanently to these colours, just as electricity or magnetism polarizes itself into distinct forms. But colours exist only on the boundary between brightness and darkness, a circumstance which Newton himself admits (p. 199). Before light can determine itself to colour, an external determination or condition must always be present, like the infinite resistance-principle in Fichte's idealism, a condition moreover which is specific. If light could spontaneously obscure (*trüben*) itself, it would be the inwardly differentiated Idea; light, however, is only an abstract moment, the selfhood and centrality of gravity which has attained to abstract freedom. What must be settled *philosophically* is this—from what standpoint is light to be considered. Light, therefore, lies still outside of the physical (*das Physicalische*). Brightness, fixed corporeally, is *white*, which is not as yet a colour; darkness, materialized and specified, is *black*. Colour lies between these two extremes; it is first produced by a combination of light and darkness, a combination which is specific. Outside this relation, darkness is nothing, but neither is light anything. Night contains the self-dissolving ferment and destructive conflict of every power, it is the absolute possibility of everything, Chaos, without material being which, just because it destroys all, contains all. Night is the mother who nourishes all that is, and light is the pure form which first possesses being in union with night. The terror of night is the silent trembling and stirring of each power; the brightness of day is the self-externality of night which can retain no inwardness, but which, as spiritless, powerless actuality, is shaken out and lost. But the truth is, as we have seen, the unity of both: light, which does not shine into darkness but, penetrated by darkness as its essence, is thereby made substantial, material. It does not shine into darkness, does not light it up, is not broken in it; but the inwardly ruptured Notion, as the unity of both, displays in this substance its Self, the differences of its moments. This is the gay realm of colours and their animated movement in the *play of colours*. Everyone knows that colour is darker than light; but on Newton's theory, light is not light but intrinsically dark: and light exists only when these various colours, supposedly original, are mixed. To quarrel with Newton may appear presumptuous but the matter is one that can only be settled empirically, and that is what

Goethe has done, whereas Newton obfuscated it by his ossified reflective concepts. It is only because such ossification has made physicists blind even when watching their experiments, that the Newtonian system could survive till this day. I can be brief in dealing with this matter, since there is a hope that a special course of lectures[1] on this very interesting topic of colours will soon be given in this university, and that experiments will provide visible evidence of Newton's monstrous error and of the thoughtless, blind adherence of the physicists.

We must start our consideration of colour at the point where *transparency is conditioned by an obscuring medium* (and we must assert the prism as such to be also such a medium), at the point, therefore, where there occurs a relation of light to darkness. Colour, as this simple, free existent, requires an Other to give it actuality—a definite, uneven shape enclosed by sides forming different angles. This gives rise to brightnesses and darkenings of varying intensities which, falling on each other and thereby darkened or lightened, yield the *free colours*. To obtain these different degrees of darkening, we mostly use transparent glasses; but they are not in the least bit necessary for the production of colours, this result being a more complex, later product. Different darkenings or illuminations, like daylight and candle-light, can be made to fall straight on one another, and then we have at once coloured shadows, the dark shadow of each light being at the same time lit up by the other light; as well as the two shadows, one has, therefore, the same shadows lit up. If a number of irregular darkenings fall on each other, this yields a colourless grey, a fact familiar to us from ordinary shadows; this is an indefinite illumination. But if only a few—two distinctly different brightnesses fall on each other, then at once we have colour: a qualitative difference, whereas shadows display only quantitative differences. Sunlight is too intense to permit the appearance of any other contrasting brightness, the whole region receives a single general, dominant illumination. But if different illuminations fall into the room, even though only together with sunshine, e.g. the blue sky, then at once one has coloured shadows: so that when one begins to turn one's attention to the varied colouring of shadows, one soon finds that there are no longer any grey shadows, but everywhere coloured ones, though their colours are often so feeble as not to be individualized. Candle-light and moonlight give the most beautiful shadows. If a stick is held in these two different lights, both shadows are illuminated by both lights—the shadow of moonlight by candle-light, and conversely; one then gets a blue and a reddish yellow, while two candle-lights alone are coloured a definite yellow. This contrast also appears with candle-light at daybreak and twilight, when the sunlight is not so blinding that the coloured shadow would be suppressed by the many reflections.

Newton believes he has found a striking proof in the *spinning disc* on

[1] By Professor v. Henning.

which all the colours are painted; for when this is rotated rapidly, no distinct colour is seen but only a whitish shimmer, from which white light is inferred to consist of seven colours. But what is seen is only a grey, a wretched grey, a dirty colour, since the rapid movement prevents the eye from distinguishing colours, much as when we are seized with vertigo or a swoon, objects do not retain their clear outlines for us. Does anyone think he sees a real circle when a stone is whirled round on the end of a string? This basic Newtonian experiment directly refutes what they want it to prove; for if colours were original fixtures, it would be impossible for the obscure element involved in them to be here reduced to brightness. On the contrary, therefore, since light as such dispels darkness, as even night-watchmen sing, the dark is nothing primary. But conversely, where the dark factor preponderates, the slight illumination vanishes. Consequently, when glasses of definite colours are laid on top of one another, one sees white through light-coloured glasses and black through dark-coloured ones. This should make the Newtonians say that darkness, too, consists of colours: another Englishman did, in fact, say that black consists of all the colours. This strips colour of its particularity.

The *course of Newtonian reasoning* (*Reflexion*) runs here, as in physics generally, simply as follows:

α. Newton starts with the appearances produced by a glass prism in a completely dark room (this pedantry, like the *foramen ovale* and the like, is wholly superfluous), where he lets 'light-rays', as he calls them, fall on the prism. Various colours are then seen through the prism, the luminous image as such is seen in another place, and the colours are arranged in a particular order in this place: for example, violet at the top and red at the bottom. Such is the phenomenon in its simplicity. Newton now reasons as follows: since one part of the image is shifted more than another, and different colours are visible in the more displaced part, therefore one colour must suffer a greater displacement than another. This is expressed by saying that the intrinsic differences of colours consists in their *differing refrangibility*. Each colour is thus an original existence, already present and complete in light; the prism, e.g., does nothing beyond making visible such a pre-existent difference, which is not produced by the experiment: as is the case when we see through a microscope scales on a butterfly's wing which are invisible to the naked eye. So it is argued. And so this soft, delicate, infinitely plastic, absolutely self-identical principle of light, which yields to every impression, and whose complete indifference simply absorbs every external modification, is supposed to consist of fixed elements. One could as well argue in another sphere: When we strike different keys on a piano, we get different notes since, in fact, different strings are struck. In the organ, too, each tone has its own pipe which, when played, yields a particular tone. But when a horn or flute is played, we can hear a variety of tones though no special keys or pipes are to be seen. There is, it is true, a Russian horn-music where each note has its own horn, each player playing only one note with this horn. Now if, after hearing this Russian horn-music, we hear the same melody played on a French horn, we could argue like Newton, as follows: 'In this single horn there lie hidden several similar horns which can be neither seen nor felt, but which the player (here the prism) causes to be heard;—since he produces different notes, he must on each occasion be playing a different horn, since each note is fixed and complete in itself, having its own separate existence and its own horn.' To be sure, we also know that different notes are produced on the same horn by different movements of the lips, by inserting the hand in the instrument's mouth, and so on. This is not, however, supposed to effect anything, but to be a purely formal activity which only causes the different notes, already in existence, to be heard; it is not responsible for the difference of tone. *We* know, too, that the prism is a kind of condition, by means of which, various colours appear; the effect of the different densities presented by the prism's shape is to cause various darkenings of light to overlap. But even when we point out to the Newtonians that the colours only originate under these conditions, they still maintain that, as regards light, these different activities do not produce differences in the product, but that the products are ready and finished before their production: as if, so to speak, the notes in the French horn already had their own different sounds, whether I open or shut my lips or put my hand this way or that in the instrument's mouth; these actions are not modifications of the sound, but only repeated playings on numerous different horns. It is Goethe's merit to have overthrown the prism theory. Newton's conclusion is: 'What the prism elicits was originally there.' That is a barbarous conclusion. The atmosphere also has a darkening effect, and in different ways: the sun, e.g. is redder when it rises, for the air is then more humid. Water and glass have an even greater darkening effect. Newton, who leaves out of account the instrument's effect in darkening light, thinks that darkening which appears behind the prism consists of the original constituents into which the prism has supposedly decomposed the light. To say that the prism has dispersive power is a piece of slovenliness, since it presupposes the theory the experiment is supposed to prove. It is as if, wanting to prove that some water was not originally clear, I first foul it by stirring it with a bit of dirty rag on the end of a stick.

β. Newton further maintains that the seven colours, violet, indigo, blue, green, yellow, orange, and red, are simple and indecomposable; but no one will be persuaded to think that violet, e.g., is a simple colour, since it is a mixture of blue and a certain red. Every child knows that if you mix yellow and blue you get green: and lilac likewise, if to the blue you add less red than when you make violet: and that orange is got from yellow and red. But as green, violet, and orange are primary for the Newtonians, so, too, indigo and light blue (i.e. celadon, which has a tinge of green) are for them absolutely different, though there is no qualitative difference between them. No painter is such a fool as to be a Newtonian;

painters have red, yellow, and blue, and make their other colours from them. Even the mechanical mixture of two dried powders, one yellow and one blue, gives green. The Newtonians cannot deny that a number of colours are produced by mixture, but to save their theory of the simple nature of colour, they say that the colours produced by the prismatic spectrum (or spectre) have an original difference from other natural colours, i.e. the pigments fixed in substances. But that is an empty distinction; colour is colour, and is either homogeneous or heterogeneous —whether it originates in one way or another, or is physical or chemical. In fact, the mixed colours themselves occur in the prism as well as outside it; here we have the coming-to-be of a specific appearance *qua* appearance, and therefore, too, a pure mixture of appearance with appearance without any further combination of coloured objects. Thus, if the prism is held close to the wall, only the edges of the colour-image are coloured blue and red, the middle stays white. It is said that in the middle, where several colours come together, a white light arises. What nonsense! It is incredible to what absurd lengths men will go; and this sort of rigmarole is becoming a habit. But if the prism is shifted further away from the wall, the bands become wider until finally the white completely vanishes, and where the bands meet, green appears. In the Newtonian experiment aimed at proving that colours are absolutely simple (see above, Remark, p. 199), it is admittedly a fact that a colour cut off by a hole in a wall and falling on another wall will, when seen through a prism, not show the different colours perfectly; the edges naturally cannot be so distinct (*lebhaft*) since the background is of another colour; it is like looking at a scene through a coloured glass. We must not therefore allow ourselves to be at all impressed, either by the authority of Newton or even by the scaffolding of mathematical proof that has in recent times been built round his theory. People say, Newton was a great mathematician, as if that in itself justified his theory of colour. But it is only magnitude, not physical reality, that can be mathematically proved. Mathematics has nothing to do with colour—the case is somewhat different with optics— and there is precious little mathematics, if any, in Newton's measurement of colour. He measured the ratio of the bands, which vary in width: but says that his eyesight was not sharp enough for him to do the measurement himself, so a *good friend* with sharp eyes whom he trusted had done it for him.* Even when Newton compared these ratios with the numerical ratios of the musical notes (see above, § 280, Remark), that, too, is still not mathematical. And even if the image is large, no one with the sharpest sight can say where the various colours begin; one need only look at the spectrum once, to know that it does not provide

---

* *Newtoni Opt.* p. 120–1: *amicus, qui interfuit et cujus oculi coloribus discernendis acriores quam mei essent, notavit lineis rectis imagini in transversum ductis confinia colorum.* Newton has been such a good friend to all physicists; no one has seen the thing himself, and if he has seen it, he has spoken and thought like Newton.

definite boundaries (*confinia*) where lines could be drawn. The matter is quite absurd when one thinks that the widths of the edges differ widely according as the prism is nearer or farther away: at maximum distance, green, for instance, has the greatest width, since yellow and blue as such always get narrower as, with increasing width, their overlap increases.

γ A third theory of Newton's which Biot has further elaborated runs as follows. If one presses with a lens on a piece of glass, one sees a ring which forms several rainbows on top of one another, for the different colours have different impulses (*Triebe*). At one point, for example, a yellow ring is seen and no other colour; this, say the Newtonians, is because the yellow has an impulse to appear, while the other colours escape the 'fit' (*Paroxysmus*) and do not let themselves be seen. Transparent bodies are supposed to let certain rays pass through, but not others. The nature of colour, therefore, is this: sometimes it has the impulse (*accès*) to appear, sometimes the impulse to pass through. This is a wholly empty thought; it is mere appearance taken up into the rigid form of Reflection.

It is to *Goethe* we owe the *theory of colour adequate to the Notion*. He was early drawn to the study of colour and light, especially in connection with painting; and his pure, simple feeling for Nature, the first requirement for a poet, forced him to oppose barbarisms of Reflection such as we find in Newton. He went through all the theories and experiments which had been maintained and carried out in connection with light and colour, from Plato onwards. He grasped the phenomenon in its simplicity: and the true instinct of reason consists in grasping the phenomenon from the side where it displays itself in greatest simplicity. The entanglement of the *archetypal phenomenon* with a whole host of conditions comes later: if we start with these, it is hard to know the essence.

α Now the main feature of Goethe's theory is that light exists for itself, and that darkness is an Other outside of it: *white* is visible light, *black*, visible darkness, and *grey* is their *first*, merely quantitative relationship, and therefore a diminution or increase of brightness or darkness. But in the *second*, more determinate relationship where light and dark retain this fixed specific quality in face of each other, everything turns on which of these two forms is the ground and which is the obscuring medium. Either we have a bright ground and a darker one upon it, or conversely; and this gives rise to colour. It was Goethe's great flair which led him to say of this notional union of differents, *This is so*; only the thinking consciousness can reckon with the fact that reasonableness means identity in abiding difference. Where therefore, for instance, a thing's selfhood does not keep aloof from the object, but fuses with it, there we have only animal sensation. But if I say, I feel something warm, etc., consciousness posits an object, and despite this division, holds both terms together in a single unity. This is a relationship; 3:4 is quite different from merely putting these numbers together as 7 (3+4) or 12 (3×4) or 4−3 = 1: for in the former instance, three counts as three, and four as four. Similarly with colours, the bright and dark must be in mutual relation; medium and ground must here remain separate, the former being, in fact, a medium and not itself emitting light (*strahlend*). (αα) Otherwise I can picture a dark ground with sunlight shining on it; this, however, is not a medium. But obscuring media, too, can produce a mere grey instead of colour: e.g. if I look at a black object through transparent muslin, or at a white object through black muslin; for specific conditions are required to make colour as such definitely perceptible. Additional determining factors are differences in eyesight and setting. If nearby there is another object of some specific degree of darkness or brightness or some other pronounced colour, the weaker colour will appear as a mere grey. The eyes, too, vary greatly in their sensitivity to colours, though one's attention to colours can be sharpened; for example, the brim of a hat seen through muslin seems to me to have a bluish tinge. Colour obscuration (*Trübung*) alone, therefore, must be distinguished from (ββ) the *reciprocal showing through each other* of bright and dark. The sky is night (*Nacht*) and black: our atmosphere is, as air, transparent; if it were wholly pure we should see only black sky. But it is full of vapours (*Dunst*) and is therefore an obscuring medium, so that the sky looks coloured—*blue*; on mountains where the air is purer, the sky looks blacker. Conversely, if we have a bright background, e.g. the sun, and look at it through a dark glass, e.g. opalescent glass, it looks coloured, *yellow* or *red*. There is a certain *wood*, an infusion of which held up against a bright background is yellow, and against a dark background blue. This very simple relation is always the basis; any diaphanous medium which is still without a definite colour is active in this way. There is an opalescent glass which is yellow or red when held up to the sky, and blue when held up against something dark. Once I saw smoke rising from a chimney in front of my window; the sky was overcast and the background therefore white. As the smoke rose on this background, it was yellowish; as it fell and had behind it the dark roofs and the dark leafless trees, it looked bluish; where, lower still, it had the white walls of the houses behind it, it looked yellow again. There are beer bottles likewise which present the same phenomenon. Goethe had a Bohemian wine glass, the inside edge of which he covered half with black and half with white paper; the glass then looked blue and yellow. This is what Goethe calls the archetypal phenomenon (*Urphänomen*).

β. Another way of bringing about this colour-obscuration is by means of the prism: if we look through a prism at white paper on which there are black figures, or black paper on which there are white figures, we see coloured edges, since the prism, as both transparent and opaque, presents the object in the place where it is and at the same time in another place; the edges thereby become boundaries, overlapping each other without the occurrence of mere obscuration (*Trübung*). Newton, in the passage cited above (§ 320, Remark, p. 199), is puzzled that certain thin

lamellae (*Opt.* p. 230) or little glass balls (*Opt.* p. 217), perfectly transparent and without a trace of shadow, when seen through a prism appear
coloured (annulos coloratos exhibeant): cum e contrario, prismatis
refractione, corpora omnia *ea solummodo sui parte* apparere soleant
coloribus distincta, ubi vel *umbris terminentur*, vel partes habeant *inaequa-
liter luminosas*. But how could he see these little glass balls without their
setting in the prism? For the prism always displaces the sharp dividing
line between image and setting; in other words, it posits its limit as *limit*
(see § 92, *Zusatz*). *This is a fact, though it has not yet been fully explained*: just as in Iceland spar we have a double image: first, as transparent, it shows the natural image, and secondly, by its rhomboidal form,
it shows the same image displaced; the same sort of thing must take place
in the other glass. In the prism, therefore, I postulate two images immediately condensed into one: the ordinary image which remains in its
place in the prism, acts from this place and is projected into the transparent medium merely as an appearance, and the displaced, extraordinary image which is the obscuring medium for the first image. The
prism thus posits in light the diremption of the Notion (p. 201) which, by
way of darkness, achieves reality. But in general, the action of the prism
consists (α) in the displacement of the whole image, a displacement
determined by the nature of the medium; but (β) the shape of the prism
is also a determining factor: and in this fact we must see the reason for
the *size of the image*, for the prismatic shape is just this, that the image
fixed by refraction suffers a further displacement *within itself*; and it is
this *'within-self'* which is the real point of interest here. For since the
prism (if, e.g., the angle points downwards) is thick on top and thin
below, the light falls differently on each point of it. The prismatic shape,
therefore, produces a specific, additional displacement. Even if this is
not clear enough, the crux of the matter certainly lies in the fact that,
through the prismatic shape the image is at the same time internally set
in a second place. This internality is still further modified by the glass's
chemical composition: as in flint glass and other substances which have
their own peculiar crystallization, i.e. their intrinsic way of directing an
image.

γ. With my eyes, I see the edges and borders of objects indistinctly at a
distance of only a few feet. The wide edges of a window-frame, which on
the whole appears grey as in half-shadow, I see effortlessly and without
blinking as coloured; here, too, there is a double image. Such double
images are also found objectively in the so-called *bending* or *diffraction* of
light; a hair is seen double or even triple when light shines into a dark
room through a fine crack. Only Newton's experiment with the two
knife-blades has interest; the others which he cites, including the one
referred to above, have no significance. In the experiment with the
blades, the really remarkable fact is that the further the blade is from the
window-opening, the wider the borders become (*Newtoni Opt.* i, iii,
p. 328); from which we see that this phenomenon connects closely with

prismatic phenomena. Here, too, light appears as a limit to what is other. But light is not merely diverted by the external force of the prism: its reality is just this, to relate itself to darkness itself, to bend itself towards it and to make a positive boundary with it, i.e. a boundary where they are not cut off, but one goes over into the other. The diffraction of light occurs wherever light and darkness meet; it creates a penumbra. Light departs from its direction; and each thing goes beyond its sharp boundary into what is other. This can be compared to the formation of an atmosphere in so far as odour constitutes such a formation, as when we speak of the sour atmosphere of metals, of an electrical atmosphere, and so on. It is the emergence of the ideal element which in shape, as Thing, appears bound. The boundary thus also becomes more positive, not merely a simple mixture but a penumbra, on the light side bounded by light, but equally on the dark side separated off from the darkness by light: so that the penumbra is blackest on the light side and gets less on the side where light separates it off from the darkness. It reduces itself thus over and over again, giving rise to a series of juxtaposed shadow-lines. This diffraction of light, light's own free refracting, further requires a particular shape in order to display these syntheses, this neutrality, as qualitatively determined.

δ. We have yet to indicate the relationship which obtains between *colours in their totality*. Colour is a *determinate* colour. Now this determinateness is no longer merely determinateness as such, but as actual determinateness contains within itself the difference of the Notion; it is no longer an undetermined determinateness. Gravity, as the universal, immediate being-within-self in other-being, immediately contains difference as inessential, the difference of so much mass; great and small are completely devoid of qualitative difference. Heat, on the other hand, as inwardly negative, has difference in the diversity of temperature as heat and cold; these, in the first instance, are themselves only quantitatively different, but acquire qualitative significance. Colour, as genuine actuality, has immediate difference as posited and determined by the Notion. We know from sense-perception that *yellow*, *blue*, and *red* are the primary colours, to which must be added *green* as itself the colour obtained by mixture. The relationship is this, as shown by experience: the first colour is yellow, a bright ground and a duller medium which is *illuminated* or *lit through* by it, as Schulz expresses it. That is why the sun looks yellow to us, its obscuration (*Trübung*) being only superficial. The other extreme is blue, where the brighter medium is *shaded through* by the darker ground, to use another expression of Schulz's. It is for this reason that, where the atmosphere is misty, the sky is blue, and deep, dark blue, almost black-blue, on high mountains, e.g. the Swiss Alps, or as seen from a balloon, where one is beyond the dulling medium of the atmosphere. In blinking, one makes the eye's crystalline lens into a prism, in that one-half of it is covered; one then sees one side of a flame yellow and the other blue. Telescopes, as lenses, are likewise prismatic and therefore show colours. Perfect achromatism can be produced only by putting one prism upon another. Between the two extremes of blue and yellow, the simplest colours, lie red and green, which no longer belong to this wholly simple, general opposition. The one mediating colour is red, to which blue as well as yellow can be intensified; yellow is readily changed into red by intensified darkening. In the spectrum, red already makes its appearance in violet, and similarly, at the other end, with yellow in orange. Red appears when yellow is again 'shaded through' or blue again 'lit through'; yellow, therefore, when given a darker tinge, or blue when given a brighter tinge, becomes red. Red is *the* mediation which—in contrast to green which is passive mediation—must be signalized as active, as the subjective, individual determination of both colours. Red is the royal colour, light which has overcome darkness and completely penetrated it, this active, powerful colour which attacks the eye and is the intensity of both extremes. Green is the simple mixture, the common neutrality of yellow and blue, as we clearly see in the prism when yellow and blue coincide. As neutral, green is the colour of plants, for it is out of their green that their further qualitative moments come to birth. Yellow, as the first colour, is light as simply obscured—colour as immediately existent; it is a warm colour. The second stage of colour is the mediating stage, where the opposition itself is doubly represented as red and green; these correspond to fire and water, which we have already dealt with (§§ 283 and 284). The third stage is blue, a cold colour, a dark ground seen through something bright—a ground which does not reach concrete totality. The blue of the sky is, so to speak, the ground from which the earth proceeds. The *symbolical* meaning of these colours is as follows: yellow is the gay, noble colour which delights by its power and purity; red expresses seriousness and dignity and also affection and graciousness; blue expresses tender, profound emotions. Red and green, since they form an opposition, pass readily into each other: there is a close affinity between them. Green intensified looks red. The extract of a green plant (e.g. of sage) looks quite green. Now if this liquid, which must, however, be dark green, is poured into a glass vessel having the shape of a champagne glass and is held up to the light, the lower part will appear green and the top part the most beautiful purple. Thus, where the glass is narrow, the liquid looks green; then it changes through yellow into red. If this liquid is in a large, wide bottle, it looks red, but while being poured out it looks green. It is its intensity, therefore, which makes it red; or rather green, raised in intensity, looks red. The lower part of a flame appears blue, for there it is thinnest: the upper part appears red since there the flame is at its intensest, and also its hottest; the flame, then, is dark at the base and yellow in the middle.

  ε What is objectively necessary is also linked in subjective vision. When one colour is seen, the eye demands the other: yellow demands violet, orange blue, purple green, and vice versa. Goethe therefore calls these '*complementary*' (*geforderte*) *colours*. We can include here the yellowish or bluish shadows in morning and evening twilight, produced by the contrast of moonlight and candlelight (see above, p. 202). Following an experiment of Goethe's, if a red glass is held behind a candle-light, the illumination is red; if a second candle is added, that shadow is red on which the red light falls; the other shadow looks green, since that is the complementary (*geforderte*) colour to red. This is a physiological fact. It is now for Newton to say where the green comes from. If one looks into light and then closes one's eyes, one sees a circle of the opposite colour to the one first looked at. I will cite the following experiment regarding this subjective image. I had gazed for some time at the image of the sun in the focus of a lens. When I shut my eyes, the image which remained was blue in the centre and the rest of the concentric area a beautiful sea-green; the centre was the size of the pupil, the surrounding area larger than the iris and slightly elliptical. When I opened my eyes, the image remained: seen on a dark ground, the centre was an equally beautiful cerulean blue, and the area round it green; but seen on a light ground, the centre became yellow and the area round it red. If a stick of red sealing-wax is laid on a piece of paper, and one stares at it for some time and then looks away, a green image (*Schein*) is seen. The purplish colour (*Purpurfarbe*) of the sea in motion is the complementary (*geforderte*) colour: the lit-up part of the waves appears green in its own colour, and the part in shadow appears in the opposite colour, purple (*purpurnen*). In meadows where nothing but green is to be seen, and the sky is moderately clear, the trunks of trees and paths often have a reddish sheen. Regius Professor Schulz has carried out extremely important and interesting experiments with these physiological colours, which he has communicated to Herr v. Goethe and also to a few friends here, and which will soon be published.

It is necessary to keep to the Goethean archetypal phenomenon. Trivial phenomena obtained by intricate experiments are used as arguments against it. Newton's experiments themselves are complicated, bad, pettily done, mean, and dirty. His theory of colour is regurgitated in a hundred manuals. None the less, the theory championed by Goethe has never lacked adherents, as he himself has shown in the literature. Goethe has been assailed for being a poet, not a professor. Only those who espouse certain jargon, certain theories, belong to the guild; what others say is quite ignored as if it simply did not exist. Often, such people want to form a caste, to be in exclusive possession of science and let no one else form a judgement: jurists do so, for instance. But law (*das Recht*) is for everyone, and it is the same with colour. In such a caste (*Klasse*), certain fundamental conceptions are developed which mould everyone's thinking. If anyone does not speak as they do, he is supposed not to understand the subject; as if only the brethren of the guild had understanding of it. They are right; we do not grasp the subject in terms of *these* categories of the *Understanding*, in terms of this metaphysics that they think should govern our thought on the matter. It is philosophers mainly who are snubbed; but it is just those categories that philosophers must attack.*

(α) In the *second* place, another kind of darkening is seen in other phenomena. Since obscuration is the formless element in punctiformity, in brittleness, and in pulverization—it is, of course, only then principle, not the actual suspension of cohesion by smashing—there occurs another kind of darkening in glass rapidly cooled after rapid heating. Such glass is brittle in the highest degree; for which reason, it is also very fragile.

Here is where the *entoptic colours* come in. Goethe in his *Morphology* has expounded this stage very cleverly. The phenomenon occurs, namely, with a cube or square plate of brittle glass of this kind, but not otherwise. If one places an ordinary, not brittle, glass cube on a black base and faces the bright quarter of the sky (in the morning this is west, for the darkest part is that nearest the sun), we see the image (*Schein*) of this brightness which, falling on the glass plate, appears to the eye as a reflection (cf. above, § 278, *Zusatz*, p. 98); in summer, with the sun at its zenith, the whole horizon is bright and the phenomenon appears everywhere. Now if we use brittle glass, there are seen in addition to the brightness which appears in any glass, dark spots at the four corners of the plate, so that the (remaining) brightness forms a white cross. But if we stand at right-angles to our previous direction (i.e. looking across the plate towards the south instead of to the west), we then see, instead of four dark points, four bright ones, and a black cross instead of the white one. This is the archetypal phenomenon. If the obscuration is increased by means of reflection, coloured rings (*Farbenkreise*) appear at the four points. What we have here, then, is simply a genesis of obscuration in this state of transparency, in this brightness; this darkness is, on the one hand, produced by the plate's boundary, on the other hand, by the medium's refractive nature. Thus we have a relation of dark and bright which, further determined and differentiated within themselves and superposed on each other, gives the different colours in their order (or in the reverse order when the position is altered). Thus, if the four points are white and the cross black, the obscuration first gives rise to yellow; from which we pass to green and blue. But if the cross is white and the corners dark, then with increased darkening, blue is the first colour to appear, since the bright element is pushed into the dark background. We have here, then, in one transparent medium a further darkening which pushes on to colour and which depends on the qualitative nature of the brittle body.

(β) Allied to this phenomenon are the *epoptic* colours, which have a mechanical origin: when a lens is pressed on a glass plate (see above,

* In the lectures based on the first edition of the Encyclopaedia, this first part of the theory of colour followed directly after the doctrine of the reflection of light (see above, § 278, *Zusatz*), where this paragraph, too, was inserted. In the present paragraph, however, the exposition of the entoptic colours directly followed the doctrine of double reflection. [Michelet's note.]

pp. 206), the point of contact is at first black, but as the pressure is increased, the point spreads out into a number of rings of different colours, green, red, yellow. The same phenomenon occurs when stones are pressed on ice. Here, it is merely the mechanical pressure which produces the colours; and this pressure is nothing but an alteration of cohesion in the nearest parts, just as heat, too, is only a transformation of cohesion. As in sound, the vibration is an extension of the mechanical impression, a trembling which spontaneously passes away, so here in the glass, there is a persistent undulation—the varying resistance to pressure, a persistent inequality of cohesion, which produces a different darkening in different places. While, therefore, in the entoptic colours it was brittleness which produced the colour, here the colour is caused by the interruption of cohesion.

(γ) If the interruption of cohesion goes further, we have the *paroptic* colours. Lamellae, fine cracks are produced in such glass, and especially in calcite; there the colour often becomes iridescent, as on a pigeon's neck. Here a darkening results from the transparent body's being pressed to the point of an actual breakdown in its togetherness.

These determinations fall within the transition from brightness to darkness. In this totality of light and darkness, light has completely deviated from its Notion; it has abandoned its pure quality which constituted its essence. In other words, the physical body (*das Physicalische*) emerges as a unity pervaded by light, the substance and the possibility of gravity and process. The constant (*constanten*) physical colours which can be exhibited as pigments are, *thirdly*, this fixed darkening of bodies, which no longer appears as an external determination, as a mere play of light over the body; on the contrary, the darkness of matter in these substances is itself essentially only their interior darkening, since light has immanently pervaded the body and is specifically determined in it. How does this material colour differ from the colour which is merely more or less translucent? Seeing that the physical body has an intrinsic colour, e.g. gold is yellow, the question arises: how does light enter into this corporeality? how does light coming from outside coagulate into matter so as to become a pigment bound to the darkness of body? Just as brightness formed the starting-point of the present exposition, so it must be the starting-point in our consideration of pigment. The first characteristic of the crystal was its abstractly ideal equality, its transparency to a light falling on it from outside. All bodies are, in the first instance, bright on the surface only when illuminated; their visibility is the falling of an external light on them. The crystal, however, receives brightness into itself, for it is through and through the real possibility of being seen, i.e. of being ideally, or theoretically, in an other, or positing itself in it. Seeing that this visibility appears, not as a real brightness, but simply as this theoretical nature as such, and that shape punctualizes itself to the inner indifference of specific gravity, of being-within-self, i.e. progresses to real brittleness, to the self-existent unit: this progress of visibility to darkness is therefore a suspension of free, inner crystallization, it is colour. Colour, therefore, is the physical nature [of body] which has come forth on to the surface, which no longer has anything internal for itself, nor anything outwardly attached to it as heat is to shape, but is pure appearance; in other words, everything that it is *in itself* is also *there*. The determinate physical body has, therefore, a colour. This obscuration of shape is the suspense of its uniform neutrality, i.e. of the form which, as such, is preserved even in neutrality, for it persists as the pervasive unity of its moments whose specific distinctness it negates. Colour is the suspense of this indifference and identity to which form has brought itself; the obscuration of the form is, therefore, the positing of a single form-determination, as a suspension of the totality of differences. Body, as mechanical totality, is form developed through and through within itself. The reduction of this form to abstract indifference is obscuration, as colour in the individualized body. This posited determinateness is the liberation of singularity, in which shape now endows its parts with a point-like nature, the liberation of the mechanical mode: but a liberation which, in the continuity of shape as such, is an internal indifference within shape. The ideality and absolute self-identity of light becomes the form of material individuality, which returns into just this identity, but an identity which, as reduction of real form to indifference, is a darkening, but a specific darkening; it is the inner self-darkening crystallization, which suspends the differences of form and so returns to pure, compact indifference, to a high specific gravity. This being-within-self, this compactness of dark matter which, as internally formless identity, is merely inwardly intensive, is *metalleity*, the principle of all colouring, the luminous side of body presented as a material substance. High specific gravity is precisely the unrevealed being-within-self, the simplicity not as yet broken down; it is in metal that specific gravity has importance: in other bodies it is practically without significance.

One of the moments here posited as a distinct determinateness, is now, therefore, abstract, pure identity, which is at the same time a real identity of bodies, the light posited in the body itself as its own colour, the identity which has become material. This universal thereby becomes a particular moment, separated from the whole; and the other moment is the opposition. The transparent body is also indifference, but in virtue of its form; this indifference is thus opposed to the dead, dark indifference we now have. The former is, like spirit, light (*hell*) within itself through the dominance of form; the indifference of the dark element, mere compactness of body with itself, is rather the dominance of matter. In the eoptic and paroptic colours, we also saw the separation of matter from form as a mode of the incipient darkness and the origin of colours. That, too, is formlessness as separation into single points, but it is more an externally posited mode of darkening. But what is in itself formless, does not exist as plurality but as indifference, as unshaped; and so in the metallic body there is nothing much to distinguish. Metal is not internally manifold: it is neither combustible nor neutral.

Every metal in its pure state has its particular colour; this is a matter of experience. Schelling says that gold is congealed light. Iron, on the other hand, has its tendency to blackness since it is magnetic. Everything coloured can be represented as a metal if the colour is separated out as a pigment, and this must be a matter for empirical science. Even vegetable pigments, e.g. indigo, when crushed have a metallic sheen, in general, a metallic appearance. The redness of blood can be traced to iron, and so on. The colour of metals can, however, be modified by chemical action or even by the action of heat. As regards the latter, it is here that the infinitely fleeting aspect of colour is manifested. When silver is melted, a point is reached where it attains its brightest lustre; this is the highest degree of melting, called by metallurgists the 'silver gleam'; it is only momentary and cannot be prolonged. Before this point, it runs through all colours of the rainbow, which pass over it in waves: the sequence is red, yellow, green, blue. Goethe says, in continuance of the passage quoted above (Remark, p. 197): 'If polished steel is heated it will take on a yellow colour at a certain temperature. If it is quickly removed from the furnace it keeps this colour. As soon as the temperature is raised, the yellow becomes darker and soon changes to purple (*Purpur*). This colour is hard to retain for it rapidly changes to deep blue. This beautiful blue can be fixed if the steel is quickly removed from the heat and put into the ashes. This is how blue-coloured steel products are manufactured. If, however, the heating is continued, the steel soon becomes bright blue in colour and remains so. If a pen-knife is held in a flame, a coloured band appears across the blade. That part of the band which was deepest in the flame is a bright blue which disappears into a bluish red. The middle of the band is purple (*Purpur*), then come a reddish yellow and yellow. The explanation is found in what we said above. The blade is less hot towards the handle than at the point held in the flame; and consequently the colours, which would otherwise appear successively, must here all appear at once, and this is the best way of fixing them permanently.' Here, too, then, it is a mere alteration of density which produces the different colours; for it is the darkness of the body posited in various determinations which produces colour. The metallic principle, therefore, is this physical likeness with self (*Sichselbstgleichheit*) which has achieved stability. Metal has colour attached to itself, but colour which derives solely from light, light that is still pure and is not as yet broken up, i.e. colour as *lustre*. Metal is opaque; for transparency is a lack of light in a thing to which actual light is alien.

The chemical significance of metal is that it can be oxidized, an extreme of form as against neutrality, the reduction of form to a formal, undifferentiated identity. Metal is easily turned white by a weak acid, as lead is made into white lead by acetic acid; zinc oxide is formed similarly. Yellow and reddish yellow, on the other hand, have an affinity for acids, and blue and bluish red for alkalis. But not only metals change colour under chemical action. Goethe says (*Farbenlehre*, part ii, p. 451): 'The juices of all blue and violet flowers are turned green (and therefore made brighter) by alkalis, and a lovely red by acids. The extracts of red woods are turned yellow by acids and violet by alkalis; but decoctions of yellow plants are turned dark by alkalis and lose almost all their colour under the action of acids.' And ibid., p. 201, he says: 'Litmus is a pigment turned blue by alkalis; it is turned red by acids and back to blue by alkalis.'

Here, however, we are considering the particularization of the individual body, and therefore have to exhibit colour only as a moment, a property, but endowed with the possibility of becoming a material substance. Consequently we are not as yet concerned with colour in the separation and isolation of metals. As properties, colours are still held within individuality, though they can be exhibited as pigments; this possibility stems from the impotence of individuality, which here is still not the infinite form, to be omnipresent in objectivity, i.e. in the properties. But if properties, even in the organic sphere too, are presented as material substances, they belong to the kingdom of death. For since in the living organism the infinite form is objective to itself in its particularization, is self-identical in its properties, this particularization is here no longer separable, otherwise the Whole would be dead and dissolved.

Now colour as a property presupposes a subject, and is held in its subjectivity; but as a particular property, colour is also for an other—and every property, as such, exists only for the sense of a living creature. We are this other, the sentient subjects; our sense of sight is determined by colours. Only colours are for sight; shape belongs to touch and only discloses itself to sight through the alternation of light and shade. Physical body has withdrawn into itself from touch, from existence in which all quality is lacking; it is reflected into self, is in its other-being. Gravity, like heat, pertains to touch; but colour is a universal presence, a being-for-another, a propagation, which heat and gravity also have, though with colour the property at the same time remains immediately objective. Nature, which at first developed its sense of touch, now develops its sense of sight; from this it passes on to smell and taste. Colour is for an other, but this other must leave colour to the body; thus the other has only a theoretical, not a practical relationship to colour. The sense (of sight) leaves the property as it is; true, the property is for sense, but the latter does not seize the property for itself. Since, however, the property belongs to Nature, this relationship must also be physical, not purely theoretical, as it is to the sense of a living creature; as, therefore, the property does belong to the thing, it must also be related to an other within the inorganic sphere itself. This other to which colour is related is light, as a universal Element; it is the other of *itself*, i.e. the same principle, but that principle in so far as it is not individual but simply free. The universal, then, is the power over this particular, and perpetually consumes it; all colours are bleached by light, all colours, that is, in inorganic objects. It is otherwise with the colours of living organisms; these perpetually renew their colours. This bleaching is not as yet a chemical process, but a silent, theoretical process, for the particular can oppose nothing to this its universal essence.

> For the Elements hate
> The work of human hands,[1]

and generally of anything individualized, and break it up. But equally, too, the abstract, universal ideality of the Element is always individualized in colour.

2. *Properties of the Opposition*

§ 321

a. The principle of one of the aspects of Difference (being-for-self) is fire (§ 283), but not yet as a real chemical process (§ 316) in the individual body, nor any longer as mechanical brittleness, but in physical particularity it is combustibility as such. This principle, which is also externally different, is a relationship to the negative side of elemental universality, to air, the invisible destroyer (§ 282); it is the process of air on material body: it is specific individuality as a *simple* theoretical process, the invisible volatilization of body in air—*Odour*.

Remark

The property of odour possessed by bodies, conceived as a separately existent *odorous matter*, is *oil*, matter which burns as flame. As merely a property, odour exists, e.g., in the unpleasant smell of metals.

Zusatz. The second moment, that of opposition, as exhibited in the individual body, is Odour and Taste; they are the senses of Difference and belong already to self-developing process. They are very closely allied and in Swabia not distinguished, so that there one has only four senses. For one says, 'The flower *tastes* good', instead of 'It smells good'; we Swabians therefore smell, as it were, with the tongue too, so that the nose is superfluous.

[1] Schiller's *Das Lied von der Glocke.*

If we want to understand the *transition* more precisely it is as follows. Since the undifferentiated dark element of metalleity at which we have arrived is, chemically speaking, the combustible element, i.e. the absolutely oxidizable, it is a base, an extreme, which is merely *capable* of being brought into active opposition by something outside of it, which must therefore be another differentiated body (oxygen, etc.). This abstract possibility of combustion is combustible only when it has been oxidized, only as lime; not till the acid has oxidized the metal does it achieve neutrality with metal (therefore with metal as oxide, not as metal); that is, the metal must first be determined as one side of the opposition before it can be neutralized. The metal as such is therefore capable of forming one side in the chemical process; its indifference is only a one-sided aspect, an abstract determinateness, and for that reason essentially a relation to an opposition. But this opposition, into which we enter from indifference, is, in the first instance, total opposition; for we are not yet dealing with the one-sided opposition of the chemical process, each side of which already itself is a corporeal reality. Because the opposition here is total, it is not the possibility of representing only one side (*Teil*) as in combustion; we have, on the contrary, a material for the whole process. This material is combustible in a different sense from metal, which is combustible in the ordinary sense, i.e. it is only one of the distinct sides of the process. But the material which is the total possibility of the opposition is the fundamental principle for smell. Smell is our sensation of this silent process, immanent in body, in which body is consumed in the air, which itself has no odour for the very reason that in it everything passes off in odour, all odours are dissolved in air as colours fade away in light. But whereas colour is only the abstract identity of bodies, odour is their specific individuality concentrated in their difference, it is their entire specific character turned outwards and consuming itself in the process; for when a body has lost its odour, it is flat and lifeless. This consuming of bodies is a process which is no process, it is not a relation to fire like a flame; for this latter is the consuming of an individual body itself in its individual shape. In the inorganic sphere, however, such concentration occurs mostly only in the form of fire; pleasant odours occur more commonly in the organic sphere, e.g. in flowers. Metals, consequently, which are not total bodies, do not smell as such, but only in so far as they are integrated with other bodies, have in some measure surrounded themselves with an atmosphere, and in this way consume themselves; they then become poisonous and therefore also have an unpleasant taste. This does not, however, happen so readily with precious metals, simply because they do not so easily lose their pure form; it is for this reason that they are mostly used as dishes for food. Just as light has a particular existence in metal, fire has a particular existence in odour; but it is not the real existence of a separate matter, sulphur, but exists here only as an abstract property.

§ 322

(b). The other moment of the opposition, *neutrality* (§ 284), is individualized to the specific physical neutrality of salinity and its determinations, acid, etc.;—*to taste*, to a property which, at the same time, remains in relationship with the *Element*, with the abstract neutrality of water, in which body, as merely neutral, is *soluble*.[1] Conversely, the abstract neutrality contained in body is separable from the physical constituents of its concrete neutrality and can be exhibited as *water of crystallization*, though this, of course, does not exist as water in the still unresolved neutral body (§ 286, Remark).

Zusatz. The water of crystallization first comes into existence as water in the process of decomposition. It is supposed to be latent again in the crystal; but water is not present, as water, in the crystal at all, for no moisture whatever can be discovered in it.

Taste, which is the third particularity of body, has, as a neutral pro-perty, also again sublated this relationship to the Element and drawn away from it; that is, the process does not always have immediate exis-tence as has odour, but rests on a contingent encounter of the two sides. Water and salt consequently exist in a state of mutual indifference, and taste is real process among individual bodies, not among individual bodies and Elements. Whereas, therefore, in the process of combustible matter the sides are united and not distinguished, the neutral body can be decomposed into acid and base (p. 218). As abstract neutrality, water again is tasteless; taste first appears with individualized neutrality, the unity of opposites which have collapsed into passive neutrality. It is there-fore only neutral bodies such as salts, which decompose into their oppo-sites, which have a definite taste. We call it taste with reference to our sense, but the other moment here is still the Element; for the solubility of bodies in water simply means that they can be tasted. Metal is not, like salt, soluble in water because, unlike salt, it is not the unity of oppo-sites, and is in general an incomplete body which first attains complete-ness in, e.g., an ore; we shall say more of this later when we consider the chemical process.

Colour, odour, and taste are the three determinations of the particu-larization of individual body. With taste, body passes over into chemical, real process; but this transition still lies some way ahead. Here, as properties of bodies, these determinations are, in the first instance, in relation to the universal Elements; and this is the beginning of their dissolution. The power of the universal is an oppositionless penetration

---

[1] Solution and resolution are chemically different. Resolution is separation into elements, solution occurs simply in water.

and infection, because the universal is the essence (*Wesen*) of the particular itself, is already contained *in principle* (*an sich*) in it. In the organic
sphere, it is the genus, the inner universal, which brings about the
destruction of the individual (*das Einzelne*). In chemical process, we
shall come across these same bodies, but as independent existences (see
§ 320, *Zusatz*, p. 215), in process with *one another*, no longer with the
Elements. This already begins in electricity, to which, therefore, we must
now make a *transition*. The properties in question, as individual realities,
likewise stand in relation to one another. Because *we* put them in relation
through our comparison, it does at first seem as if this concerns us alone;
the deeper significance is, however, that the individual bodies themselves, just inasmuch as they are particular, put themselves into relation with others. Individualized bodies, therefore, do not merely have
an indifferent existence as in the immediate totality of the crystal, nor do
they merely have physical differences as differences in their relation to
the Elements; they also have a relation to one another, and this in twofold manner. These particularizations are, in the first place, only superficially related to one another and preserve their independence; this is the
phenomenon of electricity, which is thus manifest in the total body. But
the real relation is the passing of these bodies into one another; that is the
chemical process, which expresses the deeper side of this relationship.

3. *The Totality in Particular Individuality: Electricity*

§ 323

Bodies stand in relationship with the *Elements* according to their
specific particularity; but as wholes possessing shape, they also
enter into relationship with each other as *physical* individualities.
In conformity with their particularity which has not as yet
entered into the chemical process, bodies are mutually *independent*
and *preserve* themselves in mutual indifference, a wholly mechanical relationship. In the mechanical sphere, bodies manifest their
self in an ideal movement, in the *internal* oscillation of sound; but
now, in their reciprocal *physical* tension, they manifest their *real*—
although still only abstractly real—selfhood as their *light*, but as a
light which is pregnant with *difference*: this is the *electrical*
relation.

Zusatz. Electricity is a notable phenomenon which formerly seemed as
isolated as magnetism, and, like the latter, was regarded as an appendage
(see above, § 313, *Zusatz*, p. 171). We have already (preceding *Zusatz*)
pointed out the connection between electricity and the phenomena most

closely connected with it; now, we want to compare it with an earlier stage, with sound. With sound, we entered the sphere of shape; the final stage, before the dissolution of shape in the chemical process, is shape as pure, self-identical form: and this it is as electric light. In sound, body manifests its abstract soul (*Seele*); but this manifestation of its selfhood belongs entirely to the field of mechanical cohesion, body in its perpetually self-returning movement appearing as a mechanical totality. Here, on the other hand, we have not such a merely mechanical self-preservation, but a self-preservation as regards physical reality. Electrical tension is a physical existence. As sound depends on a stroke from another body, so electricity too is conditioned by the fact of needing two bodies to produce it. But there is this difference, that with electricity both bodies are differently disposed to each other, so that the exciting body, too, enters into the difference; in sound, on the other hand, only one of the bodies sounds, or if both sound, the sounding of each is indifferent to the other's. The ground of this progress lies in the fact that physically individualized bodies, as the totality of their properties, now behave differently towards one another. While to our senses, these separate properties fall apart from each other, the individual body is their unifying bond; precisely as our conception of things recombines them into a unity. Now this individual totality stands in a relationship, and it is this relationship which we must consider from this standpoint. But as developed totality, body is a differentiated totality; and this difference, in remaining a totality, is only difference as such, which therefore necessarily requires two terms mutually related.

As physical body is now before us as physical totality, this immediately presupposes a plurality of such bodies; for the multiplication of the Oue is made evident by Logic (§ 97, *Zusatz*). Now though these many bodies are also, in the first instance, mutually indifferent, this indifference is eliminated in their actively different behaviour towards one another: because they have to be the positing of their totalities. In this positing relationship and in this self-demonstration as physical individualities mutually related, they must at the same time remain what they are, since they are these Wholes. Their relation is thus at first a mechanical one, just because they remain what they are; the bodies touch each other, *rub* each other. This is brought about by an external force; but as they are to remain totalities, this external relation is not the contact we had previously. It is not a destructive shattering of bodies in which the resistance of cohesion is the determining factor; nor is it a sound-producing relation or a force which generates heat or flame, and which consumes bodies. It is, therefore, only a slight friction or pressure of surfaces—their thrust, which puts *one* of the indifferent bodies where the other is: or it is a blow to shape, an incitation of sound, the positing of the existence of the body's inner, pure negativity, its vibration. In this way there is posited a unity of two terms, and of terms which are independent and indifferent: a magnet, both poles of which are free shapes in which opposition is so divided that the middle term exists as a pure negativity which itself has no outer reality but is only present in its members. Electricity is the pure goal of shape from which it has freed itself: shape which has begun to sublate its indifference; for electricity is the immediate emergence from shape, or the existence which still has its origin in shape, is still conditioned by it. Or we may say that it is not the dissolution of shape itself, but the superficial process in which the differences abandon shape but are conditioned by it, and are not yet in themselves completely independent. This relationship seems contingent since it is only in principle (*an sich*) necessary. The relationship is not difficult to grasp; but that it must be electricity may at first occasion surprise: in order to demonstrate it, we must compare our notional determination with the phenomenon.

§ 324

In mechanical contact, the physical difference of one body is posited in the other. As the bodies at the same time remain mechanically independent of each other, this difference is a *tension* of the bodies in their mutual opposition. This tension consequently does not involve the physical nature of the body in its concrete determinateness: individuality is manifested and involved in the process only as a reality of the *abstract* self, as *light*, and as light pregnant with opposition.—The other moment of this superficial process, the removal of the diremption, has as its product an undifferentiated light which, being incorporeal, immediately vanishes; apart from this abstract physical manifestation, the only other significant outcome of the process is the mechanical effect of shock.

Remark

The difficulty in grasping the *Notion* of electricity stems, in the first place, from the fundamental determination of inertia, both physical and mechanical, ascribed to the individual body in this process. This is why electrical tension is attributed to another special matter to which the light belongs which manifests itself in abstract separation from the concrete reality of the body, the latter remaining aloof in its independence. The difficulty is, in the second place, the general one of the Notion as such, the difficulty of grasping light in its relationship as *moment* of a totality and here no longer in freedom as solar light, but as a moment of a particular body; in this it is *implicitly* present as the pure selfhood of the body and enters into existence as a product of the body's own inwardness. Primordial light, that of the sun (§ 275), proceeds only from the Notion as such; here, however (as in § 306), we have a *coming-to-be* of light, but of differentiated light, from an existence which is the Notion existing as a particular body.

It is a familiar fact that the former distinction of *vitreous* and *resinous* electricity, in which the difference is defined in terms of specific, sensuous existence, has with the advance of empirical science been converted into the *conceptual distinction* of *positive* and *negative* electricity; a remarkable instance of the way in which empiricism, whose primary aim is to grasp and retain the universal in sensuous form, itself transforms its own sensuous stuff. There has been much talk recently of the *polarization of light*: it would have been more correct to reserve this expression for electricity than to apply it to the phenomena observed by Malus, in which transparent media, reflecting surfaces and their various mutual inclinations, and other extraneous circumstances, produce an *external* difference in the *shining* of light, but not a difference in light itself (§§ 278, 319, and 320).—The conditions for generating positive and negative electricity, a smoother or rougher surface, e.g., a puff of air, etc., are evidence of the *superficial character* of the electrical process, and show how little the concrete, physical nature of body enters into it. Similarly, the faint coloration of the two electrical lights and the smell and taste of positive and negative electricity, indicate only an *incipient* bodily nature in the abstract self of the light in which the tension of the process is contained, a process which, though physical, is still not concrete. The negativity, viz. the removal of the tension between the opposed bodies, is mainly a *shock*; the self which has posited itself as self-identical out of its diremption, is still, as this totalization, confined within the external sphere of *mechanics*. The light of the spark discharged hardly begins to develop into *heat*; and the *combustion* which can arise from the so-called discharge is, according to Berthollet (*Statique chimique*, partie i, sect. iii, not. xi), rather a direct *effect* of shock than the result of light developing into the reality of fire.

In so far as positive and negative electricities are kept apart from each other in different bodies, there comes into play, as in the case of magnetism (§ 314), the specific function of the Notion, viz., the positing of the opposed as identical and of the identical as opposed. This is, on the one hand, the mechanistic activity of *spatial* attraction and repulsion—in so far as this can occur as a separate phenomenon, it establishes the connection between electricity and magnetism as such; on the other hand it acts physically in the interesting phenomena of electrical *transmission* as such or of *conduction*, and of *distribution* (*Verteilung*).

Zusatz. This electrical relationship is activity, but an abstract activity, since it is not yet product; it is present only where the tension, the contradiction, is not yet resolved, so that each side contains its opposite and yet remains independent.

Now this tension is no mere internal mechanical tension of the parts but one that essentially must express itself. This expression must be different from the corporeality of the individual body, for this, in becoming different, remains what it is. At first, therefore, it is only the universal individuality of the body which is manifest, without the body's real corporeality entering into this process; this expression is therefore still only abstractly physical, i.e. the body shows its difference only by its general shining (*sein allgemeines Scheinen*). Thus the body shows its physical soul (*Seele*) as light; but whereas the solar light (*die Sonne*) is immediate and free, this light is rather called forth by the power of another body. Light, then, is in this case the mode of existence of bodies opposed to each other; this tensed light has the urge to differentiate itself upon the other body. But the differentiated bodies appear as light only in their vanishing, simply because the difference is as yet not independent but only abstract. What appears here consequently is not such a flame as results from friction, where light is the triumphant climax in the consuming of body; even the spark struck from a stone is a suspension of cohesion and a concentration of parts in a point. Here, however, ideality is manifest as preserving body—it is a gentle fire; the spark is cold, a mere light which as yet has no nutriment. For the specific materiality of the tensed body has not as yet entered into the process but is determined only in elemental fashion, in soul (*Seele*). But as differentiated, light is no longer pure but already coloured; the negative spark has a tinge of red, the positive a bluish hue. And since light is ideality breaking forth from physical body, the other physical determinations of total individuality, odour and taste, begin to be manifest, but in a quite ideal, immaterial way. Electricity smells; when close to one's nose it smells rather like cobwebs; one also notices a taste, but a bodiless one. The taste is in the sparks; one tastes more acid, the other more alkaline.

Lastly, in addition to taste, figures too appear: positive electricity has a longish, radiating spark, the negative spark is more concentrated into a point; this is seen when both sparks are made to strike on colophonium powder.

Reflection is accustomed to thinking of the individual body as something dead, which has only external, mechanical contacts, or chemical relationships, with other bodies. The expression of tension which we have here is accordingly not ascribed to the body itself but to another body, of which the former is only the vehicle; this other body has been called 'electrical matter'. This theory regards body as merely a sponge which lets such matter circulate within it, since body remains what it is, merely taking in more or less of this matter; this would be no immanent activity of body but only a transmission. Electricity is further made responsible for everything in Nature, and especially for meteorological phenomena. But the part electricity is supposed to have played in all this cannot be demonstrated. Since it is not matter, nor a propagation of things (*Dingen*), it appears, like magnetism, to be on the whole rather superfluous. In both cases, activity appears to be very restricted in scope; for if magnetism is the peculiar property of iron to point north, electricity merely is the making of a spark. But this is met with everywhere; and that is all, or almost all, there is to it. Electricity thus appears as an occult agent, like the occult properties assumed by the Scholastics. If it is present in thunderstorms, we do not see why it should be present elsewhere. But we must not think of such great natural phenomena as thunderstorms on the analogy of our chemical laboratories. For how can clouds rub against one another, being at least softer than a sponge? And since it lightens when it is already raining and when the whole sky is wrapped in a veil of moisture, all electrical tensions would necessarily be immediately neutralized, since the falling rain which connects the cloud with the earth is a perfect conductor (see above, § 286, p. 115). But even if electricity is present here the End, that is, the necessary linkage and connection of electricity with physical Nature has not been demonstrated. Electricity is, of course, the universal scapegoat, everything is electrical; but such a statement is vague, and leaves the function of electricity unspecified. We, however, see in electricity body's own selfhood which, as a physical totality, preserves itself when in contact with another body. It is body's own upsurge of anger which we see; no one else is there but body itself, least of all any foreign matter. Its youthful courage lashes out, it raises itself on its hind legs; its physical nature rouses itself to struggle desperately against the connection with an other, and it does so as the abstract ideality of light. It is not only we who compare bodies, they themselves compare themselves, and in doing so preserve their physical nature; it is a beginning of organic being which likewise preserves itself against the means of nutrition. The essential point here is that what is active is body's own immanent physical refractoriness.

It must be observed in this connection that what at first was an

I

immediate determination is now a posited one. Shape, namely, as crystal, was immediately transparent, just as the celestial bodies, being self-subsistent, were immediately lights. Now individual body is not immediately luminous, is not itself a light, since as Shape it is not an abstract ideality; on the contrary, as an explicated and developed unity, it includes the determination of the celestial bodies as a property in its individuality; immediately, therefore, it is only as the shining of an other in it, through it. In the crystal, it is true, form has brought the difference of material being-for-self back to unity; but this unity of form in its determinations is still not physical ideality, but only immanently determined mechanical totality. Light, on the other hand, is physical ideality; the crystal, therefore, not being self-luminous, is this ideality only *in principle* (*an sich*), since it manifests the latter only when reacting to an other. But what the crystal is in itself (*an sich*) must now be posited: thus this ideality, posited in developed totality, is no longer merely a shining of body as visible (*bloß ein Scheinen des Gesehenwerdens*), an alien incident light, but the simple totality of the shining of the self in the face of an other. That is to say, since the unity of form with itself is now posited, the crystal here constitutes itself a sun; the light which proceeds from it as a differentiated self, only[1] displays the crystal's totality in its peculiarity as a simple, physical existence.

How does electrical opposition (*Differenz*) arise? and how is it related to the physical properties of bodies? Electricity makes an appearance wherever two bodies come into contact, especially when they are rubbed. Electricity, therefore, does not merely attach to the electrical machine; but every pressure, every blow, produces electrical tension; contact, however, is the condition for this. Electricity is not a specific, particular phenomenon which occurs only in amber, shellac, etc.; it attaches, on the contrary, to every body in contact with another body; it is only a question of having a very fine electrometer to convince oneself of this. The angry self of body comes forth from every body when excited; they all exhibit this vitality towards one another. Now although positive electricity appears primarily in glass, and negative in resin (Biot and the French generally, still speak of *électricité résineuse et vitreuse*), this is a very narrow distinction, simply because all bodies are electrical: metals also are so, only they must be insulated. Negative electricity can also be produced in glass; for the kind of electricity produced depends on whether the glass plate is polished or rough: and this difference reveals different electricity, and so on. Haüy (*Traité de minéralogie*, part i, p. 237) says: 'Electricity divides the mineral kingdom into three great divisions which correspond to the general classes of minerals. Almost all stones and salts are made positively electric by friction, provided they have a certain degree of purity. Combustible substances such as resin, sulphur, also diamonds, are, on the other

[1] '*nur*' in the text is probably a misprint for '*nun*' and 'only' should read 'now'.

hand, negatively electric. The metals are conductors.' A neutral substance, therefore, has positive electricity: a differentiated substance
belonging to fire, to negative, self-subsistent being, exhibits negative
electricity: a substance without immanent difference, whose nature is
completely uniform, is fluid and a conductor. Thus almost all liquids are
conductors; oil alone is a bad conductor on account of its combustibility.
In general, electricity has this general connection with the specific
Qualities of Nature (*Natur-Qualitäten*); it is at the same time so superficial that even the slightest modification (*Unterschied*) of bodies is
sufficient to produce an alteration in electricity. Wax and silk, e.g., are
bad conductors; but if the former is melted and the latter heated, they
become good conductors, since heat makes them fluid. Ice is a good
conductor: dry air and dry gases, on the other hand, are very bad conductors. Polished glass, when rubbed with woollen stuff, becomes positively
electrical, negatively so when rubbed with a catskin. Silk rubbed with
resin yields negative electricity, with polished glass, positive. If two
quite similar glass tubes are rubbed together, one becomes negatively, the
other positively, charged; of two sticks of sealing wax, one likewise is
positively, the other negatively, charged. A silk ribbon when stroked
crosswise becomes negatively electrical, but if a similar ribbon is stroked
lengthwise, its electricity is positive. If two persons are insulated—if not,
their electricity goes to earth and they do not count as individuals—and
one of them holds a catskin in his hand and rubs the clothes of the other
with it, the first will be positively, the other negatively, charged. The
difference is due to the action of one of the parties. If molten sulphur is
poured into insulated metal vessels, the sulphur will acquire positive, the
metal negative, electricity; sometimes, however, the reverse also happens.
A principal factor is the one adduced by Biot (part ii, pp. 356–9): 'When
the surfaces of bodies are rubbed together, that surfaces seems to become
positive whose particles are least separated and deviate less from their
natural position relatively to each other. That surface, conversely, whose
particles are more scattered by the other's roughness, tends more strongly
to become negatively charged. This tendency is increased if the surface
actually expands. If an animal or vegetable substance, solid and dry, is
rubbed against a rough metallic surface, it becomes negatively charged
since its particles are more disarranged. But if, on the other hand, such a
substance is rubbed on very smooth metal which only slightly modifies
its surface, the effect being restricted to pressure and separation of
isolated particles, the substance then either gives no sign of electricity or
gives signs of positive electricity. If a catskin is rubbed on a polished or
unpolished metallic surface, the hairs can only yield to the pressure
without losing their relative position: they are therefore positively electrified. But if these same hairs, in the form of a woven material (which
involves their being crushed, twisted, and pressed back on themselves)
are rubbed against an unpolished metallic surface, they are not only compressed but separated from each other and pulled apart by the roughness

of this surface; this makes them negatively electrical, save when the metallic surface has a certain degree of smoothness.' Colour, too, makes a difference: 'Black silk material, if new, when rubbed against a white silk ribbon acquires negative electricity: plainly, because the black colouring of the material's surface makes it rougher. If, however, the black material has been used and its colour rubbed off, it acquires positive electricity if rubbed against a white ribbon. A white' (?silk) 'ribbon, rubbed against white woollen material, gives signs of negative electricity: rubbed against black woollen material, it shows positive electricity.' The difference, therefore, can be produced either by essential or by superficial qualities.

Pohl says in his review of Gehler's *Physical Dictionary*, published by Munke in three volumes (*Berliner Jahrbücher für wissenschaftliche Kritik*, 1829, October, No. 54, pp. 430 et seq.): 'We must recognize that electrical opposition, hardly less than the opposition of colours, comes close to the chemical opposition of oxidation and deoxidation, except that the latter opposition is extremely mobile (*beweglich*) and is often quite independent of the state of the mass and its more solid, internal qualitative relationships. We must recognize, too, that where two substances are interacting reciprocally in apparently similar conditions, and where the most delicate, careful observation is unable to detect further modifications, it requires but little effort on the part of Nature, in her active, playful urge towards manifestation, to cast the $+$ and $-$ of electrical opposition, now on one side and now on the opposite side; just as from the same seed of an individual plant, it sends forth the same species sometimes with a red, and sometimes with a blue, corolla.

'The commonest and at the same time most harmful consequence of the false supposition of causal relationships existing in isolation, a supposition imported without question into phenomenology, has reached an extreme in the case of electrical phenomena through the idea, everywhere rampant, of electricity as in a state of motion, as a current. In supposing that something which, in its true meaning, is only the first stirring of an incipient chemical process, is an isolated, independent fluid something which persists throughout the flux of phenomena, one no longer thinks of following up the process as such in its further development, and of recognizing the determinations which belong to it in their natural context. Instead, that which constitutes the veritable inner movement and development of the process itself is now, in accordance with the said fixed idea, straightway placed under the empty schema of a merely external movement of the said fictitious electric fluid, and viewed as a current which, next to the manifestation in the original form of tension, is exclusively asserted to be a second species of activity of this fundamental electrical substrate.

'This standpoint denotes a complete divergence from a natural view of phenomena and has initiated a series of shallow and erroneous conclusions, the baneful influence of which has hitherto infected all theories of electricity and galvanism, both generally and in their particular observations, up to the most recent researches in galvanism and electro-chemistry, which teem with all sorts of deceptions and absurdities.

'Even though before Oersted's discovery, the assumption that electri-city was actively present where the most sensitive electrometer gave not the least sign of its presence, could not properly be held to have an empirical basis, it is quite unjustifiable to stick to this assumption now that, in addition to the absence of any response from the electrometer, we see the magnetic needle immediately indicate the presence there, not of the electricity so long assumed to be present, but of magnetism.'

Electricity is the infinite form which is immanently differentiated and is the unity of these differences; and thus the two bodies are inseparably bound together, like the north and south poles of a magnet. But in magnetism there is only a mechanical activity, an opposition therefore only in the activity of movement; there is nothing to see, smell, taste, or feel—that is, no light, colour, odour, or taste. But in electricity, these variable (*schwebenden*) differences are physical, for they are in the light; if they were a further particularization of the bodies, we should have the chemical process. Of course, so far as in electricity the element of differ-ence is active and as such still remains active, this activity, too, can consist only in mechanical movement. It is an approach and a withdrawal, as in magnetism; this accounts for electrical rain, electrical chimes, etc. Negative electricity is attracted by positive, but repelled by negative. The different elements, in thus forming a unity, communicate themselves to each other; but as soon as they form a unity, they again flee from each other, and conversely. In magnetism, only one body is required, one which does not as yet possess physical determinateness but is only a substrate of this activity. In the electrical process, each of the two different bodies has a different determination, which is posited only by the other body; but as opposed to this, the rest of the body's individuality remains free and distinct. Both kinds of electricity therefore require for their existence an individual body of their own; or we may say that one electrical body has only one kind of electricity, but causes another body outside of it to be charged with the opposite kind: and where we have one kind of electricity, the other is at once also present. But the same body does not polarize itself inwardly, as is the case in magnetism. Electricity, therefore, although it has the same fundamental syllogistic determination as magnetism, has raised the *opposition* to an existence of its own. Schelling therefore called electricity 'ruptured magnetism'. As a process it is more concrete than magnetism, but less concrete than chemi-cal process. The tensed extremes still fail to make up an actual, total process; they are still independent, so that their process is only their abstract self. For physical difference does not constitute the entire nature of body; and for this reason electricity is only the abstract totality of the physical sphere. What, therefore, magnetism is in the sphere of shape, that electricity is in the sphere of physical totality.

When a body is electrically charged, its electricity can be communicated, especially to conductors, like metals, for example; though metal, when insulated, can equally well acquire its own electricity as self-differentiating; so, too, can glass, only it is not a conductor. But as communicated, the electricity of each body is of the same kind; such bodies then repel each other. Physicists further distinguish between electricity which is communicated and electricity distributively manifested (*sich durch Verteilung zeigt*). The latter is as follows: A body *A* is charged with positive electricity. A cylinder *B*, an insulated conductor, is placed close to it without touching it, with the result that the conductor, too, is electrified, but in such a way that the end turned towards body *A* is negatively charged, the opposite end positively charged, while the middle is neutral. Two different cases are to be noticed: (α) when *B* is removed from the electrical sphere of *A*, its electricity vanishes. (β) But if it is still near to *A* and its positive end is brought into contact with a third body *C* (which through this communication takes the positive charge from *B*), then when *B* is removed from the sphere of *A*, it is still electrified but only negatively. The reason for this is that to fix electricity, two individual bodies are required, one for positive and the other for negative electricity. Now so long as body *B* has not been touched, it contains tension and difference within itself, like magnetism, though this does not constitute its individual determinateness; but, being brought into proximity with another body which is already self-determined, it has its determination only through another. In all this it remains, as a conductor, indifferent; but because it is also in the electrical sphere it can, as extended, display differing determinations. Although, therefore, it possesses both electricities, electricity still does not exist as attaching to body itself; it is not till the body has only one of the electricities, that electricity enters upon individual existence: this requires that the body should be opposed by another body. Now since through this contact the indifference of body *B* is removed, and the opposite electricity to that which it turns to body *A* passes into body *C* with which it is in contact, body *B*, on the other hand, becomes charged with the other electricity. Also, since the proximity of the bodies is already a binding (*Binden*) of their opposition, the negative electricity of body *B* is stronger, the greater its distance from *A*; and its intensity diminishes the nearer it is brought to *A*. Two glass plates rubbed against each other and insulated, show no trace of electricity when brought near each other; but when separated they do. This is not true of metal plates, even when insulated, since their electricity is also implicitly neutralized. If two spheres of the same size, and having similar electricity, are brought into contact, then the intensity at the point of contact = o, and is stronger at the remote points of the spheres. If spheres of unequal size and similar electricity are used, then the electricity is likewise = o at the point of contact; but when they are separated, there is negative electricity at the point of contact of the smaller sphere. If, however, the distance is increased, this determination vanishes, and the whole of the smaller sphere is positively charged. Here, it is the inequality of the amount which posits this opposition. Haüy (*Traité de minéralogie*, part i, p. 237) also remarks that tourmaline and many other crystals with asymmetrical forms, when placed in warm water or even over a fire, acquire electric poles at just those parts of their extremities which violate symmetry, whereas in the middle they are indifferent.

As regards the *effects* of electricity, these are shown principally in the removal of the tension. If the electrified body is connected with water, the tension ceases. The amount of electricity a body can take up depends on its surface. A bottle can be electrified up to the point where it bursts; i.e. the glass can no longer resist the increased tension. The capital instance of the removal of tension is when the two electricities come into contact. Each is incomplete without the other, and they want to totalize themselves: they remain in a forced state if kept apart. The substanceless opposites have no enduring existence; they form a tension which is spontaneously self-resolving. As thus collapsing into their unity, they are the electric light which in appearing vanishes. But the essence of this light is the negativity of the indifferent existence of shape, and this negativity itself has existence. The light forces its way into the shape and, shattering its indifference, it is inner and outer form concentrated into unity. The form which has become like itself is the light which breaks forth from within and flows into the light outside: the being-within-self of gravity which, in destroying itself, and in its vanishing, just becomes powerless, simple light, i.e. is simply one with the outer light; it is thus that Plato grasps Seeing as a fusion of inner and outer light. Through the connection established between the tensed bodies, one difference hurls itself into the other, the two electricities reciprocally completing each other. This product, however, is only a play, the loss of two abstract determinations—the interpenetration of these sparks. The main result is the destruction of the bodies brought into contact: electricity shatters pieces of wood, kills animals, breaks panes of glass, heats and fuses metal wire, melts gold, etc. That the effects of electricity can just as well be produced by mechanical pressure is shown by the electric pistol: this is charged with two volumes of hydrogen and one of oxygen, which are transformed into water by the electric spark. The chemical side of the electrical process is the decomposition of water. As it is not the individuality of the body which enters into the tension, electrical action can only produce a physical result in the Element of abstract neutrality, water. It has the power of decomposing water into hydrogen and oxygen, though we already know (see above, § 286, *Zusatz*, p. 117) hat these are not the ingredients of water but only the abstract forms in which water is manifested. For in the galvanic process, no bubbles are seen moving about in the glass tube, nor is there any change in an acid placed in the middle of the tube—though this would be inevitable if these gases did pass through the tube.

§ 325

The *particularization* of the individual body does not stop at an inert diversity of properties and their own, separate activities, from which in the (electrical) process the abstract, pure selfhood of body, the light-principle, first issues in the tension of opposed moments and then resolves the latter in their indifference. Since the particular properties are only the reality of this simple Notion, the body of their soul, of *light*, and since the complex of the properties, the particular body, is not truly independent, the *entire* corporeality therefore enters into tension, into a process which is at the same time the *becoming* of the individual body. Shape, which at first only proceeded from the Notion and therefore was posited only *in principle* (*an sich*), now issues from an existent process and presents itself as the posited outcome of an existence—the *chemical process*.

Zusatz. We began with Shape in its immediate form, and its necessity has been ascertained from the Notion. But Shape must in the end also display itself as existing, i.e. as the outcome of a process. Body, as immediate, presupposes the real chemical process. Parents are thus the immediate from which one begins: but as regards their existence they, too, are characterized as posited. Shape, in conformity with its Notion, passes into this third stage; but this is rather the First from which what was previously the First, first proceeds. This is founded in the deeper logical advance. Particularization does not stop at the moment of difference as the tension of abstract selfhood. Body as particular is not independent, not self-subsistent, but a link in the chain and in relation to what is other. This is the omnipotence of the Notion which we already saw in the electrical process; in this excitation of a body by an other, it is only the abstract selfhood of the bodies which comes into play and is manifest. But the process must become a real process of the bodily determinations, their whole corporeality entering into the process. The relativity of body must be manifest, and this manifestation is the alteration of body in the chemical process.

C. THE CHEMICAL PROCESS

§ 326

In individuality developed into a totality, the moments themselves are determined as individual totalities, as whole particular bodies which, at the same time, are in relation only as different towards each other. This relation, as the identity of non-identical, independent bodies, is contradiction, and hence is essentially *process*, the function of which, in conformity with the Notion, is the positing of the differentiated as identical, the removal of difference, and the differentiation of the identical, the enlivening and dissociation of it.

Zusatz. To understand the *general position and nature of the chemical process*, we must look forwards and backwards. Chemical process is the third stage in the process of shape. The second was differentiated shape and its abstract process, electricity. We also had a process in shape before it achieved completeness and neutrality, namely, magnetism. If shape is the unity of Notion and reality, then magnetism, as at first only abstract activity, is the Notion of shape; the second stage, the particularization of shape within itself and against an other, is electricity; the third stage is the self-realizing unrest of the chemical process, as the veritable reality of the Notion in this sphere. As in magnetism, there is one form which sunders itself into differences and exists as a unity; yet it does not stop there. In magnetism, the difference is manifest in one body. In electricity, each difference belongs to a separate body; each difference is self-subsistent, and the whole shape does not enter into this process. Chemical process is the totality of the life of inorganic individuality; for here we have whole, physically determined shapes. Bodies enter into the process not merely as having odour, taste, and colour, but as being odorous matter, tasting and coloured matter. Their relation is not one of movement but of alteration of the entire different matters, the vanishing of their distinctive characteristics. The abstract relation of the body which is its light, is not only abstractly, but essentially, this particular relation; the whole corporeality therefore enters this process, and the chemical process is consequently the *real* electrical process. Thus we have the whole shape, as in magnetism, though not one whole but distinct wholes. The two sides into which the form sunders itself are thus whole bodies, such as metals, acids, and alkalis; their truth is that they enter into relation. The electrical moment in the process is that these sides separate themselves out to have their own independent existence; this did not happen in magnetism. The inseparable unity of magnetism likewise dominates the two sides; this identity of both bodies which makes them return once more to the magnetic relation is absent from the electrical process.

The chemical process is thus the unity of magnetism and electricity, which are the abstract, formal sides of this totality and are for that reason not the same process. Every chemical process contains magnetism and electricity in principle (*an sich*). But they cannot appear in their distinctiveness in the, so to speak, saturated course of the process; they can do so only when the chemical process is itself an abstract manifestation,

when it does not attain its full reality. This is so in the universal individuality of the Earth. The fully realized (*für sich*) chemical process is the
universal process of the Earth; but we must distinguish between the process of the individuality proper and the universal individuality. In the
latter, which is self-maintaining, even the chemical process, though
spontaneous (*lebendig*), can only manifest itself in an abstractly universal
way. The Earth-individuality is not a particular individuality which can
resolve itself and achieve real self-neutralization with another. For as a
universal individuality, Earth endures and does not therefore enter into
the chemical process which affects a whole Shape; only in so far as its
existence is not universal, i.e. in so far as it divides itself into particular
bodies, does it enter into chemical process. The chemistry of Earth, then,
is what we have seen the meteorological process to be, the process of
physical Elements as universally determined matters which are not yet
individual corporealities. Since the chemical process exists here thus
abstractly, its abstract moments come to view here, too. It is on Earth,
consequently, which has alteration outside it, that magnetism makes its
appearance, and likewise the electric tension of the thunderstorm. The
electricity of Earth, which includes lightning, the northern lights, etc.,
however, differs in kind from ordinary electricity and is not tied to the
same conditions (see above, § 286, *Zusatz*, p. 115; § 324, *Zusatz*, p. 225).
Magnetism and electricity are merely borne by the chemical process;
it is through the universal process of Earth that they themselves are first
posited. The magnetism which determines a single magnetic needle is
subject to alteration and depends on the inner process of Earth and the
meteorological process. Parry, on his expedition to the north pole, found
that there the magnetic needle became quite indefinite; e.g. in a thick fog
its direction northwards was quite indifferent; the needle lost its activity
and could be pushed in what direction one wished. Electrical phenomena
such as the northern lights, etc., are considerably more variable. The
northern lights have been seen near midday south of England, even
south of Spain. They are, then, only moments of the total process, on
which they depend. Electrical tension also arises in the chemical process,
especially when this is galvanic; but it also carries magnetic tendencies
with it. This dependence of magnetism on chemical process is a remarkable recent discovery. The general revolution of the Earth, its rotation
about its axis, which is the east–west polarity, determines the south–north
polarity, the direction of the stationary axis. Oersted found that electrical
and magnetic activities, in so far as they are related as spatial directions,
are also opposites which cross one another. Electricity runs in an east-
to-west direction, while magnetism runs from north to south; but this
can also be reversed (cf. *supra*, § 313, *Zusatz*, p. 172). Magnetism,
however, is essentially mere spatial activity, whereas electricity has a
more physical character. This discovery also shows the simultaneous
togetherness of these moments in the chemical process of the individual
corporeality, and it does so by showing them to issue from the galvanic

process as separate and distinct manifestations of electricity and chemical action.

The difference of the philosophically systematic mode of treatment from the empirical is that it does not treat levels of concrete existences in Nature as totalities, but as levels of characters, determinations. Thus when we have first considered the Earth as a planet, its concrete nature has not been exhausted; a further determination of physical moments is, on the contrary, a further determination of Earth, so far as such determinations are proper to Earth as a universal individuality, for the finite relationships of individual bodies do not concern Earth. This is precisely the case with the relationships here. The hierarchy of these relationships and their inter-relatedness is one thing, but the consideration of a concrete, individual body as such is another. The individual body unites all these determinations within itself and is like a bouquet in which they are bound together. To apply these observations to the present case, Earth as a self-subsistent individuality opposed to the Sun does in fact exhibit chemical process, but only as a process of Elements. At the same time, the chemical process of Earth is to be grasped only as a past process, for these giant members [the Elements], enjoying a separate and independent existence, remain at the stage of diremption, not passing over into neutrality. On the other hand, process as it comes to view in particular corporeal individualities brings about their reduction to neutral existences which can be taken apart again. This process is inferior to the universal process; *we* are restricted to it, whereas the meteorological process is the great chemistry of Nature. But on the other hand, it ranks higher, since it immediately precedes the vital process. For in the latter, no member can endure or exist as a part, but endures only in the subjective unity; and it is the subjective unity which is the actuality of the vital process. The process of the heavenly bodies is, on the other hand, still abstract since they remain in their independence; the individual chemical process therefore is deeper, since in it the truth of particular bodies becomes actual, namely, that they seek and attain their unity.

This is the position of the chemical process in the whole. We must distinguish in it the process of the Elements and the particular process, simply because particular bodies are not only particular but belong also to the universal Elements. Consequently, when they are in process as particular bodies, the universal meteorological process must also be manifest in them, simply because it is the universal process. All chemical processes are bound up with the general process of the Earth. The galvanic process is also determined by the seasons and time of day; this is especially noticeable in the electrical and magnetic sides of the process, each in its own way. These activities have their periods, apart from other variations: these periodic variations have been accurately observed and reduced to formulae. Something of the kind has also been observed in the chemical process, but not to the same extent: e.g. Ritter found that a solar eclipse produced variations. But this connection is more remote; it is not the case that the Elements as such enter into this process. There is, however, in every chemical process, a determination of the universal Elements, for the particular formations are only subjectivized forms (*Subjectivi*^e*rungen*) of the universal Elements which still stand in relation to them. If, therefore, particular qualities are altered in the chemical process, this also involves a determining of the universal Elements. Water is essentially a condition or a product; fire, similarly, is a cause or an effect.

As in this way the Notion of the chemical process is in general to be totality, we have to think of the Notion as wholly immanent in its differences: i.e. in positing itself as the negative of itself, it remains quite at home with itself. Each side, therefore, is the whole. As one side of the process, the acid is, of course, not what the alkali is, and vice versa; both are thus one-sided. But the further point is that each side is also in itself the other, the totality of itself and the other; this is the thirst of the alkali for the acid, and conversely. The moment the bodies are activated (*begeistet*), they seize hold of each other; if they can find nothing better, they enter into process with the air. That each is in itself the other, is demonstrated by each seeking the other; each is therefore the contradiction of itself: but everything only has an impulse in so far as it is this self-contradiction. This first begins in the chemical process, for here, this contradiction of being *in itself* neutral, *in itself* the whole, brings about the infinite urge; in Life, this is further brought *to view*. The chemical process is thus an analogue of Life; the inner restlessness (*Regsamkeit*) of Life, there before our eyes, may astonish us. If the chemical process could carry itself on *spontaneously*, it would be Life; this explains our tendency to see Life in terms of chemistry.

§ 327

First of all, we must set aside the *formal* process which is a combination of merely different, unopposed bodies; such bodies do not require a Third, or middle term, in which they could be *virtually* (*an sich*) one. The determinateness of their existential relationship consists in their common nature or genus; their combination or dissociation is immediate and the properties of the bodies are preserved. Such combinations of bodies chemically inactive towards each other are amalgams and other alloys of metals, mixtures of acids with each other, of alcohol, etc., with water, and so forth.

Zusatz. Winterl* has called this process *synsomaty*; this name is not

* He was a professor at Pesth, and at the beginning of this (19th) century, had

found elsewhere and has accordingly been omitted from the third edition. These synsomaties are combinations formed directly without any intermediary which would produce and itself undergo change; they are still, in consequence, not strictly chemical processes. Fire certainly is involved in metallic amalgams, but it is not an intermediary which itself enters the process. When various incomplete bodies are made to form a unity, we ask what it is in them that has been changed. We must reply: That which makes them these particular bodies. Now the first, original determinateness which renders them particular bodies is their specific gravity, and next their cohesion. The combination of such bodies belonging to the same class is, therefore, no mere mixture, since their specific difference suffers modification in their combination. But since these determinatenesses belonging to the general particularity of bodies lie beyond the sphere of real physical difference, their alteration is still not a characteristically chemical change, but the alteration of the substantial inwardness of the body which does not yet reach to external existence of specific difference as such. We must therefore distinguish this particular mode of alteration from the chemical process; for though it occurs in every chemical process, it must also have a special, free existence of its own. The mixture is not external, but a genuine combination. Thus, water and alcohol mixed together, completely permeate each other; true, the weight is the same as when they were separate, but the specific density differs from the quantitative unity of both since they now occupy a smaller space. Similarly, gold and silver melted together occupy a smaller space. That is why the goldsmith who was given gold and silver by Hiero to make a crown was suspected of fraudulently keeping part of it for himself; for Archimedes had calculated the weight of the whole mixture on the basis of the specific weight of the two bodies. But Archimedes may well have done the goldsmith an injustice. Not only do specific gravity and cohesion alter, but colour also. In brass, which is an alloy of copper and tin, the red colour of the copper turns to yellow. With mercury, which readily amalgamates with gold and silver but not with iron and cobalt, there is a specific ratio in which each metal saturates itself with the other. For example, if too little silver has been taken, the unsaturated portion of the mercury runs off; or if there is too much silver, part of it does not enter into the change. Some combinations also have greater hardness and density than the metals taken singly; this is because difference represents a higher being-within-self, whereas the undifferentiated body is lighter. At the same time, amalgams are more fusible than the individual metals of which they are composed would argue, since, on the contrary, a body immanently differentiated is more open to chemical change and offers less resistance to it: just as the strongest natures are most obstinate in the face of violence, but freely

an urge towards deeper insight into chemistry. He claimed to have discovered a particular substance, *Andronia*, but his claim has not been substantiated.

and unreservedly yield themselves to those of kindred spirit. D'Arcet's alloy (*Schnellloth*), a mixture of 8 parts bismuth, 5 parts lead, and 3 parts tin, melts at a temperature below the boiling-point of water, will in fact melt in a warm hand. There are also earths, not by themselves fusible, which become so in combination, a fact of some importance in metallurgy, where it facilitates operations in foundries. Here we also must include the refining of metals, since this rests on the diversity of melting-point in combinations. Silver, e.g., combined with copper, is refined with the aid of lead: the heat which melts the lead carries the silver off with it; but the gold remains combined with the copper if any is present. Aqua regia is a combination of hydrochloric and nitric acids: the separate acids do not dissolve gold, but only when thus combined. These synsomaties, therefore, are alterations only of the inner, implicit (*an sich seienden*) difference. The chemical process proper, however, presupposes more determinate opposition; from this a still greater activity and a more specific product are born.

§ 328

The *real* process is, however, also connected with chemical difference (§§ 200 ff.), the whole concrete totality of the body at the same time entering into it (§ 325). The bodies which enter into the real process are mediated in a third body distinct from them. This third is to the two extremes their abstract, merely at first *implicit*, unity which the process brings into existence. It accordingly comprises only *Elements*, these being distinguished as the Element of combination (*des Vereinens*), abstract neutrality as such—*water*; and as the Element of differentiation and dissociation—*air*. As, in Nature, the different moments of the Notion acquire separate existence, so here too the dissociative and neutralizing sides of the process are each in themselves twofold, each, namely, has a concrete and an abstract side. *Dissociation* is, on the one hand, a splitting up of neutral corporeality into material constituents, and on the other, a differentiation of the abstract physical Elements into the four yet more abstract chemical moments of Nitrogen, Oxygen, Hydrogen, and Carbon, which together constitute the totality of the Notion, determined in accordance with its moments. We have accordingly as the chemical elements: 1. the abstraction of indifference, *Nitrogen*; 2. the two elements of opposition, (*a*) the element of self-subsistent difference, *Oxygen*, the consuming element, and (*b*) the element of indifference which belongs to the opposition, *Hydrogen*, the combustible element; 3. the abstraction of their *individual* element, *Carbon*.

Combination similarly is, on the one hand, a neutralizing of concrete corporealities, on the other, a neutralizing of these abstract chemical elements. The concrete and abstract sides of the process are, furthermore, as much united as distinct; it is from the differences of the physical Elements, which are the mean of the extremes of the process, that the indifferent concrete corporealities are activated; i.e. their chemical difference acquires an existence which presses on to neutralization and passes over into it.

Zusatz. The general nature of the chemical process is, as a totality, the double activity of dissociation and the reduction of the separated parts to unity; and since the shaped bodies which take part in the process must come into contact with each other as totalities, so that their essential determinatenesses touch—which is not possible if they only attack each other by friction as mechanically indifferent bodies do in the superficial electrical process—they must meet in what is indifferent which, as their indifference, is an abstract, physical Element—water as the principle of affirmation, and air as the principle of fire, of being-for-self, of negation. The Elements which form this middle term take part in the process and determine themselves to differences; equally, they again fuse together into the physical Elements. Here, therefore, the Element is either the active principle in which individual bodies first display their activity towards each other, or else it is manifest as passive determination, as a transformation into abstract forms. The extremes are, however, combined to form the middle term; or if they are neutral bodies, e.g. salts, they are decomposed into extremes. The chemical process is therefore a *syllogism*; and not merely the beginning of the process but its entire course is syllogistic. For the process requires three terms, namely, two self-subsistent extremes, and one middle term in which their determinatenesses come into contact and they are differentiated: whereas in the merely formal chemical process (see preceding §) only two terms were needed. Fully concentrated acid, which as such contains no water, when poured on metal either fails to dissolve it or else has only a weak action on it; if, on the other hand, it is diluted with water, it attacks the metal vigorously, simply because the process calls for three terms. It is the same with air. Trommsdorff says: 'Even in dry air, lead soon loses its lustre, but it does so even more quickly in moist air. Pure water does not act on lead if air cannot get to it: if therefore a piece of freshly melted lead which is still very lustrous is put into a glass which is filled up with freshly distilled water and then sealed, the lead remains quite unchanged. Lead, on the other hand, which lies under water in vessels open to the air, soon loses all its lustre.' The same is true of iron: rust, consequently, is formed only when the air is moist; if the air is dry and warm, the iron is not affected.

The four chemical elements are the abstractions of the physical Elements, whereas these latter are real in themselves. For some time it was thought that all bases were composed of such simple substances, just as they are now supposed to be composed of metallic substances. Guiton supposed lime to be composed of nitrogen, carbon, and hydrogen: talc, of lime and nitrogen, potassium, of lime and hydrogen, and sodium, of talc and hydrogen. In vegetable and animal organisms, Steffens again tried to find the opposition of carbon and nitrogen, and so on. Such abstractions, however, appear on their own as chemical differences in individual bodies only because process gives the universal physical Elements, as a middle term, the character of existing differences, and thereby separates them into these abstractions. Water is thus differentiated into oxygen and hydrogen, Just as it is not permissible to represent water as *consisting* of oxygen and hydrogen (as physicists do), a point to which we drew particular attention in connection with meteorology (§ 286, *Zusatz*, p. 117), so air, too, must not be thought of as consisting of oxygen and nitrogen, for these too are only the forms under which air is posited. These abstractions, then, are not integrated through one another, but in a third term, in the extremes, which have got rid of their abstraction and have completed themselves into the totality of the Notion. As regards the chemical elements, they are called substances (*Stoffe*) after their bases, regardless of their form. Yet with the exception of carbon, none of them can be kept on its own as a substance (*Stoff*) but exhibited only in the form of a gas. Yet they are, as such, material, ponderable existences, since, e.g., metal, when oxidized by the addition of oxygen, also gains in weight; and white lead, for instance, i.e. lead in combination with the abstract chemical element of oxygen, weighs more than lead in its pure state. Lavoisier's theory is based upon this. The specific gravity of the metal is, however, reduced; it loses its indifferently solid character.

These four elements constitute a totality in the following manner: (α) Nitrogen is the dead residue, corresponding to metalleity: it cannot be inhaled, nor does it burn; but it can be differentiated, oxidized—the air of the atmosphere is an oxide of nitrogen. (β) Hydrogen is the positive side of the determinateness in the opposition, the differentiated nitrogen-gas; it is incapable of supporting animal life and animals are soon suffocated in it. Phosphorus does not catch fire in it and it extinguishes a light or any burning substance plunged into it; but it is itself combustible and can be made to burn as soon as the air of the atmosphere or oxygen-gas has access to it. (γ) The other side of the determinateness, the negative, the activating principle, is oxygen; it possesses a characteristic smell and taste and activates the former two elements. (δ) The fourth element in the totality is the defunct individuality, carbon—ordinary coal, the chemical, terrestrial element. In its transfigured form it is the diamond, which is held to be pure carbon and is, as rigid terrestrial Shape, crystalline. Whereas carbon alone can exist independently, the other elements achieve separate existence only by force and so only exist momentarily. It is these chemical determinations which make up the forms out of which solid substances are in general integrated. Only nitrogen remains outside the process; but hydrogen, oxygen, and carbon are the differing moments which are beaten into physically individual bodies, whereby these lose their one-sidedness.

§ 329

The process is *abstractly* the identity of judgement (*Urteilens*) and the unification (*In-Eins-Setzen*) of the terms distinguished by the judgement; and in its course, the process is a totality returning into itself. But its *finitude* consists in this, that the moments of the process also possess bodily independence, so that the totality contains the *presupposition* of *immediate* corporealities, which, however, are equally only the products of the process. Because of this immediacy, the bodies appear to exist outside of the process, and the process to come to them. For the same reason, too, the *moments in the course* of the process fall apart into immediate and distinct processes; the course of the process as a real totality becomes a circle of *particular processes*, each of which presupposes the other but is itself initiated from without and becomes extinct in its particular product, without from its own resources continuing itself and passing immanently into the process which forms the next moment of the totality. In one of these processes, the body appears as condition. and in another as product; and its specific chemical nature is determined by the particular process in which it occupies one or the other position. Only on the basis of these positions in the particular processes can a classification of bodies be founded.

The two sides of the process are: (1) the passage from the indifferent body, through its activation, to neutrality; and (2) from this combination (*Vereinung*) back to dissociation into indifferent bodies.

Zusatz. The chemical process is still *finite* in comparison with the organic process: (α) since the unity of the diremption and the diremption itself, which are absolutely inseparable in the vital process (for in this, the unity perpetually converts itself into object; and what it thus separates off from itself perpetually converts into its own self), this infinite activity still falls apart into two sides in the chemical process. That the differentiated sides can be brought together again is, for them, an external and indifferent affair; with the diremption, one process was finished, and a new one can now begin. (β) The finitude of the chemical process consists further in the fact that although each one-sided chemical process is again also the totality, still it is so only in a formal way: combustion, for example, i.e. the positing of a difference, oxidation, finishes as diremption; but with such a one-sided process there is also produced a neutrality: water, too, is generated. And conversely, in the process which culminates in the neutral body, there is also differentiation, but only in an abstract manner, gases, namely, are developed. (γ) The shapes, then, which appear in the process are in the first instance stable (*ruhend*); the process consists in the positing of such distinct formations into a unity, or in forcing them out of their indifferent existence into difference, without the body being able to preserve itself. The implicit unity of the distinct sides is, it is true, the absolute condition; but since they still appear as distinct bodies, they are only in principle, or notionally, one, and their unity has not yet come into existence. Acid and caustic potash are in principle (*an sich*) identical, the acid is in itself (*an sich*) alkali; and that is why it thirsts for the alkali, as caustic potash thirsts for acid. Each has the urge to integrate itself, i.e. each is in itself neutral, but it does not yet exist as neutral. The finitude of the chemical process here, therefore, is that the two sides of Notion and existence do not yet correspond to each other, whereas in the living creature the identity of the differences also *exists*. (δ) True, in the chemical process, the differences sublate their one-sidedness; but this sublation is only relative, a lapse into another one-sidedness. The metals become oxides, a substance changes to acid: neutral products which again are always one-sided. (ε) It follows from this, too, that the totality of the process breaks up into distinct processes. The process whose product is one-sided, is itself incomplete, is not the total process. The process is finished when one determinateness has been posited in the other; therefore this process is not itself the genuine totality, but only one moment of the whole, total process. In itself, each process is the totality of the process; but this totality breaks up into distinct processes and products. The Idea of the chemical process in its entirety is thus a series (*Verlauf*) of broken processes which represent the various stages and transitional points of that series.

(ζ) Another feature of the finitude of the chemical process is that it is to these same stages of this process that the particular individual corporeal forms belong: in other words, the particular corporeal individualities are determined according to the stage of the process to which they belong. The superficiality of the electrical process still has a very slight connection with the individuality of the body, in that the smallest determination will cause a body to become charged with positive or negative electricity; it is in the chemical process that this connection first becomes important. In the various chemical processes there are a host of sides and substances which can be distinguished. Before one can grasp this complex, one must distinguish in each process, which substances are active and which are not; and the two must not be set on the same level but must be kept well apart. The nature of a body depends on its position in relation to the various processes in which it plays the part of generator, determinant, or product. True, it is also capable of entering into still other processes, but it is not the determining factor in them. Thus in the galvanic process, pure metal is the determining factor; it does indeed also pass over into the process of fire as alkali and acid, but these do not give it its place in the total process. Sulphur also has a relationship to acid and is effective as so related; but it is in its relationship to fire that it is a determining factor. This gives it its place. In empirical chemistry, however, bodies are described by their reactions to all chemical substances. If a new metal is discovered, its reactions to the whole range of chemical substances are gone through. A glance at textbooks of chemistry to ascertain how the various bodies are classified, shows the main distinction to be between so-called simple bodies and those which are combinations of such bodies. Lumped together under the former heading one finds Nitrogen, Hydrogen, Oxygen, Carbon, Phosphorus, Sulphur, Gold, Silver, and the rest of the metals. But one sees at the first glance that these things are quite heterogeneous. Compounds also are certainly products of the process; but the so-called simple bodies also result from the more abstract processes. Finally, for chemists, it is the dead product resulting from this or that process that is the main thing described. But in truth, the main thing is the process and the sequence of stages of the processes; its course is the determining factor, and the determinatenesses of the individual bodies have significance solely in its distinct stages. This, however, is the finite, formal process in which each body through its particularity exhibits a modified course of the total process. It is precisely the particular behaviour of the body and its specially modified process, which is the subject-matter of chemistry, which presupposes the body's determinatenesses as given. Here, on the contrary, we must consider the process in its totality, how it distinguishes the classes of bodies, and characterizes them as stages of its course, stages which become fixed.

The process in its *totality*, in which it fixes its stages in particular individual bodies, causes these stages themselves to appear as processes of a particular kind. The totality of these is a chain of particular processes; they are a circle whose periphery is itself a chain of processes. The totality of the chemical process is thus a system of particular modes of the process: (1) In the formal process of the synsomaties with which we have already dealt (§ 327), the difference is not yet a real one. (2) In the actual process, the crucial point is the mode in which the activity exists: (a) in galvanism it exists as a diversity of indifferent bodies; here, too, the difference is not yet present as a reality, but the mere diversity is posited by the activity of the process as a real difference. Thus we have metals here whose differences are in contact; and because in this association they are active, i.e. are really different, we have process there. (b) In the process of fire, the activity has independent existence apart from the body; for fire is this immanently negative, destructive being-for-self, the restless, really different Element whose outcome is the positing of difference. This process is in the first instance elemental and abstract; its outcome, which is to give fire a bodily existence, is the transition to the caustic alkalis, to active acids. (c) The third stage now is the process of these active substances, whereas the first was the positing of the oxide, the second the positing of the acid. The differentiating activity now exists in bodily form. This production is the reduction to neutrality, the production of salts. (d) Finally, we have the return of the neutral substance to its beginnings, to acid, to oxide, and to radical. The process starts with the indifferent body, then comes the positing of the differentiated bodies, then their opposition, and lastly, the neutral body as product. But since the neutral body is itself one-sided, it is in turn reduced to an indifferent one. The indifferent body is the presupposition of the chemical process and this presupposition is the product of the process. In empirical treatment the forms of the substances (Körper) are the main thing; but the starting-point must be the particular forms of process and these must be distinguished. It is only in this way that the empirically endless variety of substances can be grouped into a rational system, and that one can avoid that abstract universality which chaotically lumps everything together.

1. *Combination* (Vereinung)

§ 330

(a) Galvanism

The *beginning* of the process, and consequently of the *first* particular process, is made by *metal*; metals are, in regard to form, *immediate*, indifferent corporealities in which distinct properties are as yet undeveloped and concentrated into the *simple* determination of specific gravity. Metals—the *first* kind of bodies, distinguished only inactively one from the other—initiate the process by imparting to each other their immanent determinateness and difference, through this compact unity of their nature (they are *in principle* fluid and are conductors of heat and electricity). In doing so, they enter into a state of tension towards each other, for they are at the same time independent; the tension is thus still *electrical.* But in the neutral, hence separable, medium of water, in combination with air, their difference can actualize itself. Through the neutrality of water, and hence of its real capacity for differentiation—the water may be pure, or salt, etc., may be added to make it capable of a more concrete action—a real (not merely electrical) activity develops between the metal in its state of tension and the water; with this, there is a transition from the *electrical* to the *chemical* process. Its production is oxidation generally, and deoxidation or hydrogenation of the metal (if the process goes so far), or at least the generation of hydrogen gas and likewise oxygen gas: that is, a positing in abstract, independent existence (§ 328) of the differences into which the neutral Element has been sundered; just as, at the same time, their union with the base comes into existence in the *oxide* (or *hydrate*): the *second* kind of corporeality.

Remark

On this exposition of the process, in so far as it is present in its *first* stage, there is no difficulty either in distinguishing between the electrical and chemical aspects of the process in general, and of the galvanic process in particular, or in grasping their connection. But physicists persist in seeing only electricity in the galvanic *process*, so that the difference between the extremes and middle term of the syllogism is grasped merely as a difference between dry and wet *conductors*, extremes and middle term being alike classed as *conductors*. It is not necessary here to take account of further modifications of the process: e.g. the extremes can be different fluids and the middle term a metal; in some cases, the form of electricity (as stated in the Paragraph) can be held to, and sometimes made to predominate, whereas sometimes the chemical action can be intensified; also whereas metals are so independent that they can be differentiated only by the help of water and other more concrete neutral substances or by substances such as acids or alkalis which are already in a state of chemical opposition, in order to pass over into oxides, the *metalloids*, by contrast, so lack independence that their differentiation is set off simply by contact with the air, which converts them into *earths*, etc. These and many other particularities do not alter the basic phenomenon of the galvanic process, which we shall call by its first, well-deserved name, but on the contrary, tend to confuse our treatment of it. The fundamental affliction which has killed a clear and simple treatment of the process, once its simple chemical character had been shown up in the voltaic pile, has been the conception of *wet conductors*. This has resulted in the ignoring, the giving up, of the conception, of the simple, empirically evident fact that water, the middle term of the process, is originally and manifestly *active*. It is regarded not as an active, but as a passive *conductor*, with the consequence that electricity, too, is regarded as something complete in itself and as only flowing through water as it does through metals; for metals, too, are in this connection seen only as *conductors*, and in comparison with water, as first-class conductors. However, the *active* relationship of water in the process, ranging from the simplest relation, i.e. between water and a single metal, to the complex relations arising from modified conditions, is to be found demonstrated *empirically* yet with all the force of intuition and with the Notion of a living natural activity, in Pohl's work: *The process of the galvanic circuit* (Leipzig, 1826). Perhaps this higher demand addressed to the instinct of Reason, to grasp the course of the galvanic and the electrical process as such, conceived as a totality of natural activity, is responsible in part for the fact that the lesser demand, viz., simply to take notice of empirically demonstrated *facts*, has up till now met with scant compliance.

An outstanding example of the ignoring of facts in this field is the idea of a *decomposition* of water into oxygen and hydrogen when the former appears at one pole of the battery in whose sphere of action the water is placed, and the latter at its opposite pole. In this idea, water is regarded as *consisting* of oxygen and hydrogen, and its *decomposition* is represented as happening as follows. From the pole where the oxygen is developed, the other constituent of water, hydrogen, is mysteriously *transmitted* across the medium, which still exists as water, to the opposite pole, and reciprocally, the oxygen is similarly transmitted from the pole where the hydrogen is developed to the opposite pole; also, the two gases are represented as passing through each other in their passage from one pole to the other. Not only does the inherent fallacy of this conception pass unnoticed, but it is also overlooked that in dividing the material substance of the two portions of water—a division which is, however, so arranged that there is still a connection, but only by a metal conductor—the production of oxygen gas at one pole and of hydrogen gas at the other, *takes place in the same manner* under conditions which render impossible this intrinsically groundless, mysterious passage of gases or molecules through each other to their respective sides. (Cf. § 286, *Zusatz*, p. 117; § 324, *Zusatz*, p. 231; § 328, *Zusatz*, p. 240.) A similar ignoring of experience occurs in connection with the neutralization of an acid and an alkali when one is placed at an opposite pole to the other. Here, too, the neutralization of the alkali is represented as due to a portion of the acid being transferred to the alkali from the opposite pole—as conversely the neutralization of the acid is represented as due to the transfer of a portion of the alkali from the opposite side—yet when a litmus solution is placed between them, no trace can be perceived in this visible medium of any action, and consequently not of the presence, of the acid which is supposedly passing through it.

It is also in place here to mention that the treatment of water as a mere *conductor* of electricity—with the experience of the weaker action of the pile with such a medium than with other, more concrete agents—has produced the original conclusion that '*l'eau pure* qui transmet une électricité forte, telle que celle que nous excitons par nos machines ordinaires, devient *presqu'isolante* pour les faibles forces de l'appareil électromoteur' (in this theory, the name of the voltaic pile) (Biot, *Traité de phys.* tom. ii, p. 506). Only the obstinate adherence to a theory which can disregard such consequences can have the audacity to make water an insulator of electricity.

But as regards the central feature of the theory, viz. the *identification* of electricity and chemical action, the difference between these two processes is so striking that the theory is almost forced to beat a retreat, but then soothes itself by admitting that this difference is inexplicable. Certainly it is! If an identification is presupposed, this very circumstance makes difference inexplicable. The superficiality and inadequacy of equating the chemical properties and relationships of bodies with positive and negative electricity should be at once plain: in comparison with chemical relationships, tied though these are to external conditions, e.g. temperature, and otherwise relative, electrical phenomena are wholly transient, unstable, and liable to reverse by the slightest circumstance. Whereas, also, the bodies of one side of the chemical relation, e.g. acids, are exactly distinguished from each other by their quantitative and qualitative ratios of saturation by an alkali (§ 333, Remark), in the case of the merely electrical opposition, even were this more stable, no such kind of distinction is possible. But even if the entire visible course of real material change in the chemical process is ignored and attention fixed only on the product, it is impossible to avoid expressing surprise at the striking difference between this product and that of the electrical process, after the previous identification of the two forms. I will confine myself to quoting the naïve expression of this surprise in Berzelius's work: *Essai sur la théorie des proportions chimiques etc.* (Paris, 1819). He says (p. 73): 'Il s'élève pourtant ici une question qui *ne peut* être *résolue* par *aucun phénomène* analogue à *la décharge électro-chimique* (the expression 'chemical combination' is dropped in favour of 'discharge') — ils restent dans cette combinaison *avec une force*, qui est supérieure à toutes celles qui peuvent produire une séparation mécanique. Les phénomènes électriques *ordinaires* — *ne nous éclairent pas* sur la cause *de l'union permanente* des corps avec une si grande force, après que l'état d'opposition électrique est détruit.' The changes in specific gravity, cohesion, shape, colour, etc., occurring in the chemical process and, in addition, in the acid, caustic, alkaline, and suchlike properties, are all set aside and submerged in the abstraction of electricity. Let philosophy no more be reproached with 'its ignoring of particularity and its empty generalities', when all the physical properties just mentioned can be disregarded in favour of positive and negative electricity. A former style of Philosophy of Nature 'potentialized'—or rather dissipated and attenuated— the system and process of animal reproduction to magnetism and the vascular system to electricity: such schematism was not more superficial than this reduction of concrete, corporeal opposition to electricity. In the former case, such a summary method of dealing with concrete phenomena to the neglect, by abstraction, of their characteristic features, was rightly rejected. Why not also in the present instance?

But there is a remaining point of difficulty in the difference between the concrete process and the abstract schema, viz. the *strength of the combination* of the substances formed into oxides, salts, etc., as a result of the chemical process. This strength, of course, offers a marked contrast to the result of the merely electrical discharge, which leaves the positively and negatively charged bodies in just the same state, and so separate and uncombined as they were before and during the process of being rubbed together; while the spark has disappeared. It is the spark which is really the result of the electrical process; it is with the spark, therefore, that the result of the chemical process should be compared in respect of the difficulty arising from the alleged likeness of the two processes. Should it not be possible to remove the difficulty by assuming the positive and negative electricity to be combined in the discharge spark with the same strength as, say, acid and alkali are combined in the salt? The spark, however, has disappeared, so that it can no longer be compared; but the main point is that a salt or oxide is manifestly a further resultant step than an electric spark. The light and heat generated in the chemical process are also improperly ascribed to such a spark. Berzelius says the following about the alleged difficulty: 'Est-ce l'effet d'une force *particulière* inhérente aux atomes, comme la polarisation électrique?' —i.e. is there not a difference between chemical and electrical action in bodies? Undoubtedly and obviously! 'Où est-ce une propriété électrique qui *n'est pas sensible* dans les phénomènes *ordinaires*?'—i.e. as above (p. 248), in strictly electrical phenomena. This question also is to be answered with a simple affirmative, viz. that in electricity as such, chemical action is not present, and is for that reason *not perceptible*, and that it is only perceptible at the stage of chemical process. However, as regards the first possibility, that of a *difference* between the chemical and electrical determination of a body, Berzelius rejoins: 'La permanence de la combinaison *ne devait pas être soumise* à l'influence d'électricité.' That is, two properties of a body, because they are different, must *not stand in any kind of relation* to each other: the specific gravity of a metal is not to be connected with its oxidation, nor its metallic lustre or colour with its oxidation, neutralization, etc. It is, on the contrary, the commonest experience that the properties of bodies are essentially *subject* to the *influence* of the action and change of other properties. It is the dry abstraction of Understanding that insists on the *complete separation* and *independence* of properties which are *different*, even when they belong to the same body. As regards the other possibility, viz. that electricity has the power to break up strong chemical compounds, though this power cannot be perceived in *ordinary* electricity, Berzelius observes: 'Le rétablissement de la polarité électrique devrait détruire même la plus forte combinaison chimique'; and adduces in support the special instance of a voltaic pile (here called an *electric battery*) consisting of 8 or 10 pairs of silver and zinc plates the size of a five-franc piece, which pile, with the aid of mercury, is able to decompose potash, i.e. to preserve the radical of potash in an amalgam. The difficulty was caused by *ordinary* electricity *not* showing the power in question, as distinct from the action of a galvanic pile. Now for ordinary electricity there is substituted the action of such a pile, with the simple modification that it is called 'batterie électrique', whereas previously (p. 247) the name for it in the theory was 'appareil électromoteur'. This turn of expression, however, is all too transparent and the proof too easily taken, since in order to resolve the difficulty which stood in the way of identifying electricity and chemistry, one again straightway presupposes that the galvanic pile is merely an electrical apparatus and its activity merely the production of electricity.

Zusatz. Each single process starts from something seemingly immediate which, however, at another point in the run-round of the periphery, is in its turn a product. The beginning, properly speaking, is with a *metal* as a substance inwardly stable whose apparent difference from another metal results from comparison: thus gold is indifferent to its difference from zinc; it is not immanently distinguished like the neutral substances or oxides, i.e. it cannot be decomposed into opposed sides. Metals are thus, in the first instance, only inertly different from one another; but they are also not only different for us, for if they come into contact with each other (and this contact is itself contingent) they distinguish themselves from each other. The continuity of metals is the condition that makes it possible for their difference to become active, so that the difference of each can be posited in that of the other. But a *third* substance is required, capable of a real differentiation in which the metals can integrate themselves; it is on this third substance that the difference of each metal feeds (*ihre Nahrung hat*). Metals are not brittle like resin or sulphur where the determination posited in them is restricted to one point; in metals, the determinateness is communicated to the whole body, and the difference of each is open to the other, each making its difference felt in the other. The *difference* of metals, then, is revealed by their relationship in process, which relationship is, in general, the antithesis of their inherent preciousness, solidity, ductility, and fluidity, to their brittleness and their readiness to form oxides. The precious metals such as *gold*, *silver*, and *platinum*, are not oxidized when heated and exposed to air; their process in an open fire is a burning without a burning up. They do not decompose into the extremes of base and acid, which would fix them as belonging to one of these sides; all that happens is a non-chemical change of shape from the solid to the molten state. This comes from their lack of difference. The Notion of this solid, simple nature of metals seems to be represented in its purest form by gold; that is why gold does not rust and old gold coins are still untarnished. *Lead* and other metals are, on the contrary, attacked even by weak acids. The still more numerous metals known as *metalloids* are those which are hardly ever found in their pure state and are oxidized merely by exposure to the air. Gold, silver, and platinum, even when oxidized by acids, can be restored to their original state without adding any combustible substance such as coal; they return to their pure form merely by being brought to a red heat in the furnace. *Mercury*, it is true, can be vaporized by heat; and when shaken and pounded under exposure to the air, admittedly does change into an imperfect, greyish-black oxide, and by continuous heating into a more complete dark red oxide with a sharp, metallic taste. But as Trommsdorff observes, when mercury is shut up in dry air and left to stand, its surface does not suffer change and does not rust; yet 'he had seen a phial of mercury which old Büttner had kept goodness knows how many years' (perforated paper allowing air to enter) which had oxidized, and which had on top a thin layer of red mercuric oxide. However, this and all other oxides of mercury can be brought back to mercury in its pure form by making them red-hot and without adding combustible substances. Schelling, therefore (*Neue Zeitschrift für spec. Phys.* vol. i, pp. 3 and 96) regards these four, gold, silver, platinum, and mercury, as precious metals, because in them is posited the indifference of essence (gravity) and form (cohesion); on the contrary, those metals are not to be regarded as precious in which form is most separated out of indifference with the essence, and in which selfhood or individuality is the predominant feature, as in *iron*: nor are those metals precious in which the incompleteness of form vitiates the essence, making them impure and bad, like lead, etc. But this is not enough. It is not simply their high degree of continuity and solidity, but also their high specific gravity which makes metals precious. Platinum, it is true, has a greater density than gold, but it is a unity of several metallic moments, osmium, iridium, and palladium. Steffens, even before Schelling, maintained that density stands in inverse ratio to cohesion; but this is true only of some precious metals such as gold, for example, whose specific cohesion is less than that of the less precious, less brittle metals. Now the greater the difference between metals, the *more active* they are, too. If we put gold into contact with silver, copper, or zinc, or silver into contact with zinc, and put a third substance between them, a drop of water (but there must be air, too), we at once have a process and one of considerable activity. This is a *simple* galvanic circuit. It was accidentally discovered that the circuit must be closed; if it is not closed, there is no active difference and no action takes place. The process is usually represented in this way: that the bodies are merely there, and in their contact only press against each other as heavy matter. But we saw that even in electricity, bodies act on each other according to their physical determinateness. Here with the metals, it is similarly their diverse natures, their specific gravities, which are in contact.

Since the simple galvanic circuit is no more than the connection of opposites by a third, a solvent, neutral substance in which the difference can enter into existence, metalleity is not the only *condition* of this activity. Liquids, too, can have this form of the process; but it is always their simple, distinctive difference which is the active principle of the process, as it is with the metals. Charcoal, too, which Ritter looked on as a metal, can enter into the galvanic process; charcoal is burnt-up vegetable matter, and as such a residue in which determinateness is extinguished charcoal, too, has the same indifferent character. Even acids, on account of their fluidity, can produce the galvanic process. If soapy water and ordinary water are connected by a piece of tin, a galvanic current is produced; if the soapy water is touched with the tongue and the ordinary water with the hand, then with the closing of the circuit the organs of taste are affected; but if the circuit is alternately opened and closed, they are affected when it is opened. Humboldt observed simple galvanic circuits produced by hot and cold zinc and moisture. Schweigger constructed similar piles from heated and cold copper dishes filled with dilute sulphuric acid. Such differences too, therefore, induce the action. When the body in which the effect is produced is as delicate as muscle-tissue, the difference can be much slighter.

Now the *activity* of the galvanic process has its origin in the immanent contradiction which arises from the effort of each particularity to posit itself in the other. But the activity itself consists in the positing of the inner, merely implicit unity of these inner differences. In the galvanic process, electricity is still predominant since what is posited as different are metals: i.e. they are indifferent, independent existences which hold to themselves even in being changed: the very thing which characterizes electricity. On the one side there must be a negative pole, and on the other a positive one: or in chemical terms, oxygen must be developed here and hydrogen there. These phenomena were associated in the conception of electro-chemistry. Some physicists went so far as to believe that electricity was tied to chemical action. Wollaston even said that electricity was only present where there was oxidation. It was properly objected to this that when catskin is rubbed on glass, electricity is produced without oxidation. The metal is neither dissolved nor decomposed by the chemical action, so that it proves to be a neutral substance in its own self: but the real difference exhibited by the metal in oxidation is a difference added to it, for the metal is combined with something else.

The two metals are combined in the first instance without the existence of a *middle term*; this middle term is only notionally present in their contact. But the real middle term is what the difference has to bring into existence; this term which, in the logical syllogism, is the simple *medius terminus*, is a duality in Nature itself. In this finite process, the mediating term, which is turned towards the two one-sided extremes, and from which these extremes are to integrate themselves, must be not merely a notionally distinct substance, but its difference must actually exist; that is to say, it is precisely the middle term which must have a break in its existence. Galvanic action also requires the *air* of the atmosphere or oxygen gas. If the galvanic pile is insulated from the atmospheric air it remains inactive. Trommsdorff adduces the following experiment by Davy: 'If the water between the plates is perfectly pure and the outside air is kept from the volume of water by a coating of resin, then no gas is released in the water, and no oxide formed, and the zinc in the pile is hardly affected.' Biot (vol. ii, p. 528) urged against Davy that beneath an air-pump a voltaic pile still produces gas, though more feebly: this, however, is because the air cannot be completely exhausted. The fact that the middle term is a duality explains why the activity is much intensified if, instead of sheets of cardboard or cloth, hydrochloric acid or sal ammoniac is put between the metals; such a mixture is already in itself chemically complex.

This activity is called galvanism because Galvani first discovered it; Volta, however, first understood it. Galvani at first made quite a different use of it; it was Volta who first freed the phenomena from organic associations and reduced the activity to its simple conditions, though he took it to be mere electricity. Galvani found that when the spinal nerves of a frog were exposed and connected with the leg muscles by different metals (or even only a silver wire), convulsive movements occur which manifest the activity which is the contradiction of these differences. Aldini showed that one metal was sufficient to produce the effect, namely, pure mercury, and that often a wet hempen cord was sufficient to effect this active connection between the nerve and the muscle. He ran such a cord, 250 feet long, round his house with successful results. Someone else found that in large, vigorous frogs, the mere contact of the leg with its nerve would produce jerks without this armature. According to Humboldt, where two like metals are used, the metallic stimulus can be evoked simply by breathing on one of them. If two parts of one and the same nerve are covered by two different metals and connected by a good conductor, this too will produce convulsive movements.

This was the first form; it was called animal electricity because it was thought to be restricted to organisms. Volta used metals instead of muscles and nerves; and he thus made up galvanic batteries out of a whole number of such pairs of plates. Each pair has the opposite determinateness of the following pair, but the activity of these pairs is summed up: so that at one end there is all the negative, at the other end all the positive activity, the middle being the point of indifference. Volta also distinguished between wet conductors (water) and dry conductors (metal)—as if nothing but electricity were present here. But the difference between water and metal is something quite different; and neither of them plays the part of a mere conductor. It is easy to separate electrical from the chemical activity. The greater the surface area of the plates, say 8 square inches, the more brilliant is the electric spark produced. The size of the surface appears to have but little influence on the other phenomena; on the other hand, with only three pairs, sparks are produced. If, in a battery constructed of 40 pairs of this size made of zinc and copper, the silver [sic] pole and zinc pole are connected by an iron wire, at the moment of contact a rose of fire appears, 3 to $3\frac{1}{2}$ inches in diameter, some of the rays being quite $1\frac{1}{2}$ to $1\frac{3}{4}$ inches long, in some places linked together and having little stars at their tips. The communicating wires are so firmly welded by the spark, that a considerable force is required to separate them. In oxygen, gold and silver behave as they do in atmospheric air, iron wires catch fire and burn away, and lead and tin burn very vigorously and with vivid colours. Now if chemical action here is reduced, it becomes distinct from combustion, for with electricity, too, vigorous combustion occurred but as a melting by heat, not as a decomposition of water (see above, § 324, p. 231). Conversely, the chemical action is increased and the electrical action diminished, if the plates are smaller but more are used, 1,000 pairs, for example. However, the two activities are also combined, so that water is decomposed by a powerful electric discharge. For Biot (*Traité de physique*, part ii, p. 436) says: 'Pour décomposer l'eau, on s'est d'abord servi de violentes décharges transmises à travers ce liquide, et qui y produisaient des explosions accompagnées d'étincelles. Mais Wollaston est parvenu à produire le même effet, d'une manière infiniment plus marquée, plus sure et plus facile, en conduisant le courant électrique dans l'eau par des fils tressés, terminés en pointes aiguës', etc. Ritter, of the Munich Academy, has constructed dry batteries where electrical activity is insulated.—Now since it has been observed that with water alone chemical action is not strong in a battery which, with a different construction, could produce strong chemical action and high electrical tension, chemists have concluded that water here acts as an electrical insulator which prevents the transmission of electricity; for since without this obstacle there would be a stong chemical action, and the action here is weak, the inference is that the transmission of electricity which gives rise to the chemical action is prevented by the water. But nothing more absurd could be imagined, since water is the most powerful conductor, more powerful than metal; and this absurdity comes from attributing chemical action solely to electricity and from thinking merely in terms of conductors.

Galvanic action is manifest both as *taste* and *light*. If, for example, a strip of tinfoil is placed under the tip of the tongue and on the lower lip, so that it projects from it, and if the upper surface of the tongue and the tinfoil are touched with silver, then the moment the metals touch, a pronounced alkaline taste is experienced like that of sulphate of iron. If I hold in my wet hand a tin saucer filled with lye and touch the liquid with the tip of my tongue, I get an acid taste on that part of my tongue which has touched the alkaline liquid. If, on the contrary, I place a tin, or better still a zinc, dish on a silver foot and fill it with clean water, then stick the tip of my tongue in the water, it has no taste; but if at the same time the silver foot is held in a thoroughly moist hand, a weak acid taste is at once felt on the tongue. If a bar of zinc is put in one's mouth between the upper jaw and left cheek, and a bar of silver between the lower right jaw and the right cheek, so that the bits of metal stick out of the mouth, and their ends are brought together, then one has in the dark the sensation of light when the metals make contact. Here the identity is subjectively present in sensation, without the production of an external spark though this does of course happen with powerful batteries.

Now the *product* of the galvanic action is, in general, this, that that which is in itself or has only notional existence—the identity of the particular differences which in metals are also bound up with their indifferent self-subsistence—attains to an existence, as does also the difference of one metal in the other, and the indifferent is therefore posited as different. The process still cannot go on to the production of a neutral substance, for there are still no existent differences. Now since these differences are not yet bodies themselves but only abstract determinatenesses, the question arises, in what forms should they come into existence here. The abstract existence of these differences is elemental in nature and we see it manifested as aeriform, gaseous substances; here, then, we have to speak of abstract chemical elements. Thus because water is the mediating neutral term between the metals, in which these differences can come into contact (as it is also that in which the differences of two salts, e.g., are dissolved), it follows that each metal takes its existent difference from water, and determines water, on the one hand, towards oxidation and on the other, towards hydrogenization. But since the character of water generally is to be neutral, the activating, differentiating principle does not exist in water but in air. The air does, indeed, seem to be neutral, but it is the stealthily destructive activity; the metals, therefore, must take from the air the activity which they display and that is why the differences appear in gaseous form (*Form der Luftigkeit*). In this process, oxygen is the activating, differentiating principle. The more specific result of the galvanic process is the *oxide*, a metal posited with a real difference—the first real difference we have; the indifferent body becomes a totality, although still not a complete totality. But though the product is at once also dual, oxidation and hydrogenization, the outcome is not two differentiated bodies. On one side we have oxidation, e.g. zinc is oxidized. The other side, the gold, silver, etc., holds out in its solidity (*in dieser Gediegenheit*) against its opposite, retains its pure form: or if it has been oxidized, it is deoxidized, restored to its pure form. Since the activation of zinc cannot be the positing of a one-sided difference, and can, on the other side, perhaps not be deoxidized, the other side of the opposition appears only under the other form of water, namely, as hydrogen. It can also happen that instead of oxidized metals, hydrogenized metals are produced, a fact established by Ritter. But the specific difference as opposition is alkali and acid, something different from that abstract differentiation. But even with such a real differentiation the opposition is mainly brought about by the oxygen. To the metal oxides which result from the galvanic process also belong the *earths*: silica, calcite, barytes, sodium, potassium; for the earths have in general a metallic base. It has been possible to demonstrate the metallic nature of these bases, although many have only slight indications of a metallic base. Now though this metallic nature cannot always be preserved in its independence, as happens with the metalloids, it is exhibited in amalgams with mercury; and only metallic substances can form amalgams with mercury. In the metalloids, therefore, metalleity is only a moment; they rapidly become oxidized again, wolfram, e.g., being obtained in its pure state only with difficulty. A specially noteworthy feature of ammoniac is that, on the one hand, it can be demonstrated that its base is nitrogen, its other constituent being hydrogen,[*] but also that it has a metallic base, ammonia; here the metalleity is carried to the stage where it is also manifested as a chemically abstract substance, as a gas.

The process terminates in the product of oxidation. The opposition to this first, abstract, general negation is the free negativity, self-subsistent negativity in contrast to negativity paralysed in the indifference of the metal. The opposition is necessary in principle (*an sich*) or in conformity with the Notion; but its existence, as fire, is brought about contingently.

§ 331

(b) The Process of Fire

The activity which, in the previous process, was only *implicit* in the differentiated determinateness of the metals brought into relation, when posited as an independent existence, is *Fire*, whereby what is in itself combustible (like sulphur)—the *third*

---

[*] The German text has '*Sauerstoff*'.

kind of corporeality—is *kindled into flame*: whereby also, in general, those bodies in which difference is still indifferent and inert (as in neutrality), are energized into the *chemical opposition* of *acid* and (caustic) *alkali*—not so much to a peculiar kind of real corporeality, for they cannot exist independently, as merely to a peculiar *posited being* of the corporeal moments of the *third* form.

Zusatz. With the cessation of the galvanic process in the production of the metallic oxide, of earth, the course of the chemical process is interrupted. For chemical processes do not hang together, otherwise we should have Life, the circular return of a process. If, now, the product is to be carried further, activity must come in from outside, just as the metals, too, were brought together by an external activity. It is only the Notion, the inner necessity, which therefore carries the process forward; it is only in principle (*an sich*) that the process is carried onward into a circular totality. Since the new form we introduce has its genesis only in us, comes to be only in principle or in itself (*an sich*), we must take the bodies entering into the process as they naturally are. It is not the same existing product (here, therefore, the oxide with which the galvanic process closed) that would receive further treatment, as it were only by other reagents; as in itself determinate, the object of the process must rather be taken up as something original, not something which has come into existence. That it has come into existence is a characteristic it possesses as a simple, inner, notional determinateness.

One side of the process is fire as flame, in which the unity of the difference which resulted from the galvanic process, exists for itself, namely in the form of free, restless activity, of self-destruction. The other side, the combustible substance, is the object of fire, of the same nature as fire, but in the form of a physically existent body. The product of the process, then, is that on the one hand fire exists as a physical quality: or conversely, that in the material substance there is posited what already constitutes its natural determinateness, namely, fire. As the first process was the process of what is heavy, so here we have the process of what is light, in which fire assumes the bodily form of an acid. The physical body, as the possibility of being consumed and activated, is not a mere lifeless reduction to passive indifference, but itself burns. Now because the material thus activated is inwardly a sheer opposition and so self-contradictory, it stands in need of its other, and only *is* in real connection with its other. The combustible substance thus has two different forms, since this being-for-self of the negative, in determining itself as different, posits itself in its own differentiation. One form is the ordinary combustible substance, sulphur, phosphorus, etc.: the other form is a neutral substance. It is not the nature of either, but only a mode of existence, to persist tranquilly: whereas in the galvanic process, the metal's indifference constitutes its very nature. A more remarkable feature of these substances is their mere shining without burning, the phosphorescence shown by a number of minerals; when they are scratched or scraped or even exposed to sunlight, they remain phosphorescent for quite a time. It is the same sort of transient light-phenomenon as electricity but without dualism. The range of primary combustible substances is limited; it embraces sulphur, bitumen, and naphtha. It is the brittle body without a firm indifferent base, which does not receive difference from outside by combining with an actively different body, but which develops the negativity immanent in itself as its own self. The body's indifference has passed into a chemical difference. The combustibility of sulphur is no longer the superficial possibility which *remains* possible in the process itself; such an indifference is actually abolished. The combustible substance burns, fire is its actuality; it does not merely burn, but burns up, it ceases to be indifferent—has become an acid. Indeed, Winterl has maintained that sulphur is as such an acid; and in fact it is, since it neutralizes saline and earthy bases and the metals, even without making use of the water base (hydrogen) required by the rest of the acids. The second form of combustible substance is the formally neutral body; and the existence of this, too, is only a form not constitutive of its nature; if it were, it might survive the process. The formally neutral bodies (salt is the physically neutral body) are lime, barytes, potash, in a word the earths, which are nothing but oxides, i.e. they have a metal for their base; a discovery brought to light by the galvanic battery, whereby alkalis (*Kalisches*) are deoxidized. The alkalis, too, are metal oxides: animal, vegetable, or mineral. The other side to the base, e.g. in lime, is the carbonic acid we produce by heating charcoal, a chemical abstraction, and not an individual, physical body. Lime is thus neutralized, but it is no real neutral body, such neutrality being effected only in an elemental, general way. Barytes, strontium, are not regarded as salts since they are not neutralized (*abstumpft*) by a real acid, but by this same chemical abstraction which appears as carbonic acid. These are the two combustibles constituting the other side of the process.

The substances in conflict with each other in the process of fire come together only externally; this is conditioned through the finitude of the chemical process. They are mediated with each other by Elements, i.e. *air* and *water*. To produce the acid of sulphur, wet partitions and air are used. The whole process thus has the form of a syllogism with a broken middle term and two extremes. The more particular forms of this syllogism concern (*a*) the modes of the activity, and (*b*) that to which the middle term is determined by the extremes in order to integrate themselves from it. To deal with this more closely would involve going into refinements of detail which would make us digress too far. Every chemical process would have to be set forth as a series of syllogisms, where what was at first an extreme, becomes a middle term, and the middle term gets posited as an extreme. What in general happens is that the combustible substance: sulphur, phosphorus, or some formally neutral substance, is activated in the process. It is thus that earths are made caustic by fire, whereas in their previous state, as salts, they were mild. Metals (*Metallisches*), too (especially bad metals, the calcareous metals), can be so activated by burning that they do not become oxides but are driven straight on to become acids. The oxide of arsenic is itself arsenious acid. Alkali if activated is corrosive, caustic: acid, too, attacks and destroys bodies. Since sulphur (and similar substances) contain no indifferent base, water here becomes the basic bond (*basische Band*) so that the acid can, even though only for a moment, exist independently. But when an alkali becomes caustic, the water which, as water of crystallization (which is no longer water) was the bond of neutralization, loses its formally neutral shape under the action of fire; such an alkali already has on its own account an indifferent metallic base.

§ 332

(c) Neutralization, Water-Process

Body thus differentiated is in a state of sheer opposition to its other; this is its quality, so that it essentially *is*, only in its connection with its other. It is only by violence, consequently, that its corporeality has an independent, separate existence; in its one-sidedness it is, in its own self, the process of positing itself as identical with the negative of itself: even if this process is only with the air, in which acid and caustic alkali lose their strength (*sich abstumpfen*), i.e. are reduced to formal neutrality. The product is the concrete *neutral* body, a *salt*, which is the *fourth* kind of body and in the form of a real body.

Zusatz. A metal is only implicitly (*an sich*) different from its other; the other is contained in the Notion of the metal, but only in its Notion. Since, however, each side now exists as an opposite, this one-sidedness is no longer merely implicit but posited. The individualized body, therefore, is the urge to overcome its one-sidedness and to posit the totality which, in its Notion, it already is. Both sides are physical realities: sulphuric or some other acid but not carbonic acid; and oxides, earths, alkalis. These opposites thus activated, do not need the presence of a third substance in order to become active. Each has in its own self the restless urge to sublate itself, to integrate itself with its opposite and neutralize itself: but they are not capable of independent existence since they are incompatible with themselves. Acids get hot, catch fire, when water is poured on them. Concentrated acids give off fumes, absorb water from the air: concentrated sulphuric acid, for example, increases its volume in this way, occupies more space, but becomes weaker.

Acids kept in air-tight vessels attack the latter. Caustic alkalis similarly lose their causticity; it is then said that they absorb carbonic acid from the air, but this is hypothetical. The truth rather is that they first form carbonic acid from the air in order to neutralize themselves.

What activates both sides is a chemical abstraction, the chemical element of oxygen as the differentiated abstraction; the bases (even if only water) are the indifferent subsistence, the bond. The activation of both acids and alkalis is therefore an oxygenation. But the difference of acid and alkali is something relative, as already appears in the opposition of positive and negative. Thus in arithmetic, the negative is to be taken partly as negative in its own self and partly as merely the negative of another: so that it does not matter which is negative and which positive. The case is similar in electricity with its two opposite directions, where the movement to and fro brings one back to the same standpoint, and so on. Acid, therefore, is certainly in its own self what is negative; but the relativity of the relationship also makes its appearance. What from one side is an acid, is from another side an alkali. Sulphuret of potash, for example, is called an acid although it is hydrogenated sulphur; here, then, an acid is a hydrogenization. Admittedly, this is not so in every case, and is here due to the combustibility of sulphur. Through oxidation, however, sulphur becomes sulphuric acid, which shows that it is capable of both forms. The same is true of a number of earths which fall into two groups: (α) lime, barytes, strontium are alkaline and metallic oxides; (β) in the case of silica, clay, and talc, this may be conjectured, partly by analogy and partly from traces of galvanic process in the amalgam. Steffens, however, opposes talc and silica to the alkaline series. According to Schuster, alum also reacts to alkalis, i.e. is acid; on the other hand, its reaction to sulphuric acid is that it takes up the position of base; clay in solution in alkalis is precipitated by acids and therefore behaves as an acid. The double nature of alum is confirmed by Berthollet (*Statique chimique*, part ii, p. 302): 'L'alumine a une disposition presqu'égale à se combiner avec les acides et avec les alcalis'; p. 308: 'L'acide nitrique a aussi la propriété de cristalliser avec l'alumine; il est probable que c'est également par le moyen d'une base alcaline.' 'Silica', says Schuster, 'is an acid, though a weak one; for it neutralizes the bases and then combines with potassium and sodium to form glass', and so on. Berthollet (part ii, p. 314) remarks, though, that they merely have a stronger tendency to combine with alkalis than with acids.

Here, too, air and water act as the middle terms, for anhydrous, completely concentrated acid (although it can never be *quite* waterless) has a much weaker action than dilute acid, especially if air is excluded, for then action can cease altogether. The general, abstract result is that acid combines with an alkali which has not been brought to the activated stage, to form a neutral substance as such, which is, however, not an abstract indifference but a unity of two existent substances. They sublate their opposition, their contradiction, since they cannot endure it;

and in thus sublating their one-sidedness, they posit what they are in their Notion, both the one and the other. It is said that an acid does not act directly on a metal, but first turns it into an oxide, into one of the sides of the existing opposition, and then neutralizes itself with this oxide which, though differentiated, is not activated to the point of being caustic. It is the salt which, as product of this neutralization, first is the chemical totality, the centre; but it is still not as yet the infinite totality of Life, but a totality come to rest and circumscribed by other totalities.

§ 333

(d) The Process in its Totality

These neutral bodies, returning into mutual relation, form the chemical process in its *complete reality*, for the sides of the process are such real bodies. Their mediation requires water, the abstract medium of neutrality. But the sides, being neutral on their own account, are not differentiated as against each other. Here we have the *particularization* of general neutrality, and with it also the particularization of the differences of the chemically active bodies in their mutual opposition. This is the so-called *elective affinity*—the formation of other particular neutralities through the break-up of those already present.

Remark

The most important step towards simplification of the details of elective affinity is the law discovered by Richter and Guiton Morveau, which states that neutral compounds suffer *no alteration* in regard to their *state of saturation* when they are mixed in solution, and the acids exchange bases with each other. It is on the basis of this law that the quantitative scale of acids and alkalis has been constructed, according to which each particular acid is saturated by a specific quantity of each alkali; so that if the alkalis are arranged in a series according to the amounts with which they saturate the same quantity of a particular acid, then *for every other acid*, the *alkalis* retain among themselves the *same ratio* for the saturation of this acid, as for the first one: all that varies is the quantitative unit of the acids combining with this constant series. In the same way, the acids bear a constant ratio to each other, relative to the various alkalis.

Elective affinity itself is, however, only an *abstract* relation of acid to base. The chemical body in general, and especially the neutral body, is at once a concrete physical body having a definite specific gravity, cohesion, temperature, etc. These strictly physical properties and their alterations in the process (§ 328) enter into relation with the chemical moments of the process, and thereby impede, obstruct or facilitate, and so modify the chemical action. Berthollet, in his famous work *Statique chimique*, while fully recognizing the serial law of elective affinity, has brought together and investigated the circumstances which produce alterations in the results of chemical action, results which are often one-sidedly attributed only to elective affinity. He says, 'the superficiality which these explanations have introduced into the science is especially regarded as progress.'

Zusatz. The immediate self-integration of the opposites, the alkali and the acid, into a neutral substance, is not a process; the salt is a process-less result, like the adherence of a magnet to the north and south poles, or the spark in an electric discharge. If the process is to be carried further, then the salts, being indifferent and not in need (*unbedürftig*), must be brought together again in an external manner. The activity is not in them but is brought forth again only by contingent circumstances; substances which are indifferent to each other can come into contact only in a third substance, which here again is water. It is here especially that formation (*Gestaltung*) and crystallization have their seat. The process, in general, is this: one neutrality is sublated, but another one is brought forth in its place. The neutrality is therefore here engaged in conflict with itself; for the neutrality which is product is mediated by the negation of neutrality. We have, therefore, particular neutralities of acids and bases in mutual conflict. The affinity of an acid for a base is negated; and the negation of this affinity is itself the relation of an acid to a base, or is itself an affinity. This affinity is equally the affinity of the acid of the second salt for the base of the first, as it is also the affinity of the base of the second salt for the acid of the first. These affinities, as negating the first affinities, are called elective affinities, which means no more than that here, as in magnetism and electricity, opposites—acid and alkali—posit themselves as identical. The way in which this process exists, appears, acts, is the same. One acid expels another from a base, as the north pole of a magnet repels the north pole, but each remains linked with the same south pole. Here, however, the comparison of the acids with each other takes place in a Third; each particular acid has *its* opposite which is *more* its base than another: the determination does not result merely from the general nature of opposites, since the chemical process is the sphere of kinds, which are qualitatively active against each other. The main thing, therefore, is the *strength* of the affinity, but no affinity is one-sided: the degree of *my* kinship with another is the degree of *his* kinship to me. The acids and bases of two salts break up their combination and form fresh salts, the acid of the second salt combining more readily with the base of the first and expelling its acid, while this acid has the same relationship to the base of the second salt: in other words, an acid abandons its base when offered another base to which it has a greater affinity. The result is another neutral reality; the outcome, therefore, is of the same kind as the beginning—formal return of the neutral substance to itself.

The law of elective affinities discovered by Richter, to which we referred in our Remark, remained unknown till the English and French (Wollaston and Berthollet) talked of Richter and made use of his work and so made it important. The same thing will happen with Goethe's theory of colour: it will not succeed in Germany till a Frenchman or an Englishman takes it up or else expounds the same theory himself and gains acceptance for it. It is no use complaining of this; it is always that way with us Germans, unless indeed some trashy theory like Gall's phrenology is propounded. Now this principle of *stoichiometry* of Richter's, expounded by him with a wealth of erudite reflections, can be most easily pictured by the following comparison. If I buy various goods with gold coins (*Friedrichsd'ors*), then for a certain quantity of the first article, for example, I require one gold coin, for the same quantity of the second article, two gold coins, and so on. Now if I buy with silver coins (*Thalern*), I need more of these, namely, $5\frac{2}{3}$ silver coins instead of 1 gold coin, $11\frac{1}{3}$ instead of two, and so on. The values of the goods preserve the same ratio with one another; an article having twice the value of another always keeps that relative value, no matter in what coinage it is measured. And the different kinds of coins likewise stand in a specific ratio; according to their relative values they therefore cover the cost of a certain portion of each article. If, therefore, the gold coin is $5\frac{2}{3}$ as much as one silver coin, and one silver coin covers the cost of 3 parts of a particular article, then the gold coin covers the cost of $5\frac{2}{3} \times 3$ parts. Berzelius adopted the same point of view in connection with the degrees of oxidation and sought to reduce them to a general law; for in this process, one substance uses up more oxygen than another. For example, to saturate 100 parts of tin as protoxide, 13·6 parts of oxygen are required, as white deuteroxide, 20·4 parts, as yellow hyperoxide, 27·4 parts. Dalton first investigated this question, but he wrapped up his conclusions in the worst sort of atomistic metaphysics. He laid down that the first elements or the simple, first quantity, was an atom, and he went on to talk of the weight and weight-ratios of these atoms: they were supposedly spherical and in part surrounded by a more or less dense atmosphere of caloric; and he then taught us how to determine the relative weights and diameters of these atoms and their number in compound bodies. Berzelius again, and Schweigger in particular, concoct a hotch-potch of electro-chemical relationships. But the formal moments of magnetism and electricity cannot appear in this real process, or if they do so appear, then only in a limited way. Only if the process is not completely real, are these abstract forms specially prominent. Thus Davy was the first to show that two substances which have a *chemically opposite action* are electrically opposite. If sulphur is melted in a vessel an electrical tension is produced between them, since this is not a real chemical process. It is for the same reason that electricity is most obviously present in the galvanic process; for which reason, too, it also disappears when the process assumes a more chemical nature. Magnetism, however, can appear only in the chemical process, when difference must present itself spatially; this again occurs principally in the galvanic form, which is precisely not the absolute activity of the chemical process.

2. *Dissociation*

§ 334

The dissociation of the neutral body is the beginning of its reversion to particular chemical bodies, back to their indifference through a series of processes which are, on the one hand, peculiar; each such dissociation is, on the other hand, itself inseparably linked with a combination, and similarly, the processes classified as processes of combination also directly contain the other moment, that of dissociation (§ 328). To determine the *peculiar place* occupied by each particular form of the process and also which is the *specific* product, it is necessary to consider the *concrete* agents and *concrete* products involved. Abstract processes where the agents are abstract (e.g. water alone acting on a metal, or simply gases, and so on), certainly contain *in themselves* the totality of the process, but they do not exhibit its moments explicitly.

Remark

In empirical chemistry, interest mainly centres in the *particularity* of the *substances* and *products* grouped together according to superficial, abstract determinations in such fashion that no order is brought into their particularity. In this grouping, metals, oxygen, hydrogen, etc., metalloids (formerly called earths), sulphur, and phosphorus, are placed side by side as *simple* chemical bodies and on the same level. The great physical diversity of these bodies is such that it straightway arouses opposition to such grouping; no less varied, too, is their chemical origin, the process from which these bodies result. But in equally chaotic fashion, the more abstract processes are put on the same level as those that have more reality. If scientific form is to be introduced into this sphere, each product must be defined according to the stage of the concrete, fully developed process from which it essentially results and from which it has its peculiar significance; for this purpose it is equally essential to distinguish between the stages of abstraction or reality of the process. *Animal* and *vegetable* substances, moreover, belong to a quite different order; their nature, far from being understood from the chemical process, is rather destroyed in it; what we grasp therefrom is only the way of their death. But these substances should principally serve to counteract the metaphysics prevalent both in chemistry and physics, the thoughts, namely, or rather muddled conceptions, of the *immutability* of *substances* in all circumstances, and the categories of the *composition* of bodies and their *constitution* out of such substances. It is readily granted that chemical substances in combination lose the properties they show in separation, and yet men imagine that they are the same things *without* these properties that they are *with* them, and that their *possession* of such properties is no consequence of their being products of process. The affirmative determination of the still indifferent body, the metal, is physically such that its properties appear in it as *immediate*. In the case of further determined bodies, however, their behaviour in process cannot be thus presupposed; their primary, essential determination springs solely from their place in the chemical process. A further matter is the empirical, quite special particularity of reaction shown by bodies to all other particular bodies; a knowledge of this involves going through the same litany of reactions to every re-agent.

What is most striking in this respect is to see the four chemical elements (oxygen, etc.), placed, as *substances*, on the same level with gold, silver, etc., sulphur, etc., as if they had the same kind of independent existence as gold, sulphur, etc., or as if oxygen had an existence like that of carbon. Their place in process indicates their subordinate, abstract character which distinguishes them in kind from metals and salts, and shows that they certainly do not belong together with such concrete bodies; this place has been dealt with in full in § 328. The *abstract* middle term which is *internally broken* in two (cf. § 204, Remark), to which, therefore, *two* elements belong—water and air—being abandoned as a middle term, becomes the source from which the original, at first merely *implicit*, difference between the real syllogistic extremes acquires *existence*. This moment of difference, thus developed into an existence *of its own*, constitutes the chemical element as a completely abstract moment; these substances, far from being primary, substantial foundations, as the term 'element' at first suggests, are rather difference in its most extreme forms.

Here, as in general, the chemical process is to be taken in its complete totality. The isolation of particular parts, of formal and abstract processes, leads to the abstract conception of the chemical process as being in general merely the action of one substance on another, with the result that such numerous other phenomena as occur—abstract neutralization (production of water) and abstract dissociation (development of gas) which occur in every process—seem almost secondary or accidental consequences, or at least as only externally connected with the process, and are not treated as essential moments in the relationship of the whole. A full exposition of the chemical process in its totality would, however, require it, as a real syllogism, to be explicated also as a *triad* of closely interlinked syllogisms; syllogisms which are not merely a simple connection of their termini but which, as active processes, are negations of their specific forms (cf. § 198) and they would have to exhibit the interrelationship of combination and dissociation knit together in a single process.

Zusatz. Whereas the first process led to combination, the processes of the neutral bodies against each other are, at the same time, their diremptions or decompositions, and the separations of the abstract bodies from which we started. In this way, the pure metal with which we began, taking it as immediately given, is now a result produced from the total body towards which we were advancing. What is here decomposed, the concrete middle term, is a real neutral substance (the salt), whereas in galvanism the formal middle term which was decomposed was water, and in the process of fire, air. The forms and stages of this reduction vary:

particularly the process of fire and also that of the salt. For example, if the salt is brought to a red heat, the weak (*abgestumpft*) acid is made strong again; in the same way, lime gives off carbonic acid, since at this temperature lime is supposed to have a greater affinity with caloric than with carbonic acid. It is in this way that metals are finally reduced: when, for example, sulphur, which as acid combined with a base, is driven off and the metal assumes a pure form. Few metals are found pure in Nature; most of them are only separated off by chemical action.

This is the complete cycle of the chemical process. Before we can determine to which stage of the process individual bodies belong, we must establish the definite order in which the stages of the chemical process succeed one another; otherwise we shall be dealing with a multitude of substances which, taken on their own, remain an unsystematized hotch-potch. The individualized bodies (*Körperindividualitäten*) acquire their specific character in the process as follows (they are moments and products of the process and they form the following system of determinate, i.e. differentiated, corporeality as the concrete Elements now determined to the stage of individuality):

(a) Individualized and differentiated air yields the different kinds of *gases*, air itself being the totality of the four: (α) *nitrogen*, the abstractly indifferent gas; (β) *oxygen* and *hydrogen*, the opposed forms of air—the former kindling and activating in opposition, the latter positive and indifferent in it; (γ) *carbonic acid gas*, the earthy moment, because it appears partly as earthy (*irdisch*) and partly as gas.

(b) One of the moments of the opposition is the *cycle of fire*, the individual, realized fire and its opposite, the *combustible substance*. It, too, forms a totality: (α) the *basis*, the intrinsically combustible substance which is, in itself (*an sich*), fiery; this is neither the indifferent substance to be posited only in a determination as difference, nor the positive which is only to be limited by difference, but it is negativity in itself, Time which is inwardly realized but still *sleeps* (as fire itself can be called *active* (*rege*) Time)—the quiescent existence of this sleeping Time being only form, so that this negativity is its quality, not a mere form of its being, but its very being as this form—*sulphur* as the earthy basis, hydrogen as the aeriform basis, naphtha, the vegetable and animal *oils*, and so on; (β) the *acids*, namely, (αα) *sulphuric acid*, the acid of the combustible earthy substance, (ββ) *nitric acid* with its various forms, (γγ) *hydrochloric acid* (I consider hydrogen to be its radical: the indifferent moments of air-individuality must be activated into acid: they are potentially combustible, not such as metals are, since they are abstract existences, but because, as indifferent, they have combustible matter within themselves, not like oxygen which must obtain it from outside), (δδ) the *earthy acids*, (1) the *abstract*, earthy, *carbonic acid*, (2) the *concrete*, arsenious acid, etc., (3) the vegetable and animal acids (citric acid, blood acid (*Blutsäure*), formic acid); (4) in opposition to acids, the oxides and alkalis generally.

(c) The other moment of the opposition is *realized water*, the neutralities of acids and oxides—*salts, earths, stones*. It is here, strictly speaking, that total body comes to view; the various gases are airs (*Lüfte*), the cycle of fire has not yet reached the stability of the totality, sulphur is suspended in it as a basis over the other earthy bodies. The *earths* are white, simply brittle, the individual body as such, possessing neither the continuity of metal and its passage through process, nor combustibility. There are four main earths. These earthy, neutral substances are differentiated into a double series: (α) those whose neutrality has its base only in the abstractness of water and which exist as neutral products of both acids and alkalis; this transition is formed by silica, clay, and talc. (αα) *Silica* is, as it were, the earthy metal, the pure case of brittleness which, through the abstraction of its singularity (*Einzelnheit*), combines specially with potassium to form glass; and as metal represents the process of melting in colour and solidity, so does silica represent it in singularity; silica is the colourless substance in which metalleity has died away into pure form and whose inwardness is absolute discreteness. (ββ) As silica is the immediate, simple, unexplicated Notion, so *clay* is the first earth with a difference, the possibility of combustibility. As pure clay, it absorbs oxygen from the air, but generally in its combination with sulphuric acid, it is an earthy fire, *porcellanite*. It is to fire that it owes its hardness and crystallization: water plays a less significant part than external cohesion. (γγ) *Talc* or *bitter earth* is the Subject of salt; to this the bitterness of sea-water is due. It is an intermediate taste which has become the principle of fire and is precisely the return of the neutral substance to that principle. (β) Finally, we have the antithesis to this, the genuinely real neutral or *calcareous substances* (*Kalkgeschlecht*), the alkaline, differentiated substances which decompose their earthy principle afresh and only need the physical Element to constitute a process—the extinguished process which reinstates itself; lime is the principle of fire which is generated by the physical body in its own self.

(d) The earthy element, all of whose determinations other than gravity now fall outside of it, and in whose case gravity is identical with light, covers the metals. As gravity is the being-within-self in indeterminate externality, so this being-within-self in light has reality. Thus metals do possess colour, but on the other hand their lustre is this indeterminate, self-propagating pure light which destroys colour. The different states of metal, first continuity and solidity, and then readiness to enter into process, brittleness, punctiformity, capacity for oxidation, all these are passed through by the metal within itself: (α) thus some metals are found in a pure state; (β) others occur only in the form of oxides or mixed with earths, hardly ever in a pure state, and when they do, they are powdery, like arsenic for example; antimony and similar metals are so brittle and hard that they are easily pulverized. (γ) Finally, metal occurs as scoria, vitrified, and has the mere form of sameness of texture (*Zusammenhang*) as in the case of sulphur.

§ 335

The chemical process is, in fact, in general terms, Life; for the individual body in its immediacy is not only *produced* by the process but also *destroyed* by it, so that the Notion no longer remains at the stage of inner necessity but is made *manifest*. But on account of the *immediacy* of the corporealities entering into chemical process, the Notion is everywhere infected with division. As a result, its moments appear as external *conditions*, and what is dissociated falls apart into mutually indifferent products, the fire and activation (*Begeistung*) are extinguished in the neutral body and not spontaneously rekindled in it. The *beginning* and *end* of the process are separate and distinct; this constitutes its finitude which keeps it far from Life and distinguishes it there-from.

Remark

Certain chemical phenomena have led chemistry to apply the determination of *teleology* in explaining them. An example is the fact that an oxide is reduced in the chemical process to a lower degree of oxidation than that at which it can combine with the acid acting on it, while a part of it is more strongly oxidized. There is here a rudimentary self-determination of the Notion from its own resources in its realization, which is thus not determined solely by conditions which are already *outwardly* to hand.

Zusatz. True, an appearance of vitality is there, but it is destroyed in the product. If the products of the chemical process spontaneously renewed their activity, they would be Life. To this extent, then, Life is a chemical process made perpetual. The determinateness of the species of a chemical body is identical with its substantial nature; we are accordingly here still in the realm of fixed species. In the organic realm, on the other hand, the determinateness of the species is not identical with the substantial nature of an individual; on the contrary, the individual is, in keeping with its determinateness, finite, but just as much infinite. In the chemical process, the Notion exhibits its moments discontinuously: the whole of the chemical process contains, on the one side, fixed determinateness in the mode of indifference, and on the other side, the urge to be internally opposed to self, an opposition in which indifference falls away. But quiescent being and this urge are distinct sides; the totality is posited only in itself or in principle. The unity in which both determinations are at once present does not come to existence; this unity, as existent, is the determination of Life, and towards this Nature strives. Life is present in principle (*an sich*) in the chemical process; but inner necessity is not yet existent unity.

§ 336

The nature of the chemical process is, however, to posit as negated these immediate presuppositions, the basis of its externality and finitude, to alter at a later stage of the process the properties of bodies which appeared as results of an earlier stage, and to reduce those conditions to the rank of products. What is thus posited in general in the chemical process is the *relativity* of the immediate substances and properties. Body as an indifferent existence is thereby posited as a mere *moment* of the individuality, and the Notion is posited in *the reality which corresponds to it*: this *concrete unity* with self, self-produced into unity from the particularizing of the different corporealities, a unity which is the activity of negating this its one-sided form of reference-to-self, of *sundering* and particularizing itself into the moments of the Notion and equally of bringing them back into that unity, is *the organism*—the infinite process which spontaneously kindles and sustains itself.

Zusatz. We have now to make the *transition* from inorganic to organic Nature, from the prose to the poetry of Nature. In the chemical process, bodies alter not merely superficially but on all sides: every property is effaced, cohesion, colour, lustre, opacity, resonance, transparency. Even specific gravity, which seems the deepest and simplest determination, does not survive. It is precisely in the chemical process that the relativity of the apparently indifferent determinations of the individuality which is the essence in this flux of accidents comes to light; body reveals the transiency of its existence, and its relativity is its being. If we are to describe what a body *is*, the whole cycle of its alterations must be stated; for the true individuality of body does not exist in a single state but is exhausted and displayed only in this cycle of states. The totality of Shape does not survive, just because it is only a particular totality; the individual body thus receives its due, i.e., because it is finite, it does not endure. Thus there are metals which, as oxides or neutralized by acids, run through the whole gamut of colours; they can also form transparent, neutral salts, salts generally being the death of colour. Brittleness, solidity, smell, and taste, equally disappear; it is this ideality of the particular that is here displayed. Bodies pass through the whole cycle of such possible determinations. Copper, e.g., in its pure form as a metal is red in colour, but copper sulphate gives a blue crystal, copper hydrate as a precipitate is ultramarine, and a muriate of copper is white; other oxides of copper are green, dark grey, reddish brown, etc.; azurite has still another colour, and so on. The reaction varies according to the agent, and the chemical body is only the sum of its reactions. That is to say, the totality of the reactions exists only as a sum, not as an infinite return-into-self. In all reactions in which the body combines with others, in synsomaties, in oxidation, and in neutrality, it preserves its specific nature, but only implicitly (*als an sich seiende*) not existently; iron always remains in itself iron, but only in itself, not in the manner of its existence. But it is in the preservation of existence, not of being-in-itself, that we are interested, more precisely, that what is in itself should exist or that what exists should be in itself. The cycle of particular reactions constitutes the universal particularity of a body, but this exists only implicitly or in itself, and is not a universal existence. Only in the process of fire is activity immanent—an instant of spontaneous life, whose activity, however, hastens to its death. But because the immediate shape in which particular determinations are present here is destroyed, we here have a transition in which the implicit universal of the determinateness also comes into existence; and this is the self-preservation of the organism. It acts, and reacts against, the most diverse powers (*Potenzen*); in each reaction it is differently determined, but equally also remains a single unity with itself. This implicit determinateness of a kind now also exists; it enters into relationship with an other, but also breaks off this involvement, and is not neutralized in it: it preserves itself, on the contrary, in the process which, none the less, is determined by it and its other. The infinite form as the soul (*Seele*) of individuality is still materialized in shape, and so reduced to a unity which is not an infinitely free form within itself, but is in its existence a quiescently enduring being. This quiescence, however, is contrary to the infinite form, for this is unrest, movement, activity; only as such does it manifest what it is in and for itself. The persistence of the moments of the infinite form in Shape, each of which moments can have an independent material existence, is of course also the entering into existence of the infinite form; but here the unity of the form does not yet have the truth which it is. But now since the chemical process precisely represents the dialectic through which all the particular properties of bodies are brought to destruction (it is the negating of the immediate presuppositions which are the principles of its finitude): what alone endures is the self-subsistent infinite form, the pure immaterial individuality which is for itself, and for which material existence is alterable through and through. The chemical process is the highest to which inorganic Nature can reach; in it she destroys herself and demonstrates her truth to be the infinite form alone. The chemical process is thus, through the dissolution of shape, the transition into the higher sphere of the organism where the infinite form makes itself, as infinite form, real; i.e. the infinite form is the Notion which here attains to its reality. This transition is the raising of existence to universality. Here, therefore, Nature has risen to the existence (*Dasein*) of the Notion; the Notion is no longer merely immanent, is no longer submerged in Nature's mutual externality of being. It is a free Fire (α) as purged of matter, and (β) as materialized in existence (*Dasein*). The moments of what exists are themselves raised to this ideality, have only this being of ideality, and do not fall back into the restricted forms of existence: we thus have objective Time, an imperishable Fire, the Fire of Life; Heraclitus, too, declared the soul to be Fire, and the dry souls to be the best.

SECTION THREE ✦ ORGANICS

§ 337

The real totality of body as the infinite process in which individuality determines itself to particularity or finitude, and equally negates this and returns into itself, re-establishing itself at the end of the process as its beginning, is thus an elevation into the first ideality of Nature, but an ideality which is *fulfilled* (*erfüllt*), and as self-related *negative* unity, has essentially developed the nature of *self* and become *subjective*. This accomplished, the *Idea* has entered into existence, at first an immediate existence, Life. This is:

firstly, as Shape, the universal image of Life, the *geological* organism;

secondly, as particular, formal subjectivity, the *vegetable* organism;

thirdly, as individual, concrete subjectivity, the *animal* organism.

The Idea has truth and actuality only in so far as it is determined as *subjective* (§ 215); Life, as only the *immediate* Idea, is therefore external to itself, is non-life, only the corpse of the life-process, the organism as totality of inanimately existing, mechanical and physical Nature.

Distinguished from this stage is the beginning of subjective vitality, the living organism in the *vegetable* kingdom: the individual, but, as external to itself, still falling apart into its members which are themselves individuals.

It is first in the *animal* organism that the differences of Shape are so developed as to exist essentially only as its members, thereby constituting it *subject*. Vitality, as natural, falls apart into the indeterminate plurality of living things which, however, are in themselves subjective organisms, and it is only in the Idea that they are *one* Life, one organic system of Life.

Zusatz. Let us look back for a moment at the preceding exposition. In the first Section we saw (α) matter, the abstract asunderness, as space; matter, as the abstract being-for-self of asunderness and as offering resistance, is completely separated into units (*vollkommen vereinzelt*), atomistic through and through. This atomistic matter, because of its sameness, is still completely indeterminate; but it is absolutely atomistic only for Understanding, not for Reason. (β) Next we had particular masses determined over against one another: and lastly (γ) gravity, which constitutes the fundamental determination in which all particularity was sublated and ideal (*ideell*). This ideality of gravity which, in the second Section, was transformed into light and then into shape, is now restored. The matter there individualized contains: (α) the free determinations as we saw them in the Elements and their process; it then unfolds itself to become (β) the realm of Appearance (*Erscheinung*), i.e. it develops into the opposition of self-subsistence and reflection-into-other, as specific gravity and cohesion; till (γ) in individual shape, it develops into totality. But since the particular body is just this, to sublate the different modes of its existence, this ideality is now result—an unclouded unity and self-sameness, like light, but at the same time as proceeding from the totality of particularizations which are compressed and taken back into the first indifference. Individuality is now within itself heavy and light-like (*lichtig*)—the triumphant individuality, the unity which, as process in all particularities, brings forth and preserves itself; and this is the subject-matter of the third Section. The living body is always on the point of passing over into the chemical process: oxygen, hydrogen, salt, are always about to appear, but are always again sublated; and only at death or in disease is the chemical process able to prevail. The living creature is always exposed to danger, always bears within itself an other, but can endure this contradiction which the inorganic cannot. But life is also the resolving of this contradiction; and it is in this that the speculative consists: it is only for Understanding that the contradiction is unresolved. Life, therefore, can be grasped only speculatively; for it is precisely in life that the speculative has an existence. The perpetual action of life is thus Absolute Idealism; it becomes an other which, however, is always sublated. If life were a realist (*Realist*), it would have respect for the outer world; but it always inhibits the reality of the other and transforms it into its own self.

Thus it is in life that what is the *True* first exists; it is superior to the stars and the sun which last is, indeed, an individual but not a subject. As unity of the Notion and outwardly turned existence in which the Notion preserves itself, life is Idea; and in this sense Spinoza, too, termed life the adequate notion, an expression which is of course still quite abstract. Life is the union of opposites generally, not merely of the opposition of Notion and reality. Wherever inner and outer, cause and effect, end and means, subjectivity and objectivity, etc., are one and the same, there is life. The true determination of life is that the reality in the unity of Notion and reality, no longer exists in an immediate manner, no longer exists independently as a plurality of properties existing outside one another, but that the Notion is absolute ideality of their indifferent subsistence. Since the ideality we encountered in the chemical process is here posited, individuality is thus posited in its freedom. The subjective, infinite form is now also in its objectivity; this was not yet so in shape, because in this, the determinations of the infinite form still have a fixed determinate being as matters. The abstract Notion of the organism, on the contrary, is that the existence of the particularities conforms to the unity of the Notion since they are posited as transient moments of one Subject: whereas in the system of the heavenly bodies, all the particular moments of the Notion are freely existent, independent bodies, which have not yet returned into the unity of the Notion. The solar system was the first organism; but it was only implicitly (*an sich*) organic, not yet an organic existence. These giant members are independent shapes, and the ideality of their independence is merely their motion; they form only a mechanical organism. But the living creature possesses these giant members of Nature in one body, in which everything particular is posited as Appearance (*als erscheinend*). Thus in life, light completely masters gravity; the living creature, therefore, is individuality which has subdued within itself the further particularizations of gravity, and is active within itself. It is only as self-sublating reality that the self-preservation of the Notion is posited. The individuality of the chemical body can fall victim to an alien power; but life has its other within itself, is in its own self a single rounded totality—or it is its *own end* (*Selbstzweck*). The first part of the Philosophy of Nature was Mechanics, the second part, in its conclusion, was the Chemical Process, and this third part is Teleology (see § 194, *Zusatz* 2). Life is means, but not for an other but for this Notion; it perpetually brings forth its infinite form. Kant already had defined the living creature as an end for itself. Alteration occurs only for the purpose of the Notion, is only an alteration of the otherness of the Notion; and it is in this negation of the negative, in this absolute negativity alone that the Notion can remain at home with itself. The organism is already in itself what it is actually; it is the movement of its becoming. But that which is result is also that from which it has resulted—beginning and end are the same; this, which was hitherto only our knowing, has now entered into existence.

Since life, as Idea, is the movement of itself whereby it first constitutes itself subject, it converts *itself* into its other, into its own obverse (*Gegenwurf*); it gives itself the form of object in order to return into itself and to be the accomplished return-into-self. Thus it is only in the third part that we have life as such, since its principal determination is subjectivity; the earlier stages are only imperfect steps in that direction. And consequently we have the three kingdoms: the living (*lebendige*) *mineral kingdom*, the *vegetable kingdom*, and the *animal kingdom*.

Life, which presupposes itself as the other of itself, is, firstly, geological Nature; and as such it is only the ground, the basis (*Boden*) of life. True, it ought to be life, individuality, subjectivity, but it is not veritable subjectivity, it does not bring back its different members (*Gegliederung*) into unity. In the sphere of life, the moments of individuality and of the return into self or subjectivity must indeed be present; but as immediate, these sides are estranged from each other, i.e. they fall outside of each other. On one side stands individuality, on the other, the process of it; individuality does not yet exist as active, idealizing life, has not yet determined itself to individuality, but is a frozen (*erstarrte*) life, over against the process of life. It, too, contains activity, but partly only as a potentiality (*an sich*), partly as outside itself; the process of subjectivity is divorced from the universal subject itself, for we have not as yet an individual which is, in principle (*an sich*), already self-active. Immediate life is therefore life which is estranged from itself; and thus it is the non-organic nature of subjective life. For all externality is non-organic: as, e.g., for the individual, the sciences are his non-organic nature, in so far as he is not yet familiar with them, but they are stirring in him and are his implicit rationality which he has only to make his own. The earth is a whole, the system of life, but, as crystal, it is like a skeleton, which can be regarded as dead because its members seem still to subsist formally on their own, while its process falls outside it.

The second part is the stage of Reflection, an incipient, truer vitality, in which the individual is intrinsically its own activity, the life-process, but only as subject of Reflection. This formal subjectivity is not as yet the subjectivity that is identical with objectivity, with the articulated system of its members. This subjectivity is still abstract because it issues only from that estrangement: it is the brittle (*spröde*), punctiform, merely individual subjectivity. True, the subject particularizes itself, preserves itself as subjectivity in its connection with its other, articulates itself into members which it pervades; but what makes it only a formal subject is that it does not truly preserve itself in this connection but is still drawn out of itself. The plant is still not veritable subjectivity because the subject, in distinguishing itself from itself and making itself into its own object, cannot trust itself to the truly articulated differences; but it is the return out of these differences which first constitutes true self-preservation. The plant therefore does not advance beyond a formal distinguishing of itself from itself, and it can remain only in formal communion with itself. It unfolds its parts; but since these its members are essentially the whole subject, there is no further differentiation of the plant: leaves, root, stem, are themselves only individuals. Since the real differences (*das Reale*) which the plant produces in order to preserve itself are completely similar to itself, it does not develop true members. Each plant is therefore only an infinite number of subjects; and the togetherness whereby it appears as one subject is only superficial. The plant is thus impotent to hold its members in its power, for these, as self-subsistent, escape from it; and the innocence of the plant is the same impotence of self-relation to inorganic being in which the plant's members become, at the same time, other individuals. This second kingdom is the Water-Kingdom, the kingdom of neutrality.

The third kingdom is the Fire-Kingdom, individual subjectivity as vitality in its completeness—the unity of the plant and the differences. This subjectivity is shape, like the first system of forms; but at the same time the members are not parts, as they still are in the plant. Animal life preserves itself in its otherness, but the latter is an actual difference; and at the same time, the system of these its members is posited as ideal (*ideell*). Only then is the living organism subject, soul (*Seele*), an ethereal being (*das Aetherische*), the essential process of articulation and expansion, but in such a manner that though this shaping is immediately posited in time, the difference is eternally retracted. Fire releases itself (*entläßt sich*) into members, there is a perpetual passage into a product; and this is perpetually brought back to the unity of subjectivity, for the self-subsistence [of the members] is immediately consumed. Animal life is therefore the Notion which displays itself in space and time. Each member has within itself the entire soul (*Seele*), is not self-subsistent but exists only as bound up with the whole. Feeling, the finding of self in self, is the highest achievement and occurs here for the first time; it is to remain one with self in determinateness, in determinateness to be freely at home with oneself. The plant does not find itself within itself because its members are self-subsistent individuals over against it. The explicated Notion of life is animal nature; here for the first time we have vitality in its true form.—These three forms constitute life.

GEOLOGICAL NATURE

§ 338

The first organism, just because it is at first determined as immediate organism or as only *implicitly* organism, does not exist as a *living creature*; for as subject and process, life is essentially a self-*mediating* activity. Considered from the standpoint of subjective life, the first moment of *particularization* is that the organism makes itself into its own *presupposition*, in this way giving itself the form of *immediacy* in which it sets itself over against its condition and outer subsistence. The *inwardization* (*Erinnerung*) of the Idea of Nature within itself to subjective vitality, and still more to spiritual vitality, is the *judgement* or partition (*Urteil*) of the Idea into itself and into this processless immediacy. This immediate totality presupposed by the *subjective* totality is only the *shape* of the organism—the Earth-body as the *universal system* of individual bodies.

Zusatz. In the chemical process, the earth is already present as this totality; the universal Elements enter into the particular corporealities of the totality and are partly causes, partly effects, of the process (§ 328, *Zusatz*, p. 239). But this movement is only abstract, because the corporealities are only particular. Now the earth, it is true, is totality; but because it is only implicitly (*an sich*) the process of these bodies, the process falls outside of its product which is perpetually renewed. As regards the content, none of the determinations belonging to life may be lacking; but as they exist outside of one another, the infinite form of subjectivity is lacking. The earth, thus presupposed by life as its own basis, is posited as not posited; for the positing is concealed by the immediacy. The next stage, then, is that this presupposition resolves itself.

A. HISTORY OF THE EARTH

§ 339

The members of this merely implicit organism do not therefore contain the life-process within themselves, and constitute an external *system* whose forms exhibit the unfolding of an underlying Idea, but whose *process of formation* lies in the *past*. The *powers behind this process*, which Nature leaves behind as selfsubsistences beyond the earth, are the connection of the earth with the solar system and its position therein, its solar, lunar, and cometary life, the inclination of its axis to the orbit, and the magnetic axis. Standing in closer relationship to these axes and their polarization is the *distribution of sea and land*, the compact *spreading* of the land in the *north*, the *division* and sharp tapering of the parts towards the *south*, and then the separation into an *Old* and a *New* World, and the further division of the former into continents distinguished from one another and from the New World by their physical, organic, and anthropological character, to all of which is joined a continent even younger and more immature than the New World; *mountain ranges*, etc.

Zusatz. 1. Whereas the powers behind this process appear as selfsubsistent over against their product, the animal, in its own self-process, has its powers within itself; its members are the potencies (*Potenzen*) of its process. The earth, on the other hand, is merely this, that it has such and such place in the solar system, occupies a place in the series of planets. But in the animal, the whole is present in each member, and consequently in the soul (*Seele*), spatial asunderness is sublated; the soul is omnipresent in its body. But to speak in this way is again to postulate a spatial relationship which, however, is not the true relationship for the soul; the soul is everywhere present, it is true, but undivided, not as an asunderness. But the members of the geological organism are, in fact, outside of one another and are therefore without soul. The earth is the most excellent of all the planets, the mean, the individual: this its existence it owes solely to this permanent togetherness (*Zusammenhang*) of its moments; if one of these were lacking, the earth would cease to be what it is. The earth appears as the dead product; but it is preserved by all these conditions which constitute a single chain, one whole. Because the earth is the universal individual, such moments as magnetism, electricity, and the chemical process are manifested, each in its freedom and independence, in the meteorological process; the animal, on the other hand, is no longer magnetism, and electricity is a subordinate phenomenon in it.

Zusatz. 2. The process of formation, then, is not in the earth itself, simply because this is not a living subject. Therefore the earth does not come to be through this process as does the living creature; it endures, it does not produce itself. For the same reason, the earth's members also endure, and this is no advantage; the living creature, on the other hand, has the advantage of coming to be and passing away. As an individual, the living creature is a manifestation (*Erscheinung*) of the genus, but it is also in conflict with the genus which manifests itself through the destruction of the individual. The process of the earth, in so far as the earth exists for itself as a universal individual, is as such only an inner necessity, for the process is present only in principle (*an sich*) and does not exist in the members of the organism; whereas in the animal, each member is product and also productive. In so far as we are to *consider* the process in the individuality of the earth, we are to *regard* it as a process which is past and which leaves its moments beyond the earth as self-subsistences.[1] *Geognosy* seeks to expound this process as a conflict of the Elements of difference: of Fire and Water. One system, *vulcanism*, maintains that the earth owes its shape, stratification, species of rocks, and so on, to fire. The other system, *neptunism*, asserts equally one-sidedly that all is the result of the action of water (*Wasser-Processes*). Forty years ago,[2] in Werner's time, this was the subject of a great deal of controversy. Both

[1] Now this does not mean, say, that moon and comet, as also the immature and aging (*überreifen*) planets, those three earlier moments, are empirical residues of the earth-process, which the earth has thrown off, nor that the last-mentioned moment, the aging planets, prefigure the state which will be reached in any given time by the earth. On the contrary, as I understand Hegel and the matter, it means that the separate stages of the process which the earth must be *represented* as having passed through, and having still to pass through, have their stereotyped representation (*Vorbild*) in these abstract heavenly bodies. [Michelet's note.]

[2] From the Lectures of 1830.

principles must be recognized as essential; but taken in isolation they are one-sided and formal. In the crystal of the earth, fire is still just as active as water: in volcanoes, springs, and in the meteorological process generally.

Three sides must be distinguished in the earth-process: (a) the universal, absolute process is the process of the Idea, process in and for itself, through which the earth is created and preserved. But the creation is eternal, it is not an event which once happened; it is an eternal generation, for the infinite creative power of the Idea is a perennial activity. We do not, therefore, see in Nature the coming-to-be of the universal; that is, the universal side of Nature has no history. The sciences, political constitutions, etc., on the other hand, have a history, for they are the universal in the sphere of Mind. (b) The process also exists on the earth, but only in a general way, since it does not produce itself as subject. It is the vivifying and fructifying of the earth generally, i.e. the possibility which the living subject takes to itself from this animate being. This process through which the earth makes itself the animate ground and basis of the living subject is the meteorological process. (c) The earth must, of course, be considered as having come to be and as passing away, just as we read in the Scriptures: 'Heaven and earth shall pass away.' Earth and the whole of Nature are to be considered as product; this is necessary according to the Notion.[1] The next step then is the empirical demonstration of this determination in the constitution of the earth; this is chiefly the subject-matter of geognosy. That the earth has had a history, i.e. that its constitution is the result of successive changes, the direct evidence of this is in this constitution itself. It points to a series of tremendous revolutions belonging to a remote past, and which probably also have a cosmic connection, in that the position of the earth with regard to the angle made by the axis with its orbit could have been altered. At the surface of the earth lie buried the flora and fauna of a past world: (α) at great depth, (β) in huge stratifications, (γ) in localities where these species of animals and plants are now extinct.

This state of the earth, according to Ebel's description in particular

---

[1] The seeming contradiction in this—that here the earth is maintained to be something that has come to be and will pass away, whereas a little way back (a) it is supposed not to come to be but to be eternally created—this contradiction can be easily resolved if we recall what was said in the Introduction (§ 247, p. 15) about the eternity of the world; there it was said that though Nature, as the manifestation of the Idea, has eternally flowed from the latter's creative activity, yet the finite, individual side of Nature, owing to its positedness and dependence on the Idea, must also have come to be. In the Notion of Nature, to be the Idea in the form of otherness, is implied the necessity for considering the earth, too, as having originated. None the less, the empirical demonstrations of this origination never get beyond showing that the earth owes its present constitution to a great upheaval, but not that the earth as this universal individual as such has originated. [Michelet's note.]

(*On the Structure of the Earth*, vol. ii, pp. 188 et seq.), is roughly as follows: Already in fletz formations one finds petrified wood, in fact entire trees, dendrolites, etc., but on an even greater scale in alluvial terrains. Huge forests which have been flattened down lie buried under masses of debris the depth of which varies from 40 to 100 feet and sometimes even from 600 to 900 feet. Many of these forests are in their vegetable state, undecayed and intact with bark, roots, branches, filled with resin and making excellent fuel; others are petrified into quartz-agate (*Kiesel-Agat*). Most of the species of these trees are still identifiable, e.g. palm trees, and among others a fossil forest of palm tree trunks in the Neckar valley not far from Kannstadt, and so on. In Holland, in the region of Bremen (*im Bremischen*), the trees of the forests there are usually found intact, lying flat firmly joined to their root-stocks; elsewhere the trunks are broken off cleanly and separated from their rootstocks which lie close by, still firmly stuck in the ground. In East Friesland, in Holland, and in the region of Bremen, all the tree-tops lie pointing to the south-east and north-east. These forests have grown here, but on the banks of the Arno in Tuscany one finds fossil oaks (with palm trees over them) lying in a confused mass and mixed up with petrified shell-fish and huge bones. These immense forests are found in all the alluvial terrains of Europe, North and South America, and northern Asia. As regards animal life, shell-fish, snails, and zoophytes come first in respect of quantity in Europe wherever there are fletz formations, consequently in countless localities in this continent; similarly in Asia, Anatolia, Syria, Siberia, Bengal, China, etc., in Egypt, Senegal, in the foothills at the Cape of Good Hope, and in America. They are found not only at great depths, in the first fletz formations covering the primitive rocks, but also at the greatest heights, e.g. on Mount Perdu, the highest part of the Pyrenees, 10,968 feet high (Voltaire's explanation of this is that travellers took fish, oysters, and the like up with them as provisions), on the Jungfrau, the highest peak of the limestone Alps, 13,872 feet high, and on the Andes in South America, which are 12,000–13,242 feet above sea-level. Such remains are not scattered throughout the whole mass of the mountain but occur only in individual strata, often in the greatest order, as if in families, and as well preserved as if they had peacefully settled there. In the very oldest stratified formations lying directly on the primitive rocks there are, on the whole, very few fossils of sea-animals, and those only of certain species; but in the later deposits their number and variety increase and sometimes, though very rarely, fossil fish, too, are found. Fossil plants, on the other hand, occur only in the more recent strata, and the bones of amphibians, mammals, and birds, only in the most recent strata. Most remarkable, in fact, are the bones of quadrupeds, elephants, tigers, lions, bears, in species now extinct. All these huge animals lie not far below the surface, under sand, marl, or loam, in Germany, Hungary, Poland, Russia, especially in Asiatic Russia where there is a considerable trade in the tusks they dig up. Humboldt found mammoth bones in the

Valley of Mexico and in the valleys of Quito and Peru, always at heights of 7,086 to 8,934 feet above sea-level, and in the River Plate he found the skeleton of a huge animal 12 feet long and 6 feet high. But not only these remains of the organic world, but the geognostic structure of the earth, too, and generally the whole formation of the alluvial terrains, bear the stamp of violent upheaval and external formation. In mountain chains there are entire formations which themselves form solid mountains and mountain ranges, composed entirely of boulders and debris all stuck together in a conglomerate. The nagelfluhe in Switzerland is a species of rock consisting of smooth pebbles cemented together again by sandstone and limestone. The stratifications of the nagelfluhe deposit are very regular: one layer, e.g., consists of big stones almost all of which are 6 inches thick, the next layer of smaller stones and the third layer of still smaller ones; this is now followed by another layer of larger stones. The constituents are the most varied assortment of debris: granites, gneisses, porphyries, amygdaloids, serpentines, silicious schists, hornstones, flints, saline and compact limestones, argillaceous and ferruginous stones, and alpine sandstones. In one nagelfluhe there is more of one species, and in another more of another species. One such nagelfluhe forms a mountain chain with a breadth of 1 to 3 leagues; it rises to a height of 5,000 to 6,000 feet above sea-level (the Rigi is 5,723 feet high), which therefore is above the tree-line in Switzerland. With the exception of the Alps and the Pyrenees they are higher than all the other mountains in France and England; and even the highest peak of the Giant Mountains in Silesia is only 4,949, and the Brocken only 3,528 feet high. Lastly, all primitive rock masses, granite mountains and rocks, bear in themselves the terrible traces of frightful poundings and upheavals; they are intersected lengthwise and crosswise by innumerable valleys and ravines superposed one on top of the other by stages, and so on.

All of this which belongs to the sphere of history must be accepted as fact; it does not pertain to philosophy. If, now, this is to be explained, we must understand the way in which this must be treated and considered. Formerly, history applied to the earth, but now it has come to a halt: a life which, inwardly fermenting, had Time within its own self; the Earth-spirit which has not yet reached the stage of opposition—the movement and dreaming of one asleep, until it awakes and receives its consciousness in Man, and so confronts itself as a stabilized (*ruhige*) formation. As for the empirical side of this past state, it is considered that the main interest for geognosy lies in the determination of Time, in knowing which stratum of rocks is the oldest, etc. To explain the geological organism usually means to make the order in which these different formations succeeded one another the chief business; but this kind of explanation is only external. It is said that first the granitic primitive rocks, the deepest strata, came into being one after the other in time, then, regenerated, dissolved granite which was precipitated again. The upper strata, e.g. the fletz formations, are supposed to have been deposited later in time, and the solution (*Brei*) is supposed to have run into the fissures, and so on. This mere 'happening', which involves only a difference of time, this temporal succession of the strata, does not explain anything at all; or rather it completely ignores the necessity of the process, the comprehension of it. The solvent effects of water or fire are wholly separate factors which do not express organic fermentation: any more than when we understand it as the process of oxidation and de-oxidation, or quite superficially reduce it to the opposition of the carbon and nitrogen series. The whole style of explanation is nothing more than a transformation of spatial juxtaposition into temporal succession: as if, seeing a house a house with a ground floor, first and second floors and a roof, I now reflect with profound wisdom, and conclude that therefore the ground floor was built first, and after that the first floor, and so on. Why is the limestone later? Because here limestone overlays sandstone. This is a facile insight. This transformation has really no rational interest. The process has no other content than the product. It is an indifferent curiosity which wants to see also in the form of succession what exists as a justaposition. One can have interesting thoughts about the long intervals between such revolutions, about the profounder revolutions caused by alterations of the earth's axis, and also those caused by the sea. They are, however, hypotheses in the historical field, and this point of view of a mere succession in time has no philosophical significance whatever.

But in this sequence there does lie a deeper meaning. The meaning and spirit of the process is the inner coherence, the necessary connection of these formations, and nothing is added to this by the succession in time. The general law of this sequence of formations can be recognized without any reference to the historical aspect; that is the essential point—this is the rational element which alone has interest for the Notion: to recognize in this sequence the characteristics of the Notion. It is Werner's great merit to have drawn attention to this sequence and to have looked at it, on the whole, from the correct point of view. The inner coherence exists in the present as a juxtaposition, and it must depend on the constitution, on the content, of these formations themselves. On one side, therefore, the history of the earth is an empirical matter, and on the other, a reasoning from empirical data. The point of interest is not to determine how things were millions of years ago (and in the matter of years one can be generous); the interest is confined to what is there before us—to this system of distinct formations. It is a very complex empirical science. Everything in this corpse cannot be explained, for contingency plays its part in it: any more than it is the concern of philosophy to acquaint itself with the rational system of legislation in its obscure rudimentary state, or to get to know in what chronological order and in what external circumstances such a system has come into existence.

The production of the living thing is represented in general as an evolution out of chaos, where plant and animal life, organic and inorganic, were in a single unity. Or it was imagined that there was a general form of life and that this split up into the many species of plants and animals, into the races of mankind. But we must not assume a sensuous process of differentiation appearing in time, nor the existence in time of a universal Man (*General-Mensch*). To postulate such a monster is to give rein to empty imagination. The natural, living thing is not mingled, is not a medley of all different forms as in arabesques. There is essentially *Understanding* in Nature. Nature's formations are determinate, bounded, and enter as such into existence. So that even *if* the earth was once in a state where it had no living things but only the chemical process, and so on, yet the moment the lightning of life strikes into matter, at once there is present a determinate, complete creature, as Minerva fully armed springs forth from the head of Jupiter. The Mosaic story of creation is still the best in its quite naïve statement that on this day plants came into being, on another day the animals, and on another day man. Man has not developed himself out of the animal, nor the animal out of the plant; each is at a single stroke what it is. In this individual, evolutionary changes do occur: at birth it is not yet complete, but is already the real possibility of all it is to become. The living thing is the point, this particular soul (*Seele*), subjectivity, infinite form, and thus immediately determined in and for itself. Already in the crystal, as a point, the entire shape is at once present, the totality of the form; the crystal's capacity for growth is only a quantitative alteration. Still more is this the case in the living thing.

3. The particular formations of the earth are the subject-matter of *physical geography*. The self of the earth, as diversity of formation, is a quiescent exposition (*Auslegung*) and self-subsistence of all its parts. It is the solid structure of the earth which does not yet possess its life as soul (*Seele*), but as universal life. It is the inorganic earth which, as an inanimate (*unbegeistet*) shape, sets forth (*auslegt*) its members like a rigid body. Its separation into water and land (which first unite with and permeate each other in the living subject), into continents and islands, and the shaping and crystallization of these into valleys and mountains, all this belongs to its purely mechanical formation. With regard to this, one may well say that in one place the earth is more contracted, and in another more spread out; but this does not tell us anything. The concentration in the north results in the products, plants and animals, sharing a common nature. At the extremities, animal life is particularized and individualized into various genera and species which are peculiar to each continent. This appears at first to be accidental; but the activity of the Notion is to grasp as necessarily determined what to sense-consciousness appears as contingent. Contingency certainly has its place, too, but only in unessentials. The north-west to south-east direction of countries and mountain ranges can also be traced back to magnetic axes; but magnetism is, in general, as a linear direction, a wholly formal moment, the force of which is already suppressed even in the globe and still more in the Subject. A rational comprehension of the configuration as a whole, would

have to consider the fixed land formations in comparison with the ocean currents rather than with the oceans, i.e. with the expression of the free movement of the earth in its own self. In general, the effort to develop a shape definitely opposed to the sphere tends to produce a pyramidal form, constructing a base in the former, a breadth which tapers off to a point on the other side; this is why the land falls away to the south. But the restless, rotatory movement of the ocean currents hollows out this shape everywhere in a west-to-east direction, as it were pushes and presses this solid land mass towards the east and distends the shape on the eastern side like a bent bow, so that to the west it is rounded and bellies out (*bauchigt*). But in general the land is split into two parts, the Old and the New Worlds. The former is shaped like a horse-shoe, the latter elongated from north to south; and this is new, not merely through the accident of being discovered later, i.e. of a later entry into the general system of peoples (although it is also new because of this very fact, since it is only in this association that its existence is actual), but everything in it is new: humanity there lacks those great weapons of civilizations against one another, the horse and iron. No part of the Old World has been conquered by the New, but the New is only a booty for Europe; its fauna is feebler, but its flora is on a vast scale. In the Old World, the mountain ranges run, on the whole, from west to east or else from south-west to north-east; by contrast, in America, the counter aspect (*Wider-lage*) of the Old World, they run from south to north; but the rivers, especially in South America, flow to the east. Altogether the New World presents an undeveloped duality—a northern and a southern part, like the poles of the magnet: but the Old World exhibits the perfect diremption into three parts, one of which, Africa, the compact metal, the lunar principle, is rigid through heat, a land where man's inner life is dull and torpid—the inarticulate spirit which has not awakened into consciousness; the second part is Asia, characterized by Bacchanalian extravagance and cometary eccentricity, the centre of unrestrained spontaneous production, formlessly generative and unable to become master of its centre. But the third part, Europe, forms the consciousness, the rational part, of the earth, the balance of rivers and valleys and mountains—whose centre is Germany. The division of the world into continents is therefore not contingent, not a convenience; on the contrary, the differences are essential.

B. STRUCTURE OF THE EARTH

§ 340

The physical organization of the earth, as immediate, does not begin with the simple, enveloped form of the germ, but with a beginning (*Ausgang*) which has fallen apart into a duality, into the concrete *granitic* principle and the *calcareous* principle: the former is the core of mountains in which the triad of moments is displayed in an already developed state, while the latter is the difference which has been reduced to *neutrality*. The development of the moments of the first principle into specific formations goes through a series of stages in which the further forms are partly transitional, the granitic principle remaining the basis, only more unlike and unformed within itself; partly a development of its moments into a more determinate difference and into more abstract mineral forms (*Momente*) such as metals and fossil objects generally, until the development loses itself in mechanical stratifications and alluvial terrains lacking any immanent formative process. Side by side with this proceeds the development of the other, the neutral principle, partly into weaker transformations and partly, in combination with the granitic principle, into formations ranging from concrescent forms down to merely external mixtures.

Zusatz. Werner's mineralogy distinguished between rock species and lodes or veins: geology treats of the former and oryctognosy of the latter. These names are no longer used in textbooks of mineralogy; it is only miners who retain the distinction. The rocks comprise the concrete mass and geology studies the further formation of a fundamental form of rock species and its modifications, in which the rocks remain concrete formations. From this develops the other, more abstract side, the veins, which, too, form themselves into mountains, so that generally the two sides cannot be exactly separated. Such abstract formations are crystals, ores, metals, where the moment of difference has developed. They have made themselves into neutral substances capable of forming concrete shapes; for it is precisely in such abstract forms that shape becomes free. The types of vein are seams in the mountains consisting of a specific medley of rocks and earths; they have a definite grain or inclination, i.e. they make an angle with the horizon. Now these rock strata are cut by the veins at various angles and it is these veins which are important in mining. Werner thought of these veins as fissures filled up with a different mineral from that of which the mountain was composed.

The physical formation of the earth is so constituted that its surface erupts into organic centres, into points of totality, which unite within themselves the whole and then let it fall apart, displaying it in individual products. This contraction, in unfolding outwards, passes over into a scattering abroad of the moments. These centres are a kind of cores which, in their shells and husks, represent the whole and which pass through these to blend with the general soil (*allgemeinen Boden*) as their element.

The core and root of these formations is not a simple self but the developed totality of the formation which contains within itself the already separated moments—the existence of the organic unity as it is able to exist in this universal individuality. This core is *granite*, which is so blended, so hard, so solid, that the individual parts are not easily separated out of it in their pure form. Everywhere there is an incipient *crystallization*. In the whole, granite is the innermost, the mean, the basis, and it is to its traits in two directions that the other formations first attach themselves. It has three constituents although it is itself primary; but these three constitute a single, quite hard mass. Granite, as we know, is composed of (α) *silica, quartz*, absolute earth, the rigid, punctiform principle, (β) *mica*, the surface which has developed to the stage of opposition, the punctiform principle which has unfolded itself, the moment of combustibility which contains the germ of every abstract form, and lastly (γ) *felspar*, the adumbrated (*angedeuteten*) but still undeveloped neutrality and crystallization of lime in the siliceous earths, for two to three per cent of lime (*Kali*)* is found in it. This is the simple, earthy triad which now develops *in accordance with its different sides*, and more specifically, in the two directions of the process: on the one hand, this whole is to contain the differences as its form and is to remain the whole, only with a variously modified content; and on the other, the differences are to permeate the substance (*Substanz*) and become simple abstract isolates; the former is the formation as it appears at this point, and the latter is difference, but a difference which has lost all chemical significance and is just the formation of simple physical bodies. More precisely, we have: (α) the external forming of the primitive rock; (β) the extirpation of the existent moments of the totality and the separation of them in their purity (*die reine Ausscheidung*) as abstract isolates—fletz-formation; this is followed by (γ) decay into an indifferent existence—alluvial terrain.

1. In *primitive rock*, as throughout all the further formations, we find the antithesis of (α) the *siliceous*, and (β) the *argillaceous* and its cognate forms, and (γ) the *calcareous*. The antithesis to granite is primitive lime-stone (*Urkalk*); so that the siliceous and the calcareous series form an essential antithesis. Steffens in his earlier writings has drawn attention to this; and it is one of his best inspirations among the otherwise crude and immature observations of his undisciplined imagination. In primitive rock, the different character of these sides is well marked and a determining factor. The calcareous side is the total neutrality, and its modifications concern more the outer formation than the inwardly self-specifying diversity. In siliceous formations, on the contrary, where granite forms the basis, a more definite difference is present.

(*a*) The granite rocks which form the beginning have the greatest

* *Kali*, misprint for *Kalk*.

height; the other rocks are supported on the granite in such a way that the rocks of greatest height are always the undermost stratum, the others in turn resting on them. The next rock formations are modifications of granite, further developments of one side of it, where now one and now the other side predominates. The granitic rocks are surrounded by beds of *gneiss, syenite, mica schist*, and so on, which are nothing but slight modifications of granite. 'One species of rock', says Ebel, 'passes by gradual modification of its composition into the rock species of another slab of rock. In this way, compact granite passes over into veined granite and gneiss, and the hardest gneiss passes over through varying combinations of its constituents into the softest mica schist, which itself passes over into argillaceous schist', and so on. The latter species are quite contiguous so that the passage of one into the other is readily seen. In the study of geology, then, we must first direct our attention to the general mass of rocks and the Notion of the moments, rather than thoughtlessly enumerate the different kinds, straightway converting a small difference into a fresh genus or species. What is most important is to follow the transitions from one layer to another. Nature keeps to this order only in a general way and numerous variations occur although the basic features of the order persist. But while Nature juxtaposes the species as parts indifferently, she indicates the necessity by the transition of the different species into one another: but the difference in kind comes to view not only by a mere lessening of difference but by a differentiation in accordance with the Notion. Nature marks these transitions as a mingling of the qualitative and the quantitative, or shows that the one species differs from the other in kind. In the one rock there are nascent formations of the other rock in the form of globules, clusters, centres, partly mingled with the first rock, partly also externally separated off in it. Heim, with a truly philosophical view of the matter, has very clearly exhibited this transition, the breaking forth of one rock in another. Syenite is the rival of granite; instead of mica it contains only hornblende which is more argillaceous than mica but resembles it. From mica schist the next stage is a definite loss of depth (*Verflachung*); quartz disappears from view and clay becomes predominant, until thin sheets (*Fläche*) and clay entirely predominate in argillaceous schist, in schistous formation generally, which is the next change of form; here the peculiar nature of quartz, felspar, mica, and hornblende formations is dissipated and lost. Further down, formlessness remains predominant, the transformation of granite progressing from this point onwards; there are a number of other formations still belonging to this stage but they are degenerate forms of granite.—Mica schist is transformed into porphyry which consists mainly of clay and also of another mineral (chert), throughout which grains of felspar and quartz are dispersed. Old porphyry still belongs to the primitive rocks. Schist assumes different forms; becomes harder, more like quartz in siliceous schist, and more sandy in greywacke schist and greywacke, so that the clay is no longer predominant. Greywacke, e.g. in the Harz mountains, is an inferior reproduction of granite, looks like sandstone, and is a mixture of quartz, argillaceous schist, and felspar: this is truer still of greenstone which consists of hornblende, felspar, and quartz, the first-named being the principal constituent. Joined on to these are the entire further ascending series of trap rocks, but here everything is more mixed. That is the limit of these absolute rocks.

So the development, starting from granite, proceeds, as we have said, to the stage where its particular constituents are no longer visible. The triad forms the basis; but these moments become separated and one or the other emerges. Basalt is the central point where the elements completely permeate one another again; it contains 40 parts of silica, 16 of clay, 9 of potash, 2 of talc, 2 of natron, and the rest is manganese oxide and water. Its alleged volcanic origin has this much truth in it, that it belongs to the igneous principle—but it owes its origin as little to fire as to water. An internal deformation is found in it and still more in amygdaloid, olivine, augite, etc., which are abstract formations completely particularized in themselves. From this point onwards we meet with only a formal mixture or formal decomposition of these elements. The further details must be classified in accordance with this principle: (α) one line of development is only a modification of granite where traces of the triple basis are still always present: in gneiss, mica schist, porphyry, right down to greenstone, greywacke, basalt, amygdaloid, and even ordinary sand. (β) The other line is the splitting up of the concrete mass into abstract forms. Here, especially, we find the antithesis of the siliceous and the calcareous series: ($\alpha\alpha$) in mountain ranges, ($\beta\beta$) within these in the formerly so-called gangues.

(b) So far, we have described mainly the siliceous formations; but on the other side, the whole passes over into the talc-form of saline earth (*der salzigen Erde*), the igneous principle (*das Brennliche*) which has unfolded itself to the point of bitterness (serpentine and the like), and which appears sporadically here and there.

(c) Over against this igneous form, then, is the calcareous as such, the neutral substance which, however, permeated by metalleity, contains qualitative unity and consequently is wholly permeated by organic development. The primitive limestone (*Urkalk*) is already associated with granite and is just as compact as granitic rock. Thus the primitive rocks are surrounded by limestone formations (*Kalkgebirgszüge*); this primitive limestone is fine-grained, crystalline. Primitive limestone, the opposite of granite, meets up with a more unfolded limestone in *transitional* limestone. Formations also occur where granite and limestone are piled in a confused mass: thus primitive limestone, e.g., permeates mica. Von Raumer in his *Geognostic Essays* (p. 13) says: 'Primitive limestone accompanies schistous rocks with which it mixes, alternating with them in thin layers, in beds, in huge deposits, and sometimes forming chunks of rock in which the schist is almost completely suppressed.'

2. These principal formations pass over into so-called fletz-formation and alluvial rock, where these moments, separated out almost as pure earths, represent the completely resolved totality: layers of sandstone, beds of clay and loam, coal-seams, peat-beds, bituminous schists, beds of rock-salt; finally, limestone strata mixed in with the last-named, gypsum and marl. As the granitic principle becomes more of an indeterminate mixture, the separate parts of what is differentiated now appear in greater abstract isolation, and this is an obliteration of differences as in trap and greywacke which belong to the transitional and fletz species. But in the process in which granite and its cognate forms gathers itself up into abstract isolation, the more it loses its compactness, its firmly knit totality, and flattens out, the more, on the other hand, do the self-separating ores and their accompanying crystals unfold themselves (iron at a particularly early stage), and these are found disseminated throughout entire rock masses and strata and especially in seams and fletz formations. The interior is opened up and reveals abstractly distinct formations. These seams are the outward formations of particular elements from the rock species which are more concrete; and in attaining to a freer outward formation they yield these manifold crystalline products and pure forms. In granite they do not occur at all or only rarely; only tin occurs. It is only when the primary rock has unfolded further to the stage of secondary (*mittlern*) limestone (for metals, too, are not found in primary limestone) that metal appears. These abstract isolations can appear only in rocks which are themselves more abstract or are mixed. Cavities open up where rock-crystal formations have reached their characteristic shape and have detached themselves from their inner connection with the rock.

The lodes are regarded as nests and containers of these minerals; in a purely mechanical manner these lodes traverse the rock-mass. Drying-out is supposed to have caused a fissure, a crevice in the rock into which the metallic solution flowed (*der aufgelöste Brei von Metallen u. s. f.*): this is the theory specially favoured by the neptunists and it provides a very plausible explanation of the subsequent closing-up of such rock-wounds. But it is a thoughtless conjecture; the relationship is not mechanical but is, in truth, physical, one in which the parts of the totality simplify themselves and sublate their developed determinate being, and for this very reason now expel it in abstracted form. The lodes mostly run counter to the direction of the rock—they form, as it were, fault-planes (*Bruch-flächen*), not merely in spatial form but in a physical [i.e. non-mechanical] sense. According to Trebra's observations, the lodes follow the gentler slopes.

These lodes must not be regarded as contingently connected with the rock species; for though contingency necessarily also plays a great part here, yet we must not fail to recognize the essential connection between them. Miners have varied experiences in this regard. One of the most important aspects of this connection concerns the range of metals and other minerals found in association. Gold, e.g., is always found with quartz, either alone or with copper and lead, with silver and zinc, and so on: not with mercury, tin, cobalt, molybdenum, wolfram. Silver is freer in its associations (*geselliger*), is found much oftener with other metals, most commonly with galena and accompanied by zinc ore. Mercury is found with quartz, calcareous spar, iron, and therefore with sparry iron ore, too; copper is rarely found with mercury. The various kinds of mercury are usually found together and all of them mainly in clayey soils. Copper with its various ores is accompanied by few minerals. Tin is not found with silver, lead, cobalt, calcareous spar, gypsum, etc. There are metals which occur in all rock-formations, such as iron, for example; others such as molybdenum, titanium, tantalium, wolfram, uranium, tin, are more confined to the primitive rocks. Molybdenum and wolfram, for instance, disappear with the primitive formations. Gold occurs most frequently near the equator. Other noteworthy relationships which hint at a higher connection are the lodes which contain sometimes precious and sometimes base metals. The cobalt formations at Riegelsdorf and Saalfeld in the Thuringian Forest only become rich in this mineral when the lodes are set in the primordial (lower new red)[1] sandstone formations. At Andreasberg in the Harz the rock is schist and greywacke, and the lodes contain base metal when set in beds of siliceous schist, in Klaustal this happens when the lodes run through fissures in clay or loam, and in the Freiburg area, when they run through porphyry. Metals occur, too, at specific depths. Horn-silver, white antimony ore, occur only in the upper strata. In the Tyrol, a bed of sparry iron ore, clayey ironstone, and brown-spar appears where copper pyrites peters out. At La Gardette in Dauphine, gold nuggets lie near the surface and especially where the ground is traversed by rifts containing iron-ochre. The veins differ according to the thickness of the rifts. At Sayn-Altenkirchen, iron-glance is always found where the lode narrows, and where it widens limonite, black magnetite, and sparry iron ore are found. 'Topazes occur in a greasy mica which has been modified into lithomarge, and in a friable lithomarge which is sometimes pure and sometimes mixed with a good deal of iron-ochre; this lithomarge also owes its formation to mica and is accompanied by quartz and china-clay. Both on the topazes and euclase, very clear imprints can be seen of very fine scales of lithomarge which could be sufficient evidence of the simultaneous formation of these minerals. It is the same with the emeralds found around Salzburg. In gneiss, the mica separates itself and forms huge seams up to several feet in thickness. Emeralds are rarely found in gneiss but always in mica, never in a compact cluster but scattered unevenly through the mica. The emeralds, too, have imprints of scales of the mica surrounding them.'[2]

[1] (*totliegende*).
[2] Spix and Martius, *Travels*, vol. i, p. 332. (Cf. Frischholz in Molls, *New Yearbooks*, vol. 4, no. 3.)

3. The last moment, the transition from fletz-formations to alluvial terrain, is a mixture, an abstract stratification of clay, sand, lime, marl, the completely formless minerals.—Such are the general outlines of the advance founded on the determinations of the Notion. The primitive rock develops itself to the point where it loses its mineral state and joins on to a vegetable state. Argillaceous earth and coal formations become transformed unmistakably into peat, where mineral and vegetable are no longer distinguishable; for peat has a vegetable origin and yet all the same still belongs to the mineral kingdom. On the other side, it is the limestone formations which, in their ultimate formations, tend towards the osseous nature of the animal. The limestone is in the first instance granular, marble, mineral through and through; but in its further forms it belongs partly to fletz-formation and partly to alluvial terrain, and passes over into forms of which it cannot be said whether they are mineral or animal (molluscs). They are not yet shells which could be regarded as the remains of an extinct animal world; although, of course, that is one explanation of the petrified animal forms which are found in abundance in limestone-pits. But, on the other hand, there are limestone formations which are not the remains, but only the beginnings, of animal form in which the limestone terminates. This is, therefore, an intermediate stage between limestone and petrifaction proper, but a stage which must be regarded only as a further development of the nature of mollusca, of what is purely mineral, for such forms have not yet attained to the fulness of animal life. The opposition of the siliceous and calcareous series hints, in this way, at a superior organic difference, since their boundaries are linked on the one hand with the vegetable kingdom, and on the other, with the animal kingdom. This side, too, has been clearly brought out by Steffens, but he has gone too far in treating these formations (*a*) as originating from a vegetable and animal process of the earth, and (*b*) as if the former were the carbon series and the latter the nitrogen series.

As regards the rudimentary organic forms in the geological organism, these belong principally to clay schists and limestone stratifications, partly as scattered animal and plant forms, but mainly in entire huge masses organically shaped through and through: they are also found in coal measures in which the tree-form is very often distinctly recognizable; so that if the breccias are included in the reckoning, there is present as much organically shaped matter as pure mineral. It is easy enough to postulate here the earlier existence of an organic world which was submerged by water. But then where did this world come from? It has arisen out of the Earth, but not historically; it perpetually proceeds from the Earth and has its Substance in it. These organic forms, especially where they occur singly and do not constitute the entire rock-mass, are present where beds pass over into one another. The boundary where the moments, which processless Nature lets fall apart, are posited in a unity, is pre-eminently the site of organic forms, of petrifactions, and of those products which are neither animal nor plant forms, but which

transcend the crystalline forms and are playful essays in organic formation. It is especially in schistous and calcareous formations that the
inorganic unfolds itself. For the former, in partly transforming its earthy
nature into the sulphurous principle, but partly retaining in itself metalleity, sublates its fixed subjectivity. Its punctiform nature, opened up by
bitumen and containing differentiation generally, receives in metalleity
the continuity of an absolute subject and predicate, is infinite, and fluctuates between the organic and inorganic. Similarly, the calcareous
formation as the neutral substance (*das Neutrale*), has in its sides the
moment of reality—they persist: and simple metalleity, through the
simplicity of its continuity, manifests itself as the qualitative unity which
cancels the indifference of the sides; a unity which contains the sides of
the neutral substance, and a neutral substance which has unity. The
calcareous formation thus represents the transition to organic being: on
the one side, arresting the leap into dead neutrality, and on the other side,
into lifeless and unitary abstraction. *These* organic forms (not all, of
course, but those others are not in question) are not to be thought of as
having once actually lived and then died: on the contrary, they are
stillborn. To suppose otherwise is like supposing that bone-fibres were
once veins or nerves, and subsequently hardened. It is organoplastic
Nature which generates the organic in the element of immediate being
and therefore as a dead shape, crystallized through and through, like the
artist who represents human and other forms in stone or on a flat canvas.
He does not kill people, dry them out and pour stony material into them,
or press them into stone (he can do this too, for he pours models into
moulds); what he does is to produce in accordance with his idea and by
means of tools, forms which represent life but are not themselves living:
Nature, however, does this directly, without needing such mediation.
That is, the Notion is not present as something conceived or imagined,
while the thing stands over against the thinker and is fashioned by him;
the Notion has not the form of consciousness but is immediately in the
element of being, not detached from it. The Notion has the material for
its work, where the moments of the organic are present in their totality;
the question is not of a universal life of Nature, of Nature being everywhere alive, but of the essence of life: this essence is to be comprehended,
to be exhibited in the moments of its actuality or totality, and these
moments are to be demonstrated.

C. LIFE OF THE EARTH

§ 341

This crystal of life, the inanimate organism of the earth which has
its *Notion* in the sidereal connection outside it, but possesses its
own peculiar process as a presupposed past, is the *immediate*

subject of the meteorological process, through which, this subject, as *in itself* the totality of life, no longer becomes merely an individual shape (§ 287) but is fructified into vitality.—Land and especially sea, as thus the real possibility of life, perpetually erupt at every point into punctiform, transient forms of life: lichens, infusoria, and in the sea countless hosts of phosphorescent points of life. But it is just because *generatio aequivoca* has this objective organism outside it that it is restricted to this punctiform organization, does not develop internally into a specifically articulated organism, or reproduce itself *ex ovo*.

Zusatz. Whereas the geological organism of the earth was at first a product in the formative process of its shape, now, as the underlying productive individuality, it overcomes its rigidity and unfolds into subjective vitality which, however, it excludes from itself and delivers over to other individuals. In other words, because the geological organism is only implicitly (*an sich*) vitality, the truly living organism is an other than the geological organism itself. But since this is in itself the negativity of itself, is the sublating of its immediacy, it posits the inwardness of itself but as a being which is the other of it: that is, the earth is fertile—fertile simply as the ground and basis (*Boden*) of the individual vitality upon it. But the earth is vitality only in an indeterminate mode; true, this vitality erupts at all points, but only feebly. This universal life of the earth has living parts which are the Elements, i.e. are its universal, its inorganic nature. But as the earth is also a particular body over against its satellite and the sun and comets, it is the perpetual generation, i.e. the conservation, of this system of differences, is the absolutely universal chemical process. Since, however, the giant members of this diremption are free, independent individuals, their connection exists purely as the free process of motion: while the comets themselves are a fresh, perpetual generation of this process. The reality of this process, then, the destruction of seemingly independent forms and the consequent emergence of real individual unity, this is first reached in the individual chemical process, which for this very reason is profounder and more fundamental than the universal process. But because the universal process of the Elements is that of material substances, the individual process cannot be without it. The free, independent members of the universal process, sun, comet, and moon, are now, in their truth, the Elements: Air as atmosphere, Water as the sea, but Fire as a terrestrial Element contained in the fructified, dissolved (*aufgelösten*) earth and separated off as a fructifying sun. The life of the earth is the process of atmosphere and sea in which it generates these Elements, each of which is an independent life for itself while all of them constitute only this process. Here the chemical process has lost its absolute meaning and is present only as moment: it is reflected into self-subsistence, subdued by the subject in which it is held fast and powerless. Each Element, through its substance, is itself related as a free subject to the other, and the formation of the organic earth contains the modes of existence of its organic life.

1. Its first determinate life is now the atmosphere. But the meteorological process is not the life-process of the earth, although the earth is vivified by it; for this vivification is only the real possibility of subjectivity emerging on the earth as a living being. As pure motion, as ideal substance, the atmosphere does contain the life of the celestial motion; but at the same time, it materializes this motion in its element. The atmosphere is the earth in its state of dissolution, of pure tension, the relation of gravity and heat; it runs through the period of the year as well as of the month and day, and expresses it as variations of heat and gravity. This periodical fluctuation in turn splits into two: where the axial rotation preponderates, the diurnal period has the ascendancy, and therefore at the equator there is a daily variation, a daily rise and fall of the barometer level; but this fluctuation is not seasonal. It is otherwise in the temperate zone where the daily rise and fall is not so noticeable and the variations are all linked more with the phases of the moon.

The gravity is interior gravity, elasticity as pressure, but essentially alteration of specific gravity: a movement, an undulation, of the atmosphere which goes together with an alteration of temperature; but so that this alteration has the opposed meaning, viz. of being ordinary temperature and light-temperature (*Lichttemperatur*)—the former, heat given out [by the atmosphere] and the latter freely added to the atmosphere by light. The latter is, in general, clearness and pure elasticity of the air, high barometer-level: while the former belongs to the formative process (*Gestaltung*) and is present when the elasticity of the air passes over into rain or snow.* It is in the air that these abstract moments return into themselves.

Just as the celestial motion materializes itself in the air, so on the other side sea and earth invade the air and volatilize themselves into it: a processless, immediate transition. The air individualizes both within itself: partly into the universal atmospheric process in which it displays its greatest independence, resolving water and earth into odours and also discharging itself and passing over into water; partly in transforming itself into meteors as transitory comets—into earths which it generates, i.e. aerolites: partly into noxious airs, miasmas, harmful to animal life: and partly into honey-dews and mildews—animal and vegetable airs.

2. But the neutral earth, the sea, is equally the movement of ebb and flow, a composite movement resulting from the changing positions of sun and moon and from the shape of the earth. Just as the air, as universal Element, takes its tension from the earth, so, too, it is from the earth that the sea takes its neutrality. The earth, relatively to the air, evaporates

* That is why rain is followed sometimes by a fall and sometimes by a rise in temperature. [Note by Michelet.]

as sea (*Die Erde dünstet gegen die Luft aus, als Meer*); but relatively to the sea, the earth is the crystal which discharges its superfluous water, into springs which collect to form rivers. But this is, as fresh water, only abstract neutrality, whereas the sea is the physical neutrality into which the crystal of the earth goes over. We must not, therefore, explain the origin of inexhaustible springs by mechanically and quite superficially attributing them to percolation; any more than we must use a similar kind of explanation, on the other side, to account for volcanoes and hot springs. On the contrary, just as springs are the lungs and secretory glands for the earth's process of evaporation (*für die Ausdünstung der Erde*), so are volcanoes the earth's liver, in that they represent the earth's spontaneous generation of heat within itself. Everywhere we see tracts, especially sandstone beds, which are always giving off moisture. I regard mountains, therefore, not as gatherers of rainwater which penetrates into them; on the contrary, the genuine springs which generate rivers like the Ganges, Rhone, and Rhine have an interior life, a striving and a stirring, like naiads; the earth discharges its abstractly fresh (*süßes*) water which, in these outpourings, hastens to its concrete life, to the sea.

The sea itself is this higher vitality (*Lebendigkeit*) than the air; it is the subject of bitterness and neutrality and dissolution—a living process which is always on the point of breaking forth into life but again perpetually falls back into water because this contains all the moments of that process: the point of the subject, neutrality, and the dissolution of this subject into neutrality. Fruitful as is the solid earth, the sea is no less so and in a still higher degree. The general mode of vivification (*Belebung*) displayed by land and sea is *generatio aequivoca*, whereas in the sphere of vitality proper, the existence of an individual presupposes another of the same kind (*generatio univoca*). It was assumed that *omne vivum ex ovo*; and then when the origin of certain animalcules could not be accounted for, recourse was had to invention. But there are organisms which originate immediately and do not procreate further; infusoria agglomerate and give rise to another shape, so that they serve only as a transitional stage. This universal vitality is an organic life which inwardly stimulates itself, acts as a stimulus on its own self. The sea, which is something other than fresh and salt water, which contains not merely common salt but also sulphate of magnesia (*Bittersalz*), is concrete salinity as an organic being which reveals itself at all points as procreative: just as water generally always has the tendency to pass away and to transform itself, for it is only the pressure of the atmosphere which preserves it in the form of water. The sea has this characteristically putrid smell—a life which, as it were, is always putrefying. Sailors speak of the blossoming of the sea in summer. In July, August, and September, the sea becomes polluted (*unrein*), turbid, slimy, and to the west in the Atlantic, this occurs a month earlier than in the Baltic. The sea is filled with vegetable life in the form of innumerable points, threads and surfaces; there is a tendency to break forth into vegetable life. When this tendency is intensified, vast tracts of sea break out into phosphorescent light—a superficial life which gathers itself into a simple unity but equally into a unity which is also completely reflected into self. For this luminosity is often present in fish and other creatures which already belong to the sphere of living subjectivity. But the whole surface of the sea, too, is partly an infinite shining, partly an immeasurable, immense sea of light which consists purely of points of life lacking any further organization. If such water is taken from the sea, the vitality dies away immediately and there remains a gelatinous slime, the beginning of vegetable life, with which the sea is filled from its surface to its depths. Already in every fermentation, animalcules reveal their presence. Lastly, the sea develops further to determinate shapes, to infusoria and mollusca which are transparent and have a longer life but which are still quite rudimentary organisms. For instance, de Chamisso made the fine discovery of a salpa which was so fertile that its numerous progeny, like the free petals of a plant clustered round its stem, were arranged in tiers one on top of the other forming a garland or circle where many have a single life, like the polyps, and then come together again in a single individual. Since this inferior animal world, which includes a host of luminous species, only gets as far as a momentarily existing slime, the subjectivity of animal life can make that life here merely a luminosity, the external show of self-identity. This animal world cannot hold its light within it as an inner self, but the light breaks forth only as a transient physical light; and the millions of rudimentary lives rapidly drift away to be dissolved again in the watery element. In this way, the sea reveals a host of stars, densely crowded together in 'milky ways' which are as good as the stars in the sky; for these are only abstract points of light, but the former come from organic forms. In the sky, light is in its first, undeveloped crudity, but here it bursts forth from animal life as an animal product, like the phosphorescence of decaying wood—a flicker of life and an emergence of soul (*Seele*). It has been rumoured round the town that I have compared the stars to a rash on an organism where the skin erupts into a countless mass of red spots; or to an ant-heap in which, too, there is Understanding and necessity (see above, § 268, *Zusatz*, p. 62). In fact I do rate what is concrete higher than what is abstract, and an animality that develops into no more than a slime, higher than the starry host. And even without counting fish, the marine world contains polyps, corals, lithophytes, zoophytes, etc.; each drop of water is a living globe (*Erdball*) of infusoria, etc. The sea contains within it the principle of life (*Lebendigkeit*) in a more immanent manner than does the land, in so far as its fluid nature does not allow the punctualization of this principle into a living being which could break free from the sea and inwardly maintain itself over against it. The neutrality of the sea wrests this incipient subjectivity back into its indifferent womb, and thus makes the vital force which this subjectivity has taken for itself melt away again into the universal. The most ancient teaching, it is true, made all living creatures come forth from the sea; but this very coming-forth from the sea is a breaking away from it, and the living being exists only as tearing itself away from the sea and maintaining its own independence in face of the neutrality. The sea, therefore, in its fluidity remains at the stage of elemental life; and when subjective life is cast back, drawn back, into the sea again (like whales which yet are mammals), it feels, even with a more developed organization, the presence of this undeveloped torpidity.

3. The land, as the giant corpse of the life which was formerly immanent in it but which has now fled, is this individual concretion (*Konsistenz*) which has wrested itself free from neutrality, the solid crystal of the lunar Element, while the sea is the cometary Element. Since, however, in the subjective living being these two moments interpenetrate, the slime becomes the casing (*Gehäuse*) of light which remains interior. Earth, like water, displays infinite, universal fecundity; but whereas the sea brings forth mainly animal life, the earth tends rather to bring forth vegetable life. The sea is more animal because neutrality is an interior propagation: earth is primarily vegetative as holding to a punctiform development (*als sich in Punktualisierung haltend*). Everywhere the earth covers itself with green vegetation—indeterminate formations which can equally be classed with animal life. Individual vegetation, must, of course, be generated from seeds of the same species; but universal vegetation is not so individual. Such are lichen, moss, into which every stone breaks forth. Wherever earth, air, and moisture are present, there we find plant life. Wherever something weathers away, at once a vegetable form, mould, or mildew makes its appearance; fungi, too, spring up everywhere. This vegetation, as not yet shaped by individuality, consists of inorganic-organic forms like lichens and fungi which one does not rightly know how to classify—peculiar, tough substances coming near to animal life. Rudolphi says (*Anatomie der Pflanzen*, § 14 and § 17): 'In lichens we can find nothing which we might assume characteristic of plant structure; they definitely do not possess true parenchyma, tubes or vascularity, and all writers are agreed on this. I have nowhere found any proof that the so-called reproductive organs are really such; and it is perhaps more likely that they are germination-buds (*Knospenkeime*) by which the lichens propagate themselves in a way similar to that of a number of true plants; so that this proves nothing. In a number of them their pigments, their gummy and resinous constituents, the sugary mucilage and tannin, point to a vegetable nature.—Fungi are entirely different in structure from plants. I have examined a good many and find that their substance is of a kind that could rightly be called animal. In the softer fungi there is a fibrous, mucous tissue which closely resembles that of animals but which is completely different from the rigid cellular structure of plants. In *Boletus cetotaphorus* there is a lanuginous tissue which is definitely not vegetable in nature but which forms a clear transition from the soft to the ligneous fungi, and which might be compared to the stem of the gorgonias.' 'If one considers the animal composition (*Mischung*) of fungi and

its behaviour in galvanization', says von Humboldt (*Experiments on stimulated muscle and nerve fibres* (Berlin, 1797), pp. 171–80), 'we shall more readily discard the opinion that fungi belong to the vegetable world and are true plants. Above all, their mode of origin is confirmation of this, for when animal or vegetable matter putrefies or decomposes, this very putrefaction gives rise to fresh forms; *Clavaria militaris*, for example, originates only on dead maggots.' This infinite host of shapes does not get to the point of a germ or a seed, which exists only where subjectivity is attained. Fungi do not, so to speak, grow but suddenly shoot forth as crystals do. We must not think of such vegetation as coming from seeds, any more than we must think of seeds or spores as the origin of the host of imperfect animal forms: infusoria, intestinal worms, swine-gargets, etc. This universal vitality is found not only in sea and on land, but also in independent, living subjectivity. The definition of what a plant or an animal is, is based on statements about cell-tissue, seeds, eggs, growth, and so on. But an exact definition cannot be established and there is none; for fungi, lichens, and the like belong, in general, to the vegetable king-dom although the specific determinateness is lacking, because Nature in its manifestations does not hold fast to the Notion. Its wealth of forms is an absence of definiteness and the play of contingency; the Notion is not to be based on them, rather it is they which are to be measured by the Notion. Such indefinite (*verschwemmte*) intermediate beings, which are neither fish not flesh, are moments of a total form, but isolated moments.

§ 342

This division between the universal, self-external organism and the merely punctiform, transient subjectivity just dealt with, is in virtue of the implicit identity of their Notion, overcome in the *existence* of this identity, in the *vivified organism*; this is the subjectivity which differentiates itself into members and which excludes from itself, as an objectivity confronting it, the merely *implicit* organism, physical Nature in its universal and individual forms. But at the same time, it has in these natural powers the condition of its existence, the stimulus, and also the material of its process.

Zusatz. What is lacking in this display of organic being, or immediate organic being as such, is that the Notion here is still immediate, is only as internal End in the element of indifference, but that its moments are physical realities which are not reflected into themselves, do not form a One confronting that indifference. But the universal, the End, expands into these moments and returns into itself; their indifference is the one-sided moment which gathers itself together into negativity and is an individual. The substance divides itself not only into different sides but into absolute opposites, such that each of them is the totality, is a being reflected into itself, indifferent to the other, a One by its very nature—and not only by its own nature since the division is into sides whose very reality is this oneness, this negativity, i.e. whose existence is the process contained in it.

Life, therefore, is essentially this perfectly fluid pervasion of all its parts, i.e. of parts indifferent to the whole. They are not chemical abstractions but have a substantial, whole life of their own; a life of the parts which, inwardly restless, resolves itself and brings forth only the whole. The whole is the universal substance, the ground as well as the resultant totality; and it is this totality as an actuality. It is the One which contains bound within itself the parts in their freedom; it sunders itself into them, endows them with its universal life and as their negative, holds them within itself as the power over them. This is posited in the form of an independent circulation in and through the parts, but this movement is at the same time the sublation of their particularity and the becoming of the universal. This is the universal circle of movement in the individual Actual, a circle which, more accurately, is the totality of three circles, the unity of universality and actuality: the two circles of their opposition and the circle of their reflection-into-self.

First. The organic being is the Actual which sustains itself and in its own self runs through its process; it is its own universal, and this sunders itself into its parts which sublate themselves in their production of the whole. The genus here stands on the side of the organic being. The conclusion [of the syllogism] is that the genus is directly united with its non-organic nature; the organic being sunders itself therefore into two universal extremes, the non-organic nature and the genus, of which it is the middle term (U–I–P), and with each of which it is still immediately one, being itself genus and non-organic nature. Thus the individual still has its non-organic nature within it, and feeds on itself in that it consumes itself as its own inorganicity (*Anorganität*). But in so doing, it develops members within itself, i.e. it sunders its universality into its differences—the course of the process within the individual itself as a diremption which does not exclude the differences, and as a relation of the organic being to itself. The universal has to actualize itself in its own self; and it is precisely through this movement in which it becomes for itself that it gives itself its self-feeling. The organic being is turned against itself as this immediate universal, as this organic genus. This is its process of individualization; it opposes itself to itself internally, as later it will oppose the external world; but as yet, the other is still held in check by the Notion. However, in so far as the individual is already presupposed, it unites here the genus which is its universality with the particularized universal. This latter is one of the extremes, that which, taken up into the absolute genus, becomes absolute particularity and singularity. This is the particular delivering, the becoming, of the moment of individuality, which enters the process as already in being. Nothing comes out of the process but what is already there. It is the process of the digestion of itself and the development of the moments as members, the shaping of them; the members are no less generated than consumed, and in this general unrest, what abides as simple is the soul (*Seele*). In this process, the individual succeeds through the genus in breaking loose from the latter; it is the process in the genus which makes the genus into a One which is charged with negativity, and so is opposed to the genus as to the universal.

Secondly. The universal is a real existence (*Daseiendes*) and the organic One (*Eins*) is the power over this negative of itself, this external being, and consumes it so that it exists only as sublated. The organic being is immediately unity of individuality and universality, organic genus: it is an exclusive One and excludes the universal from itself—the genus as abandoned by the power of negativity, by life; in other words, the organic posits for itself its non-organic nature. The genus is the absolute universal which posits the abstract universal as its opposite; but in doing so, it has also liberated the moment of singularity which is the negative relationship to this non-organic nature. Whereas previously the individual was the middle term and the sides the universal extremes, now it is the genus which is the middle term (*das Element*); here, therefore, it is through the genus that the organic being is mediated with its non-organic nature (P–U–I). The former is the power over the latter, because it is the absolute universal; this is the *process of nutrition*. The non-organic nature is the universality as the non-actual genus, which is subject partly to individuality as such, to the earth, and partly to the singularity which frees itself from it; this universality is mere passivity. But in its actuality, as it is in its own self, the universality is the sunderance (*Auseinandertreten*) of organic Nature and its non-organic nature: the former being the form of individuality and the latter the form of universality. Both are abstractions; the substance is the same in both forms (*Arten*) into which it has differentiated itself.

(α) The determinateness remains a universality, is one with the element and principle; *for the organic being, there is nothing which it is not itself*. The reflection-into-self of the organic being means that its non-organic world is no longer in itself (*an sich*); this exists only as sublated and the organism is the positing and sustaining of it. But to take this activity alone, would be equally one-sided. The truth is rather that the earth makes the sun and its Elements, as it makes everything organic, because it is this universal organic being; but it is equally in itself both of these sides. This positedness of the non-organic is its sublatedness; it is not in itself (*an sich*). The organic being is self-subsistent; but the non-organic as an in-itself for the organic being is, in the first instance, the indifferent existence of both; but it then passes over into an existence which is a tension, into the form of being-for-self appropriate to the organic being.

(β) That immediate being of the organism as genus is equally the outcome of sheer mediation through the non-organic world: it exists only through this otherness, this antithesis to itself as abstract universality; it is the genus which has been released from the individuality. But because that abstract universality is in its own self also life, it makes the transition through its own self to organic being in the *generatio aequivoca*; in general, the existence of organic being is the act of the whole earth, in which it individualizes and contracts itself, the reflection-into-self of the universal. But equally it becomes a stabilized reflectedness into-self; and the higher plants and animals are this established reflectedness-into-self, which does not shoot up out of the earth like fungi, like unindividualized jelly or lichens which are only organic life in general (*überhaupt*) with but a meagre internal organization. But the abstract universality in its real existence only reaches as far as a general reflection and begins here its immediate becoming. This life which is a reflectedness-into-self is now established as an independent existence passing through its own cyclic process, and it has its own existence which remains opposed to that other reality and holds fast to its negative nature, denies its origin, and displays its own becoming.

Thirdly. This actual being thus brought forth is the genus, the power over the individual and the process of that power; it sublates this individual, brings forth another which is the actuality of the genus, but just for that reason is also a tearing itself apart from the non-organic nature to which the genus relapses. The organic being which is thus mediated through the non-organic nature with the genus (I–P–U) is the sex-relation.

The conclusion [of the syllogism] is the connection of the two sides which are the whole organic being, or the diremption of this whole into opposed, self-subsistent sexes; the sublation of the individual and the resultant being of the genus, but of the genus as an individual actual being which initiates the cycle again. The result is, therefore, that the individual has separated itself off from the genus. This self-subsistent individual is therefore related to a being to which, as genus, it is indifferent; the genus has sundered itself into self-subsistent beings, each of which as this whole is object to itself, but outside of itself. In the first process we have being-for-self, in the second, the representation and knowledge of an other, in the third, the unity of both, of the other and itself. It is the true actualization of the Notion, the complete self-subsistence of both, in which each also knows itself in the other as its own self; it is the relation which has become purely ideal, so that each is ideal to itself, is in itself a universal—the pure non-objectivity is set up in the self as such.

The organic being begins with singularity and rises to the genus. But just as immediately this course is the reverse: the simple genus descends to singularity, for the consummation of individuals in the genus resulting from their sublation, is no less the becoming of the immediate singularity of the child. The other to the universal life of the earth is thus the truly organic form of life which continues itself in its genus. This is, in the first instance, the vegetable world, the first stage of being-for-self, of reflection-into-self: but only immediate, formal being-for-self, not yet the genuine infinity; the plant discharges its moments from itself as free members and is only the subjective point of life. Plant-life therefore begins where the vital principle gathers itself into a point and this point sustains and produces itself, repels itself, and produces new points.

THE PLANT NATURE

§ 343

The *subjectivity* in virtue of which organic being exists as a *singular*, unfolds itself into an *objective* organism in the shape of a body articulated into parts which are *separate and distinct*. In the plant, which is only the *first, immediate* stage of subjective vitality, the objective organism and its subjectivity are still immediately identical. Consequently the process whereby the plant differentiates itself into distinct parts and sustains itself, is one in which it comes forth from itself and falls apart into a number of individuals, the whole plant being rather the basis (*Boden*) for these individuals than a subjective unity of members; the part—bud, branch, and so on, is also the whole plant. A further consequence is that the *difference* of the *organic parts* is only a superficial *metamorphosis* and one part can easily assume the function of the other.

Zusatz. Whereas the geological organism is the mere system of shape devoid of ideality, with the subjectivity of plant-life ideality now enters in. But as the ideality present in all its members, life is essentially a living being; and this is merely excited by the outer world. Here, therefore, the causal relation falls away, and generally in the sphere of Life, all the categories of the Understanding cease to be valid. If, however, these categories are still to be employed, then their nature must be transformed; and then it can be said that life is its own cause.—The proposition can be advanced that everything lives in Nature; this is sublime and is supposed to be speculative. But the Notion of life, i.e. life *in itself*, which of course is found everywhere, is one thing: real life, the subjectivity of the living organism, in which each part *exists* as vivified, is another. Thus the geological organism is alive, not in its separate parts (*im Einzelnen*) but only as a whole: it is only potentially (*an sich*) alive, not in present existence. But the living organism, too, differentiates itself into a subjective and a dead being: on the one hand, in its woody structure, in its bones, it makes itself the presupposition of its frame (*Gerüste*) in the individual, as is the case in the geological organism as a whole; but on the other hand, the living organism is the shape which is inhabited by the substantial form; this is determinative not only in respect of the spatial relationships of the separate parts, but is equally the unrest of the process in which the form determines the physical properties out of itself so that, from that process, it may produce shape.

The plant, as the first self-subsistent subject that still has its origin in immediacy, is, however, the feeble, infantile life that has not yet developed within itself the moment of difference. Like every living organism, the nature of a plant is particularized; but whereas in the animal the particularity is at the same time a particularity in contrast with which the subjectivity as soul (*Seele*) is also a universal, in the plant the particularity is quite immediately identical with the plant's vitality in general. It does not exist as a state distinct from the plant's inner life; on the contrary, the quality of the plant completely pervades its general vegetative nature, instead of being distinct from it as in the animal. In the plant, therefore, the members are particular only in relation to each other, not to the whole; the members themselves are in turn wholes, as in the dead organism where in sedimentary strata they are also external to each other. Although then the plant posits itself as the other of itself in order perpetually to idealize this contradiction, this differentiation is only formal; what it posits as the other is not a veritable other but the same individual as the subject.†

In plant-life, therefore, growth is predominantly an increase of the plant itself, as an alteration of form: whereas animal growth is only an alteration of size but at the same time remains one shape, because the totality of the members is taken up into the subjectivity. The growth of the plant is an assimilation into itself of the other; but as a self-multiplication, this assimilation is also a going-forth-from-itself. It is not a coming-to-self as an individual, but a multiplication of the individuality: so that the one individuality is only the superficial unity of the many. The individuals remain a separated plurality, indifferent to each other, which do not proceed from their substance as from a common essence. Schultz therefore says (*Die Natur der lebendigen Pflanze*, vol. i, p. 617): 'The growth of plants is a perpetual addition of new parts which did not exist previously.' Bound up with the homogeneity of the parts of the plant, therefore, is their falling asunder, because they are not related to each other as inner, qualitative differences—in other words, the organism

† Goethe, *Zur Morphologie* (1817), vol. i, pp. x–xi: 'The more imperfect a creature is, the more do the parts resemble each other, and the more are they like the whole. The more perfect the creature is, the more dissimilar its parts become. In the first case, the whole is more or less like the parts; in the second, the whole is dissimilar to the parts. The more the parts resemble each other, the less they are subordinated to each other. Subordination of the parts betokens a more perfect creature.' [Footnote by Michelet.]

has not at the same time acquired a system of viscera. It is a production of itself in externality, but all the same, a growth altogether from within outwards (*aus sich*) not a sort of external accretion as in crystallization (*ein äußerliches Ankrystallisieren*).

§ 344

The process of formation and of reproduction of the *singular* individual in this way coincides with the process of the genus and is a perennial production of new individuals. Because the selflike (*selbstische*) universality, the subjective One (*Eins*) of the individuality, does not separate itself from the real particularization but is only submerged in it, so that the plant is not yet a self-subsistent subjectivity over against its *implicit* organism (§ 342), therefore it can neither freely determine its place, i.e. *move from the spot*, nor is it for itself, in face of the physical particularization and *individualization* of its implicit organism. Consequently its nutrition is not an interrupted process but a continuous flow, and it relates itself not to individualized inorganic Nature but to the universal Elements. Still less is it capable of animal heat and feeling, for it is not the process in which its members—which are rather mere parts, and are themselves individuals—are brought back into a negative, simple unity.

Zusatz. Everything organic is an immanent differentiation which preserves the manifoldness in the unity. Animal life, however, as the truth of the organic sphere, advances to a higher specific difference, such that the difference which is pervaded by the substantial form is only one side, and the other side is constituted by the substantial form on its own, over against this submergence in the difference; the animal consequently has sensation. But the plant has not developed to this difference within itself, to the stage, that is, where the selflike (*selbstische*) point of unity and the organic crystal would already be the two sides of its life. Accordingly the vital principle, which in the animal is soul (*Seele*), is in the plant still submerged in the process of the mutually external parts. In the animal, on the contrary, the one vital principle is doubly present: (α) as indwelling and vivifying, (β) as a selflike unity which exists as simple. It is true that both moments, and their relation, must also be present in the plant; but one part of this difference falls outside of its existence, whereas in the animal there is present the absolute return of the living organism as *self-feeling*. The existent plant, on the other hand, is only one bodily organism, in which the pure selflike unity-with-self is not yet present as a reality but only in the Notion, because it has not yet become objective. In the plant, therefore, the body with its members is not yet the objectivity of the soul (*Seele*); the plant is not yet objective to itself. Therefore for the plant, the unity is something external, just as the process of the organism of the earth falls outside of it; and this outer, physical self of the plant is light towards which it strives, in the same way that man seeks man. The plant has an essential, infinite relationship with light; but at first it is a quest for this its self, like heavy matter. This simple principle of selfhood (*einfache Selbstischkeit*) which is outside of the plant is the supreme power over it; Schelling therefore says that, if the plant had consciousness, it would worship light as its god. The process of self-preservation is to attain the self, to satisfy oneself, to come to self-feeling; but because the self is outside of the plant, the latter's striving after the self is rather a being-drawn-out-of-itself, so that its return into itself is a perpetual forth-going, and conversely. Thus the plant preserves itself by multiplying itself (§ 343). The externality of the subjective, selflike unity of the plant is objective in its relation to light, in the same way that light appears externally in the jelly-like forms of marine life (see § 341, *Zusatz*, p. 296) and also in the colours of birds in the tropics (see *Zusatz* to § 303, p. 149); so that here, even in the animal world, the power of light is visible. Man fashions the self in more interior fashion, although in southern latitudes he, too, does not reach the stage where his self, his freedom, is objectively guaranteed. It is from light that plants first get their sap, and in general, a vigorous individualization; without light they can, indeed, grow bigger, but they remain without taste, colour, and smell. They therefore turn to the light: potato-plants sprouting in a cellar creep from distances of several yards across the floor to the side where light enters through a hole in the wall and they climb up the wall as if they knew the way, in order to reach the opening where they can enjoy the light. Sunflowers and a host of other flowers follow the motion of the sun in the sky and turn towards it. In the evening, if one enters a meadow full of flowers from its east side, only a few flowers, or perhaps none, will be seen, because they are all turned towards the sun; but looked at from the west they all make a splendid show. In the early morning, too, when one enters the meadow from the east, no flowers are seen; not until the sun shines on them do they turn towards the east. 'Some', says Willdenow *Grundriß der Kräuterkunde*, edited by Link (6th edition, 1821, p. 473), 'do not open out to the Sun until noon, like *Portulaca oleracea, Drosera rotundifolia*; some only at night', like the magnificent torch thistle (*Cactus grandiflorus*, which only blooms for a few hours.

(α) Now because, as we have said, the subjective One of the plant is fused with its very quality and particularization, and consequently the negative selfhood (*Selbstischkeit*) of the plant is not yet self-related, therefore this self, too, does not yet exist as a purely non-sensuous being, the name of which is simply soul (*Seele*), but is still sensuous; no longer, it is true, as a material plurality, yet still as a sensuous unity of material parts. Now the sensuous element which remains for the unity is space. Since the plant thus cannot entirely destroy the element of sense, it is not yet pure time within itself; for this reason, the plant is in a specific place which it cannot get rid of, although it unfolds itself within it. The animal, however, as process, opposes itself to its place, gets rid of it, even though it does posit it afresh. Similarly, the ego wills to move itself, the point: that is to say, it wills to change its place, i.e. its sensuous, immediate existence as point; or the ego wills to distinguish itself as ideality of the One, from itself as a sensuous One. In the heavenly motions, the bodies of the one system have indeed a free motion, but it is not a contingent motion; their place is not determined by them as particulars, but by the time of the system which is rooted by law in the sun. Similarly, in magnetism, the opposed qualities are the determining factors. But in the subjectively living being which is its own time, there is negation of place, a negation posited in an absolutely indifferent manner, or as an inner indifference. The plant, however, is not yet this mastery over the indifferent, mutually external existence of parts in space, and its space is consequently still an abstract space. The movement of pistils and anthers towards each other, the oscillatory movements of conferva, etc., these are to be understood only as a simple growth without any contingent determination of place. The movement of plants is determined by light, heat, and air. Treviranus† points this out, e.g., in *Hedysarum girans*: 'At the end of each stem of this plant there is a larger leaf, elliptical and lanceolate in shape, and on each side of this and attached to the same main stem are two smaller petiolate stipules (*Nebenblätter*). The movements of the main stems and leaves are different from those of the stipules. The movement of the main stems and larger leaves consists in an erection in the light and in a drooping down in the dark; it occurs in the joints which join the leaf with the stem and the latter with the branch. Even the reflection of sunlight from a wall twenty yards away produced a distinct erection of the leaves, and also the screening of sunlight by an opaque body or by a passing cloud resulted in their drooping again. At high noon, and by focusing sunlight through a burning-glass, Hufeland observed a trembling movement of the main leaves and of the whole plant. Moonlight and artificial light had no influence on this movement. The second movement, which is made only by the small folioles (*Seitenblätter*) consists in the alternate erection and drooping of each pair of these leaves which face each other on the same branch; the movement ceases only with the death of the plant. There are no external causes immediately producing this effect, but it is most marked at the time of fertilization.' Treviranus, however, attributes to the zoospores (*Körnern*) of the conferva an arbitrary (*willkürliche*) movement even after they have become detached from these plants (ibid., vol. ii, pp. 381 et seq. and 507; vol. iii, pp. 281 et seq.). Some of the movements

† *Biologie oder Philosophie der lebenden Natur*, vol. v, pp. 202-3.

of the conferva are said to be oscillatory: 'Their separate threads bent their free ends in a series of jerks from right to left and from left to right; often they twisted in such a way that their free end seemed to describe a circle.' But movement of this kind is still not a voluntary movement.

(β) The relationship of the plant to the outer world could be an interrupted relationship only if the plant existed as something subjective, only if, as a self, it had a relation to its self. The reason, therefore, why the introsusception of the plant is not interrupted is simply that its nature is not to be a veritable subjectivity, but its individuality always falls apart into its particularity, and so does not hold on to itself as an infinite being-for-self. It is only when the self exists *qua* self that it is exclusive in its relationship to the outer world and, precisely as such, is the soul of this relationship as reference-to-self: and since in this self-reference the self forms both sides of the relation, this latter is a circle within the soul which holds itself aloof from its non-organic nature. But as the plant is not such a self, it lacks the inwardness which would be free from the relationship to the outer world. Thus air and water are perpetually acting on the plant; it does not take sips of water. True, the action of light is interrupted or weakened externally at night and in winter; but this is not a difference of the plant itself, but is external to it. It is possible, therefore, gradually to change the plant's activities by putting it at night into a lighted room, and in a darkened room during the day. De Candolle in this way changed the period of sleep of mimosas and several other plants after only a few nights by leaving lamps alight. The rest of the plant's behaviour depends on the seasons and the climate; plants from northern latitudes, which sleep through the winter, gradually change this habit in southern latitudes. Similarly, the plant does not yet enter into relationship with what is individual, also because its relationship is not that of self to self; its other, therefore, is not individual, but what is elementally inorganic.

(γ) A number of experiments have been carried out on heat in plants and the subject has aroused much controversy: Hermbstädt in particular has devoted much attention to it (*cf.* Treviranus, ibid., vol. v, pp. 4 et seq.; Willdenow, ibid., pp. 422–8). It has indeed been claimed that in plants a slightly higher specific heat has been detected than in their environment; but that does not settle the matter. Heat is a conflict of altered cohesion; but plants lack this alteration of cohesion in themselves, they are devoid of this internal inflammatory process, this interior fire which constitutes animal life. True, a thermometer placed in a hole bored through a tree revealed a significant difference between the outside and inside temperatures, e.g. of $-5°$ Réaumur and $+2°$, of $-10°$ and $+1°$, etc. This, however, is because wood is a bad conductor of heat, and also the trunk gets its heat from the earth. Besides, says Treviranus (ibid., vol. v, p. 16) 'there are more than 4,600 experiments of Fontana which show that the heat of plants depends entirely on the temperature of the medium in which they are situated'. Treviranus continues (p. 19):

'There are some species of plants which, in certain circumstances, can in fact generate heat and cold, and thus withstand the influence of the outside temperature. Several investigators have observed on the surface of the spadix of *Arum maculatum* and other varieties, at the time when it begins to break out of its spathe, a heat which increased over a period of four to five hours (in *Arum maculatum* between 3 and 4 o'clock in the afternoon), and which diminished over a similar period; the maximum temperature exceeded that of the air outside, in the case of *Arum maculatum* by 15°–16° F. and of *Arum cordifolium* by 60°–70° F.† The ice-plant (*Mesembryanthemum crystallinum*) develops cold, undoubtedly from its saltpetre content. But in the former instance, the heat probably no more serves to protect the plant from cold at the time of fertilization, than in the second instance, the cold serves to protect the plant from heat.' The plant is therefore none the less devoid of this internal process, for in its movement outwards it only gets benumbed and rigid (*erstarrt*): the animal, on the other hand, is this fluid magnet whose differentiated parts pass over into one another and so develop heat, the principle of which resides precisely only in the blood.

(δ) That the plant has no feeling is again a consequence of the fusion of the subjective One with the quality, the plants own particularization: the being-within-self is not yet self-subsistent in face of the outer world as a nervous system, as it is in the animal. Only that which possesses sensation (*Empfindung*) can tolerate itself as other, can, with the hardiness of individuality, assimilate it and venture into conflict with other individualities. The plant is the immediate, organic individuality in which the genus has the preponderance, and the reflection is not individual, the individual does not as such return into itself but is an Other and therefore has no self-feeling. The sensitivity of certain plants does not come under this head, and is only a mechanical elasticity, like the action of light in connection with the sleep of plants. On this point Treviranus says (loc. cit., vol. v, pp. 206–8): 'There has been a tendency to regard the sensitivity to external, purely local stimuli and the movements of reaction to them, as sensation; and, of course, the resemblance of this to the contraction of animal muscle-fibres is unmistakable', but this can also take place without sensation. 'Pollination mechanisms in particular display such sensitivity: the pollen is scattered from the anthers when the stamens are touched, the pistils and stamens move in response to mechanical stimuli, and the filaments, especially, move towards the pistils when they are touched.' But the externality of the cause of this sensitivity is demonstrated particularly by the observations of Medicus cited by Treviranus (loc. cit., p. 210): 'that a number of plants in colder latitudes

† Link, *Grundlehren der Anatomie und Physiologie der Pflanzen* (Göttingen, 1807) p. 229, remarks on this that 'the flower has a very offensive smell; in my opinion, the sole cause of the generation of heat is the release and decomposition in the air of the oil or carburetted hydrogen which produces the stench.'

show no sensitivity in the afternoon when the weather is hot and dry, but in the morning after a heavy dew, and during the whole of the day with a gentle rain, they are very sensitive; plants in warmer climates display their sensitivity only when the sky is bright; and all plants are most sensitive when the pollen ripens and the pistil is covered with a lustrous oil.' With regard to the sensitivity of the leaves, the most notable plants are some of the mimosa species and other plants which, like these, belong to the family of legumes: 'The *Dionaea muscipula* has a large number of leaves arranged in a circle round the stalk, and the leaves of *Oxalis sensitiva* consist of twelve pairs of oval-shaped leaflets; when they are touched they fold up their leaves. The leaves of *Averrhoa carambola* are pinnate and droop when their stalk is touched' (Treviranus, ibid., vol. v, pp. 217–19). The anatomical observations of Rudolphi and Link demonstrate this fact. Rudolphi (*Anatomie der Pflanzen*, p. 239) says: 'These plants have an articulation of the leaf-stalk and of the partial leaf-stalks peculiar to them. At the base, the leaves are contracted, while in other pinnate leaves the base is widened or at least is not thinner. The stalk, which is thick above the joint, in these plants becomes much thicker than in the other parts, and this makes the contracted joint still more visible. Moreover, this thickening consists only of cell-tissue which usually soon lignifies. When saxifrage, lupins, etc., are cut, all the parts very soon close up as when the plants are asleep, and they do not reopen. A fresh mimosa will droop at the slightest touch, and, if it is quickly lifted up again while it is sick or exhausted, it can be stimulated for a long time in vain, and a long time, too, can elapse before it lifts up the drooping parts. Desfontaine, as Mirbel relates, carried a mimosa with him on a journey. At the first movement of the carriage it closed all its leaves, but subsequently they opened again imperceptibly, and did not close again on the journey, almost as if they had got used to the swaying of the carriage.' Link says (ibid., p. 258): 'In the wind, the leaves close, but open up again in spite of the wind, and finally become so used to it that the wind ceases to have any effect on them;' and in the *Nachträge zu den Grundlehren* (i, p. 26): 'The sensitivity is confined to the area of shock. A leaflet can be subjected to very violent action without the leaves near by being affected by it; each stimulus seems to be confined to, and to affect, only the place where it is produced.' Here, then, we have nothing more than the simple phenomenon of contraction and expansion which occurs more rapidly and suddenly than in the change in plant activity mentioned above, (β), where the action was slower.

§ 345

But the plant, as organic, also essentially articulates itself (*sich gliedert*) into a variety of structures, some abstract (*cells, fibres*, and the like), and some more concrete, which, however, remain in their original homogeneity. The *shape* of the plant, as not liberated out of individuality into subjectivity, is still closely related to geometrical forms and crystalline regularity and the products of its process are even more closely related to chemical products.

Remark

Goethe's *Metamorphose der Pflanzen* marks the, beginning of a rational conception of the nature of plant-life, in that it has forced attention away from a concern with mere details to a recognition of the *unity* of life. The *identity* of the organs is predominant in the category of metamorphosis; but the other and necessary side to this substantial unity is the specific difference and characteristic function of the members through which the life-process is posited. The *physiology* of the plant necessarily appears more obscure than that of the animal body because it is simpler, assimilation passes through fewer intermediary processes, and alteration occurs as *immediate infection*. As in every natural and spiritual life-process, the main point in both assimilation and secretion is the *substantial* alteration, i.e. the *immediate* transformation of an external or particular material as such into another; the attempt to follow up the mediation as a series either of chemical or mechanical *gradations* meets a point where it breaks down and becomes impossible. This point is everywhere present in the process and pervades it, and it is the ignorance of, or rather the failure to recognize, this simple identification as well as the simple diremption, which makes a physiology of the organism impossible. Interesting information on the physiology of the plant is given in the work of my colleague Prof. C. H. Schultz (*Die Natur der lebendigen Pflanze, oder die Pflanzen und das Pflanzenreich*, 2 vols.), a work which I am the more bound to mention here, as some of the special features of the life-process of the plant referred to in the following Paragraphs have been taken from it.

Zusatz. The objectification of the plant is wholly formal, is not a veritable objectivity: not only does the plant outwardize itself simply as such, but its self is preserved as an individual only by a perennial positing of a fresh individual.

(α) The type of the whole plant is simply this: there is a point (utricle), a germ, a grain, a node, or whatever you may call it. This point puts out threads, develops into a line (you can call this magnetism if you like, but there is no polar opposition); and this linear movement outwards stops again, develops a fresh grain, a fresh node. By this process of self-repulsion these nodes continue to be formed, for inside a thread the plant splits up into a number of germs which, in turn, are whole plants; thus members are produced, each of which is the whole. It is at first a matter of indifference whether these nodulations (*Verknotungen*) keep within a single individual or whether they split up into several individuals. This reproduction is thus not mediated by opposition, is not a coming together resulting from it, although the plant can also rise to this. The veritable separation of the sides of the opposition in the sex-relation belongs, however, to the sphere of animal force; and it is only a superficial form of this which is found in the plant, about which we shall speak later. The simplest and quite immediate example of this plant-type is found in the Conferva, which are nothing else but green threads devoid of any further developed structure—the first rudiments of aquatic vegetation. Treviranus thus describes them (ibid., vol. iii, pp. 278–83): 'The Conferva in fountains and spring water (*Conferva fontinalis*, *L.*) propagate themselves by an oval bud (*Knöpfchen*) into which the tip of the delicate thread of which this plant consists, swells up. After a while, this bud separates from the thread, establishes itself in the nearest spot, and soon puts out a tip which prolongs itself into a complete thread. The propagation of all the species classed by Roth under the genus *Ceramium* takes place in a similar simple manner. On the surface of their stem or their branches there are formed at certain periods, but mostly in the spring, bacciform bodies which usually contain one or two smaller grains. When these bodies are fully ripe they either fall off or open and release their seed. In the Conferva proper (*Conferva R.*), in *Hydrodictyon R.*, in Rivularia and many Tremella, the reproductive organs (?)* are found in the substance of the plant; and they are of two kinds. They consist either of small grains arranged regularly side by side in rows, which are already present in the plant from its first formation: or of larger, ovular bodies of the same diameter as the inner tube of the Conferva, which appear only at a certain period in the life of these Phytozoa. In some Conferva, the former are arranged in a zig-zag or in a spiral; in others, in star-shaped figures, right-angled parallelograms, etc.; or they are ranged side by side in the shape of branches which form a whorl round a common stem. They flow away and are the beginnings of fresh Conferva. Very different from these smaller grains is a larger variety of round' (ovular and bacciform) 'bodies which are formed in some articulated (*gegliederten*) Conferva (*Conferva setiformis*, *spiralis* and *bipunctata R.*), and propagate only at a certain period in their life (in May, June, and July). At this time, the smaller, original grains leave

* Michelet's question-mark.

their normal position and unite to form larger oval or spherical bodies. With the formation of these, the Conferva loses its green colour, and all that is left is a transparent, colourless skin which contains in each of its articulations a brownish fruit. When at last this membrane has disintegrated, these fruits fall to the ground, where they rest until the following spring, when a Conferva of the same species develops from each of them in a manner which seems to bear more resemblance to an animal coming out of its shell than to the germination of a grain of seed.' In the same work (pp. 314 et seq.) Treviranus credits the conferva with copulative procreation.

(β) In the higher plants, especially in shrubs, the immediate growth occurs as a simultaneous division into twigs and branches. In the plant we distinguish roots, stem, branches, and leaves. But there is no more familiar fact than that each branch and twig is a complete plant which has its root in the plant as in the soil; if it is broken off from the plant and put as a slip into the ground, it puts out roots and is a complete plant. This also happens when branches are accidentally severed from the plant. Treviranus says (ibid., vol. iii, p. 365): 'The propagation of plants by division never occurs spontaneously (*von freien Stücken*) but always artificially or by chance. The ability to propagate itself in this way is possessed to a remarkable degree by *Tillandsia usneoides*, a parasitic plant of the Bromeliaceae. If any part of this plant is torn off by the wind and caught up in the branches of a tree, it at once takes root and grows just as well as if it had sprung from seed.' Strawberries and a number of other plants, as we know, put out runners, i.e. creeping stalks which grow out of the root. These filaments or leaf-stalks form nodes (why not from 'free portions'?); if these points touch the earth they, in turn, put out roots and produce new, complete plants. Willdenow states (ibid., p. 397): 'The mangrove tree (*Rhizophora mangle*) bends down its branches perpendicularly to the ground and turns them into trunks; so that in tropical latitudes in Asia, Africa, and America a single tree will cover the moist banks of rivers or lakes for a mile or more with a forest consisting of numerous trunks which meet at the top like close-clipped foliage.'

(γ) The branches grow from buds (gemmulae). 'From each bud', quotes Willdenow (ibid., p. 393) from Aubert du Petit Thouars, 'vessels are prolonged and go down through the plant, so that the wood is strictly a product of the root-fibres of all the buds, and the woody plant is an aggregate of a number of growths (*Gewächse*).' Willdenow then continues: 'If a grafted tree is opened up at the side of the graft, fibres from the graft will, of course, be found running for a short distance into the main stem, as both Link and myself have observed.' He speaks at length about this process of grafting (pp. 486–7): 'We know that a bud from a shrub or a tree when grafted on to another trunk develops on it and is to be regarded as a separate plant. Its nature does not change at all, but it continues to grow as if it were in the earth. Agricola and Barnes were even more fortunate in this kind of propagation. They set the buds straight in the earth and raised perfect plants from them. A noteworthy feature of this kind of artificial propagation is that where the branches or eyes (*gemmae*) are made into fresh plants by layering, grafting, inoculation, or any other way, the plant from which they were taken propagates itself not only as a species but also as a variety. The seed only propagates the species, which can bring forth by various methods (*unter mancherlei Ansehen*) from the same seed, a variety. Consequently the Borstorf apple must always remain the same when grafted and inoculated; but from the seed quite different varieties will be obtained.' Such buds retain their individuality to such a degree when they form a branch of another tree that from a single tree one can grow, e.g., a dozen varieties of pears.

Bulbs, too, are such seed-buds (namely in monocotyledons) and similarly divide themselves. Treviranus says (ibid., vol. iii, pp. 363-4): 'Bulbs are peculiar to the monocotyledons. They grow sometimes on the upper part of the root and sometimes in the angle between the stem and the leaf-stalk as in *Lilium bulbiferum* and *Fritillaria regia*, and sometimes in the flowers, as in several species of *Allium*. Those plants whose roots bear bulbs' (i.e. simply divide themselves) 'usually produce infertile seeds; but these become fertile if the young bulbs are destroyed as they appear. In *Fritillaria regia* each leaf, even when detached from the stem, is capable of producing bulbs. A leaf of this plant cut off close to the bulb in autumn, lightly pressed in blotting paper and kept in a warm place, puts out fresh bulbs at the lowest extremity where it was joined on to the root, and the development of these bulbs proceeds *pari passu* with the gradual dying off of the leaf. In some plants whose bulbs are produced in the axils of the leaves or on the stems, the bulbs spontaneously detach themselves from the parent stem and, separated from it, put out roots and leaves. Such plants especially deserve to be called viviparous. In *Lilium bulbiferum*, *Poa bulbosa* and several species of *Allium*, this phenomenon occurs without artificial aid. In *Tulipa gesneriana*, *Eucomis punctata* and a number of other succulent monocotyledons, it can be produced artificially if the flowers are removed from these plants before fertilization occurs and the stalk with the leaves on it is put in a shady place.' Willdenow actually remarks (ibid., p. 487): '*Pothos* and *Plumiera* can even be propagated from leaves;' to which Link adds: 'This property is particularly remarkable in *Bryophyllum calycinum*.' A leaf placed horizontally on the ground puts out threads and rootlets all round its edge. Link says (*Grundlehren*, p. 181): 'Thus we have examples of rooting buds which grew from the leaf-stalk; Mandirola was the first to propagate trees artificially from leaves. It is possible for a bud to grow from any part which contains only spiral vessels and cellular tissue. In short, any part of the plant can exist immediately as a complete individual; this can never be the case in animals with the exception of the polyps and other quite undeveloped (*unvollständigen*) species of animals. Strictly speaking, then, a plant is an aggregate of a group of individuals which form a single individual, but one whose parts are completely self-subsistent. This self-subsistence of the parts is the impotence of the plant; the animal, on the contrary, has viscera, members which are not self-subsistent, which can exist only and solely in unity with the whole. If the viscera are injured (that is, the vital internal organs) then the life of the individual is destroyed. Of course, the animal organism, too, can be deprived of organs, but organs of this kind are the only ones possessed by the plant.

Accordingly Goethe with his great insight into Nature has defined the growth of plants as a metamorphosis of one and the same formation. His work, *The Metamorphosis of Plants*, which appeared in 1790, has been treated with indifference by botanists who did not know what to make of it just because it contained the exposition of a whole.* The going forth of the plant from itself into several individuals is at the same time a total structure, an organic totality which, in its completeness, has root, stem, branches, leaves, blossom, fruit, and of course also posits a difference in the plant which we shall develop in the sequel. But what Goethe aims to do is to show how all these different parts of the plant are a simple, self-contained basic life, and all the forms remain only outer transformations of one and the same identical fundamental nature, not only in the Idea but also in their existence, so that each member can quite easily pass over into the other; a spiritual, transient adumbration (*Hauch*) of forms which does not attain to qualitative, fundamental difference, but is only an ideal metamorphosis in the material aspect of the plant. The parts exist as intrinsically the same and Goethe† grasps the difference between them merely as an expansion or contraction. It is well known, for example, that trees have been planted upside down, the roots up in the air and the branches and twigs in the ground, with the result that the former put out leaves, buds, blossoms, etc., and the latter have become roots. Double flowers, e.g. in roses, are nothing else but flowers in which extra nourishment has changed the stamens, anthers, and in the wild rose the pistil too, into petals, either entirely or still leaving traces of their original form. Many of these petals retain the nature of the stamen, so that on one side they are petal and on the other side stamen; for the stamens are simply nothing else but contracted leaves. Tulips which are called monstrosities have petals which hover between petals and sepals. The petals themselves are nothing but leaves of the plant, only refined. The pistil, too, is only a contracted leaf; also the pollen which in the rose-bush is a yellow powder, has the leaf-nature. The same is true of the capsule and the fruit, and sometimes on the back of the fruit leaves can still be seen. The leaf-nature can also be recognized in the stone of the fruit. The thorn of wild plants becomes a leaf in the cultivated plant; in poor soils apple, pear, and lemon trees have thorns, but cultivation turns these into leaves.[1]

---

* Goethe, *Zur Morphologie*, vol. i (1817); *Die Metamorphose der Pflanzen*, pp. 66, 70, 126.

† Ibid., p. 58.   [1] Cf. Willdenow, ibid., p. 293.

In this way, the whole growth (*Production*) of the plant shows the same uniformity and simple development; and this unity of form is the leaf.[1] One form can thus readily pass over into the other. Even the seed bears within itself the characteristic of the leaf, with its cotyledons or seed-leaves, which are just leaves composed of cruder material and not elaborated. The next stage in the development is the stalk, which puts out leaves which are often pinnate and so approximate to flowers. When this prolongation goes on for some time (as in the Conferva), the stalk-leaves develop nodes: and from the nodes grow leaves which, lower down on the stalk, are simple, and then notched, separating and dividing themselves; in the former, those lower on the stalk, the periphery, the edge, is not yet developed.[2] Goethe, in this picture which he gives of an annual plant, continues therefore: 'However, the further development of the plant stretches continuously from node to node through the leaf. From this point onwards, the leaves appear indented, deeply notched, or composed of several leaflets; in the latter instance, we are presented with complete little branches. The date-palm provides a striking example of such an excessive and extreme diversification of the simplest leaf-shape. In a sequence of several leaves, the midrib is carried forward; the fan-like simple leaf is torn and divided, and there is developed an extremely complex leaf vying with a branch' (Goethe, ibid., p. 11). The leaves are now more finely elaborated than the cotyledons, for they draw their sap from the stem which already possesses an organization (ibid., p. 12).

In this connection, I make the following observation which has an important bearing on the difference of species, namely that this course of leaf-development, which can be seen in one species, is also the principal determinant in the different species themselves; so that the leaves of all the species together exhibit the complete development of a leaf: as can be seen, for example, in a series of pelargoniums in which the leaves, in the first instance very diverse, pass one into the other through a series of transitions. 'It is well known that botanists find the specific difference of plants mostly in the formation of the leaves. Consider the leaves of *Sorbus hybrida*. Some of these leaves are still almost completely anastomosed; and it is only the somewhat deeper notches of the indented edge between the lateral veins which hint that Nature here is striving towards a more marked separation. In other leaves these indentations, mainly at the base and the lower half of the leaf, become deeper; and it is unmistakably evident that each lateral vein is meant to become the midrib of a separate leaflet. In other leaves the lowest lateral veins are already clearly detached to form separate leaflets. In the following lateral veins the deepest indentations have already achieved this; and we recognize that here, too, a freer impulse towards ramification would have overcome anastomosis. Now this is achieved in other leaves where, from below

[1] Goethe, *Zur Morphologie*, pp. 59, 83–5.
[2] Ibid., pp. 7–10.

upwards, two, three, or four pairs of lateral veins are detached, and the original mid-rib by a speedier growth pushes the leaflets apart. Thus the leaf is now half pinnate and half still anastomosed. According to whether the tree is younger or older, and to its condition, and even according to the kind of year, we see a predominance sometimes of the process of ramification and sometimes of anastomosis; and I possess leaves which are almost entirely pinnate. Now if we turn to *Sorbus aucuparia*, it becomes evident that this species is only a continuation of the evolutionary history of *Sorbus hybrida*, and that these two species are distinguished only by the fact that *Sorbus hybrida* strives to develop a more compact tissue, and *Sorbus aucuparia* strives to achieve more freedom to germinate.' (Schelver's *Kritik der Lehre von den Geschlechtern der Pflanzen: Erste Fortsetzung* (1814) pp. 38–40.)

Goethe then passes from the leaves to the calyx (ibid., pp. 15–20): 'The transition to the flowering phase occurs sometimes more rapidly, sometimes more slowly. In the latter case, we usually observe that the stalk-leaves begin to draw in again from their periphery and in particular to lose their various peripheral divisions, while on the other hand, a varying measure of expansion is shown in the lower parts of these leaves where they are joined to the stalk. At the same time, we see that even where the interval from node to node is not markedly increased, nevertheless the stalk assumes a much finer and slenderer shape than it had before. It has therefore been remarked that excess of nourishment hinders inflorescence of the plant. Often we see this transformation occur rapidly: and in this case the stem, above the bud of the last-formed leaf, suddenly shoots upwards, becoming longer and slenderer and gathering at its apex a number of leaves round a centre; the calyx. Its leaves are the same organs as the stalk-leaves, but now gathered round a common centre. Further, in many flowers we see unaltered stalk-leaves directly beneath the corolla drawn together in a kind of calyx. Since they still completely retain their leaf-form, we need only appeal here to ocular evidence and to botanical terminology which designates them "floral leaves" (*folia floralia*). Where the stalk-leaves gradually draw close together, they become transformed, and gently insinuate themselves, as it were, into the calyx. These leaves become still less recognizable when, as often happens, they are united and their sides have grown together. The leaves thus pushed and crowded together present us with the bell-shaped or so-called monophyllous calyces which are more or less incised from the top inwards. The way therefore in which Nature forms the calyx is to join together round a single centre a number of leaves, and then a number of nodes which she would otherwise have produced one after the other, and at some distance from one another; in the calyx, therefore, Nature produces no new organ.' On the contrary, the calyx is merely a point round which are gathered in a circle what previously were distributed throughout the whole stalk.

The flower itself is only a duplication of the calyx; for the petals and sepals are very similar to each other. Here, too, in the 'transition of the calyx to the corolla', Goethe does not find any pronounced antithesis: 'Although the colour of the calyx usually stays green and similar to the colour of the stem-leaves, yet it often changes in one or the other of its parts, at the apices, the edges, the back, or even on its inner side, while the outer side still remains green; and all the time we find this change of colouring associated with a refinement (*Verfeinerung*) of the form. In this way, ambigenous calyces arise which can equally correctly be regarded as corollas. Now the corolla again is produced by an expansion. The petals are usually larger than the sepals; and it can be observed that the organs which were in a state of contraction in the calyx, are now expanded again as petals in a higher degree of refinement. Their finer texture, their colour, their smell, would quite disguise their origin from us if we could not see Nature at work in a number of unusual instances. Thus, e.g., inside the calyx of a pink, there is sometimes to be found a second calyx which in part is completely green, and looks like an incipient monophyllous incised calyx; and in part, is jagged and remodelled at its points and edges into actual rudimentary petals, spread out and coloured and of a delicate texture. In several plants the leaves appear more or less coloured even long before inflorescence; others are completely coloured at the approach of inflorescence. Sometimes, too, on the tulip-stem appears an almost completely developed and coloured petal; and even more remarkable is the case when such a leaf is half green, with its green half belonging to the stem and remaining firmly attached to it, while its coloured half is carried up with the corolla, and the leaf is torn into two pieces.[1] It is a very likely conjecture that the colour and smell of the petals derive from the presence of the male fertilizing substance (*männlichen Samens*) in them. Probably it is present in them in a form not yet sufficiently isolated, but only mixed and diluted with other juices. And the beautiful appearance of the colours leads us to think that the substance with which the leaves are filled, although possessing a high degree of purity, does not yet possess it in the highest degree, in which it appears white and colourless.' (Goethe, ibid., pp. 21–3).

Fructification is the supreme development of light in the plant; and here, too, Goethe points out 'the close affinity of the petals with the organs of pollination'. 'This transition is often a normal occurrence, e.g. in *Canna*. A true petal, slightly modified, contracts in its upper margin and an anther appears in which the rest of the petal takes the place of a filament. In flowers which are often double, we can observe this transition in all its stages. There are several varieties of roses in which, inside the perfectly formed and coloured petals, other petals can be seen which are contracted, sometimes in the centre and sometimes at the side. This contraction is caused by a small callosity which appears as a more or less complete anther. In some double poppies, fully formed anthers

---

[1] Which is just what happens in the monstrosities referred to on p. 315.

are borne on slightly modified petals of strongly double corollas. The organs designated nectaries' (better *paracorolla*) 'are gradual transitions between the petals and the stamens. Some of the petals carry little grooves or glands which secrete a honey-like sap which has not yet been perfected into a fertilizing fluid. At this point there is a complete absence of all the factors which caused expansion of the stem-leaves, sepals, and petals and a feeble, extremely simple filament develops. Those very vessels which would otherwise have grown longer and broader, and again sought each other out, are now present in an extremely contracted condition.' Thus the pollen acts all the more powerfully outwards, on the pistil, which Goethe also traces back to the same type: 'In many cases the pistil almost resembles a stamen without anthers. In the light of the close affinity of the female part with the male, which this examination has made clearly evident, we see no objection to calling fertilization an immaterial (*geistige*) anastomosis, and we believe that we have, for a moment at least, brought closer together the concepts of growth and generation. We often find that the pistil has grown together out of several separate pistils. The pistil of the Iris with its stigma, presents to our eyes the complete form of a petal. The umbelliform stigma of *Saracenia* does not, indeed, reveal itself so strikingly as compounded of several leaves, but its green colour does not belie the idea.' (Goethe, ibid., pp. 23–6 and 30–4.) A physiologist says of the anthers: 'In the formation of the anthers, the edges of the sepals curled inwards, so that at first a hollow cylinder was formed, at the top of which there was a tuft of fine hairs. These dropped off later as the anthers became more perfect and fuller. A similar transformation appeared in the style (*stilus*) where one sepal, often several, curled inwards at the edge to form an arc (*arcuarentur*); from this there developed first a simple cavity and later the ovary. The tuft of hairs seated at the top of the cavity did not wither as did those on the anthers but, on the contrary, grew into a perfect stigma.'†

The fruit and the capsule can similarly be shown to be transformations of the leaf: 'We are speaking specifically of those seed-vessels which Nature forms to enclose the so-called covered seeds, . . . In pinks the seed-capsules are often changed back into calyx-like leaves: indeed, there are pinks in which the seed-vessel has changed into a genuine and perfected calyx. In these instances, the apical notches of the calyx still bear delicate remains of the styles and stigmas, and, in place of seeds, a more or less perfect corolla is developed from the interior of this second calyx. Furthermore, in regular and constantly recurrent forms, Nature herself has revealed to us, in very diverse ways, the fertility that is latent in a leaf. Thus a leaf of a lime tree—modified, but still completely recognizable—will produce from its midrib a little stalk, and on it a perfect flower and fruit. . . . The direct fertility of leaves is presented to us even more forcefully and, as it were, monstrously, in ferns, which develop and scatter

† H. F. Autenrieth, *De Discrimine sexuali etc.* (Tübingen, 1821), pp. 29–30.

countless seeds capable of growth. In the seed-vessels, we cannot fail to recognize the leaf-shape. Thus the legume, for example, is a simple, folded leaf; the siliquas consist of several leaves superposed and fused. Nature obscures this similarity to the leaf most effectually when she forms soft and sappy or woody and tough seed-containers. . . . The relationship of the seed capsules to the preceding parts shows itself also in the stigma which, in many instances, is sessile and inseparably bound up with the seed-vessel. We have already indicated the relationship of the stigma to the leaf-form. . . . It can be observed in various instances that the seed transforms leaves into its immediate integuments. . . . In many winged seeds, of the maple, for example, we can detect traces of leaf-forms which are imperfectly fitted to the seed. . . . To avoid losing hold of the thread which we have once grasped, we have throughout considered the plant only as an annual; we have observed only the transformation of the leaves associated with the nodes and have derived all forms from them. But to give this essay the necessary completeness, we must now also speak of the buds. . . . The bud needs no cotyledons', etc. (Goethe, ibid. pp. 36-40, 42-3). Later, we shall come to speak of the impulses and processes of perennial plants.

These are the main concepts of the Goethean metamorphosis of plants. Goethe has ingeniously represented the unity of the plant as a spiritual conductor (*geistige Leiter*). But metamorphosis is only one side which does not exhaust the whole; we must also pay attention to the difference of the organs, with which difference the vital process proper first makes its appearance. We must therefore distinguish two things in the plant: (α) this unity of its entire nature, the indifference to a change of form of its members and organs; (β) the diversity of its development, the course of the vital process itself—an organization which is an elaboration up to the stage of sexual differentiation, even though this is only an indifferent and superfluous affair. The vital process of the plant is an independent process of the plant in each part; branches, twigs, leaf, each possesses an entire independent process, because each is also the whole individual. The plant's vital process is thus complete in each part, because the plant is particularized through and through without the process having already differentiated itself into a number of different processes. Consequently the process of the plant as an immanent differentiation, appears both in its beginning and in its end-product only as a development of shape (*nur als Gestaltung*). In this respect the plant stands midway between the crystal of the mineral sphere and the free, animal shape; for the animal organism has the oval, elliptical form, and the crystal the straight-line form of the Understanding. The shape of the plant is simple. The Understanding is still dominant in the straight line of the stem, and altogether in the plant the straight line is still very preponderant. In the interior of the plant are cells, in part like those in a honey-comb, and in part elongated; and then fibres which, it is true, do intertwine in spirals but then spontaneously resume their linear form without developing inwardly into a rounded shape. In the leaf, surface predominates: the various forms of leaves, both of the plant and of the flower, are still very regular; and a mechanical uniformity is noticeable in their definite indentations and taperings. The leaves are dentate, jagged, pointed, lanceolate, scutiform, heart-shaped—but yet their regularity is no longer an abstract one: one side of the leaf is not the same as the other, one half is more contracted, the other more expanded and rounded. Finally, in the fruit the spherical shape is dominant, but the roundness is commensurable, not yet the higher form of the roundness of the animal structure.

Numerical determinations, also characteristic of the Understanding, still play a dominant part in plants, e.g. the number three or six; in bulbs it is the latter. In the calyx of flowers the numbers six, three, and four are dominant, although the number five also occurs: in such a way, too, that if the flower has five filaments and anthers, there are also five or ten petals, and the calyx then also has five or ten sepals. Link says (*Grundlehren*, p. 212): 'Strictly, only five leaves seem to constitute the complete whorl. If there are six or more, two or more whorls will certainly be noticed, one inside the other. Four leaves in a whorl leave a gap for a fifth, three indicate a less perfect form, and two or even only one, likewise leave gaps for two or a third.'

Like its shape, the plant's juices, too, stand midway between chemical and animal matter. The process itself, too, still hovers between the chemical and animal spheres. Plant products are acids (e.g. citric acid)—substances which, though no longer wholly chemical but already more indifferent, have not yet the indifference of animal matter. These products cannot be accounted for simply by oxygenation and hydrogenation: and this applies even more in the sphere of animal life, e.g., in connection with respiration. Water which has become organic, pervaded by life and individualized, escapes from the domain of chemistry—the bond is spiritual.

§ 346

The process which is vitality, although a unity, must no less explicate itself as a triad of processes (§§ 217–20).

Zusatz. In the process of the plant, which splits up into three syllogisms, the *first*, as already stated (§ 342, *Zus.*), is the universal process, the process of the vegetable organism within itself, the relation of the individual to itself in which the individual destroys itself, converts itself into its non-organic nature, and through this self-destruction comes forth into existence—the process of formation. *Secondly*, the organism has its other, not within it, but outside of it, as a self-subsistent other; it is not itself its non-organic nature, but it finds this already confronting it as object, an object which it seems to encounter only contingently. That is the specialized process towards an external Nature. The *third* is the process of the genus, the union of the first two; the process of the individuals with themselves as genus, the production and the preservation of the genus—the destruction of the individuals for the preservation of the genus as production of another individual. The non-organic nature is here the individual itself, its nature, on the other hand, is its genus: but this too is also an other, its objective nature. In the plant, these processes are not so distinguished as they are in the animal, but coincide; and this precisely is the source of the difficulty in expounding the nature of the vegetable organism.

A. THE PROCESS OF FORMATION

§ 346a

The *inner* process of the plant's *relation* to *itself* is, in keeping with the simple nature of the vegetable organism itself, immediately a relation to an outer world, and an externalization. On the one side it is the *substantial* process, the *immediate* transformation, partly of the absorbed nutriment into the specific nature of the plant species, and partly of the internally transformed fluid (the *vital sap*) into organs (*Gebilde*). On the other side, as self-*mediation* (*a*), the process begins with the simultaneous *outward* diremption into *root* and *leaf*, and the inner, abstract diremption of the general *cellular tissue* into *woody fibre* and '*vital vessels*', the former likewise being related to the outer world, and the latter containing the plant's *internal circulation*. The *preservation* of the plant in this self-mediating process is (*β*) *growth* as production of fresh formations, diremption into *abstract* self-reference, into the *hardening* of the *wood* (which goes as far as *petrifaction* in *bamboo* and similar plants) and the other parts, and into the *bark* (the permanent leaf). (*γ*) The unification (*Zusammennehmen*) [of the moments] of self-preservation is not a union of the individual with itself but the production of a fresh plant-individual—the *bud*.

Zusatz. In the process of formation we begin with the germ of the organism, the immediate form of the latter. But this is only a posited immediacy, i.e. the germ is also a product; this determination, however, appears only in the third process. The process of formation ought to be only an interior process of the plant, as a production of the plant from within itself; but because in the plant world the plant produces itself by coming out of itself, what it produces is an other—the bud. This too, is directly involved with the process outwards; the first process, therefore, cannot be grasped without the second and third. The process of formation in its developed form (*für sich*), which would be the visceral process of the individual with itself, is lacking in the plant, just because it has no viscera, but only members with a relationship to the outer world. However, an essential side of the organic process generally is that it destroys, infects, and assimilates what comes to it from outside. Water, in being absorbed, is at once affected by the vital force of the organism, so that it is at once posited as a fluid pervaded by organic life. Does this take place immediately, or is there a sequence of transformations? The main thing in the plant is that this transformation takes place without mediation. But in more highly organized plants this process can also be traced as passing through many intermediate stages: as it does in the animal organism. Yet here, too, the direct transformation into lymph (*Infizieren zu Lymphe*) occurs without the intermediation of the organs. In plants, especially in the lower forms, there is no mediation through opposed sides, no coming together out of opposition, but nutrition is a transformation devoid of any process. Consequently, the inner physiological construction of the plant is also quite simple. Link and Rudolphi have shown that it consists only of simple cells and spiral vessels and tubes.

1. The germ is the unexplicated being (*das Unenthüllte*) which is the entire Notion; the nature of the plant which, however, is not yet Idea because it is still without reality. In the grain of seed (*Samenkorn*) the plant appears as a simple, immediate unity of the self and the genus. Thus the seed, on account of the immediacy of its individuality, is an indifferent thing; it falls into the earth, which is for it the universal power. A good soil means simply that it is this unlocked, organic power or possibility—just as a good head means no more than a possibility. The seed, as essentially power, through its being in the earth surmounts its existence as earth and actualizes itself. But this is not the opposition of an indifferent outer existence (*Dasein*), like the opposition to its non-organic nature; on the contrary, putting the seed in the earth means that the seed is power. This hiding of the seed in the earth is therefore a mystical, magical act which signifies that in it there are secret forces which are still slumbering, that, in truth, the seed is something quite other than what it is as it lies there: just as the infant is not only this helpless human shape which gives no indication of Reason, but is in itself the power of Reason, something quite other than this creature which cannot speak or perform any rational action; and baptism is precisely this solemn recognition of fellowship in the realm of spirits. The magician who endows this seed, which I crush in my hand, with quite another significance—he for whom a rusty lamp is a mighty spirit—this magician is the Notion of Nature; the seed is the power which conjures the earth to serve it with *its* power.

(*a*) The development of the germ is at first mere growth, mere increase; it is already in itself the whole plant, the whole tree, etc., in miniature. The parts are already fully formed, receive only an enlargement, a formal repetition, a hardening, and so on. For what is to become, already is; or the becoming is this merely superficial movement. But it is no less also a qualitative articulation (*Gegliederung*) and shaping, and therefore an essential process. 'The germination of the seed first takes place through the agency of moisture. In perfect plants, the future stem can be distinctly seen in the future plant or embryo, and it forms the conical part which is usually called the radicle (*radicula, rostillum*); the pointed part is lower down, and from this grows the future root. It is only rarely that the upper part is very elongated; this elongation is usually called a stalk (*scapus*). Sometimes, too, on this part there is an indication of a plumule (*plumula*). From the sides of the embryo there often grow the two seed-lobes or cotyledons which later develop and represent the seed-leaves. It is incorrect to regard the radicle as the future, actual root; it is only the stem growing downwards. If we carefully examine the larger plant-seeds, e.g. of wheat, pumpkin, or beans, during germination, we shall see how from the seed (the wheat-grain is divided into three parts) the true roots emerge, much thinner and more delicate.'[1] If the pointed part is turned up, it germinates, but grows in an arc and turns its tip downwards. 'The germ consists of the radicle (*rostillum*) and the plumule (*plumula*). From the former grows the root and from the latter the part of the plant above ground. If the seed is put in the ground upside down so that the radicle is turned towards the surface, it will never grow upwards. It grows longer, but into the ground and turns the seed over in order to come into its proper position.'[2] On this subject, Willdenow has made the following discovery: 'The water-chestnut (*Trapa natans*) has no radicle. These nuts put out a long plumule which grows in a perpendicular direction towards the surface of the water and puts out at wide intervals along its sides capillaceous, branching leaves; some of these leaves bend over and take firm root in the ground. This shows that some seeds can dispense with a radicle; but a fertile seed without plumule and cotyledons is quite unthinkable. No one has ever yet presumed to deny the existence of a plumule in any seed whatever. It is noteworthy that in bulbiferous plants, the radicle is changed into the bulb; in some which have a middle stem' (i.e. a stem 'which belongs neither to the descending nor ascending stem, and has the appearance sometimes of a root and sometimes of a stem, in the first case being tuberous and then either like a turnip or a bulb, e.g. in *Ranunculus bulbosus*', etc.) the radicle is changed into this stem, e.g. in cyclamens; lastly, in some plants the radicle disappears soon after the seed has sprouted and the true root develops at the side.'[3] This diremption of the one seed in two directions, towards the earth as the ground, the concrete universal, the universal individual, and towards the pure abstract ideal being, towards light, this can be called polarization.

---

[1] Link, *Grundlehren*, pp. 235–6 (236 to § 6).
[2] Willdenow, *Grundriß der Kräuterkunde*, pp. 367–9.
[3] Ibid., pp. 370–1, 380 (p. 31).

Between leaf and root, the *first* diremption, is the stem: for fungi and the like do not come under this head. The stem, however, is not altogether essential; the leaf can grow directly from the root, and many plants are restricted to these two principal moments (leaf and root). This is the great difference between the monocotyledons and the dicotyledons. The first class includes bulbous plants, grasses, palms—the *Hexandria* and *Triandria* of Linnaeus who had not yet drawn attention to this difference (it was Jussieu who first did so) and who ranged all plants in a single row. The question, namely, is whether the leaflet (χοτυληδών) put out by the seed, is double or single. In the monocotyledons, the root and leaf, which constitute the first antithesis, represent the primary, compact nature of the plant, a nature which does not advance to the opposition in which an Other, the stem, appears between root or bulb and leaf. True, palms have a stem; but this is formed solely by the attachment of the leaves to one another at their base; this can be seen quite easily from the outside. 'Palms have no branches except at the top of the trunk, and there are only twigs to support the blossom. It seems as if the excessive size of the leaves has absorbed the branches. This is precisely the case too with ferns. Even in our indigenous grasses and many bulbous plants, one rarely sees branches other than those bearing flowers.' (Link, *Grundlehren*, p. 185.) The antithesis of cells and woody fibres is possessed by them only interiorly in their substance, but they have no medullary rays (*Spiegelfasern*). The leaf-veins are not curved, or only slightly so, and in grasses they grow in straight lines. The monocotyledons not only lack a proper stem, they also do not produce a completed, flat leaf; they are always this enveloped bud which, though it opens, never completely develops. Consequently, they never produce fertile seed; their root and entire stem is pith. The stem is a continuation of the root, has neither buds nor branches, but continues to put out fresh roots which die off and are bound together by woody fibres. The overwhelming power of light prevents the internalization of the plant into wood; the leaf does not die off but puts out new leaves. But just as in the palm the leaves seem to be trunk and branches, so also, conversely, there are varieties of stem where the stem remains one with the leaf, as, e.g., in the cactus, where stem grows out of stem: 'The joints which are commonly regarded as leaves are parts of the stem. The leaves of this plant are subulate, fleshy tips which are often surrounded at their base with small prickles. They fall off directly after the development of the part' (i.e., off course, the joint) 'and the place they occupied is indicated by a scar or a tuft of prickles.' (Willdenow, ibid., p. 398.) These plants remain fleshy leaf which withstands light; and, instead of wood, they produce only prickles.

(*b*) The general texture of the plant is formed by cellular tissue which, as in the animal organism, consists of small cells; it is the universal animal and vegetable product—the fibrous constituent (*Moment*). 'Each cell is separate from the others and has no community with them. In the bast, the cells assume an oval, pointed-oval or elongated form.' The vesicles and elongated cells are differentiated in the basis itself of the plant. (α) 'The regular cellular tissue is (αα) the parenchyma, the loose, spongy cellular tissue which consists of broad cells; it is very easily recognized and it occurs especially in the bark and pith of the trunk. (ββ) The bast, the fibrous, tight, cellular tissue proper, is found principally in the stamens, in the pistil-support and similar parts; it has very long, narrow, but still clearly distinguishable cells. It is only in the inner bark, in the wood, in the nerves of the leaves, that it is very difficult to recognize the structure of the bast or fibrous tissue. It consists of extremely slender and narrow cells which assume an elongated, pointed-oval form. (β) Irregular cellular tissue occurs in those plant species in which only a pericarp (*sporangia*) and the rest of the supporting body (*thallus*) are distinguished externally. The lichens have either a crustlike or leaflike *thallus*; the crust consists entirely of round vesicles or cells of widely varying sizes, irregularly heaped together. The algae are quite different from lichens. If the thallus is cut through its thickest part, there will be found very distinct but, as it were, jelly-like threads tangled in all directions. The basis of some algae is a membrane, often slimy, often jelly-like, but never soluble in water. The tissue of fungi consists of fibres which are readily recognized as cells. Between this fibrous tissue, grains lie scattered everywhere just as they are in lichens where they can be taken for gemmae. This concerned the outer form of the cellular tissue. Now how does this cellular tissue develop and alter? It is apparent that new cellular tissue is formed between the old cells. The grains in the cells might be the starch of the plant.'†

Whereas the first diremption was directly related to the process outwards, the root being in reciprocal relation with the earth and the leaf with air and light, the *second*, more intimate diremption is the plant's own separation of itself into woody fibres or active spiral vessels and into other vessels which Prof. Schultz has called 'vital vessels'; his well-founded experiments are in keeping with his philosophical grounding of the subject, even though one might disagree with him about the details of the latter. This separation of the plant in its inner structure, the production of spiral vessels, etc., this, too, is an immediate production, generally a mere multiplication. The medullary cells multiply, and with them also the spiral vessels, the woody fibres, etc. Link makes this particularly clear: 'The spiral vessels are bands which are rolled spirally to form a tube. The spiral vessels are transformed into "stairways" (*Treppengänge*), the coils of the spiral vessels growing together in pairs; the stairways cannot be uncoiled. Through the accretion of neighbouring parts the spiral vessels become taut or compressed; this produces the wavy curves of the cross-bands (*Querstreifen*) and the apparent splitting of the cross-lines (*Spaltungen der Querstriche*) when two coils have been pushed one over the other—perhaps, too, there are actual (*wahre*) splits.

† Link, *Grundlehren*, pp. 12 (*Nachträge*, vol. i, p. 7), 15–18; 20–6; 29–30, 32.

The vessels which have such bands or points are the stippled vessels which I hold to be similar in kind to the stairways.' At first, there remain only the cross-lines; and coils of the spiral vessels which have grown quite close to each other exhibit only dots instead of lines, indentations and cross-lines. 'The ring-vessels (*Ringgefäße*) arise from the rapid growth of the adjacent parts, the coils of the spiral vessels being torn apart and left standing singly. It is no wonder that in the rapidly growing roots and other parts where such spiral vessels in quantity must fulfil their functions, there are also to be found more old, modified vessels than in those parts where growth proceeds at a gentler pace. The spiral vessels are disseminated in almost every part of the plant and form its skeleton. The reticulated bunches of spiral vessels present in the leaves, after they have been freed from all the intervening cellular tissue, are actually called the leaf-skeleton. *It is only in the anthers and the pollen that I have never found spiral vessels.* They are everywhere accompanied by bast; and the bundles of vessels mixed up with bast we call wood. The cellular tissue which surrounds the wood is called bark; and that which is completely surrounded by wood, pith.'†

'In many plants all these vessels are missing: they have never been found in plants with anomalous cellular tissue, in lichens, algae and fungi. The genuine plants with regular cellular tissue either possess spiral vessels or do not. To the latter belong mosses and liverworts and a few aquatic plants like *Chara*. How the spiral vessels originate I do not know. Sprengel says that since they are present in the form of cellular tissue, they must surely have developed from it. This does not seem to me to follow; my belief is that they are developed between the cells of the bast from the sap discharged there. Anyhow, the spiral vessels do grow; and new ones grow between them. Apart from these vessels which can be given the general name of spiral vessels (I call them *true* vessels in contrast to the "stairways" and stippled vessels) I have not observed any vessels in plants.'[1] But where are the vital vessels to be found?

From what Link says in the *Nachträge* (vol. ii, p. 14), it could be inferred that the spiral vessels develop from the linear-shaped woody fibres: 'I find myself compelled to accept again an old opinion, namely that in plants there exist simple, long *fibres*; whether they are solid or hollow cannot easily be seen. The simple fibre without a trace of branches, by no means extends throughout the whole plant. Where branches enter the stem, it can be seen distinctly that their fibres adhere to those of the stem and form, as it were, a wedge in the stem. Even in the same stem and branches they do not seem to advance uninterruptedly. The fibre-vessels always lie in bundles which are heaped together in the oldest stems together with the bast in the form of rings. Usually they surround a bundle of spiral vessels; although in some plants there are

† Link, *Grundlehren*, pp. 46–9, 51–8, 64–5.
[1] Ibid., pp. 65–8.

also simple fibre-vessels without any trace of spiral vessels. These vessels lie in straight lines and are almost parallel in these bundles. In tree-trunks and in roots they tend to diverge and are, as it were, inter-laced. They are found in most plants and are general in the phanero-gams. In many lichens and algae there can be seen only threads coiled together and in fungi these can often be clearly seen. Yet there are fungi, lichens and algae in which *not a trace of them can be found, but only vesicles and cells.*' Thus we see the original antithesis of grain or node and simple length in the antithesis of utricle and fibre, while the spiral vessels strive to attain to roundness.

Oken expounds this transition of cellular tissue into spiral vessels on the lines of the principles outlined above (*Zus.* to § 344, p. 305) but he decks it out with the formalism of the philosophy of Nature of his time as follows: 'The spiral vessels are the light-system (*Lichtsystem*) in the plant. I am well aware how much this doctrine conflicts with what has been accepted up till now; but I have collected all the facts, weighed opinions and experiments, and can confidently state that they all corro-borate this result of construction by philosophy of Nature.' This construc-tion, however, is merely an assertion. 'If they are the light-system, then their function in the plant is *spiritual* or the function of simple polariza-tion. The spiricle (*Spiralfaser*) arises from the opposition between light and the cellular tissue, or from the opposition of the sun to the planet. A light-ray travels through the utricle or the germ. The utricles or cells or the points of slime (*Schleimpunkte*) (originally the plant is this in the seed) gradually arrange themselves side by side along this polar line. In the conflict between the sphere and the line introduced into it by light, the globules of slime although placing themselves side by side in a line, get continually dragged down into the circle of chemism by the planetary process of the cellular tissue, and it is from this conflict that the spiral form arises. The part played by the sun's revolution whereby at any moment another part of the plant is lit up and another is left in shadow, so that the parts become in turn stem and root, this is a topic I do not pretend to have done more than briefly touch on.'†

(*c*) The other side to this is *finally* the process itself, the activity in the first determination, universal life; this is the formal process of merely immediate transformation, this infection as the infinite power of life. The living creature is a being, stable and determined in and for itself. Anything from outside acting chemically on it is immediately transformed by this contact. The living creature, therefore, directly overcomes the presumptuous chemical action and in being brought into contact with an other, preserves itself. It poisons, converts this other in an immediate manner: just as spirit, in envisaging something, transforms it and makes it into its own; for it is *its* picture. In the plant, this process is again to be grasped in its two aspects: (α) as the action of the woody fibres which is

† Oken, *Lehrbuch der Naturphilosophie* (1st ed., vol. ii, p. 52).

absorption, and (β) as the action whereby the sap in the vital vessels acquires the vegetable nature. Absorption and the circulation of the sap with its vegetable-organic nature are the essential moments of the Notion, even though there might be variations in particular instances. Now the leaf is the principal seat of the action of the vital sap: but it absorbs, just as well as the root and the bark, since it already stands in a reciprocal relation with the air; for in the plant, each member does not have such a special function as is the case in the animal. 'One of the most important functions of leaves', as Link says (*Nachträge*, vol. i, p. 54), 'is to prepare the sap for other parts.' The foliage is the pure process; and so, according to Linnaeus, the leaves can be called the lungs of the plant.

About the functions of the vessels and the cellular tissue generally, Link remarks: 'Uninjured roots do not absorb coloured liquids; nor can these penetrate the coloured cuticle (*Oberhaut*). The nutritive sap therefore at first passes through *imperceptible* openings in the cuticle and fills the cells at the tip of the roots before it is absorbed by the vessels. The saps pass through the various vessels, especially through the ducts in the cellular tissue which are not enclosed by any special skin, exude through the spiral vessels, etc. There is air in the spiral vessels and all the associated vessels; the sap which is in the fibre-vessels exudes from them into the cells, spreads in all directions. The fibre-vessels everywhere accompany the air-vessels (*Luftgefäße*). The pores on the cuticle still seem to me to have the function of excretory glands.' (*Nachträge*, vol. ii, pp. 18, 35.) For 'oils, resin, and acids are secretions and waste products of plants'.[1] Spix and Martius, too, in their *Travels to Brazil* (vol. i, p. 299) speak of the gum produced between the bark and the wood of the tree *Hymenaea courbaril L.*, which over there is called *jatoba* or *jatai*: 'By far the greatest part of the resin appears under the tap-roots of the tree when the earth is cleared away from them, and this, as a rule, can only be done after the tree has been felled. Under old trees, pale yellow round cakes, weighing six to eight pounds, are sometimes found, which have been gradually formed by the oozing of the liquid resin. This formation of resinous masses between the roots seems to throw some light on the origin of amber, which had been accumulated in this way before it was taken from the sea. Insects, too, especially ants, are found in bits of *jatai* resin as they are in amber.'

Now if the spiral vessels carry out the first function, namely, to absorb moisture *just as it is*, the second function is the elaboration of the sap into an organic form. This elaboration, in keeping with the nature of the plant, takes place in an immediate manner. The plant has no stomach, etc., as the animal has. This sap circulates through the entire plant. This quivering of vitality within itself belongs to the plant because it is alive— restless Time. That is the blood-circulation in plants. As early as 1774,

[1] Schultz, *Die Natur der lebendigen Pflanze*, vol. i, p. 530.

the Abbe Corti[1] had observed a kind of circulation of the sap in the Conferva *chara Lin.* Amici[2] observed it afresh in 1818 and with the aid of the microscope made the following discoveries: 'In every part of this plant, not only in the finest green threads of the stem and branches, but equally in the most delicate root-fibres, there can be seen a regular circulation of the sap. There is an uninterrupted circulation of white, transparent globules varying in size, in a constant, regular flow, the velocity gradually increasing from the centre to the lateral partitions; they circulate in two currents flowing alternately in opposite directions, one up and the other down, and through the two halves of a simple, cylindrical canal or vessel without any partition. This canal runs lengthwise through the plant-fibre, but is interrupted at intervals by nodes, and is closed by a partition which bounds the circulation. Often, too, the circulation is spiral. Thus the circulation goes through the entire plant and in all its fibres from one node to another, and in each such bounded section is a separate process, independent of the others. In the root-fibres, only one such simple circulation occurs, for only one such central vessel can be seen; but in the green filaments of the plant the vessel is multiple, for the large central vessel is surrounded by several small similar vessels each of which is separated from it by a partition. If such a vessel is loosely tied underneath, or bent at a sharp angle, the circulation is interrupted as if by a natural node, and then continues to circulate above and below the ligature or bend, through the whole section as before; if the vessel is restored to its former state, the original circulation is also restored. If we make a cross-section of such a vessel, its sap does not immediately and entirely flow away, but only the sap from one of the two halves, that sap namely which is flowing towards the section, while the other sap continues its circulatory course.[3] Professor Schultz has observed this flow in some developed plants, e.g. in *Chelidonium majus* (celandine), which has a yellow sap, and also in euphorbia. The description which Schultz gives of this is simply the activity of the Notion (*nur die Regsamkeit des Begriffs*); what has been intuitively apprehended in thought is represented outwardly. The flow is a movement from the centre to the partitions, and from the partitions to the centre again; and, together with this horizontal flow, there is the flow upwards and downwards. The process in relation to the partitions is such that these, too, are not fixed (*fest*), but everything is produced from them. The flow is perceptible through the tendency to form a globule which is always

[1] Osservazioni microscopiche sulla Tremella e sulla circolazione del fluido in una pianta aquajuola dell'Abate Corti. Lucca, 1774. 8.

[2] Osservazioni sulla circolazione del succhio nella Chara. Memoria del Signor Prof. G. Amici. Modena, 1818. 4; with an engraving.

[3] *Wiener Jahrbücher 1819*, vol. v, p. 203. (Martius' Abh. über den Bau der Charen in: *nova acta physico-medica* der Leopold. Karol. Akademie der Naturforscher, Bd. i, Erlangen, 1818; 4. L. E. Treviranus' zu Bremen Beob. über d. Chara in Webers Beiträgen zur Naturkunde, part ii, Kiel, 1810. 8.)

dissolved again. If the plant is cut in two, and the sap is allowed to run into water, then globules are seen like blood corpuscles of animals. This flow is so slight (*zart*) that it cannot be perceived in every species. In the plants investigated by Professor Schultz, the flow was not through a single tube as in the *chara*, but there are two vessels for the ascending and descending movements. Research would be necessary to find out whether this circulation is interrupted or not in trees which have been grafted. Now it is through this circulation which traverses the entire plant that the many individuals which form a plant are combined into a single individual.

(α) Schultz (ibid., vol. i, pp. 488, 500) now describes this double process (see above, p. 329) as follows: First 'the wood-sap is the still imperfectly assimilated' (less particularized) 'food of the plant which will not be more highly organized and carried over into the circulatory system until later. The wood is the system for assimilating air and water; this assimilation is a vital activity.' The wood, which consists of cellular tissues and spiral vessels, absorbs water through the woody fibres of the roots, and above ground absorbs air. 'The papillae, clearly visible at the tips of many roots, have the function of absorbing the nutritive sap; and then the spiral vessels receive it from them in order to carry it further.'[1] Capillaries and their law of capillary action are not adequate explanations in connection with plants; the plant wants water, is thirsty and so absorbs it.

(β) The other point is the quite original and very important discovery by Schultz, the movement of a sap which is now assimilated; although it cannot be demonstrated in every plant because the movement is difficult to observe. The wood-sap still has only a slight taste, is only slightly sweet, and is not yet elaborated into the peculiar character of the plant which has a particular smell, taste, etc. Schultz now says of this vital sap (ibid., p. 507, 576, 564): 'The circulation in plants which goes on during the whole of winter is the movement of a fully organized sap, a movement which takes place in a closed system in every external part of the plant: in the root, stem, flowers, leaves and fruits; similarly all these parts have their assimilative function which, however, is always in polar opposition to the circulation, and in which the movement of the wood-sap is quite different from the movement in the circulatory system. Also the passage of wood-sap into vital-sap takes place only in the extremities of the external parts of the plant, and particularly in those parts where leaves are present, in the leaves themselves and also in the flowers and the parts of the fruit. On the other hand, wood-sap does not pass directly from any bundle of wood-fibres into the vital vessels. The passage of wood-sap into the bark is by way of the leaves.' That is why the bark, which has no direct connection with buds or leaves, dies. On this subject, Link cites the following experiment: 'Meier isolated portions of bark by cutting

[1] Link, *Grundlehren*, p. 76.

away strips of bark round them, and he noticed that those portions on which there were a bud, etc., survived, but those which had none soon withered. I have repeated these experiments on apricot trees and confirmed them. A piece of bark without buds and leaves, isolated in this way, soon withered and dried up, nor did it exude any gum. Another piece, isolated, with three torn-off buds and leaves, dried up more slowly, and also exuded no gum. A third piece, with three undamaged buds and leaves, did not dry up, remained green all over, and from its lower portion exuded gum. On a piece of detached bark, a layer of parenchyma is first formed, a fresh pith, as it were; this was followed by a layer of bast with individual spiral vessels and "stairways": and all was covered by the new bark from the parenchyma, which therefore is produced first and also forms the basis of the young stem and the embryo. There was formed in some measure a new pith, new wood and new bark.'[1]

(γ) Thirdly, the plant's vital sap becomes a product: 'With the breaking-out of the leaf, the bark is easily separated from the wood in every part of the plant; and this is a result of a delicate, soft substance found between them, i.e. cambium which only comes into being with the leaf. The vital sap, on the other hand, is not between the bark and wood but in the bark.' This third sap is the neutral substance: 'The cambium does not move and has a periodic existence in the plant. Cambium is the residuum of the entire individual life (as the fruit-formation is of the generic life); it is not a fluid like the other plant-juices, but the delicate embryonic shape of the whole, already formed plant-totality, the unexplicated totality, like a woodless plant (or like animal lymph). Now the cambium is formed from the vital sap of the bark by the circulation; and from this also comes the wood and the layer of bark. The cellular tissue, too, is developed from the undifferentiated cambium. As, therefore, in the vascular system of the circulation, we have the antithesis of vital vessels and vital sap, in the assimilative system the antithesis of spiral vessels and wood-sap, so in the cellular tissue there appears the antithesis of the cell and its fluid content. With the lengthening of the roots and branches, the new embryonic formations are deposited on their tips, those which come from the homogeneous substance going upwards, and those from the cambium going to the side, although there is no essential difference between them. In ferns, grasses and palms one node forms on top of another: in bulbous plants the nodes are formed side by side, and from one side of them grow the roots, and on the other side the buds. In the higher plants, this external nodulation (*Verknotung*) is no longer so evident, but instead there is seen the formation of wood and bark at the tips of the nodes.'†

Now, summarizing the foregoing, we have to distinguish the following three moments in the interior formative process of the plant: (α) the

---

[1] Link, *Nachträge*, vol. i, pp. 49–51.

† Schultz, *Die Natur der lebendigen Pflanze*, vol. i, pp. 632, 636, 653, 659.

diremption into root and leaf, as itself a relation outwards, is the interior nutritive process—the wood-sap; (β) the relation to its interior, the pure, immanent process, is the vital sap; (γ) the general product is ($\alpha\alpha$) the cambium of the botanists, ($\beta\beta$) the dead secretion into etheric oils and salts, ($\gamma\gamma$) the internal diremption of the plant into wood and cortical substance. Then secondly, we have the formation of nodes as a generic multiplication of the plant, and lastly, the bud, which hints at the process of sexual difference.

2. The sap which has been endowed with a vegetable nature, and its product, the division of what was previously undifferentiated into bark and wood, can be compared to the diremption of the individual which takes place in the universal life-process of the Earth, namely, into the vital activity as such, which lies in the past and outside it, and into the system of organic formations as the material substrate and residue of the process. The plant, like the animal, perpetually destroys itself, in that it sets up an opposition between itself and being; in the plant it is the formation of wood, and in the animal it is the skeletal system. The latter is the supporter of the animal organism, but, as abstract, immobile being, is the excreted, calcareous moment. The plant, too, posits within itself its inorganic basis, its skeleton. The unreleased power, the pure self, which simply, on account of its immediate unitary nature, sinks back into the inorganic sphere, is the woody fibre; looked at chemically it is carbon, the abstract Subject which, in the root, remains in the earth as pure wood without bark and pith. Wood is combustibility as potentiality of fire without itself being heat; for this reason it often develops a sulphurous nature. In some roots fully formed sulphur is produced. In the root, surface and line are so crumpled and effaced, so knotted, that the former dimension is suppressed, and is a solid continuity, which is on the point of being wholly inorganic and without any distinction of shape. Oken considers the woody fibres to be nerve-threads: 'The spiral vessels are for the plant what nerves are for the animal.'[†] But the woody fibres are not nerves but bones. The plant only gets as far as this simplification as abstract reference-to-self; this reflection-into-self is a dead substance because it is only abstract universality.

The process of wood-formation in its further details is very simple. Link describes it in his *Grundlehren* (pp. 142–6) as follows: 'In the monocotyledons, the inner structure of the stem differs considerably from that in the dicotyledons. In the former, the woody rings which separate the pith from the bark are absent; the woody bundles are dispersed in the cellular tissue in larger quantities towards the bark, and in smaller quantities towards the centre. In the dicotyledons, all the woody bundles are disposed in a circle, although, since Nature nowhere draws precise boundaries, such scattered bundles are found in *cucurbitaceae* and a few other plants. Usually bast accompanies the cellular tissue, but there are

† Oken, *Lehrbuch der Naturphilosophie*, vol. ii, p. 112.

some cases where bundles of very narrow, elongated cellular tissue or bast occur in the stem fairly remote from the vascular bundles. Thus some *labiatae* have such bundles of bast in the four corners of the stem, and many *umbelliferae* in the projecting edges. Now the growth of the stem and the formation of layers of wood in the monocotyledons takes place in a simple, ordinary manner. Not only do the parts become longer and wider, but new parts appear between the old—cells between cells, vessels between vessels. The cross-section of an older stem resembles that of a younger stem in every part. In the arborescent grasses the parts harden in an extraordinary way.' 'In many grasses', remarks Willdenow (ibid., p. 336), 'silica has been found, in bamboo cane (*Bambusa arundinacea*), etc.; it also forms an ingredient of plant-fibre, e.g. in hemp and flax. It also seems to be present in the wood of *Alnus glutinosa* and *Betula alba* for when this wood is turned on the lathe it often emits sparks.'

Link continues: 'Things are quite different in the dicotyledons. In the first year, the woody bundles form a circle, separated from each other, and surrounded by parenchyma. At this earliest age, they contain only bast and a bundle of spiral vessels inside. It is mainly the bast which adnates and inserts itself between the parenchyma'; thus giving rise to alternate layers of fibres and parenchyma. 'The woody bundles spread laterally, compress the parenchyma and finally form a closed ring which envelops the pith. Now the bast of this woody bundle is alternately dense and loose; it is probable, therefore, that new bast has inserted itself between the old. Inside the woody ring, and against the pith, there are still individual woody bundles disposed in a circle. The medullary rays (*sogenannte Spiegelfasern*) originate in the alternate layers of bast as well as in the compressed parenchyma.' They are, therefore, prolongations of the pith, and they grow outwards towards the bark, are found between the elongated fibres, and are not present in the monocotyledons. 'It is the woody ring which first separates the pith from the bark. Later the woody bundles spread inwards; the woody ring grows wider. Rows of scalariform tissues are seen radiating towards the pith' (but undoubtedly in a vertical direction). 'On the inner side of the ring round the pith there is a circle of separated bundles of spiral vessels. But the medullary cells have become, not smaller, but larger, although the amount of pith in relation to the thickness of the stem has diminished. The amount of pith has therefore decreased, the outer part being diminished and compressed laterally into rays; but this reduction is not the result of the pith being compressed into a smaller space at the centre. Consequently the first (innermost) bundles of spiral vessels are not pushed inwards by the adnate wood; on the contrary, fresh bundles are continually being formed in the pith, and those already existing have spread themselves laterally and compressed the parenchyma. The scalariform tissues were formed from the spiral vessels; and as the spiral vessels are, in the first instance, slightly separated from each other, so now the scalariform vessels too, lie in rows running inwards. It is evident from all this that the woody layer is formed by scattered bundles of spiral vessels and bast meeting and joining together at the sides, and also by the constant growth, in a circle on the inside, of fresh bundles of spiral vessels, which likewise join together at the sides.'†

'In each of the following years a fresh layer of wood is inserted between the bark and the wood. As in the first year, layers grow on to the woody bundles, thus enlarging them, and so it is extremely probable that in successive years a similar fresh layer of wood attaches itself round the wood. Similarly fresh layers of parenchyma are deposited in the outer bark, and fresh layers of bast in the inner bark. But the precise, uninterrupted passage of one layer into the other shows that the new growth also takes place in the interstices of the vessels and of the cellular tissue of the older layer: in the pith, too, until it is completely filled out. Everywhere fresh parts are interpolated, but only on the outside in amounts large enough to make the increase easily perceptible. In the growth itself, there is no difference between the layers, everywhere the wood grows uniformly and uninterruptedly; and there is no difference whatever except in the denseness or looseness of the layers. The older layers, however, do not retain their thickness, but get continually thinner, and finally so thin that they can hardly be distinguished and counted any longer. There takes place, therefore, a genuine contraction which narrows the bast-cells. In the interior of the wood, growth finally ceases when all the pith is exhausted (*verzehrt*). From May to June, I examined almost daily branches of the previous year, and for a long time found no trace of a second-year ring. Then suddenly it appeared, and when it did it was already a respectable size. It seems to me, therefore, that the annual ring was made by a sudden contraction of the wood; this contraction must occur about or after St. John's Day, and has no connection with the annual growth of wood. If what takes place is only the accretion of a fresh ring round the outermost layer, then one could not fail to notice the annual ring of the previous year in the spring and summer.'†† Therefore even the development of the annual ring in the plant is always a fresh production, not, as in the animal, a simple conservation.

3. With this production is also bound up the taking back of the individuality into itself; and this is the production of the bud. It is a fresh plant on the old one, or, at any rate, the simple return of the old plant into the tendency to become a new one: 'Each bud unfolds a stem with leaves, and at the base of each petiole is a fresh bud. That is the way in which growth in general takes place. The development from bud to bud would, however, continue unchecked, were it not that each bud, as soon as it has produced blossom, dies after the blossom and fruit have completed their development. The opening of the flower and of the fruit which follows it constitutes the insurmountable barrier to the growth of the

† Link, *Grundlehren*, pp. 146–51 (*Nachträge*, vol. i, pp. 45–6).
†† Link, *Nachträge*, vol. i, pp. 46–8; vol. ii. pp. 41–2 (*Grundlehren*, pp. 151–3).

branches.'¹ The blossom is thus an annual plant.² With this, the process of the plant is closed; the plant preserves itself by the reproduction of itself, which is at the same time the production of another plant. The process is thus mediated by the moments indicated; it is still the *formal* process with regard to production, as a simple bursting forth of what was enveloped in the initial main impulse of the plant.

B. THE PROCESS OF ASSIMILATION

§ 347

2. The process of formation is directly connected with the second process, *the self-specifying process of the plant outwards*. The seed germinates only when stimulated from outside; and, in the process of formation, the diremption into root and leaf is itself a diremption into the direction of earth and water and that of light and air: into the absorption of water and its *assimilation* through the intermediation of leaf and bark and of light and air. The return-into-self in which assimilation terminates, does not have for result the *self* as inner, subjective universality over against externality, does not result in self-feeling. Rather is the plant drawn out of itself by light, by its self which is external to it, and climbs towards it, ramifying into a plurality of individuals. *Inwardly*, the plant draws from light its specific energy (*Befeuerung*) and vigour, the immaterial quality of scent and of flavour, the splendour and depth of colour, and the compactness and robustness of shape.

Zusatz. The coincidence of the process outwards with the first process, being such that the process of root and leaf in their vital existence exists only as a process outwards, the only distinction between the two processes is partly that this outward-turned side must become more definitely marked, but also and principally that the return-into-self as the becoming of the self—self-feeling, the satisfaction of the self from the overcoming of (its) inorganic nature—has here the peculiar form of being also a development outwards. The self present in the shape enters into the process outwards in order, through this self-mediation, to come to itself, to bring the self before the self. But the self does not authenticate itself; in the plant, this self-satisfaction does not become a union-with-self, but a fashioning of itself into a light-plant (*Lichtpflanze*). This takes the place

---

¹ Willdenow, *Grundriß der Kräuterkunde*, pp. 402–3.
² Goethe, *Zur Morphologie*, p. 54.

of the senses. In its existence, in its shape, the self is reflected into itself: this means here, that its existence, its shape, is, in all its parts, a complete individual, is itself something that simply is *(ist selbst ein Seiendes)*; but, in its existence, it is not itself a universal individual, in which it would be the unity of itself and of the universal; but the other individual to which it stands in relation is only a part of the whole, and is itself a plant. The self does not become object of the self, of its own self; on the contrary, the second self with which the plant, in conformity with its Notion, must enter into relation, is outside of it. The self does not become *for* the plant, but the plant becomes a self to itself only in light; its lighting-up, its becoming light *(ihr Erleuchten, Lichtwerden)*, does not mean that the plant itself becomes light, but that it is only in light *(am und im Licht)* that it is produced. Consequently the selflike character of light as an objective presence *(gegenständliche Gegenwart)* does not develop into vision: the sense of sight remains merely light, colour, in the plant, not the light which has been reborn in the midnight of sleep, in the darkness of the pure ego—not this spiritualized light as existent negativity.

This closed circle of the outward-turned process is annual, even though in other respects the plant, as a tree, is perennial; and the same is true, not only of the opening of the flower-bud, but also of all the parts and organs which are involved in the rest of the process, the roots and leaves. The leaves fall 'in northern climates', says Willdenow (ibid., pp. 450–1), 'in the autumn, but in others they live several years'. But whereas Willdenow attributes the shedding of leaves to the stoppage of sap (p. 452), Link *(Nachträge* vol. i, p. 55) postulates an opposite cause: 'The shedding of leaves seems to be preceded rather by a superabundance of sap than by a lack of it. This shedding was furthered by complete ringing of the bark which prevented the return flow of the sap in the bark. It now seems to me that the primary cause of leaf-shedding is a weakening of the bark, partly by the growth of the trunk and partly by cold.' The roots too die off and fresh ones grow: 'The plant-root is constantly changing. Fibres and hairs are perpetually dying and being replaced by others. The quantity of fibres and hairs which grow out of the root are enticed out by moisture, and they spread in all directions; and in this way the root is drawn away into moist surroundings. The roots also exude moisture, and this probably accounts for the sand clinging to them. The older roots, it seems, soon become useless, perhaps because of the excessive dislocation of the spiral vessels, and so they manure and corrupt the soil. The main root seldom lasts more than a few years; it dies after it has put out branches and stems with new roots. In trees, the trunk grows into the earth and finally takes the place of the root. For it is not only the root which tends to grow downwards, this tendency is by no means absent in the stem, too; a few days after germination it can be found to have penetrated already well into the ground.'†

† Link, *Grundlehren*, pp. 137 *(Nachträge*, vol. i, pp. 39, 43), 140.

External Nature with which the plant stands in relationship is not Nature as individualized, but the Elements. The plant enters into relation with (α) light, (β) air, (γ) water.

1. While the process of the plant involved with the Elements of air and water is general, the relation with light is displayed particularly in the opening of the flower-bud; but this, as production of a fresh shape, also belongs to the first process, and, as indicating sexual difference, to the third process too, thus demonstrating how the different processes of the plant interpenetrate and are only superficially distinct. It is in light that all the plant's energies develop, and it acquires scent and colour; it is light that endows the plant with these qualities, and also holds it upright. 'In light, the leaves grow green; but there are also green parts of the plant which lie completely hidden from the light, e.g. the inner bark. Young leaves raised in the dark are white; but when they are larger and stronger they take on a greenish colour in the same darkness. But flowers become more beautifully coloured in the light, and there is an increase of aromatic oils and resins. In the dark, colour, scent and vigour all diminish. In hot-houses, plants throw out long shoots; these, however, are feeble, without colour and scent, so long as they are deprived of light.'† The bark and leaf, which are the self of the process, are still unseparated (noch in ihrer Ungeschiedenheit), and for that very reason are green. With the neutrality of water, this synthesis of blue and yellow is broken up and split into blue and yellow, the yellow later turning to red. Horticulture consists in making flowers grow in all these colours and their combinations. In this relation of the plant to its self which is outside of it, the plant does not behave chemically, but appropriates this self and possesses it inwardly, as is the case in vision. In light, and in the relationship with it, the plant is for itself; and the plant constitutes itself an independent being in face of this absolute power of light over it, in face of light's very own identity. Just as a human being in his relationship to the State, which is his ethical, substantial nature, his essence and the absolute power over him, becomes in this very identity independent and for himself, a mature and substantial being, so too does the plant in its relation with light give itself its particularity, its specific and robust quality. These aromatic plants grow especially in southern latitudes; one of the Spice Islands spreads its scent many miles out to sea and has a magnificent display of flowers.

2. The specifying of air within the plant in the air-process is manifested by the plant giving out the air again as a specific gas, for, in appropriating the elemental matter, it differentiates it. This process comes closest to being chemical. Plants exhale; they convert air into water, and, conversely, water into air. This process is a breathing-in and a breathing-out: during the day, the plant breathes out oxygen and at night, carbon dioxide.†† This process is obscure because of the sealed reticence of the

† Link, *Grundlehren*, pp. 290–1.
†† Ibid., p. 283.

plant (*verschlossenen Ansichhaltens der Pflanze*). If intussusception is understood as a taking-up of parts already formed (*fertig*), only the heterogeneous element being separated from them, this amounts to saying that the plant draws in carbon dioxide from the air, and leaves the rest, the oxygen, etc., outside. This supposedly philosophical way of looking at the matter is based on experiments in which plants under water and exposed to light give off oxygen; as if this were not just as much a process with the water, as if plants do not also decompose the air and take in oxygen. But the process does not get as far as a chemical existence; if it did, organic life would be destroyed. In the transformation of air into water, it is useless to look for a chemical explanation of the passage of nitrogen into hydrogen, for these substances are immutable from that standpoint. The transformation is brought about by oxygen which is the negative self. However, the process does not stop here: it returns into carbon, the solid element (*das Feste*) and conversely, the plant equally resolves this punctiform element (*das Punktuelle*) by the opposite path into air and water. The plant maintains the moisture in the atmosphere and equally absorbs water from it; everything negative is equally positive. But in the plant itself, this process is its formation, which contains three moments: the plant becomes (α) a solid self, a woody substance, (β) a water-filled, neutral existence, (γ) an aeriform, purely ideal process.

Link gives the following account of this process of the plant with the air: 'I found that oxygen is indispensable to the life of the plant, but that the plant does not grow in it at all; on the other hand, carbon dioxide mixed in the ratio of 1:12 with oxygen promotes an excellent growth of the plant in the light; carbon dioxide is decomposed and oxygen is liberated. In the dark, carbon dioxide is harmful. According to Saussure's experiments, plants absorb oxygen, convert it into carbon dioxide, and, after decomposing it, breathe out oxygen. Parts which are not green do not absorb oxygen, they convert it straightway into carbon dioxide. The extract of fertile soil serves as nourishment for plants. Oxygen takes the carbon from it to form carbon dioxide. Soil taken from far below the surface is no good for feeding plants, but it becomes so after long exposure to the air.' A shower of rain then puts everything right. 'Saussure observed that bare roots, which withered when they were exposed to irrespirable gases, and their tips were dipped in water, lived on in oxygen. This they converted into carbon dioxide; but, if the stalk were still attached, they absorbed carbon dioxide and developed oxygen from the leaves.'[1] The process with the air, therefore, must certainly not be represented as an appropriation by the plant of something already formed which it increases only mechanically. Such a mechanical representation is altogether to be rejected; what occurs is a complete transformation, an operation accomplished by the majesty of the living organism, for organic life is just this power over the inorganic to transform it.

[1] Link, *Nachträge*, vol. i, pp. 62–3; *Grundlehren*, pp. 284–5.

Besides, where else is the potash supposed to come from which is so often found particularly in unripe plants, in grapes for example.[1]

The organs of this process of the plant with the air are described by Willdenow as follows (ibid., pp. 354–5): 'The apertures (*pori, stomata*) are seen on the cuticle (*Oberhaut*) of plants; they are extraordinarily delicate, oblong fissures which open and shut. As a rule they are open during the morning and closed in the heat of the midday sun. They are found in every part of the plant which is exposed to the air and has a green colour, and are more abundant on the underside of leaves than on the upper side. They are lacking on the leaves of aquatic plants below the surface of the water, and on the surface of leaves which float on the water; they are missing in water-algae, mosses, lichens, fungi and cognate plants. But there is no canal running inwards from this pore, and therefore no tubes to be found connected with it; the pore culminates, without any further mechanism, in the closed cell.'

3. Next to the air-process, the water-process is of cardinal importance, for it is moisture which first makes the plant fertile; there is in the plant no independent impulse to germinate, and without water the seed remains inanimate. 'There lies the grain of seed—perhaps for countless years—without any vital impulse, inert and locked up within itself. Its awakening is for it a lucky chance, without which it would remain still longer in its indifference or finally perish. To liberate this growth from earthy influences, and to grow from the food which it has itself grown, this is the urge of the sprouting stem. To liberate the growth from the plant's own food resources (the root), from the accident of what is already a growth, and to achieve its own measure, the circumscribed form over against the abundance of earthy influences, this is the life of the leaf.'[2]

Most plants do not require soil for their nourishment; they can be planted in powdered glass or in pebbles which remain unaffected by them, i.e. the plants cannot draw any nourishment from them. The plant gets on just as well with water, although, if possible, it should contain an oily substance. 'Helmont was the first to find that a tree in a pot filled with earth increased its weight by much more than the loss in weight of the earth; and he concluded from this that water is the proper food of plants. Duhamel grew an oak tree in water alone, and it continued to grow for eight years. Schrader, in particular, has carried out accurate experiments on the growth of plants in flowers of sulphur sprinkled with pure water; but the plants do not bear ripe seeds. It is no wonder that plants raised, not in their proper soil, but either in water alone, or sand, or sulphur, do not come to perfection. A plant from chalky soil never thrives in sand; and conversely, sand plants put into rich soil as a rule do not bear ripe seeds. It may well be that salts really act as manure and not

---

[1] Cf. Link, *Nachträge*, vol. i, p. 64.

[2] Schelver, *Kritik der Lehre von den Geschlechtern der Pflanze: Erste Fortsetzung:* vol. i, pp. 23 and 78.

merely as stimulants to growth; but in larger amounts they are harmful. The insoluble basis of the soil is not a matter of indifference as regards plant growth, nor is its action to be measured merely by its capacity to hold water or let it pass through. Sulphur accelerates the germination of seeds in the air, so too does lead monoxide and without any trace of deoxidation.'[1] 'When moisture begins to fail, plants often feed on themselves, as is shown by bulbs laid out to dry, which grow leaves and flowers, but, in doing so, use up the entire bulb.'[2]

The process outwards is introduced, on the one hand, through the root, and on the other, through the leaf, it is the digestive life of the plant drawn outwards, and indeed, in *Chelidonium* and other plants, the circulation extends from the root to the leaf. The product of this process is the formation of nodes (*Verknoten*) in the plant itself. This development and movement outwards of the plant, which results in this product, can be expressed as a ripening of the plant internally. But in doing so, the plant also arrests this movement outwards; and this is precisely the plant's reproduction of itself in buds. Whereas the first impulse is the purely formal increase of what is already in existence, a mere continued sprouting (for example, the bud often produces leaves, too, and these in turn a bud, and so on *ad infinitum*), the flower-bud is at once an arrest and retraction of the movement outwards, of growth as such, and that, too, as soon as inflorescence takes place. 'With us, every shrub or tree makes two growths (*Triebe*) annually: one, the main growth, occurs in spring; it is formed by the quantity of sap which the root has absorbed during the winter. With us, it is not until about St. Sebastian's Day, 20th January, that we find sap in trees when they are tapped; if mild days follow, the sap does not flow, but only when there is another spell of cold weather. From late autumn to the middle of January the sap does not flow at all.' Nor will it flow again later when the leaves have come out: therefore it flows only once when the root begins to be active in January, and then for as long as the leaves are still active in feeding the bark. 'The second impulse is not so strong, and occurs near the longest day, i.e. St. John's Day; that is why it is also called St. John's sap (*Trieb*). It is produced by the moisture absorbed in spring. In warm latitudes, both growths are equally strong, with the consequence that plants there grow more luxuriantly.'[3] In those latitudes, therefore, there are two different impulses; but in such tropical plants, growth and suspended growth occur at the same time, whereas with us when one impulse is present the other is not. Since the reproduction of the living organism is exhibited as the repetition of the whole, the formation of fresh buds is also accompanied by the formation of a fresh annual ring (*Holzring*), or a fresh diremption within the plant; for as next year's buds form about St. John's Day, so

[1] Link, *Grundlehren*, pp. 272–4; 278–9.
[2] Willdenow, ibid., pp. 434–5.
[3] Ibid., pp. 448–9 (pp. 419–21).

too does the new wood, as we have already seen above (§ 346a, *Zusatz*, 2. p. 335).

Now as the fruitfulness of trees is increased generally by arresting the growth outwards, so it is also increased particularly, by grafting, simply because the foreign branch remains more apart from the life of the entire plant, which just consists in the growth outwards. The tree therefore bears (α) more fruit because, as independent, it is relieved from simply sprouting, and in its own peculiar life can devote itself more to fruit-bearing; (β) also cultivated fruit of finer quality because, as Schelver says (ibid., p. 46): 'The root of the wild stock which serves the cultivated plant is always presupposed, and the organ which is grafted is also already presupposed by the cultivated plant.' Ringing the bark of olive trees also arrests growth and makes the tree fruitful; root growth is also promoted by ringing.

In general, however, the character of this process is not an endless growth outwards, but rather the plant takes hold of itself, returns into itself; the blossom itself is just this moment of return, of being-for-self, although the plant can never really develop into a self. The flower is this node, not the bud which merely grows; but as this nodulation which arrests growth, it is the assemblage of leaves (*petala*) which are more delicately developed. From the punctiform basis of the cellular tissue or from the first seed, through the linear form of the woody fibre and the surface of the leaf, the plant has achieved in the flower and fruit the fully rounded shape; the plurality of leaves is concentrated again into one point. As the shape which has been raised into light, into the self, it is the flower above all which possesses colour; already in the calyx and still more in the flower, the merely neutral green takes on colour. Also the flower does not smell only when it is bruised, like the leaves of trees, but it gives out a scent. Finally, in the blossom, there occurs the differentiation into organs which have been compared to the genitals of the animal; and these are an image of the self generated in the plant itself, which brings itself into relationship with the self. The flower is the plant life which has clothed itself, which forms a garland round the seed as an inner product, whereas previously its activity was directed only outwards.

C. THE GENUS-PROCESS

§ 348

The plant also brings forth its light as *its own* self in the *blossom*, in which the neutral colour green is then further specified. The *genus-process*, the relation of the individual self to the self, as a return into itself, *arrests* the growth of the plant as an unrestrained sprouting from bud to bud. But the plant does not attain to a relationship between individuals as such but only to a difference, whose sides are not at the same time in themselves whole individuals, do not determine the whole individuality; therefore the difference, too, does not go beyond a beginning and an adumbration of the genus-process. The *germ* is to be regarded here as one and the same individual, whose life runs through this process, and through return into itself has not only advanced to the maturity of a seed, but equally has preserved itself; but this process is, on the whole, superfluous since the process of formation and assimilation is itself already reproduction as production of fresh individuals.

Zusatz. The final act of the plant is the opening of the blossom whereby the plant makes itself objective, assimilates light, and produces this external element as its own. That is why Oken says (*Text-book of the Philosophy of Nature*, vol. ii, p. 112) that the flower is the brain of the plant;† others, however, from the same school opined that the plant has its brain, the root, in the ground, but its sexual organs turned towards the sky. The flower is the plant's highest subjectivity, the contraction of the whole as in the individual, its opposition within itself and to itself— but at the same time to itself as an externality, for this development of inflorescence is itself in turn a succession (*Succession*): 'The stem flowers earlier than the branches, the main branch earlier than the side branches, and so on. On one and the same branch, flowering is earlier on the lower part than on the upper part.'[1] But furthermore, since the plant, in producing other individuals, at the same time preserves itself, the significance of this fruitfulness is not merely that the plant, by its constant budding (*Verknoten*), transcends itself, but rather that the cessation of growth, the arrest of this sprouting (*Hinaussprossen*), is the condition for that fruitfulness. Now if this negation of the plant's coming-out-of-itself is to attain *existence* in the plant, this means nothing more than that the self-subsistent individuality of the plant, the substantial form which constitutes its Notion and exists for itself throughout the whole plant— the *idea matrix* of the plant, becomes isolated as a separate existence. True, the outcome of this isolation is only the production of a fresh individual, but this, just because it arrests reproduction, is only a differentiation within itself; and that is what takes place in the plant if we consider the fate of the sexual parts. It is of no use here, as in the generative process generally, to investigate what is in the unfertilized seed and what is added to it by fertilization. The process eludes the crude methods

† Schelling says the same: *Zeitschrift für speculative Physik*, vol. ii, No. 2, p. 124.   [1] Link, *Nachträge*, vol. i, p. 52.

of chemistry, which destroys the living organism and deals only with inanimate matter, not living substance. The fertilization of the plant consists solely in this, that the plant endows its moments with an abstract existence in which they exist separately, and posits them as a unity again through contact (*Berührung*). This movement, as a movement between abstract, differentiated, activated, but existent moments, is the plant's actualization of these abstractions, a process which it displays within itself.

1. Since Linnaeus, this display has been regarded generally as a sexual process; but it could be this only if the moments of the process were not merely parts of the plant by whole plants. It is therefore notoriously a moot point among botanists whether there is actually in plants, as in animals, first, sexual difference, and secondly, impregnation.

(a) To the first question we must answer: The difference reached by the plant, which is a difference of one plant self from another plant self, each of which has the urge to identify itself with the other—this determination exists only as an analogue of the sexual relationship. For the sides of the relation are not two individuals. There are only a few plants where the difference of sex occurs in such a manner that the separate sexes are distributed in two separate and distinct plants. These are the *Dioecia*, of which the most important are palms, hemp, hops, etc. The *Dioecia* thus provide the chief proof of impregnation. In the *Monoecia*, however, such as melons, pumpkins, hazels, firs, oaks, the male and female flowers are found on the same plant; i.e. such plants are hermaphrodites. To this class belong also the *Polygamia*, plants which bear flowers, some of which are hermaphroditic and some not.[1] But these differences are often very changeable while plants are growing: in dioecious plants like hemp, *Mercurialis*, etc., a plant will show, for example, an early disposition to be female and yet subsequently become male; thus the difference is only a quite partial one. The different individuals cannot therefore be regarded as of different sexes because they have not been completely imbued with the *principle* of their opposition—because this does not completely pervade them, is not a universal moment of the entire individual, but is a separated part of it, and the two enter into relation with each other only in respect of this part. The sexual relationship proper must have for its opposed moments entire individuals whose determinateness, completely reflected into itself, spreads through the whole individual. The entire habit (*habitus*) of the individual must be bound up with its sex. Only when the inner, generative forces have reached complete penetration and saturation, does the individual possess the sexual impulse, only then is it awakened. That which in the animal is sexual right from the beginning, which merely develops itself, becomes a force, an impulse, but is not the formative principle of its organs, that in the plant is an external product.

---

[1] Willdenow, *Grundriß der Kräuterkunde*, pp. 235–6.

The plant therefore is asexual, even the *Dioecia*, because the sexual parts form a closed, particular circle apart from their individuality. On the one side, we have filaments and anthers as male sexual parts, and on the other, seed-bud and pistil as female sexual parts, which Link describes as follows (*Grundlehren*, pp. 215–18, 220): 'I have never found vessels in the anthers; these consist for the most part of large, round and angular cells: these are longer and narrower only where nerves' (?) 'are to be seen. The pollen is found in the anther, mostly loose in tiny globules. Only rarely is it fixed to a fine thread; in some plants it is resinous, in others, of an animal substance, phosphate of lime and phosphate of magnesia. The anthers of moss have in their outer form, in the regular arrangement of leaves round them, a great similarity to stamens. The vascular fascicles never run from the peduncle, or the middle of the seed-bud, straight into the pistil, but they meet in the pistil after coming from the outer coverings of the fruit or from the surrounding fruits. Accordingly, the base of the pistil sometimes seems to be hollow, and a strong slender strip of cellular tissue runs through the middle of the seminal passage (*Staubweg*). There is no other canal running from the stigma to the seeds to fertilize them.' (Does not this cellular tissue then actually go to the seeds?) 'Often the vessels do not reach as far as the stigma; or else they go from the stigma past the seed into the fruit outside, and from there to the peduncle.'

(b) To the first question, whether the plant has veritable sexual organs, is linked the second: whether copulation as such occurs. That actual fertilization does occur is proved by the following account which is well known in Berlin: 'In the botanical garden there, is a female *Chaemerops humilis* which for thirty years had borne flowers but never any ripe fruit. In 1749, Gleditsch fertilized it with pollen from a male plant which was sent to him from the Bosischen Garten at Leipzig, and obtained ripe seeds. In the spring of 1767, Kölreuter sent part of the pollen of *Chaemerops humilis*, gathered in the Karlsruhe botanical garden, to Gleditsch in Berlin, and the rest to Eckleben the head gardener in St. Petersburg. At both places the pollination of the female palm was successful. The palm in St. Petersburg was already a hundred years old, and had always blossomed in vain.'[1]

(c) Now though this compels us to admit the occurrence of an actual fertilization, there still remains the third question, whether it is *necessary*. Since buds are complete individuals, and plants propagate themselves by stolons, and leaves and branches need only come into contact with the earth in order to be themselves fertile as distinct individuals (§ 345, *Zus.*, p. 313), it follows that the production of a new individual through the union of the two sexes—generation—is a play, a luxury, a superfluity for propagation; for the preservation of the plant is itself only a multiplication of itself. Fertilization by sexual union is not necessary, since the

[1] Willdenow, ibid., p. 483; Schelver, ibid., pp. 12–13.

plant organism, because it is the whole individuality, is already fertilized on its own account even without being touched by another plant. Thus many plants have fertilizing organs but produce only sterile seeds: 'Some mosses can have stamens without needing them for propagation, for they can reproduce themselves sufficiently by buds. But ought it not to be possible even for unfertilized plants, at least over several generations, to bear germinating seeds, as they do plant-lice? Spallanzani's experiments seem to prove that it is.'[1]

Now if we ask whether a plant can bear ripe seeds without the pistil receiving pollen from the filaments and anthers, the answer is that in some instances the plant does not bear ripe seeds, but in others it certainly does. The position generally is, therefore, that in most plants *contact* of the pistil with the pollen is a condition of fertilization, but that in many plants fertilization occurs without contact being necessary. And the reason for this is that, although the feeble life of the plant attempts to advance to the stage of sexual difference, but does not quite succeed, the nature of the plant being, on the whole, indifferent to this distinction, yet some plants do mature and develop even when the anthers and stigma are nipped off, and the life of the plant has in consequence been injured; they therefore achieve consummation on their own account, and in this way the seed is not superior to the bud. In hermaphrodites like melons and pumpkins, the two parts are not ripe at the same time, or else at such a distance and in such a position that contact between them is impossible. Thus in many flowers, especially the *Asclepias*, one cannot see how the pollen can get on to the pistil.[2] This must be effected in some instances by insects, the wind, etc.

2. Now where sexual difference and the genus-process are present, the further question arises, how ought this process to be understood, since it is not necessary for the ripening of the seed; and also, whether it is to be taken as a complete analogue of the genus-process in the animal.

(a) In plants the genus-process is *formal*; it is only in the animal organism that the process has its true meaning. Whereas in the genus-process of the animal the genus, as the negative power over the individual, is realized through the sacrifice of this individual which it replaces by another, in the plant this positive side of the process already exists in the first two processes, since the relationship with the outer world is already a reproduction of the plant itself and therefore coincides with the genus-process. It is for this reason that, strictly speaking, the sex-relationship should be regarded as just as much, or as even more, a *digestive process*; here digestion and generation are the same. Digestion produces the individual itself; but in the plant it is another individual that is produced, as in the immediate digestion of growth, this very growth is a process of bud-formation. All that is necessary for the production and ripening of the buds is the arrest of luxuriant growth; through this, the whole plant

---

[1] Link, *Grundlehren*, p. 228.   [2] Cf. Ibid., p. 219.

recapitulates itself in the bud and in the fruit, and falls asunder into many seeds which are capable of existing independently. The genus-process therefore has no importance for the nature of the plant. It shows that the reproduction of the individual is *mediated*, is even a complete process, although, nevertheless, in the plant all this again is equally an immediate production of individuals, the difference of the sexes as well as the production of the seed.

(b) But where there is actual contact, what does happen? The anther bursts open, the pollen flies out and touches the stigma on the pistil. After this release of the pollen, the pistil withers and the seed-bud, the seed and its case, swell up. But all that is necessary for the production of individuals is merely the negation of growth; even the fate of the sexual parts is only an arrest, a negation, a falling into dust, a withering away. Arrest, negation, is also necessary in animal life. Each sex negates its being-for-self, posits itself as identical with the other. But it is not through this negation alone that this living unity is posited in the animal; the affirmative realization (*Gesetztwerden*) of the identity of both, the realization brought about by this negation, is also a necessary factor. This is the accomplished fertilization, the germ, the product. But the reason why *only* the negation is necessary in the plant, is that the affirmative identity of the individuality, the germ, the *idea matrix*, is already everywhere present in principle in the plant itself; for the plant's identity is original, since each part is already an individual. In the animal, on the other hand, the negation of the independent existence of the individuals also becomes an affirmation as a sense of unity. Now this negative side, which is alone necessary in the plant, exists precisely in the turning to dust of the pollen which goes together with the withering of the pistil.

(c) Schelver has gone even further in regarding this negative side as a poisoning of the pistil. He says: 'If the anthers are removed from tulips, the latter produce neither capsules nor seeds but remain sterile. But from the fact that the anthers are necessary to the consummation of the fruit of the plant, and must not be snipped off' (although this is not true in every case as we have seen, p. 346) 'it still does not follow that they are the fertilizing sex. Even if they did not serve the purpose of fertilization, they still would not on that account be a superfluous part which can be removed or damaged without injuring the life of the plant. Also the removal of the petals and other parts can harm the development of the fruit; and yet we do not therefore say that in removing them the fertilizing sex of the fruit has been removed. Could not the pollen, too, be a necessary excretion prior to the ripeness of the germ? Anyone who considers the matter without prejudice will, on the contrary, probably find that in some climates there are also plants in which the removal of the stamens can be just as beneficial to fertilization, as in others and generally, it is harmful. Often, too, sterile plants can be made fertile by pruning the roots and branches, by tapping the bark, drawing off sap, etc. But Spallanzani has broken off the male flowers in monoecious plants, e.g. the "shield-melon" (*Schildmelone*) and water-melon, also without causing injury, and has obtained from the non-pollinated fruits ripe seeds which germinated again.'[1] The same result was obtained in dioecious plants whose female flowers were enclosed in glass vessels. Such pruning of trees, roots, etc., in order to get more fruit, is a withdrawal of excess nourishment which can be regarded as an arboreal venesection. Now a number of experiments and counter-experiments were made, some successful and others not so. 'If the fruit is to ripen, then the plant must stop growing and sprouting; for, if the plant is continually making fresh efforts to grow from within outwards with new, youthful vigour, then necessarily there can be no arrest of growth, and maturation, the formation of the fruit, cannot come to completion. That is why, in general, young plants and all those rich in sap and richly nourished, seldom bear ripe fruit. It often happens that even the already partly formed fruit falls off or is changed into shoots, as in so-called perfoliate flowers and fruits. As such a lethal poison does the pollen act on the stigma, arresting growth. For the pistil always withers as soon as the germ begins to swell and to ripen. Now if this death does not occur as a result of the turning inwards of the plant-process, then the germ will not ripen without help from outside. But this help is in the pollen, because this is itself the eruption and the manifestation of the climax of the growth-impulse, the disruption of the process of growth (an outgrowing of self). This power in the pollen which is fatal to growth is chiefly the oil in it.' For the plant produces for itself a combustible being-for-self. 'In every part of the plant the oil, wax, resin, is the shiny outer covering which bounds it. And after all, is not oil in itself the limit of vegetable matter, the highest, ultimate product which, striving almost to surpass the plant-nature, is analogous to animal matter, to fat? With the passage into oil, the plant-nature perishes, and that is why the oil contains the power to subdue the fresh sprouting of the germ. That pollen can also fertilize other plants is shown by the so-called hybrids.'[2] Fertilization, as the contact of the stigma with the oily substance, is thus only the negation which overcomes the separateness of the sexual parts, but not as a positive unity. In the new number of his periodical,[3] Schelver deals with the superficial character of the experiments on this subject.

3. The result of this destructive process is the formation of the *fruit*— a bud which is not immediate, but is posited by the developed process, whereas the earlier bud is only the formal repetition of the whole. The fruit, however, is expressly the production of a seed; consequently in the fruit the plant achieves its consummation.

(a) The seed which is produced in the fruit is a superfluity. The seed,

---

[1] Schelver, *Kritik der Lehre von den Geschlechtern der Pflanze: Fortsetzung* I, pp. 4–7 (14–15).   [2] Ibid., pp. 15–17.
[3] Ibid. *Fortsetzung* II. (1823).

qua seed, is not superior to the bud, for what is to be produced is only something new. But the seed is the digested plant, and in the fruit the plant demonstrates that it has brought forth its own organic nature from itself and by itself: whereas in many plants which have no seeds, the preservation of the genus is not effected in this way, but the genus-process has already coincided with the process of the individuality.

(b) The seed is the seed as such, and the pericarp is its covering—husk or fruit or more woody case, a rounded shape into which the entire nature of the plant is finally concentrated. The leaf which, from the seed, from the simple Notion of the individual, has reached out into line and surface, has concentrated itself into an aromatic (*würziges*), powerful leaf in order to be the covering of this seed. In the seed and the fruit the plant has produced two organic beings (*Wesen*) which, however, are indifferent to each other and fall apart. The power which gives birth to the seed becomes the earth; it is not the fruit that is the womb.

(c) The ripening of the fruit is also its downfall; for injury to the fruit assists its ripening. True, it is said that, where insects have conveyed the pollen to the female parts, no fruits are formed. But Schelver has shown that in figs it is precisely the injury which causes the fruit to ripen. He quotes (ibid., pp. 20–1) from Julius Pontedera (*Anthologia*, Patavii 1720, c. XXXII) on caprification: 'As with us the fruits of most plants soon ripen and fall off if they have suffered external injury, apple and other fruit-bearing trees whose fruits fall off before ripening, have been helped by placing (*induntur*) stones on them and fastening the roots (*fixa radice*). This method often prevents the loss of fruit. The peasants often obtain the same result in almond trees by driving in an oak wedge. In others, plugs (*caulices*) are bored into the trees as far as the pith, or the bark is ringed. I believe that in this way a particular kind of fly (*culicum*) is produced which breeds on the blossom of the barren' (i.e. male) 'palms; this insect penetrates to the embryos of the fertile trees, boring into them and attacking them with, as it were, a helpful bite (*medico morsu*) so that all the fruit stays on the tree and ripens.'

Schelver continues (pp. 21–4): 'In the case of the fig tree which is supposed to be fertilized by *Cynips Psenes*, and which seems to have first made celebrated this art of insects, the transference of pollen is the less to be suspected because this caprification is made necessary only by the climate.' Caprification owes its name to the fact that this insect which has to puncture the good fig tree so that it will bear ripe fruit, is found only on another species of wild fig tree (*caprificus*) which is there-fore planted near by. 'These insects', says Johann Bauhin, 'which have bred from the rotting fruit of the wild fig tree, fly on to the fruit of the cultivated tree (*urbanae*), and in biting these open *draw off the super-fluous moisture*, and in doing so promote and hasten ripening. Pliny (XV. 19) says that a dry soil, on which the figs soon dry and burst open, produces the same effect on fertilization as that contributed by the in-sects: that in districts where a lot of dry dust from the roads gets on to the trees, and the superfluous sap is absorbed, caprification is unnecessary. In our regions where the male tree and the insect are missing, fig seeds do not come to maturity, because the figs do not ripen completely. But that in hot countries, figs which ripened without caprification were only a ripe container which did not contain any ripe seeds, that is a mere assertion.' A lot therefore depends on the warmth of the climate and the nature of the soil. Caprification is an arrest in the nature of the fruit; and this heterogeneous, lethal influence fashions (*herausbildet*) the reproduction of the plants themselves and completes it. The insect punctures the fruit, and brings it to maturity by doing so, not by conveying pollen from elsewhere: and generally, fruit which has been punctured drops off and ripens more quickly.

'The flower, the pollination and the fruit, however, lie dormant (*ruhen*) so long as the lower life is in control. But when the flower opens, the mystery is everywhere unfolded to its fullest extent; growth and germination are suspended, and the colouring and scent of the flower are then often developed in every part. When pollination dominates, the flower which, in opening has achieved its consummation, dies away: all its parts then begin to wither, the leaves drop soon after, the outer bark dries and becomes loose, and the wood hardens. When finally the fruit dominates, the same vital spirit (*Lebensgeist*) enters into every part, the root puts out runners, buds spring up in the bark; in the axils of the leaves new leaves begin to grow. Pollination is in its own self an End of vegetation, a moment of the entire plant life which passes through every part of the plant and finally, breaking through to an existence of its own, only attains to a separate manifestation in the anthers.'[1]

§ 349

But what has been posited in the Notion is that the process displays the return into itself of the individuality, and shows that the parts—which in the first instance are individuals—belong also to the mediation, and are transient moments in it, and consequently that the immediate singularity and externality of plant life are sublated. This moment of negative determination is the basis for the transition to the veritable organism, in which the outer formation accords with the Notion, so that the parts are essentially members, and subjectivity exists as the One which pervades the whole.

Zusatz. The plant is a subordinate organism whose destiny is to sacrifice itself to the higher organism and to be consumed by it. In the same way

[1] Schelver, *Kritik der Lehre von den Geschlechtern der Pflanze: Zweite Fortsetzung* (1823), pp. 56-7, 69.

that light in the plant's colour is a being-for-other, and the plant in its airy form is an odour-for-other, so the fruit as etheric oil concentrates itself into the combustible salt of sugar and becomes a fermented liquid. The plant now reveals itself here as the Notion which has materialized the light-principle and has converted the watery nature into a fiery one. The plant is itself the movement of the fiery nature within itself: it proceeds to ferment; but the heat which it gives out from itself is not its blood, but its destruction. This animal process which is higher than that of the plant is its ruin. Now since the stage of flower-life is only a relationship to an other, whereas life consists in being self-related in its self-distinguishing, this contact within the flower, whereby it becomes for itself, is its death; for it is no longer the principle of the plant. This contact is a positing of the individual, of the singular, as identical with the universal. But the singular is thereby degraded to being no longer immediately for itself, but only through negation of its immediacy; but thus it is raised into the genus, which now comes into existence in it. With this, however, we have reached the higher Notion of the animal organism.

THE ANIMAL ORGANISM

§ 350

The organic individuality exists as *subjectivity* in so far as the externality proper to shape is *idealized* into members, and the organism in its process outwards preserves inwardly the unity of the self. This is the *animal* nature which, in the actuality and externality of immediate singularity, is equally, on the other hand, the *inwardly reflected* self of *singularity*, *inwardly* present *subjective* universality.

Zusatz. In the animal, light has found itself, for the animal arrests its relationship to an other; it is the self which is for the self—the existing unity of distinct moments which are pervaded by it. The goal of the plant's development is to become for-itself, but it does not transcend the stage of two independently existing individuals, viz. the plant itself and the bud, which are not in the form of ideal moments: these two posited in a unity are the animal nature. The animal organism is therefore this duplication of subjectivity, which no longer, as in the plant, exists as duplicated, but only as the unity of this duplication. There thus exists in the animal the veritable subjective unity, a unitary soul (*Seele*), the immanent infinitude of form which is set forth in the externality of the body; and this soul in turn stands in relationship with an inorganic Nature, with an outer world. But the subjectivity of the animal consists in preserving itself in its bodily nature and in its contact with an outer world and, as the universal, remaining at home with itself. The life of the animal as this highest point of Nature is thus the absolute idealism of possessing within itself the determinateness of its bodily nature in a perfectly fluid form—the incorporation of the immediate into the subject and its possession as incorporated.

Here, therefore, heaviness is first truly overcome; the centre has become a filled centre, which has itself for fulcrum and first, as such, is a truly self-subsistent centre. In the solar system we have the sun and other members which have an independent existence, and are related to each other, not according to their physical nature, but only according to the nature of space and time. Now if the animal organism, too, is a sun, then in it the stars are related to each other according to their physical nature, and are taken back into the sun, which holds them within itself in one individuality. The animal is the existent Idea in so far as its members are purely and simply moments of the form, perpetually negating their independence and bringing themselves back into their unity, which is the reality of the Notion and is for the Notion. If a finger is cut off, it is no longer a finger, but a process of chemical decomposition sets in. In the animal, the fully achieved unity is for the implicit unity, and this latter is the soul (*Seele*), the Notion, which is present in the body in so far as this is the process of idealization. The asunderness of spatial existence has no truth for the soul, which is unitary, finer than a point. People have been at pains to find the soul; but this is a contradiction. There are millions of points in which the soul is everywhere present; and yet it is not at any one point, simply because the asunderness of space has no truth for it. This point of subjectivity is to be adhered to, the others are only predicates of life. But this subjectivity is not yet for-itself as pure, universal subjectivity; it is not aware of itself in thought, but only in feeling and intuition. That is to say, it is only reflected into itself in the individual which, reduced to a simple determinateness, is posited as ideal; it is objective to itself only in a specific, particular state and is the negation of any such determinateness, but does not transcend it—in the same way that sensual man can indulge every appetite, but not get beyond it in order to grasp himself in thought as universal.

§ 351

The animal has freedom of *self-movement* because its subjectivity is, like light, ideality freed from gravity, a free time which, as removed from real externality, *spontaneously determines its place.*

Bound up with this is the animal's possession of a *voice*, for its *subjectivity* as *real* ideality (soul), dominates the abstract ideality of time and space and displays its self-movement as a free vibration *within itself*; it has animal *heat* as a permanent *process of the dissolution* of cohesion and of the enduring self-subsistence of the parts in the permanent preservation of shape: further, [it nourishes itself by] an *interrupted intussusception* as a self-individualizing relationship to an individual, non-organic nature. But above all, as the individuality which in determinateness is for itself, immediately *universal*, simply abiding with itself and preserving itself, it has *feeling*—the *existent* ideality of being determined.

Zusatz. Because in the animal the self is for the self, it at once follows that it possesses the wholly universal determination of subjectivity, that of sensation, (*Empfindung*), which is the *differentia specifica*, the absolutely characteristic feature of the animal. The self is ideal (*ideell*), is not poured out and immersed in materiality but is only actively present therein, at the same time finding itself within itself. This ideality which constitutes sensation is, in Nature, the supreme wealth of existence because in it everything is compressed. Joy, pain, etc., assume, it is true, a bodily form; but all this corporeal existence is still distinct from the simple independent existence as feeling (*Gefühl*) into which they are taken back. In seeing and hearing, I am simply in communion with myself (*bei mir selbst*); and they are in me only a form of my pure transparency and clarity. This point, which yet is infinitely determinable, which remains thus unclouded in its simplicity, this point, because it has itself for its object, is the subject as self = self, as self-feeling. The animal, in its possession of sensation, has a theoretical relationship to its other, whereas the plant bears itself either indifferently or practically towards the outer world, and in the latter case does not leave it in existence, but assimilates it to itself. True, the animal, like the plant, also comports itself towards the outer world as to something ideal; but, at the same time, the other is left free, remains in existence, and withal is still in relation with the subject, without remaining indifferent to it. This is a disinterested (*begierdeloses*) relationship. The animal as sentient is inwardly satisfied when it is modified by an other; and it is precisely this inner satisfaction which is the basis of the theoretical relationship. That which enters into a practical relationship is not inwardly satisfied, since an other is posited in it: on the contrary, it must react to this modification posited in it, must sublate it and identify it with itself, for it was a disturbance. But the animal in its relationship to the other is still inwardly satisfied; and this is because at the same time it posits as ideal the externally caused modification, and can therefore tolerate it. The other determinations are merely the consequences of sensation.

(α) The animal as sensuous is heavy, remains tied to the Centre; but the particular place it occupies is not determined by gravity. Gravity is the universal determination of matter, but it also determines the *particular* place; the mechanical relationship of gravity consists precisely in this, that something, in being determined in space, has its determination therein only in something outside it. But the animal, as self-related singularity, does not occupy this particular place as the result of an external determination, because, as a singularity which is turned back into self, it is indifferent to non-organic Nature, and in free movement is merely related to it by space and time generally. The particularization of place lies therefore in the animal's own power, and is not posited by an other; it is the animal itself which gives itself this place. In any other thing, this particularization is fixed, because the thing is not a self which is for itself. True, the animal does not escape from the general determination of being in a particular place; but *this* place is posited by the animal itself. And it is for this very reason that the subjectivity of the animal is not simply distinguished from external Nature, but the animal distinguishes itself from it; and this is an extremely important distinction, this positing of itself as the pure negativity of *this* place, and *this* place, and so on. The whole of Physics is the form which develops in contradistinction to gravity; but in Physics the form does not yet attain to this freedom in face of the torpor (*Dumpfheit*) of gravity, and it is in the subjectivity of the animal that this being-for-self over against gravity is first posited. The physical individuality, too, does not escape from gravity since even its process contains determinations of place and gravity.

(β) Voice is a high privilege of the animal which can appear wonderful; it is the utterance of sensation, of self-feeling. The animal makes manifest that it is inwardly for-itself, and this manifestation is voice. But it is only the sentient creature that can show outwardly that it is sentient. Birds of the air and other creatures emit cries when they feel pain, need, hunger, repletion, pleasure, joyfulness, or are in heat: the horse neighs when it goes to battle; insects hum; cats purr when pleased. But the voice of the bird when it launches forth in song is of a higher kind; and this must be reckoned as a special manifestation in birds over and above that of voice generally in animals. For while fish are dumb in their element of water, birds soar freely in theirs, the air; separated from the objective heaviness of the earth, they fill the air with themselves, and utter their self-feeling in their own particular element. Metals have sound, but this still is not voice; voice is the spiritualized mechanism which thus utters itself. The inorganic does not show its specific quality until it is stimulated from outside, gets struck; but the animal sounds of its own accord. What is subjective announces its psychic nature (*als dies Seelenhafte*) in vibrating inwardly and in merely causing the air to vibrate. This independent subjectivity is, quite abstractly, the pure process of time, which in the concrete body, is self-realizing time, vibration, and sound. Sound belongs to the animal in such a manner that it is the animal's own activity that makes the bodily organism vibrate. But nothing is outwardly altered thereby; there is only movement, and the movement produced is only abstract, pure vibration, and this produces only an alteration of place, but an alteration which is equally cancelled again—a negation of specific gravity and cohesion which, however, are equally reinstated. The voice is the closest to Thought; for here pure subjectivity becomes objective, not as a particular actuality, as a state or a sensation, but in the abstract element of space and time.

(γ) With voice there is linked animal heat. The chemical process also yields heat which can rise to the intensity of fire, but it is transitory. The animal, on the other hand, as the lasting process of self-movement, of consuming and producing itself, perpetually negates and reproduces what is material and must therefore perpetually generate heat. This is especially true of warm-blooded animals in which the opposition between sensibility and irritability has reached a more highly developed stage (see below § 370, *Zusatz*), and irritability is established in its own independent character in the blood, which can be called a fluid magnet.

(δ) Because the animal is a true, self-subsistent self which has attained to individuality, it excludes and separates itself from the universal substance of the earth which is for it an outer existence. This external world which has not come under the domination of the self, is, for the animal, a negative of itself, an indifferent existence; an immediate consequence of this is that the animal's non-organic nature has become individualized in relation to it: for it is at no distance from the Element. And it is this relationship to non-organic nature which is the general Notion of the animal; it is an individual subject which enters into relationships with individual objects as such, not like the plant, merely with the Elements, or with another subject, except in the genus-process. The animal also has the plant-nature, a relationship to light, air, and water: but in addition it has sensation, to which is also added in man, thought. Aristotle thus speaks of three souls, the vegetable, animal, and human, as the three determinations of the development of the Notion. As a unity of different individualities reflected into self, the animal exists as an End which spontaneously produces itself—is a movement which returns into *this* individual. The process of the individuality moves in a closed circle which, in organic being in general is the sphere of being-for-self; and because this is its Notion, its essence (*Wesen*), its non-organic nature is individualized for it. But because as a self-subsistent self it is equally in relationship with itself, it posits its being-for-self as distinct from [its] non-organic nature, in relationship with it. It interrupts this relationship with the outside world because it is satisfied, because it is sated—because it has sensation, is a self for itself. In sleep, the animal submerges itself in its identity with universal Nature, in the waking state it forms relationships with individual organisms but also breaks off this relationship; and the life of the animal is the alternating fluctuation between these two determinations.

§ 352

The animal organism as living universality is the Notion which passes through its three determinations as syllogisms, each of which is *in itself* the same *totality* of the substantial unity, and, at the same time, in keeping with the determination of the form, *transition* into the others, so that the totality as existent *results* from this process. It is only as this self-reproductive being, not as a mere being (*nicht als Seiendes*), that the living creature *is* and *preserves itself*; it only is, in making itself what it is, and is the antecedent End which is itself only result. The organism is therefore, like the plant, to be considered (a) as individual Idea which in its process is only *self*-related, and inwardly coalesces with self— Shape; (b) as Idea which enters into relationship with its other, its non-organic nature, and posits this inwardly as ideal—Assimilation; (c) Idea as entering into relationship with an other which is itself a living individual, so that in the other it is in relationship with itself—the Genus-process.

Zusatz. The animal organism is the microcosm, the centre of Nature which has achieved an existence for itself in which the whole of inorganic Nature is recapitulated and idealized; this will be worked out in the detailed exposition to follow. Since the animal organism is the process of subjectivity, of self-relation in an outer world, the rest of Nature is therefore here present for the first time as outward, since the animal preserves itself in this relation with the outer world. Now the plant is drawn towards the outer world but without truly preserving itself in connection with what is other, and consequently the rest of Nature is still not present for it as outer. As its own product, as self-end, animal life is End and Means at the same time. End is an ideal determination which is already existent beforehand; so that, in the process of realization which must fit in with what exists determinately beforehand, nothing new is developed. The realization is equally a return-into-self. The accomplished End has the same content as that which is already present in the agent; the living creature, therefore, with all its activities does not add anything to it. As the organization [of life] is its own End, so too it is its own Means, it is nothing merely there. The viscera, the organs generally, are perpetually posited as ideal, for they are active against each other: and just as each, as centre, produces itself at the expense of all the others, so it exists only through the process; in other words, that which, as sublated, is reduced to Means is itself End, is itself product. As that which develops the Notion, the animal organism is the Idea manifesting only the differences of the Notion; and thus each moment of the

Notion contains the others, is itself system and totality. These totalities, as determinate, produce in their transition the whole which each system is in itself, as a One, as subject.

The first process is that of the self-related, self-embodying organism which contains the other within itself: while the second, that which is directed against non-organic nature, i.e. against its in-itself in the form of an other, is the judgement (*Urteil*) of the living creature, its active Notion; the third process is the higher one, that, namely, of singularity and universality, of the individual against itself as genus with which it is implicitly identical. In the perfect animal, in the human organism, these processes are developed in the fullest and clearest way; this highest organism therefore presents us in general with a *universal type*, and it is only in and from this type that we can ascertain and explain the meaning of the undeveloped organism.

A. SHAPE (STRUCTURE)

§ 353

1. *Functions of the Organism*

Shape is the animal subject as a whole which is *related only to itself*. It exhibits the developed *determinations* of the Notion as existent within it. Although these, as existent within the subject, are inwardly concrete, they are here present only (a) as its simple elements. The animal subject is consequently: (1) its simple, *universal being-within-self* in its externality whereby the real determinateness is *immediately* taken up as a particularity into the universal: and this latter in it is an undivided identity of the subject with itself—*sensibility*; (2) Particularity as a capacity for being stimulated from outside and the subject's own reaction outwards to the stimulation—*irritability*: (3) the unity of these moments, the *negative* return to itself from its relation with the outside world, and, through this, the production and positing of itself as a singular—*reproduction*, which is the reality and the basis of the first two moments.

Zusatz. The plant lets its wood, its bark, die and sheds its leaves; but the animal is this negativity itself. The former can counter the becoming-other of itself only by leaving this other lying there indifferently. The animal is the negativity of itself which transcends its shape; it does not let the arrest of its growth issue only in the digestive and sexual processes, but as the negativity of itself, in its own inner process it gives itself form in its viscera. In thus shaping itself as an individual, it is a unity of shape and individuality. The simple identity of the universal subjectivity of the Notion with itself, the sentient creature—which in the sphere of spirit is the ego—is sensibility; if an other is brought into contact with it, it transforms this directly into itself. The particularity, which in sensibility is at first only ideally posited, receives its due in irritability, where the activity of the subject consists in repelling the other with which it is in relation. Irritability is also sensation, subjectivity, but in the form of relation. But whereas sensibility is only this negative relationship to other, reproduction is this infinite negativity of transforming what is outside me into myself, and myself into externality. Only then is universality real and not abstract—developed sensibility. Reproduction passes through sensibility and irritability and absorbs them; it is thus derived, posited universality which, however, as self-producing, is at the same time concrete singularity. It is reproduction which is first the whole—the immediate unity-with-self in which the whole has at the same time entered into relationship with itself. The animal organism is reproductive; this it is essentially, or this is its actuality. The higher forms of life are those in which the abstract moments of sensibility and irritability have separate existences of their own; whereas the lower forms of life remain at the stage of reproduction, the higher forms of life possess within themselves the profounder differences, and preserve themselves in this more intense diremption. Thus there are animals which are nothing more than a reproductive process—an amorphous jelly, an active slime which is reflected into self and in which sensibility and irritability are not yet separated. These are the general animal moments; but they are not to be regarded as properties, as if each acted, as it were, in its own special way, as colour acts specially on sight, taste on the tongue, and so on. Nature does, it is true, give the moments an indifferent, separate existence, but only and solely in the shape, i.e. in the dead being, of the organism. The animal is intrinsically the most lucid existence in Nature, but it is the hardest to comprehend since its nature is the speculative Notion. For, although this nature is a sensuous existence, it must nevertheless be grasped in the Notion. Although in sensation the animal is utterly simple, in contrast to the separation of qualities characteristic of inorganic Nature, yet the animal is also the most concrete, for it allows the moments of the Notion, real in a single subject, to have determinate existence; the inorganic, on the other hand, is abstract. In the solar system, sensibility corresponds to the sun, the moments of difference are comet and moon, and reproduction is the planet. But whereas there each member is a separate existence, here they are held in a single subject. This idealism which recognizes the Idea throughout the whole of Nature is at the same time realism, for the Notion of the organism is the Idea as reality, even though in other respects the individuals correspond only to one moment of the Notion. What philosophy recognizes in the real, the sensuous world, is simply the

Notion. One must start from the Notion; and even if, perhaps, the Notion cannot yet give an adequate account of the 'abundant variety' of Nature so-called, we must nevertheless have faith in the Notion though many details are as yet unexplained. The demand that everything be explained is altogether vague; that it has not been fulfilled is no reflection on the Notion, whereas in the case of the theories of the empirical physicists the position is quite the reverse: these must explain everything, for their validity rests only on particular cases. The Notion, however, is valid in its own right; the particulars then will soon find their explanation (see § 270, *Zusatz*, p. 82).

§ 354

2. *The Systems of Shape (Structure)*

These three moments of the *Notion* are (β) not merely concrete elements in principle, but have their reality in three systems, namely, the *nervous* system, the *circulatory* system, and the *digestive* system, each of which, as totality, is inwardly differentiated according to the relevant determinations of the Notion.

1. The system of sensibility is differentiated into
   αα. the extreme of *abstract* self-reference, which is a transition into *immediacy*, into non-organic being, and an absence of sensation, but a transition which remains incomplete—the *osseous* system, a covering for what is *inner*, and a firm support for the inner against the *outer*;
   ββ. the moment of irritability, the cerebral system and its further ramifications in the nerves, which similarly have an inward and an outward reference—the sensory and motor nerves respectively;
   γγ. the system pertaining to reproduction, the sympathetic nerves and the ganglia, the sphere of dull, indeterminate self-feeling, devoid of will.

2. Irritability is just as much a capacity for being stimulated by an other and the reaction of self-maintenance against it, as it is also, conversely, an active maintenance of self, in which it is at the mercy of an other. Its system is
   αα. *abstract (sensible)* irritability, the *simple* conversion of receptivity into reactivity—*muscle* in general; this gains

an outer hold on the skeleton (immediate reference-to-self leading to its own division) and is differentiated first into extensors and flexors, and then, further, into the special systems of the extremities.

ββ. Irritability as independent of, and opposed to, an other, and as concretely self-related and self-contained, is inward activity, *pulsation*, living self-movement, the material of which can be only a *fluid*, the living *blood*, and which itself can only be circulation: this, in keeping with the *particularity* of its origin, is in its own self immediately specified into the duality of the pulmonary and the portal systems, in which the circulation at the same time has an *outward* reference: in the former system the blood takes fire within itself, and in the latter it kindles itself against its other.

γγ. Pulsation, as irritable, self-coalescing totality, is the circulation which, from its centre, the *heart*, returns in the dual system (*Differenz*) of arteries and veins into itself, and is equally an *immanent* process, in which the blood generally is delivered up for the reproduction of the other members which take their nourishment from it.

3. The digestive system, as a system of glands with skin and cellular tissue, is *immediate*, vegetative reproduction, but in the system proper of the intestines, it is *mediating* reproduction.

Zusatz. Since sensibility also has an existence of its own in the nervous system, irritability in the system of the blood, and reproduction in the digestive system, 'the bodies of all animals can be analysed into three different constituents of which all the organs are composed: into cellular tissue, muscle fibre, and nerve pulp (*Nervenmark*)'†—the simple, abstract elements of the three systems. But since, all the same, these systems are not separate, and each point contains all three in immediate unity, they are not the abstract Notion-moments of universality, particularity, and singularity. On the contrary, each of these moments exhibits the totality of the Notion in its determinateness, so that the other systems actually exist in each: blood and nerves are everywhere present, and everywhere, too, there is a glandular, lymphatic substance, that which constitutes reproduction. The unity of these abstract moments

† Treviranus, *Biologie*, vol. i, p. 166.

is the animal lymph from which the internal organs are developed; but along with its inner differentiation, it also surrounds itself with skin, which forms its surface, with the general relationship of the vegetable organism to [its] non-organic nature. Now, although each system, as the developed whole, contains the moments of the other systems, yet in each one form of the Notion remains predominant. The immediate shape is the dead, quiescent organism which, for the individuality, is its non-organic nature. Because it is this inert thing, the Notion, the self, is not yet actual, the production of the self is not yet posited: or we may say that this self is merely an inner self, and it is we who have to apprehend it. The function of this outer organism is to relate itself to other equally indifferent shapes; it is the mechanical side of the whole which is articulated into its persistent (*bestehenden*) parts.

Sensibility, as self-identity of sensation, if reduced to abstract identity, is insensibility, the inert, dead side of the organism, the deadening of itself which, however, still falls within the sphere of vitality; and this is the production of bone, whereby the organism presupposes its own basis. Thus the osseous system itself still participates in the life of the organism: 'In old age the bones get smaller, the skull bones, the cylindrical bones get thinner; their medullary cavity seems' as it were 'to get larger at the expense of the bony substance. The entire, dry bony skeleton of an old person becomes relatively lighter; accordingly old people get shorter, even without taking account of their bent backs. Bones, simply on account of the larger number of their blood vessels, in general possess more vitality' (in comparison with cartilages); 'and this is evidenced by their susceptibility to inflammation and pathological changes, by their reproduction; also by the absorptive power of their pointed extremities and their readier arousal of sensation, and finally even by their composite structure.'† Bone, i.e. the sensibility belonging to shape as such, is, like the wood of the plant, the simple and therefore dead force which is not yet a process, but abstract reflection-into-self. At the same time, however, it is the dead force reflected into self; or it is the vegetative burgeoning which produces itself in such wise that the product is an other.

(1) Its shape is, in the first instance, a bony nucleus (*Knochenkern*); for that is how all bones begin. The bony nuclei multiply and grow lengthwise like the plant node which becomes a woody fibre. The bony nuclei are found at the extremities of the limbs; they contain the marrow which is not yet expressly developed into their nerves. Bone marrow is fat; and that is why there is little marrow or liquid marrow in thin people, and plenty of marrow in fat people. The periosteum is the life proper of the bone, a production directed entirely outwards, which consequently dies away in itself and lives only on the surface of the bone—the dull force within the bone itself; the osseous system, together with the system

† Autenrieth (Johann Heinr. Ferd.), *Handbuch der Physiologie*, part ii, § 767, §772.

of the skin, thus falls under reproduction. The bone, in developing towards totality from nucleus and line, breaks open; and in place of the marrow there appears the nerve, which is a nucleus (*Kern*) shooting out lengthwise from its centre. But, with this totality, the bone ceases to belong to the shape as such; its marrow becomes living sensibility, a point which expands in lines and from which, as from the totality, the dimensions proceed. As nucleus, the bone is the immediately sensible moment of shape; but, as bony skeleton, its first and more precise function is to be, in relation to the outer world, the stable, merely firm, hard element of the body, to give itself its own firmness, to attain mechanical objectivity and thus win a fulcrum against the earth which is the absolutely firm, fixed body.

(2) The prolongation of the bone is the *middle* term, the transition in which the shape sinks to the level of an outer whose inner is an other. In the limbs, the bone is the inner moment, what is immediately firm and solid: but for the rest, it ceases to be inner. Just as wood is the plant's inner being and the bark its exterior (though in the seed, the wood is overcome and it is only the outer husk of the seed): so bone becomes the outer covering for the viscera, a covering which no longer has its own centre, but is at first still discontinuous and held together by its own line (*sternum*), still has its own articulation. Finally, however, it again becomes a pure surface without internality of its own—a reversion to point or line, from which lines radiate and become flattened out into what is merely an enclosing surface. This is the totality which has not yet rounded itself off into a whole, but which is still turned outwards. Thus the *second* determination of the bone is to be controlled by an other, to have an other as subject within it, and to terminate outwardly in firm *points d'appui* like horns, claws, nails, etc.: it is the indestructible element in the organism since, after everything else in a corpse has turned to dust, skin is often still visible on some parts.

(3) At the same time, since in the vertebra the bony centre is pierced, the bone, now returning into itself, is, *thirdly*, the hollow *cranium*. The form of the spinal column is the basis of the skull-bone and the one can be explained from the other. But the *os sphenoidum* is directed towards completely overcoming the centre, and reducing the cranium to a surface without centre of its own. But at the same time this complete overcoming of nuclearity passes over into the reinstatement of the nuclei; the teeth are this return of nuclei into themselves, which pass through the moments of the process, i.e. they are negative, active, effective, and therefore cease to be a merely passive separated organ (*Absonderung*): it is immediate sensibility which has become irritability. In the teeth, the periosteum is no longer an outer, but only an inner membrane. The bones, like the periosteum, are without sensation; but they acquire sensation in the (syphilitic) lymphatic diseases.

The basic organism of the bone is the spinal vertebra, and all else is merely a metamorphosis of it, a tube directed to the interior of the body and continuations of the tube directed outwards. It was Goethe† in particular who, with his organic feeling for Nature, saw this to be the fundamental form of bone-structure and followed out the transitions in full detail in a treatise written as early as 1785 which he published in his *Morphology*. Oken, to whom Goethe had communicated the treatise, paraded its ideas as his own in a programme he wrote on the subject, and so gained the credit for them. Goethe showed (it is one of the finest intuitions he has had) that the cranial bones are developed solely out of this form: the *os sphenoidum*, the *os zygomaticum* (the cheek-bone) up to the *os bregmatis*, the frontal bone which is the hip-bone in the head. But here, as in the plant, the identity of form is insufficient to explain such a transformation of the bones, how it is that, instead of being an inner centre, they now become an enclosing structure, and are determined as external fulcras for the extremities, arms, legs, etc., combining with each other and being at the same time movable. This other side of metamorphosis, the introjection (*Hereinwerfen*) of the spinal vertebra into the separate bones was not developed by Goethe although it was by Oken. The spinal vertebra is the centre of the osseous system, a centre which splits into the extremes of the cranium and the extremities and which at the same time joins these together: in the former we have a hollowing out which, by uniting surfaces, excludes the outer world, while the latter is a development in length which takes up a middle position [in the limbs] and is fastened, essentially by cohesion, along the length of the muscles.

The moment of difference in sensibility is the nervous system which is directed outwards and is involved in external relationships: sensation as determinate—either as immediately posited from outside or as self-determination. The motor nerves mostly start from the spinal cord, and the sensory nerves from the brain: the former are the nervous system in its practical function, the latter are that system as receptive of determinations, and to this the sense organs belong. But in general the nerves are concentrated in the brain, from which they ramify into every part of the body. The nerve is the condition for sensation where the body is touched; it is also a condition of the will, and generally of any self-determining end. Apart from this, we still know very little about the organization of the brain. 'Experience teaches that there is a partial or total cessation of the function of the motor organs which carry out voluntary actions and the capacity of these organs for sensation, when the nerves coming from them, or the spinal cord, the cerebellum or cerebrum connected with those nerves, is damaged or destroyed. The individual nerve-fibres with their sheaths are joined together in bundles by cellular tissue, and these bundles are more or less tightly combined into a larger, palpable cord. Even the individual medullary fibres (*Markfasern*) of the nerves are everywhere closely interconnected by small lateral canals filled with medullary substance which, at their points of contact, seem to form very

† Cf. *Zur Morphologie*, pp. 162, 248, 250–1, 339.

fine tiny knots; and in this respect a nerve-bundle resembles a very expanded net pulled lengthwise like a piece of knitting, the threads of which are now almost parallel.'† We must not represent the communication between the brain and another part of the body as if, when the nerves in that part have been affected, the impression is propagated by these particular nerve-fibres on their own, or as if an impression was made by the brain on a particular nerve-fibre according to the external association of the nerves; on the contrary, communication occurs through the common nerve-trunk and yet achieves determination through the universal presence of the will and consciousness. The nerve-fibre is connected with many others, and when it is affected these, too, are affected: although this does not produce a plurality of sensations, nor conversely does the general nerve-trunk from the brain set in motion all the associated nerves.

The sensibility which has withdrawn into itself, the innermost point of the sentient creature in virtue of which it no longer is abstract, the system of ganglia generally, and especially of the so-called sympathetic nerves, a system not yet separated out, not developed into specific sensory forms, this system forms ganglia which can be regarded as little brains in the abdomen; they are, however, not absolutely independent and for themselves, i.e. are not without connection with the nerves directly connected with the brain and those of the spinal cord, but have at the same time their own place in the nervous system, and are distinct from the nerves of the cerebro-spinal system both in function and structure.[1] This division into the brain of the head and the brain of the abdomen is the reason why headaches originate in the abdomen. 'It is remarkable that in the stomach, one could almost say at its upper opening, the development of the eighth nerve descending directly from the brain stops, its place being taken by the sympathetic nerve, so that there is here, as it were, the boundary of a more distinct feeling. This upper opening plays a marked and significant role in many diseases. Autopsies show that inflammation is found more often near this opening than in any other part of the stomach. Nature leaves us a free choice in the matter of selecting food, mastication, deglutition, and finally, in the evacuation of the useless, major part, but the business of digestion proper is withdrawn from our control.'[2] In the somnambulistic state, where the outer senses are cataleptically rigid, and self-consciousness is turned inwards (*innerlich ist*), this internal vitality passes into the ganglia and into the brain of this dark, independent self-consciousness. Richerand[3] therefore says: 'Through the sympathetic nerves, the internal organs are withdrawn from the dominance of the will.' The system of these ganglia is irregular.[4]

† Autenrieth, *Handbuch der Physiologie*, part iii, § 824, § 866, § 868.
[1] Cf. ibid., § 869.
[2] Ibid., part ii, § 587.
[3] Nouveaux éléments de physiologie, vol. i, Prolegom. CIII.
[4] Autenrieth, ibid., part iii, § 871.

Bichat[1] says: 'The system of the ganglia can be divided into the ganglia of the head, throat, thorax, abdomen and pelvis.' They are found therefore throughout the body, though principally in the parts belonging to the internal structure, especially in the abdomen. 'A series of these ganglia lies on either side in the openings between the vertebrae, where they are formed by the posterior roots of the nerves of the spinal cord.'[2] Through their interconnections they form the so-called sympathetic nerves, then the *plexus semilunaris, solaris, splanchnicus*, and finally the communication of the semi-lunar ganglion, through its ramifications, with the thoracic ganglia. 'In many subjects the so-called sympathetic nerve is found to be interrupted, that is, the part in the thorax is separated from that in the abdomen (*pars lumbaris*) by an interstice. Often, after having provided a number of threads to the neck, the nerve is thicker than before. The nerve-threads of this system are very different from those of the cerebro-spinal system. The latter are thicker, not so numerous, whiter, denser in tissue, and exhibit little variety in structure. The distinguishing marks of the ganglia, on the other hand, are extreme tenuity, very large numbers of threads, especially near the plexus, greyish colour, considerable softness of tissue, and extraordinary variety in different subjects.'† There is controversy as to whether these ganglia are independent, or whether they originate in the brain and spinal cord. This expression 'originate' is a dominant conception in the relation of nerves to brain and spinal cord, but it is without definite meaning. It counts as an undoubted truth that the nerves originate in the brain. But if here they are in identity with the brain, they are also separate from it; although not in the sense that the brain is antecedent to the nerves, these coming later—any more than the fingers originate in the palm of the hand, or the nerves originate in the heart. Individual nerves can be severed, and the brain still lives, just as parts of the brain can be removed without destroying the nerves.

The sensibility of the outer organism having passed over into irritability, into difference, its unitary nature now overcome, passes over into the opposition of the muscular system. The burgeoning (*Knospen*) of the bone has been taken back into the simple difference of the muscle, whose activity is the real, material relationship with inorganic nature, the process of mechanism with the outer world. Organic elasticity is the softness which, when stimulated, withdraws into self, equally negates this yielding and reinstates itself, pushing against itself in a linear movement. The muscle is the unity of this dual activity, and both moments also exist as kinds of movement. Treviranus[3] puts forward the proposition 'that contraction is accompanied by an actual increase in cohesion'.

---

[1] Recherches physiologiques sur la vie et la mort (§ 4. ed. Paris, 1822), p. 91.
[2] Autenrieth, ibid., part iii, § 870.
† Bichat, loc. cit., pp. 90, 92.
[3] *Biologie*, vol. v, p. 238.

This is demonstrated particularly by the following experiment. 'Erman (Gilbert's *Annalen der Physik*, Jahrgang 1812, part i, p. 1) took a glass cylinder open at both ends, closed the bottom end with a cork through which passed a platinum wire, and filled the cylinder with water. He introduced into the water a part of the tail of a live eel, and then closed the top of the cylinder likewise with a cork through which passed a platinum wire and, in addition, a narrow glass tube open at both ends. When the latter cork was pressed, water entered the glass tube, its level being accurately marked. Now Erman observed that, whenever he connected the spinal cord with one wire and the muscles with the other, and brought both wires into contact with the poles of a voltaic pile, the water in the tube fell in jerks to the extent of four or five lines (*vier bis fünf Linien*) each time.'[1] Also, the muscles are spontaneously irritable, e.g. those of the heart, even when the cardiac nerves are not stimulated: similarly in the galvanic circuit, the muscles are set in motion without the nerves being touched.[2] Treviranus also maintains (vol. v, p. 346) that his 'hypothesis that the transmission of voluntary stimuli to the muscles, and the conveyance of external impressions to the brain, are the action of different nerve-constituents, the former being performed by the nerve-sheaths (*Nervenhäute*), the latter by the nerve-pulp (*Nervenmark*)' has not yet been refuted.

Muscular movement is the elastic irritability which, a moment of the whole, posits a peculiar, self-dividing movement which arrests the circulatory flow and, as a self-contained movement, posits and generates from within itself a fire-process which overcomes (*aufhebt*) this inert persistence. This dissolution of this persistence is the pulmonary system, the true, ideal process with the outer world of inorganic Nature, with the Element of air; it is the organism's own self-movement which, as elasticity, draws in air and expels it. The blood is the result, the organism which through its own interior process returns into itself, the living individuality which makes members (*Glieder*) into viscera. The blood as axially rotating, self-pursuing movement, this absolute interior vibration, is the individual life of the whole in which there is no distinction—animal time. This axially rotating movement then splits up into the cometary or atmospheric process and the volcanic process. The lung is the animal leaf which enters into relationship with the atmosphere and forms this self-suspending and self-restoring process of outbreathing and in-breathing. The liver, on the other hand, is the return from the cometary process into being-for-self, into the lunar process; it is the being-for-self which seeks its centre, the heat of being-for-self, the rage against other-ness and the consuming of it. The processes of lung and liver are most intimately connected; the transient, eccentric (*ausschweifend*) lung-process tempers the heat of the liver, and the latter vivifies the former. The lung is in danger of passing over into liver, of becoming nodulated (*sich*

[1] Treviranus, *Biologie*, vol. v, p. 243.   [2] Ibid., vol. v, p. 291.

zu verknoten) in order then to consume itself when it receives into itself the heat of being-for-self. The blood divides itself into these two processes. Its real process, therefore, is to be this threefold circulation: one is its own proper circulation, the second is the pulmonary circulation, and the third is that of the liver. Each is a separate circulation on its own: for what appears as an artery in the pulmonary circulation appears as a vein in the portal system, and conversely, the veins entering the portal system appear as arteries. This system of living movement is the opposite of that of the outer organism; it is the *power* of digestion—the power of overcoming the outer organism. This inorganic nature is here necessarily threefold: (αα) the outer, universal lung; (ββ) the specified (*besonderte*) lung, the universal reduced to an organic moment, the lymph and the entire organism in its immediate aspect (*seiende Organismus*); (γγ) the individualized lung. The blood elaborates itself from the air, the lymph, and the digestion, and is the transformation of these three moments. From the air it takes pure dissolution, the light of the air, oxygen; from the lymph, the neutral fluid: from digestion, the moment of singularity, the substantial moment. And as thus the whole individuality, the blood opposes itself to itself afresh and generates shape.

(1) The blood in the pulmonary circulation, having its own movement, is this purely negative immaterial life for which Nature is air and which has here the sheer victory over it. The infant's first breath is its own individual life; up till then the infant floated in the lymph and absorbed nutriment in vegetative fashion. Emerging from the ovum or the womb, the creature breathes; it enters into relationship with Nature which for it has become air, and it is not this continuous flow (of air) but its interruption—the simple organic irritability and activity through which the blood demonstrates itself to be pure fire and becomes such.

(2) It is the blood which sublates the neutrality, the floating in the lymph; it overcomes this, stimulating and exciting the whole outer organism and impelling it to return into itself. This movement, too, is a digestive system, a cycle of distinct moments. Everywhere the lymphatic vessels construct for themselves ganglia (*Knoten*), stomachs, in which the lymph is digested and finally conducted into the *ductus thoracicus*. It is in this process that the blood acquires its fluid nature as such: it cannot be rigid. From its watery neutrality, the lymph changes into fat (bone-marrow is this same fat) and does not therefore become more animalized but becomes a vegetable oil and serves as nutriment. Consequently, hibernating animals grow very fat in summer, and in winter live on their own resources so that in spring they are quite thin.

(3) Lastly, blood is the digestive process proper of the individual, and this is the peristaltic movement generally. As this process of singularity, blood splits up into the following three moments: (αα) the dull, interior being-for-self—the state of becoming hypochondriacal and melancholic, its slumber, the venous blood in general, which becomes this

nocturnal force in the spleen. In this, blood is said to be carbonized; this carbonization is precisely the process in which it becomes earth, i.e. absolute subject. (ββ) From here, its centre is the portal system where its subjectivity is movement and becomes an active process, a consuming volcano. As thus active in the liver, it operates on the chyme prepared in the stomach. Digestion begins in the stomach after the food has been masticated and steeped in the salivary lymph. The gastric and pancreatic juices are, as it were, the solvent acids which induce fermentation in the food; this action of the lymph and the generation of heat constitute the chemico-organic moment. (γγ) It is in the duodenum that the proper, complete mastery over the food is achieved by fire, by the bile, which is produced by the venous blood of the portal vein. The outward-turned process which is still active in the lymph develops into being-for-self and is now transformed into an animal self. The chyle, this product of the blood, returns into blood: the latter has produced itself.

This is the great, interior circulation of the individuality whose centre is the blood itself; for it is the individual life itself. Blood in general, as the universal substance of every part, is the irritable concentration of everything into the interior unity: it is heat, this transformation of cohesion and specific gravity—but not merely the dissolution produced by heat but the real, animal dissolution of everything. Just as all food is converted into blood, so, too, blood is dispensed as the source from which everything takes its nutriment. That is what pulsation (*Pulsieren*) is in its complete reality. It has been said that the juices, because they are secreted (*das Ausgeschiedene*) are inorganic and that life belongs solely to the solid parts. But in the first place, such distinctions are in themselves meaningless, and secondly, blood is—not life, but the living subject as such, in opposition to the genus, the universal. Those feeble flowery folk the Hindus do not eat animals but let them live in complete freedom; the Hebrew law-giver forbade only the eating of the blood of animals, the reason given being that the life of the animal is in its blood. The blood is this endless, unbroken unrest of welling forth, whereas the nerve is at rest and remains where it is. The endless process of division and this suppression of division which leads to another division, all this is the immediate expression of the Notion which is, so to speak, here visible to the eye. In the description of it given by Professor Schultz it presents itself as a visible phenomenon: blood has a tendency to form globules but does not actually do so. If blood flows into water it forms globules; but blood itself in its living state does not do so. Thus blood-globules only appear when blood is dead, when it is exposed to the atmosphere. Their *existence* is therefore an invention, like that of atoms, and is based on misleading phenomena, those which occur when blood is forcibly withdrawn from the organism. This pulsation remains blood's chief characteristic; this circulation is the vital point where none of the mechanical explanations of the Understanding are of any use. It eludes the finest anatomical and microscopic investigations. The inward ignition of the blood through its contact with air is explained as an inhalation of the atmosphere and an exhalation of nitrogen and carbon. But these chemical conceptions explain nothing; it is no chemical process, but life, which is perpetually interrupting such a process.

The concentration of this internal differentiation into a single system is the heart, the vital muscular principle (*Muskulosität*)—a system which is everywhere connected with reproduction. No nerves are found in the heart, but what pulsates is the pure vitality of irritability present as muscle in the centre. As absolute motion, the natural living self, process itself, the blood is not moved but *is* motion. Physiologists search for all kinds of forces to explain its movement: 'The cardiac muscle first drives the blood outwards, and is helped in this by the walls of the arteries and veins and the pressure of the solid parts which impel the blood onwards; admittedly the cardiac impulse is no longer operative in the veins, so that the effect must be produced solely by the pressure of the walls of the veins.' But all these mechanical explanations of the physiologists are inadequate. For whence comes this elastic pressure of the walls and the heart? 'From the irritation (*Reiz*) of the blood' they reply. According to this, therefore, the heart moves the blood, and the movement of the blood is, in turn, what moves the heart. But this is a circle, a *perpetuum mobile*, which would necessarily at once come to a standstill because the forces are in equilibrium. But, on the contrary, this is precisely why the blood must be regarded as itself the principle of the movement; it is the 'leaping point' (*punctum saliens*), in virtue of which the contraction of the arteries coincides with the relaxation of the ventricles of the heart. There is nothing incomprehensible or unknowable about this *self-movement* unless we mean by 'comprehension' that something else, the cause, is assigned by which the movement is effected. This, however, is only outer necessity, i.e. no necessity at all. The cause is itself again a thing, the cause of which has in turn to be asked for, and so on to another cause, *ad infinitum*, the spurious infinity which is the incapacity to think and conceive the universal, the ground, the simple, which is the unity of opposites and consequently the immovable which yet moves. This is the blood, the subject, which no less than the will initiates a movement. As the whole movement, the blood is the ground and the movement itself. But also, it steps to one side as *one* moment, for it is the distinguishing of itself from itself. The movement is precisely this stepping aside of itself whereby it is subject, a Thing, and the supersession of its standing aside, so that it overlaps itself and its opposite. But it appears as a part and a result just because the opposite intrinsically sublates itself and it is from *its* side that the return takes place. Thus does the living and vivifying power of blood develop from shape; and its interior movement also demands real, mechanical, external movement. It moves, embraces the parts in their negative, qualitative difference, but requires the simple negativity of external movement: an invalid who has remained immobile for a long while, e.g. after an amputation, develops ankylosis; the synovial fluid diminishes, the cartilages become ossified, and the muscles flaccid† as a result of this bodily inactivity (*äussere Ruhe*).

The course of the flow itself is, in one regard, the general circulation through which each part participates in this circular movement; but it is no less completely elastic within itself and is not merely this circular movement. Even in different parts of the body the circulation varies somewhat: in the portal system and inside the cranium, it is slower than in the other parts, in the lungs, on the other hand, the flow is more accelerated. In a whitlow (*panaricium*) the artery (*radialis*) has a hundred pulse-beats to the minute, while the artery on the healthy side has only seventy, synchronizing with the heart-beats. Further, the passage of the arteries and veins into each other is made by the finest canals (capillaries) some of which are so fine that they do not contain any red blood-corpuscles but only yellowish serum. 'It seems', says Sömmering (§ 72), 'that in the eye the arteries are continued into finer branches which no longer contain red blood; these at first join on to a similar vein (*Vene*) but finally on to a venule carrying red blood.' Here, therefore, there is no passage of the thing that is properly called blood: but there is a movement in which it vanishes and reappears, or an elastic vibration which is not an advance. The passage, then, is not directly perceptible, or only rarely so. In addition, there are abundant anastomoses of the veins and more particularly of the arteries; some of these form larger branches, others form entire large plexuses where, therefore, circulation, strictly speaking, is inconceivable. In the anastomosed branch, the blood flows in from both sides; there is an equilibrium which is not a flow in one direction but only an internal oscillation. It might perhaps be thought that here in one branch, one direction had a preponderance; but with several whole festoons, plexuses, of anastomosed blood-vessels, one direction cancels out the other and converts the movement into a general interior pulsation. 'When an *artery* is opened, the blood spurts much further at the moment that the heart contracts than when it is distended. In the arteries, the period of contraction lasts a little longer than the period of distension; in the heart the converse is true. But we must not conceive the live arterial system as if the blood moved on in a succession of rounded waves, or as if an artery, laid bare along its whole length, rather resembled a string running through a garland of roses. On the contrary, the arterial system throughout its entire length and in all its branches appears always cylindrical, oscillating delicately with every heart-beat and expanding uniformly laterally, yet so slightly as to be hardly perceptible and that only in the larger branches, while during the contraction of the heart a shortening, as it were, takes place.'* Circulation, then, does indeed occur but it is an *oscillatory* circulation.

The distinction between arterial and venous blood takes on reality in the lungs and liver; it is the same opposition as that of the extensor and

† '*weiss*' in the text is presumably a misprint for '*weich*'.

* Autenrieth, *Handbuchder, Physiologie* part i, §§ 367–9.

flexor muscles. The arterial blood is the outgoing, solvent activity: the venous blood is the inward-going activity; the lungs and liver are, as a system, their peculiar life. According to chemistry the difference is that the arterial blood contains more oxygen which makes it bright red: venous blood contains more carbon and when shaken in oxygen also becomes bright red: a difference which expresses only the fact (*Ding*), not the nature of the arterial and venous blood and their relation in the whole system.

The general process is this return of self to self after running its cometary, lunar, and terrestrial course, from its viscera back to unity. This return is, then, its general digestion, and thus returned, its existence is quiescence; i.e. it returns to mere shape which is its result. This process of nutrition which supersedes shape and which only splits itself up into the viscera, but in so doing shapes itself, is the alimentary process whose product is likewise shape. Now this alimentation does not consist in the arterial blood throwing off its oxygenated fibrin. On the contrary, the arterial exhalations are rather a finely elaborated exudation: a wholly universal aliment from which each individual part of the body takes what it needs and converts it into whatever part it is in the whole. This lymph, born from the blood, is the vivifying aliment: or rather it is the general vivification, the being-for-self of each organ, which enables it to transform into itself its non-organic nature, the universal organism. The blood does not conduct material to each organ but vivifies the latter, the form of the organ being the main thing; and this is done not only by the artery but by the blood in its twofold nature as venous and arterial. Thus the heart is everywhere, and each part of the organism is only the specialized force of the heart itself.

Reproduction or the system of digestion is not present, strictly speaking, as a developed, articulated whole (*als ausgebildete Gegliederung*). For whereas the systems of sensibility and irritability are developed into distinct organs, reproduction does not create any structure, nor is it the total [bodily] structure except merely formally, and consequently it does not reach the stage of a differentiation into characteristic forms. The system of reproduction can here only be called abstract since its function is [the general one of] assimilation.

(α) Reproduction in its crass, *immediate* form is the cellular tissue and the glandular organs, the skin, a simple animal gelatine together with tubes; in animals which are no more than this there is an absence of developed differences. The organic activity of shape or structure operates through the skin; connected with this is the lymph, the contact of which with the outer world is the entire process of nutrition. The immediate return of the exterior organism into itself is the skin, in which it becomes actively related to itself; it is, at first, still only the Notion of the interior organism and is therefore the exterior aspect of shape or structure. The skin can be and become everything, nerves, blood-vessels, etc.; as *absorbent*, it is the universal digestive organ of the *vegetative* organism.

(β) But the skin, which in claws, bones, and muscles has acquired a relation involving real difference, now interrupts the process of absorption and enters into individual relationship with air and water. The organism relates itself to the external world not only as to a universal element but to this element as a separate, detached existence, even though it is only a draught of water. The skin thus turns back on itself towards the organism's interior; in addition to being a general orifice, it is now a single orifice, the mouth, and non-organic nature is seized and ingested as an individual thing. The individual organism seizes it, crunches and destroys it as a purely external structure and transforms it into itself, not by immediate infection but in virtue of a mediating activity (*Bewegung*) which makes it pass through the different moments; *reproduction* in *opposition*. Immediate, simple digestion becomes explicit in the higher species of animals in a system of viscera: the bile, the liver, the pancreas or gastric gland, the pancreatic juice. Animal heat derives, in general, from the fact that the structures it overcomes are individual structures. This heat is the absolutely mediating activity of the organism reflected into itself, the organism which possesses the Elements within itself and through these goes into action, bringing them all into action to attack the individual [bit of food]: (1) it infects it with organic lymph, the saliva; (2) it works on it with the neutrality of the alkaline and acid principles, with the animal gastric and pancreatic juices; (3) lastly, it attacks it with the bile, the onslaught of the fiery element on the ingested food.

(γ) The inward-turned or visceral reproduction is the stomach and intestinal canal. Immediately, the stomach is this digestive heat as such, and the intestinal canal is the separation of what is digested: (1) into entirely inorganic matter which is to be excreted; and (2) into completely animalized matter which is both the unity of the enduring structure and of the heat of dissolution—the blood. The simplest animals are merely an intestinal canal.

§ 355

3. *The Total Structure*

But for the structure [of the animal subject] we have, on the one hand, the differences of the Elements and their systems uniting to produce a general, concrete interpenetration of one another so that each part (*Gebilde*) of the structure contains these systems linked together in it; and on the other hand, structure divides *itself* (*insectum*) into (a) the centres of the three systems of the head, thorax, and abdomen, with the addition of the extremities for mechanical movement and prehension, these latter constituting the moment of singularity positing itself as distinct from the *outer world.* (*b*) Structure differentiates itself in accordance with abstract difference into the two directions of *inward* and *outward.* Each structure shares in the inward and outward aspects of each system; the outward aspect, as in its own self different, exhibits this difference through the symmetrical duality of its organs and limbs (Bichat's *vie organique et animale*).[1] (3) The whole, as structure completely developed into a self-subsistent individual, is, in this self-related universality, at the same time *particularized* into the *sex*-relation, into a relation outwards with another individual. Structure, being self-enclosed, points within itself to its two directions outward.

Zusatz. Sensibility, irritability, and reproduction, brought together into the concrete unity of total structure, form the outer configuration of the organism, the crystal of vitality.

(α) These determinations are, first of all, merely forms, as in insects where they are cut up into separate parts; each moment is a total system as a given determinateness, or under one given form. Thus the head is the centre of sensibility, the thorax of irritability, and the abdomen of reproduction, and these contain the precious viscera, the interior side of the organism: while the extremities, hands, feet, wings, fins, etc., represent the behaviour of the organism in relation to the outer world.

(β) Secondly, these centres are also developed totalities, so that the other determinations have the character, not of mere forms, but are displayed and contained in each of these totalities. Each abstract system permeates, and is connected with, them all, each displays the entire structure; therefore the systems of nerves, veins, blood, bones, muscles, skin, glands, etc., are each an entire skeleton; and this gives interconnection to the organism, for each system is dominated by the others with which it is interlaced and at the same time maintains within itself the total connection. The head, the brain, has viscera of sensibility, bones, nerves; but there also belong to it all the parts of the other systems,

[1] Bichat, *Recherches physiologiques sur la vie et la mort* (Paris, 1800), p. 7: 'Les fonctions de l'animal forment deux classes trèsdistinctes. Les unes se composent d'une succession habituelle d'assimilation et d'excrétion. Il ne vit qu'en lui, par cette classe de fonctions; par l'autre, il existe hors de lui. Il sent et apperçoit ce qui l'entoure, réfléchit ces sensations, se meut volontairement d'après leur influence, et le plus souvent peut communiquer par la voix ses désirs et ses craintes, ses plaisirs ou ses peines. J'appelle *vie organique* l'ensemble de fonctions de la première classe, parceque tous les êtres organisés, végétaux ou animaux, en jouissent. Les fonctions réunies de la seconde classe forment la *vie animale*, ainsi nommée parcequ'elle est l'attribut exclusif du règne animal.' To have brought to notice this distinction in the organism, which Bichat with his great insight into Nature has done, reveals a penetrating glance.

blood, veins, glands, and skin. Similarly, the thorax has nerves, glands, skin, etc.

(γ) In addition to these two distinct forms of these totalities, there is the third form of the totality which belongs to sensation as such, where therefore the psychic character (*das Seelenhafte*) of the organism constitutes the main feature. These higher unities which gather round themselves organs of all the totalities and have their unifying point in the feeling subject, still present great difficulty. There are connections of particular parts of one system with particular parts of the same or another system or systems which, in respect of their functions, are linked together, seeing that on the one hand they form a concrete centre, and that on the other hand, the essential nature (*Ansich*) of their unities, their profounder determination, is to be found in the sentient creature—they are, so to speak, psychic ganglia (*seelenhafte Knoten*). The soul (*Seele*), as self-determining, is as such present in the body: it does not merely conform to the specific pattern of physical relationships in the body.

(1) Thus, e.g., the mouth belongs to a particular system, that of sensibility, for it contains the tongue, the organ of taste, as a moment of the theoretical process: further, the mouth has teeth which appertain to the extremities, for their function is to seize outside things and to crunch them: in addition, the mouth is the organ of the voice, of speech: other cognate sensations, e.g. that of thirst, also have their seat there: laughing, and kissing too, are also done with the mouth; and thus the expressions of many sensations are unified in it. Another example is the eye, the organ of sight, which also sheds tears, as animals also do. Sight and weeping which are functions of a single organ, may seem remote from one another, but both have the inner ground of their connection in the sentient nature [of the creature], and have therefore a higher link which cannot be said to lie in the process of the living organism.

(2) There are also connections of another kind where phenomena are manifested in the organism in widely separated parts, phenomena connected not physically but only in principle (*an sich*): so that it is said there is a sympathy between such parts, a sympathy which was supposed to be explained by the nerves. But this connection is possessed by every part of the organism, so that such an explanation is inadequate. The connection is grounded in the specific nature of the sensation, and in man, in his spiritual nature. Such a connection is found in the development of the voice and of puberty, a connection which is rooted in the interior aspect of sentient nature; similarly with the tumescence of the breasts in pregnancy.

(3) As the sentient creature produces relationships here which are not physical, so too it isolates again parts which are physically related to each other. One wills, e.g., to be active in some part of the body, and this activity is brought about by means of the nerves; but these are themselves branches of nerves connected with many others with which they unite to form a single stem which is connected with the brain. The sentient

creature is here, of course, active in all this, but sensation isolates this point of activity; so that the activity results from or by means of these nerves without the rest of the bodily system being involved. Autenrieth (loc. cit., part iii, § 937) cites the following example of this: 'It is harder to explain crying by internal causes; for the nerves connected with the lachrymal glands belong to the fifth pair which also serve so many other parts in which feelings of sadness fail to produce changes as they do in the lachrymal glands. But the soul has the capacity to act in certain directions from within outwards, even though the direction is not determined by the anatomical connection of the nerves. Thus we can move particular parts of the body in a certain direction by particular muscles connected with many other muscles by common nerve-stems, without all these other muscles taking part in the action. And yet it is abundantly clear that the will, in such a case, acts solely through the nerve-stem common to them all, the separate fibres of which are interlaced in so complex a fashion that if the nerve is cut or ligatured, the soul no longer possesses any influence on the muscles served by it, even when all the other kinds of connections of these muscles with the rest of the body, e.g. by vessels, cellular tissue, etc., remain undamaged.' The factor therefore which stands supreme over the organic interconnection and efficacy of the systems is the essential nature (*Ansich*) of the sentient creature, which forms relationships which have no physical reality, or, conversely, intercepts or interrupts relationships which have such reality.

There is also symmetry in this structure, but only in its outward-turned aspect;[1] for in the relation to an other, self-identity manifests itself only as exact likeness. The distinct moments of structure which go inwards are not only not symmetrically duplicated, but anatomists come across 'many other diversities in form, size, position, and direction of the internal organs, of the spleen, liver, stomach, kidneys, salivary glands, and the lymphatic vessels in particular, since the number and volume of these are seldom the same in two subjects'.[2] In the system of sensibility, observes Bichat (loc. cit., pp. 15–17) quite correctly, the sensory and motor nerves are symmetrical, for they have two similar pairs on each side: similarly with the sense organs we have two eyes, two ears, and the nose too, is double, and so on; the osseous system also is extremely symmetrical. In the system of irritability the muscles, the female breasts, etc., are symmetrical. Similarly the members of the extremities which subserve locomotion, voice, and mechanical prehension are a pair of similars, such as arms, hands, and legs. The frequent asymmetry of the larynx is described by Bichat (loc. cit., p. 41) as an exception: 'Most physiologists, Haller in particular, have stated that the cause of a lack of harmony in the voice is the disparity between the two symmetrical sides of the larynx, the inequality of strength in the muscles

---

[1] Bichat, loc. cit., p. 14.　　　　[2] Ibid., p. 22.

and nerves', etc. On the other hand, the brain, heart, lungs, ganglia, the internal venous system of reproduction, the abdominal muscles, the liver, and the stomach lack symmetry. The ganglia in particular are signalized by their quite irregular arrangement, i.e. they are not separated into two sides: 'The sympathetic nerve', says Bichat (ibid., pp. 17-18), 'whose sole function is to serve the interior life, shows an irregular distribution in most of its branches; the *plexus solaris*, *mesentericus*, *hypogastricus*, *splenicus*, *stomachicus*, etc., are examples of this.'

These symmetrical pairs are not, however, perfectly symmetrical. In human beings particularly, this evenness of configuration is again made asymmetrical by occupation, habit, activity, and intelligence in general. As an intelligent being, man concentrates his efforts mainly on a single point, comes to a point, as it were; but not merely to a mouth for animal nourishment (like the animal's mouth which Nature has shaped to a point); on the contrary, man alters his shape, turning his individuality outwards and so individualizing his bodily strength at one point of his body and concentrating it on one side—for a particular purpose, e.g. writing—rather than holding it in equilibrium. Thus human beings are more dexterous with the right arm than with the left, and with the right hand likewise; this naturally has its basis in the position of the right arm in relation to the whole, since the heart is on the left side and is always held back and defended by the right. Similarly, people seldom hear equally well with both ears; the eyes, too, often have different visual acuity and in human beings the cheeks are seldom quite similar in shape. In animals this symmetry is more marked. Thus there is similarity in limbs and strength, but agility varies. But exercises in which intelligence plays a small part preserve symmetry in their movements. 'Animals leap with the greatest skill from crag to crag where the very slightest slip would hurl them into the abyss, and they walk with marvellous precision on surfaces which are hardly as wide as the extremities of their limbs. Even those animals which are very ungainly do not stumble as often as man. In them, equilibrium in the motor organs of both sides' is even more rigidly maintained than it is in man, who voluntarily introduces inequality. When people acquire intellectual and special skills, e.g. writing a great deal, cultivating music, the fine arts, technical skills, fencing, etc., equilibrium is lost.† On the other hand, cruder, merely physical, exercises like drilling, gymnastics, running, climbing, walking on narrow surfaces, jumping and vaulting preserve this equilibrium: but they do not fit in with the other practices. Because they are thoughtless activities they are in general obstacles to mental composure and collectedness.

In this Paragraph we considered structure, first as quiescent, and secondly, in its connection with an other outside it. The third moment is the connection of structure with an other, which at the same time be-

† Cf. Bichat, *Recherches physiologiques sur la vie et la mort* (Paris 1800), pp. 35-40.

longs to the same genus, and in which the individual achieves self-feeling in the act of feeling itself in the other. Through the male and female natures, there emerges a determination of the entire structure, a different *habitus* which, in man, also extends to the spiritual sphere and becomes a distinct natural feature.

§ 356

4. *The Structural Process*

Structure, as alive, is essentially process, and it is, as such, *abstract process*, the *structural process within structure itself*, in which the organism converts its own members into a non-organic nature, into *means*, lives on itself and produces its own self, i.e. this same totality of articulated members, so that each member is reciprocally end and means, maintains itself through the other members and in opposition to them. It is the process which has for result the simple, immediate *feeling of self*.

Zusatz. The structural process is, as the first process, the Notion of the process, formation as an unrest but only as a general activity, as a general animal process. It is true that, as this abstract process, it resembles the process of vegetable life with the external world, in so far as the living creature's power is the immediate transformation into animality of what is external to it. But since the organism, as a developed being, expresses itself in a special articulation, not containing independent parts, but only moments in a living subjectivity, these moments are sublated, negated, and posited by the organism's vitality. This contradiction, that they are and are not, that they have come forth from subjectivity and yet are contained in it, manifests itself as a perpetual process. The organism is the unity of internal and external, so that (α) as internal, it is the structural process, in which the structure is a sublated moment which remains enclosed within the organism's self; the external, the other, the product, has, in other words, returned to that which brought it forth. The organic unity brings itself forth without becoming another individual like the plant; it is a circle which returns into self. (β) The otherness of the organism or the organism as external, is free, quiescent (*seiende*) structure, the quiescence or repose which is opposed to the process. (γ) The organism itself is the higher repose as a unity of both—the restless Notion which is self-identical. Now the general structural process consists in this, that the blood in its exhalation (*Aushauchen*) lets itself be reduced to lymph, but that the sluggish, indeterminate fluidity of the lymph strengthens and organizes itself; on the one hand, it becomes split in the opposition inherent in muscle, an opposition which is a movement immanent in its structure, and on the other hand, withdraws into the immobility (*Ruhe*) of bone. Fat, bone-marrow, is this vegetable substance which goes on to become oil and excludes the neutral from itself, not as water but as an earthy (*erdigte*) neutrality, as lime, in the same way that the plant goes on to produce silica. Bone is this dead neutrality set between lymph and bone-marrow.

The individual, however, does not merely convert itself into an object, but equally idealizes this reality. Each part is hostile to the others, maintains itself at their expense, but delivers itself up to them. Nothing in the organism endures, but everything is reproduced, not excepting the bones. Richerand therefore says of bone-formation (loc. cit., part ii, p. 256): 'If the inner *periosteum* is destroyed with a stylet, the outer *periosteum* separates itself from the bone which it covered, appropriates the phosphate of lime brought by the vessels spread through its tissues and forms a new bone round the other.' Each organ is so determined as to serve only the general end, the development of the whole living creature. Each member draws on the others for its own needs, for each secretes animal lymph which, discharged into the blood-vessels, is brought back into the blood; from this secretion each takes its nourishment. The structural process is thus conditioned by the consumption of the products [of the organism]. When the organism is restricted to this process, as e.g. in disease, where its interaction with the outer world is interrupted, the human being consumes himself, converts himself into aliment. This is the cause of emaciation in disease, for the organism no onger has the power to assimilate its non-organic world but can only digest its own self. Thus in Blumauer's *Aeneid*, the companions of Aeneas consume their stomachs; and in starving dogs the stomach has been found actually eaten and partly absorbed by the lymphatic vessels. The process in which the organism expends itself and inwardly collects itself goes on without ceasing. It is said that after five, ten, or twenty years the organism no longer contains its former substance, everything material has been consumed, and only the substantial form persists.

The higher unity is, in general, that in which the activity of one system is conditioned by that of an other. Many experiments have, e.g., been conducted to determine to what extent digestion, circulation of the blood, etc., are independent of nervous activity, or respiration is independent of the brain, etc., and the one or the other way round, and whether, therefore, life can still persist if one or the other is stopped: also what kind of influence respiration has on the circulation of the blood, etc. In this connection Treviranus (loc. cit., vol. iv, p. 264) cites the case 'of a child born without heart and lungs, but which had arteries and veins'. In the womb it could, of course, have lived in that condition, but not outside it. Now from this example it was concluded that Haller's assertion, 'that the heart is the sole mainspring of the circulation of the blood' was false; this was indeed a fundamental question. But it is questionable whether the blood does still circulate after the heart has been extirpated. Treviranus (loc. cit., vol. iv, pp. 645 et seq.) has carried out a large number of experiments especially on frogs' hearts; but they have yielded nothing except details of the way in which he tortured these animals. Contrary to Haller's opinion that the beating of the heart produces the circulation of the blood, Treviranus asserted 'that the blood has a motive power of its own dependent on the nervous system, whose continuance requires the uninterrupted influence of this system, especially of the spinal cord'. For if the nerve-trunk and spinal cord of a limb are severed, the blood ceases to circulate in this part; from which, therefore, it follows that 'each part of the spinal cord and each nerve-trunk from it sustains the circulation of the blood in those organs which it provides with nerve-branches'. Legallois, who 'does not seem to have dreamed of the possibility of any other theory than Haller's regarding the circulation of the blood', opposes to Treviranus the hypothesis that 'the circulation of the blood depends solely on the contractions of the heart, and that partial destruction of the nervous system enfeebles or stops the circulation only through its influence on this organ'; in general, he maintains that the heart draws its force from the whole of the spinal cord.[1] Now the experiments made by Legallois on rabbits and also on cold-blooded animals led him to the following conclusion: Any part of the spinal cord, that, e.g., in the neck, the chest, or the lumbar region, is certainly very closely connected with the circulation of the corresponding part of the body which receives its motor nerves from that part. But the destruction of such a part has a twofold effect on the circulation of the blood: (α) it weakens the general circulation, since the heart is deprived of the contingent of forces received from the extirpated part of the spinal cord; (β) it at once weakens the circulation in the corresponding part, and then forces the heart, though no longer having the force of the entire spinal cord, to do the same amount of work throughout the extent of the circulation. If, on the other hand, a ligature is applied to the arteries in the part, e.g. the lumbar region, where the spinal cord is destroyed, circulation is no longer necessary there; and since there is spinal cord in the rest of the body, the heart and circulation remain in equilibrium. Life indeed persists in this remaining part for an even longer period; and when Legallois destroyed the brain and the cervical spinal cord, circulation continued through the jugular arteries. Thus a rabbit survived more than three-quarters of an hour after decapitation and prevention of haemorrhage, since an equilibrium was produced; these experiments were made on rabbits aged three, ten, up to fourteen days at the most, death occurring earlier in older rabbits.[2] In these last, life has a more intensive unity, whereas in the younger animals life still is more like the life of polyps (*polypenartig*). The conclusions of Legallois were refuted by Treviranus mainly on experiments showing that even if the

---

[1] Treviranus, loc. cit., vol. iv, pp. 653, 272, 266–7, 269–70, 273, 644.

[2] *Moniteur universel*, 1811, No. 312 (cf. Treviranus, loc. cit., vol. iv, pp. 273–5).

circulation of the blood has been arrested by destroying the spinal cord, the heart still continues to beat for a time; from which, at the close of his investigation, he concludes, in opposition to Legallois, that 'Haller's teaching that the heart-beat is not *directly* dependent on the action of the nervous system is therefore not refuted'.[1] Whatever importance is attached to these determinations and conclusions, the only inference that can be made is that, e.g., if the heart is extirpated, digestion still continues, and so on. But this continuance is of such short duration that neither function can be regarded as at all independent of the other. The more perfect the organization, i.e. the more separate and distinct are the functions, the more are these dependent on each other; that is why the more rudimentary (*unvollkommnen*) animals are more tenacious of life. Treviranus (loc. cit., vol. v, p. 267) cites amphibia as examples, 'toads and lizards which were found in completely closed cavities in stones'— which therefore may well have been present at the creation of the world! 'Recently in England note was taken of two lizards discovered at Eldon in Suffolk in a chalk cliff fifteen feet below the surface. These at first seemed to be completely lifeless, but began gradually to show signs of life, especially after being exposed to the sun. The mouth in both creatures was sealed with a sticky substance which prevented their breathing. One of the lizards was put in water and the other left in the dry. The former succeeded in freeing itself from the sticky substance and lived for several weeks, but finally died. The other died the following night.' There are even more remarkable facts in connection with molluscs, insects, and worms, which can go without food for months and years. Snails can live headlessly for more than a year. Some insects can be frozen for the whole of their life without suffering vital injury, other animals can do without atmospheric air for lengthy periods, others again can live in very hot water. Rotifers have been resuscitated after four years, etc.[2]

B. ASSIMILATION

§ 357

The self-feeling of the individuality is also directly exclusive and in a state of tension with a non-organic nature which stands over against it as its *external* condition and material.

Zusatz. The process outwards is the *real* process in which the animal no longer, as in disease, converts its own nature into a non-organic one; on the contrary, the organism must also release the other which is a moment within itself to exist as the abstraction of an immediately present outer

---

[1] Treviranus, *Biologie*, vol. iv, pp. 651-3.
[2] Ibid., vol. v, pp. 269-73 (vol. ii, p. 16).

world with which it enters into relation. The standpoint of life is precisely this judgement (*Urteil*) of expelling the sun and everything from itself in this way. The Idea of life is this inner unconscious creative principle—an expansion of Nature which, in the living being, has returned into its truth. But for the individual, its non-organic nature becomes a presupposed world already in existence; and this constitutes the finitude of the organism. The individual exists for itself over against this non-organic nature, but in such a way that the connection between them is altogether absolute, indivisible, inner, and essential, for the organism has negativity within itself. The only determination or destiny of the outer is to be for the organism; and the organism is that which preserves itself in face of the outer world. Now since the organism is directed towards the outer world as well as being inwardly in a state of tension towards it, we have the contradiction of a relationship in which two independent terms appear mutually opposed while at the same time the outer must be sublated. The organism must therefore posit what is external as subjective, appropriate it, and identify it with itself; and this is *assimilation*. The forms of this process are threefold: first, the theoretical process; secondly, the real, practical process; thirdly, the unity of both, the ideally real process, the adaptation of the non-organic to the purposes of the living creature—in other words, instinct, including the constructive instinct.

1. *The Theoretical Process*

§ 357a

Since in this external relation the animal organization is *immediately* reflected into self, this ideal relationship (*Verhalten*) is the *theoretical* process, sensibility as outward process, a *determinate feeling*, which differentiates itself into the manifold sensory approaches to its non-organic nature.

Zusatz. The self of the organism is the unity of its blood or pure process, and of its structure; and because this latter is completely sublated in the fluidity of the blood, the self contains being as a sublated moment. The organism is thus raised into pure ideality, perfectly transparent universality; it is space and time, and at the same time neither spatial not temporal: it intuits something which is spatial and temporal, i.e. which is distinct from itself, an other, yet which is immediately not an other. This movement of intuiting is the universal element of *sense*. Sensibility was just this vanishing of determinateness into pure ideality which, as soul or ego, remains at home with itself in the other; the sentient subject is thus the self which is for the self. But the animal in sentience does not merely sense itself, but itself as determined in a particular way; it senses a particularized form of itself. That the animal in sensation becomes a particularized form of itself, is what distinguishes the sentient creature from the non-sentient; the sentient creature therefore contains a relation to an other which is immediately posited as mine. The object which is hard, warm, etc., exists independently outside of me: but equally it is immediately transformed, made ideal, a determinateness of my feeling; the content within me is the same as the content outside of me, only the form differs. Thus spirit has consciousness only as self-consciousness: in other words, in being related to an external object, I am at the same time for myself. The theoretical process is the free, disinterested one of sensation which also leaves the existence of the external object unaffected. The different determinations we have found in inorganic nature are also a diversified relationship to it of the organism, as modifications of sensation; and that is why they are called senses.

§ 358

The senses and the theoretical processes are therefore: (a) the sense of the mechanical sphere—of gravity, of cohesion and its alteration, and of heat—feeling as such; (b) the senses [coming under the moment] of opposition, (1) of the particularized principle of air, and (2) of the likewise realized neutrality of concrete water, and of the opposed moments of the dissolution of concrete neutrality—smell and taste. (c) The sense of ideality is likewise twofold, since the moment of particularization indispens-able to the ideality as abstract self-reference, falls apart into two indifferent determinations: (1) the sense of ideality as a manifes-tation of the *outer* for the outer, of light as such, and more pre-cisely of light as being determined in the concrete outer world, i.e. colour, and (2) the sense of the manifestation of the organism's *inwardness* expressed as such in its utterance, the sense of sound: the two senses, then, of sight and hearing.

Remark

Here we see how the threefold moments of the Notion become fivefold. The more general reason for the transition we have here is that the animal organism is the reduction of inorganic nature, sundered into separate moments, into the infinite unity of *subjectivity*, in which, however, it is at the same time that nature's developed totality, the moments of which exist separately because the subjectivity is still a *natural* one.

Zusatz. Sense—the immediate unity of the being of the organism and its object (*des Seins und des Seinen*)—is in the first place feeling, the non-objective unity with the object, in which, however, the latter also retains its own independence. This unity is therefore double: the sense of shape as shape, and the sense of heat. The differentiation here is only vague, since the other is only the other in general, lacking distinction within itself. The difference therefore—the positive and the negative—falls asunder as figure or shape, and heat. Feeling is thus the sense of the earthy element, of matter, of what offers resistance, in accordance with which I exist immediately as an individual, and the other in its contact with me is also an individual, a material object existing independently, which is how I, too, feel it. Matter yearns for a centre, a yearning which is first satisfied in the animal, which has its centre within itself. It is just this drivenness of matter, as lacking a self, towards an other, which I sense. Here, too, belong the particular ways of offering resistance: softness, hardness, elasticity, smoothness or roughness of surface; figure and shape, too, are simply nothing else than the way is which this resistance is spatially limited. In feeling, these determinations, treated by us in their various spheres, are bound together as in a bouquet; for as we have already seen (*Zusatz* to § 355, p. 374), sentient Nature has just this power of binding together several disparate spheres.

Smell and taste have a close affinity, even in regard to their organs, for nose and mouth are intimately connected. Whereas feeling is the sense of the indifferent existence of things, smell and taste are the practical senses, whose object is the real being of things for an other by which they are consumed.

In light a thing only manifests itself immediately as an immediate existence. But the manifestation of the organism's inwardness, namely, sound, is the explication, the bringing forth, the manifestation of the inwardness as inwardness. In sight, the physical self manifests itself spatially, and in hearing, temporally. In hearing, the object ceases to be a thing. We see the same thing with two eyes because they see the same thing, they make their sight of the object into one sight, as many arrows hit only one point; it is precisely the unity of direction which cancels the diversity of sensation. But it is just possible to see an object doubled if in the field of vision the eyes are fixed on something else. If I, for example, fix my eyes on a distant object and at the same time pay attention to my finger, I am aware of my finger without changing the slant of my eyes and see both objects at once; this awareness of the whole field of vision is 'unfocused vision'. There is an interesting essay on this by Regius Professor Schulz in *Schweigger's Journal* (1816).

The tetrad, as the developed totality of the Notion in Nature, goes on to become a pentad in so far as its moment of difference appears not only doubled but even as tripled. We could also have begun with the sense of ideality; it manifests as a duality because, though abstract, it should also be the totality. If, therefore, we began in Nature with the ideal asunder-ness of space and time, which are Two because the Notion is concrete (its moments are there in their completeness but they appear in that abstract sphere thrown apart, the content not yet having been posited in its concreteness): so we have now, on the one hand, the sense of physi-cally determined space, and on the other hand, the sense of a physical time. Space is here determined in accordance with the physical abstrac-tion of light and darkness, time as an inner vibration, the negativity of the organism's inwardness. The second member in the grouped totality of the senses, smell and taste, retains its place; and feeling is then the third. The arrangement is more or less immaterial; the main point is that the senses, as rational, constitute a totality. Because, therefore, the sphere of the theoretical process is determined by the Notion, there cannot be more senses, though some can be missing in the lower animals.

The sense organs *qua* feeling constitute the general sense of the skin: taste is the muscle of the *tongue*, the neutrality which connects itself with the mouth, i.e. with the incipiently internalized *skin*, or with the retracted vegetative universality of the entire surface; the nose, *qua* organ of smell, is connected with the principle of air (*Luftigkeit*) and with breath-ing. Whereas feeling is the sense of shape in general, taste is the sense of digestion, of the passage inwards of what is outer; smell belongs to the inner organism as the principle of air. Sight as a sense does not spring from an earlier function but is, like hearing, a sense of the brain; in eye and ear sense is related to its own self—but in the former case, the exter-nal object is an indifferent self, while in the latter, it is a self-sublating self. The voice, as active hearing, is the pure self positing itself as uni-versal, expressing pain, desire, joy, contentment. Every animal suffering violent death has a voice, and thereby declares its own supersession. In voice, sense returns to inwardness and is negative self or desire—the feeling of its insubstantial nature as mere space, whereas the senses are saturated, filled space.

2. *The Practical Relationship*

§ 359

The *real* process or *practical* relationship with non-organic nature begins with the diremption of the organism within itself, with the feeling of externality as *negation* of the subject, which is at the same time positive self-relation and the certainty thereof in face of this its negation: in other words, the feeling of *lack* and the *urge* to get rid of it. In this there is manifest a condition of an *external stimulation* and the negation of the subject posited in it in the form of an object against which the subject is braced.

Remark

Only what is living feels a *lack*; for in Nature it alone is the *Notion*, the unity of itself and its specific opposite. Where there is a limitation, it is a negation only for a third, for an external comparison. But it is a *lack* only in so far as the lack's overcoming is equally present in the same thing, and contradiction is, as such, immanent and explicitly present in that thing. A being which is capable of containing and enduring its own contradiction is a *subject*; this constitutes its infinitude. Even when reference is made to *finite* Reason, Reason demonstrates its infinitude in the very fact that it characterizes itself as finite; for negation is finitude, a lack only for that which is its accomplished sublation, *infinite* self-reference (cf. § 60, Remark). Thoughtlessness stands still at the abstraction of the *limitation*, and in life, too, fails to grasp the Notion though in life the Notion enters into *existence*; it sticks to the determinations of ordinary thought (*Vorstellung*) such as impulse, instinct, need, etc., without inquiring what these determinations in themselves are. But the analysis of their concept will show that they are negations posited as contained in the affirmation of the subject itself.

An important step towards a true conception of the organism is the substitution of the concept of stimulation by external potencies for that of the action of external causes. The former concept contains the seed of idealism, which asserts that nothing whatever can have a positive relation to the living being if this latter is not in its own self the possibility of this relation, i.e. if the relation is not determined by the Notion and hence not directly immanent in the subject. But of all the concoctions of external reflection in the sciences, none is more unphilosophical than the introduction of such formal and material relationships in the theory of stimulation as have long been regarded as philosophical, the introduction, for example, of the wholly abstract opposition of receptivity and active capacity, which are supposed to stand to each other as factors in inverse ratio of magnitude.[1] The result of this is to reduce all distinctions within the organism to the formalism of a merely *quantitative* difference, a matter of increase or decrease, of intensification or attenuation; depriving them, in other words, of every possible trace of the Notion. A theory of medicine built on these arid determinations of the Understanding is complete in a half dozen propositions; it is no wonder that it spread rapidly and found many adherents. The cause of this aberration lay in the fundamental error of first defining the Absolute as the absolute indifference of subject and object, and then treating all determinations as only *quantitative* differences. The truth is rather that the absolute form, i.e. the Notion and principle of life, has for its soul only and solely the qualitative difference which sublates itself, the dialectic of absolute opposition. The failure to recognize this genuine negativity can lead to the belief that it is impossible to hold fast to the absolute identity of life without converting the moment of difference into a product of merely external reflection— as is the case with Spinoza's attributes and modes which present themselves in an external intelligence, with the result that life then altogether lacks the *punctum saliens* of selfhood, the principle of self-movement, of self-differentiation.

Another crude and thoroughly unphilosophical procedure was that which simply substituted carbon and nitrogen, oxygen and hydrogen, for the determinations of the Notion, and then further defined the difference hitherto characterized as intensive, as a more or less of one or the other substances, the active and positive relation of the external stimulus, however, being defined as an addition of a deficient substance. In an asthenia, e.g. a nervous fever, the nitrogen in the organism is supposed to have the upper hand because brain and nerve generally are supposed to be 'potentiated' nitrogen, *chemical* analysis having shown this to be the principal ingredient of these organic structures; the ingestion of carbon is therefore supposed to be indicated in order to restore the balance of these substances, i.e. health. The remedies which empirical medicine has found effective in the treatment of nervous fever are, on these same grounds, regarded as belonging to the

[1] Schelling, *Erster Entwurf eines Systems der Naturphilosophie*, p. 88. [Note by Michelet].

carbon side; and this kind of superficial collocation and mere opinion is put forward as philosophical construction and proof. The crudity of this procedure consists in taking the *caput mortuum* in its ultimate form, the dead substance, the life already destroyed, on which chemistry has inflicted a second death, for the essence of a living organ, and, indeed, for its Notion.

It is this ignorance and contempt for the Notion which, in general, gives rise to the facile formalism that, in place of the determinations of the Notion, makes use of sensuous materials such as chemical substances, as well as relationships belonging to the sphere of inorganic Nature, such as the north and south poles of the magnet, or even the difference between magnetism itself and electricity, a formalism which, in its apprehension and exposition of the natural universe, attaches externally to its various spheres and differences a ready-made schema compounded of such material. For this purpose, a great variety of forms is possible, for it remains a matter of choice whether one employs for the schema determinations as they appear in the *chemical* sphere, e.g. oxygen, hydrogen, etc., transferring them to magnetism, mechanism, vegetable and animal life, etc., or whether one takes opposites from any one sphere, e.g. magnetism, electricity, male and female, contraction and expansion, and then applies them to the other spheres.

Zusatz. The practical process, it is true, is an alteration and overcoming of the outer inorganic nature in its independent material existence, but it is none the less a process of unfreedom, because in animal appetite the organism directs itself outwards. People believe that it is in the will that they are free, but it is just in willing that they are in relationship with a reality outside them. It is only in the reasonable will, which is theoretical, as in the theoretical process of the senses, that man is free. What is primary, therefore, in animal appetite is the subject's feeling of dependence, that it is not for itself, but stands in need of an other which is its negative, and this not contingently but necessarily; this is the unpleasant feeling of need. The defect in a chair which has only three legs is in us; but in life, the defect is in life itself, and yet it is also sublated because life is aware of the limitation as defect. It is thus a privilege of higher natures to feel pain; the higher the nature, the more unhappiness it feels. The great man has a great need, and the urge to rid himself of it. Great deeds come only from profound mental suffering; here may be found the solution to the problem of evil, etc. The animal is thus, in the negative, at the same time positively at home with itself; and this, too, is the privilege of higher natures, to exist as this contradiction. But equally, too, the animal restores its lost harmony and finds satisfaction within itself. Animal appetite is the idealism of objectivity, so that the latter is no longer something alien to the animal.

The external manner of apprehension referred to in the Paragraph plays a part even in Schelling's philosophy, in that he often carries his parallels too far. Oken, Troxler, and others lapse completely into an empty formalism, as when Oken, as we have already seen (§ 346, *Zusatz*, p. 333), calls the woody fibres of plants their nerves, or when the roots of the plant are called its brain (see § 348, *Zusatz*, p. 343): similarly, the brain is supposed to be the human sun. In order to express the concept of an organ of vegetable or animal life, the name is taken, not from the sphere of thought, but from elsewhere. But one should not fall back again on sensuous forms for the purpose of determining other forms; it is from the Notion that they must be derived.

§ 360

Need is something specific and its determinateness is a moment of its universal Notion, though particularized in an infinite variety of ways. An urge is the activity of getting rid of the defect of such determinateness, i.e. getting rid of its initially merely *subjective* form. In that the content of the determinateness is primary, and *preserves* itself in the activity through which it is only carried into effect, it is *end* or *purpose* (§ 204), and the urge, as only in the living being, is *instinct*. This formal defect is the inner stimulus, whose determinateness, specified in accordance with the content, is at the same time a relation of the animal to the particular individualized forms of the various spheres of Nature.

Remark

The mystery thought to occasion the difficulty in understanding instinct is simply this, that an *end* can be grasped only as an inner *Notion*, so that explanations and relationships stemming from mere Understanding soon reveal their ineptness in regard to instinct. The basic determination of the living being seized on by Aristotle, that it must be conceived as acting purposively, has in modern times been almost forgotten till Kant, in his own way, revived this concept in his doctrine of *inner* teleology, in which the living being is to be treated as its own end (*Selbstzweck*). The difficulty here comes mainly from representing the *teleological* relationship as *external*, and from the prevalent opinion that an *end* exists *only* in *consciousness*. Instinct is purposive activity acting unconsciously.

Zusatz. Since an urge can be carried out only by quite specific actions, this appears as instinct, in that it seems to be a choice guided by a purpose. But because the urge is not a known *end*, the animal still does not know its ends as ends; and that which unconsciously acts in accordance with ends Aristotle calls φύσις.

§ 361

In so far as a need is a connection with the *universal* mechanism and abstract powers of Nature, instinct is only an *inner*, not even a sympathetic stimulus (as in sleeping and waking, climatic and other migrations, etc.). But, as the animal's relation to *its* non-organic *individualized* nature, instinct as such is *determinate* and in its further particularization is restricted to only a limited sphere of the universal non-organic nature. Instinct is a *practical* relationship to this, an inner stimulus associated with the show of an external stimulus, and its activity is partly a *formal* and partly a *real assimilation* of non-organic nature.

Zusatz. Waking and sleep are not the result of an external stimulus but are an unmediated participation in the life of Nature and its changes, a resting of the organism within itself and a separation of itself from the outer world. Similarly, the migrations of animals, e.g. of fishes to other seas, are a participation in the life of Nature, a movement (*Zug*) within Nature itself. Sleep is not preceded by a need, by a feeling of lack; one falls asleep without actively setting about doing so. It is rightly said that animals sleep out of instinct and also gather food for the winter; this, too, is the same kind of participation as waking. The lower the organism, the more it participates in this life of Nature. Primitive peoples are sensitive to the course of Nature, but Spirit turns night into day; and so, too, the moods of the seasons have less influence on higher organisms. Intestinal parasites, found at certain seasons of the year in the liver and brain of the hare or deer, are a weakness of the organism in which one part develops a separate life of its own. Because the animal lives sympathetically in the universal course of Nature, it is not so absurd to speak of a connection of animal life with the moon and with terrestrial and sidereal life, and to see a presage in the flight of birds, e.g. at time of earthquakes. Thus certain creatures have a foreknowledge of the weather; spiders and frogs, for example, are weather prophets. Man, too, feels a coming change in the weather in a weak spot, e.g. a scar; the change is already there and manifests itself in man, even though it has not yet come into existence as a change of weather.

An urge in a particular animal is wholly determinate; each animal has only a restricted sphere for its non-organic nature, which exists for that animal alone and which it must seek out by instinct from its complex environment. In the lion, it is not merely the sight of a deer that awakens the desire for it, nor the sight of a hare in the case of the eagle, nor corn, rice, grass, oats, etc., with other animals, nor is the desire a choice; the urge is rather so immanent in the animal that this specific determinateness of the grass, and moreover of this grass, this corn, etc., is in the animal itself for which everything else simply does not exist. Man, as the universal thinking animal, has a much more extensive environment and makes all objects his non-organic nature and objects for his knowing. Undeveloped animals have only elemental Nature—water—for their non-organic nature. Lilies, willows, fig trees have their own particular insects whose non-organic nature is entirely restricted to such plants. The animal can be stimulated only by *its* own non-organic nature, because for the animal, the opposite can be only *its* opposite; what is to be recognized is not the other as such, but each animal recognizes its own other, which is precisely an essential moment of the peculiar nature of each.

§ 362

Instinct, in so far as it is directed to formal assimilation, impresses its specific nature (*Bestimmung*) on the details of its outer world and gives them, as material, an *outer* form appropriate to the end, leaving their objectivity untouched (as in the building of nests and other resting-places). But it is a *real* process in so far as it individualizes inorganic things or relates itself to those already individualized and assimilates them, consuming them, and destroying their specific qualities—the process with *air* (breathing and skin process), with *water* (thirst), and with individualized *earth*, i.e. particular formations of it (hunger). Life, the subject of these moments of the totality, develops inwardly a tension between itself as Notion, and the moments of a reality external to itself and is the perpetual conflict in which it overcomes this externality. In this relationship, the animal comports itself as an immediate singular, and because it can only overcome single determinations of the outer world in all their variety (this place, this time, etc.), its self-realization is not adequate to its Notion and the animal perpetually returns from its satisfaction to a state of need.

Zusatz. The animal itself determines its place for resting, sleeping, and bearing its young; it not only changes its place but makes its own place. In doing so, the animal is practically related to the outer world and this purposive determining is its inner urge put into action.

The real process is at first a process with the Elements, for the outer world itself is, in the first instance, universal. The plant stops at this process with the Elements; but the animal goes on to the process of singularity. We could also include in these processes the relation to light, for this too, is an outer, elemental power (*Potenz*). But for animal and man, light as such is not the same power as it is for the plant nature; on the contrary, because man and animal *see*, light, this self-manifestation of objective form, is external to them, but in the theoretical process their relation to it is ideal (*ideell*). It is only on the colour of feathered creatures and on the colour of animal's pelts that light exerts an influence: the black hair of the negro, too, is an effect of climate, of heat and light: the blood of animals and their coloured fluids are also subject to this influence. On the colour of plumage, Goethe has remarked that this is determined by the action of light as well as by internal organization. Speaking of the colours of organic structures in general, he says: 'White and black, yellow, orange (*Gelbrot*) and brown, alternate in a variety of ways; yet their appearance is never[1] such as to remind us of the elementary colours. They are all rather a mixture of colours resulting from an organic concoction: and they indicate more or less the level of development of the creature to which they belong. . . . Markings on the skin are connected with the internal parts which they cover.' Molluscs and fish have more elementary colours. 'Warmer climates which affect even the water, bring out the colours of fishes, beautify and intensify them. In Otaheiti, Forster saw fish whose surface showed a beautiful play of colour, especially at the moment of death. The fluid in molluscs has the peculiar property of appearing, when exposed to light and air, first yellowish, then greenish; it then turns to blue and from blue to violet, but always[2] assumes a deeper red, and finally, under the action of the sun, especially when spread on cambric, takes on a pure, deep red hue. The action of light on the plumage of birds and their colours is altogether remarkable. In certain parrots, for example, the breast feathers are really yellow; but the part which stands out like a scale and which catches the light is intensified from yellow into red. Thus the breast of such a bird looks deep red; but if one blows into the feathers, the yellow colour appears. There is thus a very marked difference between the uncovered part of

---

[1] Goethe's *Farbenlehre* reads 'never' which Hegel misquotes as 'not'.

[2] The *Farbenlehre* reads '*immer*' which is misquoted as '*weiter*'.

the plumage and the part covered up and not in movement; so that, e.g., in ravens it is, in fact, only the uncovered part which has coloured feathers, and, using this as a guide, it is possible to rearrange at once in their proper order the tail feathers, if they have been thrown into a heap.'[1]

While the process with light remains this ideal process, the process with air and water is a process with material substance. The skin-process is the advancing vegetative process which erupts into hair and feathers. The human skin is less hirsute than that of the animal; but bird-plumage especially is a taking-up of vegetable life into animal life. 'The quills not only grow to a considerable size but they are all covered with branches (barbs) and this makes them true feathers; many of these branches and tufts are subdivided again (barbules), everywhere reminding us of the plant . . . the surface of the human being is smooth and clean (*rein*) and in the finest specimens allows the beautiful form to be seen, except for a few places which are more decorated with, than covered by, hair . . . an excessive amount of hair on chest, arms and legs is an indication of weakness rather than strength; for it is probably only the poets who, misled by the appearance of a nature in other respects intensely animal, have occasionally brought such hirsute heroes to honour among us.'[2]

The respiratory process is a spontaneously interrupted continuity. Exhalation and inhalation is a volatilization (*Verdunsten*) of the blood, the volatilizing irritability (*verdunstende Irritabilität*) (§ 354, *Zusatz*, p. 371); the transition into air is started and retracted. 'The mud-fish *Cobitis fossilis*) breathes through the mouth and exhales through the anus.'[3] The gills by which fishes decompose water are also a secondary, respiratory organ analogous to the lungs. The entire bodies of insects are pierced by air-passages with openings on both sides of the stomach; some which live under water collect a supply [of air], keep it under their wing-coverings or in the fine hair on the abdomen.[4] Now why is the blood connected with this ideal assimilation of the abstract Element? The blood is this absolute thirst, its unrest within itself and against itself; the blood craves to be ignited (*hat Hunger nach Befeuerung*), to be differentiated. More exactly, this assimilation is at the same time a mediated process with air, namely, a conversion of air into carbon dioxide and venous (dark, carbonated) blood, and into arterial, oxygenated blood. The activity and animation of the arterial blood I attribute not so much to its material alteration as to its satiation, that is to say the blood, after the manner of the other digestive process, perpetually appeases its hunger or quenches its thirst (call it what you will) and achieves being-for-self through negativity of its otherness. Air is in itself the fiery and negative element; the blood is the same thing, but as a developed unrest—

[1] Goethe, *Farbenlehre*, vol. i, §§ 664, 644, 645, 641, 660, 661.
[2] Ibid., §§ 655, 669.
[3] Treviranus, *Biologie*, vol. iv, p. 146.
[4] Ibid., p. 150.

the burning fire of the animal organism which not only consumes itself but also preserves itself as fluid and finds in air its *pabulum vitae*. Venous blood injected into arterial blood therefore paralyses action. In corpses, in place of red blood, almost pure venous blood alone is found; in apoplexy, it is found in the brain. This is not caused by a trifle more or less of oxygen or carbon.[1] In scarlet fever, on the contrary, the venous blood too is scarlet-red. But now the true life of the blood is the continuous conversion of arterial and venous blood into each other, in which process the small vessels develop the greatest activity.[2] 'In various organs, there occurs a more rapid transformation of arterial blood into venous blood, and often into venous blood whose characteristic properties (blackness, lesser density when left to stand) are present in a higher degree than elsewhere, as, e.g., in the spleen, without the walls of the vessels showing in a higher degree the normal influence of the oxygen of the arterial blood; on the contrary, they are softer, almost pulpy. The thyroid gland, taken as a whole, possesses greater arteries than any other part of the human body. This gland in its own small space converts large quantities of arterial blood into venous.'[3] Since the vessels of this gland do not get harder, as they should, what becomes of the oxygen of the arterial blood? For it does not exercise any external chemical action.

The process with water is the demand for the neutral Element: on the one side, to counteract the abstract heat within itself, and on the other, to counteract the specific taste of which one wants to get rid; for that is why one drinks.—Urge is only instinct when it relates itself to an individualized object. But whereas in such relationship the momentarily satisfied need always recurs, spirit finds its satisfaction in the cognition of universal truths, in a universal manner.

§ 363

The process begins with the *mechanical seizure* of the external object; *assimilation* itself is the conversion of the externality into the self-like unity. Since the animal is subject, unitary negativity, the nature of assimilation can be neither mechanical nor chemical, for in these processes both the material substances and the conditions and activity *remain external* to each other and lack living, absolute unity.

Zusatz. The appetitive organism which knows itself as the unity of itself and the object confronting it, and so sees into the determinate being of the other, is structure turned outwards and provided with weapons,

[1] Cf. Bichat, loc. cit., pp. 329 et seq.
[2] Autenrieth, loc. cit., part iii Index, p. 370.
[3] Ibid., part i, § 512 (391); §§ 458–9.

whose bones and skin have made themselves into teeth and claws respectively. The process with claws and teeth is still mechanical, but the saliva already makes the process organic. It has long been the fashion to give a mechanical explanation of the process of assimilation, as also of the circulation of the blood; or to explain the action of the nerves as if they were taut strings which vibrated; but a nerve is quite slack. Another explanation is that the nerves are a series of globules which when pressed, push and displace one another, the last globule impinging on the soul. The soul, however, is omnipresent in the body and its ideality is such that the outer separated existence of bones, nerves, and veins has no significance for it. To assign finite relationships to life is therefore even more strikingly out of place than when, as we saw in the case of electricity, it is imagined that the processes in the upper atmosphere are similar to those carried out in a laboratory. Similarly, attempts have been made to reduce digestion to a matter of pressing, pumping, and so on; but in that case it would imply an external relationship of inner and outer, whereas the animal is the absolute self-identity of life, not a mere composition or aggregate. Recently, chemical relationships have been employed; but assimilation cannot be a chemical process either, because in the living being we have a subject which preserves itself and negates the specific quality of the other, whereas in the chemical process, each of the substances taking part, acid and alkali, loses its quality and is lost in the neutral product of the salt or returns to an abstract radical. There the activity is extinguished, but the animal, on the contrary, is a lasting unrest in its self-relation. Digestion can, indeed, be grasped as a neutralizing of acid and alkali: it is correct to say that such finite relationships begin in life, but life interrupts them and brings forth a product which is other than chemical. Thus there is moisture in the eye which refracts light; these finite relationships can therefore be pursued up to a certain point, but then there begins a quite different order of things. Again, chemical analysis can discover a good deal of nitrogen in the brain: similarly, analysis of exhaled air reveals ingredients other than those contained in inhaled air. The chemical process can thus be followed up even to the point of decomposing the separate parts of the living being. None the less the processes themselves should not be regarded as chemical, for chemistry applies only to what is lifeless, and animal processes always sublate the nature of what is chemical. The mediations which occur in the living being, like those in the meteorological process, can be followed up for some distance and demonstrated; but this kind of mediation cannot be imitated.

§ 364

Because the living being is the *universal* power over its outer [non-organic] nature which is opposed to it, assimilation is, first, the *immediate* fusion of the ingested material with animality, an infection with the latter and *simple transformation* (§ 345 Remark, § 346). Secondly, as *mediation*, assimilation is *digestion*—opposition of the subject to the outer world, and, as further differentiated, the process of animal *water* (of the gastric and pancreatic juice, animal lymph as such) and of animal *fire* (of the gall, in which the accomplished return of the organism into itself from its concentration in the spleen is determined as *being-for-self* and as an active consuming): processes which are, all the same, particularized infections.

§ 365

But this *involvement* with the outer world, the stimulus and the process itself, has likewise the determination of *externality over against the universality* and *simple* self-relation of the living being. This involvement itself therefore constitutes, properly speaking, the object and the negative over against the subjectivity of the organism, which the latter has to overcome and digest. This inversion of attitude is the principle of the organism's reflection into itself; the return-into-self is the negation of its outward-directed activity. It has a double determination: on the one hand, the organism separates from itself the activity in which its conflict with the externality of the object is manifested, and on the other, as immediately identical with this activity, it has become *for itself*, has in this means reproduced itself. The process outwards is thus transformed into the first, formal process of simple reproduction from its own self, into the uniting of itself with itself.

Remark

The chief moment in digestion is the *immediate* action of life as the *power* over its non-organic object which it presupposes as its stimulus only in so far as it is *in itself* identical with it, but is, at the same time, its ideality and being-for-self. This action is *infection* and immediate transformation; to it corresponds the *immediate* seizure of the object pointed out in the exposition of purposive activity (§ 208). This immediacy with which the living being as a *universal, continues itself into its food without any further mediation,* by its mere contact with it and by simply taking it into the heat of its own sphere, has also been empirically demonstrated and shown to accord with the Notion by the experiments of Spallanzani[1] and others and by recent physiology—a refutation of the theory of a merely mechanical and fictitious sorting out and separating of parts already assimilable, and of the theory of a chemical process. But investigations of the intermediary processes have not revealed more specific moments of this transformation (as is found, for example, in vegetable substances where it is exhibited in a series of *fermentations*). It has, on the contrary, been shown, e.g., that a great deal of food passes straight from the stomach into the mass of gastric juices without having passed through the other intermediate stages, that the pancreatic juice is nothing more than saliva and the pancreas could quite well be dispensed with, etc. The final product, the chyle which is received into the thoracic duct and discharged into the blood, is the same lymph which, secreted (*excerniert*) by each intestine and each organ, is obtained from every part of the skin and the lymphatic system in the immediate process of transformation and is everywhere found already prepared. The lower forms of animal life which, moreover, are nothing more than lymph coagulated into a membranous point or tube—a simple intestinal canal—do not go beyond this immediate transformation. The *mediated* digestive process in more highly organized animals is, in respect of its *characteristic product*, just such a superfluity as, in the plant, the production of seeds through the so-called difference of sex. The *faeces* often show, especially in children, in whom moreover the increase of material is most prominent, the greater part of the food unchanged, mixed mainly with animal substances, bile, phosphorus, and the like, and the chief action of the organism to be to overcome, and get rid of, what is has itself produced.

The syllogism of the organism is, therefore, not the syllogism of *external teleology*, for it does not stop at directing its activity and form against the outer object but makes this very process, which is on the point of lapsing into a mechanical and chemical one, into

[1] Spallanzani, Lazzaro, 1729–99; Professor of Natural History in Modena and Pavia (since 1769).

an object. This behaviour was expounded as the second premiss in the universal syllogism of purposive activity (§ 209). The organism is a uniting of itself with itself in its outward process; from it, it takes and wins nothing but chyle, its general animalization referred to above, and as the self-existent living Notion, it is thus no less a disjunctive activity which rids itself of this process, draws away (*abstrahiert*) from its *anger* towards the object, from this one-sided subjectivity, thereby becoming *explicitly* what it is implicitly—the subjective, not neutral, identity of its Notion and its reality—and thus finds the end and product of its activity to be that which it already is at the beginning and originally. In this way, the *satisfaction conforms to Reason*; the process outwards into external difference is converted into the process of the organism with itself, and the result is not the mere production of a means but of the end—union of the organism with itself.

Zusatz. Here the alimentary process is the main thing; the organism is in a state of tension with its non-organic nature, negates it and makes it identical with itself. In this immediate relation of the organic to the non-organic, the former is, as it were, the direct melting of the non-organic into organic fluidity. The ground of every reciprocal relation between these two is just this absolute unity of the substance through which the non-organic is thoroughly transparent, ideal and non-objective for the organic. The alimentary process is merely this transformation of the non-organic nature into a corporeality belonging to the subject: but then it also manifests itself as a process passing through a number of phases (*Momente*), a process which is no longer direct transformation but seems to employ means. The animal nature is the universal over against particular natural existences which, in this animal nature, are in their truth and ideality; for the animal nature is actually what these forms are implicitly. Similarly, because all men are implicitly rational, they are subject to the power of that man who appeals to their instinct of Reason, since what he reveals to them is something corresponding to this instinct, something which can harmonize with the Reason he has explicated. Because the people directly accept what is imparted to them, Reason manifests itself in them as a propagation and infection; and so the rind, the illusion, of a separation, which had previously obtained, vanishes. This power of animality is the substantial relation, the main thing in digestion. If, therefore, the animal organism is *substance*, then the non-organic is merely *accident*, whose peculiarity is only a form which it immediately surrenders. 'We know from experience that sugar, vegetable gums and oils, nutritious substances, therefore, which contain little or no nitrogen, are none the less converted into animal substance which contains a large quantity of nitrogen. For there are whole races which live solely on a vegetable diet, just as others live entirely on meat. But the temperate nature of the former demonstrates that their body does not merely retain that small ingredient in their food resembling animal substance which is present in every plant, and excretes the remainder, but that it elaborates a large part of this vegetable food into nutriment appropriate to its organs.'[1] The animals and plants which the animal consumes, are, it is true, themselves organic structures, but for this animal they are relatively its non-organic nature. What is particular and external has no enduring existence of its own, but is a nullity as soon as it comes into contact with a living being; and this. ransformation is merely the revelation of this relationship.

It is on this immediate transition and transformation that all chemical and mechanical explanations founder and in which they find their limit, for such explanations take into account only those data which are already externally similar. The truth is rather that the two sides exist in complete freedom from each other. Bread, e.g., has in its own self no connection with the body: or the chyle, the blood, is something wholly different. Neither chemistry nor mechanics can follow empirically the alteration of food to the point where it is changed into blood, no matter what methods they employ. True, chemistry extracts something of a similar nature from both of them, possibly albumen, perhaps iron, too, and the like, or oxygen, hydrogen, nitrogen, etc.: or it extracts from the plant substances also found in water. But the two sides are at the same time simply different, and therefore wood, blood, flesh, are still not the same thing as these other substances; and blood which has been analysed into these constituents is no longer living blood. The quest for what is similar and the continued pursuit of it is abruptly halted, for the reality of the substances completely vanishes. If I decompose a salt, I obtain again the two substances of which it was composed; the salt, therefore, is thereby explained and the substances have not become something else in the salt but have remained the same. In the organism, however, this becoming-something-else on the part of non-organic (*seienden*) substances is made explicit. Because the non-organic being is only a sublated moment in the organic self, it has to be taken into account, not as what it immediately is, but as what it is in its Notion; but in its Notion, it is the same as organic being.

This is exhibited in organic assimilation. Food which is subjected to the influence of organic life is dipped in this fluid and itself becomes this dissolved fluid. Just as a thing becomes an odour, a dissolved matter, a simple atmosphere, so, in the organic sphere, it becomes a simple organic fluid in which nothing more is to be found of the thing or its constituents. This organic fluid which remains selfsame is the fiery nature of the non-organic which therein directly returns into its Notion;

[1] Autenrieth, *Handbuch der Physiologie*, part ii, § 557.

for eating and drinking convert non-organic things into what they are in themselves. It is an unconscious seizure (*Begreifen*) of them; and the reason why they become such sublated moments is that they are such in themselves. This transition must also exhibit itself as a mediated process in which the terms of its opposition are developed. But the basis of it is that the organism directly draws the non-organic into its organic matter because it is the genus as a simple self and hence is the power over the non-organic. If the organism does bring the non-organic into an identity with itself gradually through separate stages (*Momente*), this complex arrangement of digestion through the intermediation of several organs is, *for the non-organic*, indeed superfluous: but it is not so for the organism which progresses through these moments within itself *for its own sake* in order to be movement and consequently actuality; just as the strength of the spirit is measured only by the extent of the opposition it has overcome. But the fundamental relation of the organism is this simple contact in which the other is transformed directly and at a stroke.

The lower animals are still without any special organs like bile, gastric juice, for the special activities connected with the assimilation of food. Water is already absorbed through the skin in the process with air as is seen in many worms and zoophytes: thus water on which polyps, e.g., feed is directly turned into lymph, jelly. 'The simplest mode of nutrition through a single mouth is found in hydra, brachiopoda, and vorticella. The hydra feeds on small aquatic animalcules which it seizes with its tentacles. The sack-shaped receptacle which comprises most of its body opens and receives the prey. This has hardly been swallowed before it is changed: it is transformed into a homogeneous mass and continually loses volume in the process; finally the polyp opens its mouth again and evacuates part of the ingested food along the same way in which it entered the hydra's stomach. This rapid decomposition of what has entered the stomach takes place even when, as not infrequently happens, the creatures swallowed are long worms only half of which can be contained by the stomach. The one half then often still tries to escape, the other half being already digested. In fact, the polyp is also able to digest with its outer surface. It can be turned inside out' like a glove, 'and the inner surface of its stomach made the outside: and yet the phenomena referred to still take place as before.'[1] An intestine of this kind is merely a canal of so simple a structure that one cannot differentiate between oesophagus, stomach, and intestines. But 'after the alimentary canal, there is no vital organ so common throughout the whole animal kingdom as the liver. It is found in every mammal, bird, amphibian, fish, and mollusc. Even in the class of worms, the *aphrodites* seem to possess bile-secreting organs in the pockets containing a dark green bitter juice, which border both sides of their intestinal canal. There are similar pockets on the alimentary canal of the sea-cucumber; and again an

[1] Treviranus, loc. cit., vol. iv, pp. 291–2.

actual liver is found in the star-fish (*asterias*). In insects, the vessels which can be regarded as biliary vessels seem to take the place of the liver.'[1] Others attribute another function to these vessels. 'Although with many zoophytes there is no visible excrement, there can be no doubt that in all of them an evacuation of gaseous matter connected with nutrition takes place through the skin and the respiratory organs. Nutrition and respiration are thus closely connected.'[2]

Also higher up the scale of animal life we find this immediate assimilation. It is a familiar experience in the catching of thrushes and fieldfares that when they are quite thin, on a misty morning, they get quite fat in the space of a few hours; this is a direct transformation of this moisture into animal matter which takes place without any further elaboration (*Abscheidung*) or passage through the separate moments of the process of assimilation. Man, too, directly assimilates as is shown by the account of the English ship at sea, the crew of which, having used up all their water, and finding the rain-water laboriously collected in the sails inadequate, quenched their thirst by moistening their shirts and even dipping themselves in the sea: their skin, therefore, had absorbed pure water from the sea without the salt. In animals provided with specific (*vermittelnden*) digestive organs there occurs partly this general assimilation as such and partly a special separate digestive process; in the latter, it is organic heat which initiates assimilation. But the stomach and intestinal canal are themselves nothing else but the outer skin, only reversed and developed and shaped into a peculiar form. The more detailed comparison of these various membranes is to be found in Treviranus (loc. cit., vol. iv, pp. 333 et seq.). Ipececuanha, opium, rubbed in on the outside of the stomach has the same effect as when taken internally; but ipececuanha has also been rubbed in the shoulder and has been equally well assimilated. 'It has been observed that small bits of meat enclosed in small linen bags and placed in the abdominal cavity of a live cat, were dissolved, down to tiny bits of bone, into a pap in a similar way as if in the stomach. The same thing happened when such meat was conveyed subcutaneously on to bare muscles of live animals and left there for a time. This seems to resemble what happens in leg-fractures where Nature discharges a quantity of moisture round the fracture, softening and quite dissolving the sharp ends of the bones: and another instance is that congealed blood in contused parts of the body which have healed over, is gradually dissolved and liquefied, finally being reabsorbed. The gastric juice does not act therefore as a quite special kind of fluid different from any other kind of animal fluid, but only as a watery fluid plentifully supplied to the reservoir of the stomach by the exhalatory arteries (*aushauchenden Schlagadern*). It is a secretion from the arterial blood which shortly before had been exposed in the lungs to the action of

---

[1] Treviranus, *Biologie*, vol. iv, pp. 415–16.
[2] Ibid., pp. 293–4.

oxygen from the air.'[1] Treviranus (loc. cit., vol. iv, pp. 348–9) also remarks: 'Bones, flesh, and other animal parts which P. Smith introduced into the abdominal cavity or under the skin of live animals, were there completely decomposed (*Pfaffs und Scheels Nordisches Archiv für Naturkunde usw*, vol. iii, part 3, p. 134). This affords an explanation of a remarkable observation made by Cuvier on *Salpa octofora*. He found in the interior of many of these creatures, but outside of the stomach, parts of an *Anatifera* all of which, down to the outer skin, had decomposed and vanished and which presumably had entered through the orifice through which the *Salpas* take in water (*Annales du Muséum d'Histoire naturelle*, part iv, p. 380). These creatures have, indeed, a stomach. But perhaps they digest quite as well outside as inside it and form the transition to those organisms in which respiration, digestion, and several other functions take place through one and the same kind of organ.'

Spallanzani's experiments were aimed at finding an answer to the question whether digestion is effected by solvent juices or by trituration performed by the stomach muscles—or by both. To decide this, he administered food to turkeys, ducks, chickens, etc., in latticed or perforated metal tubes or spheres so that the gastric juice could reach it; since the grain was never digested but only became more bitter, he concluded that digestion results from the violent pressing and pushing of the walls of the stomach. Now since in these experiments the hardest bodies like metal tubes and glass balls, even pointed and cutting objects, were triturated by the stomachs of these creatures, it was believed that the many small stones, as many as two hundred even, which are often found in the stomachs of such animals help to triturate the food. Now to refute this hypothesis, Spallanzani took young pigeons which could not yet have swallowed any stones from their parents' beaks; he also saw to it that their food contained none, and shut them up to prevent them from looking for any: and yet even without the stones the birds were able to digest food. 'I began to mix hard objects with their food, some iron tubes, glass balls, small bits of glass; and although not a single small stone had been found in the stomachs of these pigeons, yet the metal tubes were worn away, and the glass balls and bits of glass broken up and rubbed smooth without leaving the slightest trace of injury to the walls of the stomach.'[2]

Drinks in particular are digested in two different ways. Drink exudes through the walls of the stomach and the cellular tissue to the urinary vessels and is excreted through them. There is a fund of experience on this subject. Beer is a diuretic. Asparagus imparts a special odour to the urine only a few minutes after ingestion; this is the effect of immediate assimilation by the cellular tissue. Afterwards the smell passes off and

[1] Autenrieth, loc. cit., part ii, §§ 597–8.
[2] *Expériences sur la digestion de l'homme et de différentes espèces d'animaux, par l'abbé Spallanzani* (par Jean Senebier, Geneva, 1783) pp. 1–27.

does not reappear until eight to twelve hours later when digestion proper and the discharge of excrements is completed. Another instance of this immediate assimilation is that cited by Treviranus (loc. cit., vol. iv, p. 404): 'Of five ounces of water injected into a dog, two were vomited: one was still left in the stomach, so that two must have found an exit though the walls of the stomach.' The greater the homogeneity of the food, e.g., meat dishes, the easier is immediate assimilation. Animal lymph, as the universal element of animality, is that into which the non-organic is directly transformed. The animal digests the food from outside just as well as it digests its own viscera, muscles, nerves, etc., even absorbing bones, which are phosphate of lime, e.g. bone-splinters in a fracture. It destroys the specific particularity of these products and turns them into the general lymph, into blood; and this it specifies again into particular products.

The other form of digestion involves mediation and this occurs only in more highly organized animals. Its proximate moments are also, of course, actions of the organism against the outer world; but it is no longer a general but a particular operation of particular animal products like the bile, pancreatic juice, etc. However, this mediatory activity is not merely a passing through the organism like, e.g., the passage through the four stomachs in ruminants: nor does it consist of distinct operations and changes, of various stages of organic cooking (*Kochung*) which the food passes through as if it had been softened and seasoned (*gewürzt*); nor is it an alteration as the action of one specific substance on another. For in that case the relationship would only be chemical and the effect nothing more than a neutralization. The most that chemical researches on gastric juice and bile have been able to demonstrate is that the chyme in the stomach is made slightly acid (not putrid, rather resisting putrefaction) and that the acidity is removed by the bile. When the bile is mixed with chyme, 'a white precipitate like a thick slime is formed' which is no longer acid although milk curdles in the stomach.[1] But even this is not quite certain, nor is it the specific point; for if the precipitate were freed from acidity, it would be the same as before. The bile is thus opposed to the pancreatic juice which comes from the great gland, below the stomach, the pancreas, and which, in the higher animals, takes the place of the lymph in the glands without being essentially different from it.

Now the whole process of digestion consists in this, that the organism in angrily opposing itself to the outer world is divided within itself. The final product of digestion is chyle; and this is the same as the animal lymph into which the animal organism, in its immediate operation, transforms what is offered to it, or what it offers to itself. Just as in the lower animals immediate assimilation prevails, so in animals with a developed organization, digestion consists in the organism relating itself

[1] Treviranus, *Biologie*, vol. iv, pp. 467–9.

to the outer world, not through its immediate, but its specific, activity. Now the process is not very complicated: first, the food is mixed with saliva, with the general animality; in the stomach the pancreatic juice is added and lastly, the bile, which plays the chief part and has a resinous, inflammable nature. Chemical analysis of the bile yields nothing more specific than that its tendency is to inflame. We know besides that in anger, bile flows into the stomach; and the connection between bile, stomach, and liver is therefore a familiar fact. A physiology which investigated such connections would be very interesting: e.g. why shame is accompanied by blushing of the face and bosom. Just as anger is the feeling of being-for-self which flares up in a person when he is insulted, so bile is the being-for-self which the animal organism turns against this 'potency' (*Potenz*) placed in it from outside; for the pancreatic juice and the bile attack the chyme. This active destruction, this turning in on itself of the organism which the bile is, originates in the spleen, an organ which presents difficulties for physiologists; it is this sluggish organ belonging to the venous system and connected with the liver, whose sole function seems to be to bring the inertia of the venous system to a focus in opposition to the lungs. Now this sluggish being-within-self which has its seat in the spleen, when ignited (*befeuert*) is the bile. As soon as animals acquire a developed nature and do not merely have an immediate digestion or remain simply at the lymphatic stage, they have both liver and bile.

The main point, however, is that the organism, although exercising a mediating, distinctive activity, none the less remains in its universality, while at the same time its outward-turned action is chemical: just as crystals when fractured reveal their characteristic inner formation as a particular mode of their existence. The animal, because it behaves as actively different, in so doing becomes different *within itself*. In other words, because the animal is involved in a struggle with the outer world, its relation to the latter is untrue, since this outer world has already been transformed in principle (*an sich*) by the power of the animal lymph; the animal therefore in turning against this food, fails to recognize its own self. But the immediate result of this is simply that when the animal comes to itself and recognizes itself as this power, it is angry with itself for getting involved with external powers and it now turns against itself and its false opinion; but in doing so it throws off its outward-turned activity and returns into itself. The triumph over the non-organic 'potency' is not a triumph over it *qua* non-organic 'potency', but a triumph over animal nature itself. The true externality of animal nature is not the external thing, but the fact that the animal itself turns in anger against what is external. The subject must rid itself of this lack of self-confidence which makes the struggle with the object appear as the subject's own action, and must repudiate this false attitude. Through its struggle with the outer thing, the organism is on the point of being at a disadvantage; it compromises its dignity in face of this non-organic being. What the organism has to conquer, is, therefore, this its own process, this entanglement with the outer thing. Consequently its activity is directed against the direction outwards, and is the means to which the organism lowers itself in order that, by repudiating and rejecting that means, it can return into itself. If the organism were actively hostile to the non-organic, it would not come into its own, for the organism is precisely the mediation which consists in involving itself with the non-organic and yet returning into itself. This negation of the outward-turned activity has this double determination: first, of the repudiation by the organism of its hostile activity towards the non-organic, and the positing of itself as immediately self-identical, but secondly, of reproducing itself in this self-preservation.

The Notion of digestion, therefore, is that after its mediating process has merely explicated what already exists in principle (*an sich*)—the triumph over the food which has entered the atmosphere (*Dunstkreis*) of the living animal—the organism, returning into itself out of the opposition, now concludes by laying hold of (comprehending) itself; the phenomena corresponding to this Notion have already been mentioned (p. 402). Through this process of assimilation, therefore, the animal becomes in a real way *for itself*; for by particularizing itself into the main differences of animal lymph and bile in its behaviour towards the individual thing itself it has proved itself to be an animal individual; and by the negation of its other, it has posited itself as subjectivity, as real being-for-self. The animal having now become, in a real way, for itself, i.e. individual, this self-relation is immediately a diremption and division of itself, and the organism in constituting itself a subjectivity is immediately a repelling of itself from itself. Thus the differentiation does not take place only within the organism itself; on the contrary, the nature of the organism is to produce itself as something external to itself. Like the plant which, in its differentiation, breaks up into parts, the animal, too, differentiates itself but with this difference, that the self-subsistent being from which the animal distinguishes itself is posited not merely as something external, but also as identical with the animal. This real production in which the animal, in repelling itself duplicates itself, is the final stage of animality as such. This real process has in its turn three forms: (α) the form of abstract, formal repulsion, (β) the constructive instinct, and (γ) the propagation of the species. These three seemingly heterogeneous processes are essentially connected with one another in Nature. In many animals the organs of excretion and the genitals, the highest and lowest parts in the animal organization, are intimately connected: just as speech and kissing, on the one hand, and eating, drinking and spitting, on the other, are all done with the mouth.†

The animal's abstract repulsion of itself by which it makes itself external to itself is excretion, the conclusion of the process of assimilation.

† Cf. *Phänomenologie d. Geistes*, p. 254 (Hoffmeister's edition). (Baillie's translation, p. 372.)

Since it only makes itself into an external thing, this latter is [for the animal] something non-organic, an abstract other in which the animal is not identical with itself. The organism in thus separating itself from itself is disgusted with itself for not having more self-confidence; this is what it does when it abandons the struggle, rids itself of the bile which it has discharged. Excrement has, therefore, no other significance than this, that the organism recognizing its error, gets rid of its entanglement with outside things; and this is confirmed by the chemical composition of the excrement. Usually, the moment of excretion is regarded only as the rejection by the organism of useless and unusable material; but the animal did not need to ingest anything useless or superfluous. And even if indigestible material is contained in excrement, the latter consists mainly of digested matter or what the organism itself has added to the ingested material, namely, the bile, whose function it is to mingle itself with the food. 'The healthier the animal and the more digestible the food consumed, the smaller the amount of undecomposed food evacuated through the rectum and the more homogeneous is the excrement. Yet even in the healthiest animals the excrement always contains a fibrous residue of the ingested food. But the principal ingredients of the excrement are substances originating in the gastric juices, especially in the bile. Berzelius found in human excrement undecomposed bile, albumen, biliary gum (*Gallenharz*) and two peculiar substances, one of which looked like glue: the other substance is formed from the biliary gum and biliary albumen only in contact with the air. The human body evacuates through the rectum: bile, albumen, two peculiar animal substances, biliary matter (*Gallenstoff*), sodium carbonate, sodium chloride and sodium phosphate, phosphate of magnesia, and phosphate of lime; and through the urinary organs: mucus, lactic acid, uric acid, benzoic acid, sodium chloride, ammonium chloride, phosphate of lime, and fluorated lime, etc. All these substances are not merely heterogeneous, inassimilable matter; they are the same ingredients of which the animal organs consist. The constituents of the urine are met with again mainly in the bones. Many of these substances also enter into the composition of the hair, others into that of the muscles and brain. A cursory examination of these facts seems to lead to the conclusion that in digestion, a larger quantity of matter is assimilated than the organs to be nourished by it are able to appropriate, and that it is this unchanged surplus which is evacuated by the excretory organs. Closer investigation, however, reveals disparities between the constituents of the food, the assimilated material, and the substances excreted, which render this assumption untenable.' What follows certainly shows disparities between the food and the assimilated material but not so much between the assimilated material and the substances excreted. 'These disparities are particularly evident in phosphoric acid and lime. Fourcroy and Vauquelin found more calcium phosphate in horse-dung and more calcium carbonate and calcium phosphate in bird-excrement, than could be extracted from the food. On the other hand, in birds a certain quantity of silica in the food disappears. The same perhaps might be found true of sulphur' which is also found in the excrement. 'Sodium, however, is also found in the bodies of herbivorous animals whose food does not contain any significant quantity of this salt. On the other hand, the urine of lions and tigers contains in place of sodium (*Natron*) a large quantity of potassium. So it is more than likely that generally in all living organisms decompositions and combinations occur which exceed the powers of chemical agents *hitherto known*.'[1] And so, in spite of all the evidence, these processes are supposed to be chemical and nothing more! But in truth, the activity of the organism is purposive; for it consists precisely in discarding the means after the end has been attained. Bile, pancreatic juice, etc., are therefore nothing else but the organism's own process which it gets rid of in material shape. The result of the process is satiation, the self-feeling which feels completeness in place of the previous lack. The Understanding will always hold to the mediations as such, regarding them as external relationships mechanical and chemical in nature; but they are none the less subordinate in comparison with free vitality and self-feeling. The Understanding pretends to know more than speculative philosophy and loftily looks down on it; but it remains confined within the sphere of finite mediation, and vitality as such is beyond its grasp.

3. *The Constructive Instinct*

The constructive instinct is not to be understood here as it is by Blumenbach, who means by it principally reproduction. The artistic impulse as instinct is the third phase—the unity of the ideal theoretical process and the real process of digestion: but in the first instance it is only the relative totality, since the veritable, interior totality is the third phase in the whole, the generic process. Here, an external object, something belonging to the animal's non-organic nature, is assimilated: but in such a manner that at the same time it is also left to remain as an external object. Thus the constructive instinct, too, like excretion, is a self-externalization, but as a building of the form of the organism into the outside world. The object is shaped in a way in which it can satisfy the animal's subjective need; but here there is not a mere hostile relationship of appetite to the outside world, but a peaceful attitude to outer existence. Appetite is thus at the same time satisfied and restrained; and the organism objectifies itself only by disposing of inorganic matter for its own purposes. Here, then, the practical and theoretical relationships are united. The instinct can be satisfied by the form, without doing away with the object; but this is only one side of the constructive instinct. The other side is that the animal

---

[1] Treviranus, *Biologie*, vol. iv, pp. 480-2; 614-28.

excretes products of its own activity, but not out of disgust, not to get rid of them; on the contrary, the externalized excrement is fashioned by the creature to satisfy its need.

This artistic instinct appears as a purposive action, as wisdom of Nature; and it is this category of purposiveness which makes instinct difficult to comprehend. It has always appeared a most remarkable phenomenon because it has been customary to grasp rationality only as external purposiveness and to contemplate vital phenomena in general merely from the standpoint of sense-perception. The constructive instinct is in fact *analogous* to the Understanding as a self-conscious entity; but one must not therefore, in thinking of purposive action in Nature, think of self-conscious Understanding. Not a step can be made in the contemplation of Nature if what an end is has not been comprehended; for an end is precisely that which is predetermined, is active, enters into relationship with an other in which it preserves itself by assimilating it. The Notion is the connection of these moments: a fashioning of the external object or of the secretions which have a connection with the creature's need. But as artistic impulse, this Notion is only the inner in-itself of the animal, only the unconscious overseer (*Werkmeister*); it is only in Thought, in the human artist, that the Notion is for itself. Cuvier therefore says that the higher the forms of animal life, the less instinct they have; the insects have most. In accordance with this inner Notion everything is a means, i.e. is connected with a unity; so that the unity (here the living being) would not exist without this means (*Ding*), which is at the same time only a moment in the whole, a sublated moment, not something independent, in and for itself: just as the sun even is a means for the earth, or each line in the crystal is a means for its immanent form. The living being has this higher nature, to be the activity which fashions the things outside of it, at the same time leaving them in their externality because, simply as purposive means, they have a connection with the Notion.

The first form of the artistic impulse which we have already touched on is the instinctive building of nests, lairs, shelters, in order to make the general totality of the animal's environment, even though only in respect of form, its own (see above, § 362): and then the migration of birds and fishes as expressing their feeling of climate, the collection and storage of food for the winter, so that what the animal will eat later on already belongs to its habitat (see above, § 361). Animals thus have relationships with the ground on which they lie, which they want to make more comfortable; in the satisfaction of this need to lie down, the thing, unlike food, is not used up but is merely fashioned and so preserved. True, food too is fashioned but it completely disappears. This theoretical side of the constructive instinct which entails a check on appetite is lacking in plants which, unlike animals, cannot restrain their impulses because they have no sensation, no theoretical relationships.

The other side of the artistic impulse is that many animals have first to prepare their weapons, e.g. the spider its web, as a means of catching their food: just as other animals with their claws and feet, or the polyp with its tentacles, extend the range within which they feel and seize their prey. Such animals which arm themselves with weapons they have elaborated out of themselves, excrete these from themselves—productions of the animals themselves which separate themselves from the animal and are also separated by the animals from themselves. 'In crabs and branchiopods, caecal appendages (*villi*) in the intestinal canal take the place of liver and pancreas and generally of the entire apparatus of glandular organs which, in the higher classes of animals, promote digestion and nutrition.' (The oesophagus, stomach, intestinal canal, is one long tube: it is however, 'divided by contractions and sphincter muscles into several sections of varying length, width and texture.) In insects, not only does the same thing occur, but here there is no trace whatever even of glands. Such' (interior) 'intestinal-like blind sacs provide in spiders the material for webs, and in caterpillars and leaf-insects the substance for the cocoon,' for pupation: 'in the fork-tailed caterpillar they supply the juice which it squirts out when excited, and in the bee, the poison which comes from the sting of this insect. In addition, it is such sacs which in insects elaborate all the juices required for procreation. On both sides of the body in the male, there lies an organ (*Körper*) consisting of a very long but also very delicate and narrow coiled-up canal; and it is this organ which corresponds to the epididymus in mammals. From it another tube goes to the penis. In the female there is a double ovary, etc. The complete absence of genitals is peculiar to all insects in their larval state and to some, worker-bees for example, throughout their whole life.' The building of cells and the excretion of honey by these asexual bees is the sole mode by which they produce themselves: they are, as it were, sterile flowers which do not attain to propagation of the species. 'With regard to this point there is a remarkable law: among insects, all asexual individuals have, instead of genitals, certain other organs which supply a substance for making artificial products. The converse of this law, however, is not true: spiders, for example, construct their webs from a substance elaborated by their own organs but they are not therefore asexual.'[1] Caterpillars merely eat and excrete and have no external genitals; the next stage, the spinning of the cocoon round the pupa, pertains to the constructive instinct, and copulation is the function of the butterfly. 'There are some insects which retain throughout their whole life the same shape with which they emerge from the egg. These insects comprise all the species of the family of spiders and several species from the classes of woodlice and mites. All other members of this class undergo a partial or total metamorphosis during their life. Where metamorphosis is only partial, the larva is distinguished from the pupa, and the latter from the developed insect,

[1] Treviranus, *Biologie*, vol. i, pp. (364) 366–7; 369–70.

mostly only by the smaller number or slighter development of their organs. On the other hand, where there is total metamorphosis, the perfect insect no longer bears any trace of what it was in its larval state. The innumerable muscles of the larva have disappeared and quite different ones have taken their place; similarly head, heart, trachea, etc. have a completely different structure.'[1]

In the constructive instinct the creature has produced itself as an outer existence and yet remains the same immediate creature; here, then, it first attains to self-enjoyment, to the specific feeling of self. Previously it had only an enjoyment of external things, the immediate sensation was only an abstract being-within-self in which the creature felt only in what way it was determined. The animal *is* satisfied when its hunger and thirst are appeased; but so far, it *has not* satisfied *itself*, it is only now that it does this. In adapting its environment to its own needs, it is present to itself externally and enjoys itself. To the artistic impulse also belongs the voice, by which the creature gives itself form in the air, in this ideal subjectivity, and perceives itself in the outer world. Birds, especially, achieve this blithe self-enjoyment: with them, voice is not a mere declaration of a need, no mere cry; on the contrary, bird-song is the disinterested utterance whose ultimate determination is the immediate enjoyment of self.

§ 366

Through the process with external Nature, the animal endows its self-certainty, its subjective Notion, with truth and objectivity as a *single* individual. This *production* of itself is thus self-preservation or *reproduction*; but further, subjectivity has become *in principle* (*an sich*) a product, and at the same time is sublated as *immediate*. The Notion, thus united with its own self, is determined as *concrete universal, genus*, which enters into relationship and process with the singularity of subjectivity.

Zusatz. The satisfied appetite does not have the significance here of the individual producing itself as this singular, but as a universal, as ground of the individuality, for which it is only a form. It is therefore the universal which has returned to itself, in which individuality is immediately present. The theoretical return (of sense) into self produces only a lack in general, but in the case of the individuality the lack is a positive being. The individual which feels a lack is filled with its own self; it is a dual individual. The animal is at first restricted to itself; secondly, it produces

---

[1] Treviranus, loc. cit., vol. i, pp. 372–4.

itself at the expense of its inorganic nature by assimilating it. The third relationship, the union of both, is the genus-process in which the animal relates itself to itself, to one of its own kind; it relates itself to a living being as in the first process and, at the same time, as in the second process, to a being already confronting it.

C. THE PROCESS OF THE GENUS

§ 367

The genus is in an *implicit*, simple unity with the singularity of the subject whose concrete substance it is. But the universal is disjunction or judgement (*Urteil*), in order to issue from this its diremption as a *unity for itself*, give itself an existence as a *sub-jective* universality. This process of its closing with itself contains the negation of the merely inner universality of the genus, and also the negation of the merely immediate singularity in which the living being is still only a natural being; the negation of this singularity exhibited in the preceding process (§ 366) is only the first, immediate negation. In this process of the genus, the merely natural being only perishes, for, as such, it does not transcend the natural. But the moments of the process of the genus, since their basis is still not the subjective universal, still not a single subject, fall apart and exist as a plurality of particular processes which culminate, in one way or another, in the *death* of the creature.

Zusatz. The individual which has established itself through its self-feeling, has acquired solidity and, so to say, breadth; its immediate singularity is sublated and the individual no longer needs to be in rela-tionship with a non-organic nature. With the vanishing of its determination as an exclusive singularity, the Notion acquires the further determina-tion that the subject determines itself as a universal. This determination is again disjunctive (*urteilend*), again excludes what is other; but it has the determination of being identical for this other and existing for it as identical. Thus we have the genus, whose determination is to attain to an existence distinct from singularity; and this is the genus-process as such. True, the genus still does not attain to a free existence in the individual, not to universality; but even though it is here, on the one hand, still only immediately identical with the individual, yet, on the other hand, it has already attained to a differentiation of individual subjectivity from the genus. This difference is a process, the outcome of which is that the genus as universal comes to itself, and immediate singularity is negated. This extinction [of immediate singularity] is the death of the individual; with this, organic Nature ends, for with the death of the individual the genus comes to its own self and thus becomes its *own* object: this is the procession of spirit. This extinction of the singularity in the genus we have still to consider. But because the genus is related to the individual in a variety of ways, we have also to distinguish the particular processes, which are the different ways, in which the living creature meets its death. Thus the genus-process, in its turn, has three forms. The first is the sex-relation: what the genus brings forth is the procreation of individuals through the death of other individuals of the same genus; the individual, after reproducing itself as another individual, perishes. Secondly, the genus particularizes itself, divides itself into its species; and these species, behaving as mutually opposed individuals, are, at the same time, nonorganic nature as the genus against individuality—death by violence. The third form is the relation of the individual to itself as genus within a single subjectivity, either as a transitory disharmony in disease, or else ending with the preservation of the genus as such through the transition of the individual into existence as a universal; this is natural death.

1. *The Sex-Relation*

§ 368 (§ 369 in 3rd ed. of *Encyclopaedia*)

This first diremption of the genus into species and the further determination of these to the point of immediate, exclusive being-for-self of *singularity*, is only a negative and hostile attitude towards others. But the genus is also an essentially affirmative relation of the singularity to itself in it; so that while the latter, as an individual, excludes another individual, it continues itself in this *other* and in this *other* feels its own self. This relationship is a *process* which begins with a *need*; for the individual as a *singular* does not accord with the genus immanent in it, and yet at the same time is the identical self-relation of the genus in *one* unity; it thus has the *feeling* of this defect. The genus is therefore present in the individual as a straining against the inadequacy of its single actuality, as the urge to obtain its self-feeling in the other of its genus, to integrate itself through union with it and through this mediation to close the genus with itself and bring it into existence—*copulation*.

Zusatz. The process of the animal with its non-organic nature has made the ideality of the latter explicit, and the animal has thereby demonstrated in its own self its self-feeling and its objectivity. It is not merely an implicit self-feeling, but a self-feeling which exists and is alive. The division of the sexes is such that the extremes are totalities of self-feeling; the animal's instinct is to produce itself as a self-feeling, as totality. Now in the constructive instinct, the organic became a dead product, freely released, it is true, from the organism, but only a superficial form imposed on an external material, and this did not therefore confront itself as a free, indifferent subject: here, on the contrary, both sides are independent individuals as in the process of assimilation, but with this difference, that they are not related to each other as organic and non-organic beings; on the contrary, both are organisms and belong to the genus, so that they exist only as one species. Their union is the disappearance of the sexes into which the simple genus has developed. The animal has an object with which it feels itself immediately identical; this identity is the moment of the first process (of formation) which is added to the determination of the second (of assimilation). This attitude (*Verhalten*) of an individual to another of its kind is the substantial relation of the genus. The nature of each permeates both; and both exist within the sphere of this universality. The process consists in this, that they become in reality what they are in themselves, namely, one genus, the same subjective vitality. Here, the Idea of Nature is actual in the male and female couple; their identity, and their being-for-self, which up till now were only for us in our reflection, are now, in the infinite reflection into self of the two sexes, felt by themselves. This feeling of universality is the highest to which the animal can attain; but its concrete universality never becomes for it a theoretical object of intuition: else it would be Thought, Consciousness, in which alone the genus attains a free existence. The contradiction is, therefore, that the universality of the genus, the identity of individuals, is distinct from their particular individuality; the individual is only one of two, and does not exist as unity but only as a singular. The activity of the animal is to sublate this difference. The genus, as the foundation, is one extreme of the syllogism, for every process has the form of the syllogism. The genus is the impelling subjectivity into which is placed the vitality which wants to produce itself. The mediation, the middle term of the syllogism, is the tension between this essential nature of the individuals and the incongruity of their single actuality; and it is this which impels them to have their self-feeling only in the other. The genus, in giving itself actuality, which, because it has the form of immediate existence is, of course, only a single actuality, closes itself with the other extreme, that of singularity.

The *formation of the differentiated sexes* must be different, their determinateness against each other must exist as posited by the Notion, because, as differentiated moments (*Differente*), they are an urge (*Trieb*). But the two sides are not merely, as in the chemical sphere, implicitly neutral; on the contrary, on account of the original identity of formation, the same type underlies both the *male and female genitals*, only that in one or the other, one or the other part predominates: in the female, it is necessarily the passive moment (*das Indifferente*), in the male, the moment of duality (*das Entzweite*), of opposition. This identity is most striking in the lower animals: 'In some grasshoppers (e.g. *Gryllus verruccivorus*) the large testicles, composed of vessels rolled together in bundles, resemble the ovaries which are equally large and composed of bundles of similarly rolled-up oviducts. Also in the male horse-fly, not only does the outline of the testicles present the same shape as the thicker (*gröbere*) larger ovaries, but they, too, consist of almost oval, elliptical, delicate vesicles which, with their base, stand up on the substance of the testicles like ova on an ovary.'[1] The greatest difficulty has been experienced in discovering the female uterus in the male genitals. The scrotum has ineptly been mistaken for it,[2] simply because the testicles present a definite correspondence to the female ovary. But it is rather the prostate in the male which corresponds to the female uterus; in the male, the uterus is reduced to a gland, to an indifferent generality. This has been very well demonstrated by Ackermann in his hermaphrodite, which has a uterus as well as other, male, organs (*Formationen*); but this uterus not only occupies the place of the prostate, but the ejaculatory ducts also pass through its substance and open into the *crista galli* in the urethra. Also, the female *labia pudendi* are shrunken scrota: consequently, in Ackermann's hermaphrodite, the *labia pudendi* were filled with a kind of testicular secretion. Lastly, the medial line of the scrotum is split in the female and forms the vagina. In this way, a complete understanding is obtained of the conversion of one sex into the other. Just as in the male, the uterus is reduced to a mere gland, so, on the other hand, the male testicle remains enclosed in the ovary in the female, does not emerge into opposition, does not develop on its own account into active brain; and the clitoris is inactive feeling in general. In the male, on the other hand, we have instead active feeling, the swelling heart, the effusion of blood into the *corpora cavernosa* and the meshes of the spongy tissue of the urethra; to this male effusion of blood correspond the female menses. In this way, the reception (*Empfangen*) by the uterus, as a simple retention, is, in the male, split into the productive brain and the external heart. Through this difference, therefore, the male is the active principle, and the female is the receptive, because she remains in her undeveloped unity.

Procreation must not be reduced to the ovary and the male semen, as if the new product were merely a composition of the forms or parts of both sides; the truth is that the female contains the material element, but the male contains the subjectivity. *Conception* is the contraction of the whole individual into the simple, self-surrendering unity, into its representation (*Vorstellung*); the seed is this simple representation itself—simply a

[1] Schubert, *Ahnungen einer allgemeinen Geschichte des Lebens*, part i, p. 185.
[2] Ibid., p. 205–6.

single point, like the name and the entire self. Conception, therefore, is nothing else but this, that the opposite moments, these abstract representations, become one.

§ 369 (§ 370 in 3rd ed. of *Encyclopaedia*)

The *product* is the *negative identity* of the differentiated individuals and is, as *realized* (*gewordene*) *genus*, an asexual life. But on its *natural* side, this product is only *in principle* (*an sich*) this genus, distinct from the individuals whose difference [from one another] has perished in it and is itself an immediate *singular*, destined to develop into the same natural individuality, into the same difference and perishable existence. This process of propagation spends itself in the spurious infinite progress. The genus preserves itself only through the destruction of the individuals who, in the process of generation, fulfil their destiny and, in so far as they have no higher destiny, in this process meet their death.

Zusatz. Thus the animal organism has run through its cycle and is now the asexual and fecund universal; it has become the absolute genus which, however, is the death of this individual. The lower animal organisms, e.g. butterflies, die, therefore, immediately after copulation; for they have sublated their singularity in the genus and their singularity is their life. Higher organisms survive the generative act since they possess a higher kind of independence; and their death is the culmination of the process in their structure, which we shall come across later as disease. The genus, which produces itself through negation of its differences, does not, however, exist in and for itself but only in a series of single living beings: and thus the sublation of the contradiction is always the beginning of a fresh one. In the genus-process the separate individual creatures perish; for they are distinct only outside of this unity of the process, which is the true actuality. Love, on the other hand, is the feeling in which the self-seeking of the individual and its separated existence is negated, and the individual form (*Gestalt*) therefore perishes and cannot preserve itself. For only that preserves itself which, as absolute, is self-identical; and that is the universal which is for the universal. But in the animal, the genus does not exist as such but only in principle (*an sich*); it is only in spirit that it exists in and for itself in its eternity. The transition to the existent genus takes place in principle (*an sich*), in the Idea, in the Notion, that is to say, in the eternal creation; but there the sphere of Nature is closed.

§ 370 (§ 368 in 3rd ed. of *Encyclopaedia*)

2. *Genus and Species*

The genus, in its implicit universality, *particularizes* itself at first simply into *species*. At the base of the *different forms* and *classes* of animals is the universal *type of the Animal*, determined by the Notion, Nature exhibits this type, partly in the various *stages of its development* from the simplest organization to the most perfect, in which it is the instrument of spirit, and partly in the various *circumstances* and *conditions* of *elemental Nature*. An animal species, developed to the point of singularity, distinguishes itself from others in and through its own self, and through the negation of them is *for itself*. The natural fate of the individuals in this hostile relationship, in which others are reduced to an inorganic nature, is a *violent* death.

Remark

Zoology, like the natural sciences generally, has concerned itself mainly with the search for sure and simple *signs* of classes, orders, etc., of animals for the purpose of a subjective recognition of them. Only since giving up this attempt to construct so-called artificial systems for classifying animals has the way been opened for a more comprehensive view directed to the *objective nature* of the organisms themselves. Of the empirical sciences, hardly one has in recent times expanded as much as zoology through its auxiliary science of *comparative anatomy*: an expansion not mainly in the sense of accumulated observations—for none of the sciences has lacked these—but in the sense of an arranging of its material to conform to the Notion [of the animal]. Just as the ingenious approach to Nature—especially of the French naturalists—has adopted the division of plants into monocotyledons and dicotyledons, so, too, it has adopted the *fundamental distinction* in the animal world made by the absence or presence of a *backbone*; in this way, the *fundamental classification* of animals has been reduced in its essentials to that which had already been perceived by Aristotle.

In addition, the habit (*habitus*) of individual animals, as a coherent whole determining the construction of *every part*, has been made the main point, so that Cuvier, the great founder of comparative anatomy, could boast that from a single bone, he could learn the essential nature of the whole animal. Also the general type of the animal has been traced in the most imperfect and disparate forms and recognized in the barest suggestions; and in the intermixture of organs and functions, too, their significance has been recognized, so that in this way the animal has been raised above and out of its particularity into its universality.

A cardinal feature of this method of treatment is the recognition of how Nature shapes and adapts this organism to the particular element in which it is placed, to climate, to a particular form of food, in general, to the environment into which it is born, an environment which can also be one particular species of plant or another species of animal (see § 361, *Zusatz*). But for the special determination, a correct instinct has hit upon taking the distinguishing characteristics of the species also from the *teeth*, *claws*, and the like, i.e. from the animal's *weapons*; for it is through these that the animal itself establishes and preserves itself as an independent existence, that is, distinguishes itself from others.

It is on account of the *immediacy* of the Idea of life that the Notion does not *exist* as such in life, and its existence is therefore subjected to the manifold conditions and circumstances of external Nature, and can appear in the most inadequate forms. The fecundity of the Earth causes life to break forth *everywhere* and in every way. Almost less even than the other spheres of Nature, can the animal world exhibit within itself an independent, rational system of organization, or hold fast to the forms prescribed by the Notion, preserving them, in face of the imperfection and medley of conditions, from confusion, degeneration, and transitional forms. This impotence of the Notion in Nature generally, subjects not only the development of individuals to external contingencies—the developed animal (and especially man) can exhibit monstrosities—but even the genera are completely subject to the changes of the external, universal life of Nature, the vicissitudes of which are shared by the life of the animal (cf. Remark, § 392), whose life, consequently, is only an alternation of health and disease. The environment of external contingency contains factors which are almost wholly alien; it exercises a perpetual violence and threat of dangers on the animals' feeling which is an *insecure, anxious,* and *unhappy* one.

Zusatz. The animal, *qua* a *natural* life, is still essentially an immediate existence, and therefore is determinate, finite, and particular. Life (*Lebendigkeit*), tied to the infinitely many particularizations of inorganic and vegetable Nature, exists always as a limited species; and these limitations the living creature cannot overcome. The particular character does not have for its determination the universality of existence (that would be Thought); on the contrary, the animal in its relationship to Nature attains only to particularity. Life, which receives these powers of Nature (*Naturpotenzen*) into itself, is capable of the most diverse modifications of its structure (*Bildung*); it can adapt itself to every condition and still pulsate among them, although the universal powers of Nature (*Naturmächte*) always retain their complete mastery.

In studying the classification of animals, the method followed is to search for a common feature to which the concrete forms (*Gebilde*) can be reduced, that is, to a simple, sensuous determinateness which, therefore, is also an external one. But there are no such simple determinations. For example, if we take the general concept 'fish' as the common feature of what this name connotes in our concept, and ask, 'What is the simple determinateness in fish, their one objective property?', the answer, 'Swimming in water', is insufficient, since a number of land animals do this, too. Besides, swimming is not an organ or a structure, and in general, is not any specific part of the shape of any fish, but a mode of their activity. A universal of this kind, like fish, simply as a universal, is not linked to any particular mode of its external existence. Now the assumption that there must definitely exist such a common feature in a simple determinateness, fins, for example, which yet cannot be found, makes the work of classification difficult. This is based on the kind and manner of the individual genera and species, and laid down as a rule; but the variety and profusion of living forms does not admit of any general feature. Consequently, the infinity of forms of animal life is not to be rigidly conceived as if they conformed absolutely to a necessary principle of classification. On the contrary, therefore, it is the general determinations which must be made the rule and natural forms compared with it. If they do not tally with it but exhibit certain correspondences, if they agree with it in one respect but not in another, then it is not the rule, the characteristic of the genus or class, etc., which is to be altered, as if this had to conform to these existences, but, conversely, it is the latter which ought to conform to the rule; and in so far as this actual existence does not do so, the defect belongs to *it*. Some amphibians, for example, are viviparous—and breathe with lungs like mammals and birds; but, like fishes, they have no breasts and a heart with a single ventricle. If we admit that the works of man are sometimes defective, then the works of Nature must contain still more imperfections, for Nature is the Idea in the guise of externality. In man, the source of these imperfections lies in his whims, his caprice and negligence: e.g. when he brings painting into music, or paints with stones in mosaic, or when epic poetry is introduced into drama. In Nature, it is external conditions which distort the forms of living creatures; but these conditions produce these effects because life is indeterminate and receives its particular determinations also from these externalities. The forms of Nature, therefore, cannot be brought into an absolute system, and this implies that the species of animals are exposed to contingency.

The other side to this is that the Notion, of course, also exerts its influence, but only to a certain degree. There is only one animal type (§ 352, *Zusatz*, p. 356) and all the varieties are merely modifications of it. The principal varieties have for basis the same determinations which we saw earlier in inorganic Nature as the Elements. These grades, then, are also grades of the development of the animal type as such; so that the grades of animal species can be recognized in those determinations. There are thus two distinct principles which determine the difference between the classes of animals. One principle of classification, and this is closer to the Idea, is that the later grade is only a further development of the one type of animal; the other is that the scale of development of the organic type is essentially connected with the Elements into which the forms of animal life are cast. Such a connection, however, exists only in the more highly developed forms of animal life; the lower forms have little relation to the Elements and are indifferent to these great differences. Apart from these chief moments in the grouping of the classes of animals, there are distinctions connected with the climatic factor: we have already remarked (§ 339, *Zusatz*, p. 284) that because in the northern hemisphere the continents are more compact, plant and animal life there are not so varied (*mehr verbunden*); whereas the further south one goes in Africa and America, where the continents divide, the greater is the variety of animal species. While climatic differences thus determine the animal, man lives everywhere; but here, too, Eskimos and other extreme types differ from the types in the temperate zone. But still more is the animal subject to such [climatic] determinations and localities, to mountains, forests, plains, etc. One must not therefore seek notional determinations everywhere, although traces of them are everywhere present.

In the scale of development formed by genera and species, one can begin with the undeveloped animals in which the differences do not as yet exist definitely in the three systems of sensibility, irritability and reproduction. Then man, as the most perfect living organism, is the highest stage of development. In recent zoology especially, this form of classification according to the grades of development, has held the field; for it is natural to progress from the undeveloped to the higher organism. But in order to understand the lower grades, one must know the developed organism, since it is the standard or archetype (*Urtier*) for the less developed animal; for in the developed animal, every function has attained to a developed existence, and it is therefore clear that it is only from this animal that undeveloped organisms can be understood. The infusoria cannot form the basis, for in this torpid life the rudiments of organic life are still so feeble that they can only be grasped by reference to more developed animal forms. But to say that the animal is more perfect than man, is inept. In one or other respects, the animal can, indeed, be better developed; but perfection consists precisely in the harmony of the organism. The universal type which forms the basis, cannot, of course, as such exist; but the universal, because it *exists*, exists in a *particular form* (*Particularität*). Similarly, perfect beauty in art must always be individualized. It is only in spirit that the universal, as ideal (*Ideal*) or Idea, exists as universal.

We have now to see how the organism is determined in these particular forms. The organism is alive and its viscera are determined by the Notion; but then it also develops entirely in accordance with this particularity. This particular determination permeates every part of the structure and harmonizes the parts with one another. This harmony is present mainly in the limbs (not the viscera); for particularity is precisely the tendency outwards, towards a specific inorganic nature. But the higher and more developed the animal is, the more marked is the thoroughness of the particularization. Now Cuvier has developed this side, to which he was led by his studies of fossil bones; for in order to find out to what animal they belonged, he had to study their formation. He was thus led to consider the appropriateness of the individual members in relation to one another. He says in his *Discours préliminaire* to the *Recherches sur les ossements fossiles des quadrupèdes* (Paris, 1812, pp. 58 et seq.): 'Every organized creature forms a whole, a *unified* and closed system, all the parts of which mutually correspond, and by reciprocal action on one another contribute to the same purposive activity. None of these parts can alter without the others altering too; and consequently each of them, taken on its own, suggests and gives all the others.

'If, therefore, the viscera of an animal are so organized that they can digest only raw meat, then the jawbones, too, must be adapted for swallowing the prey, the claws for seizing and tearing flesh, the teeth for biting it off and chewing it up. In addition, the whole system of the motor organs must be adapted for pursuing and securing the prey: and the eyes, too, for seeing it at a distance. Nature must even have implanted in the brain of the animal the necessary instinct to conceal itself and to ensnare its victims. These are the general conditions of the *carnivora*; each carnivore must, without fail, combine these within itself. But particular conditions like the size, kind, and haunt of the prey, also result from particular circumstances within the general forms; so that not only the class, but also the order, the genus, and even the species, is expressed in the form of each part.

'In fact, in order that the jawbone can seize the prey, the condyle'—

the organ which moves the jawbone and to which the muscles are attached —'must have a particular shape. The temporal muscles must possess a certain bulk, and this requires a certain hollowing of the bone in which they are inserted and of the process of the cheek-bone (*arcade zygomatique*) under which they pass. This latter must also have a certain strength in order to afford sufficient support to the masticatory muscle (*masseter*).'

The same principle applies throughout the entire organism: 'In order that the animal can carry away its prey, the muscles which lift the head' (the neck muscles) 'must have a certain strength; this in turn affects the form of the dorsal vertebra to which the muscles are attached, and the form of the occiput in which they are inserted. The teeth must be sharp in order that they can cut flesh and must have a solid base so that bones can be crushed. The claws must have a certain mobility'—accordingly their muscles and bones must be developed; similarly with the feet, etc.

This harmony, however, also leads on to correspondences which have an inner connection of a different kind, a connection which is not always so easy to recognize: 'We quite see, e.g., that the ungulata must be *herbivorous* since they have no claws for seizing prey. We also see that, because their forefeet can only be used to support their bodies, they do not require such large shoulder-blades. Their herbivorous diet will demand teeth with a flat crown for grinding grain and herbage. Grinding requires that this crown shall make horizontal movements, therefore the condyle of the jawbone must not be such a tight hinge as in the carnivora.' Treviranus says (loc. cit., vol. i, pp. 198–9): 'In the lower jawbone of horned animals, there are usually eight incisors; the upper jawbone, on the other hand, instead of incisors, has a cartilaginous pad. Most of them lack canines; in all of them the molars are grooved by serrated, transverse furrows, and their crowns do not lie horizontally but are notched obliquely, in such a way that in the molars of the upper jaw it is the outer side which is highest, but in those of the lower jaw it is the inner side, that which is turned towards the tongue.'

The following observations of Cuvier also present no difficulties: 'It is fitting that those species with less perfect teeth should have a more complex digestive system'; such are the *ruminants*, which require a more complex system mainly because herbivorous food is itself harder to digest. 'But I doubt whether anyone who had not learned by observation would have guessed that all ruminants have cloven hoofs: that therefore the dental system is more perfect in the ungulata which are not ruminants, than in cloven-hoofed animals, that is in ruminants. It is noticeable, too, that the development of the teeth is in thorough-going sympathy with the greater development in the osteology of the feet.' According to Treviranus (ibid., vol. i, p. 200), most horned animals lack fibulas (Coiter: *De quadrupedum sceletis*, ch. 2; Camper's *Natural History of the Orangutang*, p. 103). Cuvier continues the passage quoted as follows: 'It is impossible to give the reasons for these connections; but that they are not accidental is evident from the fact that whenever an animal with cloven hoofs shows an approach to the non-ruminants in the arrangement of its teeth, it also shows it in the arrangement of its feet. Camels, for example, which have eye-teeth (canines) and even two or four incisors in the upper jawbone, have an extra bone in the tarsus' in comparison with other animals with a less developed dental system. Similarly in children, teething, the ability to walk and also to talk, all develop simultaneously, namely, in the second year.

The particularity of the determination brings, therefore, a harmony into all the parts of the animal: 'The smallest facet of bone, the least apophysis, has a specific character in relation to the class, order, genus, and species, to which it belongs; so that if one has only a well-preserved splinter of bone, it is possible with the aid of analogy and comparison to determine everything else with the same certainty as if one possessed the entire animal'—*ex ungue leonem*, as the proverb says. 'I have tried out this method many times on parts of known animals before putting my whole trust in it for fossils; but I have always had such infallible success that I no longer have the slightest doubt of the certainty of the results it has yielded me.'

But although there is a universal type underlying the various species of animals, a type which Nature works out in them in such a way that the result conforms to the particularity of the species, we must not think that everything found in the animal serves a purpose. In many animals, we find rudiments of organs which belong only to the universal type, not to the particularity of these animals, and which therefore have not been developed because the particularity of these animals does not need them; consequently, too, it is only the higher organisms, not these lower ones, that can afford an explanation of such rudiments. For example, reptiles, snakes, fish, show rudimentary feet which have no meaning, and the whale has undeveloped teeth which serve no purpose, being merely rudimentary teeth concealed in the jawbones. Conversely, in man, there are some organs which are only necessary in the lower animals: he has, e.g., a gland in his neck, the so-called thyroid gland, the function of which is not understood but which is really obliterated and past; but in the foetus in the womb, and still more in the lower species of animals, this organ is active.

Now further consideration of the scale of development which provides the basis for the general classification of animals shows that, as the animal is both an unmediated production of itself (in its internal organization) and a production mediated by its inorganic nature (in its articulation connecting it with the outer world), therefore the distinction between the forms of the animal world is that either these two essential sides are in equilibrium, or else that the animal exists more in accordance with one side than with the other—so that while one side is more developed, the other plays a subordinate part. It is this one-sidedness which makes one animal stand lower in the scale than another, although in no animal can one side be completely lacking. In man, who is the fundamental type of organism, since he is the instrument of spirit, all sides attain their most perfect development.

The ancient classification of animals belongs to Aristotle, who divides all animals into two main groups, into those with blood (ἔναιμα) and those without it (ἄναιμα); and he enunciates as a general proposition based on observation, that 'all animals which have blood have an osseous or bony spine'.† This is the great, veritable difference. To be sure, it has been possible to raise many objections to it: e.g. that there are animals which by nature (*habitus*) should be bloodless and yet have blood, like leeches and earth-worms which have a red fluid (*Saft*). In general, the question posed is, What is blood? and in the end, the difference is one of colour. The vagueness of this division caused it to be abandoned, and Linnaeus opposed to it his well-known six classes. But just as the French rejected the Linnaean system of plant classification, a mere rigid product of Understanding, in favour of Jussieu's classification into monocotyledons and dicotyledons, so too, following Lamarck, a gifted Frenchman, they reverted to the Aristotelian division of animals, but in this form, that animals are classified, not according to blood, but into vertebrates and invertebrates. Cuvier united both principles of classification for, in fact, the vertebrates have red blood, and the others white blood and no inner skeleton, or at least, only an inarticulated one, or else an articulated but external skeleton. It is in the lamprey that we first see a backbone which, however, is still only a tough leathery substance and in which the vertebrae are indicated merely by grooves. The vertebrates are mammals, birds, fish, and amphibians: the invertebrates comprise molluscs, crustacea, which have a carapace separated from the fleshy skin, insects and worms. The general appearance of the animal world at once shows this huge difference which prevails between the two groups into which it is divided.

This difference also corresponds to the previously mentioned classification based on the relation between the organization of the organism's viscera and the organic articulation connecting it with the external world, a relation which, in turn, is based on the fine distinction of *vie organique* and *vie animale*. 'In the invertebrates, therefore', says Lamarck (*Éléments de zoologie*, part i, p. 159), 'the basis for a proper skeleton is also lacking. Nor have they true lungs consisting of cells; consequently neither do they have a voice or vocal organ.' Aristotle's classification according to blood is, on the whole, confirmed by this. The invertebrates, Lamarck continues, at the place quoted, 'do not possess true blood, which should be red' and warm; it is more like lymph. 'Blood owes its colour to the intensity of animalization', which, therefore, is also lacking in these animals. 'Such animals, on the whole, also lack a genuine circulation of the blood; nor have they an iris in the eye, nor kidneys. Also they have no spinal cord, nor the great sympathetic nerve.' The

† Aristotle's *Hist. animal.* I, 4; III, 7: πάντα δὲ τα ζῶα, ὅσα ἔναιμα ἐστιν, ἔχει ῥάχιν ἤ ὀστώδη ἤ ἀκανθώδη.

_orates, therefore, have a greater development, an equilibrium of _ner and outer; in the other group, on the contrary, the one is developed at the expense of the other. Accordingly, of the invertebrates, two classes in particular must be mentioned, worms (molluscs) and insects; the former have more developed viscera than the insects, but these have a more delicately fashioned exterior. To the invertebrates also belong polyps, infusoria, etc., which are completely undeveloped, consisting merely of skin and jelly. Polyps, like plants, are a collection of several individuals and can be cut up into pieces; even the garden snail grows a new head. But this reproductive strength is a weakness of the substantiality of the organism. In the invertebrates, one sees a gradual disappearance of heart, brain, gills, circulatory vessels, the organs of hearing, sight, and sex, and finally of sensation altogether, and indeed even of movement (Lamarck, loc. cit., p. 214). Where the interior life predominates as an independent activity, there is development of the digestive and reproductive organs as the concrete universal in which, as yet, there is no difference. It is only where the animal kingdom has relationships with the outer world, with the emergence of sensibility and irritability, that a differentiation takes place. While therefore in the invertebrates, organic and animal life stand opposed to each other, in the vertebrates, where both moments are in a single unity, the other essential basis of determination must come into play, namely, the particular element for which the animal is destined, whether it is a land animal, an aquatic creature, or a creature of the air. The invertebrates, on the contrary, do not exhibit this connection of their development with the Elements, because they are already subordinated to the other basis of classification. But naturally there are also animals which are intermediate forms; the reason for this lies in the impotence of Nature to remain true to the Notion and to adhere to thought-determinations in their purity.

a. In worms, molluscs, shell-fish, etc., the organism is internally more developed but its exterior is formless: 'In spite of the outer difference which distinguishes molluscs from the higher animals', says Treviranus (loc. cit., vol. i, pp. 306–7), 'we find in their internal structure in some measure, the organization of the latter. We see a brain resting on the oesophagus; a heart with arteries and veins, but no spleen and pancreas. The blood is white or bluish in colour; and the fibrin is not formed in the cruor, but its threads swim freely in the serum. In only a few are the male and female sexual organs found in separate individuals; and in these, the structure of the organs is so peculiar that often their function (*Bestimmung*) cannot even be guessed.' 'They breathe through gills', says Lamarck (loc. cit., p. 165), 'and have a nervous system but the nerves are not nodulated, that is they do not present a series of ganglia; and they have one or more hearts which, although possessing only one ventricle, are well developed.' The system of external articulation in molluscs is, on the other hand, much more undeveloped than in insects: 'Here', says Treviranus (loc. cit, vol. i, pp. 305–6), 'the difference of head, thorax, and

abdomen, of which there are still traces in fish and amphibian.
pears completely. Molluscs do not have a nose; most of them h.
external limbs at all and they move either by alternately contracting
relaxing their stomach muscles or else are quite incapable of any forwa.
movement.'

b. The organs of movement in insects are far superior to those in
molluscs, which, in general, have only a few motor muscles; for insects
have feet and wings, and the head, thorax, and abdomen are quite
distinct in them, too. On the other hand, their interior structure is
correspondingly less developed. The respiratory system permeates the
whole body and coincides with the digestive system, as in some fishes.
The blood-system has only a few developed organs and even these can
hardly be distinguished from the digestive system, whereas the external
articulation, e.g. the masticatory organs, etc., are correspondingly more
developed. 'In insects and other lower classes of animals', says Autenrieth (loc. cit., part i, § 346), 'a movement of the fluids seems to take
place without circulation and in the following way: fluids are received
into the body only from the surface of the alimentary canal, and after
being used for nourishing the various parts are gradually excreted as
waste matter through the surface or in other ways.' These are the principal classes of invertebrates; according to Lamarck (loc. cit., p. 128) there
are fourteen of them.

c. As regards the further classification of animals, this is based more
simply on the Elements of their inorganic nature: earth, air, and water,
that is, they are either land animals, birds, or fish. This is a convincing
distinction and one directly appealing to a naïve apprehension of Nature,
whereas in the preceding classifications, the distinction became a matter
of indifference. For many beetles, for example, have webbed feet but
live as well on land and also have wings for flying. Now there are, of
course, even in the higher animals transitions from one class to another
which nullify that distinction. Life, which exists in different Elements, is
united in a single organism just because it is unable to discover in the
representation of the land animal, the single determinateness which
ought to contain the simple, essential character of the animal. Only
Thought, Understanding, can make fixed distinctions: and only spirit,
just because it is spirit, can produce works which conform to these
rigid distinctions. Works of art or of science are so abstractly and essentially individualized that they remain faithful to their character (*Bestimmung*) and do not confuse essential differences. If these differences are
mixed in art, as happens in poetic prose and prosaic poetry and in
dramatized history, or if painting is introduced into music or poetry, or
if painting is done in stone and, e.g., shows curly hair in a statue (bas
relief is also a painting in sculpture), then the essential character of the
art is violated; for genius can produce a genuine work of art only by
expressing a specific individuality. It is the same when one man wants to
be poet and painter and philosopher. In Nature, this is not so: a creature

can develop in two directions. But the fact that in the cetacea, the land animal falls back again into the water; that in the amphibians and reptiles the fish again climbs on to the land, where it presents a sorry picture, snakes, for example, possessing the rudiments of feet which serve no purpose; that the bird becomes an aquatic bird and in the duck-billed platypus (*ornithorynchus*) even crosses over to the class of land animals, and in the stork becomes a camel-like animal that is covered more with hair than with feathers; that the land animal and the fish attain to flight, the former in vampires and bats, and the latter in the flying fish: all this does not efface the fundamental difference, which is not a common, a shared difference, but a difference in and for itself. The great distinctions must be adhered to in face of these imperfect products of Nature, which are only mixtures of such determinations, like a humid air or a moist earth (i.e. mud), and the transitional forms must be interpolated as mixtures of the differences. The true land animals, the mammals, are the most perfect; then come birds, and the least perfect are fish.

α. The natural element of *fishes* is water, as their whole structure shows; articulation is restricted by the element and accordingly is forced inwards. Their blood has little warmth, for its temperatures differ only slightly from that of the element in which they live. Fish have a heart with a single ventricle, or else with several, which then are directly interconnected. Lamarck, describing the four higher classes of animals, says of fish (loc. cit., pp. 140 et seq.): 'They breathe through gills, have a smooth or scaly skin, fins, no trachea, no larynx, no tactile sense, and probably no sense of smell either.' Fish, and [some] other animals, simply abandon their young, and have no concern for them at all, right from the start; such creatures, therefore, do not yet attain to a feeling of unity with their young.

β. *Reptiles*, or *amphibians*, are intermediate forms which belong partly to land and partly to water; and that is why there is something repulsive about them. They have only one cardiac ventricle, an imperfect pulmonary respiration, and a smooth, or else scaly, skin; frogs, before reaching maturity, do not have lungs but gills.

γ. *Birds*, like animals, have feeling for their young. They provide them with their food in the egg: 'Their foetus', says Lamarck (loc. cit., p. 146), 'is contained in an inorganic envelope (the egg-shell), and soon ceases to have any connection with the mother but can develop inside the shell without drawing nourishment from her.' Birds use their own warmth to keep their young warm, share their food with them and also feed their females; but they do not sacrifice their own lives for their young as insects do. By building nests, birds display the artistic and constructive instinct and thus attain to a positive self-feeling in that they make themselves into an inorganic nature for an other; and this other, their young, they put forth directly from themselves. Lamarck (loc. cit., p. 150) proposes the following classification of birds from this standpoint: 'If one bears in mind that aquatic birds like the palmipedes, for example, sandpipers, and gallinaceous birds, have the advantage over all other birds that their young, as soon as they emerge from the egg, can walk and feed themselves, it will be seen that they must form the first three orders, and that the Columbidae, Passeres, birds of prey, and climbers must form the last four orders of this class; for their young, when they have emerged from the egg, can neither walk, nor feed themselves.' But this very circumstance can be regarded as a reason for placing these latter in front of the others, not to mention that the palmipedes are mongrels (*Zwitter*). Birds are positively distinguished by the connection between their lungs and membraneous air-pockets (*Luftbehälter*) and big, marrow-less cavities in their bones. They have no breasts, for they do not suckle their young, and are bipeds; and the two arms or forefeet are transformed into wings. Because this form of animal is cast into the air, and the abstract Element thus lives in birds, the vegetative principle fluctuates and develops on their skin in the form of plumage. Also, since birds belong to the air, their thoracic system, too, is specially developed. Consequently, many birds not only have, like mammals, a voice but they also sing, the inner vibration developing in the air as in its element. Whereas the horse neighs and the ox bellows, the bird continues this cry as an ideal enjoyment of itself. On the other hand, the bird does not roll about on the ground, the expression of a crude self-feeling; it clings only to the air and in this element attains to self-feeling.

δ *Mammals* have breasts, four articulated extremities, and all their organs are developed. Because they have breasts, they suckle and feed their young from themselves. These animals thus attain to the feeling of the unity of the one individual with the other, to the feeling of the genus, which achieves an existence in the progeny in which the two individuals are precisely the genus, even though, in Nature, this unity of the indivi-dual with the genus falls back again into singularity. But the perfect ani-mals still behave as genus to this existence, for in it they find their universal; these are the mammals, and those birds which hatch out their young. Of all animals, monkeys are the most docile (*bildsamsten*) and have most affection for their young; the satisfied sexual instinct persists for them in objective form, for they have passed over into an other, and in caring for the needs of their young, they have the higher, disinterested intuition of this unity. Although in mammals the skin partakes of a vege-tative nature, the vegetative life is far from being as powerful as it is in birds. In mammals, the skin continues its growth into wool, hair, bristles, spines (in the hedgehog), and even into scales and armour (in the arma-dillo). Man, on the other hand, has a skin which is smooth, pure, and much more animalized and which also sheds anything of an osseous nature. Woman has a more luxuriant head of hair. In the male, an abundance of hair on the chest and elsewhere is regarded as a sign of strength; it is, however, a relative weakness of the cutaneous organization (see *supra*, § 362, *Zusatz*, p. 392).

Further essential classifications have been based on the behaviour of animals as individuals, to other animals: that is, on their teeth, feet, claws, and beaks. It was a correct instinct which led to the choice of these parts, for it is by them that animals themselves distinguish themselves from other animals: if the difference is to be a true one, it must not be simply a sign which *we* have picked out, but a difference of the animal itself. By opposing itself as an individual to its non-organic nature through its weapons, the animal demonstrates that it is a subject for itself. On this basis, the classes of mammals are very accurately distinguished: αα. into animals whose feet are *hands*—man and the *monkey* (the monkey is a satire on man, a satire which it must amuse him to see if he does not take himself too seriously but is willing to laugh at himself); ββ. into animals whose extremities are *claws*—dogs, wild beasts like the *lion*, the king of beasts; γγ. into *rodents* in which the *teeth* are specially shaped; δδ. into *cheiroptera*, which have a membrane stretched between the toes, as occurs even in some rodents (these animals come nearer to dogs and monkeys); εε. into *sloths*, in which some of the toes are missing altogether and have become claws; ζζ. into animals with *fin-like* limbs, the *Cetacea*; ηη. into *hoofed* animals, like *swine, elephants* (which have a trunk), *horned cattle, horses*, etc. The strength of these animals resides in the upper part of the body, most of them can be tamed to work; and the formation of the extremities shows a special relationship to the animals' non-organic nature. If the animals under ββ, γγ, δδ, εε, are grouped together as *animals with claws*, then we have four classes: 1. *Animals with hands*, 2. *with claws*, 3. *with hooves*, which work for man, 4. *with fins*. Lamarck (loc. cit., p. 142), following this classification, grades the mammals in descending order as follows: 'The unguiculate mammals have four limbs, flat or pointed claws at the tips of their toes which latter do not envelop the claws. The limbs are, in general, fitted for seizing, or at least hanging on to, objects. These animals include those which are most highly organized. The *hoofed* mammals (*Ungulata*) have four limbs, the toes of which are completely surrounded at their extremities by a rounded, horny substance called a hoof (*sabot*). Their feet can be used only for walking or running on the ground; they cannot be used for climbing trees, or for seizing an object or prey, or for attacking and rending other animals. They are completely herbivorous. The mammals without hooves have only two extremities, and these are very short and flat, and shaped like fins. Their toes, covered by skin, have neither claws not hooves (*corne*); they are the least highly organized of all the mammals. They have neither a pelvis, nor hind legs; they swallow their food without masticating it; lastly, they usually live in water but come up to the surface to breathe air.' As regards the further subdivisions, these must be left to the chance and contingency proper to Nature, that is, to be determined by external factors. Climate, however, still constitutes the great determining factor. In southern latitudes, the animal kingdom is particularized more according to differences of climate and country than it is in northern latitudes: thus the Asiatic and African elephants are essentially distinct from each other, while in America there are none; lions and tigers, etc., are similarly distinguished.

3. *The Genus and the Individual*

§ 371

a. The Disease of the Individual

In the two preceding relationships, the self-mediation of the genus with itself is the process of its diremption into individuals and the sublation of its difference. But since the genus also (§ 357) assumes the shape of external universality, of an inorganic nature against the individual, it attains to existence in the latter in an abstract, negative manner. In this relationship of an external existence, the individual organism can just as well not conform to its genus as preserve itself in it through its return into self (§ 366). It finds itself in a state of *disease* when one of its systems or organs, *stimulated* into conflict with the inorganic power (*Potenz*), establishes itself in isolation and persists in its particular activity against the activity of the whole, the fluidity and all-pervading process of which is thus obstructed.

Zusatz. While the division of animal life is the animal type in its self-particularization, so now, in disease, the individual organism, too, is capable of one particularization which does not accord with its Notion, i.e. with its total particularity. Here too, therefore, the deficiency of the individual subject in face of the genus is still not removed, but the individual is, both in its own self and in its opposition to itself, genus; it is itself alone the genus, and has it within itself. This is the disharmony to which the animal is now subjected and with which it comes to an end.

Health is the *due relation* (*Proportion*) of the organic self to its real existence (*Dasein*), that is, all its organs are fluid in the universal; it consists in the commensurate relationship of the organic to the non-organic, so that for the organism there is nothing non-organic which it cannot overcome. Disease does not consist in an irritation (*Reiz*) being too great or too small for the susceptibility of the organism, rather is its *Notion* a *disproportion* of its being and its self—not a disproportion between factors which exist separately within the organism. For factors are abstract moments, and cannot exist apart from each other. To talk of an increase of irritation and a decrease of susceptibility—as if an increase in the one were accompanied by a corresponding decrease in the other, the latter falling as the former rises—this quantitative contrast is inevitably at once suspect. Nor is it a question of *disposition*, as if someone could be diseased in principle (*an sich*) without being actually infected (*ange-steckt*), without being ill; for it is the organism itself which makes this reflection, namely, that what is in itself is also actual. Disease arises when the organism, as simply immediate (*als seiend*), is separated from its inner sides—which are not factors, but whole, real sides. The cause of disease lies partly in the organism itself, like ageing, dying, and congenital defects: partly also in the susceptibility of the organism, in its simply immediate being, to external influences, so that one side is increased beyond the power of the inner resources of the organism. The organism is then in the opposed forms of *being* and *self*; and the *self* is precisely *that* for which the negative of itself *is*. A stone cannot become diseased, because it is destroyed in the negative of itself, is chemically decomposed and its form does not endure: because it is not the negative of itself which overlaps (*übergreift*) its opposite, as in illness and in self-feeling. Appetite, too, the feeling of a lack, is to its own self the negative, relates itself to itself as a negative: is itself and is also in relation to itself as a being feeling a lack; but with this difference, that in appetite this lack is something external, that is, the self is not turned against its structure (*Gestalt*) as such, whereas in disease the negative thing is the structure itself.

Disease, therefore, is a *disproportion between irritation and the capacity of the organism to respond*. Because the organism is an individual, it can be held fast in one of its external sides, can exceed its measure in a particular respect. Heraclitus says (144b): 'Excess of heat is fever, excess of cold, paralysis, excess of air, suffocation.'[1] The reason why the organism can be irritated beyond its capacity is that, being equally the complete unity of possibility and actuality (of substance and the self), it is wholly under each of the two forms. The opposition of sex separates efficacy and stimulus (*Wirksamkeit und Reize*), distributing them between two organic individuals. But the organic individual is itself both; and this is the possibility of its death, a possibility immanent in it, namely, that the organic individual itself separates itself into these forms. In the sex-relation, it has surrendered its essential determinateness outwards in so far as it is in the relation; but now, it has this determinateness in its own self, mating, as it were, with itself. The union is not consummated in the genus because life is tied to one singular (*Einzelheit*): and in many animals copulation is even the terminal point of existence. But even though others survive, so that the animal overcomes its non-organic nature and its genus, yet all the same, the latter remains master over it. Into this reversal [of the relationship] falls disease. Whereas in health, all the vital functions are held in this ideality, in disease the blood, e.g., is heated, inflamed; and then it is active on its own account. Similarly, the bile can become over-active and, for example, generate gall-stones. When the stomach is overloaded, the digestive apparatus functions as an isolated, independent activity, makes itself the centre, is no longer a moment of the whole but dominates it.

[1] Heraclitus, 144b, ὅσα ἐν ἡμῖν ἑκάστου κράτος, νόσημα· ὑπερβολὴ θερμοῦ, πυρετός· ὑπερβολὴ ψυχροῦ, παράλυσις· ὑπερβολὴ πνεύματος, πνῖγος.

This isolated functioning (*Isolieren*) can go so far that animals are generated in the intestines; all animals, at certain times, have worms in the heart,
lungs, and brain (see § 361, *Zusatz*). In general, the animal is feebler than
man, who is the strongest animal; but it is a false hypothesis that tape-
worms in human beings are the result of swallowing the eggs of such
creatures. The restoration of health can consist only in the overcoming of
this particularization.

A Dr. Goede, in *Isis* (vol. vii, 1819, p. 1127), has attacked this doctrine
in a rigmarole which purports to be profoundly philosophical, even
'saving the unity of the Idea, the *essence*, the comprehension of life and
disease in the essence'. It is very pretentious to try to disprove a theory
about mere *appearance* and *externality* with the loftiness and frankness
appropriate to truth: 'This definition of disease has missed the point; only
the external appearance of fever, only its symptom, has been grasped.'
He continues (p. 1134): 'That which, in life, is blended into a unity and
internally concealed, appears in the phenomenal world as a particularity,
i.e. as developing and exhibiting, in a peculiar way, the essence of the one
organism and its Idea. Thus life's inner essence appears externally as its
character. Where all is, where all lives from one Idea, from one essence,
there all opposition is only a semblance and external, is only for appearance
and reflection, not internally for life and Idea.' The truth is rather that
the living being itself is reflection, diremption. These philosophers of
Nature mean only an external reflection; but life is just this, to appear.
Life is beyond their comprehension because they do not get as far as its
appearance, but stop short at dead gravity. Dr. Goede seems, in particular,
to fancy that the diseased organ does not come into conflict with the
organism, but, at first, with *its own essence*: 'The total activity of the
whole is only a consequence and a reflex of the arrest of free movement
in the individual.' By this, he fancies he has said something really speculative. But then, what is essence? Just vitality. And what is actual vitality?
Just the whole organism. To say, therefore, that the organ is in conflict
with its essence, with itself, is to say that it is in conflict with the totality,
which is in it as vitality in general, as the universal. But the reality of this
universal is the organism itself. Fine philosophers these, who fancy that
in essence they have the truth, and that if only they keep on saying 'essence', then this makes it the inner truth of the matter! I have not the
slightest respect for their talk of essence, for it is nothing but an abstract
reflection. To explicate essence, however, is to make it appear as a real
existence.

There are various ways in which subjectivity can be deranged through
failure of the bodily activities to preserve their ideality. The principal
grounds from which disease originates are, on the one hand, air and
moisture, and on the other hand, the stomach and the skin-process.
More precisely, the types of disease can be reduced to the following.

(α) One type of disease is the *injurious affection* which is, in the *first*
instance, a *general* determinateness lying in the non-organic nature as such.

Such injurious affection is a simple determinateness which, though it must be considered as coming from outside and as inflicted on the organism, can at the same time also appear as something placed in the organism itself, no less than in its natural environment. For diseases such as *epidemics* or *plagues* are not to be thought of as something particular, but as a whole of the determinateness of external Nature, to which the organism itself also belongs; they can be called an infection of the organism. Various circumstances contribute to such afflictions which are of an elemental, climatic nature, and therefore also have their seat—namely, their origin—in the elemental determinateness of the organism; they exist therefore, at first, obscurely in the general foundations of the organism which are not as yet a developed, formed system, that is chiefly in the skin, the lymph, and the bones. Such diseases are not only climatic but also historical, since they appear at certain periods of history, and then disappear.† They can also come about through the transference of an organism accustomed to one climate, to another climate. Historical researches have not resulted in any well-founded conclusions, e.g. on syphilis or venereal disease. When this disease first appeared, there had been contact between European and American organisms; but it has not been proved that the disease was brought over here from America, and it is no more than a theory that it came from there. The French call it *mal de Naples* because it appeared when they captured Naples, although no one knew where it came from. Herodotus reports that a nation migrated from the Caspian Sea to Media and there caught a disease; it was the mere change of place (*Wohnsitz*) which caused the disease. With us, too, cattle from the Ukraine were brought into South Germany, and although they were all healthy, the mere change of place gave rise to a murrain (*Pestseuche*). Many nervous diseases were the result of Germans coming into contact with miasmas in Russia; and a thousand healthy Russian prisoners were attacked by a terrible outbreak of typhus. Yellow fever is endemic in America and in a number of maritime

† *Spix and Martius' Travels*, part i, p. 114. 'Small-pox, which has been almost only sporadic during the last ten years, does not run a very virulent course in the organisms of the inhabitants of Rio de Janeiro, because the hot climate and the flabbiness of the body are favourable to the development of the disease. However, there can be no doubt that this disease runs a much milder course in people of the Caucasian race than in negroes and especially American negroes. In the Indians [of South America], who are very susceptible to small-pox, the small-pox matter is assimilated only with the greatest difficulty and they very frequently succumb to the disease. This is attributed mainly to the thickness and hardness of their skin. The physician who compares some of the diseases in Brazil, such as small-pox and syphilis, with those in other parts of the world, is led to observe that just as each individual is subject to particular diseases in each phase of his development, so, too, whole nations, according to their state of culture and civilization, are more readily susceptible to, and develop, certain diseases.'

districts, in Spain, for example, and does not spread from there; for the inhabitants protect themselves against it by going several miles inland. Such diseases are dispositions of elemental Nature in which the human organism participates, although one cannot say that it is infected by the disease, since the dispositional change is in it, too; but, of course, infection does also occur. It is therefore idle to dispute whether disease originates spontaneously or is caused by infection. Both cases exist; if it does develop spontaneously, it also develops through infection after it has penetrated into the lymphatic system.

(β) Another general type of disease is that which is caused by *particular*, external harmful influences with which the organism comes into contact, and then it is one of the particular systems of the organism—e.g. the skin or the stomach—which is affected. This system is then particularly active (*beschäftigt*) and so acts only for itself, in isolation from the rest of the organism. Now here we must distinguish two forms of disease, the acute and the chronic, and it is the former which *medicine* knows best how to treat.

1. When one of the systems of the organism is diseased, cure mainly depends on the possibility of the entire organism becoming morbidly affected, because then the activity of the whole organism too, can be released, thus facilitating the cure of the disease; and this is *acute disease*. Here, the organism is shut off from the outer world, has no appetite or muscular movement, and in so far as it lives, it lives on its own resources. Now it is just because acute diseases are in this way seated in the organism as a whole, not apart from the whole in one of its systems, but in the so-called humours (*Säften*), that the organism can free itself from them.

2. If, however, the disease cannot become a disease of the whole organism, then I regard it as *chronic*, e.g. hardening of the liver or phthisis, etc. In such diseases, appetite and digestion remain quite unimpaired and the sexual instinct retains its strength. Here, because one system has made itself the independent centre of activity, and the organism can no longer be raised above this particular activity, the disease remains in one organ, since the organism too can no longer, as an independent whole, come to itself. Cure is therefore difficult and the difficulty increases in proportion to the severity of the attack and the extent to which this organ or system is affected.

(γ) A *third* form of disease is that which originates in the universal subject, especially in man. These are *diseases of the soul* (*Seele*), which are caused by terror, grief, etc., and which can even result in death.

§ 372

The characteristic *manifestation* of disease is, therefore, that the identity of the entire organic process displays itself as the *successive* course of the vital movement through its distinct moments: sensibility, irritability, and reproduction, i.e. as *fever*, which, however, as process of the *totality* in opposition to the *isolated (vereinzelte)* activity, is just as much the effort towards, and the beginning of, *cure*.

Zusatz. We have seen that the Notion of disease is that the organism separates itself into its separate moments; now we have to consider in more detail the course of disease.

(α) The first stage of disease is that it is *virtually (an sich)* present, but without any actual morbidity.

(β) In the second stage, the disease becomes *for* the self: i.e. there is established in the self and in opposition to it as universal, a determinateness which makes its own self into a fixed self; in other words, the self of the organism becomes a fixed existence, a specific part of the whole. Up to this point, the systems of the organism had a selfless existence; but now, the actual beginning of disease consists in this, that the organism, being irritated beyond its capacity to respond, one particular part, a single system, gains a foothold in opposition to the self. The disease can begin in the organism as a whole, can be an indigestibility in general (for after all, it is digestion which is involved): or in a particular part which establishes itself, for example, in the process of the gall or the lungs. The simply affirmative determinateness is a single determinateness which, usurping the self, takes possession of the whole organism. In this immediate, isolated form, the disease is, as physicians say, in its first stages; this is, so far, nothing more than the first conflict, the running riot of the particular system. But so far as the determinateness has become the centre, the self of the whole organism, so far as the organism is dominated, not by the free self, but by a determinate self, then we have disease proper. On the other hand, so long as the disease is peculiar to one particular system and is confined within that system, it is easier to cure because only one organ is irritated or depressed. The system has only to be extricated from its entanglement with its non-organic nature and kept within bounds, and so external remedies can also be of assistance here. Generally, in this case, the remedy can be restricted to the stimulation of the system concerned. Appropriate remedies in this second stage are emetics, purgatives, venesection, and the like.

(γ) But the disease also spreads into the general life of the organism; for when one organ is affected, there is also an infection of the whole organism. The entire organism, therefore, is involved and its activity deranged because one wheel (*Rad*) in it has made itself the centre. But at the same time, the entire vitality of the organism is turned against it, so that the isolated activity shall not remain an excrescence but a moment of the whole. For if, e.g., digestion isolates itself, then the circulation of the blood, muscular energy, etc., are also affected; in jaundice the whole body secretes bile, is liver through and through, and so on. The third stage of the disease, then, is *coction*, which consists in the affection of the one system becoming an affection of the whole organism; here the disease is no longer in the particular system external to the whole, but the whole life is concentrated in it. Here, too, as we saw in connection with acute disease (p. 432), cure is always easier than when, as in chronic diseases, for example of the lungs, the disease is no longer capable of becoming a disease of the whole organism. With the entire organism thus infected (*affizirt*) with a particularity, a *dual life* begins to be manifested. In opposition to the stable (*ruhigen*) universal self, the whole organism becomes a *differentiating movement*. The organism posits itself as a whole against the determinateness; here the physician can do nothing, and, as a matter of fact, the whole of medicine does no more than assist the forces of nature. Indeed, since the particular morbid affection has become an affection of the whole, this disease of the whole organism is itself at the same time a cure; for it is the whole which is set in motion and, in the circle of necessity, breaks asunder. The true *constitution* of disease consists, therefore, in the organic process now taking its course in this fixed shape, in this persistence (*Bestehen*): i.e. the harmonious processes of the organism now form a *succession*, that is to say, the general systems, torn apart, are no longer immediately a One, but display this unity through the passage of one into the other. Health, which is at the same time in the organism, but arrested, cannot exist in any other way than by a succession of activities. The total process, health, is not in itself abnormal in relation to the kind or system, but only through this succession. This movement, now, is fever. This, then, is disease in its pure, proper form, or the diseased, individual organism liberating itself from its specific disease, as the healthy organism does from its specific processes. Fever being thus the pure life of the diseased organism, its appearance first makes possible the recognition of a specific disease. Not only is fever this succession of the functions but it also makes them fluid, so that through this movement the disease is at the same time sublated, digested; it is an interior process directed against the organism's non-organic nature, a digestion of medicine. Therefore, even if fever is, on the one hand, a morbid state and a disease, yet on the other hand, it is the way in which the organism cures itself. This, however, is true only of a severe, violent fever which lays hold of the whole organism; but a creeping, consuming fever which does not develop into a true fever is, on the other hand, a dangerous sign in chronic diseases. Chronic diseases are, therefore, of a kind which fever cannot subdue; a creeping fever, in its course, does not gain the mastery, but all the separate processes of the assimilating organism function disconnectedly and each on its own account. Here, therefore, fever runs only a superficial course which does not overcome these separate parts (*Teile*). In burning, violent fevers it is chiefly the vascular system which is attacked, and in asthenic fevers, the nervous system. In a true fever, then, the entire organism subsides (*fällt*), first into the nervous system, into the general organism; then into the interior organism, and finally into the [outer] structure.

1. Fever is, at first, shivering, heaviness of the head, headache, twinges in the spine, twitching of the skin, and shuddering. In this activity of the nervous system, the muscles are left free and consequently their own irritability functions as an uncontrolled trembling and powerlessness. Heaviness of the bones sets in, tiredness of the limbs, withdrawal of the blood from the skin, a sensation of cold. The simple subsistence of the organism, wholly reflected into self, isolates itself and has the entire organism in its power. The organism dissolves all its parts within itself in the simplicity of the nerve, and feels itself withdrawing into the simple substance [of its being].

2. But secondly, as a dissolution of the whole, this very process is the negative power; though this Notion, this organism which is concentrated in its nervous system (*nervigte Organismus*) passes over into the organism of over-heated blood—delirium. It is this very withdrawal which is the transformation into *heat*, *negativity*, where the blood is now the dominating factor.

3. Thirdly, this dissolution passes over finally into the process of shape-formation (*das Gestalten*), into product. The organism in the reproduction of itself reduces to lymph; this is *sweat*, the existence of the organism in fluid form. The significance of this product is, that in it, the isolation, the single system (*das Einzelne*), the determinateness, ceases, for the organism has produced itself as a whole, in general, has digested itself; sweat, to use an expression of the ancient physicians, is *cooked morbid matter*—an excellent notion. Sweat is the *critical secretion*; in it, the organism attains to an excretion of itself, through which it eliminates its abnormality and rids itself of its morbid activity. The *crisis* is the organism which has gained the mastery over itself, which reproduces itself, and exercises this power by sweating. Of course, what is secreted is not the *morbid matter*: as if the body would have been healthy if this matter had not been present in it or could have been emptied out with a spoon. On the contrary, the crisis, like digestion generally, is at the same time a secretion. But the product is double. Consequently, critical secretions are very different from secretions arising from exhaustion, which are not strictly secretions but a dissolution of the organism and therefore have the very opposite significance.

The process of recovery implicit in fever consists in the totality of the organism becoming active. In so doing, the organism raises itself out of its submergence in a particularity; it is alive as a total organism. It subdues the particular activity and then also gets rid of it. Having thus recovered itself, the organism now exists as a universal and is no longer diseased. The determinateness is transformed at first into movement, necessity, into total process, and this in turn into total product, and accordingly also into total self, since the product is simple negativity.

§ 373

b. Therapy

The medicine provokes the organism to put an end to the *particular* irritation in which the formal activity of the *whole* is fixed and to restore the fluidity of the particular organ or system within the whole. This is brought about by the medicine as an irritant, but one which is difficult to assimilate and overcome, so that the organism is confronted by something alien to it against which it is compelled to exert its strength. In acting against something external to it, the organism breaks out from the limitation with which it had become identified and in which it was entangled and against which it cannot react so long as the limitation is not an object for it.

Remark

The main point of view from which medicine must be considered is that it is an *indigestible* substance. But indigestibility is a relative term; not, however, in the vague sense that only what is tolerable by weaker constitutions is to be called easily digestible; on the contrary, such substances are indigestible for the stronger individuality. The immanent *relativity*, that of the *Notion*, which has its actuality in life, is of qualitative nature and consists, when expressed quantitatively (so far as this standpoint is valid here), in the *homogeneity* being greater, the more the opposed terms are intrinsically *self-subsistent*. For the lower forms of animal life which have not attained to a *difference* within themselves, the digestible nutriment is the unindividualized neutral Element of water, as is the case with plants; for children it is in part the completely *homogeneous* animal lymph, mother's milk, a food which is already digested or rather has been directly converted into animal substance as such and is not further differentiated within itself, and in part the least individualized of the more heterogeneous (*differenten*) substances. Substances of this kind are, on the other hand, indigestible for mature and robust constitutions which more easily digest individualized animal substances or plant juices which sunlight has matured to a more powerful individuality and which are therefore called *spirituous*, than, for example, those vegetable products which are still only neutral in colour [green] and stand closer to the chemical process proper. Substances of the former kind, on account of their more intensive selfhood (*Selbstigkeit*), form a correspondingly greater contrast, but for that very reason are more homogeneous irritants. Medicines are, so far, *negative* irritants, poisons; the organism, estranged from itself in disease, is given an irritant which is at the same time an indigestible substance alien and external to it, and to counter it the organism must gather up its strength and enter into process against it in order thereby to regain its self-feeling and its subjectivity. Brown (in his *Elementa medicinae*, 1780) reduced the classification of diseases to sthenia or asthenia, the latter being subdivided into direct and indirect asthenia, and the efficacy of remedies was restricted to their fortifying or debilitating action; furthermore, to give these distinctions an air of natural philosophy, they were traced to the action of carbon and nitrogen, oxygen and hydrogen, or magnetic, electrical, and chemical factors and the like. Now this theory of Brown's regarded as a complete system of medicine, was simply an empty formalism; but on the other hand it did also serve to direct attention beyond what was merely particular and specific both in diseases and remedies, to the *universal* in them as the essential element. Through its opposition to the more *debilitating* (*asthenisierende*) method on the whole practised up till then, it was shown that the organism does not react to the most opposite kind of treatment in such an opposite way, but frequently, at least in the final results, reacts in a similar and hence *general* way; also that the *simple identity* of the organism with itself as the substantial and truly efficacious activity combating a particular disequilibrium of one of its systems, is demonstrated in specific irritants. The definitions and statements put forward in the Paragraph and the Remark are general and, in comparison with the very complex phenomena of disease, insufficient: but none the less it is only the firm foundation of the Notion which can furnish a clue to the maze of particulars and also really clarify those phenomena of disease and its treatment which, to those who are steeped in the externalities of the particular, appear extravagant and bizarre.

Zusatz. Our conception of healing must follow the lines of our treatment of digestion. The organism does not will to subdue something external to it; but it is healed by disentangling itself from something which is particular and which it must regard as beneath its dignity, and by coming to itself. This can happen in various ways.

(α) One way is that the determinateness which holds sway in the organism is given to the latter in the form of something inorganic and selfless to which the organism reacts; thus administered as a determinateness opposed to health, it is for the organism *medicine*. The instinct of the animal feels the determinateness placed in it; the instinct of self-preservation, which is just the total, self-relating organism, has the definite feeling of its deficiency. It therefore proceeds to consume this determinateness, seeking it in the form of an edible, inorganic nature; the determinateness thus exists for the animal in a less powerful, in a simple, passive form. *Homeopathy*, in particular, prescribes remedies which are able to produce the same disease in the healthy body. The effect of introducing into the organism this poison, something simply inimical to it, is that this particularity in which the organism is fixed becomes for it something external: whereas the particularity, as disease, is still a property of the organism itself. Since, therefore, the medicine is the same particularity, although with this difference, that it now brings the organism into conflict with its determinateness as with something external, the effect now is to stimulate the healthy energy of the body into an outward activity and to force it to rouse itself, to come out of its self-absorption and not merely to concentrate itself inwardly but to digest the external substance administered to it. For every disease (but especially acute illnesses) is a hypochondria of the organism, in which the latter disdains the outer world which sickens it, because, restricted to itself, it possesses within its own self the negative of itself. But now the medicine excites the organism to digest it, and the organism is thus drawn back again into the general activity of assimilation; a result which is obtained precisely by administering to the organism a substance much more indigestible than its disease, to overcome which the organism must pull itself together. This results in the organism being divided against itself; for since what was initially an immanent involvement is now an external one, the organism has been made dual within itself, namely, as vital force and diseased organism. This action of medicine can be called *magical*, like that of animal magnetism in which the organism is brought under the power of another person; for through the medicine the organism as a whole is subjected to this specific determination and it succumbs, therefore, to the power of a magician. But if the organism, in virtue of its diseased state, is in the power of something other than itself, yet at the same time, as in animal magnetism, it also has a world beyond, free from its diseased state, through which the vital force can restore itself. That is, the organism can sleep within itself: for in *sleep*, the organism is alone with itself. Now while the organism is thus internally at variance with itself, its vital force endows it with an existence of its own; and possessing such an independent existence, it has saved its general vitality as such and got rid of its entanglement in this particularity. Since this no longer has any power to affect the organism's inner life, the latter is, in consequence, restored, just as in magnetism, the inner life retains its vitality in face of the controlling influence. It is just this extrication from the entanglement, therefore, which permits and brings about the return of the organism into itself by way of assimilation; and recovery simply means that in this accomplished withdrawal into itself, the organism digests itself.

Now to say which are the right remedies is a difficult matter. *Materia medica* has not yet uttered a single rational word on this connection between a disease and its remedy; experience alone is supposed to decide this. And so experience with chicken dung has as much value as that with medicinal plants; for in order that medicine should be nauseating, human urine, chicken dung, and peacock dung were formerly used. Thus there is not a specific remedy for each particular disease. If there were, it would mean finding the connection between the two, i.e. the form in which a determinateness is present in the organism and the form in which it occurs in vegetable Nature, or simply as a dead, externally applied irritant. Thus cinchona, leaves, green plants, seem to have a cooling action on the blood. Soluble salt, saltpetre, must be administered, it seems, to counteract excessive irritability. As the organism in disease is still alive and merely obstructed, easily digested foods can suffice to maintain its vitality and often, therefore, even to effect a cure. When the disease is not located in a particular system but in the digestive system generally, vomiting can occur spontaneously and especially in children who vomit very easily. The reaction to an inorganic remedy like mercury, for example, can be an inordinate intensification of a partial activity; the action is, on the one hand, specific, but there is also a general stimulation of the organism. In general, the relationship of disease to medicine is magical. The irritant, the poison administered, can be called, as Brown calls it, a *positive irritant*.

(β) The remedy can, however, be more in the nature of a *negative irritant*, like, e.g., hydrochloric acid. Its purpose, then, is to depress the activity of the organism so that in eliminating from it all activity, that of the diseased system, too, is eliminated. Thus, on the one hand, the organism has to exert its activity since it must direct itself outwards: on the other hand, the activity of the conflict is weakened, e.g., by venesection, or ice in cases of inflammation, or by paralysing the digestion by salts; in this way, the ground is cleared for the functioning of the inner vitality, for there is no longer any external object. Thus fasting (*Hungerkur*) as a debilitating treatment has come into fashion; and in so far as homeopathy is concerned mainly with *diet*, that, too, falls into this class. The simplest kind of food, like that received by the infant in the womb, is intended to make the organism live on its own resources and so overcome the abnormality. In general, remedies have tended to become more general in character. In many cases, a general shock to the organism is all that is necessary, and physicians themselves have admitted that one remedy is as efficacious as its opposite. Both methods, therefore, the debilitating and the fortifying, although opposed, have in this way demonstrated their efficacy; and ailments which, since Brown, have been treated with opium, naphtha, and brandy, were formerly treated with emetics and laxatives.

(γ) A third way of healing, corresponding to the third type of disease (see § 371, *Zusatz*, p. 431), is that which acts on the universal aspect of the organism. It is here that *magnetism* has its place. The organism, as immanently universal, is to be raised above itself and brought back to itself, and this can be brought about externally. Since, therefore, the self, as simple, falls outside the diseased organism, it is the finger-tips of the magnetizer which conduct this magnetism thoughout the whole organism and which, in this way, fluidify it. Only sick persons can be magnetized, can be put to sleep in this external manner; sleep is just this gathering itself together of the organism into its simplicity, whereby it is brought to the feeling of its inner universality. But instead of this magnetically induced sleep, a healthy sleep, too, can produce this turning-point in an illness, i.e. the organism can then spontaneously gather itself together into its substantiality.

§ 374

In disease, the animal is entangled with a non-organic power (*Potenz*) and is held fast in one of its particular systems or organs in opposition to the unity of its vitality. Its organism, as a determinate existence, has a certain quantitative strength and is, indeed, capable of overcoming its dividedness; but the organism can just as well succumb to it and find in it the manner of its death. The animal, in overcoming and ridding itself of particular inadequacies, does not put an end to the general inadequacy which is inherent in it, namely, that its Idea is only the *immediate* Idea, that, as animal, it stands *within Nature*, and its subjectivity is only *implicitly* the Notion but is not *for its own self* the Notion. The inner universality therefore remains opposed to the natural singularity of the living being as the *negative* power from which the animal suffers violence and perishes, because natural existence (*Dasein*) as such does not itself contain this universality and is not therefore the reality which corresponds to it.

Zusatz. The organism which is abandoned by self brings about its own death. But disease, strictly speaking, in so far as it is not a fatal process, is the outer, existent course of this movement from the singular to the universal. In the organic sphere, the necessity of death, as of all else, does not consist in particular causes; for it lies in the nature of the organism itself that the cause be something external. There is always a remedy for a particular disease; for the latter as such is weak and cannot be the ground of death. The ground is the necessity of the transition of the individuality into universality; for the living being, as alive, is the one-sidedness of existence as a self; but the genus is the movement of just sublating the individual, merely immediate (*seiende*) self, and then relapsing into this sublation—a process in which the merely immediate singular perishes. Death, simply from old age, is an impotence, a general, simple state of decline. The outer signs of this are an increasing ossification and the slackening of muscles and tendons, bad digestion, feeble sensation, a retreat from the individual to the merely vegetative life. 'If the soundness of the heart in old age to a certain extent increases, its irritability diminishes and finally ceases altogether.'[1] There is also noticeable a 'shrinking in size in extreme old age'.[2] This merely quantitative behaviour, but as qualitative, as a specific process, was strictly speaking the disease—not weakness or excessive strength, which is a completely superficial explanation.

§ 375

c. The Self-induced Destruction of the Individual

The universality which makes the animal, as a singular, a *finite* existence, reveals itself in it as the abstract power which terminates the internal process active within the animal, a process which is itself abstract (§ 356). The disparity between its finitude and universality is its *original disease* and the inborn *germ of death*, and the removal of this disparity is itself the accomplishment of this destiny. The individual removes this disparity in giving its singularity the form of universality; but in so far as this universality is abstract and immediate, the individual achieves only an *abstract objectivity* in which its activity has become deadened and ossified and the process of life has become the inertia of *habit*; it is in this way that the animal brings about its own destruction.

Zusatz. The organism can recover from disease; but disease is in its very nature, and herein lies the necessity of death, i.e. of this dissolution in which the series of processes becomes the empty process which does not

---

[1] Autenrieth, *Handbuch der Physiologie*, part i, § 157.
[2] Ibid., part ii, § 767.

return into itself. In the opposition of sex, it is only the separated sexual organs—parts of the plant—which die in an immediate manner: here, they die through their one-sidedness, not as a totality; as a totality, they die through the opposition of the male and female principles which each has within it. Just as in the plant, the stamens swell up into the passive receptacle, and the passive side of the pistil swells up into the generative principle, so now, each individual is itself the unity of both sexes. But this is its death; for it is only an individuality, and this is its essential determinateness. Only the genus is the unity of complete wholes in a single unity. Just as at first, we had the opposition of male and female unsublated in the organism, so now we have the opposition in a more determinate form, that of the abstract forms of the whole which occur in fever and are filled with the whole. The individuality cannot divide itself in such a manner because it is not a universal. In this general inadequacy lies the separability of soul and body, whereas spirit is eternal, immortal; for because spirit, as truth, is itself its object, it is inseparable from its reality—it is the universal which is objective to itself as the universal. In Nature, on the other hand, universality is manifested only negatively, in that subjectivity is sublated in it. The form in which this separation is accomplished is, precisely, the consummation of the singular, which converts itself into the universal but cannot endure this universality. In life, the animal maintains itself, it is true, against its nonorganic nature and its genus; but its genus, as the universal, in the end retains the upper hand. The living being, as a singular, dies from the habit of life, in that it lives itself into its body, into its reality. Vitality makes itself, for itself, into the universal, in that the activities become universal; and it is in this universality that the vitality itself dies; for since vitality is a process, opposition is necessary to it, and now the other which it should have had to overcome is for it no longer an other. Just as in the spiritual sphere, old people dwell more and more within themselves and their kind, and their general ideas and conceptions tend to occupy their interest to the exclusion of what is particular, with the result that tension, *interest* (*inter esse*) falls away and they are contented in this processless habit: so, too, it is in the physical sphere. The absence of opposition to which the organism progresses is the repose of the dead; and this repose of death overcomes the inadequacy of disease, this inadequacy being therefore the primary cause of death.

§ 376

But this achieved identity with the universal is the sublation of the *formal opposition* between the *immediate* singularity of the individuality and its *universality*; and this is only one side, and that the abstract side, namely, the *death of the natural being*. But in the

Idea of life, subjectivity is the Notion, and it is thus *in itself* the absolute *being-within-self* of *actuality* and concrete universality. Through the sublation of the *immediacy* of its reality just demonstrated, subjectivity has coalesced with itself; the last *self-externality* of Nature has been sublated and the Notion, which in Nature is present only *in principle* (*an sich seiende Begriff*), has become *for itself*. With this, Nature has passed over into its truth, into the subjectivity of the Notion whose *objectivity* is itself the sublated immediacy of singularity, is *concrete universality*; so that the Notion is posited as having for its *determinate being* the reality which corresponds to it, namely, the Notion—and this is *spirit*.

Zusatz. Above this death of Nature, from this dead husk, proceeds a more beautiful Nature, *spirit*. The living being ends with this division and this abstract coalescence within itself. But the one moment contradicts the other: that which has coalesced is for that reason identical—Notion or genus and reality, or subject and object, are no longer divided; and that which has repelled and divided itself is for that very reason not abstractly identical. The truth is their unity as distinct moments; therefore in this coalescence and in this division, what is sublated is only *formal* opposition because of the intrinsic identity of the moments, and similarly, what is negated is only *formal* identity, because of their division. That is to say, in more concrete terms, the Notion of life, the genus, life in its universality, repels from itself its reality which has become a totality within it, but it is in itself identical with this reality, is Idea, is absolutely preserved, is the Divine, the Eternal, and therefore abides in this reality; and what has been sublated is only the form, the inadequacy of natural existence, the still only abstract externality of time and space. The living being is, it is true, the supreme mode of the Notion's existence in Nature; but here, too, the Notion is present only in principle (*an sich*), because the Idea exists in Nature only as a singular. Certainly, in locomotion the animal is completely liberated from gravity, in sensation it feels itself, in voice it hears itself; in the genus-process the genus exists, but still only as a singular. Now since this existence is still inadequate to the universality of the Idea, the Idea must break out of this circle and by shattering this inadequate form make room for itself. Therefore, instead of the third moment in the genus-process sinking back again into singularity, the other side, death, is the sublating of the singular and therewith the emergence of the genus, the procession of spirit; for the negation of natural being, i.e. of immediate singularity, is this, that the universal, the genus, is posited and that, too, in the form of genus. *In the individuality*, this movement of the two sides is the process which sublates itself and whose *result is consciousness*, unity, the unity in and for itself of both, as self, not merely as genus in the inner Notion of the singular. Herewith, the Idea exists *in* the self-subsistent subject, for which, as organ of the Notion, everything is ideal and fluid; that is, the subject *thinks*, makes everything in space and time its own and in this way has universality, i.e. its own self, present within it. Since in this way the universal is now *for* the universal, therefore the Notion is *for itself*; this is first manifested in spirit in which the Notion makes itself objective to itself, but in doing so, the existence of the Notion, as Notion, is *posited*. Thought, as this universal which exists for itself, is *immortal being*; mortal being is that in which the Idea, the universal, exists in an inadequate form.

This is the transition from Nature to spirit; in the living being, Nature finds its consummation and has made its peace, in that it is transformed into a higher existence. Spirit has thus proceeded from Nature. The goal of Nature is to destroy itself and to break through its husk of immediate, sensuous existence, to consume itself like the phoenix in order to come forth from this externality rejuvenated as spirit. Nature has become an other to itself in order to recognize itself again as Idea and to reconcile itself with itself. But it is one-sided to regard spirit in this way as having only *become* an actual existence after being merely a potentiality. True, Nature is the immediate—but even so, as the other of spirit, its existence is a relativity: and so, as the negative, its being is only posited, derivative. It is the power of free spirit which sublates this negativity; spirit is no less *before* than *after* Nature, it is not merely the metaphysical Idea of it. Spirit, just because it is the goal of Nature, is *prior* to it, Nature has proceeded from spirit: not empirically, however, but in such a manner that spirit is already from the very first implicitly present in Nature which is spirit's own presupposition. But spirit in its infinite freedom gives Nature a free existence and the Idea is active in Nature as an inner necessity; just as a free man of the world is sure that his action is the world's activity. Spirit, therefore, itself proceeding, *in the first instance*, from the immediate, but *then* abstractly apprehending itself, wills to achieve its own liberation by fashioning Nature out of itself; this action of spirit is philosophy.

With this, we have brought our treatment of Nature to its boundary. Spirit, which has apprehended itself, also wills to know itself in Nature, to make good again the loss of itself. This reconciliation of spirit with Nature and with actuality is alone its genuine liberation, in which it sheds its merely personal habits of thought and ways of looking at things. This liberation from Nature and Nature's necessity is the Notion of the Philosophy of Nature. The forms which Nature wears are only forms of the Notion, although in the element of externality; it is true that these forms, as grades of Nature, are grounded in the Notion, but even where the Notion gathers itself together in sensation, it is still not yet present to itself as Notion. The difficulty of the Philosophy of Nature lies just in this: first, because the material element is so refractory towards the unity of the Notion, and, secondly, because spirit has to deal with an ever-increasing wealth of detail. None the less, Reason must have confidence in itself, confidence that in Nature the Notion speaks to the Notion and that the veritable form of the Notion which lies concealed beneath Nature's scattered and infinitely many shapes, will reveal itself to Reason.

Let us briefly survey the field we have covered. At first, the Idea was, in gravity, freely disbanded into a body whose members are the free heavenly bodies; then this externality fashioned itself inwardly into properties and qualities which, belonging to an individual unity, had in the chemical process an immanent and physical movement. Finally, in the living being, gravity is disbanded into members in which the subjective unity abides. The aim of these lectures has been to give a picture of Nature in order to subdue this Proteus: to find in this externality only the mirror of ourselves, to see in Nature a free reflex of spirit: to know God, not in the contemplation of him as spirit, but in this his immediate existence.

INDEX

Made in the USA
Lexington, KY
24 May 2013